CLASSICAL FOUNDATIONS OF ISLAMIC EDUCATIONAL THOUGHT

◆

This publication was funded through the support of the U.S. Congress and the Library of Congress

Classical Foundations of Islamic Educational Thought

A compendium of parallel English-Arabic texts selected and introduced by

Bradley J. Cook

with assistance from
Fathi H. Malkawi

Brigham Young University Press ♦ *Provo, Utah* ♦ *2010*

Library of Congress Cataloging-in-Publication Data is available.

ISBN: 978–0–8425–2763–7 (alk. paper)

PRINTED IN THE UNITED STATES OF AMERICA.

1 2 3 4 5 6 7 8 9 16 15 14 13 12 11 10

First Edition

Contents

Foreword to the Series

Brigham Young University and its Middle Eastern Texts Initiative are pleased to sponsor and publish the Islamic Translation Series (ITS). We wish to express our appreciation to James L. and Beverley Sorenson of Salt Lake City for their generous support, which made ITS possible, and to the Ashton Family Foundation of Orem, Utah, which kindly provided additional funding so that we might continue.

Islamic civilization represents nearly fourteen centuries of intense intellectual activity, and believers in Islam number in the hundreds of millions. The texts that appear in ITS are among the treasures of this great culture. But they are more than that. They are properly the inheritance of all the peoples of the world. As an institution of The Church of Jesus Christ of Latter-day Saints, Brigham Young University is honored to assist in making these texts available to many for the first time. In doing so, we hope to serve our fellow human beings, of all creeds and cultures. We also follow the admonition of our own tradition, to "seek . . . out of the best books words of wisdom," believing, indeed, that "the glory of God is intelligence."

—Daniel C. Peterson
—D. Morgan Davis

Note on Conventions

In this work, terms of Arabic derivation found in *Webster's Third New International Dictionary* generally follow the first spelling given and are treated as regular English words. Otherwise, Arabic or Persian words and proper names have been transliterated following, with few exceptions, the Romanization tables established by the American Library Association and the Library of Congress (*ALA-LC Romanization Tables: Transliteration Schemes for Non-Roman Scripts*. Compiled and edited by Randall K. Barry. Washington, DC: Library of Congress, 1997).

Unless otherwise indicated, all dates are "common era" (CE). Where more than one date is given for the same event (e.g. 324/935), the first is AH—*anno Hegirae* (in the year of the Hijra)—the second is CE.

Internals reference numbers (e.g., 3.45) are to chapter and paragraph. All works cited in the notes appear in short form. Full information for each citation is available in the bibliography.

Ellipses indicate portions of text that have been omitted from this edition due to space constraints.

Abbreviations

CAG Diels, H., ed. *Commentaria in Aristotelem Graeca.* Berlin: Reimer, 1882–1909.

GAS Fuat Sezgin, *Geschichte des arabischen Schrifttums.*

EI^2 *The Encyclopaedia of Islam,* Second Edition, Leiden: Brill, 1954–Present.

Introduction

Histories rarely give justice to Islam's brilliant cultural contribution and inimitable intellectual energy. To overlook the phenomenal development of the Muslim educational enterprise during Islam's classical period between the eighth and thirteenth centuries is to ignore some of the basic foundations of the Western intellectual tradition. Islam not only bridged early Greco-Hellenistic intellectualism to medieval European scholasticism but also contributed to and improved the corpus of knowledge in medicine, astronomy, philosophy, mathematics, music, architecture, cartography, and geometry. Islamic society can also be credited for conserving and transmitting large bodies of knowledge from Arabic into Latin and promulgating them throughout Europe. Great centers of learning arose throughout the Islamic world, producing scholars whose cumulative and creative genius burned with an intensity that dwarfed the intellectual backwardness of the Latin West. For centuries Islam produced scholars who were both devout Muslims and the foremost thinkers in various intellectual disciplines.

Embedded within this extraordinary, centuries-long heritage of Islamic scholarship is a remarkably rich and deep contribution to the philosophy of learning and education. The ideas of Islamic philosophers concerning education are of great significance, not only because of their innate value but also because of their impact on the development of educational institutions and theories that emerged in Europe.

The educational masterpieces included in this volume provide insights into a variety of social conditions and educational concerns of the period: curriculum, pedagogy, student-teacher dynamics, educational organization, discipline, moral and religious education, and child psychology. Some of these works are limited in the scope of their treatment of specific questions regarding educational process, while others are more comprehensive.

In the classical period, scholars who touched on issues relating to education rarely treated it as a discrete field of inquiry but rather as a subset of larger and broader philosophical and sociological discussions. Many of the works presented here are reflections on education or references to it that are quarried from larger treatises on other subjects. The works chosen for this anthology have been selected partly for their formative influence on the development of educational thought in Islam and partly for their inherent value for students of educational theory and history.

Knowledge and Islam

From its inception, Islam has valued knowledge and its transmission and has enjoyed a long and rich intellectual tradition. At the time of the Prophet Muḥammad, no organized system of education existed in the Arabian Peninsula, and illiteracy was nearly universal. Indeed, it is widely held that the Prophet himself was illiterate, as he has been called the unlettered prophet (*al-nabī al-ummī*).[1] However, from Muḥammad's first transcendent encounter with the angel Gabriel, he was enjoined: "Read! In the name of the Lord who created, created man out of a mere clot, Read! And your Lord is the Most Bountiful, who taught by the pen, taught man which he knew not."[2]

The value of knowledge (*ʿilm*), particularly religious knowledge, is significant within Islam, as evidenced by more than eight hundred references to it in the Qurʾān alone. The importance of education is repeatedly emphasized in the Qurʾān with frequent injunctions; for example, "God will exalt those of you who believe and those who have knowledge to high degrees," and "O my Lord! Increase me in knowledge," and "As God has taught him, so let him write."[3] Such verses provide a forceful stimulus for the Islamic community to strive for education and learning.

The hadith, or traditions and sayings of the Prophet, ranking second in authority to the Qurʾān, are also replete with aphorisms exalting the position of the educated and providing inspiration for acquiring and disseminating knowledge.

"A learned person is superior to a worshipper as the full moon is superior to all the stars." "The learned [scholars] are heirs of the prophets, and the prophets do not leave any inheritance in the shape of dirhams and dinars [wealth], but they do leave knowledge as their legacy. As such, a person who acquires knowledge acquires his full share."[4] "A person who goes [out of his house] in search of knowledge, he is on Allah's way and he remains so until he returns." "A person who follows a path for acquiring knowledge—Allah will make easy the passage for Paradise for him."[5] "Seeking knowledge is a religious duty for every Muslim."[6] "Seek knowledge from cradle to grave."[7] "Seek knowledge even unto China."[8] "An hour of deep thinking is better than sixty years of worship."[9] A fourteenth century treatise on education appreciatively quotes the hadith that "nothing is more powerful than knowledge: kings are rulers over people, but scholars (ulama) are the rulers over kings."[10] These examples show the high value placed on learning both within the Qur'ān and in the biographical narratives of the Prophet. In turn, this underlying philosophy gave impetus for the expansion of education in the early days of Islam.

The purpose of this book is twofold: first, to highlight the intellectual heritage bestowed by scholars and philosophers of Islam's classical period on the discipline of education; and second, to bring together some of the most influential classical Arabic texts on the topic of education for English-speaking scholars and professional educators, Muslim and non-Muslim alike. The abundance of medieval primary materials on the topic of education and learning has heretofore been moderately inaccessible to non-Arabic-speaking audiences. English secondary sources on the development and history of Islamic education are relatively plentiful and are worthy of note.[11] Besides the eight materials selected for this volume (Ibn Saḥnūn in the ninth century, Ikhwān al-Ṣafā in the tenth century, al-Qābisī and Miskawayh in the eleventh century, al-Ghazālī and al-Zarnūjī in the twelfth century, Ibn Jamā'ah and Ibn Khaldūn in the fourteenth century), other Muslim scholars have written specifically on education.[12]

The Centrality of the Qur'ān

Islamic education is unique among educational theories and practices due largely to the all-encompassing influence of the Qur'ān.[13] The Qur'ān remains for the vast majority of Muslims the immutable source for direction in all human endeavor. For Muslims, the transcendent revelations enshrined in the Qur'ān not only envelop the spiritual dimensions of faith and the religious obligations of the faithful but also contain instruction on the political, social, and economic requirements of the umma (the Islamic community as a whole). The Qur'ān serves as a comprehensive blueprint for both the individual and society: in short, it is the primary source of all knowledge.

The absolute primacy of the Qurʾān in the life of the believer induced a strong desire to learn how to read and write in a large number of Islam's early converts. Indeed, the advent of the Qurʾān was revolutionary in the predominantly illiterate Arabian society. Arab society had enjoyed a rich oral tradition, but the Qurʾān was fundamentally different in its function. The Qurʾān, as the word of God, could not be communicated indirectly as could the oral conventions of the time. It is not sufficient to receive the words of the Qurʾān through auditory means alone, it must be received in its purest form. To maximize the power of the Qurʾān, a believer must organically interact with it by reading and reciting its words. Hence, to be able to read and write for the purpose of accessing the blessings of the Qurʾān was an aspiration for most Muslims. Thus, education in Islam derives its origins from its symbiotic relationship to religious instruction.

The first teachers within Islam took as their example the Prophet Muḥammad, who frequently instructed the faithful in his home or in the mosque concerning their religious duties as contained in the Qurʾān. To strengthen the souls of the faithful, Muḥammad created a type of formalized education, held in a place attached to the central mosque in Medina. It is described in this manner:

> [It was] set apart for the lodging of newcomers and those of the local people who were too poor to have a house of their own. This was a regular residential school where reading, writing, Muslim law, memorizing of chapters of the Qurʾān, *tajwīd* (how to recite the Qurʾān correctly), and other Islamic sciences were taught under the direct supervision of the Prophet, who took pains to see after the daily requirements of the boarders. The students also earned their living by laboring in their spare hours. . . . Besides the local population, batches of students from far-off tribes used to come and stay there a while and complete their course before returning to their country.[14]

In this way, Islamic education began. Pious and learned Muslims (*muʿalim* or *mudarris*),[15] dedicated to making the teachings of the Qurʾān more accessible to the *umma,* began to teach the faithful in what came to be known as the *kuttāb* (plural, *katātīb*) or *maktab.*[16]

Primary Education: The *Kuttāb*

The *katātīb* could be located in a variety of available venues: private homes, shops, tents, or even out in the open. Due to the religious ambience of Islamic education, many of the *katātīb* were attached to the mosque.[17] Historians are uncertain as to when the *katātīb* were first established, but due to the widespread desire of the faithful to study the Qurʾān, *katātīb* were in virtually every part of the Islamic empire by the middle of the eighth century. Prior the nineteenth century the *katātīb* were generally funded and erected by wealthy families or other philanthropists through the *waqf* system.[18] The Qurʾān served as the only vehicle for formal public instruction for primary age children, and continued so to do until Western models of education were introduced in the modern period. Even at present, it exhibits remarkable durability as an important means of religious instruction in many Islamic countries.

The significance that Islam places on knowledge is a mandate for broad-based social and cultural support for education. Al-Qābisī argues that education should be available to all children of society, regardless of socioeconomic status. Since education in Islam is obligatory, parents or guardians are responsible for their children's education. If a child has no guardian, the governor of the town or local community is then responsible.[19]

Public education, like many other functions in the Muslim community, came into being gradually as Muslim society developed its various civil institutions. The Prophet Muḥammad enjoined parents to take the responsibility of educating their children as one of their most important parental duties. In one hadith, the Prophet said, "A parent would not ever give a child any thing better than good education (character)."[20] Education, then, was not only a familial duty but also a public responsibility. During the Islamic empire, a large number of institutions were established or endowed principally dedicated to the training of youth in the religious sciences. The values of Islam were such that the *kuttāb* and other public educational institutions blurred prayer and worship with the educational enterprise.

But just as ubiquitous was the personal, informal development of private education, particularly for elites. Families of the elite would hire renowned scholars to provide private education to their children. Typically these scholars provided a higher quality of training not only in religious studies but also in other fields such as literature, poetry, mathematics, and health. In most instances, private education was intended to train children for future high-level civil service positions. However, private, personalized instruction was often supplemented with instruction that involved broader social interaction for the child. The rationale is explained by Ibn Sīna (d. 1037):

> It is not advised to have one child with a private teacher as this will create mutual boredom. Having several children with the teacher motivates them to compete for good character and opens their minds. As they interact with each other their morals are refined and their vigor elevated. Then they become friends, exchange visits and generosities, and negotiate rights. This provides them with opportunities to compete, take pride, debate, and even emulate each other.[21]

Pedagogy

The early methodology for teaching the Qur᾿ān was rather simple and usually consisted of students sitting on straw mats in a circle (*ḥalqa* or *majlis*) surrounding the *mudarris* or *muᶜallim,* who recited the verses from the Qur᾿ān and the Hadith until the students memorized the material. The curriculum of the *kuttāb* was primarily directed to young male children, beginning as early as four years of age, and was centered on Qur᾿ānic studies and basic religious obligations such as ritual ablutions, fasting, and prayer. The education of girls was much more circumscribed, and typically instruction was given within their own homes by a male relative. Certain education tracts strongly cautioned against the co-education of girls and boys, because "teaching girls and mixing them with the boys . . . is a corruption for them."[22] However, while separating girls from boys was encouraged, searching for knowledge was an obligation for every Muslim, including females. Indeed, the eleventh century exegete al-Qābisī notes that "teaching a female the Qur᾿ān and learning . . . is good and of benefit to her. . . . She should be taught only things that can be expected to be good for her and protect her from temptation. . . . How should [women] not be taught the good and what helps to its attainment?"[23] Learning, according to an important educational treatise from the *Mamluk* period, was "prescribed for all of us," boys and girls alike:

> [For knowledge has an important bearing] on all other qualities [of human character] such as generosity and avarice, cowardice and courage, arrogance and humility, chastity [and debauchery], prodigality and parsimony, and so on. For arrogance, avarice, cowardice, and prodigality are illicit. Only through knowledge of them and their opposites is protection against them possible.[24]

After all, whether male or female, the "sum total of learning," asserted the celebrated eleventh century philosopher al-Ghazālī, "is to know the meaning of obedience and service [to God]" so that one may attain the eternal abode of heaven.[25]

The focus during the early history of Islam on the education of youth reflected the belief that raising children with correct principles was a holy obligation for parents and society. Many philosophers underscored this sacred responsibility by asserting that the natural state of the child is innocent, pure, and possessed of a stainless soul. A child's heart, according to al-Ghazālī, "is a precious uncut jewel devoid of any form or carving, which will accept being cut into any shape, and will be disposed according to the guidance it receives from others."[26] It was believed that every child comes into the world with a pure soul; the parents or guardians must form and mold the child into either a responsible and productive adult or one who is immoral and ill-trained.[27] The mind of the child was thought to be like a mirror in that it would reflect anything put before it and that the child would imitate whatever it watches.[28] The *tabula rasa* theory is generally consistent with classical Islamic texts on the instruction of youth. Miskawayh, for example, considered "the soul of the child as naïve and neutral, nothing printed on it [with] no specific opinion or direction to turn it from something to another. If a certain picture has been printed on it and is accepted, the child will grow with that picture and get accustomed to it."[29]

However, other Muslim scholars have thought more positively about human nature. Al-Attas, for example, has asserted that "the soul is not merely a passive recipient like the *tabula rasa,* but is also an active one in the sense of setting itself in readiness to receive what it wants to receive and to consciously strive for the arrival at meaning."[30]

The responsibility of the teacher has been particularly poignant, elevating the position to the level of the Prophet's proxy.[31] According to tradition, if parents and teachers were to raise children according to righteous principles, not only would the student live happily in this world and the next but also all involved in the child's life would enjoy God's blessings. If parents and teachers should fail, the child would inevitably make poor decisions, leading to an unhappy life. Parents and teachers who neglect their duties have sinned and must suffer unhappiness in the life to come.

The process of memorization was critical in virtually every aspect of the *kuttāb's* curriculum. Since Islamic education was essentially Qur'ānic instruction, committing large segments of the Qur'ān to memory was central to a student's educational experience, beginning often by the age of seven. Once students had memorized the greater part of the Qur'ān, they could advance to higher stages of education where the complexity of instruction increased as well as the expectation to commit larger volumes of text to memory. Students were subjected to rigorous training designed to help them memorize as many as four or five hundred lines of text per day.[32] Memorization remained central to mastering all aspects of the Islamic sciences, but it was an interactive process. Al-Zarnūjī instructed that retention is best facilitated by repeating the previous day's lesson five times, the lesson prior to that four times, the lesson before that three times, and so on until all the lessons were firmly fixed in the student's mind. Al-Zarnūjī also encouraged students to read and memorize aloud: "It is essential not to become accustomed to repeating [things] silently, since it is necessary that learning and repetition be carried on with vigor and enthusiasm."[33]

Western analysts commenting on the *kuttāb* system usually criticize two areas of its pedagogy: the limited range of subjects taught, and the exclusive reliance on memorization. Jaques Waardenburg suggests that the constrictive range of subject matter "had a narrowing effect upon the minds of educated Muslims" and that "the memorization methods, becoming habits, made independent thought impossible in practice."[34]

The contemporary *kuttāb* system still emphasizes memorization and recitation as an important modality of learning. The value placed on memorization during a student's early religious training directly influences his or her learning approach on entering formal education offered by the modern state. A common frustration of some educators in the Islamic world is that while their students can memorize copious volumes of notes and textbook pages, they often lack competence in critical analysis and independent thinking.[35]

The issue of memorization has been debated throughout Islamic society, both medieval and modern. While some scholars have argued against its efficacy, al-Jāḥiẓ concludes that memorization and comprehension are two different capabilities: "when a student perfects memorization, understanding and comprehension are not impaired." Indeed, he argues, when "memorization is neglected the meaning of things will not have permanence in the mind and heart."[36] Some contemporary educators have argued that memorization actually has positive benefits in later learning, and they point to great scholars who have exhibited sharp and critical mental capacities in various fields of language, science, technology, and medicine, who began their education in the *kuttāb* and who have relied heavily on the practice of memorization.[37]

Discipline

The philosophy of education that permeated the teaching of children, especially in the *kuttāb,* was strict, and the conditions in which young students learned were often quite harsh. Corporal punishment was often used as a remedial technique for laziness and imprecision.[38] Discipline clearly was an important and indispensable form of reinforcing learning. Further, corporal punishment was not used indiscriminately or without circumspection. Some Islamic texts carefully delineated the appropriate uses of corporal punishment and proscribed under what conditions it was to be permitted. Certain Islamic educational theorists, such as al-Qābisī, advised teachers to exercise moderation when disciplining students, limiting the punishment to only three lashes of the cane.[39] Any excess over three lashes required approval of the child's primary guardian. Al-Qābisī also urged the teacher to maintain a proper perspective when resorting to corporal punishment: "The teacher is dealing with the honor and bodies of Muslims and should not harm them unfairly and unduly." Also the teacher should avoid hitting the student on the face or head. The punishment should be painful enough to deter the student from repeating the offense in the future but not to an "extent where it causes severe pain or weakening of the body." The teacher was also advised by al-Qābisī not to punish the student when his judgment might be clouded by anger: "This is not a place for anger," he wrote.[40]

Equally destructive to the spirit of a young child is name-calling and other humiliating language. Al-Qābisī, speaking on the psychological effects of language, admonished teachers to avoid degrading language like that of "monster" or "monkey" when referring to students. Such language can wound the child's honor and damage his confidence.[41] Rather, the student should "be praised and honored for any good trait or any good deed which he may show."[42] Thus while these texts clearly valued disciplining children within the context of their education, discipline was not to be done to the extent that it broke the student's spirit, confidence, or self-esteem.

Most medieval educationists considered discipline essential to learning. Many thought it necessary to regulate the student's life in such a way that the body would be hardened and conditioned and thus subservient to the mind and spirit. More generally, writers on educational matters prescribed precise times as the best for students to study. Al-Zarnūjī and

Ibn Jamā^c^ah considered the period before sunrise to be the optimal time for memorization. The middle of day was to be dedicated to writing, while dusk and evening would be best for reading and group study.[43] Most instruction between the students and teacher happened between dawn and noon. While many classical writers warned against luxuries that would lead to laziness, they also suggested that students be allowed physical exercise and play that might "stir up the innate heat, preserve health, banish laziness, drive dullness away, arouse liveliness, and kindle the soul."[44] Continuous study, with no play, was understood to have a diminishing effect on learning and morale.

Higher Education: The Madrasa

Ahmed Shalabi, in his classic study on Islamic education, claimed that the year 1066 CE marked an important turning point in Muslim education. During that year, a new religious institution of higher learning, or "college," called *madrasa,* began to flourish.[45] The exact origins of the madrasa are not definitely known, but historians generally give credit to Niẓām al-Mulk, the vizier of the Seljuk sultan, when he founded the Madrasa al-Niẓamīyya in Baghdad in the eleventh century. The educational model in medieval Islam relied heavily on the intense, personal relationship between the student and the *mu^c^allim.* The seriousness with which a teacher must approach his craft was matched only by the seriousness with which a student must choose his.

With the increasing influx of students, education in the mosque progressively became more disruptive, which "prevented worship from being conducted properly."[46] But it was more than the nuisance of noisy students in the mosques that inspired the madrasa. Most of the existing literature cites three other reasons for its creation. First, the madrasa was used by the Seljuk Sunni regime to stem the advancement of Shi^c^i ideology being propagated by the rival Fatimid caliphs in Egypt.[47] The Sunni-Shi^c^i ideological rivalry in the Islamic world at that time generated numerous institutions, including the great educational institution al-Azhar, for propagating Shi^c^i doctrine. The madrasa was designed to revive, strengthen, and defend Sunni orthodoxy. Second, the creation of the madrasa was to train and produce loyal civil servants to feed the bureaucratic needs of the new Seljuk administration. Many of the students educated in the early madrasas became judges, ministers, administrators, and other bureaucratic functionaries of the state. Third, the madrasa served a socio-political control function by bringing the orthodox religious elite, the ulama, under tight control of the state.[48]

The establishment of the madrasa was significant in that it marked the first efforts of the state to institutionalize and standardize course content so that subjects could be taught uniformly throughout the Caliphate. It also represented a new formal educational opportunity for the post-*kuttāb* level of education.[49] Whereas the *kuttāb* was primarily directed at the youth for imparting elementary education, the madrasa was the first formal institution geared to adult and higher learning. Until the eleventh century, if a student wanted to continue formal studies past the *kuttāb* level, there were very few options available other than private instruction or apprenticeship. Attendance was not compulsory; in fact, access to the madrasa was open to anyone who wanted to attend the lectures. Examinations consisted of reading and memorizing certain written texts, for which the student received an *ijāza* (certificate) from a master, authorizing him to transmit the work to others.[50] The master bestowing the *ijāza* was either the author of the text itself or a person licensed by "the author, directly or indirectly, through a transmitter or chain of transmitters leading back to the author."[51]

The distinction between the mosque and the madrasa is, to some extent, difficult to delineate due to their overlapping roles and close proximity. In principle, however, there was little difference between the madrasa and the mosque. The mosque was a place of both worship and education, often having rooms set aside for teaching purposes. The madrasa functioned as a place of religious instruction, but also served as a place of prayer (*masjid*), sometimes as a gathering site for community prayer on Fridays. R. Hillenbrand notes, "The distinction between the madrasa and the ordinary mosque was very slight. . . . The distinction remained quite an artificial one and this is true also of the distinction between madrasa and the *jāmi*ᶜ."[52] The madrasa, however, was characterized by its specific purpose of teaching the science of Islamic jurisprudence (*fiqh*) according to one or more of the four Sunni schools of law. In fact, the word madrasa derives its meaning from the Arabic root D-R-S (to study). "A *dars,*" says Gary Leiser, "was a lesson in *fiqh; darrasa* and *tadrīs* meant to teach or teaching *fiqh,* a *mudarris* was a person who taught *fiqh,* and a madrasa was a place where *fiqh* was taught."[53] Once it had been converted to a Sunni orthodox institution in the eleventh century, the largest and most enduring madrasa was al-Azhar in Cairo.

In reviewing the existing literature on Islamic education, there appears to be a slight discrepancy as to what, if any, auxiliary subjects were taught within the madrasa outside the scope of religious studies.[54] Most of the literature suggests, however, that curriculum at the madrasa was divided into two classifications: *ᶜulūm ᶜaqlīyya,* or rational sciences, and *ᶜulūm naqlīyya,* or transmitted sciences. The core of the traditional curriculum consisted almost exclusively of subjects relating to the Qurᵓān and Sunna, which included theology (*tawḥid*), Islamic law (*fiqh*), Qurᵓānic exegesis (*tafsīr*), Qurᵓānic reading (*qirāᵓāt*), traditions of the Prophet (*al-ḥadīth*), and the Arabic language (*al-lugha*). The rational sciences included syntax (*nahw*), logic (*manṭiq*), mathematics (*rīyāḍiyyāt* or *hisāb*), medicine (*ṭibb*), philosophy (*falsafa*), and rhetoric (*balāgha*). Rational sciences were further divided into that which was considered good (*mahmūd*) and that which was considered undesirable or excessive (*madmūm*). Rational sciences that were considered *mahmūd* included such subjects as mathematics, logic, and medicine, whereas *madmūm* subjects included philosophy, chemistry, and astrology.[55] Such fields were considered undesirable and even harmful.

By the twelfth century, when Western Europe was groping in intellectual backwardness and stagnation, Islamic scholarship was flourishing with an impressive openness to the rational sciences, art, and even literature. During this period the Islamic world made most of its contributions to the scientific and artistic world. It was the Islamic world, ironically, that preserved much of the knowledge of the Greeks after it had been prohibited by the Christian world. Other outstanding contributions were in areas of chemistry, botany, physics, mineralogy, mathematics, and astronomy, as many Muslim thinkers regarded scientific truths as tools for accessing religious truth.[56] One Islamic scholar summed up the general feeling of the period when he wrote:

> Through knowledge man can get his happiness, which is either acquiring religious and worldly benefits or avoiding religious and worldly harms. To acquire conditions of knowledge, one should not leave any discipline without looking into it, so that he knows its content, purpose, and methodology. Then when he screens all disciplines, or the majority of them, he may choose the one discipline that he finds himself inclined to. . . . He should not like some and hate others, because this is a great mistake. . . . Rather he should derive from every branch of knowledge something that brings him closer to his Lord Almighty and what may benefit him in the next world, and with earning his living (in this world).[57]

Even the orthodox scholar al-Ghazālī recorded in his autobiography his search for "hidden meanings and ultimate goals" in the various branches of learning:

> As for mathematics, it includes arithmetic, geometry, and cosmography, and nothing in them touches on religion neither by way of refutation nor verification; they are verifiable sciences that nobody can reject if he really understands them. . . . Those who think to support Islam by rejecting these sciences, are committing a great crime against religion, for religion does not deal with them neither by way of refutation nor verification, nor is there anything in these sciences that touches on religion.[58]

Ultimately, the original objective of Islamic education was never abandoned, and even al-Ghazālī was cautious about pure reason and always reserved the final authority to divine revelation.[59]

The Decline of the Islamic Intellectual Tradition

Gradually the open and vigorous spirit of enquiry and individual judgment (*ijtihād*), characterized by the era of the Golden Age, gave way to a more insular, unquestioning acceptance (*taqlīd*) of the traditional corpus of authoritative knowledge. By the thirteenth century the ulama had become "self-appointed interpreters and guardians of religious knowledge. . . . Madrasa learning was confined to the transmission of traditions and dogma, and [was] hostile to research and scientific inquiry."[60] The mentality of *taqlīd* dominated all areas, and religious scholars condemned all other forms of inquiry and research.[61] Exemplifying the *taqlīd* mentality, al-Zarnūjī, wrote in the thirteenth century, "Stick to ancient things while avoiding new things," and "Beware of becoming engrossed in those disputes which come about after one has cut loose from the ancient authorities."[62] Much of what was written after the thirteenth century lacked originality, consisting mostly of commentaries on existing canonical works and lacking substantively new ideas. The closing of the Muslim mind affected not only scientific knowledge, but the religious sciences as well.

Some modern scholars of Islamic history also point out a rise of the mystical Sufi tradition, which made matters worse for the intellectual period. "Sufism," according to El-Shayyal, "became . . . a form of hallucination, and people believed greatly in the occult science and superstitions. Lunatics were taken for saints, imbeciles for respected *shaykhs*."[63]

Bayard Dodge commented, "So many Sufi scholars became teachers in the mosques and colleges that Muslim education was permeated with doctrines of mysticism. Progress gave way to fatalism, scientific study to superstition and academic initiative to imitation."[64] This form of mystical inclination developed a spiritual tradition that was egocentric and individualistic. Its prime concern was the state of consciousness of the practitioner, not of broader society (*umma*). The virtuous leaders and great minds who laid down the foundations for what later became Sufi orders did not anticipate that their followers would develop traditions that would run counter to mainstream Islam.[65] With the decline of *ijtihād,* education in the Muslim world diminished to a mere specter of what it once was. In spite of the many scientific advances Muslim scholars had once made, they soon lagged behind advances happening in Europe.

In addition to the ascendancy of *taqlīd* over *ijtihād* and other influences within Islam, the waning of the Islamic intellectual tradition was exacerbated by formidable external forces. Repeated waves of European crusaders (1095–1270 CE) weakened the Islamic empire and strengthened the growing political divisions within it.[66] Other foreign conquests, especially the Mongol invasion of the 13th century, destroyed many Islamic seats of learning, razing entire cities and burning observatories and schools. A veritable holocaust occurred in Baghdad in 1258 when the Mongol armies brutally massacred 800,000 inhabitants and burned library collections of inestimable value. When the Turks conquered much of the empire in the sixteenth century, libraries and madrasas fell into neglect and disrepair as thousands of books were lost, sold, or transferred to other countries. Many of the madrasas came to be used only as mosques.

Such was the general attitude of the Islamic world to education in the closing decades of the 18th century. The lethal combination of *taqlīd* and foreign invasion dimmed Islam's preeminence in both the artistic and scientific worlds. Nevertheless, Islam's contributions to the world cannot be minimized; it kept the intellectual torch burning at a time when Western scholarship was at a level no higher than semi-barbarism.[67] Muslim scholars laid a valuable intellectual base in the sciences, mathematics, and philosophy that provided the sparks for the European Renaissance.[68] "No people in the Middle Ages," remarks Philip Hitti, "contributed to human progress so much as did the Arabs."[69]

Educational Challenges in the Contemporary Period

Despite its brilliant legacy of earlier periods, the Islamic world seemed unable to respond culturally or educationally to the onslaught of Western advancement by the eighteenth century.[70] Contributing to the imbalance of power was the introduction of foreign modes of administration, law, and social institutions by the West. One of the most damaging aspects of European colonialism was the deliberate diminishing of indigenous cultural norms through the influence of secularism. Secularism, with its veneration of human reason over divine revelation and its precepts of the separation of religion and state, is anathema to Islam, which views all aspects of life, spiritual or temporal, as interrelated in a harmonious whole. Western institutions of education, with their pronounced secular-religious dichotomy, were infused into Islamic countries in order to produce functionaries to feed the bureaucratic and administrative needs of the state.

As Islamic countries gradually emerged from their colonial experiences, political leaders sought to modernize their countries along the lines of Western development paradigms. Government bureaucrats and officials were usually modern, educated elites who had grown affluent and comfortable with Western material culture. Most educational policy was based on perpetuating the secularized systems of which they themselves were a product in order to maintain their economic and sociopolitical advantage.[71] What the early educational framers did not fully realize was the extent to which secularized education fundamentally conflicted with Islamic thought and traditional lifestyle.[72] Religious education was to remain a separate and personal responsibility, having no place in public education. If Muslim students desired religious training, they could supplement their existing education with moral instruction in traditional religious schools—the *kuttāb* and madrasa. As a consequence, the two differing educational systems evolved independently with little or no official interface.

The imposition and lingering influence of Western secularist approaches to education have been vehemently criticized by contemporary Islamic scholarship as doing immeasurable damage to the "moral, spiritual and ethical values" of Islamic culture and heritage.[73] Having two parallel streams of secular and religious education has drawn virtually unanimous condemnation in the Islamic world as a hindrance to national development and "the epitome of Muslim decline."[74] Two prominent professors of Islamic education have described the current situation in these terms:

> There are at present two systems of education. The first, traditional, which has confined itself to classical knowledge, has not shown any keen interest in new branches of knowledge that have emerged in the West nor in new methods of acquiring knowledge important in the Western system of education. . . . The second system of education imported into Muslim countries, fully subscribed to and supported by all governmental authorities, is one borrowed from the West. At the head of this system is the modern University which is totally secular and hence nonreligious in its approach to knowledge. Unfortunately, these people educated by this new system of education, known as modern education, are generally unaware of their own tradition and classical heritage. It is also not possible for this group to provide such leadership as we have envisaged.[75]

Many Islamic educators have pointed inwards to the umma as the source of continued cultural dualism found in their countries. They level criticism at Muslim intellectual and political leaders who have neglected, intentionally or otherwise, the cultural problems associated with the dualism found in most educational systems in the Islamic world. The current leadership, noted Ibrahim Sulaiman, "continue[s] to hold the reins of government in all these [Islamic] countries in cynical and damaging succession," creating a "neo-colonial status" legacy which the umma cannot escape.[76] Al-Attas commented:

> [The] problems arising out of secularization, though not the same as those confronting the West, have certainly caused confusion in our midst. It is most significant to us that these problems are caused due to the introduction of Western ways of thinking and judging and believing emulated by some Muslim scholars and intellectuals who have been unduly influenced by the West and overawed by its scientific and technological achievements.[77]

The Islamic disposition of the general public and the Western predilection of its political and intellectual elites contribute to a state of socio-psychological dissonance. According to some, the Islamic leadership not only lacks the vision necessary for meaningful change but also perpetuates an educational system that produces students who are "deluded hybrids."[78] On one level, students of these systems remain Islamic in performing the outward duties of Muslims (i.e., prayer, mosque attendance, etc.), but they retain the trappings of Western thought, dress, and language.

Criticisms of this ilk, along with the general rise in Islamic consciousness, have forced many Islamic leaders to take a different strategy towards educational policy. The "Islamic solution" has gained greater popular and emotional appeal as disillusionment with Western-inspired socio-political systems has increased. Islam's renewed vigor has encouraged the return of many Islamic countries to traditional religious values in education. Greater attention, therefore, is being given to Islam in contemporary education policy out of sheer political expediency. Policy makers in many Islamic countries pay at least rhetorical homage to religious education in the public sector in order to alleviate extremist demands. The resultant effect has been various permutations and often superficial combinations of Islamic and Western education systems. "Despite a widespread and sometimes deep consciousness of the dichotomy of education," wrote Fazlur Rahman, "all efforts at a genuine integration have been largely unfruitful."[79] How to solve the issues related to modernity and development while at the same time maintaining the cultural and religious integrity of the umma, remains an elusive, monumental task. On a pragmatic level, modern Islamic nations still struggle to meet the scientific and technological changes demanded by the modern period. Modernity and development, in the minds of many Muslim policy makers, are still closely linked to Western modes of doing things. Herein lies the overwhelming challenge of education in the Muslim world: creating a system which gives adequate attention to religious instruction to maintain cultural values, while at the same time providing education and skills to students that would enable them to succeed individually and help meet the needs of their developing and modernizing countries. A system espousing too many Western secular values might introduce elements alien to the spirit of Islam and spark further religious opposition from Islamists. On the other hand, traditional Islamic education fails to adequately prepare students for the modern technological world. The quest is obviously modernization without Westernization, and Islamization without extremism—a complex and delicate balance.

Islamists throughout the Islamic world are calling for revolutionary educational reform to rejuvenate their societies. The governing bodies of these countries interpret educational reform along a variant Western-secular conception. Understanding Islamic educational theory will help us understand the Islamist side of the debate and appreciate the extent to which its adherents see the Islamization of education as a crucial factor in eradicating the dichotomized Western-secular influences eroding their culture.

Aims and Objectives of Islamic Education

Three terms in Arabic are used for education, differing in connotation but together embodying the various dimensions of the educational process as perceived by Islam. The most widely used word for education in a formal sense is the word *tāᶜlīm,* stemming from the root *ᶜalima* (to know, to be aware, to perceive, to learn) and relating to knowledge being sought or imparted through instruction and teaching. *Tarbīyya,* coming from the root *raba* (to increase, to grow, to rear), implies a state of spiritual and ethical nurturing in accordance with the will of the Lord (*al-Rabb*). *Tādīb* comes from the root *āduba* (to be cultured, refined, well-mannered), suggesting the social dimensions of a person's development of sound behavior. What is meant by "sound" requires a deeper understanding of the Islamic conception of the human being. Recommendations made by scholars at the First World Conference on Muslim Education comprised this definition:

> Man according to Islam is composed of soul and body. . . . He is at once spirit and matter. . . . Man possesses spiritual and rational organs of cognition such as the heart (*qalb*) and the intellect (*ᶜaql*) and faculties relating to physical, intellectual and spiritual vision, experience and consciousness. . . . His most important gift is knowledge which pertains to spiritual as well as intelligible and tangible realities.[80]

Education, as envisioned in the context of Islam, claims to be a process which involves the complete person, including the rational, spiritual, and social dimensions. As discussed previously, Islam provides a complete code of life which emphasizes a balanced, harmonious worldview, represented by the concept of *tawḥid.* The comprehensive and integrated approach to education in Islam strives to produce a well-rounded person, aiming at the "balanced growth of the total personality . . . through training Man's spirit, intellect, rational self, feelings and bodily senses . . . such that faith is infused into the whole of his personality."[81] In Islamic educational theory, the general objective of gaining knowledge is the actualization and perfection of all dimensions of the human being. Each individual is intended to act as the vicegerent of God (*khalīfat Allah*), who, in order to fulfill this holy obligation, must submit completely to

Allah.[82] Indeed, it is obedience which is the summum bonum of existence, as illustrated in the Qurʾānic verse: "I have not created *jinn* and mankind except to serve Me."[83] Perfection then, which is the ultimate aim of Islamic education, can be achieved only through a person's obedience to God.[84] While education does prepare humankind for happiness in this life, "its ultimate goal is the abode of permanence and all education points to the permanent world of eternity (*al-akhira*)."[85] In Islam, education is, or at least should be, inseparable from spiritual life.

The perfect model for humankind from an Islamic perspective was in the education of the Prophet Muḥammad through God's final message, the Qurʾān. The Qurʾān and the Sunna of the Prophet are the immutable sources for all aspects of both temporal and spiritual life. The Qurʾān is, as the founder of the International Federation of Muslim and Arabic Schools wrote, "the perennial foundation for Islamic systems of legislation and of social and economic organization. It is last but not least the basis of both moral and general education . . . and the core, pivot and gateway of learning."[86] As long as the Qurʾān remains central to the educational curriculum, there is "a guarantee that the Muslim umma will keep its integrity and authentic character."[87] The Prophet was the highest and most perfect example of *al-insān al-kamil,* and the function of education, as al-Attas remarks, "is to produce men and women resembling him as near as possible."[88] The teachings of the Qurʾān and the example of the Prophet constitute the spiritual pattern of early Islamic education, which resulted in the blossoming prosperity of Islamic civilization. Under this assumption, the current crisis in Islam and the erosion of the spiritual and moral foundations in the Islamic world may be considered the result of the umma straying from God's intended course and "from the program of [true] Islamic education."[89]

If the goal of education is the balanced growth of the human character, the heart (*qalb*), which is the seat of the spirit and affection, conscience, feelings, and intuition, should receive the same attention as the intellect (*ʿaql*), reason (*manṭiq*), and man's other rational dimensions. To ascertain truth by complete reliance on reason alone is restrictive, since spiritual and temporal reality are two sides of the same sphere. Indeed, the highest form of knowledge is the perception (*idrāk*) of God, which cannot be realized in any other way except through faith (*īmān*).[90] Revelatory knowledge is the most elevated form of knowledge not only because it relates to God and leads to an understanding of His attributes, but also because it provides an essential foundation for all other forms of knowledge.[91] To favor reason at the expense of spirituality hampers balanced growth. Exclusive training of the intellect, for example, is inadequate in developing and refining elements of love, kindness, compassion, and selflessness, which have an altogether spiritual ambiance and can only be appealed to by processes of spiritual training.[92] Separating the spiritual development of the human being from the rational, temporal aspects of the same person, said one prominent Islamic educationalist, "is the main cause for the disintegration of the human personality."[93]

Education then becomes a twofold process—acquiring intellectual knowledge (through the application of reason and logic) and developing spiritual knowledge (derived from divine revelation and spiritual experience). According to the educational worldview of Islam, provision must be made equally for both. Acquiring knowledge in Islam is not meant as an end unto itself, but only as a means to stimulate a more elevated moral and spiritual consciousness leading to faith and righteous action.

Inadequacies of Western Secular Education from an Islamic Perspective

According to many Muslim thinkers, the philosophical shortcoming of most modern systems of education in the Islamic world is that they do not reflect the fundamental aims and objectives of Islamic education. Contemporary policy makers are products of the Western social and cultural milieu, adopting Western curriculum development modes, administrative structures, and pedagogical tools. Shahed Ali comments: "Our intellect is steeped in the norms and forms evolved by the West. Systems of education in our schools, colleges and universities are mostly imported; these are not our own systems; they are fashioned after the outlook and model of Western educational systems."[94]

Because such systems do not represent the religious values implicit in Islam, they fall short in educating the whole person. Modern Western education and research are insufficient on their own in Islamic society because they "have been totally cut off from the spiritual roots."[95] The source of any system of education, according to Ali, "should be traced to its philosophy of life, and a system of education is organically connected with the ethical and moral values that spring from that philosophy. . . . When such a short-sighted policy prevails, social cohesion and collective initiative for the well-being of the community becomes a far cry."[96]

Muslim countries, according to Islamic educational theory, cannot modernize their educational systems along Western lines without seriously compromising their essential Islamic character. Western philosophies of education are fundamentally at variance with Islam because of the absence of properly integrated religion in Westernized curriculum. Scathing attacks on the dissonant influences of Western educational theory on the Muslim world have factored prominently in the literature on Islamic educational theory. Most Muslim theorists object to the Western notions of liberalism and secularism, which aim at delivering man "first from the religious and then the metaphysical control over his reason and his language."[97] It is, as Ali suggested,

> the loosing of the world from religious and quasi-religious understandings of itself, the dispelling of all closed world views, the breaking of all supernatural myths and sacred symbols. . . . [It is] man turning his attention away from worlds beyond and towards this world and this time.[98]

Thus, secular approaches to education are not only fundamentally different from an Islamic approach, they are plainly antagonistic.[99]

Western modern education relies primarily on the rational faculties for the discovery of truth. Reality is restricted to sensual experience, scientific procedure, or a process of logic. Secular education strives principally for "critical rationality," which is the "ability to critically evaluate evidence and forms of justification in order to arrive at rational acceptable conclusions."[100] Islam is not unique in claiming that this represents only one level of reality. Secular scientists and Christians in the West, for example, have been debating for centuries whether spiritual experience is a legitimate means for determining truth. In Islam, revelatory experience, intuition, and faith are not only valid but absolutely necessary in ascertaining the highest of truths—the nature of God. The Qurʾān speaks of how all natural phenomena are manifestations of God: "Surely in the creation of the heavens and earth . . . there are signs for a people having understanding."[101] Al-Attas, in particular, has expounded on the weaknesses of the secular scientific method, claiming that its preoccupation with natural phenomena unnecessarily prevents the discovery of whole truth. Fixating only on observable objects and events, argues al-Attas, limits truth because such objects and events "point to themselves as the sole reality and not to any other Reality."[102] While secular science tries to interpret reality with only the empirically verifiable, in Islam this conception of reality is defective because direct observation is no more than "outward appearances, perceived through human senses," which by the standards of experimental science are innately limited.[103] Therefore, human senses can perceive *evidences* of truth, but not the truth itself. El-Nejjar argued:

> Man cannot arrive at conclusive answers . . . because of the fact that man's observations and measurements are limited to the outer appearances of things in this universe, masked by the limitations of his senses and the relativity of his space and time. . . . To accept a measure as correct does not necessitate that we should accept what it yields. . . . Pure and experimental sciences are nothing more than outward appearances of truth as man can see it from his position in the universe and in the very limited time allocated to him, and not the truth itself.[104]

Islam does not reject science and technology per se, but rather the pervading Western philosophy of secular science. After all, at the height of its glory, the Islamic empire was considered the vanguard of science and technology. However, science and technology as presented today bear the distinct mark of a Western social and intellectual milieu, causing some Muslims to mistrust them. Badawi explains:

> This suspicion is well founded. Western science, it must be remembered, has, for historical reasons, developed in an atmosphere of hostility towards religion and has acquired a negative attitude towards religion and has in the process acquired a negative attitude towards all non-empirical aspects of belief. The basic assumptions of Western science are in reality a greater menace to Islamic culture than any hostile work by Orientalists. . . . Modern education is by definition that type of education inspired by the West. . . . The onslaught of science upon our basic belief and values is indirect and therefore too obscure for the ordinary person or even the educated to measure and rebut.[105]

Sayyid Quṭb, an influential figure in contemporary Islamic thought, argued that science itself should not be rejected but rather that its acceptance should be qualified. "Islam," he said, "is in harmony with the laws of the universe and the nature of existence" (*fiṭrat al-wūjūd*).[106] Science, pure and applied, can be accepted on the condition that it does not exceed its limits by trying philosophically to interpret what exists.[107] Quṭb argued that "man neither has knowledge, nor the ability to know the entire order of this universe," and hence, neither empiricism nor rationalism is a satisfactory instrument for the expression of complete truth[108] Islam emphasizes the concept of *tawhīd,* and as Quṭb stated, "The universe is a unity composed of [the] visible and the invisible unknown. Life is a unity of material and spiritual energies whose separation results in imbalance or disturbance."[109] Consequently, any system or philosophy that does not embrace the unity of the universe is incomplete and fragmentary.

The Western liberal perspective of education further conflicts with Islamic educational theory in its heavy emphasis on relativism. The tendency in liberal theory is to accept a pluralism of personal private beliefs, with the notion that all beliefs are equally justifiable.[110] Thus liberal educators avoid claims of absolute truth at almost every level. In a recent document on how to handle controversial subject material in British schools, the inspectors stated, "It can be very helpful for pupils to know their teachers' views, provided these are offered as one among many possible perspectives on an issue with no more weight or 'truth' than any other."[111]

The basic assumption in this relativist approach is that there are no absolutes and all truth is subjective. Islam considers this sort of relativism overtly damaging. If all positions are relative and all opinions are considered equally valid, on what basis can a society build a reliable and stable civilization? What will inevitably occur is that the "truth" of "the one who shouts loudest and longest will prevail."[112]

Islam claims to embody absolute truth, affirming that there is an innate universal truth that each person may access through the perfect essence which is borne within the depth of each being.[113] While Islam shows tolerance for differing moral, aesthetic, and cultural perspectives, "it never considers all views to be equally valid."[114] Secular values are ever changing and tentative. For a completely balanced development of a child's moral, spiritual and intellectual dimensions and for a society to be built on a foundation of righteousness and justice, "basic universal unchanging norms are necessary."[115]

Secular education is characterized by a predominant stress on individualism and on the freedom of individual choice. "What [secular education] liberates the person from," commented Charles Bailey, a noted liberal theorist, "is the limitations of the present and the particular."[116] According to most liberal theorists there are no absolute authorities in matters of morality or in ethical or effective living, and therefore education must avoid authoritarian positions.[117] Bailey explained that a liberally educated person is released from the restrictions imposed by the limited and specific circumstances in which he or she is born. Liberal education, according to Bailey, allows for

> intellectual and moral autonomy, the capacity to become a free chooser of what is to be believed and what is to be done, a free chooser of beliefs and actions—in a word, a free moral agent, the kind of entity a fully-fledged human being is supposed to be and which all too few are![118]

Islam, in contrast, puts much less stress on individual autonomy than it does on the consensus (*ijmāᶜ*) of the umma and on respect for the social contexts and traditions in which an individual originates. Education, including the acquisition of knowledge, then, is good only if it serves to engender virtue in the individual and to elevate the whole community. Islamic educators criticize the "freedom" implicit in liberal theory because, as Ashraf commented:

> By denying faith and by creating a conglomeration of multiple choices . . . with no norm to be guided by, except reason or social values or . . . fashions, the secularist educationalists create an unsettled situation for children. Doubts and skepticism are preferred and even encouraged. As a result children have no norm of good and evil, right and wrong, justice and injustice, truth and falsehood.[119]

Western liberal education encourages people to align their religious beliefs with rational principles, helping children to become free agents independent of the pressures of socialization.[120] Without this ability to make independent rational choices, people then tend toward "blind reliance on authority.[121] In Islam, however, the position is that encouraging students to question their moral beliefs may merely cause them to be confused and "unmeshed with society as it is."[122]

The unhealthy material fixation of the West, according to Islamist theorists, can be directly related to this sort of individualism. Shahed Ali stated that Western forms of education "create a capital 'I' in the psychology of man to the exclusion of the rest of the world." "Self before everything" is the only truth, disguised as "enlightened self-interest."[123] Ali claimed that if education becomes secular or irreligious, material progress and prosperity become the end all and be all of life.[124] And if an education system focuses on material pursuits to the exclusion of spiritual and moral training, it will fail to "nourish the human soul . . . [to] enrich human life with noble virtues of love, service and sacrifice."[125] Strengthening spiritual faith and virtue is imperative in any education system which seeks to possess an Islamic character.

Edition, Translation, and Acknowledgments

This anthology of readings on the topic of Islamic educational theory is the result of several years of collaboration with various Muslim and non-Muslim educationists. The editors are particularly grateful for the cooperation and insight of colleagues from the International Institute of Islamic Thought in Herndon, Virginia. Our goal was to consolidate in a single volume a collection of formative and enduring readings on the subject of Islamic educational theory to acquaint students and others with some of the most profound primary sources on the subject. The task of identifying and ultimately selecting a final list of formative works is problematic not only by its subjectivity, but also by the vast amount of material from which to choose. Given constraints of space, it is inevitable that some worthwhile works and key thinkers have been excluded. While the editors may expect to be criticized for the exclusions, it should be considerably more difficult to challenge the inclusions. Our general operating guidelines for inclusion were the power of the ideas developed by each scholar, the breadth of the overall contribution and, of course, the judgment of history. Each included work is considered something of a classic in the influence it has had for other scholars. The hundreds of citations of these works in the footnotes of other studies indicate the extent of their influence. One criterion of this project was that the selected works not have wide availability to English speaking audiences. Another criterion was that the work originate between the eighth and fourteenth centuries, as the editors wanted to focus exclusively on medieval scholarly contributions related to education. Perhaps a second volume employing more contemporary materials will be compiled at a later date.

Once the list had been distilled through scholarly consensus, many of these works needed translation. Since translating medieval philosophical texts in Arabic is not an easy undertaking, the editors preferred that the project be a collaborative effort using more than one translator. Helmut Ritter remarked, "someone who translates by himself falls all too easily into the unavoidable vicious traps waiting for translators from this harmfully deceptive language. The collaboration of two or more scholars gives at least some protection against getting lost in the Arabian Desert."[126] Thus we gratefully acknowledge the superb translating skills of Michael

Fishbein, Ruediger Arnzen, and David C. Reisman. For other selections we have chosen to obtain copyright permission to republish existing translations. Constantine K. Zurayk, G. E. von Grunebaum, and Franz Rosenthal are all widely recognized for their outstanding translations. Thus the editors felt it unnecessary to commission new translations.

We also want to acknowledge and thank Brigham Young University, Utah Valley University, and the Abu Dhabi Women's College for their moral and financial support of this project. The dedicated staff of the Middle Eastern Texts Initiative must also be recognized for their dogged persistence and professionalism. In particular, we want to whole heartedly thank Dr. Morgan Davis for his patient and methodical administration of the project.

Islamic educational thought and practice have never been limited to formal schooling. The selected reading will show that education has been considered a continuous lifetime process of physical, intellectual, and psychological development of individuals. In addition to shaping individuals, Islamic education is concerned with attitudes and behaviors of the general public. In Islamic thought, education has consistently been considered in a broader context than the aspect of schooling, and so a "philosophy of education" is generally regarded as continuous with concerns about child rearing generally, with issues of intellectual development not regarded as separate from matters of spiritual, moral, or cultural development.

Finally, this collection will satisfy, hopefully, at least in part, what Charles Stanton has hoped for:

> to unveil a part of that hidden past by celebrating the Classical Age of Islam—a brilliant chapter in the intellectual history of the human race. It has introduced the main actors in that drama and their distinguished contributions in our understanding the human condition and the physical world—men and achievements long unrecognized in Western experience.[127]

◆

The Authors

Ibn Saḥnūn

Abū ᶜAbdallāh Muḥammad ibn Saḥnūn ibn Ḥabīb al-Tanūkhī was born in Qayrawān (202/817), situated in present-day Tunisia. He was educated under his father, Abū Saᶜīd ᶜAbd al-Salām Ibn Saᶜīd al-Tanūkhī, best known as Saḥnūn (either on account of his shrewdness, or derived from the name of a bird renowned for its sharp vision), who was an illustrious scholar of *Mālikī* jurisprudence (*fiqh*). Muḥammad Ibn Saḥnūn exhibited great aptitude for learning at an early age. According to tradition, his father sent him to a local *kuttāb* with a note to the teacher requesting that his son be taught in the following manner:

> Teach my son by praising him and speaking to him softly. He is not the type of person that should be trained under punishment or abuse. I hope that my son will be unique and rare among his companions and peers. I want him to emulate me in the seeking of knowledge.[128]

Ibn Saḥnūn had the benefit of receiving instruction from a variety of scholars in the region before traveling east to receive additional learning from scholars in the Hijāz, Egypt, and Tripoli. He returned to Qayrawān where he succeeded to his father's position as the head of the incipient *Mālikī* school, upon the latter's death. Al-Khashnī described Ibn Saḥnūn as one of the most knowledgeable and learned scholars within the *Mālikī* tradition, a gifted historian and orator.[129] His scholarly production was prolific, including a large number of books and other writings covering over 180 subjects, with titles in over 40 disciplines.

Ibn Saḥnūn also contributed extensively on the subject of education, particularly with his foundational work entitled *Kitāb adab al-muᶜallimīn* (The Book of Rules of Conduct for Teachers). This book has a wide reputation among educators, perhaps because it was the first specialized book in Arabic in the field of teaching theory and learning, marking the establishment of education as an independent field of knowledge and practice. Ibn Saḥnūn focused his theoretical models on problems and questions existing in the *kuttāb* and on issues that were of concern to parents, scholars, community leaders, and concerned educators of his time, including student discipline, classroom management, educational leadership, teacher compensation, gift giving, and the limits of corporal punishment. Ibn Saḥnūn's major epistemological focus was teacher-centric: academic qualifications, personal behavior, curriculum development, and teaching pedagogy. His original approach to organizing and classifying a wide variety of educational issues qualified him as a pioneer of Islamic educational theory and inspired later authors addressing educational matters, like al-Qābisī and al-Zarnūjī, to quote him at length.

Apart from his activities in forging new ground in educational theory, Ibn Saḥnūn was a tireless promoter of the still nascent *Malīkism* of his time. Biographers record that, like his father before him, he died in defense of the Tunisian Sahel against incursions of pirates in 870.[130]

Ikhwān al-Ṣafā᾽

The Ikhwān al-Ṣafā᾽, or Brethren of Purity, were a group of philosophers who lived in the Lower Mesopotamia river port of Baṣra during the fourth century of the Hijra/tenth century of the common era. Their exact identity remains obscure, but they are thought to have been high-ranking scholars in the Shiʿa community with some connections to the Ismāʿīlī movement. Sources differ as to members' individual names, and their history remains in dispute. Perhaps this demonstrates the secrecy they sought for themselves.

The *Rasā᾽il Ikhwān al-Ṣafā᾽* is considered to be one of the great works of Arabic literature, and the Ikhwān al-Ṣafā᾽ are as well known to Arab intellectuals as Aquinas, St. Augustine, and Rousseau are to well-educated Americans or Europeans. The *Rasā᾽il* is a unique encyclopedic work consisting of approximately fifty-two epistles on a wide range of subjects, some of which are likely unacceptable to orthodox *Sunnī* Islam.

The primary aim of the work was to help Muslims secure human happiness in this life by perfecting the body, and to save the soul by perfecting the spirit. The epistles were designed to instruct the "brothers" or disciples in various dimensions of human wisdom, each commencing with the characteristic phrase: "Know, O Brother." The *Rasā᾽il* has four main sections, following a gradual progression from the concrete to the abstract: mathematical sciences (fourteen epistles), natural sciences (seventeen epistles), psychological and rational sciences (ten epistles), and theological sciences (eleven epistles). The *Ikhwān* were thoroughly dedicated to the doctrine of purity, which can, in the Brethren's view, be attained through asceticism, self-discipline, and virtuous living. The object of their work was to establish a "ship of salvation" to help humankind negotiate and survive the earthly sea of the material world to eventually attain the heavenly abode.

The seventh epistle, "On the Scientific Arts and Their Aim," is imbedded in what the *Ikhwān* called the *propaedeutic* (disciplinary or training) sciences, which are established primarily "for the necessities of livelihood and the well-being of the worldly life."[131] The seventh epistle is significant to this study in that it provides a system of scientific classification and outlines the hierarchal nature of knowledge. The *Ikhwān* wrote, "Those who seek knowledge and search for the real nature of things should first know what knowledge is, what the object of knowledge is, and how many methods of asking questions there are."[132]

The seventh epistle outlined general classifications of knowledge needed by the student to "improve the substance of the soul" through the proper sequencing of *adab*, or education.[133] It outlined three genres of sciences in which the student should be engaged: first, the *propaedeutical sciences*, which include such categories as reading, writing, language, and poetry; second, the *religious and conventional sciences*, with categories such as revelation, interpretation, and jurisprudence; and third, the *philosophical sciences*, with categories such as mathematics, logic, and metaphysics. Each of these categories within the genre were further delineated into subcategories.

The *Rasāʾil* occupies a place of the first order in Arabic literature, and the seventh epistle ranks among its most outstanding contributions to Islamic education.

al-Qābisī

Abū al-Haṣan Alī ibn Khalaf al-Qābisī was born in Qayrawān in 324/1012. In some ways his life and career parallel that of Ibn Saḥnūn. His last name was derived from his uncle, whose turban resembled that of the people of Qābis, a region in the *Maghrib*, west of Tripoli. When he traveled to the east to perform pilgrimage, he studied with various scholars in Mecca and Cairo, settling in Egypt for five years. He then returned to Qayrawān, where he began writing and teaching and became a prominent *Mālikī* scholar in *fiqh*, hadith, and Qurʾān. His written legacy is noteworthy, as he wrote more than 10 books.

In *Al-risāla al-mufaṣṣila,* al-Qābisī was heavily influenced by the educational writings of Ibn Saḥnūn and quoted him often. Today the work is considered by many to be the most complete work on education up to that point, after Ibn Saḥnūn's *Kitāb adab al-muᶜallimīn.*

The book was written primarily to deal with matters arising from the fact that teaching was a profession based on a contract, with defined conditions, between the teacher, parents, and student. Al-Qābisī's approach was juridical, adopting Malikī *fiqh* in outlining various provisions and laws on what a teacher could or could not do. The treatise was divided into three sections, each outlining various views of teacher-student-parent relationships. This book was written as a response to detailed questions indicative of issues and circumstances of the period. Al-Qābisī clearly emphasized education as a right for every child and a duty for society. If parents were not able to provide the appropriate education or fees for their children, the responsibility then fell to the state using *bayt al-māl* (public resources). This ruling was derived from the fact that education is compulsory in Islam, to teach Muslims how to better perform their religious obligations.

It is obvious that al-Qābisī was not comfortable with the educational practices of his time. He maintained that most teachers did not properly fulfill their duties when teaching young students. Accordingly, al-Qābisī admonished the teacher to stand "in *loco parentis* toward them," and should keep in mind that they were "dealing with the dignity and person of Muslims."[134]

Miskawayh

Abū ᶜAli Aḥmad ibn Muḥammad ibn Yaᶜkūb Miskawayh was born in 320/932 in al-Rayy near present-day Tehran. By the time Miskawayh was nineteen or twenty, he was serving as the secretary and librarian to various Būyid viziers of the Abbasid Empire, a testimony to his innate competence and intelligence. Miskawayh was an assiduous writer who showed scholarly interest in the varied branches of the sciences and human knowledge. It is evident that he was thoroughly in contact with the culture of his age, a period that is regarded as one of the most luminous of Islamic civilization. During this time, Muslims excelled in nearly all known branches of learning and exerted great effort in translating works from other languages into Arabic. Centers known as *Dar al-ᶜIlm* (House of Learning) and *Dar al-Hikma* (House of Wisdom) were established in urban centers such as Cordoba, Cairo, and Baghdad, where scholars gathered for academic discourse and study. For a time, Miskawayh lived and worked in Baghdad, where he became a reputable philosopher and historian. He eventually returned to Isfahān, where he died after having lived to be almost one hundred years old.

Commenting on Miskawayh's acumen as both philosopher and historian, Muhammad Arkoun writes of him as "one of the very rare intellectuals in the Arabic language who is known to have practiced the two disciplines with competence and with a resolve to embark on the most complex ethico-political reflection."[135] Like other Muslim intellectuals, Miskawayh was very much attracted to Greek philosophy, particularly to the works of Plato and Aristotle. He studied and referred to a wide variety of other non-Muslim scholars, including Porphyry, Pythagorus, Galen, Alexander of Aphrodisias, and Bryson. As a philosopher he distinguished himself particularly in the field of ethics, writing *Tahdhīb al-akhlāq wa-taṭhīr al-aᶜrāq,* which some consider "the most important book on philosophical ethics in Muslim literature."[136] The *Tahdhīb al-akhlāq* (Refinement of Character) was very influential among later Muslim thinkers, such as al-Ghāzālī (d. 1111), al-Ṭūsī (d. 1274), and al-Dawwānī (d. 1502). It was written as an ethical compendium consisting of six discourses: the Principles of Ethics, Refinement of Character, the Good and Its Division, Justice, Love and Friendship, and the Health of the Soul.

The second discourse of the *Tahdhīb,* "Refinement of Character," discusses the development of character and humanity, and expounds on the method of instructing youth—particularly boys. It is, in the words of Miskawayh, largely "copied from the work of Bryson," the obscure neo-Pythagorean philosopher of the first century CE.[137] Miskawayh's primary concern, however, was for the moral and cultural development of the child's soul while yet malleable and receptive to learning. He considered intervention in the early stages of human maturation to be essential so that the child might break free of the proclivities of the natural man: laziness, ignorance, insolence, and idleness.

Miskawayh prescribed an environment that maximized learning. The student should be praised for the good that is done, encouraged to rise above base desires, trained to admire virtuous characteristics, encouraged to be abstinent, and punished only when absolutely necessary. Miskawayh set forth various rules of etiquette for proper social interaction: to avoid evil-speaking and to be respectful of parents and elders. Miskawayh's intended audience was the children of the privileged and affluent, who valued refinement of character and good behavior over specific training in various disciplines of knowledge or crafts. He emphasized proper techniques of dining, drinking, dressing, sleeping, attaining physical fitness, and appreciating poetry and other fine arts. The basic aim of education, according to Miskawayh, was the refinement and purification of the soul, with the final aim of attaining happiness by adopting Godly attributes in this life and a hope of perfect eternal happiness.

This work differs from other works discussed in this volume in that it is more epistemologically student-centric. It discusses the training of youth while providing scant detail as to the content and curriculum of this training. Likewise, Miskawayh referred very seldom to the obligations and duties of the teacher, a difference from other authors who sought to describe the normative dimensions of the student-instructor dynamic.

al-Ghazālī

Abū Ḥāmid Muḥammad ibn Muḥammad al-Ṭūsī al-Ghazālī was born in Ṭus in Persia in 450/1058. He and his brother were orphaned at an early age but were provided the very best education available. His education began in Ṭus, but he traveled to Nīshāpūr to be trained by one of the greatest systematic theologians of the time, al-Juwaynī, Imām al-Ḥaramayn (or the Imam of the two sanctuaries, Mecca and Medina). While only 33 years old, al-Ghazālī was offered the leading teaching position at the most noted theological institute in Baghdad—perhaps in all the Islamic world at the time—the Naẓāmīyya.

Over the next four years he became one of the most prominent scholars and teachers in the Islamic world, lecturing to audiences numbering in the hundreds. Al-Ghazālī authored many foundational scholarly works, including his celebrated *Tahāfut al-falāsifa* (The Incoherence of the Philosophers), in which, by the use of logic, he directly refuted the philosophy of Neoplatonism and Arab Aristotelianism as being incompatible with Sunni Islam. Indeed, al-Ghazālī eventually considered all rational theology to be hazardous and incompatible with genuine religious faith.

At the height of his professional career as a professor, al-Ghazālī suffered a profound spiritual crisis, realizing that the worldly recognition he was receiving as a distinguished scholar was engendering vain material attachments and conceit that treacherously detracted from his spiritual welfare. He gave up his satisfying intellectual position at the Naẓāmīyya and turned to a life of asceticism by immersing himself in

Ṣūfism. He spent the next eleven years living and writing in Damascus, Jerusalem, and the Hijāz. It was during this period that he composed his magnum opus, *Iḥyāʾ ʿulūm al-dīn* (The Revival of the Religious Sciences), an extensive work of four volumes. Eventually al-Ghazālī returned to his native Persia and died in 505/1111 after a long life of wisdom seeking. His elevated and distinguished life as a theologian, mystic, and religious reformer has led some to describe him as the "second greatest Muslim after Muhammad."[138]

Among the topics he addressed in the *Iḥyāʾ*, al-Ghazālī focused on a variety of issues relating to character formation and the virtues of educating the young. Of particular note is his twenty-second book in the *Iḥyāʾ*, *Kitāb riyāḍat al-nafs wa-tahdhīb al-akhlāq wa-muʿālajat amrāḍ al-qalb* (Disciplining the Soul, Refining the Character, and Curing the Sicknesses of the Heart). But perhaps al-Ghazālī's finest composition on the moral and practical foundations of education is found in his essay *Ayyuha al-walad* (O Son!).

Al-Ghazālī's views on education were characterized by a deep spiritual and moral concern for children. In essence, al-Ghazālī believed that knowledge can be acquired in two ways: human reason and "light from God." In a proper Islamic educational environment, a balance must be found between the two. His educational philosophy emphasized the dignity of students, encouraging teachers to have compassion and to treat students with the same kindnesses with which they would treat their own children. While he did not tolerate misconduct in students, he cautioned against strong corporal punishment and abuse. The material the students learned should be commensurate with their particular ability. However, the "sum total of learning," according to al-Ghazālī, was "to know the meaning of obedience and service to God."[139]

While the search for knowledge is commendable, it was to be tempered by humility and foster spiritual development as its ultimate end. "Look into a field of learning," he wrote, "it should be something that improves your heart and cleanses your soul." He asked his students to consider what subjects might be important if they only had one week to live. He wrote, "You certainly would not concern yourself with law, and legal disputation and theory; . . . rather, you would pay attention to your heart and learn characteristics of your soul and relinquish your ties to the world and purify your soul of its reprehensible traits and turn your attention to the love of God."[140] Al-Ghazālī's philosophy of education can be noted for its balance between the rational faculties and authentic religious life. "You may be certain," he wrote, "that knowledge alone will not stand you in good stead."[141]

Al-Ghazālī's legacy is profound on many fronts, but has been particularly foundational in Islamic educational thought. Tibawi wrote, "Classical Arabic literature contains no theory of education more authoritative, systematic and comprehensive than had been bequeathed by al-Ghazālī."[142]

al-Zarnūjī

Burhān al-Din al-Zarnūjī was a scholar whose origins, education and travels have remained relatively obscure. Even the date of his birth and death are not precisely documented. There is general speculation that he was born in 539/1144 in the town of Zarnūj, a well-known town beyond the river Oxus in what is now Turkistan. Particulars about his early life are meager, but it is recorded that he studied under several illustrious Hanafī scholars, including Shaykh ᶜAlī ibn Abī Bakr al-Marghiyanī al-Rushdanī from Samarqand. Al-Zarnūjī is thought to have died in Bukhara around 620/1223.

Al-Zarnūjī is best known for writing *Taᶜlīm al-mutaᶜallim ṭarīq al-taᶜalum* (Instruction of the Student: The Method of Learning), a book with wide circulation among Muslim educators. The book has remained popular because it identified critical factors that aid or hinder the learning process from the social cognitive perspective of the learner, such as the influence of environment, school, home, peers, and instructors. Al-Zarnūjī was consistent with previous Islamic scholars in viewing the purpose of education as a means "to strive for the good will of God, . . . the removal of ignorance, . . . and the survival of Islam."[143] Thus, acquiring knowledge was viewed not as a mundane duty but as a religious obligation. Al-Zarnūjī was an avid "collector and synthesizer of the ideas of scholars and sages who had preceded him," and he quoted liberally from poetry and other literature on the value of learning.[144] He wrote that a Muslim's education should provide students with the basic skills necessary to prepare them to discharge not only their religious duties but also the duties of responsible independence: personal hygiene, awareness of civil law, and provision for and protection of family.[145]

Al-Zarnūjī considered various characteristics necessary for successful learning: respect for authority, mental alertness, diligence, and perseverance. He wrote, "All glory is attained by exertion, not by luck. Is luck without exertion of any glory?"[146] He claimed the psycho-emotional state of the student to be critical to effective learning, along with socio-environmental factors. Al-Zarnūjī expended great effort delineating the optimum conditions for learning: when to sleep, what to eat, what times should be best for memory retention, and so on. Bad habits and lack of personal hygiene he found to be distracting to meaningful study, as well as the negative effects of fatigue. Judicious time management, proper organization, and thorough selection of subject matter were also critical variables in successful scholarship.

Selecting the right teacher he claimed to be of utmost importance, advising students to choose the "most learned, the most pious, and the most advanced in years."[147] Once the student found a teacher, the student must venerate and honor his authority. The teacher should in return be patient, humble, and child-centered, but never overly permissive and lenient. He also thought the choice of peers important to the learning process. Al-Zarnūjī quoted various scholars to underscore the point that industrious, morally sound companions can be an invaluable asset to the student: "Do not associate yourself with a companion indolent in his ways. How often through corruption of another man is a pious man corrupted," he wrote. "A bad friend is worse than an evil snake."[148]

The most notable distinction between al-Zarnūjī and previous authors on the subject of education was his emphasis on learning methodology rather than on teaching theory and technique. It appears that al-Zarnūjī was addressing a more mature student and likely had the madrasa in mind rather than the *kuttāb* when he drafted the *Ta^clīm.*[149]

Ibn Jamā^cah

Badr al-Dīn Abū ^cAbdallāh Muḥammad ibn Ibrāhīm ibn Sa^cd Allāh ibn Jamā^cah al-Kinānī al-Shāfi^cī was born (639/1241) and educated in Ḥamā in northern Syria. Ibn Jamā^cah achieved recognition at an early age for his aptitude and skill in the study of the Qur^canic sciences, hadith, *tarīkh* (history), and *fiqh.* He eventually attained some of the most elevated positions in the Muslim world for a religious scholar. He was a leading exponent of Shāfi^cī *fiqh,* was appointed *khaṭīb* (deliverer of sermons) of the al-Aqṣā mosque in Jerusalem, and served as chief *qāḍī* (Justice) of Egypt three times and of Damascus twice. In addition, he was well versed in poetry and prose and he authored numerous books on Islamic law, of which the most widely recognized was *Taḥrīr al-aḥkām fī tadbīr ahl al-Islām,* a treatise on constitutional law. He commanded tremendous respect and influence throughout the Mamlūk empire, within which he established one of the leading religio-judicial dynasties.

In addition to his distinguished legal career, he had a large number of students and followers, and he was fully engaged in the academic life of teachers and students in various educational institutions. His greatest contribution to the study of education was his book *Tadhkirat al-sāmiᶜ wa-al-mutakallim fī adab al-ᶜālim wa-al-mutaᶜallim* (A Memorandum for Students and Lecturers: Rules of Conduct for the Learned and the Learning), written in 672/1273. The work was intended to be a guide for both students and teachers in improving the quality of their academic experience. He died in 733/1333 and was buried in Cairo next to the great Imām Shāfiᶜī.

The *Tadhkirat* is divided into five sections, each taking an aspect of the madrasa experience. Ibn Jamāᶜah placed a high value on the personal and professional qualifications of the teacher, including the ability to shun pride and arrogance and to greet people in an affable and pleasant manner. He considered the teacher's primary responsibility to be the students' welfare and their academic and spiritual development. Appointment of the teacher was to be made with great care. Only scholars with demonstrated expertise should be permitted to teach a particular subject. Otherwise, a mockery would be made of the educational process and students would be at risk of a fraudulent experience. The teacher carries a serious responsibility to motivate students and instill in them a love for knowledge.

As the title indicates, Ibn Jamāᶜah addressed both the instructor and the student and placed special importance on the teacher's lecture and class discussions. He recommended that teachers encourage their students to ask questions—a departure from prior works discussing pedagogy and classroom management. The instruction of the subject matter should remain appropriate for the level of the student, commencing with simple manuals and progressing in complexity. Before beginning instruction, teachers should assess their students' understanding and then modify the instructional level accordingly.

For optimal student success, the student should take his educational responsibilities seriously and commit to being sincere in purpose and fastidious in personal conduct: punctual, polite, and diligent. The students should be moderate in both their sleeping and eating habits and should always treat the teacher with the deference, not interrupting the teacher and only asking questions in a courteous manner.

The final section is particularly interesting because it presented the author's views on how one should choose an educational institution and what one might expect of residential life in the madrasa. The nature of higher educational institutions was included, along with ways a student might make the most judicious choices in programmatic selection. The social dimension of the madrasa and the conditions of residential life were also discussed, with the added admonition to choose well one's friends and roommates.

Ibn Jamāᶜah's work is important in what it taught of education as well as the insight it provided into the educational enterprise of the thirteenth and fourteenth centuries CE (seventh and eighth centuries AH). In the sphere of educational pedagogy, Ibn Jamāᶜah must be considered somewhat of a pioneer in the formulation of participation-centered pedagogy as an essential characteristic of affective and cognitive learning.

Ibn Khaldūn

ᶜAbd al-Raḥmān Abū Zayd Ibn Muḥammad ibn Muḥammad ibn Khaldūn, born in Tunis in 732/1332, would become one of the most recognized and distinguished intellectuals of Islamic-Arabic culture in the age of its decline. As a family of accomplished scholars and courtiers, his parents ensured a thorough education in Arabic, poetry, *fiqh*, Qurʾān, hadith, and Qurʾānic sciences. He studied under many famous scholars, but considered Muḥammad ibn Ibrāhīm al-Ābilī his most influential master.

He grew up in a politically volatile period at about the same time that the Black Plague ravaged the region, claiming scores of victims, including Ibn Khaldūn's parents. In his twenties, Ibn Khaldūn entered the service of the *Marīnid* Sultan in Fez and became part of the Sultan's literary circle. Of that time he wrote: "I devoted myself to reflection and to study, and to sitting at the feet of the great teachers, those of the *Maghrib* as well as those of Spain who were residing temporarily in Fez, and I benefited greatly from their teaching."[150]

Beginning in 1357, he spent nearly two years in prison for political subversion after the *Marīnid* rule was cut short. Once free, Ibn Khaldūn was appointed by the new Sultan and held several influential positions in the courts of Fez, Granada, and Bougie. His career, however, continued to be affected by the turbulent political tides of the time along with other tribulations. He retreated under the protection of the powerful tribe *Awāld Arīf* in Oran for three years and tried to occupy himself with his scholarly work. It was during this time that he began writing *Kitāb al-ᶜibar,* a history of the world. The *Muqaddima,* or introduction of the work, was intended to be a preface to the *Kitāb al-ᶜibar.* He completed the *Muqaddima* in 1377 and continued working on the history as he pursued his new career as a scholar and teacher living in Tunis, Alexandria, and Cairo. In Cairo, he was appointed to the highest academic post at al-Azhar university and was also appointed Chief *Malikī* judge of Egypt. He completed the *Kitāb al-ᶜibar* while in Egypt, which was eventually comprised of seven volumes plus the *Muqaddima.* He died in 1406 CE (808 AH) in Cairo after an illustrious and celebrated career.

Ibn Khaldūn's *Muqaddima* is arguably one of the best-known social histories of the world. He began the work with a discussion on human civilization: the effects of the physical environment on civilizations in its various locations, and the character of government and social organization. In his sixth chapter, Ibn Khaldūn explored the characteristics and conditions of urban life, portraying it as the highest form of human association, with the development of civilization, commerce, and the arts and sciences. He asserted that education and proper instruction were essential for the social health and sustainability of higher civilization.

It is perhaps appropriate that this volume ends with Ibn Khaldūn's work because of the scope of his ideas related to education. In his sixth chapter, Ibn Khaldūn engaged the educational process in multiple dimensions having to do with the nature of man and his acquisition of knowledge. First, he considered sensory perception (physical stimulus and observation) the most basic and fundamental means to learning. Second, he asserted that knowledge can also be gained by the cognitive faculties of the intellect through logic, reason, and inference. Third, he considered the highest form of perception to be through extrasensory or revelatory experiences.[151] Ibn Khaldūn wrote:

> [T]he natural means for the perception of the truth is . . . man's natural ability to think. . . . Logic merely describes the process of thinking and mostly parallels it. Take into consideration and ask for God's mercy when you have difficulty in understanding problems! Then, the divine light will shine upon you and give you the right inspiration.[152]

Using these various degrees of knowledge acquisition, he constructed a detailed and extensive classification of knowledge, each degree with its own branches, categories, and subclassifications. Nearly a third of the *Muqaddima* is dedicated to the survey and description of these various sciences. Ibn Khaldūn was not unique among Muslim scholars in attempting to classify knowledge, but his analysis is considered by many to be the finest attempt up to that period.[153]

Ibn Khaldūn also expended considerable ink on the normative dimensions of learning and teaching. He described various pedagogical techniques that maximize learning: live examples and demonstrations, gradual and sequential teaching of material, and thoughtful repetition to ensure good habits of observation.[154] He believed it important to calibrate the curriculum to the abilities of the student, cautioning the teacher not to present too many subjects simultaneously, and "not expose students to two disciplines at the same time. Otherwise he will rarely master one of them . . . and be unsuccessful in both."[155]

Ibn Khaldūn considered the teacher-student relationship to be an indispensable aspect of good teaching. A positive personal relationship between the teacher and student must exist because personal contact can enable the student to be more fully involved in the education process.

Finally, he stressed the significance and necessity of treating students, particularly children, with consideration and gentleness. Oppression in any form, he contended, may cause the students "to lose their energy, . . . makes them lazy and induces them to lie and be insincere."[156] The teacher must be firm with the student, but as much as possible "correct him kindly and gently."[157]

Ibn Khaldūn's particular contribution to the study of education was his discussions on the sociality of knowledge in that knowledge should not be viewed as merely an objective in and of itself, but rather as strongly tied to the social and cultural practices of society. Ibn Khaldūn was a social philosopher and as such he observed education as a socially conditioned process. In describing different forms of education in different parts of the world, he came to the conclusion not only that these differences were culturally conditioned, but that human learning in general—and even intelligence—were largely influenced by the social environment.

بسم الله الرحمن الرحيم

Ibn Saḥnūn

The Book of Rules of Conduct for Teachers

TRANSLATED BY MICHAEL FISHBEIN

◆

In the name of God, the Merciful, the Compassionate,
and may God bless and grant peace to our master Muḥammad
and to his family and Companions.

What has been mentioned about teaching the Mighty Qurʾān

(1) Abū ᶜAbdallāh Muḥammad ibn Saḥnūn[1] said: My father Saḥnūn[2] transmitted to me from ᶜAbdallāh ibn Wahb,[3] from Sufyān al-Thawrī,[4] from ᶜAlqamah ibn Marthad,[5] from Abū ᶜAbd al-Raḥmān al-Sulamī,[6] from ᶜUthmān ibn ᶜAffān[7] (may God the Exalted be pleased with him), that the Messenger of God (may God bless him and grant him peace) said: The most excellent among you is he who learns the Qurʾān and teaches it.

(2) Muḥammad [ibn Saḥnūn transmitted] from Abū Ṭāhir,[8] from Yaḥyá ibn Ḥassān,[9] from ᶜAbd al-Wāḥid ibn Ziyād,[10] from ᶜAbd al-Raḥmān ibn Isḥāq,[11] from al-Nuᶜmān ibn Saᶜd,[12] from ᶜAlī ibn Abī Ṭālib[13] (may God be pleased with him), who said: The Messenger of God (may God bless him and grant him peace) said: The best among you is he who learns the Qurʾān and teaches it.

محمّد بن سحنون

كتاب آداب المعلمين

بسم الله الرحمن الرحيم

« وصلى الله على سيدنا محمد وآله وصحبه وسلم »

ما جاء في تعليم القرآن العزيز

(١) قال أبو عبد الله بن سحنون: حدثني أبي سحنون، عن عبد الله بن وهب عن سفيان الثوري، عن علقمة [بن مرثد]، عن أبي عبد الرحمان السلمي، عن عثمان بن عفان رضي الله تعالى عنه أن رسول الله ﷺ قال: أفضلكم من تعلم القرآن وعلّمه.

(٢) محمد، عن أبي طاهر، عن يحيى بن حسان، عن عبد الواحد بن زياد، عن عبد الرحمان بن إسحاق، عن النعمان بن سعد، عن علي بن أبي طالب (رضي الله عنه) قال: قال رسول الله ﷺ خيركم من تعلم القرآن وعلّمه.

(3) Muḥammad [ibn Saḥnūn transmitted] from Yaᶜqūb ibn Kāsib,[14] from Yūsuf ibn Abī Salamah, from his father [Abū Salamah],[15] from ᶜAbd al-Raḥmān ibn Hurmuz,[16] from ᶜUbaydallāh ibn Abī Rāfiᶜ,[17] from ᶜAlī ibn Abī Ṭālib (may God be pleased with him), that the Prophet (may God bless him and grant him peace) said: God raises up peoples by the Qurᵓān.

(4) From Saḥnūn, from ᶜAbdallāh ibn Nāfiᶜ,[18] who said: Ḥusayn ibn ᶜAbdallāh ibn Ḍamīrah[19] transmitted to me from his father, from his grandfather, from ᶜAlī (may God be pleased with him), that the Messenger of God (may God bless him and grant him peace) said: Hold to the Qurᵓān, for it expels hypocrisy as fire expels the dross of iron.

(5) [From] Mūsá,[20] from ᶜAbd al-Raḥmān ibn Mahdī,[21] from ᶜAbd al-Raḥmān ibn Budayl,[22] from his father,[23] from Anas ibn Mālik:[24] The Messenger of God (may God bless him and grant him peace) said: To God belong certain people among men. Someone asked: Who are they, O Messenger of God? He replied: The bearers of the Qurᵓān: they are God's people and familiar friends.

(6) From Mālik,[25] from Ibn Shihāb,[26] from ᶜUrwah ibn al-Zubayr,[27] from ᶜAbd al-Raḥmān ibn ᶜAbd al-Qārī,[28] from ᶜUmar ibn al-Khaṭṭāb,[29] who said: The Messenger of God (may God bless him and grant him peace) said: The Qurᵓān was revealed according to seven modes [of reading]; so recite of it what is easiest [for you].[30]

(7) He said: Mūsá ibn Muᶜāwiyah al-Ṣumādiḥī transmitted to me from Sufyān,[31] from al-Aᶜmash,[32] from Tamīm ibn Salamah,[33] from Ḥudhayfah,[34] who said: The Messenger of God (may God bless him and grant him peace) said: Whoever recites the Qurᵓān with proper inflections shall have a martyr's reward.[35] And he transmitted to me from al-Zuhrī Aḥmad ibn Abī Bakr,[36] from Muḥammad ibn Ṭalḥah,[37] from Saᶜīd ibn Abī Saᶜīd al-Maqrubī,[38] from Abū Hurayrah,[39] who said: The Messenger of God (may God bless him and grant him peace) said: Whoever learns the Qurᵓān in his youth, the Qurᵓān becomes mingled with his flesh and blood; but whoever learns it in his old age, when it easily escapes, and does not abandon it, shall have a double reward.

(8) Mūsá[40] transmitted to me from Ibn Wahb, from Muᶜāwiyah ibn Ṣāliḥ,[41] from Asad ibn Wadāᶜah, from ᶜUthmān ibn ᶜAffān (may God be pleased with him), who said, regarding God's words "Then we bequeathed the Book to those of our servants whom we chose" [Qurᵓān 35:32]: Whoever learns the Qurᵓān and teaches it is one of those whom God has chosen from the sons of Ādam.

(٣) [محمد] عن يعقوب بن كاسب عن يوسف بن أبي سلمة، عن أبيه، عن عبد الرحمان بن هرمز، عن [عبيد الله بن أبي رافع]، عن علي بن أبي طالب (رضي الله عنه) أن النبي ﷺ قال: يرفع الله بالقرآن أقواماً.

(٤) عن سحنون، [عن عبد الله] بن نافع قال: حدثني حسين بن عبد الله بن [ضميرة]، عن أبيه، عن جده عن علي (رضي الله عنه) أن رسول الله ﷺ قال: عليكم بالقرآن، فإنه ينفي النفاق كما تنفي النار خبث الحديد.

(٥) [عن] موسى، عن عبد الرحمان بن مهدي، عن عبد الرحمان بن بُدَيْل، عن أبيه، عن أنس بن مالك، قال رسول الله ﷺ : إن لله أهلين من الناس. قيل: من هم يا رسول الله؟ قال: هم حمَلة القرآن، هم أهل الله وخاصته.

(٦) عن مالك، عن ابن شهاب، عن عروة بن الزبير، عن عبد الرحمان بن عبد القاري، عن عمر بن الخطاب قال: قال رسول الله ﷺ: أُنزل القرآن على سبعة أحرف فاقرؤوا ما تيسّر منه.

(٧) قال: حدثني موسى بن معاوية الصمادحي، عن سفيان، عن الأعمش، عن تميم ابن سلمة، عن حذيفة، قال: قال رسول الله ﷺ: من قرأ القرآن بإعراب فله أجرُ شهيد. وحدثني، عن الزهري أحمد بن أبي بكر، عن محمد بن طلحة، عن سعيد بن أبي سعيد المغربي، عن أبي هريرة قال: قال رسول الله ﷺ: من تعلم القرآن في شبيبته اختلط القرآن بلحمه ودمه، ومن تعلمه في كبره وهو يتفلت منه ولا يتركه فله أجره مرتين.

(٨) وحدثني موسى، عن ابن وهب، عن معاوية بن صالح، عن أسد بن وداعة، عن عثمان بن عفان (رضي الله عنه) في قول الله تبارك وتعالى ﴿ثُمَّ أَوْرَثْنَا الْكِتَابَ الَّذِينَ اصْطَفَيْنَا مِنْ عِبَادِنَا﴾ [فاطر ٣٥:٣٢] قال: كل من تعلم القرآن وعلمه فهو ممن اصطفاه الله من بني آدم.

(9) They also transmitted to us from Sufyān al-Thawrī, from [ᶜAṭāᵓ] ibn al-Sāᵓib,[42] who said: Ibn Masᶜūd[43] said: Three things are indispensable to men. They must have a commander to judge between them, or else they would eat one another up; they must buy and sell copies of the Qurᵓān, or else God's Book would become rare; and they must have a teacher to teach their children and receive remuneration for it, or else people would be illiterate.

(10) Ibn Wahb [transmitted] from ᶜUmar ibn Qays, from ᶜAṭāᵓ,[44] that the latter used to teach the Qurᵓān[45] during the reign of Muᶜāwiyah[46] and would stipulate [a fee]. Ibn Wahb [transmitted] from Ibn Jurayj[47] that the latter said: I asked ᶜAṭāᵓ: Shall I accept a fee for teaching the Book? He replied: Have you learned that anyone finds it offensive? He said that he had not.

(11) Ibn Wahb [transmitted] from Ḥafṣ ibn ᶜUmar,[48] from Yūnus,[49] from Ibn Shihāb, that Saᶜd ibn Abī Waqqāṣ[50] brought a man from Iraq to teach their children in Medina the Book[51] and that they used to pay him a salary. Ibn Wahb said: Mālik has said: There is no harm in a teacher's receiving something for teaching the Qurᵓān. If he stipulates something, it is lawful and permissible, and there is no harm in such a stipulation. He has a right to [special remuneration for] completion [of teaching the Qurᵓān], whether he has stipulated it or not.[52] The learned men in our country hold this opinion concerning teachers.

What has been mentioned regarding equal treatment of children

(12) Muḥammad ibn ᶜAbd al-Karīm al-Barqī[53] transmitted to me from Aḥmad ibn Ibrāhīm al-ᶜUmarī, from Ādam ibn Bahrām ibn Iyās, from al-Rabīᶜ, from Ṣabīḥ, from Anas ibn Mālik, who said that the Messenger of God (may God bless him and grant him peace) said: Any educator who takes charge of three children from this community and does not teach them equally, the poorest of them with the wealthiest, and the wealthiest of them with the poorest, will be mustered on the Day of Resurrection among those who betrayed their trust.

(13) From Mūsá, from Fuḍayl ibn ᶜIyāḍ,[54] from Layth,[55] from al-Ḥasan,[56] who said: If a teacher has been engaged for pay and does not treat them—that is, the children—equally, he is inscribed among wrongdoers.

(٩) وحدثونا عن سفيان الثوري، عن علاء بن السائب قال: قال ابن مسعود: ثلاث لا بد للناس منهم: لا بد للناس من أمير يحكم بينهم ولولا ذلك لأكل بعضهم بعضاً، ولا بد للناس من شراء المصاحف وبيعها، ولولا ذلك لقل كتاب الله، ولا بد للناس من معلم يعلم أولادهم ويأخذ على ذلك أجرًا ولولا ذلك لكان الناس أميين.

(١٠) [عن] ابن وهب، عن عمر بن قيس، عن عطاء، أنه كان يعلّم الكتْبَ على عهد معاوية ويشترط. [عن] ابن وهب، عن ابن جريج قال: قلت لعطاء أآخذ الأجر عن تعليم الكتاب؟ قال: أعلمت أن أحداً كرهه؟ قال: لا.

(١١) [عن] ابن وهب، عن حفص بن عمر، عن يونس، عن ابن شهاب أن سعد بن أبي وقاص قدم برجل من العراق يعلم أبناءهم الكتاب بالمدينة ويعطونه الأجر قال ابن أبي وهب: وقال مالك: لا بأس بما يأخذ المعلم على تعليم القرآن وإن اشترط شيئاً كان له حلالاً جائزًا. ولا بأس بالاشتراط في ذلك وحق الختمة له واجب اشترطها أو لم يشترطها، وعلى ذلك أهل العلم ببلدنا في المعلمين.

ما جاء في العدل بين الصبيان

(١٢) حدثني محمد بن عبد الكريم البرقي، قال: حدثنا أحمد بن إبراهيم العمري، قال: حدثنا آدم بن بهرام بن إياس، عن الربيع، عن صبيح، عن أنس بن مالك قال: قال رسول الله ﷺ: أيما مؤدب ولي ثلاثة صبية من هذه الامة فلم يعلمهم بالسوية، فقيرهم مع غنيهم، وغنيهم مع فقيرهم، حشر يوم القيامة مع الخائنين.

(١٣) عن موسى، عن فضيل بن عياض، عن ليث، عن الحسن قال: إذا قوطع المعلم على الأجرة فلم يعدل بينهم أي الصبيان كتب من الظَلَمة.

That it is reprehensible to erase passages of the Qurʾān, and what should be done in this regard

(14) Muḥammad ibn ᶜAbd al-Raḥmān transmitted to me from ᶜAbdallāh ibn Saᶜīd,[57] from Zayd ibn Rabīᶜ, from Bishr ibn Ḥakīm, from Saᶜīd ibn Hārūn, from Anas ibn Mālik, who said:[58] If the schoolchildren erase from their slates with their feet "a revelation from the Lord of the worlds,"[59] the teacher is casting his Islam behind his back; and when he meets God, he will be heedless of the state in which he meets Him.

(15) Someone asked Anas: How were educators in the days of the *imāms* Abū Bakr, ᶜUmar, ᶜUthmān, and ᶜAlī (may God who is exalted be pleased with them)? Anas said: The teacher would have a basin. Every day each child in turn would bring clean water, and they would pour it into the basin and wash their slates in it. Anas said: Then they would dig a hole in the ground, pour the water into it, and it would dry up.

(16) I asked:[60] Then do you think it can be licked off?[61] He said: There is no harm in that, but it should not be wiped off with the foot; it should be wiped off with a kerchief or something similar.

(17) I asked: What do you think about the [legal] maxims[62] that the pupils write out in school? He said: Let him not blot out anything from "God's memorial"[63] with his foot. There is no harm in blotting out anything else not from the Qurʾān.

(18) He also transmitted to us from Mūsá, from Juwaybir ibn Manṣūr, who said that Ibrāhīm al-Nakhaᶜī[64] used to say: It is manly for ink to be visible on a man's shirt and lips. He said that this proves that it is all right to lick it off.

What has been mentioned regarding discipline—what is permissible and what is not

(19) [Muḥammad ibn Saḥnūn] said: He also transmitted to us from ᶜAbd al-Raḥmān,[65] from ᶜUbayd ibn Isḥāq, from Sayf[66] ibn Muḥammad, who said that he had been sitting with Saᶜd al-Khaffāf[67] when the latter's son came to him crying. "Son," asked Saᶜd, "what is making you cry?" "The teacher struck me," he replied. "By God," he said, "I will

باب ما يكره محوه من ذكر الله تعالى وما ينبغي أن يفعل من ذلك

(١٤) حدثني محمد بن عبد الرحمان، عن عبد الله بن سعيد، عن زيد بن ربيع، عن بشر بن حكيم، عن سعيد بن هارون، عن أنس بن مالك، قال: إذا محت صبية الكتاب ﴿تَنْزِيلٌ مِن رَبِّ العالَمِين﴾ من ألواحهم بأرجلهم، نبذ المعلم إسلامه خلف ظهره، ثم لم يبال حين يلقي الله على ما يلقاه عليه.

(١٥) قيل لأنس: كيف كان المؤدبون على عهد الأئمَّة: أبي بكر، وعمر، وعثمان وعلي رضي الله تعالى عنهم؟ قال أنس: كان المؤدب له إجانة. وكل صبي يأتي كل يوم بنوبته ماء طاهراً فيصبونه فيها فيمحون به ألواحهم. قال أنس: ثم يحفرون حفرة في الأرض، فيصبون ذلك الماء فينشف.

(١٦) قلت: أفترى أن يلعط؟ قال: لا بأس به. ولا يمسح بالرِّجل، ويُمسح بالمنديل وما أشبهه.

(١٧) قلت: فما ترى فيما يكتب الصبيان في الكتاب من المسائل؟ قال: أما ما كان من ذكر الله فلا يمحه برجله ولا بأس أن يمحى غير ذلك مما ليس من القرآن.

(١٨) وحدثنا موسى، عن جويبر بن منصور، قال: كان ابراهيم النخعي يقول: من المروءة أن يُرى في ثوب الرجل وشفته مداد قال: وفي هذا دليل أنه لا بأس أن يلعطه يعني يلعقه.

ما جاء في الادب وما يجوز من ذلك وما لا يجوز

(١٩) قال: وحدثنا عن عبد الرحمن، عن عبيد بن اسحاق، عن سيف بن محمد قال: كنت جالساً عند سعد الخفّاف فجاءه ابنه يبكي فقال: يا بني، ما يُبكيك؟ قال ضربني

transmit a tradition to you today. ᶜIkrimah[68] transmitted to me from Ibn ᶜAbbās,[69] who said that the Messenger of God (may God bless him and grant him peace) said: The worst people of my community are their children's teachers—the least merciful to the orphan and the most unkind to the poor.

(20) Muḥammad [ibn Saḥnūn] said: That is because he strikes them whenever he becomes angry, not for their benefit, but there is no harm in his striking them for their benefit. [Saḥnūn said:][70] Let him not exceed three blows in disciplining, unless the father gives permission for more than that if [the child] hurts someone. He may discipline them for playing or idleness, but should not exceed ten blows for discipline. However, for [mistakes in] reciting the Qurʾān, his discipline should not exceed three blows.

(21) I asked: Why have you set ten as the limit of disciplining in matters other than Qurʾān, but three with regard to the Qurʾān?

(22) He replied: Because ten is the limit of disciplining. Thus I heard Mālik say that the Messenger of God (may God bless him and grant him peace) said: Let none of you strike above ten lashes, except for a *ḥadd* [punishment].[71]

(23) Muḥammad [ibn Saḥnūn] said: Yaᶜqūb ibn Ḥumayd transmitted to us from Wakīᶜ,[72] from Hishām ibn Abī ᶜAbdallāh ibn Abī Bakr,[73] from the Prophet (may God bless him and grant him peace), who said: It is not permissible for a man who believes in God and the Last Day to strike above ten lashes, except for a *ḥadd* punishment.

(24) Rabāḥ[74] ibn Thābit transmitted to us from ᶜAbd al-Raḥmān ibn Ziyād,[75] from Abū ᶜAbd al-Raḥmān al-Ḥublī,[76] who said that it had been reported to him that the Messenger of God (may God bless him and grant him peace) said: The discipline for a boy is three lashes of the whip (*dirrah*); for anything above that [the inflicter] will receive retribution on the Day of Resurrection. The discipline of a wife by her husband is six lashes of the whip; for anything above that he will be beaten on the Day of Resurrection. The discipline for a slave-girl for a matter other than *ḥadd* punishments is ten to fifteen; for anything above that, up to twenty, [the inflicter] will receive blows on the Day of Resurrection.[77]

(25) Muḥammad [ibn Saḥnūn] said: Similarly, I think that no one should strike his slave more than ten blows. Retribution will be exacted for anything above that on the Day of Resurrection, except for a *ḥadd* punishment or for repeated misdeeds; for it is not wrong to strike him more than ten times if he has not abstained from his former offense. The Prophet (may God bless him and grant him peace) permitted the

المعلم. قال: أما والله لأحدثكم اليوم: حدثني عكرمة، عن ابن عباس قال: قال رسول ﷺ: شِرار أمتي معلمو صبيانهم، أقلهم رحمة لليتيم، وأغلظهم على المسكين.

(٢٠) قال محمد: وإنما ذلك لأنه يضربهم إذا غضب، وليس على منافعهم. ولا بأس أن يضربهم على منافعهم، ولا يجاوز بالأدب ثلاثًا إلا أن يأذن الأب في أكثر من ذلك إذا آذى أحدًا. ويؤدبهم على اللعب والبطالة ولا يجاوز بالأدب عشرة. وأما على قراءة القرآن فلا يجاوز أدبه ثلاثًا.

(٢١) قلت: لم وقّت عشرة في أكثر الأدب في غير القرآن، وفي القرآن ثلاثة؟

(٢٢) فقال: لأن عشرة غاية الأدب. وكذلك سمعت مالكًا يقول. وقد قال رسول الله ﷺ: لا يضرب أحدكم أكثر من عشرة أسواط إلا في حدّ.

(٢٣) قال محمد: وحدثنا يعقوب بن حُميد، عن وكيع، عن هشام بن أبي عبد الله بن أبي بكر، عن النبي ﷺ قال: لا يحل لرجل يؤمن بالله واليوم الآخر أن يضرب فوق عشرة أسواط إلا في حد.

(٢٤) حدثنا رباح بن ثابت، عن عبد الرحمان بن زياد عن عبد الرحمان الحبُلي قال: بلغني أن رسول الله ﷺ قال: أدب الصبي ثلاث درر فما زاد عليه قوصِص به يوم القيامة. وأدب الرجل زوجته ست درر، فما زاد يُضرب به يوم القيامة. وأدب الإماء في غير الحدود عشر إلى خمسة عشرة فما زاد عنه إلى العشرين يضرب به يوم القيامة.

(٢٥) قال محمد: وكذلك أرى ألا يضرب أحد عبده أكثر من عشرة، فما زاد على ذلك قوصص به يوم القيامة إلا في حد، إلا إذا تكاثرت عليه الذنوب فلا بأس أن يضربه أكثر من عشرة. وذلك إذا كان لم يعف عما تقدم. وقد أذن النبي ﷺ في أدب

disciplining of women, and Ibn ᶜUmar[78] (may God be pleased with him and with his father ᶜUmar) is reported to have struck his wife. The Prophet said: It is better for a man to discipline his child than to give alms. Some men of learning have said that discipline should be proportional to the misdeed, but it sometimes has gone beyond the limit.[79] Among those who have said this are Saᶜīd ibn al-Musayyab[80] and others.

What has been mentioned regarding completions [of the Qurʾān] and what is owed to the teacher in the matter

(26) I asked him when special remuneration for completion [of the reading of the Qurʾān] becomes due. He said: When [the pupil] comes close to [completion] and has passed beyond two-thirds. I asked him about special remuneration for completion of half [of the Qurʾān]. He said: I do not think it necessary.

(27) Saḥnūn said: No special remuneration for completion is necessary except for the entire Qurʾān—not for one-half, one-third, or one-quarter—unless people give it of their own accord.

(28) Muḥammad [ibn Saḥnūn] said: I was present when Saḥnūn enjoined [payment of] a remuneration for completion (*khitmah*) on a man, but only in accordance with the man's wealth or poverty.

(29) Someone asked [Saḥnūn]: Do you think a teacher may give the children a vacation for a day or so? He said: That has always been common practice—a day or part of a day, for example—but the teacher should not give them more than that, except with the permission of all their fathers, because he is their employee.

(30) I asked: What if a child gives the teacher a present or gives him something and the latter gives him a vacation for it? He said: No, vacations are only for *khitmah*s—a day or so—and on feast days; otherwise, the teacher may not grant them without the fathers' permission. He said, For this reason the testimony of most teachers is invalid because they do not fulfill their obligations, except those whom God protects.[81] He said to me: This is if the teacher teaches for a fixed remuneration each month or each year; however, if he is without contract, so that he accepts whatever is given, and when nothing is given he does not ask, he may do whatever he wishes. If the children's guardians learn that he is being negligent, they may still give him something if they wish, or not give him anything if they wish.

النساء. وروي أن ابن عمر (رضي الله عنهما)، ضرب امرأته. وقال النبي ﷺ: يؤدب الرجل ولده خير له من أن يتصدق. وقد قال بعض أهل العلم إن الأدب على قدر الذنب، وربما جاوز الأدب الحد، منهم سعيد بن المسيب وغيره.

ما جاء في الختم وما يجب في ذلك للمعلم

(٢٦) وسألته متى تجب الختمة، فقال: إذا قاربها وجاوز الثلثين؛ فسألته عن ختمة النصف، فقال: لا أرى ذلك يلزم.

(٢٧) قال سحنون: ولا يلزم ختمة غير القرآن كله، لا نصف، ولا ثلث، ولا ربع الا ان يتطوعوا بذلك.

(٢٨) قال محمد: وحضرت لسحنون قضى بالختمة على رجل. وإنما ذلك على قدر يُسر الرجل وعسره.

(٢٩) وقيل له: أترى للمعلم سعة في إذنه للصبيان اليوم ونحوه؟ فقال: ما زال ذلك من عمل الناس مثل اليوم وبعضه. ولا يجوز له أن يأذن لهم أكثر من ذلك إلا بإذن آبائهم كلهم لأنه أجير لهم.

(٣٠) قلت: وما أهدى الصبي للمعلم، أو أعطاه شيئًا فيأذن له على ذلك؟ فقال: لا. إنما الاذن في الختم اليوم ونحوه، وفي الأعياد. وأما في غير ذلك فلا يجوز له إلا بإذن الآباء. قال: ومن ها هنا سقطت شهادة أكثر المعلمين لأنهم غير مؤدين لما يجب عليهم إلا من عصم الله. قال لي هذا إذا كان المعلم يعلم بأجر معلوم كل شهر أو كل سنة، وأما إن كان على غير شرطه، فما أُعطي قَبِل، وما لم يُعط لم يسأل شيئًا، فله أن يفعل ما شاء. اذا كان أولياء الصبيان يعلمون تضييعه، فإن شاؤوا أعطوه على ذلك وإن شاؤوا لم يعطوه.

What has been mentioned regarding demanding a feast-day gift

(31) I asked: Can a feast-day gift be enjoined? He said: No, and I do not know what such a thing might be, unless people give it of their own accord. He said: A teacher must not burden the children with anything above his salary in the way of a gift or anything else. He must not ask them for it. If they give him a gift on that basis, it is forbidden—unless they give without being asked, or if his asking is done politely, so that if they do nothing he does not strike[82] them for it, but if he threatens them in the matter, it is not permissible for him. Nor is it permissible for him to give them a vacation if they give him a gift, because the promise of a vacation is inducement of a gift, and that is reprehensible.

When the teacher ought to give the children vacation

(32) I asked him: How many days' vacation do you think he should allow them for feast days? He said: One day at the Feast of Breaking the Fast,[83] but there is no harm in his allowing them three days; for the Feast of Immolation[84] three days, but there is no harm in his allowing them five days.

(33) I asked: May he send one child to fetch another? He said: I do not think it permissible for him to do so, unless the children's parents or guardians give them permission, or if the places are close—the child should not be distracted with the matter. Let him personally take charge of the children at the time to return home, and he should inform their guardians if they have not come.

(34) He said: I would not have the teacher put any of the children in charge of administering blows. He should not appoint any of them to be a monitor unless the boy has finished reciting the Qurʾān, knows it, and thus needs no instruction—there is no harm in that and in the boy's assisting him, for it will benefit the boy in his education. It is not permissible for him to order one boy to instruct another, unless it brings the boy benefit in his education or the boy's father permits it.[85] Let him take charge [of instruction] himself or hire someone to assist him if the latter is as qualified as he.

ما جاء في القضاء بعطية العيد

(٣١) قلت: فعطية العيد يقضى بها؟ قال: لا. ولا أعرف ما هي، إلا أن يتطوعوا بها. قال: ولا يحل للمعلم أن يكلف الصبيان فوق أجرته شيئاً من هدية وغير ذلك ولا يسألهم في ذلك، فإن أهدوا إليه على ذلك فهو حرام، إلا أن يهدوا إليه من غير مسألة، إلا أن تكون المسألة منه على وجه المعروف. فإن لم يفعلوا فلا يضربهم في ذلك. وأيضاً إن كان يهددهم في ذلك فلا يحل له ذلك، أو يخليهم إذا أهدوا له فلا يحل له ذلك، لأن التخلية داعية إلى الهدية، وهو مكروه.

ما ينبغي للمعلم ان يخلي الصبيان فيه

(٣٢) قلت له: فكم ترى أن يأذن لهم في الأعياد؟ قال: الفطر يوماً واحداً. ولا بأس أن يأذن لهم ثلاثة أيام، والأضحى ثلاثة أيام. ولا بأس أن يأذن لهم خمسة أيام.

(٣٣) قلت: أفيرسل الصبيان بعضهم في طلب بعض؟ قال: لا أرى ذلك يجوز له، إلا أن يأذن لهم آباؤهم أو أولياء الصبيان في ذلك، أو تكون المواضع قريبة لا يشتغل الصبي في ذلك. وليتعاهد الصبيان هو بنفسه في وقت انقلاب الصبيان ويخبر أولياءهم أنهم لم يجيئوا.

(٣٤) قال: وأحب للمعلم أن لا يولي أحداً من الصبيان الضرب، ولا يجعل لهم عريفاً منهم، إلا أن يكون الصبي قد ختم وعرف القرآن وهو مستغن عن التعليم، فلا بأس بذلك، وأن يعينه فإن ذلك منفعة للصبي ولا يحل أن يأمر أحداً أن يعلم أحداً منهم إلا أن يكون في ذلك منفعة للصبي في تخريجه أو يأذن والده في ذلك. ولْيلِ هو ذلك بنفسه أو يستأجر من يعينه إذا كان في مثل كفالته.

The teacher's duty to keep close to the children

(35) It is not permissible for the teacher to become distracted from the children, except during time when he is not making them recite [individually]; there is no harm in his conversing then, if while he does so he watches the children and monitors them.

(36) I asked: Is the popular custom of banners[86] at [celebrations of] completion [of the recitation of the Qurʾān] and fruit thrown to the people permissible? He said: It is not permissible because it is plunder; and the Messenger of God (may God bless him and grant him peace) forbade eating food taken as plunder.

(37) He said: Let the teacher remain diligent and devote himself to the students. It is not permissible for him to [go to] pray at funerals, except when it is unavoidable, for people to whose affairs he is obliged to attend; for he is a hired person who cannot leave his work, follow funeral processions, or visit the sick.

(38) He should set a time for them in which he teaches them writing,[87] and he should have them compete with each other,[88] because that is something that will improve them and educate them. He may allow them to discipline each other, but it should not go beyond three [blows]. It is not permissible for him to strike a child's head or face. It is not permissible for him to deprive a child of his food and drink when they have been sent after him.

(39) I asked: Do you think that a teacher may write out books of jurisprudence for himself or others? He said: During the time when he is free from the children, there is no harm in his writing for himself and for other people, for example when he dismisses them to go home, but as long as they are around him it is certainly not permissible for him. How can it be permissible for him to leave what is his duty and attend to what is not his duty? Do you not see that it is not permissible for him to entrust the instruction of one pupil to another? How then can he busy himself with other people than his pupils?

(40) I asked: May he permit a child to write out a letter for[89] someone? He said: There is no harm in it. It is something that will educate the child, if he writes out messages. The teacher should teach them arithmetic, but it is not his duty unless it has been stipulated for him; and likewise poetry, obscure words,[90] Arabic language, calligraphy, and the whole of grammar—in these matters he acts voluntarily. It is fitting for him to teach them [the correct reading of] the case-endings[91] of [the

ما يجب على المعلم من لزوم الصبيان

(٣٥) ولا يحل للمعلم أن يشتغل عن الصبيان إلا أن يكون في وقت لا يعرضهم فيه، فلا بأس أن يتحدث وهو في ذلك ينظر إليهم ويتفقدهم.

(٣٦) قلت: فما يعمل الناس من [. . .] عند الختم، ومن الفاكهة يرمى بها على الناس، هل يحل؟ قال: لا يحل، لأنه نهبة. وقد نهى رسول الله ﷺ عن أكل طعام النهبة.

(٣٧) قال: وليلزم المعلم الاجتهاد، وليتفرغ لهم، ولا يجوز له الصلاة على الجنائز، إلا فيما لا بد له منه ممن يلزمه النظر في أمره، لأنه أجير لا يدع عمله. ولا يتبع الجنائز، ولا عيادة المرضى.

(٣٨) وينبغي له أن يجعل لهم وقتاً يعلمهم فيه الكتاب ويجعلهم يتجايرون لأن ذلك مما يصلحهم ويخرجهم ويبيح لهم أدب بعضهم بعضاً. ولا يجاوز ثلاثاً. ولا يجوز له أن يضرب رأس الصبي ولا وجهه. ولا يجوز له أن يمنعه من طعامه وشرابه إذا أرسل وراءه.

(٣٩) قلت: فهل ترى للمعلم أن يكتب لنفسه كتب الفقه أو لغيره؟ قال: أما في وقت فراغه من الصبيان فلا بأس أن يكتب لنفسه والناس، مثل أن يأذن لهم في الانقلاب، وأما ما داموا حوله فلا. أي لا يجوز له ذلك. وكيف يجوز له أن يخرج مما يلزمه النظر فيه إلى ما لا يلزمه؟ ألا ترى أنه لا يجوز له أن يوكل تعليم بعضهم إلى بعض، فكيف يشتغل بغيرهم؟

(٤٠) قلت: فيأذن للصبي أن يكتب لأحد كتاباً؟ فقال: لا بأس به. وهذا مما يخرّج الصبي إذا كتب الرسائل وينبغي أن يعلمهم الحساب، وليس ذلك بلازم له إلا أن يشترط ذلك عليه، وكذلك الشعر، والغريب، والعربية، والخط، وجميع النحو، وهو

words of] the Qurʾān—it is his duty to do so—and vocalization, spelling, good handwriting, good reading,[92] when to pause [in recitation],[93] and how to articulate clearly—it is his duty to do so. There is no harm in his teaching them poetry[94]—words and reports of the [ancient] Arabs that contain nothing indecent—but it is not incumbent upon him.

(41) It is his duty to teach them the good reading that has become well-known, namely the reading of Nāfiᶜ, but there is no harm in his having them read according to another [authority] if [the reading] is not considered disagreeable. For example, [he may mention the readings] *yabshuruka, wulduhu,* and *ḥirmun ᶜalá qaryatin,* but he should have them read *yubashshiruka, waladuhu,* and *ḥarāmun ᶜalá qaryatin,* and so forth, and [he may mention] every reading that was used by the Companions of the Messenger of God (may God bless him and grant him peace).

(42) It is the teacher's responsibility to procure the whip and the *falaqah*; it is not the responsibility of the students.[95] It is his responsibility to rent the shop; it is not the responsibility of the students. It is his responsibility to examine them on what they have been taught and to make them recite [individually]. He should set a fixed time for [individual] recitation of the Qurʾān, such as Thursday and Wednesday evening. He should give them a day off on Friday: that has always been the custom of teachers, and they have never been reproved for it.

(43) There is no harm in his teaching them homilies, if they desire.[96] I do not think that he should teach them melodies for the Qurʾān, because Mālik said: It is not permissible for the Qurʾān to be recited with melodies. I do not think that he should teach them [vocal] ornamentation, because that leads to singing, which is reprehensible, and I think should be strictly forbidden.

(44) Saḥnūn said: Mālik was asked about sessions in which people gathered to recite. He said: [They are] an [undesirable] innovation. And I think the governor ought to forbid people to do so and discipline them well. He should teach them good manners, for it his duty toward God to give good advice, protect them, and care for them.

(45) Let him hold school[97] from early morning till the time to return home. There is no harm in his having them dictate to each other, because that is a benefit to them; and let him examine their dictation. It is not permissible for him to move them from sura to sura until they memorize the sura with its case-endings and orthography, unless the parents give him leeway. If they have no parents but have legal guardians or a guardian appointed by testament, then, if payment of the teacher's

في ذلك متطوع. وينبغي له أن يعلمهم إعراب القرآن وذلك لازم له. والشكل، والهجاء، والخط الحسن، والقراءة الحسنة، والتوقيف والترتيل، يلزمه ذلك. ولا بأس أن يعلمهم الشعر مما لا يكون فيه فحش من كلام العرب وأخبارها، وليس ذلك بواجب عليه.

(٤١) ويلزمه أن يعلمهم ما علم من القراءة الحسنة وهو مقرأ نافع. ولا بأس إن أقرأهم لغيره اذا لم يكن مستبشعاً مثل: «يَبْشُرك» و«وُلْده» و«حِرْم على قرية» ولكن يقرئها «يُبَشِّرك» و«وَلَده» و«حَرامٌ على قريةٍ» وما أشبه هذا. وكل ما قرأ به أصحاب رسول الله ﷺ.

(٤٢) وعلى المعلم أن يكسب الدرة والفلقة. وليس ذلك على الصبيان. وعليه كراء الحانوت وليس ذلك على الصبيان. وعليه أن يتفقدهم بالتعليم والعرض، ويجعل لعرض القرآن وقتاً معلوماً مثل يوم الخميس، وعشية الأربعاء. ويأذن لهم في يوم الجمعة. وذلك سنة المعلمين منذ كانوا، ولم يعب ذلك عليهم.

(٤٣) ولا بأس أن يعلمهم الخطب إن أرادوا. ولا أرى أن يعلمهم ألحان القرآن، لان مالكاً قال: لا يجوز أن يقرأ بالألحان. ولا أرى أن يعلمهم التحبير لأن ذلك داعية إلى الغناء وهو مكروه، وأرى أن ينهى عن ذلك بأشد النهي.

(٤٤) قال: وقال سحنون: ولقد سئل مالك عن هذه المجالس التي يجتمع فيها للقراءة فقال: بدعة. وأرى للوالي أن ينهاهم عن ذلك ويحسن أدبهم،وليعلمهم الأدب، فإنه من الواجب لله عليه النصيحة، وحفظهم ورعايتهم.

(٤٥) وليجعل الكتاب من الضحى إلى وقت الإنقلاب. ولا بأس أن يجعلهم يملي بعضهم على بعض، لأن ذلك منفعة لهم. وليتفقد إملاءهم، ولا يجوز أن ينقلهم من سورة إلى سورة حتى يحفظوها بإعرابها وكتابتها إلا أن يسهل له الآباء. فإن لم يكن

salary comes not from the child's wealth but from the guardian's, the latter has the same right as the father to give the teacher leeway; but if the salary is paid from the child's wealth, it is not permissible for him to give the teacher leeway to have the child leave one sura until he has memorized it, as I have told you; and similarly if the father is paying out of the child's wealth.

(46) He said: I think that what the child must pay from his own wealth (if he has wealth) for the teacher's provision has the same status as [what he must pay for] his own clothing and maintenance.

(47) I asked: Suppose a child close to completing [the reading of the Qur'ān] comes under the tutelage of a [new] teacher. Can the latter demand from him [the remuneration] for completion, when the first teacher neglected to demand it? He said: If [the child] studies with the [second] teacher, [starting] from a point at which he would have owed no [remuneration for] completion to the first [teacher] had the latter claimed it (for example, more than one-third, from "Yūnus" or "Hūd," or the like),[98] the [remuneration for] completion must be paid, because in that case nothing would be awarded to the first [teacher] if he should make a claim. However, if the child comes under the tutelage of the second teacher at a time when the first [teacher] would have been owed a [gift for] completion if he had claimed it, nothing can be demanded of the newly arrived student: it is as if the first [teacher] had left the [remuneration for] completion to [the discretion of] the child's father or the child himself—unless [the father] voluntarily gives something to [the second teacher]. I consider it commendable if he gives him something voluntarily, but it is not a rule.[99]

(48) I asked: What would you think if his parent takes him out [of a teacher's tutelage] and says, "He shall not finish [the Qur'ān] with you," although the child is close to finishing, and the teacher's salary is on a monthly basis? He said: I would judge that he owes the [remuneration for] finishing, and I would not take into account whether he removed him or left him.

(49) I asked: What would you say[100] if [the parent] says, "My son does not know the Qur'ān"? Does he owe the [remuneration for] finishing? He said: If the child can read the Qur'ān from the written text, knows its letters, and correctly pronounces the case-endings, the teacher is owed the [remuneration for] finishing, even if the child cannot recite the Qur'ān from memory, for it is a rare child who can memorize the Qur'ān the first time. I asked: But if he errs in reading the written text? He said: If it is a small matter, and knowledge is predominant in him, it is all right.

لهم آباء وكان لهم أولياء أو وصي، فإن كان دفع أجر المعلم من غير مال الصبي إنما هو من عنده، فله أن يسهل للمعلم كما للأب. وإن كان من مال الصبي يعطي الأجرة لم يجز أن يسهل للمعلم أن يخرجه من السورة حتى يحفظها كما أعلمتك، وكذلك إن كان الأب يعطي من مال الصبي.

(٤٦) قال: وأرى ما يلزم الصبي من مؤونة المعلم في ماله إن كان له مال بمنزلة كسوته ونفقته.

(٤٧) قلت: فالصبي يدخل عند المعلم، وقد قارب الختمة هل له أن يقضي له عليه بالختمة وقد ترك الأول أن يطالبه؟ فقال: إن كان أخذ عنه من الموضع الذي لا يُلزمه الختمة للأول أنّ لو قام مثل أكثر من الثلث من يونس وهود ونحو ذلك فالختمة لازمة له، لأن الأول حينئذ لو قام لم يقض له بشيء. وأما إن كان دخوله عنده في وقت لو قام عليه الأول لزمته الختمة لم يقض للداخل عنده بشيء، لأن الأول كأنه إنما تركها لأبيه أو للصبي إلا أن يتطوع لهذا بشيء. واستحسن أن ترضخ لهذا بشيء استحسانا وليس بقياس.

(٤٨) قلت: أرأيت لو أن والده أخرجه، وقال: لا يختم عندك وقد قارب الختمة، وإنما كانت الأجرة على شهر؟ فقال: أقضي عليه بالختمة. ثم لا أبالي أخرجه أم تركه.

(٤٩) قلت: فما يقول إن قال: ابني لا يعلم القرآن، هل تجب عليه الختمة؟ فقال: إن قرأ الصبي القرآن في المصحف وعرف حروفه وأقام إعرابه، وجبت للمعلم الختمة، وان لم يقرأه ظاهراً، لأنه قل صبي يستظهر القرآن أول مرة. قلت: فإن كان أخطأ في قراءة المصحف؟ فقال: إن كان الشيء اليسير، والغالب عليه المعرفة فلا بأس.

(50) Saḥnūn said: It is not permissible for the teacher to send students on his errands. The teacher should command them to perform the ritual prayer when they are seven years old and beat them for [omitting to pray] when they are ten. That is what Mālik said. ᶜAbd al-Raḥmān[101] reported to us that Mālik said: Ten-year-olds are beaten for it, and [at that age] they are given separate places to sleep. I asked: [Did he mean] males and females? He said: Yes.

(51) [Saḥnūn] said: He must teach them [how to perform] the ablutions [before prayer] and the ritual prayer, because that is their religion—the number of bowings[102] and prostrations[103] in [each] prayer, the recitation [of verses from the Qurʾān] in the prayer, [the saying of] "God is great,"[104] the manner of sitting[105] [during prayer], the manner of entering a state of sacralization[106] [to commence the prayer], the salutation[107] [that concludes the prayer], and whatever is necessary for them in prayer; [how to recite] the Confession of Faith[108] and the Supplication of Standing[109] in the morning. For the latter belongs to the Sunna[110] of prayer and to what by right is an essential part of it. The Messenger of God (may God bless him and grant him peace) made it his practice until God the Exalted took him (may God's prayers, mercy, and blessings be upon him), and the leaders after his death did so too. Not one of them was known to have omitted the Supplication of Standing in the morning, being loathe to do so. They were the true believers and rightly guided ones: Abū Bakr,[111] ᶜUmar, ᶜUthmān, and ᶜAlī—all of them followed this practice, and also those who followed them (may God the Exalted be pleased with them all).

(52) Let him take care to teach them supplications,[112] that they may make their humble petitions to God; and let him teach them God's greatness and majesty, that they may magnify Him for it. If the people suffer from drought and the imam leads them in prayers for rain,[113] I would have the teacher bring the children out (those of them who know how to pray), and let them beseech God with supplications and make their humble petitions to Him, for I have been told that when the people to whom Jonah was sent (may God's blessing be upon our prophet and upon him) saw the chastisement with their own eyes, they brought out their children and entreated God by means of them, [and the chastisement was lifted].[114]

(٥٠) قال سحنون: ولا يجوز للمعلم أن يرسل الصبيان في حوائجه. وينبغي للمعلم أن يأمرهم بالصلاة إذا كانوا بني سبع سنين ويضربهم عليها اذا كانوا بني عشرة وكذلك قال مالك حدثنا عنه عبد الرحمن، قال: قال مالك: يضربون عليها بنو عشر ويفرق بينهم في المضاجع قلت: الذكور والإناث؟ قال: نعم.

(٥١) قال: ويلزمه أن يعلمهم الوضوء والصلاة، لأن ذلك دينهم، وعدد ركوعها وسجودها، والقراءة فيها، والتكبير وكيف الجلوس، والإحرام، والسلام، وما يلزمهم في الصلاة، والتشهد، والقنوت في الصبح، فإنه من سنة الصلاة ومن واجب حقها الذي لم يزل رسول الله ﷺ عليها، حتى قبضه الله تعالى صلوات الله عليه ورحمته وبركاته. ثم الأئمة بعده على ذلك لم يعلم أحد منهم ترك القنوت في الفجر رغبة عنه وهم الراشدون المهديون: أبو بكر وعمر وعثمان وعلي. كلهم على ذلك (ومن تبعهم رضي الله عنهم أجمعين).

(٥٢) وليتعاهدهم بتعليم الدعاء ليرغبوا إلى الله، ويعرفهم عظمته وجلاله ليكبروا على ذلك. واذا أجدب الناس واستسقى بهم الإمام فأحب للمعلم أن يخرج بهم، من يعرف الصلاة منهم، وليبتهلوا إلى الله بالدعاء، ويرغبوا إليه، فإنه بلغني أن قوم يونس (صلى الله على نبينا وعليه) لما عاينوا العذاب خرجوا بصبيانهم فتضرعوا إلى الله بهم.

(53) He ought to teach them the traditional usages[115] of [the five canonical] prayers, such as the two *rakᶜah*s of the dawn prayer,[116] the *witr* [prayer],[117] the prayer of the two feasts,[118] the prayer for rain, and the [prayer at an] eclipse,[119] so that he may teach them their religion whereby they worship God and the Sunna of their prophet (may God bless him and grant him peace).

(54) He [i.e., Saḥnūn] said: It is not permissible for the teacher to teach Christian children the Qurᵓān or writing.

(55) He said: Mālik said: There is no harm in the teacher's writing [text from] the Book [of God] without having performed ablutions, but he should not touch the volume of the Qurᵓān without having performed them. There is no harm if a child who has not reached puberty reads [the Qurᵓān] from his slate without having performed ablutions, if he is learning, and likewise the teacher; but the child should touch the volume of the Qurᵓān only after having performed ablutions. Let the teacher command them regarding this, so that they learn it.

(56) He said: Let them learn the prayer of funerals[120] and the supplications at them, for that is part of their religion. Let him set them on an equal footing in instruction, the eminent and the lowly, or else he betrays his trust.

(57) When Mālik was asked about teaching children in the mosque, he said: I do not think that it is permissible, because they are not careful about filth, and the mosque was not erected for teaching. Mālik [also] said: I do not think people should sleep in the mosque or eat in it, except from necessity and those who can find no alternative, such as the stranger, the traveler, and the needy person who cannot find a place.

(58) Muḥammad [ibn Saḥnūn] said: Saḥnūn transmitted to me from ᶜAbdallāh ibn Nāfiᶜ, who said: I heard Mālik say: I do not think that anyone should recite the Qurᵓān while he is walking in the street, unless he is learning it, and I do not think that he should recite it in the bath.

(٥٣) وينبغي أن يعلمهم سنن الصلاة مثل ركعتي الفجر، والوتر، وصلاة العيدين، والاستسقاء والخسوف، حتى يعلمهم دينهم الذي تعبَّدهم الله به، وسنة نبيهم ﷺ.

(٥٤) قال: ولا يجوز للمعلم أن يعلم أولاد النصارى القرآن ولا الكتب.

(٥٥) قال: وقال مالك: ولا بأس أن يكتب المعلم الكتب على غير وضوء؛ ولا يمس المصحف إلا على وضوء. ولا بأس على الصبي. إذا لم يبلغ الحلم، أن يقرأ في اللوح على غير وضوء إذا كان يتعلم. وكذلك المعلم. ولا يمس الصبي المصحف إلا على وضوء، وليأمرهم بذلك حتى يتعلموه.

(٥٦) قال: وليعلمهم الصلاة على الجنائز. والدعاء عليها فإنه من دينهم، وليجعلهم بالسواء في التعليم: الشريف والوضيع، وإلا كان خائناً.

(٥٧) وسئل مالك عن تعليم الصبيان في المسجد. قال: لا أرى ذلك يجوز، لأنهم لا يتحفظون من النجاسة. ولم ينصب المسجد للتعليم قال مالك: ولا أرى أن ينام في المسجد ولا يؤكل فيه إلا من ضرورة ولا يجد بدا منه مثل: الغريب والمسافر والمحتاج الذي لا يجد موضعاً.

(٥٨) قال محمد: وحدثني سحنون عن عبد الله بن نافع، قال سمعت مالكاً يقول: لا أرى لأحد أن يقرأ القرآن وهو مار على الطريق إلا أن يكون متعلماً. ولا أرى أن يقرأ في الحمام.

(59) Mālik [also] said: If the teacher comes to a *sajdah*[121] and the pupil recites it to him, the teacher need not prostrate himself, because the pupil is not an imam.[122] However, if the pupil has come of age, there is no harm in the teacher's prostrating himself; but if he fails to do so, he is not to be blamed, because it is not obligatory. Similarly, if the teacher himself recites [the verse containing a *sajdah*], he prostrates himself if he wishes, or he omits the prostration if he wishes. Do you not see that ᶜUmar once read [a verse containing a *sajdah*] from the pulpit and came down and prostrated himself; then he read it again and did not prostrate himself, and he said: It has not been prescribed for us.

(60) Mālik [also] said: Similarly, if a woman recites the *sajdah* to a man, the man does not prostrate himself with her, because she is not an imam. The Messenger of God (may God bless him and grant him peace) said to the man who recited to him: You were an imam, and so if you had prostrated yourself I would have prostrated myself with you.

(61) Saḥnūn said: I disapprove of a teacher's teaching girls and mixing them with the boys, because that is corruption for them.[123]

(62) Saḥnūn was asked whether the teacher should accept the children's word that one has injured another. He replied: I do not think so as a matter of rule. The teacher need discipline the children only when one of them injures another, and that, in my opinion, is when he has learned of the injury from all of them as a body or when there has been a confession—unless it is children whom he has known for honesty: then he may accept their word and punish on the basis of it. As I have told you, he should not discipline to excess. He should order them to stop injuring each other and should return what one has taken from the other, but that is not a matter of legal settlement. Thus have I heard from more than one of our companions. The testimony [of children] has been admitted in [cases of] homicide and bodily injury, so why [not] in this case? But God knows best.[124]

(٥٩) قال مالك: وإذا مر المعلم بسجدة وهو يقرؤها عليه الصبي فليس عليه أن يسجدها لأن الصبي ليس بإمام، إلا أن يكون بالغا فلا بأس أن يسجدها، فإن ترك، فلا شيء عليه، لانها ليست بواجبة. وكذلك إذا قرأها هو، فإن شاء سجد، وإن شاء ترك. ألا ترى أن عمر قرأها مرة على المنبر، فنزل فسجد، ثم قرأها مرة أخرى، فلم يسجد. وقال: إنها لم تكتب علينا.

(٦٠) قال مالك: وكذلك المرأة إذا قرأت السجدة على الرجل، لم يسجد الرجل معها لأنها ليست بإمام. وقد قال رسول الله ﷺ للذي قرأ عليه: كنت إماماً فلو سجدت سجدت معك.

(٦١) قال سحنون: وأكره للمعلم أن يعلم الجواري ويخلطهن مع الغلمان، لأن ذلك فساد لهم.

(٦٢) قال: وسئل سحنون عن المعلم: أيأخذ الصبيان بقول بعضهم على بعض في الأذى؟ قال: ما أرى هذا من ناحية الحكم، وإنما على المؤدب أن يؤدبهم إذا آذى بعضهم بعضاً. وذلك عندي إذا استفاض علم الأذى من الجماعة منهم، أو كان الاعتراف، إلا أن يكونوا صبيانًا قد عرفهم بالصدق فيقبل قولهم ويعاقب على ذلك. ولا يجاوز في الأدب كما أعلمتك ويأمرهم بالكف عن الأذى، ويرد ما أخذ بعضهم لبعض. وليس هو من ناحية القضاء، وكذلك سمعت من غير واحد من أصحابنا. وقد أجيزت شهادتهم في القتل والجراح فكيف بهذا! والله أعلم.

What has been mentioned about the teacher's remuneration and when it is obligatory

(63) [Muḥammad ibn Saḥnūn] said: Shajarah ibn ᶜĪsā[125] wrote to Saḥnūn asking him about a teacher who is hired to teach children, but one of them falls ill, or [his father] wants to take him on a journey or the like. Saḥnūn said: If the teacher has been hired for a fixed yearly remuneration, the parents must pay the remuneration whether they travel or stay. However, in this case it is divided[126] according to the pupil's condition, because some are poor and some are wealthy. Sometimes for one child the teacher receives provisions for his teaching him, while for another the teacher receives no provisions for it.[127] This needs to be taken into account.

(64) Saḥnūn also said: [If the child dies,] the remuneration owed by the child's father for the remainder of the contract is cancelled and is not binding on him; similarly, if the father dies, the remainder of the remuneration is cancelled, and this remainder becomes part of the child's property.

(65) Muḥammad [ibn Saḥnūn] said: It is like the case of nursing, if someone hires a woman to nurse his child and then the father or the child dies. ᶜAbd al-Raḥmān [ibn al-Qāsim] related from Mālik that the payment is cancelled, and the remainder becomes part of the child's property, if he has any property, and is inherited from the deceased. If the child dies, the father retains the remainder of the remuneration. Ashhab[128] related from Mālik that [the benefit of] the payment [to the wet-nurse] accrued to the child, so that if the father dies it belongs to the child; and if the child dies, the remainder is inherited from the child as if it were his property. A teacher's salary is similar to this. But God alone knows best. Muḥammad [ibn Saḥnūn] said: This is also what I hold, and it is what can be deduced by analogy.

(66) Saḥnūn said: Some scholars of the Ḥijāz, including Ibn Dīnār[129] and others, were asked about a teacher's being hired for a group, with a share [of the teacher's salary] being assessed of each member. They said that it is permissible if the parents agree to it among themselves, because it [viz. hiring a teacher to educate their children] is a necessity that people cannot avoid. This is the most likely [answer].

ما جاء في إجارة المعلم ومتى تجب

(٦٣) قال محمد: وكتب شجرة بن عيسى إلى سحنون يسأله عن المعلم يستأجر على صبيان يعلمهم فيمرض أحد الصبيان أو يريد [أبوه] ان يخرج به الى سفر أو غيره. فقال: إذا استؤجر سنة معلومة فقد لزمت آباءهم الإجارة خرجوا أو أقاموا، وإنما تكون الإجارة هنا تبعّض على حال الصبيان لأن منهم الخفيف والثقيل، وقد يكون الصبي له المؤونة في تعليمه ومنهم من لا مؤونة على المعلم فيه، ففي هذا يُنظر.

(٦٤) قال: وقال سحنون: انتقض ما ينوب أباه من إجازة في باقي الشرط، ولا يلزمه ذلك، وكذلك إن مات الأب انتقض ما بقي من الإجارة وكان ما بقي في مال الصبي.

(٦٥) قال محمد: مثل الرضاع إذا استأجر الرجل لولده من يُرضعه ثم مات الأب أو الصبي، فإن عبد الرحمن روى عن مالك: أن الإجارة تنتقض، ويكون ما بقي في مال الصبي إن كان له مال، ويكون ذلك موروثاً عن الميت. وإن مات الصبي أخذ الأب باقي الإجارة. وروى أشهب عن مالك: أن تلك العطية نفذت للصبي، فإن مات الأب كانت للصبي، وإن مات الصبي كان ما بقي موروثاً عن الصبي كأنه مال له. وكذلك أجرة المعلم مثل هذا. والله أعلم. قال محمد: وهذا قولي، وهو القياس.

(٦٦) قال سحنون: وقد سئل بعض علماء الحجاز منهم ابن دينار وغيره - أن يُستأجر المعلم لجماعة وأن يفرض على كل واحد ما ينوبه. فقال: يجوز إذا تراضى بذلك الآباء لأن هذا ضرورة ولا بد للناس منه وهو أشبه.

(67) He also said: It is as if a man should hire two slaves from two men, each of whom has a slave: the case is similar to sale. However, ᶜAbd al-Raḥmān [ibn al-Qāsim] does not permit such hiring because he does not permit it in a sale. God alone knows best.

(68) [Saḥnūn] said: There is no harm in the teacher's buying for himself such requisites as are appropriate for him if he finds no one to provide him with a sufficiency of them. There is no harm in his occupying himself with study during the times when the children have no need for him, as when they are engaged in writing and dictating to each other, when that is of benefit to them; for some of our colleagues have given the teacher leeway in this.

(69) When Mālik was asked about the teacher's appointing a monitor for the children, he said: If he is as effective as the teacher. Thus, he opened the way for it if the child benefits from it.

(70) I also heard him[130] say: Al-Mughīrah[131] and Ibn Dīnār—both were scholars of the Ḥijāz—once disputed with each other about a child who completes the Qur'ān with a teacher, but the father says that he does not know it by heart. Al-Mughīrah said: If the child has studied the entire Qur'ān with the teacher, can recite it all by looking at the text, and can pronounce its letters correctly, then, even if he makes slight mistakes that are inevitable in letters and such things, the [remuneration for] completion is owed to the teacher: from the prosperous [according to] their measure, and from the impoverished [according to] their measure. That is what I remember of the words of Mālik.

(71) Ibn Dīnār said that he had heard Mālik say that the [remuneration for] completion is owed to the teacher according to the man's degree of wealth or poverty as judged by the competent authorities.[132]

(72) I think that if the father and the teacher dispute over the child's not knowing the Qur'ān, in that case if the child recites from the Qur'ān, looking [at the text], from the point at which [remuneration for] completion would have been owed to the teacher if the child had studied under him alone, I would award it to him; I would take no account of the child's reciting nothing but that, because this teacher should not be held accountable for what the child has not studied with him. All have agreed that if the child studies one-third [of the Qur'ān], up to the Sura of the Cow[133] with him, the [remuneration for] completion is due if the child knows how to recite it as I have described to you, and the teacher is not held accountable for anything else that the child has not studied with him.

(٦٧) وقال: وهو بمنزلة ما لو استأجر رجل عبدين من رجلين لكل واحد عبد. وإنما ذلك بمنزلة البيع، وعبد الرحمن لا يجوز هذه الإجارة لأنه لا يجوز ذلك في البيع. والله أعلم.

(٦٨) قال: ولا بأس للمعلم أن يشتري لنفسه ما يصلحه من حوائجه إذا لم يجد من يكفيه. ولا بأس أن ينظر في العلم في الأوقات التي يستغني الصبيان عنه مثل أن يصيروا إلى الكتب وإملاء بعضهم على بعض إذا كان ذلك منفعة لهم، فإن هذا قد سهل فيه بعض أصحابنا.

(٦٩) وسئل مالك عن المعلم يجعل للصبيان عريفاً فقال: إن كان مثله في نفاذه فقد سهل في ذلك إذا كان للصبي في ذلك منفعة.

(٧٠) وسمعته يقول: تنازع المغيرة وابن دينار كلاهما من علماء الحجاز - عن الصبي يختم القرآن عند المعلم فيقول الأب: إنه لا يحفظ. فقال المغيرة: إذا كان أخذ القرآن كله عنده، وقرأه الصبي كله نظراً في المصحف وأقام حروفه فإن أخطأ منه اليسير الذي لا بد منه مثل الحروف ونحوها، فقد وجبت للمعلم الختمة وهو « عَلَى المُوسِعِ قَدَرُه وعلى المُقتِرِ قَدَره »، وهو الذي أحفظ من قول مالك.

(٧١) وقال ابن دينار: سمعت مالكا يقول: تجب للمعلم الختمة على قدر يسر الرجل وعسره، يجتهد في ذلك أولو النظر للمسلمين.

(٧٢) وأرى أنه إذا تنازع الأب والمعلم في الصبي أنه لا يعلم القرآن، فإنه إذا قرأ منه نظرا من الموضع الذي لو كان أخذه عنده مفرداً وجبت له الختمة، قضيت له بها، ولا أبالي أن لا يقرأ غير ذلك لأنه لو لم يأخذه عنده، لم يسأل هذا المعلم عنه. وأجمعوا على أنه إذا أخذ عنده الثلث إلى سورة البقرة، أن الختمة واجبة، إذا عرف أن يقرأ، كما وصفت لك، ولا يسأل عن غير ذلك مما لم يكن أخذه عنده.

(73) He [i.e., Saḥnūn] was asked about a teacher who dies after being hired to teach for a year.[134] He said: If he dies, the remuneration is cancelled. Similarly, if one of the children dies, remuneration in the amount of the remaining remuneration for a similar child is cancelled. Some have said that the remuneration is not cancelled: the teacher, for what is [still] due to him, must make compensation in teaching, and the child's father must bring someone for the teacher to teach to the end of the year; but if [the father] does not do so, the teacher receives the full remuneration.

(74) Muḥammad [ibn Saḥnūn] said: The first opinion is that of ᶜAbd al-Raḥmān [ibn al-Qāsim], and it is followed in practice. The case is like that of a particular riding camel: if it perishes, the hire is cancelled. It is not permissible [for the person who hires out riding animals] to bring one similar to it, and no such condition is imposed on him. But God knows best.

(75) I heard [Saḥnūn] say: All our colleagues—Mālik, al-Mughīrah, and the others—have said that the teacher is owed [remuneration for] completion even if he has been hired month by month or to teach the Qurᵓān for a set fee and is owed nothing else. They also said that if the child memorizes the entire Qurᵓān, his gift to the teacher should be greater than if he recites it looking [at the text]. However, if the child cannot spell what is dictated to him and does not understand the letters of the Qurᵓān, nothing should be given to the teacher: the teacher should be disciplined and prevented from teaching if he becomes known for this practice and his negligence becomes manifest.

What has been mentioned about renting out copies of the Qurᵓān, books of jurisprudence, and similar things

(76) Saḥnūn said: I asked Ibn al-Qāsim:[135] Do you think it right for the bound volume of the Qurᵓān to be rented out to be read from? He said: There is no harm in the practice; for Mālik said there is no harm in selling it. [According to] Ibn Wahb, from Ibn Lahīᶜah[136] and Yaḥyá ibn Ayyūb,[137] from ᶜUmārah ibn Ghaziyyah,[138] from Rabīᶜah, [Mālik] said: There is no harm in selling the volume of the Qurᵓān; only the ink, the paper, and the labor are being sold. [And according to] Ibn Wahb, from ᶜAbd al-Jabbār ibn ᶜUmar: Ibn Muṣabbāḥ used to write out

(٧٣) وسئل عن المعلم يستأجر على تعليم سنة فيموت، فقال. إذا مات الفسخت الإجارة، وكذلك إذا مات أحد من الصبيان انفسخ من الإجارة بقدر ما بقي من إجارة مثل الصبي، وقد قيل إن الإجارة لا تنفسخ، وإن على المعلم فيما له مقاصة في التعليم وعلى أبي الصبي أن يأتي بمن يعلمه المعلم تمام السنة، وإلا كانت له الإجارة كاملة.

(٧٤) قال محمد: الأول كلام عبد الرحمن وعليه العمل وإنما ذلك بمنزلة الراحلة يعينها إذا هلكت انفسخ الكراء، ولا يجوز أن يأتي بمثلها ولا يشترط عليه ذلك. والله أعلم.

(٧٥) وسمعته يقول: قال أصحابنا جميعا، مالك والمغيرة وغيرهما: تجب للمعلم الختمة، وإن استؤجر شهرا شهرا، أو على تعليم القرآن بأجر معلوم ولا يجب له غير ذلك. وقالوا: إذا استظهر الصبي القرآن كله، كان أكثر في العطية للمعلم من إذا قرأه نظرا. واذا لم يتهجأ الصبي ما يملي عليه ولا يفهم حروف القرآن لم يعط المعلم شيئا، وأُدب المعلم، ومُنع من التعليم إذا عرف بهذا، وظهر تفريطه.

ما جاء في إجارة المصحف وكتب الفقه وما شابهها

(٧٦) وقال سحنون. قلت لابن القاسم. أرأيت المصحف، أيصح أن يستأجر ليقرأ فيه؟ فقال لا بأس به، لأن مالكا قال: لا بأس ببيعه. عن ابن وهب عن ابن لهيعة ويحيى بن أيوب، عن عمارة بن غزية عن ربيعة وقال: لا بأس ببيع المصحف. وإنما يباع الحبر والورق والعمل. ابن وهب عن عبد الجبار بن عمر أن ابن مصبح كان

copies of the Qurʾān in those days and sell them. (I think he said it was in the time of ʿUthmān ibn ʿAffān, may God the Exalted be pleased with him.) No one reproved him for it, nor have we seen anyone in Medina disapprove of the practice. That is what he said, and none of them sees any harm in the practice.

(77) [Saḥnūn said:] He [viz., Ibn al-Qāsim] said: But I do not think it is permissible to rent out books of jurisprudence. Mālik disapproved of their sale because in it [viz., jurisprudence] scholars have disagreed, some allowing what others disallow.

(78) I asked: Yet you [and those who share your view] have permitted the hiring of a free man, who may not legally be sold. How is it that do you not permit the hiring out of books of jurisprudence?

(79) He replied: It is because in the case of a free man what is being hired out is something determinate: his service can be owned. In the case of books of jurisprudence [what is being hired out] is the reading, and reading cannot be owned.

(80) Muḥammad [ibn Saḥnūn] said: I see no harm in renting out and selling them if one knows the person who rents them or buys them.

(81) Muḥammad [ibn Saḥnūn] said: There is no harm in a man's hiring a teacher to teach his children the Qurʾān for a set salary until a certain date or by the month—and similarly half of the Qurʾān, one-quarter of it, or any part of it that the two specify.

(82) [Muḥammad ibn Saḥnūn] said: If a man hires a teacher for particular children, it is permissible for the teacher to teach other children with them if it does not distract him from teaching those for whom he was hired.

(83) [Muḥammad ibn Saḥnūn] said: If the teacher has been hired for particular children for a year, the children's guardians must rent a place for the teacher.

(84) [Muḥammad ibn Saḥnūn] said: If someone says to the teacher, Teach this slave boy, and you shall have half ownership of him; it is not permitted.

يكتب المصاحف في ذلك الزمان ويبيعها. أحسبه قال: في زمن عثمان بن عفان رضي الله تعالى عنه. ولا ينكر ذلك عليه أحد، ولا رأينا أحداً بالمدينة يذكر ذلك قال: وكلهم لا يرون به بأساً.

(٧٧) قال: ولا أرى أن تجوز إجارة كتب الفقه. لأن مالكاً كره بيعها لأن فيه اختلاف العلماء: قوم يجيزون ما يبطل قوم.

(٧٨) قلت: فقد أجزتم إجارة الحر وهو لا يحل بيعه، فكيف لا تجيزون إجارة كتب الفقه؟

(٧٩) فقال: لأن الاجارة في الحر معلومة، خدمته تملك. وإنما في كتب الفقه القراءة، والقراءة لا تملك.

(٨٠) قال محمد: لا أرى بأساً بإجارتها وبيعها إذا علم من استأجرها أو اشتراها.

(٨١) وقال محمد: لا بأس أن يستأجر الرجل المعلم على أن يعلم أولاده القرآن بأجرة معلومة إلى أجل معلوم أو كل شهر وكذلك نصف القرآن أو ربعه أو ما سميا منه.

(٨٢) قال: واذا استأجر الرجل معلماً على صبيان معلومين جاز للمعلم أن يعلم معهم غيرهم إذا كان لا يشغله ذلك عن تعليم هؤلاء الذين استؤجر لهم.

(٨٣) قال: واذا استؤجر المعلم على صبيان معلومين سنة فعلى أولياء الصبيان كراء موضع المعلم.

(٨٤) قال: واذا قيل للمعلم علم هذا الوصيف، ولك نصفه لم يجز ذلك.

(85) [Muḥammad ibn Saḥnūn] said: If a teacher disciplines a child whom he is permitted to discipline and accidentally puts out his eye or strikes a mortal blow, the teacher must perform expiation for homicide and his fellow tribesmen must pay blood money if he has gone beyond the rule [for teachers].[139] If he has not gone beyond what is the rule and has done what is permissible for him, he does not owe the [full] blood money; his fellow tribesmen are liable for anything amounting to one-third [or more] of [the full blood money], and whatever does not amount to one-third shall be [paid] from his own property.

(86) [Muḥammad ibn Saḥnūn] said: There is no harm in a man's hiring a man to teach his child writing and spelling, for the Prophet (may God bless him and grant him peace) used to accept as ransom [for the life of a prisoner of war] that the man should teach writing.[140]

(87) [Muḥammad ibn Saḥnūn] said: I do not think it permissible to sell books of poetry, grammar, and the like, nor is it permissible to hire someone to teach that. Mālik said: I do not think one should hire someone to teach jurisprudence or the distribution of shares in estates.

(88) Saḥnūn said: If a teacher strikes a child a permissible blow (one that a similar child would be strong enough to bear) and the child dies or suffers injury, the teacher need only perform expiation if the child dies. If the teacher acts excessively,[141] he becomes responsible for blood money from his property despite [his having struck according to] the rule—some say that [the blood money] is to be paid by his fellow tribesmen—along with expiation. If the teacher goes beyond what is the rule and the child sickens and dies because of it, if he has acted excessively with what is deemed to be intent to kill, they shall swear oaths and the next of kin may kill him [in retaliation] for the child. If the teacher has not acted excessively with what is deemed to be intent to kill and has [struck the child] only for the purpose of discipline, but was ignorant of [how to administer] discipline, [the next of kin][142] shall swear oaths and shall be entitled to blood money from [the teacher's] tribesmen, and he himself shall perform expiation. If the teacher did not administer the deed, but someone else [at his command, the teacher is liable][143] as I have explained to you, and the subordinate is not liable. However, if [the subordinate] is of age, some of our colleagues hold that his tribesmen owe blood money and that he must perform expiation. Others hold that the teacher's tribesmen owe blood money and that the person who struck the blow must perform expiation. God alone knows best.

(٨٥) قال: وإذا أدب المعلم الصبي الذي يجوز له فأخطأ، ففقأ عينه، أو أصابه فقتله، كانت على المعلم الكفارة في القتل، والدية على العاقلة إذا جاوز الأدب. وإذا لم يجاوز الأدب، وفعل ما يجوز له فلا دية عليه، وإنما تضمن العاقلة من ذلك ما يبلغ الثلث، وما لم يبلغ الثلث ففي ماله.

(٨٦) قال: ولا بأس بالرجل يستأجر الرجل أن يعلم ولده الخط والهجاء. وقد كان النبي ﷺ يفادي بالرجل يعلم الخط.

(٨٧) قال: ولا أرى أن يجوز بيع كتب الشعر ولا النحو ولا أشباه ذلك، ولا يجوز إجارة من يعلم ذلك. قال مالك: ولا أرى إجارة من يعلم الفقه والفرائض.

(٨٨) قال: قال سحنون: وإذا ضرب المعلم الصبي بما يجوز له أن يضربه إذا كان مثله يقوى على مثل ذلك فمات أو أصابه بلاء لم يكن على المعلم شيء غير الكفارة إن مات. وإن جاوز الأدب ضَمِن الدية في ماله مع الأدب. وقد قيل على العاقلة مع الكفارة، فإن جاوز الأدب فمرض الصبي من ذلك فمات فإن كان جاوز ما يعلم أنه أراد به القتل اقسموا، وقتله به الأولياء وإن كان لم يجاوز ما يرى أنه أراد به القتل إلا على وجه الأدب، إلا أنه جهل الأدب، أَقسم الأولياء واستحقوا الدية قبل العاقلة. وعليه هو الكفارة، فإن كان المعلم لم يل الفعل وإنما وليه غيره كان الأمر على ما فسرت لك، ولا شيء على المأمور. وإن كان بالغا فمن أصحابنا من رأى الدية على عاقلة الفاعل وعليه الكفارة، ومنهم من رأى الدية على عاقلة المعلم، وعلى الفاعل الكفارة والله اعلم.

(89) [Muḥammad ibn Saḥnūn] said: I heard Saḥnūn say: I do not think a teacher should teach *abū jād,*[144] and I think that teachers should be given instructions regarding this. I heard Ḥafṣ ibn Ghiyāth[145] say that *abū jād* were devils' names that they put on the tongues of the Arabs in the time of ignorance [before Islam] and so they wrote them down. Also, I heard a certain scholar allege that they were the names of the children of King Sābūr[146] of Persia that he commanded the Arabs under his authority to write down. I think no one should write them, as it is sinful. Saḥnūn ibn Saᶜīd informed me, from ᶜAbdallāh ibn Wahb, from Yaḥyá ibn Ayyūb, from ᶜAbdallāh ibn Ṭāwūs, from his father, from Ibn ᶜAbbās—may God be pleased with him—who said: People who look to the stars and write *abū jād*—such people have no share [in the world to come].[147]

(90) [Saḥnūn] said: Mālik was asked about a teacher who strikes a child and puts out his eye or breaks his hand. He answered that if the teacher strikes with the whip according to the rule [for discipline], but hits the child with its wooden rod, breaking his arm or putting out his eye, the teacher's tribesmen owe blood money if the teacher was doing what was permissible for him. If the child dies, the teacher's tribesmen owe blood money upon the sworn oaths [of the child's kin], and the teacher must perform expiation. If the teacher strikes the child with the slate or a stick, killing him, he is subject to retribution,[148] because he had no permission to hit the child with a stick or a slate.

(91) I said [to Saḥnūn]: Some Andalusians transmit [the view] that there is no harm in hiring someone to teach jurisprudence, the distribution of shares in estates, poetry, and grammar and that it is like [hiring someone to teach] the Qurᵓān.

(92) [Saḥnūn] said: Mālik and his[149] companions were averse to it. How could it be comparable to [teaching] the Qurᵓān, when the Qurᵓān has an end that can be reached, while the things you have mentioned do not have an end that can be reached—that is unknown [with regard to these things]? Also, jurisprudence and learning are matters over which there is disagreement, but the Qurᵓān is the truth in which there is no doubt. Finally, jurisprudence is not memorized like the Qurᵓān, and so does not resemble it; and it has no end or limit that can be reached.

◆

(٨٩) قال: وسمعت سحنون يقول: لا أرى للمعلم أن يعلم «أبا جاد» وأرى ان يتقدم للمعلمين في ذلك. وقد سمعت حفص بن غياث يحدث إن «ابا جاد» اسماء الشياطين ألقوها على ألسنة العرب في الجاهلية فكتبوها. قال: وسمعت بعض أهل العلم يزعم أنها أسماء ولد سابور، ملك فارس أمر العرب الذين كانوا في طاعته أن يكتبوها فلا أرى لأحد أن يكتبها فإن ذلك حرام. وقد أخبرني سحنون بن سعيد، عن عبد الله بن وهب، عن يحيى بن أيوب، عن عبد الله بن طاوس، عن أبيه، عن ابن عباس (رضي الله عنه) قال: قوم ينظرون في النجوم يكتبون «ابا جاد» أولئك لا خلاق لهم.

(٩٠) قال: وسئل مالك عن معلم ضرب صبياً ففقأ عينه، أوكسر يده، فقال: إن بالدرة على الأدب وأصابه بعودها فكسر يده، اوفقأ عينه، فالدية على العاقلة إذا عمل ما يجوز، فإن مات الصبي فالدية على العاقلة بقسامة وعليه الكفارة وإن ضربه باللوح أو بعصا فقتله فعليه القصاص، لانه لا يؤذن له أن يضربه بعصا ولا بلوح.

(٩١) قلت روى بعض أهل الأندلس انه لا بأس بالإجارة على تعليم الفقه والفرائض، والشعر والنحو. وهو مثل القرآن.

(٩٢) فقال: كره ذلك مالك وأصحابه وكيف يشبه القرآن، والقرآن له غاية ينتهي اليها. وما ذكرت ليس له غاية ينتهي إليها فهذا مجهول. والفقه والعلم أمر قد اختلف فيه. والقرآن هو الحق الذي لا شك فيه. والفقه لا يستظهر مثل القرآن فقال. فهو لا يشبهه ولا غاية له، ولا أمر ينتهى إليه.

Ikhwān al-Ṣafāʾ

The Seventh Epistle of the Propaedeutical Part on the Scientific Arts and What They Aim at

TRANSLATED BY RÜDIGER ARNZEN

◆

In the Name of the Merciful God, the Compassionate.
"Praise be to God, and peace be upon His servants whom He has chosen! Is God better, or what they associate [with Him]?"
(Qurʾān 27:59)

(1) Know, O brother—may God strengthen you and us through His spirit—that we have now finished the explanation of the numerical proportions;[1] informed about their essences, the number of their genera, and the species thereof; described how they arise from potentiality into actuality; and demonstrated that in all of them there are physical bodies as a substratum, that all that is formed out of them are corporeal substances, and that they all serve to cultivate the earth in order to perfect the living conditions of the worldly life! In this epistle we now intend to explain the scientific arts,[2] the substratum of which are spiritual substances—namely, the souls of the students[3]—and to demonstrate that the effects which these [substances] have on the students are altogether of a spiritual kind, as we have explained in the "Epistle on Logic."[4] We will also make clear the essence of the sciences and explain the number of their genera and the species thereof. In addition, we will describe how the sciences which are in the potentiality of the soul turn into actuality,

إخوان الصفا

الرسالة السابعة من القسم الرياضى
فى الصنائع العلمية والغرض منها

بسم الله الرحمن الرحيم

الحمد لله وسلام على عباده الذين اصطفى،
﴿آلله خير أما يشركون﴾ [النمل ٢٧:٥٩]

(١) اعلم أيها الأخ، أيدك الله وإيانا بروح منه، أنا قد فرغنا من ذكر النسب العددية وأخبرنا بماهياتها وكمية أجناسها وأنواع تلك الأجناس ووصفنا كيفية إظهارها من القوة إلى الفعل وبينا أن الموضوع فيها كلها أجسام طبيعية وأن مصنوعاتها كلها جواهر جسمانية وأن أغراضها كلها عمارة الارض لتتميم أمر معيشة الحياة الدنيا فنريد أن نذكر في هذه الرسالة الصنائع العلمية التى هي الموضوع فيها جواهر روحانية التي هي أنفس المتعلمين ونبين أن تأثيراتها في المتعلمين كلها روحانية كما ذكرنا في رسالة المنطق ونبين أيضاً ماهية العلوم ونذكر كمية أجناسها وأنواع تلك الاجناس ونصف أيضاً كيفية إخراج ما في قوة النفس من العلوم إلى الفعل الذي هو الغرض الأقصى في التعاليم وهو إصلاح جواهر النفوس وتهذيب أخلاقها وتتميمها

which is the ultimate goal in education. This in turn involves improving the substance of the soul, refining its morals as well as perfecting and completing it for its continued existence in the eternal abode, which is the home of the living creature insofar as it strives for knowledge, whereas those who seek to remain forever in this world disregard what concerns the hereafter.

Chapter on the Dualism of Man

(2) Know, my brother—may God strengthen you and us through His spirit—that, since man is a complex compounded of a corporeal body and a spiritual soul, and since these two are substances that differ in their qualities, are opposed to each other in their dispositions, and associate with each other in their accidental actions and temporary qualities, he tends [on one hand] to seek everlasting existence in this world and to desire to remain forever in it for the sake of his corporeal body; [on the other hand, he tends] to long for the eternal abode and to desire to enter into it for the sake of his spiritual soul! Thus most of the affairs of man and the vicissitudes of his dispositions are dualistic and opposed to each other—as life and death, waking and sleeping, knowledge and ignorance, thoughtfulness and carelessness, reasonableness and stupidity, sickness and health, dissolution and decency, miserliness and generosity, cowardice and courage, sorrow and joy—and he vacillates between friendliness and hostility, poverty and wealth, youthfulness and age, fear and confidence, honesty and deceitfulness, truth and falsehood, correctness and wrongness, good and evil, ugliness and beauty, and what corresponds to these of the opposed and contrary traits of character, deeds, and words that are manifested by man, who is a complex compounded of a corporeal body and a spiritual soul.

(3) Know, my brother, that the features we just listed should neither be assigned solely to the body nor solely to the soul but to man, who is a whole of these two and compounded of them! Man is a rational, mortal, living being, and his being alive and his rationality are due to his soul, while his mortality is due to his body; accordingly his sleeping is due to his body, while his being awake is due to his soul. By analogy all his other contrary and opposed affairs and dispositions are in part due to the soul and in part due to the body: his reasonableness, for example, as well as his knowledge, his insight, his thinking, his generosity, his courage, his

وتكميلها للبقاء فى دار الآخرة التى هي دار الحيوان لو كانوا يعلمون، والذين يريدون الخلود في الدنيا هم الغافلون عن أمر الآخرة.

(فصل فى مثنوية الانسان)

(٢) اعلم يا أخي أيدك الله وإيانا بروح منه بأن الانسان لما كان هو جملة مجموعة من جسد جسماني ونفس روحانية وهما جوهران متباينان فى الصفات متضادان فى الأحوال ومشتركان في الأفعال العارضة والصفات الزائلة صار الإنسان من أجل جسده الجسماني مريداً للبقاء فى الدنيا متمنياً للخلود فيها؛ ومن أجل نفسه الروحانية صار طالباً للدار الآخرة متمنياً للبلوغ إليها وهكذا أكثر أمور الانسان وتصرف أحواله مثنوية متضادة كالحياة والممات والنوم واليقظة والعلم والجهالة والتذكر والغفلة والعقل والحماقة والمرض والصحة والفجور والعفة والبخل والسخاء والجبن والشجاعة والألم واللذة، وهو متردد بين الصداقة والعداوة والفقر والغنى والشبيبة والهرم والخوف والرجاء والصدق والكذب والحق والباطل والصواب والخطأ والخير والشر والقبح والحسن وما شاكلها من الأخلاق والأفعال والأقاويل المتضادة المتباينة التى تظهر من الإنسان الذي هو جملة مجموعة من جسد جسماني ونفس روحانية.

(٣) واعلم يا أخي بأن هذه الخصال التى عددنا لا تنسب إلى الجسد بمجرده، ولا إلى النفس بمجردها ولكن إلى الإنسان الذي هو جملتهما والمجموع منهما الذي هو حي ناطق مائت؛ فحياته ونطقه من قبل نفسه وموته من قبل جسده، وهكذا نومه من قبل جسده ويقظته من قبل نفسه. وعلى هذا القياس سائر أموره وأحواله المتباينات المتضادات بعضها من قبل النفس وبعضها من قبل الجسد مثال ذلك عقله وعلمه وحلمه وتفكره وسخاؤه وشجاعته وعفته وعدله وحكمته وصدقه وصوابه وخيره

decency, his fairness, his wisdom, his veracity, his correctness, his good nature, and similar praiseworthy features are altogether due to his soul and the purity of its substance, while their opposites are due to the humors of his body and their [different states of] mixture.

Chapter on the Specific Qualities of Body and Soul

(4) Know, my brother, that the qualities which are specific to the body alone are the following: the body is a physical corporeal substance with taste, color, smell, weight, [states of] movement and rest,[5] softness, roughness, hardness, and pliability! It is made up of the four humors, which are blood, phlegm, and the two [sorts of] bile[6] that are generated from the food composed of the four basic elements, which are fire, air, water, and earth with their four physical dispositions: heat, coldness, moisture, and dryness. It, I mean the body, is subject to transience, change, and transition and changes back into these four basic elements after death, which is the separation of the soul from the body and the soul's leaving off using the body [as a tool].

(5) The qualities now which are specific to the soul alone are the following: it is a spiritual, celestial, and luminous substance, animated by itself, potentially knowing, acting by nature, disposed to education, acting upon the bodies and using them as a tool, perfecting the animal[7] and the vegetable bodies for a certain time, after which it leaves these bodies, separates from them, and returns, either in [the state of] enrichment and bliss or in [the state of] penitence, sorrow, and loss, to its origin, source, or principle, [being then] as it was before. It is this that is expressed by God—mighty and sublime is He—in His word: "As He gave you a beginning, so return you [to Him]. A part [of man] has He led aright, and [another] part has justly deserved to go astray" [Qurʾān 7:29–30], and where He—mighty and sublime is He—says: "As We began a first creation, We shall repeat it. [This is] a promise [binding] upon Us. Verily, We have become active!" [Qurʾān 21:104], or where He—exalted is He—says: "Did you think that We had created you for fun and that you would not be returned to Us?" [Qurʾān 23:115]. But that should be sufficient for you, my brother, as chastisement, menace, intimidation, reprimand, reminding, and warning, if you are cautious with respect to the sleep of carelessness and watchful with respect to the slumber of ignorance.

وما شاكلها من الخصال المحمودة فكلها من قبل نفسه وصفاء جوهرها وأضدادها من قبل أخلاط جسده ومزاج أخلاطه.

(فصل في الصفات المختصة بالجسد والنفس)

(٤) واعلم يا أخي بأن الصفات المختصة بالجسد بمجرده هي أن الجسد جوهر جسماني طبيعي ذو طعم ولون و رائحة وثقل وخفة وسكون ولين وخشونة وصلابة و رخاوة، وهو متكون من الاخلاط الأربعة التي هي الدم والبلغم والمرتان المتولدة من الغذاء الكائن من الأركان الاربعة التي هي النار والهواء والماء والارض ذوات الطبائع الاربع التي هي الحرارة والبرودة والرطوبة واليبوسة. وهو منفسد، أعنى الجسد، ومتغير ومستحيل و راجع الى هذه الاركان الأربعة بعد الموت الذي هو مفارقة النفس الجسد وتركها استعماله.

(٥) وأما الصفات المختصة بالنفس بمجردها فهي أنها جوهرة روحانية سماوية نورانية حية بذاتها علامة بالقوة فعالة بالطبع، قابلة للتعاليم فعالة في الأجسام ومستعملة لها ومتممة للأجسام الحيوانية والنباتية إلى وقت معلوم. ثم إنها تاركة لهذه الاجسام ومفارقة لها و راجعة إلى عنصرها ومعدنها ومبدئها كما كانت إما بربح وغبطة أوندامة وحزن وخسران، كما ذكر الله عز وجل بقوله ﴿ كما بدأكم تعودون فريقًا هدى وفريقًا حق عليهم الضلالة﴾ [الاعراف ٣٠-٧:٢٩] وقال عزوجل ﴿ كَمَا بَدَأْنَا أَوَّل خَلْقٍ نُعيدُه وَعْداً عَلَيْنا إنا كُنَّا فاعلين﴾ [الأنبياء ٢١:١٠٤] وقال تعالى ﴿أَفَحَسِبْتُم أَنَّمَا خَلَقْنَاكُم عَبَثًا وأنكم إلينا لا تُرْجَعُون﴾ [المؤمنون ٢٣:١١٥] فكفى بهذا يا أخي زجرًا و وعيداً وتهديداً وتوبيخًا ومذكرًا ونذيرًا إن كنت منتبهًا من نوم الغفلة ومستيقظًا من رقدة الجهالة.

(6) I pray [to God] that He guard you, O pious and merciful brother, against becoming one of those who are rebuked by the Lord of the worlds with the following words: "They have hearts with which they do not understand, they have eyes with which they do not see, and they have ears with which they do not hear. These are like the cattle, nay, they are further astray, these are neglectful" [Qurʾān 7:179]. You wouldn't think that they are rebuked for not taking reasonable care of the affairs of their worldly life, would you? No, surely they are rebuked, because they don't worry about what concerns the hereafter and the return [to the other world][8] and don't comprehend what they are told about the meaning of the hereafter and the path to the return [to the other world], for He says: "They know [only] what appears of the worldly life, [but] of the hereafter they are negligent" [Qurʾān 30:7], and [elsewhere] He says—mighty and sublime is He: "[As for] those who do not believe in the hereafter, their hearts deny, and they are haughty" [Qurʾān 16:22].

Chapter on the Dualism of the Habitus and the Deeds of Man

(7) Having demonstrated that most of the affairs of man and of the vicissitudes of his dispositions are dualistic and opposed to each other, since he is a complex compounded of two different substances, a corporeal body and a spiritual soul, as pointed out above, [we turn now to] his habitus, [which] has also two species—one corporeal (like wealth and worldly goods), the other spiritual, (like knowledge and religion). For knowledge is a habitus of the soul as wealth is a habitus of the body, and just as wealth enables man to enjoy the pleasures of eating and drinking in his worldly life, so he attains through knowledge the path to the hereafter; and through religion he arrives there. Through knowledge the soul becomes bright, illuminated, and sound, just as the body prospers, grows, thrives, and becomes well fed through eating and drinking. Accordingly there are also two sorts of social gathering: one for the purpose of eating, drinking, entertainment, amusement, and bodily pleasures derived from the meat of animals and the plants of the earth in order to keep this changeable, transient, and fading body in good health; the other in order to obtain knowledge, wisdom, and spiritual instruction through delight of the souls, whose substances do not perish and whose happiness shall not come to an end in the eternal abode, as explained by God—mighty is His glory—in His words: "Therein is

(٦) وأعيذك أيها الأخ البار الرحيم أن تكون من الذين ذمهم رب العالمين بقوله ﴿لَهُم قُلوب لا يَفقَهونِ بها ولَهُم أَعيُنٌ لا يُبصِرون بها ولَهُم آذانٌ لا يَسمَعونِ بها أولئك كالأنعام بل هم أضل أولئك هم الغافلون﴾ [الاعراف ٧:١٧٩] أفترى ذمهم من أجل أنهم لم يكونوا يعقلون أمر معيشة الدنيا؟ إنما ذمهم لأنهم لم يكونوا يتفكرون في أمر الآخرة والمعاد ولا يفقهون ما يقال لهم من معانى أمر الآخرة وطريق المعاد فقال ﴿يعلمون ظاهراً من الحياة الدنيا وهم عن الآخرة هم غافلون﴾ [الروم ٣٠:٧] وقال عزوجل ﴿الذين لا يؤمنون بالآخرة قلوبهم منكرة وهم مستكبرون﴾ [النحل ١٦:٢٢].

(فصل في مثنوية قنية الانسان ومثنوية الاعمال)

(٧) ولما تبين أن أكثر أمور الإنسان وتصرف أحواله مثنوية متضادة من أجل أنه جملة مجموعة من جوهرين متباينين جسد جسماني ونفس روحانية كما بينا قبل، صارت قنيته أيضاً نوعين جسمانية كالمال ومتاع الدنيا وروحانية كالعلم والدين وذلك ان العلم قنية للنفس كما أن المال قنية للجسد وكما أن الإنسان يتمكن بالمال من تناول اللذات من الأكل والشرب في الحياة الدنيا فهكذا بالعلم ينال الإنسان طريق الآخرة وبالدين يصل إليها وبالعلم تضيء النفس وتشرق وتصح كما أن بالاكل والشرب ينمى الجسد ويزيد ويربو ويسمن، فلما كان هكذا صارت المجالس أيضاً اثنين مجلس للأكل والشرب واللهو واللعب واللذات الجسمانية من لحوم الحيوان ونبات الأرض لصلاح هذا الجسد المستحيل الفاسد الفانى، ومجلس للعلم والحكمة وسماع روحانى من لذة النفوس التى لا تبيد جواهرها ولا ينقطع سرورها في الدار الآخرة كما ذكر الله جل ثناؤه بقوله ﴿فيها ما تَشتَهيه الأنفس وتلذّ الأَعيُنَ وأنتُم فِيها خالِدون﴾ [الزخرف

what the souls desire and the eyes delight in; and you will remain there [forever]" [Qurʾān 43:71]. Now, since there are two sorts of social gathering, those who ask are likewise twofold: on one hand those who ask with the intention of obtaining worldly possessions[9] in order to keep this body in good health, to bestow benefit on it, or to avert mischief from it; on the other hand those who ask in search of knowledge for the sake of the well-being of the soul, in order to free it from the gloom of ignorance or to acquire a good knowledge of the religion, trying to find the path to the hereafter, eagerly striving to arrive there and to escape from hellfire, as well as for the sake of salvation from the world of becoming and corruption, and [in order to] succeed in reaching and ascending to the world of the celestial spheres and the expanse of the heavens, and [to acquire the benefit of] wandering through the levels of the heavenly gardens[10] and inhaling the spirit and the fragrant smell that is mentioned in the Qurʾān.

Chapter on Knowledge and its Object, on Learning and Teaching,[11] and on the Methods of Asking Questions

(8) Those who seek knowledge and search for the real natures of things should first know what knowledge is, what the object of knowledge is, how many methods of asking questions there are, and what the [correct] answer to each question is, in order that they understand what they are asking about and what to answer if they are questioned; for he who asks a question without understanding what he is asking about won't understand what is stated in reply.

(9) So know, my brother, that knowledge is the form of what is known in the soul of him who knows, and that ignorance is its opposite—that is, the privation of this form in the soul![12] Know that the souls of the scholars are actually knowing while those of the students are potentially knowing, and that learning and teaching are none other than the transformation of what is potentially, I mean [what has] the possibility [to be], into actuality—that is, being! Relating this [transformation] to him who knows, you call it teaching; relating it to him who learns, you call it learning.

(10) Furthermore, know that the species of philosophical questioning are nine like the nine units: (i) whether something is, (ii) what it is, (iii) how much it is, (iv) how it is, (v) which one it is, (vi) where it is, (vii) when it is, (viii) why it is, and (ix) who it is! These can be explicated [as follows]: "Whether something is" is a question that inquires about the being or not-being of something. The answer is "Yes" or "No." The meaning of

[٤٣:٧١ فلما كانت المجالس اثنين صار أيضاً السائلون اثنين واحد يسأل حاجة من عرض الدنيا لصلاح هذا الجسد ولجر المنفعة اليه أو لدفع المضرة عنه، و واحد يسأل مسألة من العلم لصلاح أمر النفس وخلاصها من ظلمات الجهالة أو للتفقه في الدين طلباً لطريق الآخرة واجتهاداً في الوصول اليها وفراراً من نار جهنم ونجاة من عالم الكون والفساد وفوزاً بالوصول والصعود إلى عالم الافلاك وسعة السموات والسيحان في درجات الجنان والتنفس من ذلك الروح والريحان المذكور في القرآن.

(فصل فى العلم والمعلوم والتعلم والتعليم وأوجه السؤال)

(٨) وينبغي لطالبي العلم والباحثين عن حقائق الأشياء أن يعرفوا أولا ما العلم وما المعلوم، وعلى كم وجه يكون السؤال وما جواب كل سؤال حتى يدروا ما الذي يسألون وما الذي يجيبون اذا سئلوا، لأن الذي يسأل ولا يدرى أى شىء سأل فاذا أجيب لا يدرى بأى شىء أجيب.

(٩) واعلم ياأخي بأن العلم إنما هو صورة المعلوم في نفس العالم وضده الجهل وهو عدم تلك الصورة من النفس. واعلم بأن أنفس العلماء علامة بالفعل وأنفس المتعلمين علامة بالقوة وأن التعلم والتعليم ليسا شيئاً سوى إخراج ما في القوة يعنى الامكان الى الفعل يعنى الوجود، فاذا نسب ذلك الى العالم سمى تعليما وإن نسب الى المتعلم سمى تعلماً.

(١٠) واعلم بأن السؤالات الفلسفية تسعة أنواع مثل تسعة آحاد: أولها هل هو والثانى ما هو والثالث كم هو والرابع كيف هو والخامس أي شىء هو والسادس أين هو والسابع متى هو والثامن لِمَ هو والتاسع من هو. تفسيرها: هل هو؟ سؤال

"being" and "not-being" is demonstrated in the "Epistle on the Intellect and the Intelligible."[13] "What something is" is a question that inquires about the real nature of a thing. This is known either through a definition or through an outline,[14] for all things are [divided into] two species: compound and simple. To be more precise, the compound is like the body, the simple is like matter and form. The meaning of these two is demonstrated in the "Epistle on Matter."[15] As for the compounded things, their real nature is known when the things of which they are compounded are known; for example, if it is asked what the real nature of clay is, you state [that it is] a mixture of dust and water, or, accordingly, in response to the question what the real nature of oxymel is, you answer [that it is] a blend of vinegar and honey. To whatever compound this question refers, the things of which it is compounded and by which it is describable have to be mentioned in an analogous way. The philosophers call this kind of description definition; therefore they give the [following] definition of the body: it is a thing with length, breadth, and depth—where their words "a thing" refer to [its] matter while their words "with length, breadth, and depth" refer to [its] form—because the real nature of the body is exactly that which has been stated in its definition. Likewise they say that the definition of man is a rational, mortal, living being,[16] where they mean by their words "rational, living being" the soul and by "mortal" the body, because man is a complex compounded of these two—that is, a corporeal body and a spiritual soul. It is in an analogous way that the real natures of [all] compounded things are known.

(11) As for the things which are not compounded of [other] things but are invented and created in the way that their Creator and Maker—sublime is He—wanted [them to be], their real natures are known by characteristics specific to each. If, for example, it is asked what the real nature of matter is, the answer would be: [it is] a simple substance capable of receiving a form and devoid of any quality; or, if it is asked what form is, the answer would be: it is that by which something is what it is. This kind of description the philosophers call an outline. What distinguishes the definition from the outline is that the definition is taken from the things out of which the definiendum is compounded, as demonstrated [above], while the outline is taken from characteristics specific to what is outlined. Another difference [lies in the fact] that the definition [both] informs you about the substance of the defined thing and differentiates it from something else, while the outline only differentiates what is outlined from something else. So if you, O pious and merciful brother—may God strengthen you and us through His spirit—are asked about the

يبحث عن وجدان شيء أوعن عدمه والجواب نعم أولا. وقد بينا معنى الوجود والعدم في رسالة العقل والمعقول، وما هو سؤال يبحث عن حقيقة الشيء وحقيقة الشيء تعرف بالحد أو بالرسم وذلك أن الأشياء كلها نوعان: مركب وبسيط فالمركب مثل الجسم والبسيط مثل الهيولى والصورة وقد بينا معناهما في رسالة الهيولى والاشياء المركبة تعرف حقيقتها إذا عرفت الأشياء التى هى مركبة منها مثال ذلك إذا قيل ما حقيقة الطين فيقال تراب وماء مختلطان وهكذا إذا قيل ما حقيقة السكنجبين فيقال خل وعسل ممزوجان وعلى هذا القياس كل مركب اذا سئل عنه فيحتاج أن يذكر الأشياء التى هو مركب منها وموصوف بها. والحكماء يسمون مثل هذا الوصف الحد ومن أجل هذا قالوا في حد الجسم إنه الشيء الطويل العريض العميق فقولهم الشيء إشارة الى الهيولى وقولهم الطويل والعريض والعميق إشارة الى الصورة لأن حقيقة الجسم ليست بشيء غير هذه التى ذكرت في حده وهكذا قولهم في حد الانسان أنه حى ناطق مائت؛ فقولهم حى ناطق يعنون به النفس، ومائت يعنون به الجسد، لأن الإنسان هو جملة مجموعة منهما أعنى جسداً جسمانياً ونفساً روحانية وعلى هذا القياس تعرف حقائق الأشياء المركبة من شيء.

(١١) وأما الأشياء التى ليست مركبة من شيء بل مخترعة مبدعة كما شاء باريها وخالقها تعالى فحقيقتها تعرف من الصفات المختصة بها مثال ذلك إذا قيل: ما حقيقة الهيولى فيقال جوهر بسيط قابل للصورة لا كيفية فيه البتة. وإذا قيل ما الصورة فيقال هى التى يكون الشيء بها ما هو، فمثل هذا الوصف تسميه الحكماء الرسم. والفرق بين الحد والرسم أن الحد مأخوذ من الأشياء التى المحدود مركب منها كما بينا، والرسم مأخوذ من الصفات المختصة بالمرسوم، وفرق آخر أن الحد يخبرك عن جوهر الشيء المحدود ويميزه عما سواه، والرسم يميز لك المرسوم عما سواه حسب فينبغي لك أيها الأخ البار الرحيم، أيدك الله وايانا بروح منه إذا سئلت عن حقيقة شيء

real nature of a certain thing, be sure not to rush the answer, but to examine [carefully] whether this thing that you are asked about is compounded or simple, in order that you may answer accordingly.

(12) "How much something is" is a question that inquires about the quantity of a thing. There are two species of quantifiable things: continuous and discrete.[17] The continuous [quantity] has five sub-species: line, plane, solid, place, and time. The discrete has two sub-species: number and movement. Of all these things you can ask how much it is. [As for their essences,] the essence of the number is demonstrated in the "Epistle on Arithmetic,"[18] the essence of movement, time, place, and the solid in the "Epistle on Matter,"[19] and the essence of the line and the plane in the "Epistle on Geometry."[20]

(13) "How something is" is a question that inquires about the quality of a thing. There are many species of quality, which are demonstrated in the "Epistle on the Explanation of the Ten Categories,"[21] each of which is a certain genus.

(14) "Which one something is" is a question that inquires about the particular with reference to the general, or the part with reference to the whole. For example, if you say: the star is rising, it might be asked: which star is it, since there are many stars? But if you say: the sun is rising, it is impossible to ask: which sun is it, since its genus comprises no plurality, as also holds true for the moon.

(15) "Where something is" is a question that inquires about either the place of something or [its position] or its rank.[22] The difference between them is that place is a characteristic of some bodies, not of all. For example, if someone says: "Where is Zayd?" and it is answered [that he is] in the house, or, in the mosque, or, at the marketplace, or some other locality. Position, on the other hand, is a characteristic of accident. There are two species of accidents: corporeal and spiritual. The corporeal accidents inhere in bodies. For example, if someone says: "Where is the blackness?" it is answered that it inheres in the black body, and correspondingly all the other colors, the tastes, and the smells inhere in bodies with a [certain] taste, color, or smell. The analogous applies to all corporeal accidents.

(16) As for the spiritual accidents, they inhere in spiritual substances. For example, if someone says: "Where is knowledge?" it is answered that it inheres in the soul of him who knows, and likewise generosity, courage, uprightness, and similar characteristics inhere in the soul, as applies also to their opposites. It is true that many scholars who do not have experience with questions concerning the soul and do

من الاشياء أن لا تستعجل بالجواب بل تنظر هل ذلك الشيء المسؤول عنه مركب أم بسيط حتى تجيب بحسب ذلك.

(١٢) وأما كم هو؟ فسؤال يبحث عن مقدار الشيء، والأشياء ذوات المقادير نوعان: متصل ومنفصل فالمتصل خمسة انواع: الخط والسطح والجسم والمكان والزمان، والمنفصل نوعان: العدد والحركة. وهذه الأشياء كلها، يقال فيها كم هو وقد بينا ماهية العدد في رسالة الأرثماطيقي وماهية الحركة والزمان والمكان والجسم فى رسالة الهيولى وماهية الخط والسطح فى رسالة الهندسة.

(١٣) وأما كيف هو؟ فسؤال يبحث عن صفة الشيء والصفات كثيرة الأنواع وقد بيناها فى رسالة شرح المقولات العشر التى كل واحدة منها جنس الأجناس.

(١٤) وأما أي شيء هو؟ فسؤال يبحث عن واحد من الجملة، وعن بعض من الكل مثال ذلك إذا قيل طلع الكوكب فيقال أي كوكب هو لأن الكواكب كثيرة. وأما إذا قيل طلعت الشمس فلا يقال أي شمس هي إذ ليس من جنسها كثرة وكذلك القمر.

(١٥) وأما أين هو؟ فسؤال يبحث عن مكان الشيء أو عن رتبته والفرق بينهما أن المكان صفة لبعض الأجسام لا لكلها، مثال ذلك إذا قيل: أين زيد؟ فيقال فى البيت أو في المسجد أو في السوق أو فى موضع آخر. وأما المحل فهو صفة للعرض، والعرض نوعان جسماني وروحاني فالأعراض الجسمانية حالة في الأجسام مثال ذلك إذا قيل أين السواد فيقال حال فى الجسم الأسود وهكذا الألوان كلها والطعوم والروائح حالة في الأجسام ذات الطعم واللون والرائحة وهكذا حكم جميع الأعراض الجسمانية.

(١٦) وأما الأعراض الروحانية فحالة في الجواهر الروحانية مثال ذلك إذا قيل: أين العلم؟ فيقال: حال فى نفس العالم، وكذلك السخاء والشجاعة والعدل وما شاكلها من الصفات حالة في النفس وهكذا حكم أضدادها. وقد ظن كثير من أهل العلم ممن

not know its substance assume that these accidents would inhere in the body and that each of them would have a specific place [of inherence]. They maintain, for example, that knowledge is in the heart, desire in the liver, reasoning in the brain, courage in the bile, cowardice in the spleen, and analogously for the other accidents.[23] But, as we have demonstrated in the "Epistle on the Structure of the Body,"[24] these parts of the body are tools and instruments for the soul through which and from which those actions and dispositions of character in fact become manifest in the body.

(17) Rank, for its part, belongs to the characteristics of the spiritual substances. For example, if someone says: "Where is the soul?" it is answered that it [ranks] beneath the intellect and above nature. Similarly, if someone says: "Where among the numbers is the five?" it is answered that it [comes] after the four and before the six. By analogy, the same holds true for [all] spiritual substances not characterized by a certain place or position but by [their] rank, as we have demonstrated in the "Epistle on the Rational Principles."[25]

(18) "When something is" is a question that inquires about the time when something is. There are three [levels of] time: the past (such as yesterday), the future (such as tomorrow), and the present time (such as today). The same applies to the years, months, and hours. The essence of time and the different statements of the scholars about its essence are demonstrated in the "Epistle on Matter."[26]

(19) "Why something is" is a question that inquires about the cause of something caused. You should know, my brother, that for everything caused by production there are four [kinds of] causes: material cause, formal cause, effective cause, and final cause.[27] For the chair, the door, or the bed, for example, the material cause is wood; the formal cause is [their] shape and [their] rectangularity; the effective cause is the carpenter; and the final cause for the chair is to sit on it, for the bed to sleep in it, and for the door to close off the house. In an analogous way, these four [kinds of] causes apply necessarily to everything that is caused. So, if you are asked about the cause of something, first make sure about which one you are asked, in order to answer accordingly.

(20) "Who someone is" is a question which inquires about the identification of something. The grammarians say that this question is directed solely at those who are endowed with reason, others say that it refers to all [living beings] with knowledge and the ability to make distinctions.[28] The answer to this [question] consists in instructing the inquirer about

ليست له خبرة بأمر النفس ولا معرفة بجوهرها أن هذه الأعراض حالة في الجسم كل واحد فى محل مختص مثال ذلك ما قالوا أن العلم في القلب والشهوة فى الكبد والعقل في الدماغ والشجاعة في المرارة والجبن فى الطحال وعلى هذا القياس سائر الأعراض وقد بينا نحن أن هذه الأعضاء آلات وأدوات للنفس تظهر بها ومنها فى الجسد هذه الافعال والأخلاق في رسالة تركيب الجسد.

(١٧) وأما الرتبة فهي من صفات الجواهر الروحانية، مثال ذلك إذا قيل أين النفس، فيقال هي دون العقل وفوق الطبيعة وهكذا إذا قيل أين الخمسة من العدد فيقال بعد الأربعة وقبل الستة وعلى هذا القياس حكم الجواهر الروحانية التى لا توصف بالمكان ولا بالمحل ولكن بالرتبة كما بينا فى رسالة المبادي العقلية.

(١٨) وأما متى هو؟ فسؤال يبحث عن زمان كون الشيء. والأزمان ثلاثة: ماض، مثل أمس؛ ومستقبل، مثل غد؛ وحاضر، مثل اليوم. وهكذا حكم السنين والشهور والساعات وقد بينا ماهية الزمان واختلاف أقاويل العلماء في ماهيته فى رسالة الهيولى.

(١٩) وأما لم هو فسؤال يبحث عن علة الشيء المعلول. واعلم يا أخي بأن لكل معلول صناعي أربع علل: إحداها علة هيولانية والثانية علة صورية والثالثة علة فاعلية والرابعة علة تمامية. مثال ذلك الكرسى والباب والسرير فان العلة الهيولانية فيها الخشب والعلة الصورية الشكل والتربيع والعلة الفاعلية النجار والعلة التمامية للكرسى القعود عليه وللسرير النوم عليه وللباب ليغلق على الدار. وعلى هذا القياس كل معلول لا بد له من هذه العلل الأربع فاذا سئلت عن علة شيء فاعرف أولا عن أيها تسأل حتى يكون الجواب بحسب ذلك.

(٢٠) وأما من هو؟ فسؤال يبحث عن التعريف للشيء ويقول علماء النحو إن هذا السؤال لا يتوجه إلا إلى كل ذي عقل ويقول قوم آخرون إلى كل ذي علم وتمييز

one of [the following] three issues: [it] either refers to the home, or to the descent, or to the profession. For example, if someone says: "Who is Zayd?" it is answered that [he is] a Basrian, with reference to his home, or [that he is] a Hashimite, with reference to his descent, or [that he is] a carpenter, with reference to his profession.

(21) This, now, was an abridged survey of the number of questions and their answers, of the inquiries of the sciences, and of the consideration of the real natures of things, [set forth] as a kind of introduction and preliminary in order to make the consideration of philosophical logic better approachable to the discernment of the students and to familiarize them with these [matters] prior to examining the *Isagoge*—that is, the introduction into philosophical logic.[29]

Chapter on the Genera of the Sciences

(22) Having completed the explanation of the essence of the sciences, the species of questions, and what answer each of them requires, we now intend to explain the genera of the sciences and their species, in order to make available for those who seek knowledge a *vade mecum* [that directs them] to the aims of their seeking and guides them to what they are searching for, since the longing of souls for the different sciences and for the disciplines of refinement is similar to the desire of bodies for foods with various tastes, colors, and smells.

(23) So know, my brother, that the sciences in which man is engaged are divided into three genera: the propaedeutical sciences, the sciences of the canonical law of Islam, and the purely philosophical sciences.

(24) The propaedeutical sciences are the sciences[30] of refinement, most of which were established for the necessities of livelihood and the well-being of the worldly life. They comprise nine species: the science of writing and reading; the science of language and grammar; the science of reckoning and balancing; the science of poetry and prosody; the science of premonition, auspices and the like; the science of magic, conjuration, alchemy, stratagems and the like; the science of handicrafts and professions; the science of buying and selling, trade, crop and stock farming; and the science of biography and historiography.

(25) As for the sciences of Islamic law,[31] which were established as an art of healing for the souls and for the seeking after the hereafter, they comprise six species: the science of the revelation; the science of the [allegorical] exegesis; the science of the authorized transmissions and

والجواب فيه أن يعرف السؤال بأحد ثلاثة أشياء: إما أن ينسب إلى بلده أو إلى أصله أو إلى صناعته. مثال ذلك إذا قيل: من زيد؟ فيقال: البصري، ينسب إلى بلده، والهاشمي إلى أصله، والنجار إلى صناعته.

(٢١) فهذه جملة مختصرة فى كمية السؤالات وأجوبتها ومباحث العلوم والنظر فى حقائق الأشياء شبه المدخل والمقدمات ليقرب من فهم المتعلمين النظر فى المنطق الفلسفي وليوقفوا عليها قبل النظر فى إيساغوجي الذي هو المدخل الى المنطق الفلسفى.

(فصل فى أجناس العلوم)

(٢٢) وإذ قد فرغنا من ذكر ماهية العلوم وأنواع السؤالات وما يقتضى كل واحد من الاجوبة، فنريد أن نذكر أجناس العلوم وأنواع تلك الأجناس ليكون دليلا لطالبى العلم إلى أغراضهم وليهتدوا إلى مطلوباتهم لأن رغبة النفوس فى العلوم المختلفة وفنون الآداب كشهوات الأجسام للأطعمة المختلفة الطعم واللون والرائحة.

(٢٣) فاعلم يا أخي بأن العلوم التى يتعاطاها البشر ثلاثة أجناس فمنها الرياضية، ومنها الشرعية الوضعية، ومنها الفلسفية الحقيقية.

(٢٤) فالرياضية هي علم الآداب التى وضع أكثرها لطلب المعاش وصلاح أمر الحياة الدنيا، وهي تسعة أنواع: أولها علم الكتابة والقراءة؛ ومنها علم اللغة والنحو؛ ومنها علم الحساب والمعاملات؛ ومنها علم الشعر والعروض، ومنها علم الزجر والفأل وما يشاكله، ومنها علم السحر والعزائم والكيمياء والحيل وما شاكلها، ومنها علم الحرف والصنائع، ومنها علم البيع والشراء والتجارات والحرث والنسل، ومنها علم السير والاخبار.

(٢٥) فأما أنواع العلوم الشرعية التى وضعت لطب النفوس وطلب الآخرة فهي ستة أنواع: أولها علم التنزيل، وثانيها علم التأويل، والثالث علم الروايات

reports [concerning the Prophet Muḥammad and his companions];[32] the science of Islamic jurisprudence, normative traditions, and the categories of assessment;[33] the science of [religious] exhortation, parenesis, asceticism, and mysticism;[34] and the science of the interpretation of dreams. Now, the scholars of the revelation are the reciters [of the Qurʾān] and those who know it by heart; the scholars of the [allegorical] exegesis are the imams and the successors[35] of the prophets; the scholars of the [prophetic] transmissions are the representatives of [the science of] hadith; the scholars of the categories of assessment and of the normative traditions are the jurisprudents; the scholars of [religious] exhortation and parenesis are the worshipers, ascetics, monks and the like; and the scholars of interpretation of dreams are the oneirocritics.

(26) The philosophical sciences, for their part, comprise the following four species: the mathematical sciences, the logical sciences, the physical sciences, and the theological sciences.

(27) The mathematical sciences [are divided into] four species: (i) arithmetic—that is, the knowledge about the essence of number, the number of its species, the peculiarities of these species, how [the numbers] increase starting from the one which [comes] before the two, and what meanings are assigned to them when they are joined to one another; (ii) geometry—that is, surveying,[36] meaning, the knowledge about the essence of the proportions of things with [one or more] dimensions, the number of their species, the peculiarities of these species, what meanings are assigned to them when they are joined to one another, and how they are developed starting from the point, the beginning of the line (which is to the art of surveying what one is for the art of numbers); (iii) astronomy—that is, [the science of] the stars, meaning, the knowledge about the number of the spheres, the stars and the signs of the zodiac, the quantity of their distances and the proportions of their bodies, how they are composed, the velocity of their movements and how they revolve, the essence of their natures, and how they indicate what will be before it is;[37] and (iv) music—that is, the science of harmony, meaning, the knowledge about the essence of the proportions [of tones], how things of different substances, disparate forms, contrary dynamics, and opposing modes might be combined, and how they might be united and combined in a way that they are no longer opposing, but harmonize with each other, form a unity, become one single entity, and produce one single effect or a variety of effects. On each of these arts we have composed an epistle as a kind of introduction and preliminaries.

والأخبار، والرابع علم الفقه والسنن والأحكام، والخامس علم التذكار والمواعظ والزهد والتصوف، والسادس علم تأويل المنامات. فعلماء التنزيل هم القراء والحفظة، وعلماء التأويل هم الأئمه وخلفاء الأنبياء، وعلماء الروايات هم أصحاب الحديث، وعلماء الأحكام والسنن هم الفقهاء، وعلماء التذكار والمواعظ هم العباد والزهاد والرهبان ومن شاكلهم، وعلماء تأويل المنامات هم المعبرون.

(٢٦) واما العلوم الفلسفية فهى اربعة انواع: منها الرياضيات. ومنها المنطقيات، ومنها الطبيعيات، ومنها الالهيات.

(٢٧) فالرياضيات أربعة أنواع أولها الأرثما طيقي، وهو معرفة ماهية العدد وكمية أنواعه وخواص تلك الأنواع وكيفية نشوئها من الواحد الذي قبل الإثنين وما يعرض فيها من المعاني اذا أضيف بعضها إلى بعض. والثانى الجومطريا وهو الهندسة وهي معرفة ماهية المقادير ذوات الأبعاد وكمية أنواعها وخواص تلك الأنواع وما يعرض فيها من المعاني اذا أضيف بعضها إلى بعض وكيفية مبدئها من النقطة التى هي رأس الخط وهي فى صناعة الهندسة كالواحد فى صناعة العدد، والثالث الاسطرنوميا وهى النجوم وهي معرفة كمية الأفلاك والكواكب والبروج وكمية أبعادها ومقادير أجرامها وكيفية تركيبها وسرعة حركاتها وكيفية دورانها وماهية طبائعها وكيفية دلائلها على الكائنات قبل كونها والرابع الموسيقى الذي هو علم التأليف وهو معرفة ماهية النسب وكيفية تأليف الأشياء المختلفة الجواهر المتباينة الصور المتضادة القوى المتنافرة الطبائع كيف تجمع ويؤلف بينها كيما لا تتنافر وتأتلف وتتحد وتصير شيئاً واحداً وتفعل فعلا واحداً أوعدة أفعال وقد عملنا فى كل صناعة من هذه الصناعات رسالة شبه المدخل والمقدمات.

(28) The logical sciences have five species: poetics[38]—that is, the knowledge about the art of poetry; rhetoric[39]—that is, the knowledge about the art of making orations; topics[40]—that is, the knowledge about the art of debating; analytics[41]—that is, the knowledge about the art of proving; and sophistics[42]—that is, the knowledge about the art of misleading[43] in disputes and debates. The ancient and later philosophers have already spoken on these arts and sciences, and they have composed many books on them which are widespread among men.

(29) As a matter of fact, Aristotle has written three other books[44] which he constructed as preliminaries to the *Book of Demonstration*:[45] the *Categories, On Interpretation,* and the *Prior Analytics*.[46] But he bestowed the greatest care upon the *Book of Demonstration,* because the proof is the scales of the philosophers by means of which they differentiate between verity and falsity in statements, right and wrong in opinions, truth and invalidity in convictions, and good and evil in deeds, as the common people determine by means of weights, dry measures, and linear measures[47] the value of things weighed, metered, or measured when they disagree on their estimation or appraisal. Again, the scholars, who know the art of proving, determine by means of it the real natures of things when they disagree on their estimation by intellect or their appraisal by opinion, as the poets, who are versed in prosody, determine, in case of disagreement, the equal value of rhymes and of alterations of the metrical foot[48] by means of the art of prosody, which is the scales of poetry.

(30) [In addition,] Porphyry[49] has written a book entitled *Isagoge,* which is the introduction into the art of philosophical logic. But, owing to the fact that there has been more than enough talk about these books, and that they have been translated from one language into another by people who neither understood them nor the notions [used] in them, the understanding of these notions has been made inaccessible to those who examine the books and learning them has been complicated for the students. In fact, we have written on each of these arts an epistle[50] in which we explain the essential points[51] and avoid any expatiation; nevertheless we would like to explain here the aim of what is [treated] in each epistle, in order that everyone who is going to examine them already knows the aim of each of these arts before starting his examination thereof. So, we say:

(٢٨) والعلوم المنطقيات خمسة أنواع: أولها انولوطيقيا وهي معرفة صناعة الشعر. والثانى ريطوريقيا وهي معرفة صناعة الخطب، والثالث طوسيقا وهي معرفة صناعة الجدل، والرابع يولوطيقا وهي معرفة صناعة البرهان، والخامس سوفسطيقا وهي معرفة صناعة المغالطين في المناظرة والجدل. وقد تكلم الحكماء الأولون والمتأخرون في هذه الصنائع والعلوم وصنفوا فيها كتباً كثيرة وهي موجودة في أيدي الناس.

(٢٩) وقد عمل أرسطاطاليس ثلاثة كتب أخر وجعلها مقدمات لكتاب البرهان: أولها قاطيغورياس، والثاني باريمنياس، والثالث انولوطيقيا الاولى، وانما جعل عنايته أكثرها بكتاب البرهان، لأن البرهان ميزان الحكماء يعرفون به الصدق من الكذب في الأقوال، والصواب من الخطأ في الآراء، والحق من الباطل في الاعتقادات، والخير من الشر في الأفعال، كما يعرف جمهور الناس بالموازين والمكاييل والأذرع تقدير الأشياء الموزونة والمكيلة والمذروعة اذا اختلفوا في حزرها وتخمينها، فهكذا العلماء العارفون بصناعة البرهان يعرفون بها حقائق الاشياء اذا اختلف فيها حزر العقول وتخمين الرأي. كما يعرف الشعراء العروضيون استواء القوافى وانزحافها اذا اختلف فيه بصناعة العروض الذي هو ميزان الشعر.

(٣٠) وقد عمل فرفوريوس الصورى كتاباً وسماه إيساغوجي وهو المدخل الى صناعة المنطق الفلسفي، ولكن من أجل أنهم طولوا الخطب فيها ونقلها من لغة الي لغة من لم يكن عارفاً بها وبمعانيها انغلق على الناظرين فى هذه الكتب فهم معانيها، وعسر على المتعلمين أخذها وقد عملنا فى كل واحدة من هذه الصنائع رسالة ذكرنا فيها نكت ما يحتاج اليه وتركنا التطويل. لكن نريد أن نذكر غرض ما فى كل رسالة منها هاهنا ليكون من ينظر فيها قد عرف غرض كل صناعة من هذه قبل النظر فيها فنقول:

(31) The aim of what [is found] in the *Isagoge* is the knowledge about the meaning of the six [simple] concepts[52] used by the philosophers in their treatises—that is, the terms *individual, species, genus, differentia specifica, proprium,* and *accident,* as well as [the knowledge] about the essence of each of these, of how they are coordinated with one another, about the essence of their outlines[53] by which they are distinguished from one another, and about how they point to the notions that are part of the thoughts of the soul.

(32) As for the aim of the *Categories,* it is the knowledge about the meaning of the ten concepts, each of which is called a genus, about [the fact] that one of them is substance and [the other] nine accidents, as well as [the knowledge] about the essence of each of them, of the numbers of their species, of the outline of each of them by which they are distinguished from one another, and how they point to all the notions that are part of the soul's thoughts.

(33) As for the aim of what [is found] in *On Interpretation,* it is the knowledge about those ten concepts of the *Categories* and the notions they point to in case they are interlinked for the purpose of forming utterances or judgments that might be true or false.

(34) Now, the aim of what [is found] in the *Prior Analytics* is the knowledge about how those concepts are interlinked once again in order to form [logical] premises out of them, about the number of their species, and about how to employ them in order to form out of them a syllogism[54] and a combination of judgments and their conclusions. As for the aim of what [is found] in the *Posterior Analytics,* it is the knowledge about how to make use of the true syllogism and the correct proof that is without error and mistake.

(35) As for the physical sciences, they are [divided into] seven species: The first of them is the science of the corporeal principles—that is, the knowledge about [the following] five things: matter, form, time, place, and movement, and what meanings are assigned to them when they are joined to one another.

(36) The second is the science of the heavens and the cosmos—that is, the knowledge about the substances of the spheres and the stars and their number, how they are composed and why they revolve, whether or not they are subject to coming-to-be and corruption as the four elements beneath the lunar sphere are, what is the cause of the movements of the stars and of the difference between them regarding velocity and slowness, what is the cause of the movement of the spheres, what is the cause of

(٣١) أما غرض ما فى إيساغوجي فهو معرفة معاني الستة الألفاظ التي تستعملها الفلاسفة في أقاويلها، وهو قولهم الشخص والنوع والجنس والفصل والخاصة والعرض، وماهية كل واحد منها وكيفية اشتراكاتها وماهية رسومها التى تميز بعضها من بعض وكيفية دلالاتها على المعاني التى فى أفكار النفوس.

(٣٢) وأما غرض قاطيغورياس فهو معرفة معانى العشرة ألفاظ التى كل واحدة يقال لها جنس الأجناس وإن واحداً منها جوهر وتسعة أعراض، وماهية كل واحد منها وكمية أنواعها ورسم كل واحد منها المميز لها بعضها من بعض وكيفية دلالتها على جميع المعانى التى في أفكار النفوس.

(٣٣) وأما غرض ما في بارمينياس فهو معرفة تلك العشرة الألفاظ التى هي فى قاطيغورياس وماتدل عليه من المعانى عند التركيب حتى تصير كلمات وقضايا ويكون منها الصدق والكذب.

(٣٤) وأما غرض ما فى أنولوطيقا الأولى فهو معرفة كيفية تركيب تلك الألفاظ مرة أخرى حتى يكون منها مقدمات وكمية أنواعها وكيف تستعمل حتى يكون منها شىء محسوس واقتران القضايا ونتائجها. وأما غرض ما في انولولطيقا الثانية فهو معرفة كيفية استعمال القياس الحق والبرهان الصحيح الذي لا خطأ فيه ولا زلل.

(٣٥) وأما العلوم الطبيعية فهى سبعة أنواع: أولها علم المبادىء الجسمانية وهى معرفة خمسة أشياء الهيولى والصورة والزمان والمكان والحركة وما يعرض فيها من المعاني إذا أضيف بعضها إلى بعض.

(٣٦) والثانى علم السماء والعالم وهو معرفة جواهر الأفلاك والكواكب وكميتها وكيفية تركيبها وعلة دورانها وهل تقبل الكون والفساد كما تقبل الأركان الأربعة التى هى دون فلك القمر أم لا؟ وما علة حركات الكواكب واختلافها في السرعة والابطاء؟ وما علة حركة الأفلاك؟ وما علة سكون الأرض في وسط الفلك في

the immobility of the earth in the middle of the sphere, [that is,] in the centre, whether or not there is another body outside the cosmos, whether there is in the cosmos empty space without anything in it, and similar fields of investigation.

(37) The third is the science of coming-to-be and corruption—that is, the knowledge about the essence of the substances of the four elements, namely fire, air, water, and earth, about how they change from one into the other through the influence of the higher entities, [how] things arise and develop out of them, such as minerals, plants and animals, and how they change back into them at [their] corruption.

(38) The fourth is the science of weather events—that is, the knowledge about how changes in the air come about through the influences of the stars by means of their movements and through radiating their rays upon those [four] elements and [how] the latter are affected by them. [That applies] in particular to the air, for it is rich in nuances and changes through light and shade, heat and cold, alternations of winds, fogs, clouds, rains, snows, hail, lightnings, thunders, shooting stars, thunderbolts, comets, rainbows, hurricanes, haloes, and similar changes and events that occur above our heads.

(39) The fifth is the science of minerals—that is, the knowledge about the mineral substances that are bound together through gases congested in the interior of the earth and through sedimentations bound together under [the influence of] weather factors, in mountain caverns, and in the depths of the sea, such as [mineral] drugs and substances that consist of sulfates, various sorts of mercury, alunites, mineral salts, ammonia, gold, silver, copper, iron, ceruse, lead, antimony, arsenic, quartz, precious stones,[55] bezoar stones,[56] and the like, as well as the knowledge about their peculiarities and their useful and harmful qualities.

(40) The sixth is the science of plants—that is, the knowledge about all plants which are planted or sown or which grow wild on the surface of the earth, on mountain peaks, in the depth of the waters, or on the banks of rivers (such as trees, cultivated plants, legumes, weeds, herbs, or grasses). It is the knowledge [also] about the number of their species and the peculiarities thereof, about the zones where they grow, how they send out roots into the earth, bring up branches and stems into the air, and spread over the surface of the earth. [It is also knowledge about how] their branches put forth shoots[57] in [all] directions. [It is about] the shapes of

المركز؟ وهل خارج العالم جسم آخر أم لا؟ وهل في العالم موضع فارغ لا شيء فيه؟ وما شاكل ذلك من المباحث.

(٣٧) والثالث علم الكون والفساد وهو معرفة ماهية جواهر الأركان الأربعة التي هي النار والهواء والماء والأرض وكيف يستحيل بعضها إلى بعض بتأثيرات الاشخاص العالية ويكون منها الحوادث والكائنات من المعادن والنبات والحيوان وكيف تستحيل إليها راجعة عند الفساد.

(٣٨) والرابع علم حوادث الجو وهو معرفة كيفية تغييرات الهواء بتأثيرات الكواكب بحركاتها ومطارح شعاعاتها على هذه الأركان وانفعالاتها منها وخاصة الهواء، فانه كثير التلون والتغير من النور والظلمة والحر والبرد وتصاريف الرياح والضباب والغيوم والأمطار والثلوج والبرد والبروق والرعود والشهب والصواعق وكواكب الأذناب وقوس قزح والزوابع والهالات وما شاكلها مما يحدث فوق رؤسنا من التغييرات والحوادث.

(٣٩) والخامس علم المعادن، وهو معرفة الجواهر المعدنية التي تنعقد من البخارات المتقنة في باطن الأرض والعصارات المنعقدة في الأهوية وكهوف الجبال وقعور البحار من العقاقير والجواهر من الكباريت والزوابيق والشبوب والأملاح والنوشاذر والذهب والفضة والنحاس والحديد والرصاص والأسرب والكحل والزرنيخ والبلور والياقوت والبانزهرات وما شاكلها ومعرفة خواصها ومنافعها ومضارها.

(٤٠) والسادس علم النبات وهو معرفة كل نبت يغرس أو يبذر أو ينبت على وجه الأرض أو في رؤس الجبال أو قعر المياه أو شطوط الأنهار من الأشجار والزروع والبقول والحشائش والعشب والكلاء ومعرفة كمية أنواعها وخواص تلك الأنواع ومواضع منابتها من البقاع وكيفية امتداد عروقها فى الأرض وارتفاع فروعها وأصولها فى الهواء وانبساطها على وجه الأرض وتفرق فروعها في الجهات

their sprouts with respect to length and shortness, thinness and thickness,[58] straightness and crookedness; about the shapes of their leaves with respect to great or small extension, and softness or hardness; about the colors of their flowers and the tints of their blossoms as well as about the forms of their fruits, grains, seeds, resins, tastes, and smells; and [finally it is] about their peculiarities, and each useful and harmful quality.

(41) The seventh is the science of the animals—that is, the knowledge about all bodies that take nourishment, grow, and have sensual perception and self-movement, whether they walk on the surface of the earth, fly in the air, swim in the water, creep in the dust, or move inside another body (as worms inside [other] animals) or in the core of plants, fruits, grains, and the like. It is the knowledge [also] about the number of their genera, the species of these genera, and the peculiarities thereof, then the knowledge about how they are generated in the uterus, in the egg, or in putrefactive processes. It is the knowledge about how their organs are made up and their bodies are composed, [about] the difference of their forms, [how] they unite with one another in mating, [about] the diversity of their noises, [about] what they avoid by nature, the difference of their tempers and the resemblance of their actions. After that [it is] the knowledge about their rutting season and the right time for breeding, the time they take up their nesting places, raise their young ones with gentleness and look after their litter with tenderness as well as the knowledge about their usefulness and harmfulness, [about] where they should be kept and by whom, whom they regard as an enemy and whom they respect,[59] and things like that.

(42) Now, the examination of all these [questions] and their investigation belongs to the physical sciences, as do also the human and the veterinary medicines; the handling of riding animals, predatory animals, and birds; crop and stock farming; and the science of the handicrafts. All of these are part of the physical sciences.[60]

وأشكال أغصانها من الطول والقصر والدقة والغلظ والاستقامة والاعوجاج وكيفية أشكال أوراقها من السعة والضيق واللين والخشونة وألوان أزهارها وأصباغ أنوارها وكيفية صور ثمارها وحبوبها وبذورها وصموغها وطعومها وروائحها وخواصها ومنافعها ومضارها واحداً واحداً.

(٤١) والسابع علم الحيوان وهو معرفة كل جسم يغتذي وينمى ويحس ويتحرك مما يمشي على وجه الأرض أو يطير في الهواء أو يسبح فى الماء أو يدب فى التراب، أو يتحرك فى جوف جسم آخر كالديدان فى جوف الحيوان وفى لب النبات والثمر والحبوب وما شاكلها ومعرفة كمية أجناسها وأنواع الاجناس وخواص تلك الأنواع ومعرفة كيفية تكونها فى الأرحام أو فى البيض أو فى العفونات ومعرفة كيفية تأليف أعضائها وتركيب أجسادها واختلاف صورها وائتلاف أزواجها وفنون أصواتها ومنافرة طباعها وتباين أخلاقها وتشاكل أفعالها ومعرفة أوقات هيجانها وسفادها واتخاذ أعشاشها ورفقها بتربية أولادها وتحننها على صغار نتاجها ومعرفتها بمنافعها ومضارها وأوطانها وأربابها وأعدائها ومعارفها وماشاكل ذلك.

(٤٢) فالنظر في هذه كلها والبحث عنها ينسب الى العلوم الطبيعيات وكذلك علم الطب والبيطرة وسياسة الدواب والسباع والطيور والحرث والنسل وعلم الصنائع أجمع داخل في الطبيعيات.

Chapter on the Theological Sciences

(43) The theological sciences are [divided into] five species: The first is the knowledge about the Creator—mighty is His glory and all-embracing His grace—and the attribute of His unity, [about] how He is the Cause of the beings and Creator of what is created, the Emanator of the good, the Giver of being, the Origin of virtues and good deeds, the One who maintains order and sustains in perpetuity, the Director of the universe, the One who knows the hidden and the manifest,[61] [Who] does not miss the tiniest thing on the earth or in the heavens, the First of each thing as regards [its] beginning, the Last of each thing as regards [its] end, the Exterior of each thing as regards [its] potency, the Interior of each thing as regards the knowledge [of it]. He is the All-hearing, the Omniscient, the Kind, the Well-knowing, the Merciful towards mankind—sublime is His rank, mighty His power, exalted His grandeur, and mighty His glory! There is no god except Him, so, keep far aloof from what the transgressors say!

(44) The second is the science of the spiritual [substances]—that is, the knowledge about the simple, intellectual, cognitive, and acting substances which are God's angels and the purest of His servants. These are the forms that are bare of matter and which are employed by the bodies in order to conduct their actions through them, for their sake, and out of them. [It includes] also the knowledge about how the [spiritual substances] are interconnected with one another, how they emanate one into the other inasmuch as they are spiritual spheres encompassing the corporeal spheres.[62]

(45) The third is the science of the mental [entities]—that is, the knowledge about the souls and the spirits that pervade the spherical and the physical bodies, from the encompassing sphere to the most central part of the earth. It is the knowledge about how they revolve the spheres, move the stars, let animals and plants grow, and take up residence in the bodies of the animals, as well as [the knowledge about] how they are sent out after [the bodies] have died.

(46) The fourth is the science of the exercise of sovereignty[63] which is [divided into] five species: the prophetic exercise of sovereignty,[64] the monarchic exercise of sovereignty, the exercise of public sovereignty, the exercise of private sovereignty, and the exercise of sovereignty over oneself.

(فصل فى العلوم الإلهية)

(٤٣) والعلوم الالهية خمسة أنواع: أولها معرفة الباري جل جلاله وعم نواله وصفة وحدانيته وكيف هو علة الموجودات وخالق المخلوقات وفائض الجود ومعطي الوجود ومعدن الفضائل والخيرات وحافظ النظام ومبقي الدوام ومدبر الكل وعالم الغيب والشهادة لا يعزب عنه مثقال ذرة في الأرض ولا في السماء وأول كل شيء ابتداء وآخر كل شيء انتهاء وظاهر كل شيء قدرة وباطن كل شيء علماً وهو السميع العليم اللطيف الخبير الرؤوف بالعباد عز شأنه وجلت قدرته وتعالى جده وجل ثناؤه ولا إله غيره تعالى عما يقول الظالمون علواً كبيراً.

(٤٤) والثاني علم الروحانيات وهو معرفة الجواهر البسيطة العقلية العلامة الفعالة التي هي ملائكة الله وخالص عباده وهي الصور المجردة من الهيولى المستعملة للأجسام المدبرة بها لها ومنها أفعالها ومعرفة كيفية ارتباط بعضها ببعض وفيض بعضها على بعض وهي أفلاك روحانية محيطات بالأفلاك الجسمانية.

(٤٥) والثالث علم النفسانيات وهى معرفة النفوس والأرواح السارية فى الاجسام الفلكية والطبيعية من لدن الفلك المحيط إلى منتهى مركز الأرض ومعرفة كيفية إدارتها للافلاك وتحريكها للكواكب وتربيتها للحيوان والنبات وحلولها في جثث الحيوانات وكيفية انبعاثها بعد الممات.

(٤٦) الرابع علم السياسة وهي خمسة أنواع: اولها السياسة النبوية، والثاني السياسة الملوكية، والثالث السياسة العامية، والرابع السياسة الخاصية، والخامس السياسة الذاتية.

(47) As for the prophetic exercise of sovereignty, it is the knowledge about how the well-pleasing laws and the veracious [prophetic] traditions were laid down through eloquent words and about [how] to cure sick souls of [the maladies of] corrupt confessions, foolish opinions, bad habits, and unjust deeds, as well as the knowledge about how to disabuse them from such confessions and habits and [how] to obliterate from their innermost parts such opinions by explaining their shortcomings, disclosing their falsity, and curing them of the illness of such opinions as well as such habits by preventing them from backsliding into them, restoring them through the well-pleasing opinion, charming habits, veracious deeds, and praiseworthy traits of character, and by making [them] desirous of the rich reward on the Day of Returning [to the other world]. Next [it is the knowledge about] how to exercise sovereignty over the souls which have become evil through turning away from pursuing the path of true faith and following the jagged paths of sin and aberration by pressuring, reproaching, menacing, chiding, and intimidating them, in order that they might return to the paths of salvation and become desirous of the rich reward. Then [it is the knowledge about] how to awaken the distracted souls and the inattentive spirits from [their] continuous sleep and their forgetting about minding the return [to the other world][65] by reminding[66] them of the commitment [that has to be met] on the Day of Contract [fulfillment], lest they might say that they had been informed neither by prophets nor by any scripture. This now is the exercise of sovereignty that falls within the specific purview of the prophets and messengers—may God's blessing be with them!

(48) As for the monarchic exercise of sovereignty, it is the knowledge about [how] to see that the canonical Islamic law is observed by the people and [how] to keep up the [prophetic] tradition in the religious community by enjoining what is generally recognized [as right] and prohibiting what is reprehensible,[67] inflicting the canonical sanctions, executing the legal regulations prescribed by the Lord of the canonical Islamic law, checking crimes, subduing the enemies, controlling the malicious, and helping the best to triumph. This now is the exercise of sovereignty that falls within the specific purview of the successors[68] of the prophets—may God's blessing be with them—and of the rightly guided imams who are bound to truth and who act justly through it.

(٤٧) فأما السياسة النبوية فهي معرفة كيفية وضع النواميس المرضية والسنن الزكية بالأقاويل الفصيحة ومداواة النفوس المريضة من الديانات الفاسدة والآراء السخيفة والعادات الردية والأفعال الجائرة، ومعرفة كيفية نقلها من تلك الاديان والعادات ومحو تلك الآراء عن ضمائرها بذكر عيوبها ونشر تزييفها ومداواتها من سقام تلك الآراء وتلك العادات بالحمية لها من العود اليها وشفائها بالرأي المرضي والعادات الجميلة والأعمال الزكية والأخلاق المحمودة بالمدح لها والترغيب في جزيل الثواب يوم المآب وكيفية سياسة النفوس الشريرة بصدودها عن قصد سبيل الرشاد وسلوكها فى وعور طرق الغي والتمادي بالقمع لها والزجر والوعيد والتوبيخ والتهديد لترجع الى سبل النجاة وترغب في جزيل الثواب ومعرفة كيفية تنبيه الأنفس اللاهية والأرواح الساهية من طول الرقاد ونسيانها ذكر المعاد والأذكار لها عهد يوم الميثاق لئلا يقولوا ما جاءنا من رسول ولا كتاب. وهذه السياسة تختص بها الأنبياء والرسل صلوات الله عليهم.

(٤٨) وأما السياسة الملوكية فهي معرفة حفظ الشريعة على الأمة وإحياء السنة في الملة بالأمر بالمعروف والنهي عن المنكر بإقامة الحدود وإنفاذ الأحكام التى رسمها صاحب الشريعة و رد المظالم وقمع الأعداء وكف الأشرار ونصرة الأخيار وهذه السياسة يختص بها خلفاء الانبياء صلوات الله عليهم والائمة المهديون الذين قضوا بالحق وبه كانوا يعدلون.

(49) As for the exercise of public sovereignty, which is the exercise of sovereignty over groups of people such as the sovereignty that governors [exercise] over countries and cities, big landowners over the village folk, military leaders over the troops, and the like—[this kind of exercise of sovereignty] is the knowledge about the classes of the subordinates; their living conditions, descents, professions, confessions, and traits of character; the order of their ranks; [about how] to take care of their affairs, to inspect their essentials, to weld them into a whole, to establish justice between them, to unify their factions, to engage them for whatever they are suitable for, and to employ them in what fits their professions and in works that are appropriate to each of them.

(50) As for the exercise of private sovereignty, it is the knowledge about how everyone should manage his domicile; conduct his way of living; take care of what concerns his servants, his boys, his children, his slaves, his relatives, his dealings with his neighbors, and his companionship with his brothers [in faith]; [about how] to assert their rights, to inspect their essentials, and to examine whether they act for the benefit of their worldly and their otherworldly affairs.

(51) As for the exercise of sovereignty over oneself, it is the knowledge everyone should have about himself and his traits of character, the control over his deeds and his words in the states of passion, anger, or delight, as well as the examination of all his affairs.

(52) The fifth [theological science] is the science of the returning [to the other world]—that is, the knowledge about the essence of the other coming into existence,[69] [about] how the spirits shall arise from the darkness of the bodies and the souls shall awaken from [their] continuous sleep and gather on the Day of Returning [to the other world], [how] they shall stand along the right road[70] and gather for the reckoning on Doomsday, as well as the knowledge about how the righteous shall be rewarded and the evildoers punished.

(53) As a matter of fact, we have composed on each section of these sciences mentioned above a [special] epistle in which we explain some of those concepts[71] and give them an exhaustive treatment in order to awaken those who are careless, to guide the disciples,[72] to excite the interest of those who seek [knowledge], and to provide a method for the students. So, be happy with it, my brother, present this epistle to your brothers [in faith] and to your friends; excite their interest in science, prompt them to renounce this world, and show them the path to the

(٤٩) وأما السياسة العامية التى هي الرياسة على الجماعات كرياسة الأمراء على البلدان والمدن و رياسة الدهاقين على أهل القرى و رياسة قادة الجيوش على العساكر وما شاكلها فهي معرفة طبقات المرؤوسين وحالاتهم وأنسابهم وصنائعهم ومذاهبهم وأخلاقهم وترتيب مراتبهم ومراعاة أمورهم وتفقد أسبابهم وتأليف شملهم والتناصف بينهم وجمع شتاتهم واستخدامهم في ما يصلحون له من الامور واستعمالهم في مايشاكلهم من صنائعهم وأعمالهم اللائقة بواحد واحد منهم.

(٥٠) وأما السياسة الخاصية فهي معرفة كل انسان كيفية تدبير منزله وأمر معيشته ومراعاة أمرخدمه وغلمانه وأولاده ومما ليكه وأقربائه عشرته مع جيرانه وصحبته مع اخوانه وقضاء حقوقهم وتفقد أسبابهم والنظر فى مصالحهم من أمور دنياهم وآخرتهم.

(٥١) وأما السياسة الذاتية فهي معرفة كل انسان نفسه وأخلاقه وتفقد أفعاله وأقاويله فى حال شهواته وغضبه و رضاه والنظر في جميع أموره.

(٥٢) والخامس علم المعاد وهو معرفة ماهية النشأة الأخرى وكيفية انبعاث الأرواح من ظلمة الأجساد وانتباه النفوس من طول الرقاد وحشرها يوم المعاد وقيامها على الصراط المستقيم وحشرها لحساب يوم الدين ومعرفة كيفية جزاء المحسنين وعقاب المسيئين.

(٥٣) وقد عملنا فى كل فصل من هذه العلوم التى تقدم ذكرها رسالة وذكرنا فيها طرفاً من تلك المعاني وأتممناها بالجمعة ليكون تنبيهاً للغافلين وارشاداً للمريدين وترغيباً للطالبين ومسلكا للمتعلمين. فكن به يا أخي سعيداً واعرض هذه الرسالة على اخوانك وأصدقائك و رغبهم فى العلم و زهدهم في الدنيا ودلهم على طريق الآخرة

hereafter, for by doing so you shall win God's favor—exalted is He—prove yourself worthy of His pleasure, attain the bliss of the hereafter, and reach there the highest level,[73] as indicated by the Prophet's word—upon him be peace—that he who directs [others] to the good is like him who does good![74]

(54) Know, my brother, that this is the way which was taken by the prophets—may God's blessing be with them—and on which the best and outstanding scholars and wise men followed them. So, do your utmost, and perhaps you will be placed among their group as promised by God—exalted is He—in that He says "those upon whom God has bestowed favor of the prophets and the faithful and the witnesses and the righteous; good company are these! Such is the bounty of God!" [Qurʾān 4:69 f.), [and] "As for those who strive for Us, We shall surely guide them in Our ways; and verily, God is with those who do well!" [Qurʾān 29:69]. May God give you, O brother, and us success in doing the right thing, and may He lead us and you on the way of the true faith.

◆

فانك بذلك تنال الزلفى من الله تعالى وتستوجب رضوانه وتفوز بسعادة الآخرة وتبلغ به المرتبة العليا كما دل عليه قول النبى عليه السلام: الدال على الخير كفاعله.

(٥٤) واعلم يا أخي بأن هذه الطريقة هي التى سلكها الأنبياء صلوات الله عليهم واتبعهم عليها الأخيار الفضلاء من العلماء والحكماء فاجتهد لعلك تحشر فى زمرتهم كما وعد الله تعالى فقال ﴿أولئك مع الذينَ أَنعَمَ الله عَلَيهم من النِبيين والصدّيقين والشهداء والصالحين وحسن أولئك رفيقاً ذلك الفضل من الله﴾ [النساء ٤:٦٩] ﴿والذين جاهدوا فينا لنهدينهم سبلنا وإن الله لمع المحسنين﴾ [العنكبوت ٢٩:٦٩] وفقك الله وإيانا أيها الأخ للسداد وهدانا وإياك سبيل الرشاد.

al-Qābisī

A Treatise Detailing the Circumstances of Students and the Rules Governing Teachers and Students

(ABRIDGED)[1]

TRANSLATED BY MICHAEL FISHBEIN

◆

Part One

In the name of God, the Merciful, the Compassionate
in Whom is my success

(1) Abū al-Ḥasan ʿAlī ibn Muḥammad ibn Khalaf al-Maʿāfirī[2] al-Qābisī, the jurist of Qayrawān, said: "Praise belongs to God who has sent down upon His servant the Book and has not assigned unto it any crookedness; right, to warn of great violence from Him; and to give good tidings unto the believers who do righteous deeds, that theirs shall be a goodly wage, therein to abide forever; and to warn those who say, 'God has taken to Himself a son'; they have no knowledge of it, they nor their fathers; a monstrous word it is, issuing out of their mouths; they say nothing but a lie" [Qurʾān 18:1–5].

أبو الحسن علي بن خلف
القابسي

الرسالة المفصلة لأحوال المتعلمين
وأحكام المعلمين والمتعلمين

الجزء الأول

بسم الله الرحمن الرحيم

و به توفيقي

(١) قال أبو الحسن علي بن محمد بن خلف المعروف القابسي الفقيه القيرواني: ﴿الْحَمْدُ لِلَّهِ الَّذِي أَنزَلَ عَلَىٰ عَبْدِهِ الْكِتَابَ وَلَمْ يَجْعَل لَّهُ عِوَجًا. قَيِّمًا لِّيُنذِرَ بَأْسًا شَدِيدًا مِّن لَّدُنْهُ وَيُبَشِّرَ الْمُؤْمِنِينَ الَّذِينَ يَعْمَلُونَ الصَّالِحَاتِ أَنَّ لَهُمْ أَجْرًا حَسَنًا. مَّاكِثِينَ فِيهِ أَبَدًا. وَيُنذِرَ الَّذِينَ قَالُوا اتَّخَذَ اللَّهُ وَلَدًا. مَّا لَهُم بِهِ مِنْ عِلْمٍ وَلَا لِآبَائِهِمْ كَبُرَتْ كَلِمَةً تَخْرُجُ مِنْ أَفْوَاهِهِمْ إِن يَقُولُونَ إِلَّا كَذِبًا﴾ [الكهف ٥-١:١٨].

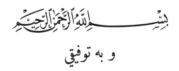

(2) And "blessed be He who has sent down Salvation upon His servant, that he may be a warner to all beings; to whom belongs the Kingdom of the heavens and the earth; and He has not taken to Him a son, and He has no associate in the Kingdom; and He created every thing, then He ordained it very exactly" [Qurʾān 25:1–2].

(3) Praise belongs to God, who is ever One, Unique, Living, and Eternal. To Him belong the Names Most Beautiful, and the Attributes Most Sublime. There is naught like unto Him. He is the All-Hearing, the All-Seeing. He has spoken by the Qurʾān, and has sent it down upon Muḥammad, the best of mankind, for mercy and clarification, with light and proof, wisdom and salvation, "to confirm those who believe, and to be a guidance and good tidings to those who surrender" [Qurʾān 16:102].

(4) And He whose praise is lofty has said: "Ṭā Hā: We have not sent down the Qurʾān upon thee for thee to be unprosperous, but only as a reminder to him who fears, a revelation from Him who created the earth and the high heavens; the All-Compassionate sat Himself upon the Throne; to Him belongs all that is in the heavens and the earth and all that is between them, and all that is underneath the soil. Be thou loud in thy speech, yet surely He knows the secret and that yet more hidden. God—there is no god but He. To Him belong the Names Most Beautiful" [Qurʾān 20:1–8].

(5) I praise Him; I believe in Him; I seek His help; in Him I trust; and I claim no power and strength other than His. I testify that there is no god but God alone, who has no partner, and that Muḥammad is His servant and messenger, the seal of the prophets; whom God sent to bring guidance and the true religion, to uplift it above every religion, though the unbelievers be averse. He delivered the message, fulfilled his trust, and counseled the community. "Grievous to him is your suffering; anxious is he over you, gentle to the believers, compassionate" [Qurʾān 9:128].

(6) Glory be to God, who is magnified by all that is in the heavens and in the earth. . . . Praise be to God, who has guided us to faith, taught us the Qurʾān, and granted us grace to follow His prophet, Muḥammad, on whom be peace. O God, be merciful to Muḥammad and the family of Muḥammad, as Thou wast merciful to Abraham. Bless Muḥammad and the family of Muḥammad, as Thou didst bless Abraham among all beings, for Thou art praiseworthy and glorious. Teach us, O God, the Book and the Wisdom that Thou didst send Muḥammad, the seal of the prophets, to bring us, and Thy signs that he recited. Purify us, for Thou

(٢) ﴿وَتَبَارَكَ الَّذِي نَزَّلَ الْفُرْقَانَ عَلَىٰ عَبْدِهِ لِيَكُونَ لِلْعَالَمِينَ نَذِيرًا. الَّذِي لَهُ مُلْكُ السَّمَاوَاتِ وَالْأَرْضِ وَلَمْ يَتَّخِذْ وَلَدًا وَلَمْ يَكُن لَّهُ شَرِيكٌ فِي الْمُلْكِ وَخَلَقَ كُلَّ شَيْءٍ فَقَدَّرَهُ تَقْدِيرًا﴾ [الفرقان ٢-٢٥:١]

(٣) والحمد لله الذي لم يزل واحداً، أحداً، حياً، قيوماً - له الأسماء الحسنى. والصفات العُلى. ليس كمثله شيء، وهو السميع البصير. تكلم بالقرآن، وأنزله على محمد خير الأنام، للرحمة والتبيان بالنور والبرهان، والحكمة والفرقان، ﴿لِيُثَبِّتَ الَّذِينَ آمَنُوا وَهُدًى وَبُشْرَىٰ لِلْمُسْلِمِينَ﴾ [النحل ١٦:١٠٢]

(٤) وقال جل ثناؤه ﴿طه. مَا أَنزَلْنَا عَلَيْكَ الْقُرْآنَ لِتَشْقَىٰ. إِلَّا تَذْكِرَةً لِّمَن يَخْشَىٰ. تَنزِيلًا مِّمَّنْ خَلَقَ الْأَرْضَ وَالسَّمَاوَاتِ الْعُلَى. الرَّحْمَٰنُ عَلَى الْعَرْشِ اسْتَوَىٰ. لَهُ مَا فِي السَّمَاوَاتِ وَمَا فِي الْأَرْضِ وَمَا بَيْنَهُمَا وَمَا تَحْتَ الثَّرَىٰ. وَإِن تَجْهَرْ بِالْقَوْلِ فَإِنَّهُ يَعْلَمُ السِّرَّ وَأَخْفَى. اللَّهُ لَا إِلَٰهَ إِلَّا هُوَ لَهُ الْأَسْمَاءُ الْحُسْنَىٰ﴾ [طه ٨-٢٠:١]

(٥) أحمده وأومن به، وأستعينه وأتوكل عليه وأبرأ من الحول والقوة إليه، وأشهد أن لا إله إلا الله وحده لا شريك له، وأن محمداً عبده ورسوله خاتم النبيين، أرسله بالهدى ودين الحق ليظهره على الدين كله ولو كره المشركون، فقام بالرسالة، وأدى الأمانة، ونصح الأمة ﴿عَزِيزٌ عَلَيْهِ مَا عَنِتُّمْ حَرِيصٌ عَلَيْكُم بِالْمُؤْمِنِينَ رَءُوفٌ رَّحِيمٌ﴾ [التوبة ٩:١٢٨].

(٦) فسبحان الله الذي سبح له ما في السموات وما في الأرض. . . . والحمد لله الذي هدانا للإيمان، وعلمنا القرآن، ومنّ علينا باتباع نبيه محمد عليه السلام. اللّهم صلّ على محمد، وعلى آل محمد، كما صليت على إبراهيم، وبارك على محمد وعلى آل محمد. كما باركت على إبراهيم، في العالمين إنك حميد مجيد. اللّهم وعلمنا ما بعثت به إلينا محمداً خاتم النبيين من كتاب وحكمة، وما تلا من آياتك، وزكّنا إنك أنت العزيز الحكيم، اللّهم وألهمنا شكر نعمتك به علينا. . . . وأيدنا على طاعتك، بأن نستعين

art the All-Mighty, the All-Wise. Inspire us, O God, with thankfulness for Thy favor to us through him. . . . Strengthen us to obey Thee, by our seeking Thy help to do so, as Thou hast commanded us. . . . Thou art the Truth, and Thy promise is Truth. There is no God but Thou, the true King who makest manifest. "Thee do we worship; Thy aid we seek. Guide us on the straight path, the path of those whom Thou hast blessed, not of those against whom Thou art wrathful, nor of those who are astray" [Qurʾān 1:5–7]—the path of the prophets, the truthful, the martyrs, and the righteous. Enable us by Thy grace and Thy mercy worthily to accompany them, for Thou art the most merciful of those who show mercy. Thou art sufficient for us—how excellent a guardian! Thou art our protector—how excellent a protector, how excellent a helper! Help us to a good outcome in what Thou hast entrusted to us and in that wherewith Thou hast tested us, of Thy mercy toward Thy righteous servants who vie in good works, outracing to them. No strength and no power is there save in God, the Most High, the Glorious.

(7) Abū al-Ḥasan [al-Qābisī] said: A certain questioner urgently asked me to reply to certain questions he had written in which he laid down certain conditions. He justified the urgency of his request by saying that he needed the answers. He desired to understand certain matters that he had been unable to understand. These matters had become incumbent on him and had descended on him; he was intimidated by them—fearful of embarking on them and fearful of the trouble of refraining from them, being far from anyone whose aid he might appropriately seek in them. I accepted his justification and was concerned not to abandon the matter, although I felt a certain timidity about replying to all he had asked. For a long time I was remiss about giving him a speedy answer, while he, for his part, continued to urge me regarding what he had sought from me. Finally, God inspired me with a willingness to answer him. I take refuge in God from being among those who pretend to know what they do not know. I ask God the Generous to bind my mind to the truth in the test which He has placed on me of speaking about religion, and that He guide me to the best speech, that I may follow it with guidance from Him, for He it is who guides to the straight path those who have believed. . . .

(8) Abū al-Ḥasan [al-Qābisī] said: You asked us to begin for you with something about the excellences of the Qurʾān. Regarding the superiority of the Qurʾān, you need only know that it is the Word of God, who is mighty and exalted. The Word of God is uncreated. God

عليها كما أمرتنا . . . . أنت الحق، و وعدك الحق، لا إله إلا أنت، الملك المبين. إياك نعبد، وإياك نستعين، ﴿اهدِنَا الصِّرَاطَ المُستَقِيمَ. صِرَاطَ الَّذِينَ أَنعَمتَ عَلَيهِمْ غَيرِ المَغضُوبِ عَلَيهِم وَلَا الضَّالِّينَ﴾ [الفاتحة ١:٥-٧]، من النبيين والصديقين والشهداء والصالحين، وأنلنا حسن مرافقتهم بفضلك و رحمتك، فأنت أرحم الراحمين، وأنت حسبنا ونعم الوكيل، وأنت مولانا، فنعم المولى ونعم النصير، فانصرنا بحسن الخلاص فيما أوليتنا وفيما ابتليتنا، برحمتك من عبادك الصالحين، الذين يسارعون في الخيرات وهم لها سابقون، ولا حول ولا قوة إلا بالله العلي العظيم.

(٧) قال أبو الحسن: قد سألني سائلٌ، وألح عليَّ أن أجيبه عن مسائل كتبها، وشرط فيها شروطاً، واعتذر من إلحاحه عليَّ، أنه مضطرٌ إليها و راغب في فهم ما تعذر عليه من فهمها، إذ هي تحلّ عليه، وتنزل به فيرهبها. ويخشى القدوم عليها، ويخاف ضيق الإمساك عنها، لبعده ممن يصلح أن يستعان به فيها، فعذرته بعذره، وأشفقت من التوقف عنه. على وجل مني في مجاوبته على كل ما سأل عنه، فتراخيت عن سرعة مجاوبته طويلاً، وهو مقيم على حفزي فيما أراد مني. حتى ألقى الله عز وجل في قلبي الانقياد إلى مجاوبته. فأعوذ بالله أن أكون من المتكلفين، وأسأل الله الكريم العصمة بالحق فيما ابتلاني به من المقالة في الدين، وأن يهديني إلى أحسن القول فأتبعه بهدى من عنده، فهو هادي الذين آمنوا إلى صراط مستقيم . . . .

(٨) قال أبو الحسن: أما سؤالك أن نبدأ لك بشيء من فضائل القرآن، فيكفيك من فضل القرآن، معرفتك أن القرآن كلام الله عز وجل: وكلام الله غير مخلوق، ثم

has praised this Qurʾān in more than one passage in it. God has said: "God has sent down the fairest discourse as a Book, consimilar in its oft-repeating, whereat shiver the skins of those who fear their Lord; then their skins and their hearts soften to the remembrance of God. That is God's guidance whereby He guides whomsoever He will; and whomsoever God leads astray, no guide has he" [Qurʾān 39:23]. And He who is exalted has also said: "*Alif Lām Rāʾ*: Those are the signs of the Manifest Book. We have sent it down as an Arabic Qurʾān; haply you will understand. We will relate to thee the fairest of stories in that We have revealed to thee this Qurʾān, though before it thou wast one of the heedless" [Qurʾān 12:1–3]. Also, "*Alif Lām Mīm* That is the Book wherein is no doubt, a guidance to the God-fearing" [Qurʾān 2:1–3]. Also, "*Alif Lām Mīm Ṣād* A Book sent down to thee—so let there be no impediment in thy breast because of it—to warn thereby, and as a reminder to believers" [Qurʾān 7:1–2]. Everything of this sort at the beginning of suras is meant to exalt the Qurʾān and acquaint believers with its superiority. Similarly, God has said: "O men, a proof has now come to you from your Lord; We have sent down to you a manifest light" [Qurʾān 4:174]. And He who is exalted has said: "There has come to you from God a light, and a Book Manifest whereby God guides whosoever follows His good pleasure in the ways of peace, and brings them forth from the shadows into the light by His leave; and He guides them to a straight path" [Qurʾān 5:15–16]. And He who is praised said to His Prophet (may God bless him and grant him peace): "And We have sent down to thee the Book with the truth, confirming the Book that was before it, and assuring it" [Qurʾān 5:48]. "And surely it is a Book Sublime; falsehood comes not to it from before it nor from behind it; a sending down from One All-Wise, All-Laudable" [Qurʾān 41:41–42]. "Surely this Qurʾān guides to the way that is straightest and gives good tidings to the believers who do deeds of righteousness, that theirs shall be a great wage; and those who do not believe in the world to come—we have prepared for them a painful chastisement" [Qurʾān 17:9–10]. "This is a Book We have sent down, blessed; so follow it, and be God-fearing; haply so you will find mercy" [Qurʾān 6:155]. There is much in the Qurʾān in this vein. It is well-known, and citing it further in this book would render the book too long. It is something clear and evident in the Qurʾān, making any book unnecessary. Praise be to God, the Lord of the worlds!

ثناء الله على هذا القرآن في غير موضع منه. قال الله عز وجل ﴿اللهُ نَزَّلَ أَحْسَنَ الْحَدِيثِ كِتَابًا مُتَشَابِهًا مَثَانِيَ تَقْشَعِرُّ مِنْهُ جُلُودُ الَّذِينَ يَخْشَوْنَ رَبَّهُمْ ثُمَّ تَلِينُ جُلُودُهُمْ وَقُلُوبُهُمْ إِلَى ذِكْرِ اللهِ ذَلِكَ هُدَى اللهِ يَهْدِي بِهِ مَنْ يَشَاءُ وَمَنْ يُضْلِلِ اللهُ فَمَا لَهُ مِنْ هَادٍ﴾ [الزمر ٣٩:٢٣] وقوله تعالى ﴿الر. تِلْكَ آيَاتُ الْكِتَابِ الْمُبِينِ إِنَّا أَنْزَلْنَاهُ قُرْآنًا عَرَبِيًّا لَعَلَّكُمْ تَعْقِلُونَ نَحْنُ نَقُصُّ عَلَيْكَ أَحْسَنَ الْقَصَصِ بِمَا أَوْحَيْنَا إِلَيْكَ هَذَا الْقُرْآنَ وَإِنْ كُنْتَ مِنْ قَبْلِهِ لَمِنَ الْغَافِلِينَ﴾ [يوسف ٣-١٢:١]. ﴿الم. ذَلِكَ الْكِتَابُ لَا رَيْبَ فِيهِ هُدًى لِلْمُتَّقِينَ﴾ [البقرة ٣-٢:١]. ﴿المص. كِتَابٌ أُنْزِلَ إِلَيْكَ فَلَا يَكُنْ فِي صَدْرِكَ حَرَجٌ مِنْهُ لِتُنْذِرَ بِهِ وَذِكْرَى لِلْمُؤْمِنِينَ﴾ [الأعراف ٢-٧:١]. وكل ما جرى في أوائل السور من هذا، فهو تعظيم للقرآن، وتعريف للمؤمنين بفضله، وكذلك قوله عز وجل ﴿يَا أَيُّهَا النَّاسُ قَدْ جَاءَكُمْ بُرْهَانٌ مِنْ رَبِّكُمْ وَأَنْزَلْنَا إِلَيْكُمْ نُورًا مُبِينًا﴾ [النساء ٤:١٧٤]. وقوله تعالى ﴿قَدْ جَاءَكُمْ مِنَ اللهِ نُورٌ وَكِتَابٌ مُبِينٌ. يَهْدِي بِهِ اللهُ مَنِ اتَّبَعَ رِضْوَانَهُ سُبُلَ السَّلَامِ وَيُخْرِجُهُمْ مِنَ الظُّلُمَاتِ إِلَى النُّورِ بِإِذْنِهِ وَيَهْدِيهِمْ إِلَى صِرَاطٍ مُسْتَقِيمٍ﴾ [المائدة ١٦-٥:١٥] وقوله سبحانه لنبيه ﷺ: ﴿وَأَنْزَلْنَا إِلَيْكَ الْكِتَابَ بِالْحَقِّ مُصَدِّقًا لِمَا بَيْنَ يَدَيْهِ مِنَ الْكِتَابِ وَمُهَيْمِنًا عَلَيْهِ﴾ [المائدة ٥:٤٨]. ﴿وَإِنَّهُ لَكِتَابٌ عَزِيزٌ. لَا يَأْتِيهِ الْبَاطِلُ مِنْ بَيْنِ يَدَيْهِ وَلَا مِنْ خَلْفِهِ تَنْزِيلٌ مِنْ حَكِيمٍ حَمِيدٍ﴾ [فصلت ٤٢-٤١:٤١]. ﴿إِنَّ هَذَا الْقُرْآنَ يَهْدِي لِلَّتِي هِيَ أَقْوَمُ وَيُبَشِّرُ الْمُؤْمِنِينَ الَّذِينَ يَعْمَلُونَ الصَّالِحَاتِ أَنَّ لَهُمْ أَجْرًا كَبِيرًا. وَأَنَّ الَّذِينَ لَا يُؤْمِنُونَ بِالْآخِرَةِ أَعْتَدْنَا لَهُمْ عَذَابًا أَلِيمًا﴾ [الإسراء ١٠-١٧:٩]. ﴿وَهَذَا كِتَابٌ أَنْزَلْنَاهُ مُبَارَكٌ فَاتَّبِعُوهُ وَاتَّقُوا لَعَلَّكُمْ تُرْحَمُونَ﴾ [الأنعام ٦:١٥٥]. ومن هذا المعنى في القرآن كثير معروف تتبع ذكره في هذا الكتاب يطيله، وهو شيء بيّن في القرآن، يغني عن كل كتاب، والحمد لله رب العالمين.

(9) As regards the merit of anyone who learns or teaches the Qur'ān, there is a well-known and widely disseminated tradition transmitted by Sa'd ibn 'Ubaydah, from Abū 'Abd al-Raḥmān al-Sulamī, from 'Uthmān (may God be pleased with him), from the Prophet (may God bless him and grant him peace), who said: "The best of you is he who learns the Qur'ān and teaches it." This Abū 'Abd al-Raḥmān [al-Sulamī] taught recitation of the Qur'ān during the reign of 'Uthmān until the time of al-Ḥajjāj, and said, "That is what has kept me seated in this seat of mine."

(10) Abū al-Ḥasan [al-Qābisī] said: "When Abū 'Abd al-Raḥmān [al-Sulamī] said, 'That is what has kept me seated in this seat of mine,' he meant that it was the tradition that 'Uthmān had transmitted from the Prophet about the merit of whoever learns or teaches the Qur'ān that caused him to sit to teach people the Qur'ān and how to recite it. . . ."

(11) The *Ṣaḥīḥ*[3] contains a tradition transmitted by Sa'īd, from Qatādah, from Anas, from Abū Mūsá, from the Prophet (may God bless him and grant him peace), who said: "A believer who recites the Qur'ān and does according to it is like a citron, whose taste and odor are good. A believer who does not recite the Qur'ān but does according to it is like a fruit whose taste is good but has no odor. The likeness of the hypocrite who recites the Qur'ān is as an herb whose odor is good but whose taste is bitter. The likeness of the hypocrite who does not recite the Qur'ān is as the colocynth whose taste is bitter or foul and whose odor is bitter."

(12) Also in the *Ṣaḥīḥ* is a tradition transmitted by Abū Hurayrah from the Messenger of God, on whom be peace, who said: "There shall be no envy save between two people: a man whom God has taught the Qur'ān, so that he recites it by night and by day; and his neighbor who hears him and says, 'Would that I had been given the like of what so-and-so has been given and could do as he does'" [*Ṣaḥīḥ al-Bukhārī*]. . . .

(13) God, who is praised, has clearly described in His Book the reciter of the Qur'ān, saying: "Surely those who recite the Book of God, perform the prayer, and expend of that We have provided them, secretly and in public, look for a commerce that does not come to naught, that He may pay them in full their wages and enrich them of His bounty; surely He is All-Forgiving, All-Thankful. And that We have revealed to thee of the Book is the truth, confirming what is before it; God is aware of and sees His servants" [Qur'ān 35:29–31]. . . .

(٩) وأما لمن تعلمه أو علمه من الفضل، ففيه حديث مشهور ومنشور، وهو حديث سعد بن عبيدة، عن أبي عبد الرحمن السُّلمي، عن عثمان (رضي الله عنه)، عن النبي ﷺ قال «خيركم من تعلم القرآن وعلمه». وأقرأ أبو عبد الرحمن في إمارة عثمان حتى كان الحجاج. قال: وذاك الذي أقعدني مقعدي هذا.

(١٠) قال أبو الحسن، قال: فأبو عبد الرحمان هو القائل «وذاك الذي أقعدني مقعدي هذا» [صحيح البخاري] يريد أن حديث عثمان (رضى الله عنه)، عن النبي ﷺ في فضل مَنْ تعلم القرآن أو علمه، هو الذي أقعده لتعليم الناس القرآن يقرئهم إياه. . . .

(١١) وفي الصحيح من حديث سعيد، عن قتادة، عن أنس، عن أبي موسى، عن النبي ﷺ قال: «المؤمن الذي يقرأ القرآن ويعمل به كالأترجة طعمها وريحها طيب، والمؤمن الذي لا يقرأ القرآن ويعمل به كالتمرة طعمها طيب ولا ريح لها. ومثل المنافق الذي يقرأ القرآن، كالريحانة ريحها طيب، وطعمها مر. ومثل المنافق الذي لا يقرأ القرآن، كالحنظلة طعمها مر أو خبيث، وريحها مر» [صحيح البخاري].

(١٢) وفي الصحيح من حديث أبي هريرة أن رسول الله ﷺ قال: «لا حسد إلا في اثنتين: رجل علمه الله القرآن فهو يتلوه آناء الليل وآناء النهار، فسمعه جار له فقال: ليتني أوتيت مثل ما أوتي، فعملت مثل ما يعمل. . .» [صحيح البخاري].

(١٣) وقد بين الله سبحانه في كتابه وصف قارئي القرآن، وذلك قوله عز وجل ﴿إِنَّ الَّذِينَ يَتْلُونَ كِتَابَ اللَّهِ وَأَقَامُوا الصَّلَاةَ وَأَنْفَقُوا مِمَّا رَزَقْنَاهُمْ سِرًّا وَعَلَانِيَةً يَرْجُونَ تِجَارَةً لَنْ تَبُورَ. لِيُوَفِّيَهُمْ أُجُورَهُمْ وَيَزِيدَهُمْ مِنْ فَضْلِهِ إِنَّهُ غَفُورٌ شَكُورٌ. وَالَّذِي أَوْحَيْنَا إِلَيْكَ مِنَ الْكِتَابِ هُوَ الْحَقُّ مُصَدِّقًا لِمَا بَيْنَ يَدَيْهِ إِنَّ اللَّهَ بِعِبَادِهِ لَخَبِيرٌ بَصِيرٌ﴾ [فاطر ٣١-٣٥:٢٩] . . . .

(14) You asked about someone who, having learned the Qurʾān, neglects it until he forgets it. If he neglects it out of disdain for it, not because of some constraint—a labor, whereby he has an excuse—I fear that what has been said about someone who learns the Qurʾān and then forgets it applies to him: "It is a bounty for which he was ungrateful." This happens in the case of someone who pretends to be too busy for it. If his distraction from it is because of some sort of fool's labor, that is even worse. How do you know whether the forgetfulness afflicted him as punishment for his neglecting the Qurʾān for the sake of ill gains? His ill gains were a sin for which he was quickly punished by his forgetting the Qurʾān after having memorized it. . . . .

(15) Abū al-Ḥasan [al-Qābisī] said: Anyone who forgets a part of the Qurʾān has been commanded not to say, "I have forgotten it." There is a . . . tradition transmitted by Shuʿbah and others, from Manṣūr, from Abū Wāʾil, from ʿAbdallāh, who said that the Messenger of God, may God bless him and grant him peace, said: "It is very bad for anyone to say, 'I have forgotten such and such a verse.' He should say that he has been made to forget. Seek to remember the Qurʾān, for it is more apt to escape from the hearts of men than are camels [from their herdsman]" [*Ṣaḥīḥ al-Bukhārī*]. . . . Let God's servant reflect on what distracted him from the Qurʾān to such an extent that he was made to forget what he did. Is there an excuse for him in that or is there not? If there be no excuse for him, let him turn to his Lord for forgiveness. God, whose name is exalted, has said to His Prophet: "We shall teach you and you will not forget, except as God wills; He knows what is manifest and what is covered" [Qurʾān 87:6–7]. The Prophet (may God bless him and grant him peace), enjoined those who memorize the Qurʾān to remember it, and he informed them that it is more apt to escape from the hearts of men than are camels from herdsmen. . . .

(16) Al-Nasāʾī[4] has related . . . from ʿĀʾishah that the Prophet (may God bless him and grant him peace), said: "The likeness of one who recites the Qurʾān, being adept at it, is with the noble and righteous scribes; but one who recites it, it being difficult for him, shall have two rewards."

(17) Abū al-Ḥasan [al-Qābisī] said: The one who is adept at the Qurʾān is commanded to chant it very distinctly. God, who is mighty and exalted, has said: "O thou enwrapped in thy robes, keep vigil the night, except a little . . . and chant the Qurʾān very distinctly. Behold, We shall cast upon thee a weighty word; surely the first part of the night is heavier

(١٤) وأما سؤالك عمن تعلم القرآن ثم ضيعه حتى نسيه، فإن كان تضييعه إياه زهادة فيه - ليس بغالب عليه عمل يقوم له به عذر - فهو الذي أخشى عليه من شيء قد جاء فيمن تعلم القرآن ثم نسيه، فهي نعمة كفرها. وإنما يكون ذلك فيمن تعمد التشاغل به عنه. فإن كان تشاغله عنه بعمل من أعمال السفهاء، كان أشد. وما يدريك أن ذلك النسيان إنما أصابه عقوبة لاشتغاله عنه بسوء الاكتساب، فكان اكتسابه السوء ذنباً منه عُجلت له عقوبته بأن نسي القرآن بعدما حفظه . . . .

(١٥) قال أبو الحسن، ولقد أمر من نسي شيئاً من القرآن ألا يقول نسيته كما في . . . حديث شعبة وغيره عن منصور، عن أبي وائل، عن عبد الله، قال: قال رسول الله ﷺ «بئسما لأحدهم أن يقول نسيت آية كيت وكيت بل نُسِّي، واستذكروا القرآن، فإنه أشد تفصياً من صدور الرجال من النعم» [صحيح البخاري] فها هنا ينظر العبد فيما يشغله عن القرآن حتى نسي ما نسي، هل له في ذلك عذر أم لا عذر له فيه، فيحسن الإنابة إلى ربه مما لا عذر له فيه، وقد قال الله عز وجل لنبيه ﴿سَنُقْرِئُكَ فَلَا تَنسَىٰ. إِلَّا مَا شَاءَ اللَّهُ إِنَّهُ يَعْلَمُ الْجَهْرَ وَمَا يَخْفَىٰ﴾ [الأعلى ٧-٦:٨٧]. وقد وصى الرسول عليه السلام أهل القرآن بالمحافظة على استذكاره، وأخبرهم أنه أشد تفضياً من صدور الرجال من النعم . . . .

(١٦) وقد قال النسائي . . . عن عائشة، عن النبي ﷺ قال «مثل الذي يقرأ القرآن وهو ماهر به، مع السفرة الكرام البررة، والذي يقرؤه وهو عليه شاق، فله أجران».

(١٧) قال أبو الحسن: والماهر بالقرآن يؤمر بترتيله، قال الله عز وجل ﴿يَا أَيُّهَا الْمُزَّمِّلُ. قُمِ اللَّيْلَ إِلَّا قَلِيلًا﴾ إلى قوله ﴿وَرَتِّلِ الْقُرْآنَ تَرْتِيلًا. إِنَّا سَنُلْقِي عَلَيْكَ قَوْلًا ثَقِيلًا. إِنَّ نَاشِئَةَ اللَّيْلِ هِيَ أَشَدُّ وَطْئًا وَأَقْوَمُ قِيلًا﴾ [المزمل ٦-١:٧٣] . قيل معنى

in tread, and more upright in speech" [Qurʾān 73:1–6]. It has been said that the meaning of this, that the Qurʾān is heavier in tread, is in the impression on your hearing and sight—that is, your understanding—so that recitation of this kind is more upright in speech. . . .

(18) You asked about what good comes to those who teach the Qurʾān to their children. The only answer you need is what the Messenger of God, may God bless him and grant him peace, said: "The best of you is he who learns the Qurʾān and teaches it" [*Ṣaḥīḥ al-Bukhārī*]. Whoever teaches the Qurʾān to his child is included in this merit.

(19) Suppose, you say, he does not undertake the teaching himself but hires someone to teach. Know, nevertheless, that he it is who is teaching his child if he expends his wealth on him to teach him the Qurʾān. Hopefully, the child, by virtue of what his father has taught him, will be among those who hasten to do good works, God permitting! Such a rank would be this father's intention in teaching his child the Qurʾān. Muslims have always desired to teach their children the Qurʾān. They rear them in accordance with it and start them with it while they are children who can neither help nor harm themselves and who know only what their parents teach them.

(20) The *Ṣaḥīḥ* contains a tradition transmitted by Hishām, from Abū Bishr, from Saʿīd ibn Jubayr, from Ibn ʿAbbās: "We memorized the *Muḥkam* during the lifetime of the Messenger of God, may God bless him and grant him peace." Asked what the *Muḥkam* was, Ibn ʿAbbās said it was the *Mufaṣṣal*.[5] According to a tradition narrated by Abū ʿAwānah, from Abū Bishr, from Saʿīd ibn Jubayr: "What you call the *Mufaṣṣal* is the *Muḥkam*." Ibn ʿAbbās said: "The Messenger of God, may God bless him and grant him peace, died when I was ten years old, and I had already memorized the *Muḥkam*."

(21) Abū Mūsá said that the Messenger of God, may God bless him and grant him peace, said: "Any man who has a slave girl and teaches her, instructing her well and instilling good manners in her, and then frees her and marries her, shall have two rewards. Any man from the People of the Book who believes in his prophet and also believes in me shall have two rewards. Any slave who does his duty to his master and his duty to the Lord shall have two rewards" [*Ṣaḥīḥ al-Bukhārī*]. Now, if anyone shall have two rewards who teaches his slave, instructing her well, and doing to her what the Prophet said in this tradition, then anyone

هذا أشد وطأ، أي مواطأة للقرآن بسمعك وبصرك، أي فهمك، فالقراءة على هذه الصفة أقوم قيلاً . . . .

(١٨) وأما سؤالك عما لمن علم القرآن ولده، فيكفيك منه قول الرسول عليه السلام « خيركم من تعلم القرآن وعلمه » [صحيح البخاري]، والذي يعلم القرآن ولده داخل في ذلك الفضل.

(١٩) فإن قلت: إنه لا يلي تعليمه بنفسه، ولكنه يستأجر له من يعلمه، فاعلم أنه هو الذي يعلم ولده، إذا أنفق ماله عليه في تعليمه القرآن، فلعله أن يكون بما علمه من ذلك، من السابقين بالخيرات بإذن الله تعالى، وتكون هذه الدرجة هي نية هذا الوالد في تعليم ولده القرآن: ما زال المسلمون وهم يرغبون في تعليم أولادهم القرآن، وعلى ذلك يربونهم، وبه يبتدونهم وهم أطفال لا يملكون لأنفسهم نفعاً ولا ضراً. ولا يعلمون إلا ما علمهم آباؤهم.

(٢٠) فقد جاء في الصحيح، من حديث هشام، عن أبي بشر، عن سعيد ابن جبير، عن إبن عباس: جمعنا المُحكَم في عهد رسول الله ﷺ، فقلت له: وما المحكم؟ قال: المُفَصَّل. وفي حديث ابي عوانة، عن أبي بشر، عن سعيد بن جبير: إن الذي تدعونه المفصل هو المُحكَم. وقال ابن عباس: توفى رسول الله ﷺ وأنا ابن عشر سنين وقد قرأت المُحكَم.

(٢١) وقد قال أبو موسى: قال رسول الله ﷺ: « أيما رجل كانت عنده وليدة فعلمها فأحسن تعليمها، وأدبها فأحسن تأديبها، ثم أعتقها وتزوجها فله أجران، وأيما رجل من أهل الكتاب آمن بنبيه وآمن بي، فله أجران، وأيما مملوك أدى حق مواليه وحق ربه، فله أجران » [صحيح البخاري]، فإذا كان لمن علم وليدة فأحسن تعليمها، وصنع فيها ما قال في هذا الحديث يكون له أجران، فالذي يعلم ولده فيحسن تعليمه، ويؤدبه فيحسن تأديبه، فقد عمل في ولده عملاً حسناً، يرجى له من تضعيف الأجر فيه، كما

who teaches his own child well and instills in him good manners does his child a good deed and can expect a double reward for it, as God has said: "Who is he that will lend God a good loan, and He will multiply it for him manifold?" [Qurʾān 2:245].

(22) The Messenger of God (may God bless him and grant him peace), is said to have passed by a woman in her litter. Someone said to her, "This is the Messenger of God." So she took the arm of a young boy she had with her, and said, "Can he make the pilgrimage?" The Messenger of God said, "Yes, and you shall have a reward." Can this woman have a reward for her child's pilgrimage except for her having brought him on that pilgrimage and taking charge of his performing it? Now, all that the child gets from that pilgrimage is the blessing of being present at a good work and the prayers of Muslims. What the child gets from being taught the Qurʾān is knowledge that remains in his possession and that is of use for a longer time and greater in benefit. This is too obvious to require further discussion.

(23) A man whose son was studying under the late Ibn Ṣaḥnūn[6] once said to Ibn Ṣaḥnūn, "I take charge of work myself, and do not distract him from what he is doing." Ibn Ṣaḥnūn said to him, "Do you know that your reward for it will be greater than for pilgrimage, guarding the borders, and jihad?"

(24) You asked whether a man who abstains from putting his child into Qurʾān school[7] may be compelled to do so by the ruler. Are male and female children equal in this? If one holds that the ruler may not compel him, should he exhort him and accuse him of sinning? What if the child has no parent, but has a guardian? Should the latter compel it by force? If the child has no guardian, may the head of the family or the ruler do it? If the child has no one, may the Muslims do it from [the child's] wealth? If he has no wealth, are the Muslims obligated to pay for him, or should he attend the school without the teacher's charging him tuition? What if he has a father who has wealth but is careless: may the ruler imprison him or flog him for it, or is it not incumbent on him? What if this takes place in a country without a ruler to compel people to do their duties and forbid them to do evil? Shall we permit a group of Muslims of approved religion to stand in for the ruler, or is this not permitted?

قال الله جل وعز ﴿مَنْ ذَا الَّذِي يُقْرِضُ اللَّهَ قَرْضاً حَسَناً فَيُضَاعِفَهُ لَهُ أَضْعَافاً كَثِيرَةً﴾ [البقرة ٢:٢٤٥].

(٢٢) وقد جاء أن رسول الله ﷺ مر بامرأة في محفّتها، فقيل لها: هذا رسول الله! فأخذت بعضد صبي معها وقالت: ألهذا حج؟ فقال رسول الله ﷺ: نعم ولك أجر [صحيح مسلم]. فهل يكون لهذه المرأة أجر فيما هو لصبيها حج، إلا من أجل أنها أحضرته ذلك الحج، ووليت القيام به فيه، وإنما له من ذلك الحج بركة شهود الخير، ودعوة المسلمين. والذي يناله الصبي من تعليمه القرآن هو علم يبقى له بحوزه، وهو أطول غناء، وأكثر نفقة. وهذا أبين من أن يطال فيه بأكثر من هذا.

(٢٣) وقد قال رجل لابن سحنون (رحمة الله عليه)، ممن يطلب ابنه العلم عنده: إني أتولى العمل بنفسي، ولا أشغله عما هو فيه، فقال له: أعلمت أن أجرك في ذلك أعظم من الحج والرباط والجهاد.

(٢٤) وأما سؤالك عن رجل امتنع أن يجعل ولده في الكتّاب هل للإمام أن يجبره؟ وهل الذكر والأنثى في ذلك سواء؟ فإن قلت لا يجبره فهل يوعظ ويؤثم، وكيف إن لم يكن له والد وله وصي، فهل يلزم ذلك بالجبر؟ فإن لم يكن له وصي فهل ذلك للولي أو للإمام؟ فإن كان لا أحد لهذا الولد فهل للمسلمين أن يفعلوا ذلك من ماله؟ فإن لم يكن له مال فهل على المسلمين أن يؤدوا عنه، أو يكون في الكتّاب ولا يكلفه المعلم إجارة؟ وكيف إن كان له أب وله مال ولا يبالي ذلك، فهل للإمام أن يسجنه أو يضربه على ذلك أو ليس ذلك عليه؟ وكيف إن كان هذا في بلد لا سلطان يكرههم على الواجبات، وينهاهم عن المنكرات، فهل نبيح لجماعة من المسلمين المرضي دينهم أن يقوموا مقام السلطان، أو ليس يجوز ذلك؟

Part Two

In the name of God, the Merciful, the Compassionate;
God Bless Muḥammad.

(25) Abū al-Ḥasan [al-Qābisī] said: What I have told you about the merit a father can be expected to acquire from teaching his child the Qur'ān should serve to encourage the father to teach his young child, who, being unable to help or harm himself and unable to distinguish for himself what to take up and what to turn away, has only his father as a refuge, whose duty it is to provide his means of support. Anything the father adds after that duty is an act of charity on the father's part to his child; it is as if he had acted charitably toward outsiders or those whom he has no obligation to support. However, a better reward may be expected for him for his charity to his child who is in need of it; for no one else is his partner therein, and the child has no expedient to rely on so as to dispense with his father's oversight in the matter.

(26) Muslims have been commanded to teach their children how to pray and how to wash themselves before prayer. They drill their children and train them so that the children feel comfortable with these things and are accustomed to them, with the result that these things are easy for them when they reach the age of obligation. If they teach their children how to pray, they must teach them something from the Qur'ān to recite during prayer.

(27) Muslims throughout their history have diligently taught their children the Qur'ān and provided them with teachers. This is something that no father refrains from doing for his child if he has the means to do so, unless he is following his soul's avarice. The latter is no excuse for him, for God, who is praised, has said: "Souls are very prone to avarice" [Qur'ān 4:128]. "And whosoever is guarded against the avarice of his own soul—they are the prosperers" [Qur'ān 64:16]. Not one father would leave off doing this, deeming its omission trivial and insignificant, except a coarse father with no desire for good. God, who is praised, has described His servants in His Book, saying: "The servants of the All-Merciful are those who walk in the earth modestly; . . . who say, 'Our Lord, give us refreshment of our wives and seed, and make us a model to the God-fearing'" [Qur'ān 25:63–74, passim]. Whoever desires that His Lord

الجزء الثاني

بسم الله الرحمن الرحيم وصلى الله على محمد

(٢٥) قال أبو الحسن: إن الذي قدمت لك مما يرجى للوالد في تعليم ولده القرآن، وإنما هو على وجه الترغيب للوالد في تعليم ولده الطفل، الذي لا يملك لنفسه نفعاً ولا ضراً، ولا يميز لنفسه ما يأخذ لها، وما يدفعه عنها وليس له ملجأ إلا لوالده، الذي تجب عليه نفقته لمعيشته. فما زاده بعد ذلك الواجب، فهو إحسان من الوالد للولد، كما لو أحسن للأجنبيين، أو لمن لا يلزمه نفقته ولكن يرجى له فيما أحسن به إلى ولده المحتاج إليه ما هو أفضل، إذ ليس يشركه فيه غيره، ولا حيلة للطفل يستعين بها فيستغني بنفسه فيها عن نظر والده له فيها.

(٢٦) وقد أُمر المسلمون أن يعلموا أولادهم الصلاة، والوضوء لها، ويدربوهم عليها، ويؤدبوهم بها ليسكنوا إليها ويألفوها، فتخف عليهم إذا انتهوا إلى وجوبها عليهم، وهم لا بد لهم إذا علموهم الصلاة، أن يعلموهم من القرآن ما يقرءونه فيها.

(٢٧) وقد مضى أمر المسلمين أنهم يعلمون أولادهم القرآن، ويأتونهم بالمعلمين، ويجتهدون في ذلك، وهذا مما لا يمتنع منه والد لولده وهو يجد سبيلاً إليه، إلا مداركة شح نفسه، فذلك لا حجة له، قال الله سبحانه ﴿وَأُحْضِرَتِ الْأَنفُسُ الشُّحَّ﴾ [النساء ٤:١٢٨] وقال تعالى ﴿وَمَن يُوقَ شُحَّ نَفْسِهِ فَأُولَٰئِكَ هُمُ الْمُفْلِحُونَ﴾ [التغابن ٦٤:١٦]. ولا يدع أيضاً هذا والد واحد تهاوناً واستخفافاً لتركه إلا والد جاف لا رغبة له في الخير. إن الله سبحانه وصف في كتابه عباده فقال سبحانه ﴿وَعِبَادُ الرَّحْمَٰنِ الَّذِينَ يَمْشُونَ عَلَى الْأَرْضِ هَوْنًا . . . .﴾ إلى قوله عز وجل ﴿الَّذِينَ يَقُولُونَ رَبَّنَا هَبْ لَنَا مِنْ أَزْوَاجِنَا وَذُرِّيَّاتِنَا قُرَّةَ أَعْيُنٍ وَاجْعَلْنَا لِلْمُتَّقِينَ إِمَامًا﴾ [الفرقان ٢٥:٦٣-٧٤]. فمن رغب إلى ربه أن يجعل له من ذريته قرة عين، لم يبخل على ولده

give him refreshment of the eye from his seed will not begrudge his child the expense of teaching him the Qurʾān. God, whose name is exalted, has said: "And those who believed, and their seed followed them in belief, We shall join their seed with them, and We shall not defraud them of aught of their work" [Qurʾān 52:21]. That is to say, We shall not diminish them aught of their work. Only a coarse or miserly man will fail to desire to instruct his family and children in what is good out of niggardliness for the expense or negligence that deprives them of this good.

(28) A child's religious status, as long as he is a minor, is the status of his father. Will the father then leave his minor child, not teaching him religion, when his teaching him the Qurʾān will make his knowledge of religion firm? Has he not heard the words of the Messenger of God, on whom be peace? "Every infant is born in a state of nature; then his parents make him a Jew or a Christian. It is just as camels are brought forth as beasts intact.[8] Do you discern any that are mutilated?" They asked him, "Messenger of God, what about those who die young?" "God," he said, "knows best what they would have done." Thus he informed us of what happens to a child because of his parents, from what they teach him. As for those who die before reaching the age of discernment, the Messenger referred their case to God's knowledge of what they would have done if they had lived.

(29) If the children of unbelievers experience harm from their parents, it behooves the children of believers to benefit religiously from their parents. The first generations of believers had no need to trouble themselves arguing about this; they made do with the desire that had been placed in their hearts; they acted according to it, and they left it as a customary practice that each generation passed on from the previous one. No father was ever reproved regarding this, nor did any father ever turn out to have omitted to do so from desire or from negligence. That is no attribute of a believing Muslim! Had it ever become evident that someone had omitted to teach his child the Qurʾān out of negligence, his condition would have been deemed one of ignorance, ugliness, and deficiency, beneath that of people of contentment and satisfaction. Sometimes, however, lack of means causes parents to lag behind in this matter; then their behavior is excusable—depending on how sound their excuse turns out to be.

بما ينفق عليه في تعليمه القرآن قال الله جل ذكره ﴿وَالَّذِينَ آمَنُوا وَاتَّبَعَتْهُمْ ذُرِّيَّتُهُمْ بِإِيمَانٍ أَلْحَقْنَا بِهِمْ ذُرِّيَّتَهُمْ وَمَا أَلَتْنَاهُمْ مِنْ عَمَلِهِمْ مِنْ شَيْءٍ﴾ [الطور ٥٢:٢١]. أي وما نقصناهم من علمهم من شيء؛ فما يدع الرغبة في تعليم أهله وولده الخير شحًا على الإنفاق أو تهاونًا به يفقدهم ذلك الخير، إلا جاف أو بخيل.

(٢٨) إن حكم الولد في الدين حكم والده. ما دام طفلاً صغيرًا، أفيدع ابنه الصغير لا يعلمه الدين، وتعليمه القرآن يؤكد له معرفة الدين؟ ألم يسمع قول الرسول (عليه السلام) كل مولود يولد على الفطرة فأبواه يهودانه أو ينصرانه كما تناتج الإبل من بهيمة جمعاء، هل تحس من جدعاء، فقالوا: يا رسول الله أفرأيت من يموت وهو صغير؟ فقال الله اعلم بما كانوا عاملين [الحديث في البخاري ومسلم]. فأخبر بما يدرك الولد من أبويه مما يعلمانه. فمن مات قبل أن يبلغ أن يعلم، رد رسول الله ﷺ أمره إلى علم الله بهم ما كانوا عاملين لو عاشوا.

(٢٩) فإذا كان ولد الكافرين يدركهم الضرر من قبل آبائهم، انبغى أن يدرك أولاد المؤمنين النفع في الدين من قبل آبائهم. ولقد استغنى سلف المؤمنين أن يتكلفوا الاحتجاج في مثل هذا، واكتفوا بما جعل في قلوبهم من الرغبة في ذلك فعملوا به، وأبقوا ذلك سنة ينقلها الخلف عن السلف ما احتسب في ذلك على أحد من الآباء، ولا تبين على أحد من الآباء أنه ترك ذلك رغبة عنه لا تهاونًا به، وليس هذا من صفة المؤمن المسلم. ولو ظهر على أحد أنّه ترك أن يعلم ولده القرآن تهاونًا بذلك، لجُهّل وقُبّح ونُقّص حاله، وَ وضُعَ عن حال أهل القناعة والرضا. ولكن قد يُخَلِّفُ الآباء عن ذلك قلةُ ذات اليد، فيكون معذورًا حسب ما يتبين من صحة عذره.

(30) If the child has property, his father or his guardian (if his father has died) should not leave him. Let him enter the primary school and engage the teacher to teach him the Qurʾān from his wealth, as is due. If the orphan has no guardian, the ruler[9] of the Muslims should oversee his affairs and proceed with his instruction as the father or guardian would have proceeded. If the child is in a town where there is no ruler, oversight would be exercised for him in a matter such as this if the town's righteous people came together to oversee the interests of the town's people, for overseeing this orphan is one of those interests.

(31) If the orphan has no property, his mother or next of kin should be encouraged to take charge of teaching him the Qurʾān. If someone else volunteers to bear the burden for them, that person shall have his reward. If the orphan has no kin to care for him, any Muslim who cares for him shall have his reward. If the teacher, reckoning on a heavenly reward, teaches him solely for God's sake, bearing it patiently, his reward for it, God willing, shall be doubled, especially since it is his craft from which he supports himself. If he prefers him before himself, he will merit, God willing, an abundant share of the rewards of those who prefer others before themselves. The words of the Messenger of God, on whom be peace, when he said to the woman, "Yes, and you shall have a reward," will sufficiently clarify to you what I have described of the recompense of those who desire to do this and hasten to do it.

(32) As for teaching a female the Qurʾān and learning, it is good and of benefit to her. However, her being taught letter-writing or poetry is a cause for fear. She should be taught only things that can be expected to be good for her and protect her from temptation. It would be safer for her to be spared learning to write. When the Prophet (may God bless him and grant him peace) permitted women to attend the festival, he commanded them to bring out adolescent girls and those who normally are secluded behind a curtain.[10] At the same time he commanded menstruating women to avoid the place where people pray. He said, "Let women be present where there is blessing and at the prayers of Muslims." On this basis it is acceptable to teach them good things that are safe for them; as for things from which harm to them can be feared, it is preferable that such things be kept away from them, and this is the duty of their guardian. Understand what I have explained to you. Seek guidance from God, and He will guide: He is a sufficient guide and helper for you.

(٣٠) وأما إن كان للولد مال، فلا يدعه أبوه أو وصيه - إن كان قد مات أبوه - وليدخل الكُتَّاب، ويؤاجر المعلم على تعليمه القرآن من ماله حسب ما يجب. فإن لم يكن لليتيم وصي نظر في أمره حاكم المسلمين، وسار في تعليمه سيرة أبيه أو وصيه، وإن كان ببلد لا حاكم فيه، نُظرله في مثل هذا، لو اجتمع صالحو ذلك البلد على النظر في مصالح أهله؛ فالنظر في هذا اليتيم من تلك المصالح.

(٣١) وإن لم يكن لليتيم مال، فأمه أو أولياؤه الأقرب به هم المرغبون في القيام به في تعليم القرآن. فإن تطوع غيرهم بحمل ذلك عنهم، فله أجره. إن لم يكن لليتيم من أهله من يعنى به في ذلك، فمن عني به من المسلمين فله أجره؛ وإن احتسب فيه المعلم فعلمه لله عز وجل، وصبر على ذلك، فأجره إن شاء الله يُضعف في ذلك، إذ هي صنعته التي يقوم منها معاشه. فإذا آثره على نفسه استأهل إن شاء الله حظاً وافراً من أجور المؤثرين على أنفسهم. ويكفيك من البيان عمّا وصفت لك من ثواب من رغب في ذلك وسارع إليه، الذي تقدم عن الرسول عليه السلام، إذ قال للمرأة: نعم، ولك أجر.

(٣٢) وأما تعليم الأنثى القرآن والعلم فهو حسن ومن مصالحها. فأما أن تُعلم الترسل والشعر وما أشبهه، فهو مخوف عليها. وإنَّما تعلم ما يرجى لها صلاحه، ويُؤمن عليها من فتنته؛ وسلامتها من تعلم الخط أنجى لها. ولما أذن النبي ﷺ للنساء في شهود العيد أمرهن أن يُخرجن العواتق وذوات الخدور، وأمر الحائض أن تعتزل مصلى الناس، وقال: يشهدن الخير ودعوة المسلمين. فعلى مثل هذا يقبل في تعليمهن الخير الذي يؤمن عليهن فيه، وما خيف عليهن منه، فصرفه عنهن أفضل لهن، وأوجب على مُتولي أمرهن. فافهم ما بينت لك، واستهد الله يهد، وكفى به هادياً ونصيراً.

(33) Know that God, who is mighty and exalted, has imposed certain duties on believing women, just as He has imposed certain duties on believing men. This may be inferred from God's words: "It is not for any believer, man or woman, when God and His Messenger have decreed a matter, to have the choice in the affair" [Qurʾān 33:36]. And, "The believers, the men and the women" [Qurʾān 9:71]. In more than one verse of His Book He has joined men and women together in being well rewarded. For example, "God has promised the believers, men and women, gardens underneath which rivers flow, forever therein to dwell, and goodly dwelling-places in the Gardens of Eden; and greater, God's good pleasure, that is the mighty triumph" [Qurʾān 9:72]. And He commanded the wives of His Prophet (on whom be peace) to remember what they had heard from the Prophet: "And remember that which is recited in your houses of the signs of God and the Wisdom" [Qurʾān 33:34]. How should they not be taught the good and what helps to its attainment? But whoever is in charge of them should turn from them anything of which one should beware on their behalf, since he is their protector and responsible for them. "Surely bounty is in the hand of God; He gives it unto whomsoever He will. . . . And God is of bounty abounding" [Qurʾān 3:73]. . . .

(34) Abū al-Ḥasan [al-Qābisī] said: I have sufficiently presented before this chapter what has come down about someone who teaches the Qurʾān. I have explained the things that stress teaching it and taking care to do so and that warn against anything that distracts from it, lest the person who has memorized it forget it. The word of God, who is mighty and exalted, to His Prophet (on whom be peace): "Say: 'What thing is greatest in testimony?' Say: 'God is witness between me and you, and this Qurʾān has been revealed to me that I may warn you thereby, and whomsoever it may reach" [Qurʾān 6:19] implies an obligation to learn the Qurʾān, so that this obligation shall be carried out by whomever it reaches until the Day of Resurrection. And the following verse implies the same: "We have made the Qurʾān easy to remember. Is there any that will remember?" [Qurʾān 54:17]. It has been made easy to remember until the Day of Resurrection. Muslims have never disagreed that the Qurʾān is God's argument against His servants and that Muslims have a duty to observe it and summon others to it until the Day of Resurrection.[11]

(٣٣) واعلم أن الله جل وعز قد أخذ على المؤمنات فيما عليهن، كما أخذ على المؤمنين فيما عليهم، وذلك في قوله جل وعز ﴿وَمَا كَانَ لِمُؤْمِنٍ وَلَا مُؤْمِنَةٍ إِذَا قَضَى اللهُ وَرَسُولُهُ أَمْرًا . . . .الآية﴾ [الأحزاب ٣٣:٣٦]. وقوله: ﴿وَالمُؤْمِنُونَ والمُؤْمِناتُ . . . .الآية﴾ [التوبة ٩:٧١] وجمعهما في حسن الجزاء في غير آية من كتابه، وفي قوله تعالى ﴿وَعَدَ اللهُ المُؤْمِنِينَ وَالمُؤْمِناتِ . . . .الآية﴾ [التوبة ٩:٧٢]، وأمر أزواج نبيه عليه السلام أن يذكرن ما سمعن منه ﷺ فقال ﴿وَاذْكُرْنَ مَا يُتْلَى فِي بُيُوتِكُنَّ مِنْ آيَاتِ اللهِ وَالحِكْمَةِ﴾ [الأحزاب ٣٣:٣٤]. فكيف لا يُعلمن الخير، وما يُعين عليه، ويصرف عنهن القائم عليهن ما يحذر عليهن منه، إذ هو الراعي فيهن والمسئول عنهن،﴿والفضل بيد الله يؤتيه من يشاء والله ذو الفضل العظيم﴾ [آل عمران ٣:٧٣] . . . .

(٣٤) قال أبو الحسن: قدمت فوق هذا الباب ما جاء لمن علم القرآن، وبينت ما يؤكد تعليمه والحرص عليه، ويحذر مما يشغل عنه لئلا ينساه من حفظ، بما فيه الكفاية، وفي قول الله عز وجل لنبيه عليه السلام ﴿قُلْ أَيُّ شَيْءٍ أَكْبَرُ شَهَادَةً قُلِ اللهُ شَهِيدٌ بَيْنِي وَبَيْنَكُمْ وَأُوحِيَ إِلَيَّ هَذَا القُرْآنُ لِأُنذِرَكُم بِهِ وَمَنْ بَلَغَ﴾ [الأنعام ٦:١٩]. ما يلزم القيام بتعلم القرآن حتى يقوم له من يبلغه إلى يوم القيامة. وكذلك قوله عز وجل ﴿وَلَقَدْ يَسَّرْنَا القُرْآنَ لِلذِّكْرِ فَهَلْ مِنْ مُدَّكِرٍ﴾ [القمر ٥٤:١٧]. وهو ميسر للذكر إلى يوم القيامة وما اختلف المسلمون أن القرآن هو حجة الله على عباده إلى يوم القيامة، وأن على المسلمين القيام به، والدعوة إليه إلى يوم القيامة.

(35) In the *Ṣaḥīḥ,* the following tradition is attributed to Ṭalḥah ibn Muṭarrif: "I asked ᶜAbdallāh ibn Abī Awfā, 'Did the Prophet (may God bless him and grant him peace) leave a testament?' 'No,' he replied. I said: 'How so? Making a testament has been prescribed for men; they have been commanded to do so—and he left no testament?' 'As his testament,' he said, 'he left the Book of God'" [*Ṣaḥīḥ Muslim*].

(36) It is widely known among Muslims that the Prophet (may God bless him and grant him peace) is reported to have said: "I have left among you two things which, if you adhere to them, you will not stray: the Book of God and my Sunna." Thus the Qurᵓān is something that must be learned. However, he who keeps it shall have his reward, and he who does not keep it will lose his portion. God forbid that Muslims should agree to cease keeping it; if that should happen, there would be ruinous destruction. . . .

(37) Know that there was not one of the religious leaders[12] of the Muslims in the first days of this community but who gave thought to what would be of benefit to Muslims in all their affairs, private and public. We have never heard that any of them appointed teachers to teach people's children in elementary schools[13] during their childhood or gave such teachers a share from the public treasury, as they did for anyone they charged to serve the Muslims either by judging between them in lawsuits, calling them to prayer in the mosque, or anything else that they established to protect Muslims and guard their affairs. They could not have neglected the business of teachers for young children. However—and God only knows—they thought it was a matter that concerned each individual personally, inasmuch as what a person taught his child was part of his own welfare that was of special concern to him. They therefore left it as one of the tasks of fathers, something that it was not fitting for someone else to do for them if they were able to do it themselves. Since the religious leaders of the Muslims had made no provision for the matter, and it was one that Muslims had to carry out for their children and without which they would not feel at ease, they got themselves a teacher for their children, someone to devote himself to them on a regular basis and to care for them as he would care for his own young children. Since it was unlikely that anyone could be found to volunteer for the Muslims, teach their children for them, devote himself entirely to them, and give up seeking his own livelihood and his profitable activities and other needs, it was appropriate for Muslims to hire someone to take care of teaching their children on a constant basis, to the exclusion of any other business.

(٣٥) وفي الصحيح لطلحة ابن مطرف قال: سألت عبد الله بن أبي أوفى: أوصى النبي ﷺ؟ قال لا، فقلت: كيف كتب على الناس الوصية أمروا بها ولم يوص؟ قال: أوصى بكتاب الله [صحيح مسلم].

(٣٦) ومشتهر عند المسلمين أنه جاء عن النبي ﷺ أنه قال «تركت فيكم أمرين لن تضلوا ما تمسكتم بهما: كتاب الله وسنتي». فهو شيء لا بد من تعلمه، ولكن من قام به فله أجره، ومن لم يقم به ترك حظه، وأعوذ بالله أن يتفق المسلمون على ترك القيام به، ولو كان كذلك لكانت الهلكة المبيرة . . . .

(٣٧) ثم اعلم أن أئمة المسلمين في صدر هذه الأمة، ما منهم إلا من قد نظر في جميع أمور المسلمين بما يصلحهم في الخاصة والعامة، فلم يبلغنا أن أحداً منهم أقام معلمين يعلمون للناس أولادهم من صغرهم في الكتاتيب، ويجعلون لهم على ذلك نصيباً من مال الله جل وعز، كما قد صنعوا لمن كلفوه القيام للمسلمين في النظر بينهم في أحكامهم، والأذان لصلاتهم في مساجدهم، مع سائر ما جعلوه حفظاً لأمور المسلمين، وحيطةً عليهم، وما يمكن أن يكونوا أغفلوا شأن معلم الصبيان، ولكنهم - والله أعلم - رأوا أنه شيء مما يختص أمره كلَّ إنسان في نفسه، إذا كان ما يعلمه المرء لولده، فهو من صلاح نفسه المختص به، فأبقوا عملاً من عمل الآباء، الذي يكون لا ينبغي أن يحمله عنهم غيرهم إذا كانوا مطيقيه. ولما ترك أئمة المسلمين النظر في هذا الأمر، وكان مما لا بد منه للمسلمين أن يفعلوه في أولادهم، ولا تطيب أنفسهم إلا على ذلك، واتخذوا لأولادهم معلماً يختص بهم، ويداومهم، ويرعاهم حسب ما يرعى المعلم صبيانه. وبَعُدَ أن يمكن أن يوجد من الناس من يتطوع للمسلمين فيعلم لهم أولادهم ويحبس نفسه عليهم، ويترك التماس ومعايشه، وتصرفه في مكاسبه وفي سائر حاجياته، صَلَحَ للمسلمين أن يستأجروا من يكفيهم تعليم أولادهم، ويلازمهم لهم، ويكتفي بذلك عن تشاغله بغيره ويكون هذا المعلم قد حمل عن آباء الصبيان مؤونة

Such a teacher would relieve the children's parents of the burden of educating them; he would make them understand how to live upright lives, and he would increase their understanding of the good and turn them away from evil.

(38) This is an occupation that few people volunteer to perform free of charge. If one had waited for people to volunteer to teach young children the Qurʾān, many children would have been neglected and many people would not have learned the Qurʾān. This would necessarily have led to loss of the Qurʾān from people's hearts. It would have caused Muslim children to be confirmed in ignorance.

(39) Yet there is no good reason to cause a shortage where there is no scarcity, and no injunction to abstain [from being paid to teach the Qurʾān] has been confirmed as coming from the Messenger of God (may God bless him and grant him peace).

(40) Al-Ḥārith ibn Miskīn, in a report dated to the year [1]73,[14] said: "Ibn Wahb[15] gave us the following report: 'I heard Mālik[16] say, "None of the scholars I have known saw anything wrong with paying teachers—teachers of the Qurʾān school."' "

(41) The following is also attributed to Ibn Wahb in his *Muwaṭṭaʾ* from ʿAbd al-Jabbār ibn ʿUmar: "No one I asked in Medina sees anything wrong in teachers teaching for pay."

(42) And the following is reported by al-Ḥārith from Ibn Wahb: Mālik was asked about a man who gives another man twenty dinars to teach his son writing and the Qurʾān until he masters it. He said, "There is nothing wrong with it, even if the man sets no time limit." Then he said, "The Qurʾān is the worthiest thing to be taught." (He may have said "the worthiest thing that has ever been taught.")

(43) Ibn Wahb also said in his *Muwaṭṭaʾ*: "I heard Mālik say, 'There is nothing wrong with receiving pay for teaching the Qurʾān and writing.' I asked Mālik, 'What if he stipulates, in addition to what he receives as his remuneration, a specified amount (to be received as a bonus) at the feasts of Fiṭr and Aḍḥā?' He said, 'There is nothing wrong with that.' "

(44) Abū al-Ḥasan [al-Qābisī] said: "Ibn Wahb was reported to me as having said: 'I was sitting with Mālik when a schoolteacher came up to him and said: "Abū ʿAbdallāh, I am a man who educates young boys. I heard something, and so I became loathe to make a contract, and now people have held back from me—they are not giving me what they used

تأديبهم، ويبصرهم استقامة أحوالهم، وما يُمني لهم من الخير أفهامهم، ويبعد عن الشر مآلهم.

(٣٨) وهذه عناية لا يكثر المتطوعون بها. ولو انتظر من يتطوع بمعالجة تعليم الصبيان القران، لضاع كثير من الصبيان، ولما تعلم القرآن كثير من الناس، فتكون هي الضرورة القائدة إلى السقوط في فقد القرآن من الصدور، والداعية التي تُثبت أطفال المسلمين على الجهالة.

(٣٩) فلا وجه لتضييق ما لم يأت فيه ضيق، ولا ثبت فيه عن الرسول عليه السلام ما يدل على التنزيه عنه.

(٤٠) ولقد ذكر الحارث بن مسكين في تاريخ سنة ثلاث وسبعين، أخبرنا ابن وهب قال: سمعت مالكاً يقول: كل من أدركت من أهل العلم لا يرى بأجر المعلمين - معلمي الكتّاب - بأساً.

(٤١) ولابن وهب أيضاً في موطئه عن عبد الجبار بن عمر قال: كل من سألت بالمدينة لا يرى لتعليم المعلين بالأجر بأساً.

(٤٢) وللحارث عن ابن وهب قال: وسئل مالك عن الرجل يجعل للرجل عشرين ديناراً، يعلم ابنه الكتاب والقرآن حتى يحذقه، فقال: لا بأس بذلك، وإن لم يضرب أجلاً. ثم قال: والقرآن أحق ما يُعلّم، أو قال عُلِّمَ.

(٤٣) وقال ابن وهب في موطئه: سمعت مالكاً يقول: لا بأس بأخذ الأجر على تعليم القرآن والكتاب. قال: فقلت لمالك: أفرأيت إذا شرط مع ما له من الأجر في ذلك شيئاً مسمى كل فطر أو أضحى؟ قال لا بأس بذلك.

(٤٤) قال، قال أبو الحسن: ولقد مرت بي حكاية تذكر عن ابن وهب أنه قال: كنت جالساً عند مالك فأقبل إليه معلم الكتّاب، فقال له: يا أبا عبد الله، إني رجل مؤدب الصبيان، وإنه بلغني شيء، فكرهت أن أشارط، وقد امتنع الناس عليّ، وليس

to give. I have a family to support and no other means but teaching." Mālik said, "Go and make a contract." The man left, and some of Mālik's companions said to him, "Abū ᶜAbdallāh, are you commanding him to stipulate payment for teaching?" Mālik said to them, "Yes, who will smooth the rough edges of our young children for us? Who will discipline them for us? Were it not for teachers, what would we ourselves be?" ' "

(45) This story about Mālik is reinforced by something that Ibn Saḥnūn mentions: "They also transmitted to us from Sufyān al-Thawrī,[17] from [ᶜAṭāᵓ] ibn al-Sāᵓib,[18] from 'Ibn Masᶜūd,[19] who said: 'Three things are indispensable to men: they must have a commander [*amīr*] to judge between them, or else they would eat one another up; they must buy and sell copies of the Qurᵓān, or else God's Book would become rare; and they must have a teacher to teach their children and receive remuneration for it, or else people would be illiterate.' "

(46) Many of our scholars have argued for the permissibility of receiving remuneration, whether stipulated or unstipulated, from the fact that people[20] have followed this practice and approved of it. They have mentioned this on the authority of ᶜAṭāᵓ ibn Abī Rabāḥ,[21] al-Ḥasan al-Baṣrī,[22] and more than one righteous scholar of old. As for anyone who claims that it is reprehensible to stipulate a remuneration, but approves of receiving an unstipulated remuneration, what is the difference between the two? Does he find stipulating a remuneration reprehensible for any other reason than that it is receiving compensation for teaching the Qurᵓān, which should be taught only for God's sake? But is it not the same if one receives remuneration not previously stipulated? And isn't someone who knows that he will be given something like someone making a stipulation? And if teaching stands in the stead of alms, which are given only for God's sake, how can it be right to receive compensation? It is something unseemly.

(47) However, the meaning of whatever is received for teaching the Qurᵓān is not that it is received as compensation in this way—because of the part of the Qurᵓān that the teacher has caused to be understood. Rather, it is compensation for the labor and the practice of teaching, as has been stated earlier.

(48) Whatever is done only for God's sake should not be done for any other compensation obtained in this world, except in the sense of not compensating for the action itself, which is done only for God. We find the following, transmitted through Abū Saᶜīd al-Khudrī, in the *Ṣaḥīḥ*: "A group of the Prophet's companions set out on a journey and halted

يعطونني كما كانوا يعطون، وقد اضطررت بعيالي وليس لي حيلة إلا التعليم. فقال له مالك اذهب وشارط، فانصرف الرجل. فقال له بعض جلسائه: يا أبا عبد الله، تأمره أن يشترط على التعليم - فقال لهم مالك: نعم فمن يُحِّط (يصلح) لنا صبياننا؟ ومن يؤدبهم لنا؟ لولا المعلمون أي شيء كنا نكون نحن؟

(٤٥) ويشد ما في هذه الحكاية عن مالك ما ذكره ابن سحنون قال: حدثونا عن سفيان الثوري، عن العلاء بن السائب، قال: قال ابن مسعود: ثلاث لا بد للناس منهم، من أمير يحكم بينهم، ولولا ذلك لأكل بعضهم بعضاً؛ ولا بد للناس من شراء المصاحف وبيعها، ولولا ذلك لبطل كتاب الله؛ ولا بد للناس من معلم يعلم أولادهم، ويأخذ على ذلك أجراً، ولولا ذاك كان الناس أميين.

(٤٦) وقد احتج كثير من علمائنا في جواز أخذ الإجارة بشرط كانت أو بغير شرط أن الناس قد عملوا به، وأجازوه، وذكروا ذلك عن عطاء بن أبي رباح، وعن الحسن البصري، وعن غير واحد من الأئمة والصالحين، فمن زعم أنه يكره الشرط فيه ويجيزه بغير شرط لم فرق بينهما؟ هل هو يكرهه إذا اشترط إلا من قبل أنه أخذ عوضاً على تعليمه القرآن وإنما يجب أن يعلم لله؟ أفليس هكذا إذا أخذه بغير شرط ومن علم أنه سيعطى أليس هو كالشرط؟ وإذا كان مقام التعليم مقام الصدقات التي إنما يراد بها وجه الله، كيف يصلح أن يؤخذ عليها عوض؟ هذا ما لا ينبغي.

(٤٧) ولكن ما يؤخذ على تعليم القرآن، ليس معناه أن يؤخذ معاوضة هكذا، لعلّة ما فَهَّم المعلم من القرآن، وإنما هو عوض من العناية بالتعليم، والقيام لرياضته حسب ما تقدم من أول.

(٤٨) وما كان إنما يُعْمل لله، لا يجوز أن يعمل لغير ذلك من الأعواض التي تنال من الدنيا، إلا على معنى غير المعاوضة من العمل نفسه الذي لا يكون إلا لله - وذكر في الصحيح من حديث أبي سعيد الخدري قال: انطلق نفر من أصحاب رسول الله

near a tribe of bedouins. They asked the bedouins for hospitality, but they refused to offer any. Then the headman of the tribe was bitten by a snake. The tribesmen did everything they could, but nothing helped. One of them said: 'Why don't you go to this group of people who have stopped here? Perhaps one of them has something?' So they went to them and said: 'People, our chief has been bitten. We have tried everything, but nothing is helping him. Does any of you have anything?' One of the men said: 'Yes, by God, I can recite a charm. However, by God, we asked you for hospitality and you offered us none, and so I won't recite the charm until you pay us a fee.' Having settled with them on a flock of sheep, he began spitting on the man and reciting, *Praise belongs to God, the Lord of all Being.*[23] It was as if the man had been released from a shackle. He started walking again with no pain. So they paid them their fee on which they had agreed. One of the group said, 'Divide it up.' But the man who had recited the charm said, 'Don't do it until we come to the Messenger of God, tell him what happened, and see what he commands us to do.' So they came to the Messenger of God, may God bless him and grant him peace, and told him. He said, 'How do you know that it was a charm?' Then he added, 'You were right. Divide it up, and give me a share with you.' And the Prophet, may God bless him and grant him peace, smiled. . . . "

(49) As for teaching law and the division of inheritances, a man may hire someone to teach his child that.[24] Ibn al-Qāsim[25] was asked about it, and said: "I heard nothing from him—meaning Mālik—about it, except that he was averse to selling books of opinion about religious law.[26] Therefore we do not like the idea of being paid to teach that, and stipulating payment for teaching it is even worse."

(50) As for Ibn Saḥnūn, he mentions in his book [how his father, Saḥnūn had mentioned] Mālik's having said, "I do not think it permissible to pay someone who teaches jurisprudence and the division of inheritances." He said to his son: "Some Andalusians transmit [the view] that there is no harm in hiring someone to teach the division of inheritances, poetry, and grammar and that it is like [hiring someone to teach] the Qurʾān." [Saḥnūn] said: "Mālik and our companions were averse to it. How could it be comparable to [teaching] the Qurʾān, when the Qurʾān has an end that can be reached, while the things you have mentioned do not have an end that can be reached—that is unknown [with regard to these things]? Also, both jurisprudence and learning are

ﷺ في سفرة سافروها، حتى نزلوا على حي من أحياء العرب فاستضافوهم، فأبوا أن يضيفوهم، فلُدغ سيد ذلك الحي، فسعوا إليه بكل شيء لا ينفعه شيء، فقال بعضهم: لو أتيتهم هؤلاء الذين نزلوا، لعله أن يكون عند بعضهم شيء. فأتوهم فقالوا: يا أيها الرهط، إن سيدنا لدغ، وسعينا له بكل شيء لا ينفعه، فهل عند أحد منكم من شيء؟ فقال بعضهم: نعم والله إني لأرقي: ولكن والله لقد استضفناكم، فلم تضيفونا، فما أنا براق لكم حتى تجعلوا لنا جعلاً، فصالحهم على قطيع من الغنم، فانطلق يتفل عليه ويقرأ الحمد لله رب العالمين، فكأنما نشط من عقال، فانقلب يمشي وما به قلبةٌ. فقال: فأوفوهم جعلهم الذي صالحوهم عليه، فقال بعضهم: قسموا. قال الذي رقى: لا تفعلوا حتى نأتي رسول الله ﷺ فذكروا له فقال: وما يدريك أنها رقية؟ ثم قال: قد أصبتم، اقسموا واضربوا لي معكم سهماً وضحك النبي ﷺ.

(٤٩) فأما تعليم الفقه والفرائض، يستأجر الرجل من يعلم ولده ذلك، فسئل ابن القاسم عنه فقال: ما سمعت - يعني من مالك - فيه شيئاً، إلا أنه كره بيع كتب الفقه، فإنا نرى الإجارة على تعليم ذلك لا تعجبني، والشرط على تعليمها أشر.

(٥٠) وأما ابن سحنون فذكر في كتابه، قال: قال مالك: لا أرى أن يجوز إجازة من يعلم الفقه والفرائض. وقال لابنه: روى بعض أهل الأندلس أنه لا بأس بالإجارة على تعليم الفقه والفرائض والشعر والنحو، وهو مثل القرآن، فقال: كره ذلك مالك وأصحابنا، وكيف يشبه القرآن، والقرآن له غاية ينتهى إليها، وما ذكرت ليس له غاية ينتهى إليها فهذا مجهول، والفقه والعلم أمر قد اختلف فيه، والقرآن هو الحق

matters over which there is disagreement, but the Qurʾān is the truth about which there is no doubt. Finally, jurisprudence is not memorized like the Qurʾān, and so does not resemble it; and it has no end or limit that can be reached."

(51) Ibn Ḥabīb said, "I asked Aṣbagh, 'How did you allow stipulating a fee for teaching poetry, grammar, and letter writing if you set no time limit? These things have no end that can be reached by a known time limit.' He said to me, 'We hold that it is known, just as with embalming and baking. Mālik permitted charging a fee for teaching embalming, baking, and similar trades. When the student reaches the level of people who know the trade, the teacher's payment comes due.'"

(52) Abū al-Ḥasan [al-Qābisī] said: As for hiring someone to teach one's child poetry, Ibn al-Qāsim said that Mālik had said about it: "This does not please me."

(53) The aforementioned people disagreed only about paying the teacher to teach something other than the Qurʾān and writing. They did not disagree about subjects meant to reinforce the Qurʾān, such as writing and penmanship.

(54) Ibn Saḥnūn mentioned: "It is fitting for the teacher to teach his students [the correct reading of] the case-endings[27] of [the words of] the Qurʾān—it is his duty to do so—and vocalization, spelling, good handwriting, good reading,[28] when to pause [in recitation],[29] and how to articulate clearly; it is his duty to do so. It is his duty to teach them the good reading that has become well-known, namely the reading of Nāfiʿ, but there is no harm in his having them read according to another [authority] if [the reading] is not considered disagreeable. There is no harm in his teaching them homilies, if they desire.[30]

(55) "He should teach them good manners, for it his duty toward God to give good advice, protect them, and care for them. The teacher should command them to perform the ritual prayer when they are seven years old and beat them for [omitting to pray] when they are ten. That is what Mālik said. ʿAbd al-Raḥmān[31] reported to us that Mālik said, 'Ten-year-olds are beaten for it, and [at that age] they are given separate places to sleep.' I asked, '[Did he mean] males and females?' 'Yes,' he said. And he must teach them [how to perform] the ablutions [before prayer] and the ritual prayer, because that is part of their religion—the number of bowings[32] and prostrations[33] in [each] prayer, the recitation [of verses from the Qurʾān] in the prayer, [the saying of] 'God is great,'[34] the manner of sitting[35] [during prayer], the manner of entering a state

الذي لا شك فيه؛ والفقه لا يستظهر مثل القرآن، وهو لا يشبهه، ولا غاية له ولا أمد ينتهى إليه.

(٥١) قال ابن حبيب: قلت لأصبغ: فكيف جوزتم الشرط على تعليم الشعر والنحو والرسائل، إذا لم تسموا لذلك أجلاً، وهو مما ليس له منتهى ينتهي منه إلى حد معروف. فقال لي: هو عندنا معروف بمنزلة الحناطة والخبز، وقد أجاز مالك الشرط على تعليم الحناطة والخبز، وما أشبه ذلك من الصناعات، فإذا بلغ من ذلك مبلغ أهل العلم به من الناس، وجب في ذلك حقه.

(٥٢) قال أبو الحسن: أما الاستئجار على تعليم الشعر لولده، فقال فيه ابن القاسم: قال مالك: لا يعجبني هذا.

(٥٣) والذي اختلف فيه من قدمنا ذكره، إنما هو في إفراد المعلم بالإجازة على غير القرآن والكتابة، فأما ما كان من معاني التقوية على القرآن، من الكتابة والخط، فما اختلفوا فيه.

(٥٤) ولقد ذكر ابن سحنون انه ينبغي إن يعلمهم إعراب القرآن، ذاك لازم له، والشكل والهجاء والخط الحسن، والقراءة الحسنة بالتوقيف والترتيل، يلزمه ذلك، ويلزمه أن يعلمهم ما علم من المقارئ الحسنة وهو مقرأ نافع، ولا بأس إن أقرأهم بغيره، إذا لم يكن مستشبعاً، ولا بأس أن يعلمهم الخُطَب إن أرادوا.

(٥٥) قال: ويعلمهم الأدب، فإنه من الواجب لله عليه، وهو من النصيحة لهم، وحفظهم ورعايتهم، وينبغي للمعلم أن يأمرهم بالصلاة إذا كانوا بني سبع سنين، ويضربهم عليها إذا كانوا بني عشر. وكذلك قال مالك؛ أخبرنا عنه عبد الرحمن وقال: قال مالك: يضربون عليها بنو عشر، ويفرق بينهم في المضاجع قلت الذكور والإناث؟ قال: نعم. قال: ويلزمه أن يعلمهم الوضوء والصلاة لأن ذلك من دينهم، وعدد ركوعها وسجودها. والقراءة فيها والتكبير، وكيف الجلوس، والإحرام،

of sacralization[36] [to commence the prayer], the salutation[37] [that concludes the prayer], and whatever is necessary for them in prayer; [how to recite] the Confession of Faith[38] and the Supplication of Standing[39] in the morning. For the latter belongs to the Sunna[40] of prayer and to what by right is an essential part of it. And he should teach them the prayer of funerals[41] and the supplications at them, for that is part of their religion. He ought to teach them the traditional usages[42] of [the five canonical] prayers, such as the two bowings of the dawn prayer, the *witr* [prayer],[43] the prayer of the two feasts,[44] the prayer for rain, and the [prayer at an] eclipse,[45] so that he may teach them their religion whereby they worship God and the Sunna of their Prophet (may God bless him and grant him peace).

(56) "Let him take care to teach them supplications,[46] that they may make their humble petitions to God; and let him teach them God's greatness and majesty, that they may magnify Him for it. If the people suffer from drought and the imam leads them in prayers for rain,[47] I would have the teacher bring the children out [those of them who know how to pray], and let them beseech God with supplications and make their humble petitions to Him, for I have been told that when the people to whom Jonah was sent (may God's blessing be upon our Prophet and upon him) saw the chastisement with their own eyes, they brought out their children and entreated God by means of them, and the chastisement was lifted. He should teach them arithmetic, but it is not his duty unless it has been stipulated for him; and likewise poetry, obscure words,[48] Arabic language, and the whole of grammar—in these matters he acts voluntarily. There is no harm in his teaching them poetry[49]—words and reports of the [ancient] Arabs that contain nothing indecent—but it is not incumbent upon him." According to Saḥnūn there is nothing wrong if the person who teaches Qurʾān and writing teaches all this, whether voluntarily or by stipulation. However, as for paying the teacher to teach these things with no intent to teach the Qurʾān and writing, Saḥnūn, as mentioned previously, rejects it based on Mālik's saying that he did not like payment for the teaching of poetry.

(57) Ibn Ḥabīb, on the other hand, said: "There is nothing wrong with paying a teacher to teach poetry, grammar, letter-writing, the Days of the Arabs, and similar things, such as the knowledge of famous men and of chivalrous knights: there is nothing wrong with paying for the teaching of all this.[50] I, however, am opposed to the teaching, learning, or recitation by an adult or child of any poetry containing accounts

والسلام، وجميع التكبير، وما يلزمهم في الصلاة، والتشهد والقنوت في الصبح؛ فإنه من سنة الصلاة، ومن واجب حقها. وليعلمهم الصلاة على الجنائز، والدعاء عليها، فإنه من دينهم؛ وينبغي له أن يعلمهم سنن الصلاة، مثل ركعتي الفجر، والوتر، وصلاة العيدين، والاستسقاء، والخسوف، حتى يعلمهم دينهم الذي تعبدهم الله عز وجل، وسنة نبيهم ﷺ.

(٥٦) وليتعاهدهم بتعليم الدعاء ليرغبوا إلى الله عز وجل، ويعرفهم عظمته وجلاله، ليكبروا على ذلك. وإذا أجدب الناس، فاستسقى بهم الإمام، فأحبُّ للمعلم أن يخرج منهم بمن يعرف ليبتهلوا إلى الله عز وجل ويرغبوا إليه، فإنه بلغني أن قوم يونس عليه السلام لما عاينوا العذاب خرجوا بصبيانهم يتضرعون إلى الله تبارك وتعالى بهم معهم، فرفع عنهم. وينبغي له أن يعلمهم الحساب، وليس ذلك بلازم له إلا أن يشترط عليه ذلك، وكذلك الشعر، والغريب، والعربية، وجميع النحو، هو من ذلك متطوع، ولا بأس أن يعلمهم الشعر مما لا يكون فيه فحش، ومن كلام العرب وأخبارها، وليس ذلك بواجب عليه. كل هذا عند سحنون لا بأس أن يعلمه الذي يعلم القرآن والكتاب، يتطوع به، أو يشترط عليه. فأما إقراره بالإجارة على تعليم هذه الأشياء، ولم يكن القصد إلى تعليم القرآن والكتاب، فسحنون يأباه، كما تقدم عنه كل ذلك، لقول مالك في الإجارة على تعليم الشعر: لا يعجبني.

(٥٧) وأما ابن حبيب فقال لا بأس بإجارة المعلم على تعليم الشعر والنحو والرسائل وأيام العرب، وما أشبه ذلك من علم الرجال وذوي المروءات، لا بأس بالإجارة على ذلك كلهن إلا أني أكره من تعليم الشعر وتعلمه وروايته الكبير والصغير، ما فيه

of unbridled violence, obscenity, or foul satire.[51] There is a sound tradition from the Messenger of God, may God bless him and grant him peace, 'Poetry is merely speech: good poetry is good, and foul poetry is foul' [*Ṣaḥīḥ al-Bukhārī*]. And the Messenger of God also said, 'Some poetry is wisdom'" [in *Bukhārī, Abū Dāwūd,* and *Ibn Mājah*]. . . .

(58) Part of a teacher's good care of his students is that he should be kind to them. It has been reported through ᶜĀʾishah, the Mother of the Believers, may God be pleased with her, that the Messenger of God, may God bless him and grant him peace, said: "O God, whosoever takes charge of any of the affairs of my nation and is kindly towards them therein, do Thou be kind to him." And he also said: "God likes kindness in everything, and God will have mercy on the merciful among His servants" [*Ṣaḥīḥ al-Bukhārī*].

(59) Abū al-Ḥasan [al-Qābisī] said: You asked whether it is desirable for the teacher to be strict with the children or whether he should be kind to them and not stern. Now as you can see, children fall under the advice given in the tradition I have just cited. However, if the teacher performs his charge well and takes proper care of them, he will set things in their proper places. He it is who is responsible for disciplining them. He sees to restraining them from what is not good for them, and undertakes to compel them to what is beneficial for them. This does not exclude them from his kindness toward them or his mercy. In fact, he stands *in loco parentis* toward them. Constant sternness on his part falls under the heading of loathsome boorishness, and the children, becoming accustomed to it, will become insolent to him. However, if he uses sternness when they deserve discipline, it will become a sign that they are being disciplined. Since they are not accustomed to sternness, it will—when used—be discipline for them, sometimes without striking; or sometimes he will accompany his sternness with beating, to the extent that the offense requires it. On the other hand, he should not always be familiar and friendly with them, without solemn reserve. By no means should he jest with one of them or smile in his face, even if he pleases him and causes him to expect good, nor should he become angry and discourage him if he does well.

ذكر الحمية والخناء، أو قبح الهجاء. قال: وقد ثبتت الرواية عن رسول الله ﷺ أنه قال: « إنما الشعر كلام فحسنه حسن وقبيحه قبيح » [صحيح البخاري] وقال رسول الله ﷺ « إن من الشعر لحكمة » [في البخاري وأبي داود وابن ماجة] . . . .

(٥٨) ومن حسن رعايته لهم أن يكون بهم رفيقاً، فإنه قد جاء عن عائشة أم المؤمنين رضي الله عنها، أن رسول الله ﷺ قال « اللّهم من ولي من أمر أمتي شيئاً فرفق بهم فيه فارفق به » [صحيح البخاري]. وقد قال رسول الله ﷺ « إنّ الله رفيق يحب الرفق في الأمر كله، وإنّما يرحم الله من عباده الرحماء » [صحيح البخاري].

(٥٩) قال أبو الحسن: فقولك هل يستحب للمعلم التشديد على الصبيان، أو ترى أن يرفق بهم ولا يكون عبوساً، لأن الأطفال كما علمت تدخل في هذه الوصية المتقدمة، ولكن إذا أحسن المعلم القيام، وعني بالرعاية، وضع الأمور مواضعها، لأنه هو المأخوذ بأدبهم، والناظر في زجرهم عما لا يصلح لهم، والقائم بإكراههم على مثل منافعهم، فهو يسوسهم في كل ذلك بما ينفعهم، ولا يخرجهم ذلك من حسن رفقه بهم، ولا من رحمته إياهم فإنما هو لهم عوض من آبائهم. فكونه عبوساً أبداً من الفظاظة الممقوتة ويستأنس الصبيان بها فيجرؤن عليه، ولكنه إذا استعملها عند إساءتهم الأدب، صارت دلالة على وقوع الأدب بهم، فلم يأنسوا إليها، فيكون فيها إذا استعملت أدباً لهم في بعض الأحايين دون الضرب، وفي بعض الأحايين، يوقع الضرب معها. بقدر الاستئهال الواجب في ذلك الجرم. ولكن ينبغي له ألا يتبسط إليهم تبسط الاستئناس في غير تقبض موحش في كل الأحايين، ولا يضاحك أحداً منهم على حال ولا يبتسم في وجهه، وإن أرضاه وأرجاه على ما يجب، ولكنه لا يغضب عليه فيوحشه إذا كان محسناً.

(60) If the student deserves beating, know that beating is from one to three strokes. Let the teacher use his judgment so as not to exceed the level deserved. This should be his discipline if the student is remiss (sluggish, for example, in paying attention to the teacher, or slow in memorizing), or makes many errors in the section he is studying, or in writing his slate (such as missing letters, misspelling, misvocalizing, or misplacing dots) and though the teacher has called attention to these things time and again, the student has been very neglectful and nothing has been gained from reproof and censure by means of words which, while threatening, involve no abuse or disrespect. The teacher must not speak like someone who does not know what is owed to children of believers. He must not say things like "You freak!" or "You ape!" He should not do this or anything of similar ugliness. If you say it once, you should ask God's forgiveness and not do it again. Foul words come from the tongue of a God-fearing man only when anger takes hold of his soul, and this is no place for anger. The Messenger of God, on whom be peace, forbade a judge to decide a case while angry. ᶜUmar ibn ᶜAbd al-ᶜAzīz,[52] may God have mercy on him, once commanded a man to be flogged, but when the man was brought to be flogged, ᶜUmar said, "Leave him alone!" Someone asked him about it, and he said, "I found myself feeling angry with him, and I did not want to flog him while I was angry."

(61) Abū al-Ḥasan [al-Qābisī] said: This is how a teacher of children ought to take care of them, so that their discipline leads to their benefit. The teacher has no right to vent his anger or to relieve his heart of rage. If he does so, he has struck Muslim children only for his own relief, and that is not just.

(62) If a child commits an offense such as harming someone, playing, running away from school, or becoming addicted to idleness, the teacher should consult with the child's father or with his guardian, if the child is an orphan, and inform him whenever the child deserves to be disciplined with more than three blows. Any punishment above what is normally given for negligence in learning will be by permission from the child's guardian, and the extra punishment will be between three and ten strokes, if the boy can bear that. The character of the blow should be painful, but it should not go beyond pain to causing a hideous effect or harmful weakness. Sometimes a teacher has a boy near puberty, badly brought up and of coarse character, who is not afraid of ten lashes. The teacher may think more stripes to be in order and be sure that the boy

(٦٠) وإذا استأهل الضرب فاعلم أن الضرب من واحدة إلى ثلاث. فليستعمل اجتهاده لئلا يزيد في رتبة فوق استئهالها. وهذا هو أدبه إذا فرط، فتثاقل عن الإقبال على العلم، فتباطأ في حفظه، أو أكثر الخطأ في حزبه، أو في كتابة لوحه، من نقص حروفه، وسوء تهجيه، وقبح شكله، وغلطه في نقطه، فنبه مرة بعد مرة، فأكثر التغافل ولم يغن فيه العذل، والتقريع بالكلام، الذي فيه التواعد من غير شتم ولا سب لعرض، كقول من لا يعرف لأطفال المؤمنين حقاً فيقول: يا مسخ، يا قرد، فلا يفعل هذا ولا ما كان مثله في القبح، فإن قلت له واحدة، فلتستغفر الله منها ولتنته عن معاودتها. وإنما تجري الألفاظ القبيحة من لسان التي تمكن الغضب من نفسه، وليس هذا مكان الغضب، وقد نهى الرسول (عليه السلام) أن يقضي القاضي وهو غضبان، وأمر عمر بن عبد العزيز (رحمة الله عليه) بضرب إنسان، فلما أقيم للضرب قال: اتركوه. فقيل له في ذلك فقال: وجدت في نفسي عليه غضباً، فكرهت أن أضربه وأنا غضبان.

(٦١) قال أبو الحسن: كذا ينبغي لمعلم الأطفال أن يراعي منهم حتى يخلص أدبهم لمنافعهم، وليس لمعلمهم في ذلك شفاء من غضبه، ولا شيء يريح قلبه من غيظه، فإن ذلك إن أصابه فإنما ضرب أولاد المسلمين لراحة نفسه، وهذا ليس من العدل.

(٦٢) فإن اكتسب الصبي جرماً من أذى، ولعب، وهروب من الكتاب، وإدمان البطالة فينبغي للمعلم أن يستشير أباه، أو وصيه إن كان يتيماً، ويعلمه إذا كان يستأهل من الأدب فوق الثلاث، فتكون الزيادة على ما يوجبه التقصير في التعليم عن إذن من القائم بأمر هذا الصبي، ثم يزاد على الثلاث ما بينه وبين العشر، إذا كان الصبي يطيق ذلك. وصفة الضرب هو ما يؤلم ولا يتعدى الألم إلى التأثير المشنع أو الوهن المضر، وربما كان من صبيان المعلم من يناهز الاحتلام، ويكون سيء الرعية غليظ الخلق، لا يريعه وقوع عشر ضربات عليه ويرى للزيادة عليه مكاناً، وفيه محتمل مأمون،

can bear it. Then there is nothing wrong, God willing, with more than ten strokes—and God knows who is doing evil and who is doing right! Yet the teacher is dealing with the dignity and person of Muslims—he should not harm them lightly and without due cause.

(63) Let the teacher administer the punishment himself. Saḥnūn thought it better not to entrust the beating to another boy.

(64) Abū al-Ḥasan [al-Qābisī] said: Saḥnūn was right in this, because anger and conflict occur among boys. A strong boy might hurt the other too much. However, if the teacher is sure that the boy is God-fearing and will not exceed the limit, he may allow it, if he has a reason for deputizing someone else to relieve him of administering the punishment himself. Let him avoid hitting the boy's head or face. Saḥnūn said that the teacher should not hit the student in either of these places. The harm of hitting there is evident—it could weaken the brain, damage the eye, or leave an ugly mark, so let the teacher avoid it. Hitting on the feet is safer and more likely to cause pain without damage.

(65) It is part of kindness toward the children that if a child is summoned to eat the midday meal, the teacher should give him leave and not hinder him from his food and drink. However, he should hold him responsible for returning promptly when he finishes his meal.

(66) The children have a right to be treated equally by the teacher. He should not prefer one to another, even if they differ in the tuition they pay and if some of them honor him with gifts and favors. In his leisure time, however, he may give preference to one he loves, after giving them all their due. This is because the person paying a small tuition has agreed that the teacher should carry out his function of fully teaching his child, just as the person paying a high tuition stipulated. An exception is if the teacher has made it clear to the children's parents that he will differentiate between them on the basis of the fee he receives from each, and they agree to this. Then he may do so, but he must fulfill what he has committed himself to do.

(67) For the good of the children and as part of his good oversight of them, the teacher should not mix boys and girls.

(68) Saḥnūn said: "I disapprove of a teacher's teaching girls and mixing them with the boys, because that is corruption for them."[53]

(69) Abū al-Ḥasan [al-Qābisī] said: The teacher should protect the children from each other whenever there is among them one whose misbehavior he fears, who is approaching puberty, or who is reckless. . . .

فلا بأس - إن شاء الله - من الزيادة على العشر ضربات، والله يعلم المفسد من المصلح، وإنما هي أعراض المسلمين وأبشارهم فلا يتهاون فيها بنيلها بغير الحق الواجب.

(٦٣) وَلْيَلِ أدبهم بنفسه، فقد أحب سحنون ألا يولي أحداً من الصبيان الضرب.

(٦٤) قال أبو الحسن: ونعم ما أحب سحنون من ذلك، من قبل أن الصبيان تجري بينهم الحمية والمنازعة، فقد يتجاوز الصبي المطيق فيما يؤلم المضروب، فإن أمن المعلم التقي من ذلك، وعلم أن المتولي للضرب لا يتجاوز فيه، وسعه ذلك إن كان له عذر في تخلفه عن ولاية ذلك بنفسه، وليتجنب أن يضرب رأس الصبي أو وجهه، فإن سحنون قال فيه: لا يجوز له أن يضرب به، وضرر الضرب فيهما بيّن، وقد يوهن الدماغ، أو يطرف العين، أو يؤثر أثراً قبيحاً، فليجتنبا. فالضرب في الرجلين آمن، وأحمل للألم في سلامة.

(٦٥) ومن رفقه بالصبيان أن الصبي إذا أرسل وراءه ليتغذى فيأذن له ولا يمنعه من طعامه وشرابه، ويأخذ عليه في سرعة الرجوع إذا فرغ من طعامه.

(٦٦) ومن حقهم عليه أن يعدل بينهم في التعليم، ولا يفضل بعضهم على بعض، وإن تفاضلوا في الجُعل، وإن كان بعضهم يكرمه بالهدايا والأرفاق، إلا أن يفضل من أحب تفضيله في ساعة راحاته، بعد تفرغه من العدل بينهم، وذلك من قبل أن القليل الجعل إنما رضي أن يؤدي أداءه ذلك على إتمام تعليم ولده، كما شرط الرفيع الجُعَل، إلا أن يبين المعلم لآباء الصبيان أنه يفاضل بينهم على قدر ما يصل إليه من العطاء من كل واحد منهم، فيرضوا له بذلك، فيجوز له، وعليه أن يفي بما التزم من قدر ذلك.

(٦٧) ومن صلاحهم، ومن حسن النظر لهم، ألا يخلط بين الذكران والإناث.

(٦٨) وقد قال سحنون: أكره لمعلم أن يعلم الجواري، ويخلطهن مع الغلمان، لأن ذلك فساد لهن.

(٦٩) قال أبو الحسن: وإنه لينبغي للمعلم أن يحترس الصبيان بعضهم من بعض إذا كان فيهم من يخشى فساده، يناهز الاحتلام، أو يكون له جرأة . . . .

(70) He should enjoin them not to injure one another. If one complains that another has injured him—Saḥnūn was asked whether the teacher should accept the children's word that one has injured another. He replied: "I do not think so as a matter of rule. The teacher need discipline the children only when one of them injures another, and that, in my opinion, is when he has learned of the injury from all of them as a body or when there has been a confession—unless it is children whom he has known for honesty: then he may accept their word and punish on the basis of it. As I have told you, he should not discipline to excess."

(71) Abū al-Ḥasan [al-Qābisī] said: Saḥnūn means from one to three strokes, as previously mentioned. If they deserve more because of the injury, the punishment should be commensurate with its severity, meaning from three to ten strokes. He should command them to stop injuring and to return anything that one has taken from another. . . .

(72) As for how the children should erase their slates and tablets—Ibn Saḥnūn mentioned the following on the authority of Anas ibn Mālik (though with a chain of transmission not going through Saḥnūn): "If the schoolchildren erase from their slates with their feet 'a revelation from the Lord of the worlds,'[54] the teacher is casting his Islam behind his back and showing no concern about the state in which he will meet God." Someone then asked Anas: "How were educators in the days of the *imāms* Abū Bakr, ᶜUmar, ᶜUthmān, and ᶜAlī (may God who is exalted be pleased with them)?" Anas said, "The teacher would have a basin. Every day each child in turn would bring clean water, and they would pour it into the basin and wash their slates in it." Anas said, "Then they would dig a hole in the ground, pour the water into it, and it would dry up."

(73) Muḥammad [ibn Saḥnūn] said: "I asked [my father] Saḥnūn, 'Do you think it can be licked off?'[55] He said, 'There is no harm in that, but it should not be wiped off with the foot; it should be wiped off with a kerchief or something similar.'

(74) "Then I asked, 'What do you think about the messages[56] that the pupils write out in school?' He said, 'Let him not blot out anything from God's memorial[57] with his foot. There is no harm in blotting out anything else not from the Qurᵓān. . . .' "

(٧٠) ويأخذ عليهم ألا يؤذي بعضهم بعضاً، فإن شكا بعضهم أذى بعض؟ فقد سئل سحنون عن المعلم يأخذ الصبيان بقول بعضهم على بعض في الأذى قال: ما أرى هذا من ناحية الحكم، وإنما على المعلم أن يؤدبهم إذا آذى بعضهم بعضاً. وذلك عندي إذا استفاض على الإيذاء من الجماعة منهم، أوكان الاعتراف، إلا أن يكونوا صبياناً قد عرفهم بالصدق فيقبل قولهم، ويعاقب على ذلك، ولا يجوز في الأدب كما أعلمتك.

(٧١) قال أبو الحسن: يريد كما تقدم من واحدة إلى ثلاث؛ فإن استأهلوا الزيادة للأذى، فعلى قدر شدة ذلك، يريد من الثلاث إلى العشر، ويأمرهم بالكف عن الأذى، ويرد ما أخذ بعضهم لبعض . . . .

(٧٢) وأما ما يضعه الصبيان من محو ألواحهم وأكتافهم، فذكر ابن سحنون فيه عن أنس بن مالك بإسناد ليس هو من رواية سحنون، إذا محت صبية الكتاب تنزيل رب العالمين بأرجلهم، نبذ المعلم إسلامه خلف ظهره، ثم لم يبال حين يلقى الله على ما يلقاه عليه. قيل لأنس: كيف كان المؤدبون على عهد الأئمة أبي بكر وعمر وعثمان وعلي رضوان الله عليهم؟ قال أنس: كان المؤدب له إنجانة، كل صبي يجيء كل يوم بنوبته ماء طاهراً فيصبه فيها، فيمحون به ألواحهم. قال أنس ثم يحفرون حفرة في الأرض، فيصبون ذلك الماء فينشف.

(٧٣) قال محمد: قلت لسحنون فترى أن يلعط؟ قال لا بأس به، ولا يمسح بالرجل، ويمسح بالمنديل وما أشبهه.

(٧٤) قلت له فما تقول فيما يكتب الصبيان في الكتف من الرسائل، فقال: أما ما كان من ذكر الله تعالى، فلا يمحه برجله، ولا بأس أن يمحى غير ذلك مما ليس من القرآن . . . .

(75) As for the children's having Friday off, Saḥnūn said: "He should give them a day off on Friday: that has always been the custom of teachers, and they have never been reproved for it." Muḥammad ibn ʿAbdallāh ibn ʿAbd al-Ḥakam is reported to have said that a teacher hired for a month has the right to take Fridays off. Any practice that people have customarily followed becomes like a stipulation. As for letting the children go free on Thursday after the afternoon prayer, that is also customary. If this is also known to be the practice of teachers, it is like their customary practice on Friday. As for their taking all of Thursday off, that is going too far. On the other hand, if the children study their portions and recite them to their teachers on Wednesday evening and Thursday morning, until the time of writing,[58] then compete with each other until before their going home at midday, then come back to school after the noon prayer and compete until the afternoon prayer, and then go home until they come back to their teacher early on Saturday—that is good, beneficial, and a kindness to children and teachers without any excess.

(76) Having the feast-days off is also a well-known custom. Ibn Saḥnūn asked his father [Saḥnūn], "How many days' leave do you think they should be given for the feasts?" Saḥnūn replied: "One day for the feast after Ramaḍān, but there is no harm in allowing them three days; three days for the Feast of Immolation, but there is no harm in allowing them five days."

(77) Abū al-Ḥasan [al-Qābisī] said: Three days at the feast after Ramaḍān means one day before the feast, the day of the feast itself, and the day after it. Five days at the Feast of Immolation means the day before the day of sacrifice, the three days of sacrificing, and the fourth day (the last of the *ayyām al-tashrīq*); then they go back to their teachers on the fifth day of the days of sacrifice. This is the best sort of kindness.

(78) As for children's having a day off on the occasion of completing the Qurʾān, Saḥnūn was asked, "Do you think the teacher should give the children a day or so off?" He replied, "That has always been common practice—a day or part of a day, for example—but the teacher should not give them more than that, except with the permission of all their fathers, because he is their employee." He was also asked, "What if a child gives the teacher a present or gives him something and the latter gives him a vacation for it?" He said, "No, vacations are only for completing the Qurʾān—a day or so—and feast-days; otherwise, the teacher may not grant them without the fathers' permission." He also said, "For this reason the testimony of most teachers is invalid because they do not fulfil their obligations, except those whom God protects."[59]

(٧٥) وأما بطالة الصبيان يوم الجمعة فقال سحنون: يأذن في يوم الجمعة، وذلك سنة المعلمين منذ كانوا، لم يُعب ذلك عليهم. وذكر أن محمد بن عبد الله بن عبد الحكم قال في المعلم يستأجر شهراً له أن يتبطل يوم الجمعة؛ وما كان الناس قد عملوا به، وجروا عليه فهو كالشرط. وأما تخلية الصبيان يوم الخميس من العصر فهو أيضاً يجري عرف الناس، إن كان قد عرف من شأن المعلمين، فهو كما عرف من شأنهم في يوم الجمعة. فأما بطالتهم يوم الخميس كله، فهذا بعيد، إنما دراسة الصبيان أحزابهم وعرضهم إياه على معلميهم في عشي يوم الأربعاء، وغدو يوم الخميس، إلى وقت الكتابة، والتخاير إلى قبل انقلابهم نصف النهار، ثم يعودون بعد صلاة الظهر للكتّاب، والخيار إلى صلاة العصر، ثم ينصرفون إلى يوم السبت يبكرون فيه إلى معلميهم. وهذا حسن نافع رفيق بالصبيان وبالمعلمين، لا شطط فيه.

(٧٦) وكذلك بطالة الأعياد أيضاً على العرف المشتهر المتواطأ عليه. وقال: ابن سحنون لأبيه، كم ترى أن يأذن لهم في الأعياد؟ فقال: الفطر يوماً واحداً، ولا بأس أن يأذن لهم ثلاثة أيام، والأضحى ثلاثة أيام، ولا بأس أن يأذن لهم خمسة أيام.

(٧٧) قال أبو الحسن: يريد ثلاثة أيام في الفطر، يوماً قبل العيد، ويوم العيد، فيوم ثانية. وخمسة أيام في الأضحى: يوم قبل النحر، وثلاثة أيام النحر، واليوم الرابع هو آخر أيام التشريق، ثم يعودون إلى معلميهم في اليوم الخامس من أيام النحر؛ وهذا وسط في الرفق.

(٧٨) وأما بطالة الصبيان من أجل الختم، فقيل لسحنون أيضاً: أترى للمعلم في إذنه للصبيان اليوم ونحوه، قال: ما زال ذلك من عمل الناس مثل اليوم وبعضه، ولا يجوز له أن يأذن لهم أكثر إلا بإذن آبائهم كلهم، لأنه أجير لهم. قيل له: ربما أهدى الصبي إلى المعلم أو أعطاه شيئاً، فيأذن لهم على ذلك؟ فقال: إنما الإذن في الختم اليوم ونحوه، وفي الأعياد، وأما في غير ذلك فلا يجوز إلا بإذن الآباء. قال: ومن ها هنا أسقط شهادة أكثر المعلمين، لأنهم غير مؤدين لما يجب عليهم، إلا من عصم الله.

Part Three

In the name of God the Merciful, the Compassionate.

. . . .

(79) You have described what takes place among you, how your teachers behave when someone gets married or when a child is born to him. They send out their pupils, who cry in a loud voice at the man's door, saying, "Our teacher!" and the people give whatever food or other things they wish. The pupils take these things to their teacher, who gives them a half or a quarter day off for their services—and all this without the parents' command. Saḥnūn gives a sufficient answer to your question. He says: "A teacher must not burden the children with anything above his salary in the way of a gift or anything else. He must not ask them for it. If they give him a gift on that basis, it is forbidden—unless they give without being asked, or if his asking is done politely, so that if they give it does not harm them. However, if he threatens them in the matter, or gives them a vacation if they give him a gift, it is not permissible for him, because [the promise of] a vacation is an inducement to a gift, and that is reprehensible." If this is the case with what Saḥnūn described of the children's bringing things, what you have described is more serious and more reprehensible. The master of the wedding feast or father of the newborn child might give what he gives only to avert harm by the teacher or his pupils or censure by the ignorant. The teacher would thereby end up eating what is unlawful.[60] Only an ignorant teacher would do this. He should be exhorted, forbidden, and reprimanded about it, until he ceases to do what you have described. It is a work of the devil, not a work of the people of the Qurʾān.

(80) As for your question about the teacher's dispatching his pupils on errands or charging them to do things for him, and whether he may occupy himself with any business that distracts him from them, Saḥnūn said: "When Mālik was asked about the teacher's appointing a monitor for the children, he said, 'If the monitor is as effective as the teacher,' thus opening the way for it if the child benefits from it." Saḥnūn also said, "There is no harm in his having them dictate to each other, because that is a benefit to them, but let him examine their dictation." Someone asked him whether a pupil should be permitted to write a letter for somebody. He replied, "There is no harm in it. It is something that

الجزء الثالث

بسم الله الرحمن الرحيم

. . . .

(٧٩) أما وصفك لما جرى عندكم من صنيع معلميكم إذا تزوج رجل، أو ولد له، فيبعثون صبيانهم فيصيحون عند بابه، ويقولون: أستاذنا، بصوت عالٍ، فيعطون ما أحبوا من طعام، أو غير ذلك، فيأتون به معلمهم، فيأذن لهم يتبطلون بذلك نصف يوم أو ربع يوم، بغير أمر الآباء، فيكفيك ما سألت عنه قول سحنون: ولا يحل للمعلم أن يكلف الصبيان فوق أجرته شيئاً من هدية أو غير ذلك، ويسألهم في ذلك، فإن أهدوا إليه على ذلك، فهو حرام، إلا أن يهدوا إليه من غير مسألة، إلا أن تكون المسألة منه على وجه المعروف، فإن فعلوا لم يضرهم في ذلك. وأما إن كان يهددهم أو يخليهم إذا أهدوا إليه، فلا يحل له ذلك، لأن التخلية داعية إلى الهدية مكروه، فإذا كان هذا كما وصف سحنون فيما يأتي به الصبيان، فالذي سألت عنه أنت أشد وأكره: لعل صاحب التزويج، أو أبا المولود، لا يعطي ما يعطي، إلا تقية من أذى المعلم أو أذى صبيانه، أو من تقريع بعض الجهال، فيصير المعلم من ذلك إلى أكل السحت، ولا يفعل هذا إلا معلم جاهل. فليوعظ فيه وليُنَهَ عنه ويزجر، حتى يترك العمل الذي وصفت، فإنه عمل الشيطان، وليس من عمل أهل القرآن.

(٨٠) وأما سؤالك عما يُصَرِّف المعلم الصبيان فيه، ويكلفهم إياه، وهو يتشاغل عنهم بشيء فإن سحنون قال: سئل مالك عن المعلم يجعل للصبيان عريفاً فقال: إن كان مثله في نفاذه، فقد سهل ذلك، إذا كان للصبي في ذاك منفعة. قال سحنون: ولا بأس أن يجعلهم يملي بعضهم على بعض، لأن في ذلك منفعة لهم، وليتفقد إملاءهم، قيل له: فيأذن للصبي أن يكتب لأحد كتاباً؟ فقال: لا بأس به. وهذا مما

will educate the child, if he writes out messages." He said, "It is not permissible for the teacher to send students on his errands." Asked whether the teacher might send one child to look for another, he said: "I do not think it permissible for him to do so, unless the children's parents or guardians give permission, or if the place is near; the child should not be distracted with the matter. Let him personally take charge of the children at the time to return home, and he should inform their guardians if they have not come. . . ." He said, "There is no harm in his occupying himself with study during the times when the children have no need for him, as when they are engaged in writing and dictating to each other, when that is of benefit to them; for some of our colleagues have given the teacher leeway in this." He said, "But let the teacher always be diligent and devote himself to them."

(81) A teacher should not go to pray at funerals, except for someone to whose affairs he must attend, for the teacher is a hired person who should not leave his work to walk in funeral processions or visit the sick.

(82) [Saḥnūn] was asked, "Do you think that a teacher may write out scholarly books for himself or others?" He said: "During the time when he is free from the children, there is no harm in his writing for himself and for other people, for example when he dismisses them to go home; but as long as they are around him, it is certainly not permissible for him. How can it be permissible for him to leave what is his duty and attend to what is not his duty? Do you not see that it is not permissible for him to entrust the instruction of one pupil to another? How then can he busy himself with other people than his pupils? . . ."

(83) You asked whether the teacher may sleep in the children's presence if sleep overcomes him or whether he should fight the urge. If this happens during the time he is teaching them and when they are in his presence, he should resist if he can. If he is overcome, he should appoint someone to fill in for him, someone as capable as he, at a wage

يخرج الصبي، إذا كتب الرسائل. قال: ولا يجوز للمعلم أن يرسل الصبيان في حوائجه. قيل له: فيرسل الصبيان بعضهم في طلب بعض؟ فقال: لا أرى ذلك له إلا أن يأذن أولياء الصبيان في ذلك، أو يكون الموضع قريباً لا يشغل الصبيان في ذلك. وليتعاهد الصبيان هو بنفسه في وقت انقلاب الصبيان، يخبر أولياءهم أنهم لم يجيئوا . . . . قال: ولا بأس أن ينظر في العلم في الأوقات التي يستغني فيها الصبيان عنه، مثل أن يصيروا إلى الكتابة، وأملى بعضهم إلى بعض، إذا كان في ذلك منفعة لهم، فإن هذا قد سهل فيه بعض أصحابنا. قال: وليلزم المعلم الاجتهاد، وليتفرغ لهم.

(٨١) ولا يجوز له الصلاة على الجنائز إلا ما لا بد منه، ممن يلزمه النظر في أمره، لأنه أجير لا يدع عمله ويتبع الجنائز وعيادة المرضى.

(٨٢) قيل: فهل ترى للمعلم أن يكتب كتب العلم له أو للناس؟ فقال: أما في وقت فراغه من الصبيان، فلا بأس أن يكتب لنفسه وللناس، مثل أن يأذن لهم في الانقلاب. وأما ما داموا حوله، فلا أراه يجوز له ذلك. وكيف يجوز له أن يخرج مما يلزمه النظر فيه إلى ما لا يلزمه؟ ألا ترى أنه لا يجوز له أن يوكل تعليم بعضهم إلى بعض، فكيف يشتغل بغيرهم! . . . .

(٨٣) وأما قولك: هل للمعلم إذا غلب عليه النوم أن ينام عندهم، أم يغالب ذلك عن نفسه؟ فإنه إن كان في وقت تعليمه إياهم. وحضورهم عنده فليغالبه إن استطاع. وإن غلب فليُقِم فيهم من يخلفه عليهم. إذا كان في مثل كفايته، بإجارة

that he pays; or the person may do it voluntarily, if he is not one of the children. If it is one of the children themselves, the rules governing this have been discussed earlier.

(84) Likewise, if the teacher falls ill or has to attend to business, he should hire someone for them of equal competence, if the time is not long. If it is long, the children's parents have a right to look into the matter and discuss it. This is because he himself has been hired, so it is not right for him to appoint a substitute except for a short time. It is considered less serious if paying the person's salary is his obligation.

(85) Similarly, if he goes on a journey and appoints someone of full competence for them—if it is a trip that he must make, a short one of one or two days—it would not be considered serious, God willing. However, if it is a long journey, or there is danger that a short journey may cause a long absence due to the accidents that happen on trips, it is not right for him to go. . . .

(86) You ask: What if he does what he has been forbidden and busies himself with his own affairs to the neglect of the children, to what does he become liable? Know, then, that some diversions are insignificant. For example, he may converse with someone while in his class, and it could distract him somewhat from the children. The importance of this and the like is small and its measure insignificant. He should ask the children's parents pardon for such things, if his wage comes from their funds. If it comes from the children's funds, I think there will be no harm if he compensates them out of his own leisure time to make up for what they missed because of his distraction. If he is absent for a whole day or more, it is too much. If he has been hired for a specified time, and he gives his pupils days off, not appointing a substitute, he loses from his salary the equivalent of the days he gave them off. On the other hand, if the hiring is unrestricted, he should be paid every month for whatever he has taught in it. However, he has no right to be habitually distracted from his work so that he is forced to appoint a substitute, because that will harm the children.

(87) You asked about things that the teacher charges the children to bring from their parents' homes—without their parents' permission—or that the children bring without the teacher's request, be it food or such, even if the quantity be small, or firewood and such. It is not lawful for teachers to command such things or to accept them if they are brought without their command, unless with the parents' permission.

يستأجره، أو يتطوع له إذا كان من غير الصبيان، وإن كان من الصبيان أنفسهم فقد تقدم من الشرائط في ذلك.

(٨٤) وكذلك إن مرض، أو كان عليه شغل، فهو يستأجر لهم من يكون فيهم بمثل كفايته لهم، إذا لم تطل مدة ذلك، فإن طالت فلآباء الصبيان في ذلك نظر ومتكلم من قبل أنه المستأجر بعينه، فلا يصلح أن يقيم عوضاً منه إلا فيما قرب، فيستخف إذا كانت الإجارة واجبة عليه.

(٨٥) كذلك إن هو سافر فأقام من يوفيهم كفايته لهم، إن كان سفراً لا بد منه، قريباً اليوم واليومين وما أشبههما فيستخف ذلك إن شاء الله، وأما إن بَعُدَ، أو خيف بعد القريب، لما يعرض في الأسفار من الحوادث، فلا يصلح له ذلك. . . .

(٨٦) فأما قولك: فإن فعل، يريد ما نهي عنه، وتشاغل عن الصبيان، ماذا عليه؟ فاعلم أنه يكون من الاشتغال الخفيف، الذي يكون في مثل حديثه في مجلسه، فيشغله من الصبيان شيئاً، فهذا وما أشبهه يقل خطبه، ويخف قدره، فيتحلل من آباء الصبيان مما أصاب من ذلك، إن كان الأجر من أموالهم، وإن كان من أموال الصبيان فلا بأس به عندي أن يعوضهم من وقت عادة راحته، ما يجبر لهم به ما نقصهم من حظوظهم باشتغاله ذلك؛ وإن كان غائباً اليوم أو أكثر اليوم، فهذا كثير. فإن كانت إجارته أجلاً معلوماً، وقد عطلهم، ولم يقم لهم عوضاً منه، فيضع من أجره ما ينوب ذلك اليوم الذي عطله. وإن كان الإجارة مطلقة، وفي كل شهر بما علم فيه: وليس له أن يعتاد التشاغل، حتى يلجئه إلى العوض، لأن ذلك يضر بالصبيان.

(٨٧) وأما سؤالك عما يكلفه المعلم الصبيان أن يأتوه به من بيوت آبائهم، يريد بغير إذن آبائهم، أو حمله الصبيان بغير تكليف من المعلم، وكان ذلك من الطعام أو غير الطعام، وإن قل قدره من حطب أو غير ذلك، فهذا لا يحل للمعلمين أن يأمروا به، ولا أن يقبلوه إن أتي به إليهم، وإن لم يأمروا به، إلا بإذن الآباء، ويسلم أيضاً من أن

Also, there should be no danger that the parents' permission was motivated by shame and fear of censure. Enough to answer your question has already been cited in Saḥnūn's section on how much vacation may be allowed—so understand!

(88) It is the teacher's responsibility to buy the whip and the *falaqah*; it is not the responsibility of the students.[61] It is his responsibility to rent the shop to be used as a classroom. These things are the teacher's responsibility according to Saḥnūn—and that is correct.

(89) Saḥnūn also said, "If the teacher has been hired for particular children for a set year, the children's guardians must rent a place for the teacher."

(90) Abū al-Ḥasan [al-Qābisī] said: This, too, is correct, for it is they who brought the teacher and put him over their children. On this basis the answer is equable.

(91) Saḥnūn said: "If a man hires a teacher for particular children, it is permissible for the teacher to teach other children with them if it does not distract him from teaching those for whom he was hired." This is the case if it has not been stipulated that the teacher should in no way exceed the specified number; however, if they stipulated that he should not exceed the specified number or that he should not mix other children with theirs, he may not do so. This is my answer to your question.

(92) As for teaching children in the mosque, Ibn al-Qāsim said that Mālik was asked whether he approved of a man's bringing a young boy into the mosque. Mālik said, "If the boy has reached the age at which he can be expected to behave well, knows what good behavior is, and does not misbehave, I see no harm; however, if he is very young, does not sit still, and misbehaves, I do not like it." Ibn Wahb transmits a similar report from Mālik. As for Saḥnūn, he said: "When Mālik was asked about teaching children in the mosque, he said: 'I do not think that it is permissible, because they are not careful about filth, and the mosque was not erected for teaching.'"

(93) Abū al-Ḥasan [al-Qābisī] said: This is a correct answer. It is wrong to seek worldly gain in a mosque. Have you not heard what ʿAṭāʾ ibn Yasār said to someone who wanted to sell merchandise in the mosque? "Go to the market-place of this world," he said. "This is the market-place of the hereafter!" So a teacher of children should not be allowed to seat the children in the mosque. If he is forced to do so because his premises become dilapidated, let him get himself a place in which to teach until what became dilapidated is repaired, if he will.

يكون ما أذن الآباء في ذلك على وجه الحياء وتقية اللائمة. وقد تقدم من قول سحنون في فصل ما يجوز من بطالتهم ما فيه الكفاية من سؤالك هذا. فافهم.

(٨٨) وشراء الدِرَّة والفلقة على المعلم، ليس على الصبيان. وكذلك كراء الحانوت لمجلس التعليم، على المعلم أن يكون. كل ذلك لسحنون، وهو صواب.

(٨٩) وقال: إذا استؤجر المعلم على صبيان معلومين سنة معلومة، فعلى أولياء الصبيان كراء موضع المعلم.

(٩٠) قال أبو الحسن: وهذا صواب أيضاً، لأنهم هم أتوا بالمعلم إليهم وأقعدوه لصبيانهم، وعلى هذا يعتدل الجواب.

(٩١) وقال سحنون: إذا استأجر الرجل معلماً على صبيان معلومين، جاز للمعلم أن يعلم معهم غيرهم، إذا كان لا يشغله ذلك عن تعليم هؤلاء الذين استؤجر لهم. ومعنى هذا: إذا كان لم يشترط على المعلم أنه لا يزيد على العدة المذكورة له، أو شرطوا عليه ألا يخلط مع صبيانهم غيرهم، فليس له ذلك، وهذا هو جواب سؤالك عندي له.

(٩٢) وأما تعليم الصبيان في المسجد، فإن ابن القاسم قال: سئل مالك عن الرجل يأتي بالصبي إلى المسجد، أتستحب ذلك؟ قال: إن كان قد بلغ موضع الأدب، وعرف ذلك، ولا يعبث في المسجد فلا أرى بأساً، وإن كان صغيراً، ولا يقر فيه ويعبث، فلا أحب ذلك. ولابن وهب عن مالك مثل معنى هذا. وأما سحنون فقال: سئل مالك عن تعليم الصبيان في المسجد فقال: لا أرى ذلك يجوز، لأنهم لا يتحفظون من النجاسة، ولم يُنصب المسجد للتعليم.

(٩٣) قال أبو الحسن: جواب صحيح، وتكسّب الدنيا في المسجد لا يصلح. ألم تسمع قول عطاء بن يسار الذي أراد أن يبيع سلعة في المسجد: عليك بسوق الدنيا، فإنما هذا سوق الآخرة. فلا يترك لمعلم الصبيان أن يجلس بهم في المسجد، وإن اضطر إلى ذلك بانهدام مكانه، فليتخذ مكاناً يعلم فيه إلى أن يصلح ما انهدم له، إن أحب.

(94) It is his responsibility to get a place for himself, be it a house or a store, unless he has been called [as a private tutor] to teach particular children. I have already cited Saḥnūn's opinion that renting in that case is the children's responsibility. If the teacher's house belongs to them—as it is they alone [whom he is teaching]—its construction is their responsibility, or they may find another place: none of it is the teacher's responsibility. The teacher is responsible for the place only if he teaches for the general public.

(95) A partnership of two, three, or four teachers is permissible, unless they are in a single place, even if one of them teaches better than the others. This is because in this way they can be colleagues and help each other. If one falls ill, the healthy one can take his place until his colleague recovers. If one of them recites like a true Arab and pronounces well[62] while the other does not, although he does not make barbarous mistakes, there is nothing wrong with it.

(96) I say: This is according to what has come down from Mālik and from Ibn al-Qāsim about two teachers who have formed a partnership. Mālik is reported to have said that [partnership on an equal basis] is not proper until the learning of both becomes equal, so that neither has an advantage over the other in his learning. If one is more learned than the other, it is not proper unless the more learned one has precedence over his colleague in earnings—otherwise it is not proper.

(97) Abū al-Ḥasan [al-Qābisī] said: However, if the only difference between the two teachers is that one pronounces his recitation like a true Arab and the other, while not pronouncing it like a true Arab, does not make barbarous mistakes, I see no reason for a discrepancy in their salaries if they become partners. Likewise, one may have a fine handwriting, while the other does not, but can write and spell. Such differences are insignificant in the partnership. Similarly, in crafts and commerce one partner may be superior to the other in what he does well, but not have precedence over the other in pay, if the two are partners. However, if one of the teachers is proficient at voweling and spelling words and knows Arabic language,[63] poetry, grammar, and arithmetic—things such that if one Qurʾān teacher alone had accumulated knowledge of them it would be permissible to stipulate his teaching them along with teaching the Qurʾān because they assist in correctly reading and understanding the Qurʾān—if such a person forms a partnership with someone proficient only at reciting the Qurʾān and writing, it is in that case, according to this report, that there may be a difference between

(٩٤) واتخاذ المكان عليه، بيتاً كان أو حانوتاً، إلا أن يدعى إلى صبيان بأعيانهم، فقد تقدم قول سحنون في كراء ذلك أنه على الصبيان. فإذا كان بيت المعلم لهم - إذ هم بأعيانهم - فبناؤه عليهم. أو يتخذوا مكاناً غيره، وليس على المعلم من ذلك شيء. إنما على المعلم المكان، إذا كان يعلم لعامة الناس.

(٩٥) وأما شركة المعلمين والثلاثة والأربعة فيه جائزة، إلا إذا كانوا في مكان واحد، وإن كان بعضهم أجود تعليماً من بعض، لأن لهم في ذلك ترافقاً وتعاوناً، ويمرض بعضهم فيكون السالم مكانه حتى يفيق. وإن كان بعضهم عربي القراءة، يحسن التقويم، والآخر ليس كذلك، ولكنه ليس يلحن، فلا بأس بذلك.

(٩٦) قلت: ذلك على ما جاء عن مالك، وعن ابن القاسم في مُعلمَين اشتركا. وقد روي عن مالك أن ذلك لا يصلح حتى يستوي علمهما، فلا يكون لأحدهما فضل على صاحبه في علمه. فإن كان أحدهما أعلم من صاحبه،لم يصاح، إلا أن يكون لأعلمهما فضل من الكسب يقدر عليه على صاحبه، وإلا لم يصلح.

(٩٧) قال أبو الحسن: أما إذا لم يكن بين المعلمين من الاختلاف إلا أن أحدهما يعرب قراءته، والآخر لا يعربها، إلا أنه لا يلحن، فما في هذا ما يوجب عندي التفاضل بين أجرتيهما إذا اشتركا. وكذلك يكون أحدهما رفيع الخط، والآخر ليس بذلك، إلا أنه يكتب ويتهجى. والاختلاف في هذا وشبهه متقارب في الشركة. وكذلك هذا في الصنائع و في التجارة يكون أحدهما أعلى من الآخر فيما يحسن من ذلك، فليس لهذا فضل على الآخر في الإجارة إذا كانا شريكين. ولكن إذا كان أحد المعلمين يقوم بالشكل والهجاء، وعلم العربية، والشعر، والنحو، والحساب، والأشياء التي لو انفرد معلم القرآن بجمع علومها لجاز أن يشترط عليه تعليمها مع تعليم القرآن، من قِبَل أنها مما يعين على ضبط القرآن، وحسن المعرفة، فهذا إن شارك من لا يحسن إلا قراءة القرآن والكتاب، فهو الذي تكون الإجارة بينهما متفاضلة على هذه الرواية، على قدر علم كل

the pay of the two, according to the extent of each man's knowledge. However, if one of them were hired to teach grammar, poetry, arithmetic, and the like, while the other were hired to teach the Qur'ān and writing, such a partnership would not be sound according to the approach of Ibn al-Qāsim or according to the position of those who disapprove of hiring to teach things other than the Qur'ān and writing. Understand this! I have explained it to you in order to deter from it anyone who wants to consume only what is legal and good.

(98) You asked whether young children or older, mature ones may recite part of a single sura as a group for the purpose of instruction. If you mean their doing so in the teacher's presence, my answer is that the teacher must consider what is best for their learning. Let him command them to do it and hold them accountable for it. Their reciting together in his presence will hide from him who is strong in memorizing and who is weak. However, if this gives relief to the children, let him tell them that he will examine each of them in his portion and discipline him for any deficiency—this as a threat, but he should administer disciplinary blows only for an offense that has become evident, as mentioned previously.

(99) As for the children's holding copies of the Qur'ān without having made ablutions, let them not do so. It is not like their holding their slates. There is no disagreement over their being forbidden to touch complete copies of the Qur'ān without having made ablutions either on the part of Mālik or on the part of those who hold his position. Saḥnūn believed that the teacher should command them to touch the Qur'ān only after having made ablution, so that they might know how to do it. This is good and correct, as Saḥnūn said, because their teacher is teaching them what will benefit their religion.

(100) Mālik was asked whether schoolchildren might be led in prayer by a boy who has not reached puberty. He said, "That has always been the case with young boys," and he made allowance for it.

(101) Abū al-Ḥasan [al-Qābisī] said: He meant that those praying with the young boy had also not reached puberty. If one of the schoolboys has reached puberty, he should be given precedence if he is fit to act as imam; if he is not fit to act as imam, he should not pray behind someone who has not reached puberty. He should not interrupt the schoolchildren's practice, so that they can advance in knowledge of the congregational prayers and know their virtue, so that they grow up with a desire to perform them. God is the best protector, and He is the most merciful of the merciful. . . .

واحد منهما، ولو كان أحدهما يُستأجر ليعلم النحو والشعر والحساب وما أشبه ذلك، والآخر يستأجر على تعليم القرآن والكتاب، ما صلحت هذه الشركة. على مذهب ابن القاسم، وعلى قول من يكره الإجارة على تعليم غير القرآن والكتاب. فافهم. بينت لك ذلك ليردع عنه من يحب أن يأكل حلالاً طيباً.

(٩٨) وسألت هل للصبيان الصغار، أو الكبار البالغين، أن يقرؤوا في سورة واحدة وهم جماعة على وجه التعليم، فإن كنت تريد يفعلون ذلك عند المعلم، فينبغي على المعلم أن ينظر فيما هو أصلح لتعلمهم، فليأمرهم به، ويأخذ عليهم فيه، لأن اجتماعهم في القراءة بحضرته يخفي عنه قوي الحفظ من الضعيف. ولكن إن كان على الصبيان من ذلك خفة، فيخبرهم أنه سيعرض كل واحد منهم في حزبه، فيؤدبه على ما كان من تقصير، تهديداً يتهددهم، ولا يوقع الضرب لأدب، إلا عن ذنب يتبين حسب ما تقدم قبل هذا.

(٩٩) وأما إمساك الصبيان المصاحف، وهم على غير وضوء، فلا يفعلون ذلك، وليس كالألواح. وما في نهيهم عن مس المصاحف الجامعة - وهم على غير وضوء - خلاف من مالك، ولا ممن يقول بقوله. ورأى سحنون أن على المعلم أن يأمرهم ألا يمسوا المصحف إلا وهم على الوضوء، حتى يعلموه. وهو حسن صواب، كما قال سحنون، لأن معلمهم يعلمهم مصالح دينهم.

(١٠٠) قد سئل مالك عن صبيان الكتاب يصلي بهم صبي لم يحتلم قال: ما زال ذلك من شأن الصبيان وخففه.

(١٠١) قال أبو الحسن: يريد الذين يصلون معه لم يحتلموا. ولو كان في صبيان الكتاب محتلم، فإن صلح للإمامة قدم، وإن لم يصلح للإمامة فلا يصلي خلف من لم يحتلم، ولا يقطع عن صبيان الكتاب عادتهم، لكي يتدرجوا على معرفة صلاة الجماعة، وليعرفوا فضلها حتى يكبروا على الرغبة فيها، والله خيرٌ حافظاً وهو أرحم الراحمين. . . .

(102) Abū al-Ḥasan [al-Qābisī] said: I have presented you with a description of what teachers may without objection take from pupils, and a description of what they may not take, and what is honest for the God-fearing among them. This should be enough to clarify what you have asked about. I have also discussed the stipulations binding on them. If any of them wants to renounce what he has entered into, or if they disagree over something, these rules should suffice for them.

(103) You asked about the special bonus for completion [of the reading of the Qurʾān], under what conditions it becomes owed to the teacher, and what the pupil's condition should be in terms of his memorization, recitation, and proficiency,[64] so that the teacher can claim it. The bonus for completion of the Qurʾān becomes owed to the teacher under two circumstances:

(104) The first is when the pupil has memorized the Qurʾān from beginning to end. The bonus (*khitmah*) is owed for this under the oversight of the Muslim official who is entrusted with oversight in the matter. The bonus will be according to the father's wealth or poverty and according to the boy's understanding of what the teacher has taught him along with his memorization of the Qurʾān. There is no fixed measure for it; rather, it is what is deemed to be obligatory according to people's customary practice regarding such a teacher, such a student, and the father's condition.

(105) The second is when the pupil has finished reading the Qurʾān from the written book, studying it, with none of its letters being obscure to him, along with such additional matters as correct spelling, correct placement of the vowels, and good handwriting. The decision about what is owed to the teacher of this pupil will also depend on people's customary practice in their circumstances. However, the bonus to the teacher for a pupil who has both memorized and also learned good handwriting, correct voweling, spelling, and to read with correct case endings is judged to be better than the bonus for a pupil who has not memorized, but has the ability to recite the Qurʾān while looking [at the book]. The more the learning of each of them falls short of what I have described to you, the lower the bonus deemed due to the teacher will be, compared to that awarded for a pupil who has perfected all these things. What the pupil owes to the teacher when he finishes memorizing the Qurʾān falls under one of these two cases.

(١٠٢) قال أبو الحسن: قد قدمت لك من وصف ما يطيب للمعلمين، يأخذونه من المتعلمين، ومن وصف ما ليس لهم أخذه، وما يكون نزاهة لأهل الورع منهم، ما فيه الكفاية والبيان لما سألت عنه، وفيه ما يوجب لهم في شرطهم، فإن أراد منهم أحد ترك ما دخل فيه، أو اختلفوا في أمر، وسعتهم الأحكام.

(١٠٣) وسألت عن الختمة متى تجب للمعلم، وعلى أي وجه تجب له، وكيف يكون حال الصبي في حفظه، وقراءته، وإجارته، فيستوجبها المعلم؟ قال: ووجوب الختمة للمعلم فيما سألت عنه على وجهين:

(١٠٤) أحدهما أن يستظهر القرآن حفظاً من أوله إلى آخره، فهذا الذي تجب له الختمة على نظر حاكم المسلمين، المأمون على النظر في ذلك. وتكون على قدر يسر الأب وعسره، وقدر ما فهمه الصبي، مما علّمه المعلم، مع استظهاره القرآن؛ وليس في ذلك حد موقت، إنما هو ما يرى أنه هو الواجب في عادات الناس في مثل هذا المعلم، بمثل هذا الصبي، وفي حالة أبيه.

(١٠٥) والوجه الآخر أن يكون الصبي استكمل قراءة القرآن في المصحف نظراً، لا يخفي عليه شيء من حروفه مع ما فهمه الصبي مما ينضاف إلى ذلك، من ضبط الهجاء، والشكل وحسن الخط. فيكون الاجتهاد في الواجب لمعلم هذا الصبي أيضاً، على قدر عادات الناس في أحوالهم، إلا أن المستظهر للحفظ مع ما صاحَبَهُ من حُسن خط، وضبط شكل، وهجاء، وإعراب قراءة، يكون في الاجتهاد أفضل جعلاً ممن لم يستظهر الحفظ، إنما قوي على تلاوة القرآن نظراً. وما نقص تعلم كل واحد منهما عما وصفت لك، كان الاجتهاد له فيما يجب من الجعل دون من استكمل ذلك. فعلى هذين الوجهين، يُحمل ما يجب للمعلم على المتعلم إذا هو استكمل ختم القرآن.

(106) This is if the teacher has not stipulated a definite payment for the *khitmah.* If he makes a stipulation, he has a right to what he stipulated, if the boy has mastered what he was taught, either by memorization or reading. If the boy's learning of what he was taught is deficient, the stipulated payment is decreased by an amount proportional to the deficiency in the boy's learning, until the boy is no longer deficient and reaches a minimum level of benefit, at which time the teacher has a right to be paid for the benefit he has done to the pupil. If for the *khitmah* nothing definite has been stipulated, such that the teacher has a right to it if he instills mastery into the pupil but the boy's mastery is so deficient—in his proficiency and knowledge of spelling and voweling—that it can hardly be called learning, and he reads from the book, how has he arrived at the level of a *khitmah*? Such a one gets no *khitmah*! Someone dictates to the boy and he cannot spell. He looks at the letters and does not pronounce them correctly. He does not continue in his recitation. If the boy's teacher knows how to teach, he has neglected him; if he does not know how to teach, he has cheated. The opinion of scholars is that such a teacher deserves to be disciplined for his neglect of the trust placed in him and for his carelessness toward his obligations: he should be forbidden to teach. The opinion is correct if the teacher's case is that of negligence or deception about his teaching, if he does not know how to teach. Another opinion is that such a teacher does not deserve to be compelled, but deserves censure, reprimand, severity, and rebuke from the just leader of the community.

(107) If the teacher pleads the boy's stupidity as an excuse and the boy is examined and found not to be able to memorize what he is taught or understand what is explained to him, the teacher should receive a fee only for the boy's board and discipline, not a fee for teaching if he has not informed the parents of the boy's lack of understanding. This is because if he had informed the father and the latter had agreed to pay him something, he would have been owed it. If he does not inform him, he has deceived him; and the deceiver deserves no payment or charity for his deception. . . .

(108) You asked about a pupil whom the teacher had taught part of the Qurʾān, then left the teacher for another teacher with whom he reached the level of *khitmah.* The question can be decided according to what I have explained to you. The first teacher receives according to what he taught—half and half, one-third and two-thirds, or one-fourth and three-fourths. The judge considers what the boy's father owes for the entire *khitmah,* according to his wealth or poverty and the level of understanding

(١٠٦) وهذا إذا لم يكن شرط المعلم للختمة جعلاً مسمى. فأما إن شرط ذلك كان له ما شرط إذا حذق الصبي الوجه الذي علم من ظاهر أو نظر. فإن نقص تعلم الصبي مما علم به، نقص من الأجر المسمى بمقدار ما نقص من تعلم الصبي، حتى ينتهي من نقص التعليم إلى أقل ما ينفعه، فيكون له بمقدار المنفعة التي له فيه. وإن كان لم يشترط للختمة شيئاً مسمى، حتى يكون للمعلم فيها إذا حذقها الصبي الاجتهاد، فنقص حذق الصبي حتى ينتهي إلى ما لا يسمى تعلماً، في إجادته، ومعرفته بالهجاء والشكل، والنظر في المصحف، فبأي شيء ختم هذا؟ ما لهذا ختمة: يملي على الصبي فلا يتهجى، ويرى الحروف فلا يضبطها، ولا يستمر في قراءتها. معلم هذا قد فرط فيه، إن كان يحسن التعليم، وإن كان لا يحسن التعليم، فقد غرر. ورأى العلماء أن مثل هذا المعلم يستأهل الأدب لتفريطه فيما وليه، وتهاونه بما التزمه، وأن يمنع من التعليم؛ وهو صواب، إذا كان شأنه التفريط أو الغرور بتعليمه وهو لا يحسن. ورأى بعضهم أن مثل هذا المعلم لا يستأهل الإلزام، بل يستأهل اللوم، والتعنيف والغلظة والتأنيب من الإمام العدل.

(١٠٧) فإن اعتذر المعلم ببله الصبي، واختبر الصبي فوجد لذلك لا يحفظ ما عُلِّمَ، ولا يضبط ما فهم، فلم يحصل لهذا المعلم إلا إجارة حوزه وتأديبه، لا إجارة التعليم إذا لم يعرِّف أباه بمكانه من فقد الفهم، لأنه لو عرف أباه، فرضي له بشيء لزمه، فإذا لم يعرفه فقد غره، والمغرر لا يستأهل على تغريره جعلاً ولا إحساناً. . . .

(١٠٨) ومسألتك في الذي عَلَّمه معلم بعض القرآن، ثم خرج من عنده إلى معلم آخر استكمل عنده الختمة، يجري على ما بينت لك: يكون للمعلم الأول بمقدار ما علم نصفاً ونصفاً، أو ثلثاً وثلثين، أو ربعاً وثلاثة أرباع، ينظر الحاكم فيما يجب على أبي هذا الصبي في الختمة كلها، على قدر يسره وعسره، وما انتهى إليه ولده من الفهم فيما تعلم. فإذا

that the boy has attained in what he has learned. When the full amount of the payment is fixed, the boy's father pays it, and the two teachers divide it according to the labor of each and the benefit that the boy has derived from each teacher's instruction. The judge decides this according to his discretion. He could award the first teacher everything, or he could deduct a little and give it to the second. This is if the first has almost reached the level of *khitmah* in teaching the boy, whether in memorization or in reading, so that the boy has become so proficient that he can do without a teacher, in which case his departure to the second teacher did not increase his knowledge because of the latter's instruction. What claim then does the latter have, save that he should have something for keeping and protecting the boy, nothing of which was incumbent on first teacher? It may be that in writing what remained for him, even *Sūrat al-Baqarah,*[65] the boy had an increase in some purposive faculty from which he benefited. This should be taken into account in determining what part of the payment should be awarded to him. It may even be that the entire payment is owed to the second teacher, with the first receiving little of it. That is because the first teacher began teaching the boy, who, having remained with him only a short time, departed, not having learned anything of benefit on account of his tortuous reading of even the easily learned suras and having neither handwriting nor spelling. So what does the first teacher deserve for his teaching? Had the boy gained some understanding of what he was taught and known what it was, the teacher would have received in proportion to that. If the second teacher was helped by anything that the first teacher taught and the pupil learned, so that he did not have to teach it, that amount should be deducted from the *khitmah* payment and the first teacher should receive it, with the rest of the payment going to the second teacher. On the other hand, if it becomes clear that the second teacher was not helped at all by what the first taught, nothing is deducted from the payment. The boy's father owes it because he voluntarily withdrew the boy from the first teacher. All of this is implied by Mālik's position.

(109) Saḥnūn, however, said: "If the first teacher teaches him [only] as far as *Sūrat Yūnus,* the *khitmah* bonus goes to the second teacher. If the first teacher goes beyond that to two-thirds or more, according to the sense of what [Mālik] said, nothing is awarded to the second. However, I consider it commendable if he is given something voluntarily, but it is not a rule.[66] This is in accord with his principle, which I have already described to you, and I have acquainted you with how I approach the question."

عُرف منتهى ذلك الجعل، غَرمه أبو الصبي، واقتسمه المعلمان، على قدر عناء كل واحد منهما، وما وصل إلى الصَبي من نفع تعليمه، يجتهد في ذلك. وربما جُعل للأول جميع ذلك، أو يُنقص منه قليل فيُعطى الثاني، وذلك إذا كان الأول قد بلغ من تعليم الصبي إلى مقاربة الختمة نظرًا أو استظهارًا؛ حتى بلغ أوان الحذق في ذلك إلى الاستغناء عن المعلم، فكان خروجه إلى الثاني لا يزيد علماً في تعليمه. فأي شيء يكون لهذا؟ إلا أن يكون له شيء في إمساكه وحياطته للصبي، فذلك ليس على الأول منه شيء. وقد يكون له في كتابة ما بقي عليه، وإن كانت سورة البقرة، زيادة فوق غرض ينتفع به. فهذا يُجتهد له فيما يُعطى من ذلك الجعل. وقد يكون الجعل يجب للثاني كله. وقلّ ما ينال منه الأول، وذلك بأن يبتدئ في تعليم الصبي، فقل ما لبث عنده حتى أخرج عنه ولم ينل من التعليم شيئاً له فيه منفعة، لعوج قراءته في سور يسيرة تعلمها، ولا خط ولا هجاء، فأي شيء يستأهل هذا في التعليم؟ ولو كان قد نال الصبي من فهم ما علم شيئاً، وعرف ما هو، لأخذ المعلم بمقدار ذلك. فإن كان فيه مرفق للمعلم الثاني بما نبه منه المعلم الأول، وخروجه فيه، نقص ما يصيب ذلك القدر من جعل الختمة، فيأخذه الأول، ويدفع سائر الجعل إلى الثاني، وإن تبين أن ليس للثاني مرفق على حال بما علمه الأول. لم ينقص من الجعل شيئاً، وكان ذلك على أبي الصبي، لأنه باختياره نزعه من عند الأول. وكل هذا مفاد مالك الذي ذهب إليه.

(١٠٩) وأما سحنون فقال: إن علمه الأول إلى يونس، فالختمة للثاني. وإن جاوز الأول ذلك إلى ثلثين أو زاد على ثلثين في معنى ما قال، لم يقض للثاني بشيء. واستحسن أن يرضخ له بشيء استحساناً، وليس بالقياس. وهذا على أصله الذي قدمت لك وصفه، وعرفتك وجه مذهبي فيه.

(110) You asked about the case of a teacher of people[67] who suffered a disaster that forced them to depart, and so they departed, some for one place and some for another; or some of them departed and others stayed in the town. What does this teacher do?

(111) The answer is that one considers the terms on which the teacher contracted with the people. If he is only teaching month by month or year by year, so that in principle he can stop teaching them whenever he wishes and they can leave him whenever they wish, the decision between them is rendered on the basis of what he has already taught them. This is in accordance with what we have already explained concerning a man who removes his child [from one teacher and sends him to another]. With such a contract no attention is paid to whether their departure was forced or not. The teacher receives in proportion to what he taught, whether they departed from him or he from them.

(112) On the other hand, if he has contracted with them for a specific year or a specific number of months, one must consider the circumstances that befell the people. If the circumstances were such that the people could not remain and had to depart—some intolerable tribulation such as civil strife or famine—they were justified in their departure, but the teacher does not have to follow them in their travels, as they did not hire him for that. If they return within the remaining time, he goes back to them during that remainder, but their payment to the teacher is reduced in proportion to the days when they could not meet, for they did not prevent him from traveling to them or keep their children from him voluntarily. They do not have to pay his fee in full when he has not completed the work for the period.

(113) On the other hand, had he settled accounts with them and dissolved the contract at the time of their departure, he would not have been required, had they returned within the remaining time, to go back to them. If their departure is voluntary, they have no right to reduce his wage. If they want to depart taking their children with them, they pay him his fee completely and then do whatever they wish. If some of them depart voluntarily and some of them remain, the judgment between him and those who depart is as stated above in the case of their all departing voluntarily, and he must fulfill the time period for those who remain, even if only one of them does. This is because he is going to receive his fee in full and he is being relieved of the care of those who are absent while they are absent.

(١١٠) وأما سؤالك عن معلم قوم نزل بهم ما اضطرهم إلى الرحيل، فرحلوا: بعضهم إلى مكان وبعضهم إلى مكان آخر، أو رحل بعضهم، وثبت بعضهم في البلدة. ما يصنع هذا المعلم؟

(١١١) فالجواب أن ينظر إلى ما عاقدهم هذا المعلم عليه. فإن كان إنما جلس على المشاهرة شهراً بشهر، أوسنة بسنة. فالحكم فيه أن يترك تعليمهم متى شاء. ويتركوه متى شاؤوا. والحكم بينهم فيما قد علم لهم. على ما قد بينا قبل هذا في الذي له أن يخرج ولده. ولا يُلتفت في هذا العقد إلى خروجهم كان بغلبة أو بغير غلبة. إنما للمعلم بقدر ما علم، رحلوا عنه، أو رحل عنهم.

(١١٢) ولو كان عقد معهم على سنة بعينها، أو أشهر بأعينها. نظر فيما نزل بالقوم، فإن كان ما لا يجدون معه ثباتاً، ولا بد لهم من الرحيل عنه، لما نزل بهم من بلاء لا يطيقونه بفتنة أو مجاعة، فهم في رحيلهم معذورون، وليس عليه أن يتبعهم في الأسفار ولم يستأجروه على ذلك، فإن رجعوا في بقية من المدة، رجع إليهم في تلك البقية، وسقط عنهم الأجر بحساب الأيام التي حيل فيها بينه وبينهم، لأنهم لم يمنعوه من السير معهم، ولا أمسكوا أولادهم عنه طوعاً، وليس عليهم أن يستكملوا له الأجر، وهو لم يستكمل عمل الأجل.

(١١٣) ولو كان قد حاسبهم عند رحيلهم وفاسخهم، لم يلزمه إن رجعوا بقية من المدة، أن يرجع إليهم، وإن كان رحيلهم طوعاً. فليس لهم أن ينقصوا إجارته. فإن أحبوا الرحيل بأولادهم دفعوا إليه أجره كاملاً، وصنعوا ما شاؤوا. فإن رحل بعضهم متطوعين، وثبت بعضهم، فالحكم بينه وبين الراحلين كما تقدم في رحيل جميعهم متطوعين، ويلزمه وفاء الأجل للثابتين، ولو لم يثبت منهم إلا واحد، لأنه يأخذ أجره كاملاً، وتخف عنه مؤونة من غاب عنه ما دام غائباً.

(114) However, if the ones who depart do so out of necessity or compulsion, taking their children with them, in my opinion that is a justification that dissolves the contract between them and the teacher. He should settle accounts with them and then look to those who remain and have not departed. If they are the majority, and he is not going to suffer a damaging reduction in income, he will complete the term for those who remain. If he finds [other] children to teach in place of the absentees, he may do so, as no harm will come from this to those who remain. However, if those who departed were the majority and so few have remained that he would suffer clear harm by remaining with them, in my opinion that is a justification for him. If he wishes to dissolve the contract with them, he may; and if he wants to stay with them, he may. If he finds replacements for those who departed, he will teach them and not be prevented from doing so.

(115) You asked about a teacher who decides to move his school from one location to another, be it close or far. Some reject this and some approve. In this case one also considers whether the teacher made a binding stipulation from which he cannot depart. If it happens that the place to which he moves causes no damage, inconvenience, or fear to those who come—it might distress a small boy or cause the family inconvenience that harms them and busies them—if, that is, nothing of the sort happens, they do not forbid someone to make this sort of move. On the other hand, if it involves harming a single one of those who object, he may not move from the place of instruction in which he concluded the contract, a place convenient for those to whose convenience he is bound, to another place that would be harmful.

(116) If a teacher dies, the contract is dissolved. No one need be hired from his estate to teach in his place. The estate may claim payment for the period that he taught and any *khitmah* bonus, according to how much of the Qurʾān he has taught, as has been explained already. Similarly, if a pupil dies, the teacher is owed only an amount of the fee proportional to how much he has taught, and similarly for any *khitmah* bonus.

(117) If a boy's father dies, the contract is not dissolved. If the teacher has not been paid anything, he collects from the estate of the deceased for the period elapsed. What falls to him for the remainder of the period will be taken from the boy's wealth, if he has any wealth

(١١٤) وأما إن كان رحيل من رحل عن قهرة غلبته على ذلك فذهب بولده، فهو عندي عذر تنفسخ به الإجارة بينه وبين الراحلين، ويحاسبهم، ثم ينظر فيمن بقي ممن لم يرحل، فإن كانوا هم مكان الأكثر، ولم ينتقص عليه ما يضرّ به، فهو يوفي الثابتين أجلهم. وإن وجد من يعلمهم مكان الراحلين كان له ذلك، إذ لا مضرة على المقيمين في ذلك. وأما إن كان الراحلون هم الأكثر ولم يبق من المقيمين إلا من عليه في الثبات معهم المضرة البينة، فهو عندي عذر له، إن شاء أن يفاسخهم فعل، وإن شاء أن يثبت معهم فعل، وله إن وجد عوضاً من الراحلين فيعلمهم، ولا يمنع من ذلك أيضاً.

(١١٥) وأما سؤالك عن معلم أراد أن يحول كتَّابه من موضع إلى موضع قريب أو بعيد، فأبى بعضهم، ورضي بعض، فهذا أيضاً إنما ينظر فيه: إذا كان شرط المعلم لازماً ليس له أن يخرج منه، فإذا كان كذلك، فإن كان المكان الذي صار إليه لا مضرة فيه على الآتين منه، ولا مشقة، ولا خوف، وقد يكون الصغير من الصبيان أن يعنته ذلك أو يكلف أهله مؤونة تضرّ بهم وتشغلهم، فإن لم يكن من ذلك، لم يمنعوا من انتقال من هذه صفته. فإن كان فيه مضرة على واحد منهم ممن أتى منه، لم يكن له التحول عن مكان على التعليم فيه وقعت الإجارة، يرفق من كان له الرفق فيه واجباً، إلى مكان يضرّ به هو.

(١١٦) وأما إن مات المعلم فالإجارة منفسخة، لا يستأجر من ماله من يعلم مكانه، وله من الإجارة بحساب ما علم من الأجل، ومن جعل الختمة بمقدار ما علم من القرآن حسب ما تقدم تفسيره، وكذلك إذا مات الصبي سواء، إنما للمعلم من الإجارة بحساب ما علَّم، وكذلك من جعل الختمة.

(١١٧) وأما إذا مات أبو الصبي فلا تنفسخ الإجارة، ولكن إن كان لم يقبض المعلم شيئاً فهو يأخذ من تركة الميت حساب ما مضى، وما بقي من الأجل فيما ينوبه،

inherited from his father or from elsewhere. If the boy has no wealth, the teacher may abrogate the contract, unless he volunteers freely to teach the boy, not pressing him for payment, hoping that he will prosper in the future—although this places no obligation on the boy. If the teacher refuses to teach voluntarily and someone else, one of the boy's guardians or another, volunteers to pay the teacher, the contract remains valid and is not dissolved. And God is the guardian of success!

(118) You asked about a boy whose father puts him into school without any conditions. Do the same terms apply to him as apply to the other schoolchildren, or are the terms different? You also asked about an orphan who presents himself at the school. Should he be charged what others are charged?

(119) Abū al-Ḥasan [al-Qābisī] said: If the orphan has wealth, he owes from it the like of what others are charged. Similarly, the father pays on behalf of his son the like of what someone like him pays, this being a contract for similar service, whether or not the stipulations differ. The difference in terms needs to be mentioned only at the time the boy is delivered to the school, the teacher being told, "We will pay you as much as you charge others monthly." Such a contract should not be concluded until it becomes clear what he charges the other boys, according to its variation.

(120) However, if the orphan has no wealth and the teacher teaches him, he can claim no fee from him; he was teaching him voluntarily and may not charge him for it. However, if the boy's mother or someone else brings the boy to the teacher and asks him to teach him, that person is responsible for paying the tuition if the orphan has no wealth—unless, that is, he explains to the teacher that the orphan has no wealth and has no one to pay for him. Then the teacher may not ask them for payment.

(121) You asked how a teacher stipulates terms. An explanation of this on the authority of Mālik and others has already been given in the legal problems mentioned above. As for the case you mentioned, that the teacher contracts to be paid in sheep or goats: if sheep or goats are set as the fee, it is permissible only if they are guaranteed to have set specifications at a certain date. In such a case a contract for delivery with prepayment is permissible.[68] It is like when someone hires himself out for a service for such a payment and begins work and likewise the teacher, if he begins teaching—or his hire is for a fixed time. When the

يؤخذ من مال الصبي إن كان له مال ورثه من أبيه، أو من غير ذلك، وإن كان لم يكن للصبي مال، فللمعلم أن يفسخ الإجارة، إلا أن يشاء أن يتطوع للصبي بذلك، ولا يتبعه بشيء رجاء أن يتيسر. هذا لا يُلزم الصبي، وإن أبى المعلم من التطوع، فتطوع غيره من أولياء الصبي، أو من غيرهم، بأن يدفع ذلك للمعلم، ثبتت الإجارة ولم تنفسخ، والله ولي التوفيق.

(١١٨) وأما سؤالك عن صبي أدخله أبوه الكُتَّاب بغير شرط، هل يلزمه ما يلزم صبيان الكتاب؟ وربما كان الشرط يختلف، وعن يتيم رمى نفسه في الكتاب، فهل يؤخذ منه مثل ما يؤخذ من غيره؟

(١١٩) قال أبو الحسن: إن كان لليتيم مال لزمه في ماله مثل ما يؤدي من هو مثله، وكذلك الأب يؤدي عن ابنه مثل ما يؤدي مثله، وذلك هو إجارة المثل، اختلف الشرط أم لم يختلف. إنما يحتاج إلى ذكر اختلاف الشرط عند إسلام الصبي للكتَّاب، فيقال له: نؤدي إليك كما تأخذ من غيرنا في الشهر. فهنالك ينبغي ألا يعقد على هذا الإجارة حتى يبين كيف أخذه من الصبيان على اختلافه.

(١٢٠) وأما إن كان ليس لليتيم مال، فعلمه المعلم، فليس له عليه أجر، هو متطوع في ذلك، ليس له أن يتبعه به. وأما إن أتت بالصبي أمه إلى المعلم أو غيرها من الناس، فسأله تعليمه، فهو المطلوب بإجارة التعليم إن كان ليس لليتيم مال، إلا أن يبين الذي جاء به للمعلم أنه ليس له مال، ولا له من يؤدي عنه، فحينئذ ليس للمعلم أن يطلب منهم إجارة.

(١٢١) وأما قولك في المعلم: كيف يشارطهم. فقد تقدم في نصوص المسائل شرح ذلك عن مالك وعن غيره، وشرطكم الذي ذكرت أنه يقع على الغَنَم، فإذا كانت الغنم مؤجرة لم يجز إلا أن تكون مضمونة. على صفة معلومة، إلى أجل معلوم، يجوز في مثله السلم، مثل ما إذا أوجر نفسه به في خدمة. وشرع في العمل؛ وكذلك المعلم إذا شرع في التعليم، أو كانت إجارته أجلاً معلوماً، فإذا حل أجل الغَنَم جاز أن يقبض من

time for the sheep or goats comes, he may take sheep instead of goats or goats instead of sheep. However, if the time has not yet come, he may not take something other than what was stipulated, just as it is not permitted in sales. Furthermore, if he hires himself out for food guaranteed or for a specified quantity of a certain food, he may not sell any of it until he receives it in full.

(122) You asked about a teacher's striking a child excessively, so that he rises to more than one blow. This happens only with a coarse and ignorant teacher. I have already told you that a teacher is forbidden to strike a child in anger. Striking in teaching is only for the pupils' mistakes. The teacher may strike them only with the whip; furthermore, it should be fresh[69] and safe, lest it leave a bad mark. I have already told you that he should avoid hitting the head and face, and he may not hit with a stick or a slate. One reads in Ibn Saḥnūn's book: "Mālik was asked about a teacher who strikes a child and puts out his eye or breaks his hand. He answered that if the teacher strikes with the whip according to the rule [for discipline], but hits the child with its wooden rod, breaking his arm or putting out his eye, the teacher's tribesmen owe blood money if the teacher was doing what was permissible for him. If the child dies, the teacher's tribesmen owe blood money upon the sworn oaths [of the child's kin], and the teacher must perform expiation. If the teacher strikes the child with the slate or a stick, killing him, he is subject to retribution,[70] because he had no permission to hit the child with a stick or a slate. . . ."

(123) You asked about a father who complains about his grown son and says that he disrespects him and his mother. Know, may God be merciful to you, that when a child matures and takes control of his own affairs, his father's oversight of him ceases. However, the child continues to have duties to his parents—he must fulfill to both parents, or to whichever of them is still with him, the obligations that God has placed upon him. God says: "Thy Lord has decreed you shall not serve any but Him, and to be good to parents, whether one or both of them attains old age with thee; say not to them 'Fie,' neither chide them, but speak to them words respectful, and lower to them the wing of humbleness out of mercy and say, 'My Lord, have mercy upon them, as they raised me up when I was little'" [Qurʾān 17:23–24].

المعز ضأناً، ومن الضأن معزاً، وما إذا لم يحل الأجل، لم يصلح أن يأخذ غير شرطه، كما لا يصح في البيوع، وكذلك لو استأجر نفسه بطعام مضمون. أو بطعم بعينه على الكيل، لم يجزله أن يبيع شيئاً من ذلك حتى يستوفيه.

(١٢٢) وأما سؤالك عما يتعدى به المعلم في ضرب الصبي، فترقى إلى ما هو أكثر من الضربة، فهذا يقع من المعلم الجافي الجاهل. وقد قدمت لك نهي المعلم عن ضرب الصبي وهو غضبان. والضرب على التعليم إنما هو لخطأ الصبيان، فما يصلح أن يضربهم به إنما هي الدرَّة، وتكون أيضاً رطبة مأمونة، لئلا تؤثر أثر سوء، وقد أعلمت أنه يجتنب ضرب الرأس والوجه، فما لهذا يضرب بالعصا واللوح، قال في كتاب ابن سحنون: سئل مالك عن معلم لو ضرب صبياً ففقأ عينه، أو كسر يده، فقال: إن ضرب بالدرة على الأدب، وأصابه بعوده فكسر يده، أو فقأ عينه، فالدية على العاقلة، إذا فعل ما يجوز. فإن مات الصبي فالدية على العاقلة بالقسامة، وعليه الكفارة. فإن ضربه باللوح أو بعصاً فقتله، فعليه القصاص، لأنه لم يؤذن له أن يضربه بعصاً، ولا بلوح . . . .

(١٢٣) وسألت عن الوالد يشكو ولده الكبير، ويذكر عنه أنه يعقّه، ويعقّ أمه. فاعلم - رحمك الله - أن الولد إذا احتلم، وملك أمره، فقد ارتفع عنه نظر والده، وبقي على الولد حق الوالدين فعليه أن يوفيهما أو من كان معه منهما ما ألزمه الله عز وجل منهما. فإنه عز وجل يقول ﴿وَقَضَى رَبُّكَ أَلَّا تَعْبُدُوا إِلَّا إِيَّاهُ وَبِالْوَالِدَيْنِ إِحْسَانًا إِمَّا يَبْلُغَنَّ عِندَكَ الْكِبَرَ أَحَدُهُمَا أَوْ كِلَاهُمَا فَلَا تَقُل لَّهُمَا أُفٍّ وَلَا تَنْهَرْهُمَا وَقُل لَّهُمَا قَوْلًا كَرِيمًا وَاخْفِضْ لَهُمَا جَنَاحَ الذُّلِّ مِنَ الرَّحْمَةِ وَقُل رَّبِّ ارْحَمْهُمَا كَمَا رَبَّيَانِي صَغِيرًا﴾ [الإسراء ٢٤-١٧:٢٣].

(124) If you see a parent complaining of his child, recite the Qurʾān to his child and remind him of what he owes to his parents. Speak gently and politely—haply he may be mindful, or, perchance, fear. Warn him about disrespecting his parents; for the Messenger of God (may God bless him and grant him peace) counted disrespect toward parents among the great sins that cause one to enter the fire of hell. Yet, as for accepting the father's word and ruling against the son on its basis—no! Only, if the father is a righteous man, and one does not suspect him of favoring another son or another wife of his who is not the son's mother, the son should be told that we do not suspect his father of lying. "There is no way in which he could think evil of you. Although no legal penalties may be imposed on you because of what he says, his speaking evil of you will disgrace you, make you detested, and turn hearts against you. You will be seen as ignorant and foolish." If the child is a person of manliness and moderation, he will change his ways, accept criticism, and clothe himself with patience toward his parents. If he is a person of foolishness, ignorance, and recalcitrance, a just Muslim ruler will examine his case well and subject him to a certain amount of rebuke for a matter where the only evidence established has been the father's complaint. Many a father of foolish character has a discerning son. Such a father in his foolishness may become insolent with the son. His complaint should not be accepted, and he should not be obeyed. He should be reprimanded until he ceases to do harm. This description, God willing, should be sufficient to answer your question. . . .

(125) May God protect us and you from temptation in our religion. May He guard us against the evil of tempters and slanderers. May He cause us to conclude our days in a way that pleases Him, so that He causes us to die in that state. Then, in His mercy, may He cause us to enter among His righteous servants. Amen, O Lord of the Worlds. And He is sufficient for us; an excellent Guardian is He.

◆

(١٢٤) فإذا رأيت والداً يشكو ولده، فاقرأ على ولده القرآن وفهّمه ما عليه لوالده، في لين و رفق، لعله يتذكر أو يخشى، وحذره عقوق والديه، فإن الرسول عليه السلام عد عقوق الوالدين مع الكبائر التي تُدخل النار. فأما أن يؤخذ بقول والده، أو يحكم بذلك عليه، فلا. ولكن إن كان والده من أهل الصلاح، ويؤمن منه أن يكون فيه انحراف لولد غيره، أو إلى زوجة له غير أمه، فيعرف الولد أن أباه لا يتهم عندنا بالكذب، ولا سبيل إلى سوء الظن به فيك. وهو إن لم تجر الأحكام بقوله، فإن قوله فيك السوء يزري بك، ويمقتك، وينفر عنك القلوب، وترى بعين الجهالة والسفه. فإن كان هذا الولد من أهل المروءة والقناعة فيُستنهى ويتأبخ ويستشعر الصبر على والديه، وإن كان من أهل السفه والجهالة والمرادة، نظر فيه حاكم المسلمين العدل بحسن النظر، و زجره عما لم يقم به عليه بَيِّنة، إلا شكوى الأب، بعض الزجر. و رب والد يكون السفه صفته وله الولد الحليم، فيعتو عليه والده بسفهه، فلا يقبل منه، ولا يطاع فيه، ويزجر عنه حتى يكف أذاه. ولك في هذا الوصف مقنع مما سألت عنه إن شاء الله. . . .

(١٢٥) عصمنا الله وإياك من الفتنة في الدين، وأعاذنا من شر الفاتنين والمفترين، وختم لنا بما يرضيه عنا، ليميتنا عليه، فيدخلنا برحمته في عباده الصالحين. آمين رب العالمين، وهو حسبنا ونعم الوكيل.

Miskawayh

From the Second Discourse of *The Refinement of Character*

TRANSLATED BY CONSTANTINE K. ZURAYK[1]

◆

The intelligent man's way to the attainment of his perfection

(1) It is necessary, therefore, for the intelligent person to understand the bodily imperfections from which man suffers, and his basic needs to remove and complete them. In the matter of food, which keeps the balance of his constitution and his life's subsistence, he should take of it only as much as is necessary for the removal of his imperfection and should not seek the pleasure [of food] for its own sake but rather for the sake of the subsistence of life, which is prior to pleasure. Should he exceed this limit slightly, let it be only in a measure that will keep his grade of manliness and save him from being accused of meanness and avarice relatively to his condition and rank among other people. In the matter of clothing [he should seek only] as much as will protect him from the harm of heat and cold and hide his nakedness. Should he exceed this limit, let it be only in such a measure that will keep him from being despised and accused of stinginess and from being degraded in the eyes of his fellows and those of his class. Finally, in the matter of sexual intercourse, his practice of it should go only as far as will preserve his kin and perpetuate his image: in other words, the begetting of offspring. Should he exceed this limit, let it be only to the extent that would not violate the religious tradition or transgress what belongs to him to what belongs to others.

أبي علي أحمد بن محمّد
مسكويه

من تهذيب الأخلاق

[سبيل العاقل الى بلوغ كماله]

(١) يجب على العاقل أن يعرف ما ابتلي به الانسان من هذه النقصانات التي في جسمه، وحاجاته الضرورية إلى إزالتها وتكميلها: إما بالغذاء الذي يحفظ اعتدال مزاجه وقوام حياته، فينال منه قدر الضرورة في كماله، ولا يطلب اللذة بعينها بل قوام الحياة الذي تتبعه اللذة، فان تجاوز ذلك قليلا فبقدر ما يحفظ رتبته في مروءته، ولا ينسب إلى الدناءة والبخل بحسب حاله ومرتبته بين الناس؛ وإما باللباس الذي يدفع به أذى الحر والبرد ويستر العورة، فإن تجاوز ذلك، فبقدر ما لا يستحقر ولا ينسب الى الشح على نفسه، وإلى أن يسقط بين أقرانه وأهل طبقته؛ وإما بالجماع الذي يحفظ نوعه وتبقى به صورته، أعني طلب النسل، فان تجاوز ذلك، فبقدر ما لا يخرج به عن السنَّة ولا يتعدى ما يملكه الى ما يملك غيره.

(2) The intelligent man should then seek virtue in his rational soul (the soul by which he has become man), examine the imperfections of this soul in particular, and strive to remedy them to the extent of his capacity and effort. For these are the goods which are not concealed, and when one attains them one does not withhold himself from them by any sense of shame or hide himself behind walls or under the cloak of darkness; on the contrary, they are always exhibited among the people and in the assemblies of men. It is because of them that some people are better than others and the humanity of some superior to the humanity of others. Further, the intelligent man should give this soul the food which suits it and remedies its imperfections, in the same way as he gives the other soul [the beastly] the food which is suitable to it. The proper food of the rational soul is knowledge, the acquisition of intelligibles, the practice of veracity in one's opinions, the acceptance of truth no matter where or with whom it may be, and the shunning of falsehood and lying whatever it may be or whence it may come.

(3) He who has the chance in youth to be trained to follow the morality of the Law and to be required to observe its duties and requirements until they become as habits to him; who later studies first the works of ethics so that these morals and fine qualities become confirmed in him by rational demonstrations, and then the science of arithmetic and geometry so that he becomes accustomed to veracity in speech and correctness in demonstration and trusts nothing but these; and who then proceeds along the way, which we outlined in our work entitled *The Order of the 'Happinesses' and the Grades of the Sciences,* until he attains the highest rank possible to man—he who follows this course, is indeed the happy and the perfect one, and it is his duty to praise God (mighty and exalted is He!) abundantly for this great gift and immense favor.

(4) He, on the other hand, who does not have this chance in his early life and whose ill luck it is to be brought up by his parents to recite immoral poetry, to accept its lies, and to admire its references to vile deeds and the pursuit of pleasures—as is found, for instance, in the poetry of Imruʾ al-Qays, al-Nābighah and their like; who later serves under chiefs who encourage him to recite such poetry or to compose its like and bestow generous gifts upon him; who has the misfortune of being associated with fellows that assist him in the quest of bodily pleasures and becomes inclined to covet excessively food, drink, vehicles, ornaments, and the possession of thoroughbred horses and handsome slaves, as was the case with me at certain times in my life; and who then indulges in

(٢) ثم يلتمس الفضيلة في نفسه العاقلة التي بها صار اِنسانا، وينظر الى النقصانات التي في هذه النفس خاصة، فيروم تكميلها بطاقته وجهده، فإن هذه هي الخيرات التي لا تستتر، وإذا وصل إليها لا يمتنع منها بالحياء ولا يتوارى عنها بالحيطان والظلمات، ويتظاهر بها أبدا بين الناس وفي المحافل. وهي التي بها يكون بعض الناس أفضل من بعض، وبعضهم أكثر انسانية من بعض. ويغذو هذه النفس بغذائها الموافق لها المتمم لنقصاناتها، كما يغذو تلك بأغذيتها الملائمة لها، فإن غذاء هذه هو العلم والزيادة في المعقولات، والارتياض بالصدق في الآراء وقبول الحق حيث كان ومع من كان، والنفور من الباطل والكذب كيف كان ومن أين جاء.

(٣) فمن اتفق له في الصبا أن يربى على أدب الشريعة، ويؤخذ بوظائفها وشرائطها حتى يتعودها، ثم ينظر بعد ذلك في كتب الأخلاق حتى تتأكد تلك الآداب والمحاسن في نفسه بالبراهين، ثم ينظر في الحساب والهندسة حتى يتعود صدق القول وصحة البرهان فلا يسكن إلا إليها، ثم يتدرج كما رسمناه في كتابنا الموسوم بترتيب السعادات ومنازل العلوم حتى يبلغ الى أقصى مرتبة الانسان، فهو السعيد الكامل. فليُكثر حمد الله عز وجل على الموهبة العظيمة والمنة الجسيمة.

(٤) ومن لم يتفق له ذلك في مبدأ نشوئه، ثم ابتلي بأن يربيه والداه على رواية الشعر الفاحش وقبول أكاذيبه، واستحسان ما يوجد فيه من ذكر القبائح ونيل اللذات، كما يوجد في شعر امرىء القيس والنابغة وأشباههما، ثم صار بعد ذلك الى رؤساء يقربونه على روايتها وقول مثلها ويجزلون له العطية، وامتُحن بأقران يساعدونه على تناول اللذات الجسمانية، ومال طبعه الى الاستكثار من المطاعم والمشارب والمراكب والزينة وارتباط الخيل الفُرَّه والعبيد الرُوقة، كما اتفق لي مثل ذلك في بعض الأوقات،

them and neglects for their sake the happiness to which he is fitted—whoever leads such a life, let him consider all this as misery rather than bliss and loss rather than gain, and let him strive to wean himself from it gradually. But what a difficult task this is! Yet it is, in any case, better than persisting further and further in the wrong way.

(5) Let it be known to the reader of this work that I in particular have gradually succeeded in weaning myself [from these things] since becoming advanced in years with well-established habits. I have struggled hard against them, and I am wishing for you, who are looking for the virtues and seeking the genuine morality, precisely what I have accepted for myself. I have even gone further in my advice by pointing out to you what I myself missed at the beginning of my life so that you may yourself achieve it, by showing you the way to safety before you go astray in the wilderness of error, and by bringing the ship to you before you sink in the sea of destruction.[2] In the name of God, I call upon you to guard your souls, brethren and children! Yield to the truth, cultivate the genuine morality rather than the false, seek consummate wisdom, follow the straight path, and consider the states of your souls and remember their faculties.

(6) Let it be known to you that the best analogy made of your three souls which were mentioned in the first discourse, is that of three different creatures[3] assembled in one place: a king, a lion, and a pig. Any of these three who overcomes by his strength the strength of the others becomes their ruler. He who reflects on this analogy should recognize that, since the soul is not a bodily substance and since it possesses none of the capacities or accidents of the body—as we have pointed out in the beginning of this work—its union and its attachment must necessarily differ from the union of bodies and their attachment one to another. Thus, when these three souls are mutually attached, they become one, yet, in spite of their being one, they remain different and preserve their respective capacities, revolting one after another as if they had not been attached to, or united with, one another. Again, each one of them seeks the help of another as if it were itself non-existent and did not have its own capacity. This is because the union of these souls does not consist in the sheer joining of their ends or the coincidence of their surfaces, as is the case with bodies. It is rather that they become one in certain conditions and remain different in others according to whether the capacities of some are agitated or quiescent.

ثم انهمك فيها واشتغل بها عن السعادة التي أهِّل لها، فليعدَّ جميع ذلك شقاء لا نعيما وخسرانا لا ربحا، وليجتهد على التدريج الى فطام نفسه منها-وما أصعب ذلك، إلا أنه على كل حال خير من التمادي في الباطل.

(٥) وليعلم الناظر في هذا الكتاب أنني خاصة قد تدرجت الى فطام نفسي بعد الكبر واستحكام العادة، وجاهدتها جهادا عظيما، ورضيت لك أيها الفاحص عن الفضائل والطالب للأدب الحقيقي بما رضيت لنفسي، بل تجاوزت في النصيحة لك إلى أن أشرت عليك بما فاتني في ابتداء أمري، لتدركه انت، ودللتك على طريق النجاة قبل أن تتيه في مفاوز الضلالة، وقدمت لك السفينة قبل أن تغرق في بحور المهالك. فالله الله في نفوسكم معاشر الإخوان والأولاد! استسلموا للحق، وتأدبوا بالادب الحقيقي لا المزور، وخذوا الحكمة البالغة وانتهجوا الصراط المستقيم، وتصوروا حالات أنفسكم وتذكروا قواها.

(٦) واعلموا أن أصح مثل ضرب لكم من نفوسكم الثلاث التي مرَّ ذكرها في المقالة الأولى مثل ثلاثة حيوانات مختلفة جمعت في رباط واحد: ملك وسبع وخنزير، فأيها غلب بقوته قوة الباقين كان الحكم له. وليعلم من تصور هذا المثل ان النفس لما كانت جوهرا غير جسم، ولا فيها شيء من قوى الجسم وأعراضه، كما بيَّنا ذلك في صدر هذا الكتاب، كان اتحادها واتصالها بخلاف اتحاد الاجسام واتصال بعضها ببعض. وذلك أن هذه الانفس الثلاث اذا اتصلت صارت شيئا واحدا، ومع أنها تكون شيئا واحدا فهي باقية التغاير باقية القوى، تثور الواحدة بعد الواحدة، حتى كأنها لم تتصل بالأخرى ولم تتحد بها، وتستخذي أيضا الواحدة للأخرى حتى كأنها غير موجودة ولا لها قوة تنفرد بها. وذلك أن اتحادها ليس بأن تتصل نهاياتها ولا بأن تتلاقى سطوحها، كما يكون ذلك في الأجسام، بل تصير في بعض الأحوال شيئا واحدا، وفي بعض الاحوال أشياء مختلفة، بحسب ما تهيج قوة بعضها أو تسكن.

(7) It is for this reason that some people assert that the soul is one but has many faculties, while others maintain that it is one in essence but many in accident and in subject. But this is a matter the discussion of which would lead us beyond the object of this work, and which you will find in its proper place. However, it does not do you any harm to hold, at this moment, any of these views you wish, provided you realize that one of these [souls or faculties] is by nature noble and moral, another is degraded and lacking morality, also by nature, and incapable of acquiring it, and the third is lacking morality but capable of acquiring it and ready to yield to the moral soul. The one which is by nature noble and moral is the rational soul; the one lacking morality and at the same time incapable of acquiring it is the beastly soul; and the one lacking morality but capable of acquiring it and of yielding to it is the irascible soul. This last soul in particular has been bestowed upon us by God (mighty and exalted is He!) in order that we may make use of it in rectifying the beastly soul which is incapable of acquiring morality.

(8) The ancients likened man and his condition with respect to these three souls to a person mounted on a vigorous beast and leading a dog or a hunting panther. Now, if he is the one who tames his horse and dog—if he commands them and they obey him in the course which he takes and in his hunting and other activities—there is no doubt that the common life of the three of them will be happy and fine. The man will get what he wants comfortably; he will let his horse, as well as his dog, run wherever he likes and as he likes, and when he dismounts and takes some rest, he will allow them to rest with him and will take good care of them and satisfy their need for food, drink, safety from enemies, and in other ways. But should the beast have the upper hand, the three would be in a bad condition. The man would become weak with respect to the beast, which would not obey its rider but would itself be master: if it saw some grass from a distance, it would run towards it haphazardly and deviate from the main road; it would rush heedlessly into valleys, pits, thorns, and trees that come across its way, and get itself into trouble in them; the rider would suffer as any similar person would in the same circumstances; and all three of them would meet such evils and such dangers of destruction as is obvious to all. The same would be true if the dog became strong. It would cease to obey its master. If it saw from a distance some prey or what it takes to be prey, it would rush towards it, dragging the rider and the horse along with it and causing all three of them to suffer harm and injury many times more than what we have described.

(٧) ولذلك قال قوم: إن النفس واحدة ولها قوى كثيرة. وقال آخرون: بل هي واحدة بالذات، كثيرة بالعرض وبالموضوع. وهذا شيء يخرج الكلام فيه عن غرض الكتاب، وسيمرُّ بك في موضعه. وليس يضرك في هذا الوقت أن تعتقد أي هذه الآراء شئت، بعد أن تعلم أن بعض هذه كريمة أديبة بالطبع، وبعضها مهينة عادمة للأدب بالطبع وليس فيها استعداد لقبول الأدب، وبعضها عادمة للأدب إلا أنها تقبل التأديب وتنقاد للتي هي أديبة. أما الكريمة الأديبة بالطبع فالنفس الناطقة. وأما العادمة للأدب، وهي مع ذلك غير قابلة له، فهي النفس البهيمية. وأما التي عدمت الأدب، ولكنها تقبله وتنقاد له، فهي النفس الغضبية، وإنما وهب الله عز وجل لنا هذه النفس خاصة لنستعين بها على تقويم البهيمية التي لا تقبل الأدب.

(٨) وقد شبه القدماء الإنسان وحاله في هذه الأنفس الثلاث بإنسان راكب بهيمة قوية، يقود كلبا أو فهدا للقنص، فان كان الإنسان من بينهم هو الذي يروض دابته وكلبه يصرِّفهما ويطيعانه في سيره وتصيده وسائر تصرفاته، فلا شك في رغد العيش المشترك بين الثلاثة وحسن أحواله، لأن الإنسان يكون مرفها في مطالبه، يجري فرسه حيث يحب وكما يحب، ويطلق كلبه أيضا كذلك، فإذا نزل واستراح أراحهما معه وأحسن القيام عليهما وأزاح علتهما في المطعم والمشرب وكفاية الأعداء وغير ذلك من مصالحهما. وإذا كانت البهيمة هي الغالبة ساءت حال الثلاثة كلهم، وكان الانسان مضعوفا عندها، فلم تطع فارسها وغلبت، فان رأت عشبا من بعيد عدت نحوه وتعسفت في عدوها، وعدلت عن الطريق النهج، فاعترضتها الأودية والوهاد والشوك والشجر فقحمتها وتورطت فيها، ولحق فارسها ما يلحق مثله في هذه الأحوال فيصيبها جميعا من أنواع المكاره والإشراف على الهلكة ما لا خفاء به. وكذلك إن قوي الكلب لم يطع صاحبه، فان رأى من بعيد صيدا أو ما يظنه صيدا أخذ نحوه، فجذب الفرس وفارسه، ولحق الجميع من الضر والضرر أضعاف ما ذكرناه.

(9) When one grasps this analogy, which was cited by the ancients, one's attention is called to the condition of these souls with respect one to another, and he is furnished with an indication of what God (mighty and exalted is He!) has bestowed upon man and what He has laid within his power and offered him. [He gets to know] also what man loses by disobeying his Creator (exalted is He!) when he neglects to follow guidance, obeys the decrees of these two faculties, and becomes enslaved by them whereas they should follow him by being subject to his command. Is there, then, a more miserable condition than that of the person who disregards the guidance of God (mighty and exalted is He!), who forfeits the favor which He has bestowed upon him, who permits these two faculties to be roused and agitated within him and to fight each other letting the master among them become a subject and the king a slave, and who allows himself to be involved with them in all sorts of perils until he, as well as they, are torn asunder? May God protect us from a relapse in character, which is caused by obedience to Satan and acquiescence to the devils! By these we mean nothing but those faculties which we have described and whose nature we have depicted. We ask from God His protection and His assistance in the refinement of these souls so that we may achieve, in what relates to them, obedience to Him, which is our welfare and in which lies our salvation and our attainment of the greatest triumph and the everlasting bliss.

(10) The philosophers have likened the person who fails to tend his rational soul and allows the sway of passion and the love of honor to gain mastery over it to a man who possesses a precious red ruby, priceless in terms of gold and silver because of its magnificence and high value, and who throws it in the blaze of a kindling fire near him, thus turning it into useless lime and losing it as well as all the profits that could be derived from it.

(11) We know now that, if the rational soul realizes its own nobility and perceives its rank with respect to God (mighty and exalted is He!), it will fulfill well its task as His deputy in ordering and tending these faculties and will rise up with the help of the power bestowed upon it by God to its place in His esteem and to its own level of sublimeness and honor. It will not submit either to the lion or to the beast, but will rather discipline the irascible soul, which we have called leonine, and lead it to morality by compelling it to good obedience. It will arouse it when the beastly soul is excited and moved to its desires, in order that, with its help, it may subdue the latter, discipline it, and repress its revolt.

(٩) وفي تصور هذا المثل الذي ضربه القدماء تنبيه على حال هذه النفوس بعضها عند بعض، ودلالة على ما وهبه الله عز وجل للإنسان ومكنه منه وعرضه له، وما يضيعه بعصيان خالقه تعالى فيها عند إهمال السياسة واتباعه أمرهاتين القوتين وتعبده لهما، وهما اللتان ينبغي أن تتبعاه بتأمره عليهما. فمن أسوأ حالا ممن أهمل سياسة الله عز وجل، وضيَّع نعمته عليه وترك هذه القوى فيه هائجة مضطربة تتغالب، وصار الرئيس منها مرؤوسا، والملك فيها مستعبدا، يتقلب معها في المهالك حتى تتمزق ويتمزق هو أيضا معها؟ نعوذ بالله من الانتكاس في الخلق الذي سببه طاعة الشياطين واتباع الأبالسة، فليست الإشارة بها الى غير هذه القوى التي وصفناها ووصفنا أحوالها. ونسأل الله عصمته ومعونته على تهذيب هذه النفوس، حتى ننتهي فيها إلى طاعته التي هي مصالحنا وبها نجاتنا وخلاصنا إلى الفوز الاكبر والنعيم السرمد.

(١٠) وقد شبه الحكماء من أهمل سياسة نفسه العاقلة وترك سلطان الشهوة ومحبة الكرامة يستولي عليها، برجل معه ياقوتة شريفة حمراء لا قيمة لها من الذهب والفضة جلالة ونفاسة، وكان بين يديه نار تضطرم فرماها في حباحبها حتى صارت كلسا لا منفعة فيها فخسرها وخسر ضروب منافعها.

(١١) فقد علمنا الآن أن النفس العاقلة إذا عرفت شرف نفسها، وأحست بمرتبتها من الله عز وجل، أحسنت خلافته في ترتيب هذه القوى وسياستها، ونهضت بالقوة التي أعطاها الله إلى محلها من كرامة الله ومنزلتها من العلو والشرف، ولم تخضع للسبع ولا للبهيمة بل تقوِّم النفس الغضبية التي سميناها سبعية، وتقودها الى الأدب بحملها على حسن طاعتها، ثم تستنهضها في أوقات هيجان النفس البهيمية وحركتها الى الشهوات، حتى تقمع بهذه سلطان تلك، وتستخدمها في تأديبها وتستعين بقوة هذه على تأبّي تلك، وذلك أن هذه النفس الغضبية قابلة للأدب، قوية على قمع

For this irascible soul is, as we said, capable of morality and able to subdue the other or beastly soul, while the latter lacks morality and is incapable of it. As for the rational (i.e., the intelligent) soul, it conforms to what Plato said in the following words: "This is like gold in its softness and suppleness, while that [the leonine soul] is like iron in its hardness and toughness." If, then, you choose to perform a good deed and the other faculty draws you to pleasure and to the opposite of what you intend, seek the assistance of the irascible faculty, which is roused and excited by a sense of indignation and enthusiasm, and subdue the beastly soul by its help. And even though, in spite of this, the beastly soul should triumph over you, if you later repent and feel indignant, then you will be in the path of righteousness. Your duty then is to build up your resolution to the utmost and to be careful lest it [the beastly soul] should come back again at you to entice and overcome you. If you are not so careful and the issue does not result in your victory, you will conform to what the first philosopher said: "I observe that most people claim that they love [to do] good deeds but, although they are convinced of their value, they do not wish to suffer the trouble which is involved in them and are overcome by the pursuit of luxury and the inclination to idleness. If they do not suffer to be patient and come to know exactly what they have chosen and esteemed, there will be no difference between them and those who do not love [to do] good deeds." Keep in mind the example of the well in which there fell a blind man and a man who is able to see. Both equally met death, but the blind man had a better excuse.

(12) Now, he who has attained in [the acquisition of] these morals a rank of which one may be proud, and has acquired through it the virtues which we have enumerated, has necessarily the obligation to educate other people and to pour out to his fellow men the gifts which God (exalted is He!) has bestowed upon him.

A section on the education of the young, and of boys in particular, most of which I have copied from the work of "Bryson."[4]

(13) We have said previously that the first faculty that appears in man when he is first formed is the faculty with which he desires the food that keeps him alive. He instinctively asks for milk and seeks it from its source, the breast, without any previous instruction or direction. Along with this, he comes to possess the faculty by which he asks for it with the voice, which is his resource and the sign with which he shows pleasure

الأخرى كما قلنا، وتلك النفس البهيمية عادمة للأدب غير قابلة له. وأما النفس الناطقة، أعني العاقلة، فهي كما قال أفلاطن بهذه الألفَاظ: أما هذه فبمنزلة الذهب في اللين والانعطاف، وأما تلك فبمنزلة الحديد في الصلابة والامتناع. فان أنت آثرت الفعل الجميل في وقت، وجاذبتك القوة الأخرى الى اللذة والى خلاف ما آثرت، فاستعن بقوة الغضب التي تثور وتهيج بالأنفة والحمية، واقهر بها النفس البهيمية. فان غلبتك مع ذلك ثم ندمت وأنفت فأنت في طريق الصلاح فتمم عزيمتك واحذر ان تعاودك بالطمع فيك والغلبة لك. فان لم تفعل ذلك ولم تكن العقبى في الغلبة لك كنت كما قال الحكيم الأول: اني أرى أكثر الناس يدّعون محبة الأفعال الجميلة، ثم لا يحتملون المؤونة فيها على علمهم بفضلها، فيغلبهم الترفه ومحبة البطالة، فلا يكون بينهم وبين من لا يحب الجميل فرق اذ لم يحتملوا مؤونة الصبر ويصيروا الى تمام ما آثروه وعرفوا فضله. واذكر مثل البئر التي تردى فيها البصير والأعمى فيكونان في الهلكة سواء، الا أن الأعمى أعذر.

(١٢) ومن وصل من هذه الآداب الى مرتبة يُعتدُّ بها واكتسب بها الفضائل التي عددناها، فقد وجب عليه تأديب غيره وافإضة ما أعطاه الله تعالى على أبناء جنسه.

فصل في تأديب الأحداث والصبيان خاصة
نقلت أكثره من كتاب بروسن

(١٣) قد قلنا فيما تقدم ان أول قوة تظهر في الانسان، أول ما يكون، هي القوة التي يشتاق بها الى الغذاء الذي هو سبب كونه حيا، فيتحرك بالطبع الى اللبن، ويلتمسه من الثدي الذي هو معدنه من غير تعليم ولا توقيف، ويحدث له مع ذلك قوة على

or pain. Then this faculty grows in him, and it induces him to continually desire its growth and to use it in the pursuit of all sorts of pleasures. Following this, he acquires the faculty with which he seeks those pleasures through the organs which are formed in him, and this is followed by the desire to perform the actions which give him those pleasures. Then he obtains through the senses the faculty of imagination, and he begins to desire the images which are formed in it. Next comes the irascible faculty by means of which he tries to ward off what injures him and to resist what hinders him from his benefits. If he is able by himself to take his revenge from what injures him, he goes ahead and does it; otherwise, he seeks the assistance of others or asks the help of his parents by shouting and crying.

(14) Following this, he acquires gradually the desire to discern those actions which are characteristically human, until he reaches his perfection in this respect, at which stage he is called a rational being.

(15) These faculties are many in number, and some of them are necessary for the formation of others, until one attains the final end, the one which is sought by man *qua* man. The first feature of this faculty which occurs in man is bashfulness, which is fear on his part lest he commit anything disgraceful. This is why we have said that bashfulness is the first sign which should be looked for in a boy and taken as a symptom of his reason. For it shows that he has begun to perceive what is disgraceful and, at the same time, to be on his guard against it, to avoid it, and to be cautious lest it appear from him or in him. If then you look at the boy and find him bashful with his eyes lowered towards the ground neither having an insolent face nor staring at you, take this as the first evidence of his intelligence and as the testimony that his soul has discerned what is good and what is bad and that his bashfulness is no more than self-restraint caused by his fear lest anything disgraceful should come out. This, in turn, is no more than the choice of the good and the abandonment of the disgraceful through judgment and reason. Such a soul is apt to be educated and fit to be taken care of. It should not be neglected or left to association with people of opposite character who would corrupt, through companionship and intercourse, anyone who has this fitness to receive virtue. For the boy's soul is still simple and has not yet received the impress of any form, nor does it possess any view or determination which would turn it from one thing to another. Should it, however, receive the impress of a particular form and assume it, the boy would grow in accordance with it and become accustomed to it.

التماسه بالصوت الذي هو مادته ودليله الذي يدل به على اللذة والأذى. ثم تتزيد فيه هذه القوة ويتشوق بها أبدا إلى الازدياد، والتصرف بها في أنواع الشهوات، ثم تحدث فيه قوة على التحرك نحوها بالآلات التي تخلق له، ثم يحدث له الشوق إلى الافعال التي تحصِّل له هذه، ثم يحدث له من الحواس قوة على تخيل الأمور وترتسم في قوته الخيالية مثالات فيتشوق إليها، ثم تظهر فيه قوة الغضب التي يشتاق بها إلى دفع ما يؤذيه، ومقاومة ما يمنعه من منافعه، فان أطاق بنفسه أن ينتقم من مؤذياته انتقم منها، وإلا التمس معونة غيره وانتصر بوالديه بالتصويت والبكاء.

(١٤) ثم يحدث له الشوق الى تمييز الأفعال الإنسانية خاصة أولا أولا، حتى يصير إلى كماله في هذا التميز، فيسمى حينئذ عاقلا.

(١٥) وهذه القوى كثيرة وبعضها ضرورية في وجود الأخرى، إلى أن ينتهي إلى الغاية الأخيرة، وهي التي لا تراد لغاية أخرى، وهي الخير المطلق الذي يتشوقه الإنسان من حيث هو إنسان. فأول ما يحدث فيه من هذه القوة الحياء، وهو الخوف من ظهور شيء قبيح منه. ولذلك قلنا: ان أول ما ينبغي أن يُتفرس في الصبي ويستدل به على عقله الحياء، فإنه يدل على أنه قد أحس بالقبيح، ومع إحساسه به هو يحذره ويتجنبه، ويخاف أن يظهر منه أو فيه. فاذا نظرت إلى الصبي فوجدته مستحييا مطرقا بطرفه إلى الأرض، غير وقاح الوجه ولا محدق إليك، فهو أول دليل نجابته، والشاهد لك على أن نفسه قد أحست بالجميل والقبيح، وأن حياءه هو انحصار نفسه خوفا من قبيح يظهر منه، وهذا ليس بشيء أكثر من إيثار الجميل والهرب من القبيح بالتميز والعقل. وهذه النفس مستعدة للتأديب صالحة للعناية لا يجب أن تهمل ولا تترك، ومخالطة الأضداد الذين يفسدون بالمقارنة والمداخلة، من كان بهذه الحال من الاستعداد لقبول الفضيلة. فان نفس الصبي ساذجة لم تنتقش بعد بصورة، ولا لها رأي وعزيمة تميلها من شيء إلى شيء، فاذا نقش بصورة وقبلها نشأ عليها واعتادها.

(16) It is appropriate, therefore, that such a soul be roused to the love of honor, especially that which comes to the boy through religion and the observance of its traditions and duties, rather than through money. Further, good men should be praised in his presence, and he himself should be commended for any good thing which he may perform and warned of reproach for the least disgraceful thing which he may demonstrate. He should be blamed for any desire on his part for food, drink, or splendid clothes, and he should hear the praise of self-restraint and of disdain of greed for food in particular and pleasures in general.

(17) He should be trained to like giving others preference over himself in food and to be content with what is moderate and frugal in seeking it. He should be taught that the people who are most fit to wear colored and embroidered clothes are, first, women who adorn themselves for the sake of men and, second, slaves and servants, and that the dress which is most becoming to noble and honorable people is white or its like. Thus, being brought up on these teachings and hearing them repeatedly from everybody around him, he should also be prevented from mixing with those who tell him the contrary, especially if they happen to be his companions or his associates and playmates of the same age. For, in his early life the boy is generally bad in all or most of his actions: he is a liar, telling and relating what he has not heard or seen; he is jealous; he steals and slanders; he is importune, meddlesome, spiteful, and malicious; and he is most harmful to himself as well as to everything that touches him. Later, under the constant influence of education, age, and experience, he changes from one state to another. That is why he should be trained as long as he is a child along the lines which we have described and are describing.

(18) He should then be required to learn by heart good traditions and poems which corroborate what he has practiced in his education, so that by reciting, learning, and discussing them, all that we have described may become confirmed in him. He should also be put on his guard against the study of frivolous poetry and what it contains about love and lovers, and against the impression which its authors give that it is a form of elegance and of refinement. For this kind of poetry has, indeed, a strong corrupting influence on youth.

(١٦) فالأولى بمثل هذه النفس أن تنبه أبدا على حب الكرامة، ولا سيما ما يحصل له منها بالدين دون المال، وبلزوم سننه ووظائفه، ثم يمدح الأخيار عنده، ويمدح هو في نفسه إذا ظهر شيء جميل منه، ويخوّف من المذمة على أدنى قبيح يظهر منه، ويؤاخذ باشتهائه للمآكل والمشارب والملابس الفاخرة، ويزين عنده ظلف النفس والترفع عن الحرص في المآكل خاصة وفي اللذات عامة.

(١٧) ويحبب إليه إيثار غيره على نفسه في الغذاء والاقتصار على الشيء المعتدل والاقتصاد في التماسه. ويعلَّم أن أولى الناس بالملابس الملونة والمنقوشة النساء اللاتي يتزينَّ للرجال، ثم العبيد والخول، وأن الأحسن بأهل النبل والشرف من اللباس البياض وما أشبهه، حتى إذا تربى على ذلك وسمعه من كل من يقرب منه وتكرر عليه، لم يترك ومخالطة من سمع منه ضد ما ذكرته، لا سيما من أترابه ومن كان في مثل سنه ممن يعاشره ويلاعبه. وذلك أن الصبي في ابتداء نشوئه يكون على الأكثر قبيح الأفعال، إما كلها وإما أكثرها، فإنه يكون كذوبا يخبر ويحكي ما لم يسمعه ولم يره، ويكون حسودا سروقا نموما لجوجا ذا فضول ومحك وكياد، أضرَّ شيء بنفسه وبكل أمر يلابسه، ثم لا يزال به التأديب والسن والتجارب حتى ينتقل في أحوال بعد أحوال. فلذلك ينبغي أن يؤخذ ما دام طفلا بما ذكرناه ونذكره.

(١٨) ثم يطالب بحفظ محاسن الأخبار والأشعار التي تجري مجرى ما تعوده بالأدب، حتى يتأكد عنده بروايتها وحفظها والمذاكرة بها جميع ما قدمنا ذكره، ويحذر النظر في الأشعار السخيفة وما فيها من ذكر العشق وأهله، وما يوهمه أصحابها أنه ضرب من الظرف ورقة الطبع، فإن هذا الباب مفسدة للأحداث جدا.

(19) The boy should also be praised and honored for any good trait or any good deed which he may show. If, at times, he violates what I have described, it is preferable that he not be reproached for it or openly told that he has committed it. One should feign not to have noticed it, as if it would not occur to him that the boy would ever dare such a thing or attempt to do it. This is especially necessary when the boy conceals it and endeavors to hide what he has done from other people. If he repeats it, let him be reproached for it secretly, shown the seriousness of his action and warned against doing it again. For if you accustom him to reproach and disclosure, you will make him impudent and incite him to repeat what he has detested. It will become easy for him to hear blame for indulging in the detestable pleasures to which his nature urges him. And these pleasures are very numerous.

(20) The training of the soul should begin with [the formation of] good manners in eating. The boy should first be made to understand that eating is meant only for health and not for pleasure and that all the kinds of food have been created and prepared for us solely to make our bodies healthy and to sustain our life. They should be considered as medicines with which we remedy hunger and the pain resulting from it. Just as we do not seek medicine for pleasure and are not driven by greed to take more and more of it, so it is also with food: we should take only as much of it as would preserve the health of the body, remove the pain of hunger, and guard against disease. Thus, the boy should be made to despise the value of food, which gluttonous people extol, and to disdain those who covet it and take more of it than is necessary for their bodies or indulge in what does not agree with them. In this way, he would get to be satisfied with only one course of food and would not desire many courses. When he sits in the company of others, he should not be the first to start eating, nor should he stare constantly and fixedly at the courses of food but should be content with whatever is near him. He should not eat in a hurry or take rapidly one mouthful after another. The mouthfuls should not be too big or swallowed before they are well chewed. He should not soil his hands, or his clothing, or his table companions, nor follow with his eyes the movements of their hands in eating. He should be trained to offer to others the food that lies near him if it is the kind that he prefers, and to control his appetite so as to be content with the least and poorest of food, eating once in a while dry bread without anything else. These manners, if commendable when shown by poor people, are even more commendable when shown by the rich.

(١٩) ثم يمدح بكل ما يظهر منه من خلق جميل وفعل حسن ويكرّم عليه، فإن خالف في بعض الأوقات ما ذكرته فالأولى أن لا يوبخ عليه ولا يكاشف بأنه أقدم عليه، بل يتغافل عنه تغافل من لا يخطر بباله انه قد تجاسر على مثله ولا همّ به، لا سيما إن ستره الصبي واجتهد في أن يخفي ما فعله على الناس، فان عاد فليُوبَّخ عليه سرا وليعظم عنده ما أتاه، ويحذر من معاودته، فإنك إن عودته التوبيخ والمكاشفة، حملته على الوقاحة وحرضته على معاودة ما كان استقبحه، وهان عليه سماع الملامة في ركوب القبائح من اللذات التي تدعو إليها نفسه. وهذه اللذات كثيرة جدا.

(٢٠) والذي ينبغي أن يبدأ به في تقويمها أدب المطاعم، فيفهم أولا أنها انما تراد للصحة لا للذة، وأن الاغذية كلها إنما خلقت وأعدت لنا لتصح بها أبداننا وتصير مادة لحياتنا، فهي تجري مجرى الأدوية يداوى بها الجوع والالم الحادث منه. فكما أن الدواء لا يراد للذة ولا يستكثر منه للشهوة، فكذلك الأطعمة لا ينبغي أن يتناول منها إلا ما يحفظ صحة البدن، ويدفع ألم الجوع ويمنع من المرض، فيحقر عنده قدر الطعام الذي يستعظمه أهل الشره، ويقبح عنده صورة من يشره إليه وينال منه فوق حاجة بدنه أو ما لا يوافقه، حتى يقتصر على لون واحد ولا يرغب في الألوان الكثيرة. وإذا جلس مع غيره لا يبادر إلى الطعام ولا يديم النظر إلى ألوانه، ولا يحدق إليه شديدا، ويقتصر على ما يليه، ولا يسرع في الأكل ولا يوالي بين اللقم بسرعة، ولا يعظم اللقمة ولا يبتلعها حتى يجيد مضغها، ولا يلطخ يده ولا ثوبه، ولا يلحظ من يؤاكله ولا يتبع بنظره مواقع يده من الطعام. ويعوَّد أن يؤثر غيره بما يليه، ان كان أفضل عنده، ثم يضبط شهوته حتى يقتصر على أدنى الطعام وأدونه، وليأكل الخبز القفار الذي لا أدم معه في بعض الأوقات. وهذه الآداب، وإن كانت جميلة بالفقراء، فهي بالأغنياء أجمل.

(21) The boy should have his full meal in the evening, for, if he has it during the day, he will feel lazy and sleepy and also his understanding will become slow. If he is forbidden to eat meat most of the time, the result will be favorable to him in [stirring] his activity and attentiveness, in reducing his dullness, and in arousing him to liveliness and agility. As for sweets and fruits, he should abstain from them entirely if possible; otherwise, let him take as little of them as possible because they become transformed in his body, thus hastening the process of dissolution and, at the same time, they accustom him to gluttony and to the desire for excessive food. He should be trained to avoid drinking water during his meals. As for wine and the different kinds of intoxicating beverages, let him indeed beware of them, for they injure him in his body and in his soul and incite him to quick anger, foolhardiness, the performance of vile deeds, impudence, and the other blameworthy dispositions. Nor should he attend drinking parties, except when the company is well-bred and virtuous; otherwise, he might hear vile speech and silly things that usually take place in such parties. [Finally,] he should not begin to eat until he has performed the educational tasks which he is pursuing and has become sufficiently tired.

(22) Furthermore, the boy should be forbidden to do anything which he hides or conceals, for, if he hides anything, it is only because he either thinks or knows that it is disgraceful. He should not be allowed to sleep too long because too much sleep makes him flabby,[5] dulls his mind, and deadens his thinking. So much for night sleep; as for sleep during the day, he should never become accustomed to it. Similarly, he should not be given a soft bed or any other means of luxury and flabbiness, so as to harden his body and to habituate him to a rough life. For the same reasons, he should be denied moistened canvas [to cool off the air] and living underground in summer, and camel furs and fire in winter. Let him develop the habits of walking, movement, riding, and exercise lest he succumb to their opposites.

(23) The boy should be taught not to uncover the extremities of his body, nor to walk fast, nor to hang his hands loose but to join them together at his chest. He should not let his hair grow long, nor adorn himself with dresses fit for women, nor wear a ring except when necessary. Let him not boast to his companions of something which his parents possess, or of his food, clothing, or the like. On the contrary, let be humble towards everybody and honor all those who associate with him. Should he possess any honor, or any power derived from his kin, he must not arouse the anger

(٢١) وينبغي أن يستوفي غذاءه بالعشيّ، فإنه إن استوفاه بالنهار كسل واحتاج الى النوم وتبلد فهمه مع ذلك. وإن منع اللحم في أكثر أوقاته كان نافعا له في الحركة والتيقظ وقلة البلادة وبعثه على النشاط والخفة. وأما الحلواء والفاكهة فينبغي أن يمنع منها البتة ان أمكن، والا فليتناول أقل ما يمكن، فانها تستحيل في بدنه فتكثر انحلاله، وتعوده مع ذلك الشره ومحبة الاستكثار من المآكل. ويعوّد أن لا يشرب في خلال طعامه الماء، فأما النبيذ وأصناف الأشربة المسكرة فإياه وإياها، فانها تضره في بدنه ونفسه وتحمله على سرعة الغضب والتهور، والإقدام على القبائح وعلى القحة وسائر الخلال المذمومة. ولا ينبغي أن يحضر مجالس أهل النبيذ إلا أن يكون أهل المجلس أدباء فضلاء، فأما غيرهم فلا، لئلا يسمع الكلام القبيح والسخافات التي تجري فيه. وينبغي أن لا يأكل حتى يفرغ من وظائف الآداب التي يتعلمها، ويتعب تعبا كافيا.

(٢٢) وينبغي أن يمنع من كل فعل يستره ويخفيه، فإنه ليس يخفي شيئا إلا وهو يظن أو يعلم أنه قبيح. ويمنع من النوم الكثير فإنه يفتّحه ويغلظ ذهنه ويميت خواطره، هذا بالليل فأما بالنهار فلا ينبغي أن يتعوده البتة. ويمنع أيضا من الفراش الوطيء وجميع أنواع الترفه والتفتح حتى يصلب بدنه ويتعود الخشونة، ولا يتعود الخيش والأسراب في الصيف، ولا الأوبار والنيران في الشتاء للأسباب التي ذكرناها. ويعوّد المشي والحركة والركوب والرياضة حتى لا يتعود أضدادها.

(٢٣) ويعوّد أن لا يكشف أطرافه ولا يسرع في مشيه ولا يرخي يديه، بل يضمهما إلى صدره، ولا يربي شعره ولا يزين بملابس النساء، ولا يلبس خاتما إلا وقت حاجته إليه، ولا يفتخر على أقرانه بشيء مما يملكه والداه، ولا بشيء من مآكله وملابسه وما يجري مجراها، بل يتواضع لكل احد ويكرم كل من عاشره، ولا يتوصل بشرف إن كان له أو سلطان من أهله إن اتفق له إلى غضب من هو دونه، أو

of those who are below him, or attempt to guide those whom he cannot divert from their whims, or deal with them high-handedly. If, for instance, his maternal uncle happens to be a vizier or his paternal uncle a sultan, this must not lead him to do injustice to his companions, or to defame his friends, or to seize the property of his neighbors and acquaintances.

(24) He should be taught, when in the company of others, not to spit, or blow his nose, or yawn, or cross his legs, or beat his chin with his forearm, or support his head with his hand, for this is an indication of laziness and a proof that he has become so flabby that he is no longer able to carry his head without the help of his hand. Further, he should be trained not to tell lies and never to swear, whether truthfully or falsely, for swearing is disgraceful to men, though they may need it at times, but it is never needed by boys. He should also be taught to keep silent, to talk sparingly, and only to answer questions. If he is in the company of older people, his duty is to listen to them and to keep silent in their presence. He should be forbidden to utter vile or improper speech, to insult, curse, or talk nonsense. On the contrary, he should be taught to utter good and elegant speech and to greet gracefully and kindly, and should not be allowed to hear the opposite of this from others. He should also be accustomed to serve himself, his master, and older people. The children of the rich and of those who live in luxury need, more than others, to cultivate these good manners.

(25) If the boy is beaten by his teacher, he should not cry or ask the intercession of any one, for such is the conduct of slaves and those who are feeble and weak. He should not reproach others except for disgraceful and bad manners. He should be accustomed not to treat other boys harshly, but to show kindness to them and to repay their favors with bigger ones lest he make it a habit to seek gain from boys and from friends. He should be made to detest silver and gold and to fear them more than he does lions, snakes, scorpions, and serpents. For the love of silver and gold is more harmful than poison. He should be allowed from time to time to play nice games in order that he may thus rest from the toil of education, but his play should not involve pain or intense fatigue. And, finally, he should be trained to obey his parents, teachers, and educators and to honor, extol, and revere them.

استهداء من لا يمكنه أن يرده عن هواه أو تطاولٍ عليه، كمن اتفق له أن كان خاله وزيرا أو عمه سلطانا، فتطرق به الى هضيمة أقرانه وثلم إخوانه واستباحة أموال جيرانه ومعارفه.

(٢٤) وينبغي أن يعوَّد أن لا يتبزق في مجلسه ولا يمتخط ولا يتثاءب بحضرة غيره، ولا يضع رجلا على رجل، ولا يضرب تحت ذقنه بساعده، ولا يعمد رأسه بيده، فإن هذا دليل الكسل، وأنه قد بلغ به التفتح إلى أن لا يحمل رأسه حتى يستعين بيده. ويعوَّد أن لا يكذب ولا يحلف البتة لا صادقا ولا كاذبا، فان هذا قبيح بالرجال مع الحاجة إليه في بعض الأوقات، فأما الصبي فلا حاجة به الى اليمين. ويعوَّد أيضا الصمت وقلة الكلام، وأن لا يتكلم إلا جوابا، وإذا حضر من هو أكبر منه اشتغل بالاستماع منه والصمت له. ويمنع من خبيث الكلام ومن هجينه، ومن السب واللعن ولغو الكلام، ويعوَّد حسن الكلام وظريفه، وجميل اللقاء وكريمه، ولا يرخص له أن يسمع أضدادها من غيره. ويعوَّد خدمة نفسه ومعلمه وكل من كان اكبر منه.

(٢٥) وأحوج الصبيان إلى هذا الأدب أولاد الأغنياء والمترفين. وينبغي إذا ضربه المعلم أن لا يصرخ ولا يستشفع بأحد فان هذا فعل المماليك ومن هو خوار ضعيف، ولا يعير أحدا إلا بالقبيح والسيء من الأدب. ويعوَّد أن لا يوحش الصبيان بل يبرهم ويكافئهم على الجميل بأكثر منه لئلا يتعود الربح على الصبيان وعلى الصديق. ويبغَّض إليه الفضة والذهب ويحذر منهما أكثر من تحذير السباع والحيات والعقارب والأفاعي، فان آفة حب الفضة والذهب أكثر من آفة السموم. وينبغي أن يؤذن له في بعض الأوقات ان يلعب لعبا جميلا، ليستريح إليه من تعب الأدب، ولا يكون في لعبه ألم ولا تعب شديد. ويعوَّد طاعة والديه ومعلميه ومؤدبيه، وأن ينظر إليهم بعين الجلالة والتعظيم ويهابهم.

The benefits of the education of the young

(26) These good manners which are useful to boys are likewise useful to older people, but to the young they are more useful because they train them to love virtue and allow them to grow up accordingly. It then becomes easy for them to avoid vices, and later to follow all the prescriptions of philosophy and the regulations of the Law and of Tradition. They thus get accustomed to control themselves in the face of the wicked pleasures towards which their natures urge them. [These good manners also] restrain them from indulging in any of those pleasures or giving much thought to them. They lead them to the high rank of philosophy and promote them to the lofty grades which we described in the beginning of this work, such as seeking proximity to God (mighty and exalted is He!) and the vicinity of the angels, as well as enjoying a good condition in this world, leading a pleasant life, gaining a fine reputation, and having few enemies, numerous praisers, and many who seek their friendship, particularly among the virtuous. If one goes beyond this grade and attains in his life to the understanding of the aims of men and the consequences of actions, one will realize that the final end of what people desire and care for—such as wealth, the acquisition of estates, slaves, horses, furniture, and the like—is nothing else but to secure the well-being of one's body, to preserve its health and keep its balance for a certain period of time, to guard it against diseases or sudden death, to cause it to enjoy the grace of God (mighty and exalted is He!) upon it, and to prepare it for the eternal world and the everlasting life. He will realize also that all bodily pleasures are in reality deliverance from pain and relief from fatigue.

(27) When the boy understands this and grasps its truth, and then becomes accustomed to it by continuous practice, the next step should be to train him in those exercises which stir up the innate heat, preserve health, banish laziness, drive dullness away, arouse liveliness, and kindle the soul. He who is rich and leads a luxurious life will find these things which I have just prescribed harder for him to perform than they are for others because of the large number of those who surround and tempt him, the fact that these pleasures agree with the nature of man at the beginning of his life, and the unanimous desire of the mass of the people to obtain as much of them as they can and to seek with their utmost

[فوائد تأديب الاحداث]

(٢٦) فإن هذه الآداب هي النافعة لهم وهي للكبار من الناس أيضا نافعة، ولكنها للأحداث أنفع لأنها تعودهم محبة الفضائل وينشأون عليها، فلا يثقل عليهم تجنب الرذائل، ويسهل عليهم بعد ذلك جميع ما ترسمه الحكمة وتحده الشريعة والسنة، ويعتادون ضبط النفس عما تدعوهم إليه من اللذات القبيحة، وتكفهم عن الانهماك في شيء منها والفكر الكثير فيها، وتسوقهم إلى مرتبة الفلسفة العالية وترقيهم إلى معالي الأمور التي وصفناها في أول الكتاب من التقرب الى الله عز وجل، ومجاورة الملائكة مع حسن الحال في الدنيا، وطيب العيش وجميل الأحدوثة، وقلة الاعداء وكثرة المداح والراغبين في مودته من الفضلاء خاصة. فإذا تجاوز هذه الدرجة وبلغ أيامه الى أن يفهم أغراض الناس وعواقب الأمور، فهم أن الغرض الأخير من هذه الأشياء التي يقصدها الناس ويحرصون عليها من الثروة واقتناء الضياع والعبيد والخيل والفرش وأشباه ذلك، إنما هو ترفيه البدن وحفظ صحته، وأن يبقى على اعتداله مدة ما، وأن لا يقع في الأمراض ولا تفجأه المنية، وأن يتهنأ بنعمة الله عليه عز وجل ويستعد لدار البقاء والحياة السرمدية، وأن اللذات البدنية كلها بالحقيقة هي خلاص من آلام وراحات من تعب.

(٢٧) فإذا عرف ذلك وتحققه، ثم تعوده بالسيرة الدائمة، عوّد الرياضات التي تحرك الحرارة الغريزية وتحفظ الصحة وتنفي الكسل وتطرد البلادة وتبعث النشاط وتذكي النفس. فمن كان متمولا مترفا كانت هذه الأشياء التي رسمتها أصعب عليه، لكثرة من يحتف به ويغويه، ولموافقة طبيعة الإنسان في أول ما ينشأ هذه اللذات، وإجماع جمهور الناس على نيل ما أمكنهم منها، وطلب ما تعذر عليهم بغاية جهدهم،

effort that which lies beyond their reach. With the poor, on the other hand, it is an easier matter. Indeed, they are close to the virtues, capable of acquiring them, and able to achieve and gain them. As for the middle class, their condition in this respect is intermediate between the two.

(28) The virtuous kings of Persia were in the habit of not bringing up their children among their retinue and their intimates for fear that they get into some of the conditions which we have described or hear what I have cautioned against. They used to send them with people whom they trusted to distant regions where those who took charge of their education were rough and hard-living people who did not experience ease or luxury. Their stories in this regard are famous, and even in our present day many of the chiefs of the Daylam remove their children, when they begin to grow up, to their own country so that they may acquire this character there and be kept away from flabbiness and the customs of the people of evil countries.

(29) Now that you know these laudable methods of educating the young, you also know their opposites. I mean that whoever grows up according to a different way or form of education has no hope of success, and one should not strive to improve or correct him. For he is in the same rank as the wild boar which nobody hopes to discipline. His rational soul has become the servant of his beastly and irascible souls and is busy trying to satisfy their whims. As it is impossible to discipline the wild beasts which do not respond to training, so also it is impossible to discipline the person who grows up in this way, gets accustomed to it, and becomes a little advanced in years, unless he is, in all his conditions, aware of the vileness of his conduct, disapproving of it, blaming himself for it, and determined to desist and to repent. For such a man, one may entertain the hope that he will depart gradually from his former character and return to the ideal way by repentance, association with good and wise men, and the diligent pursuit of philosophy.

◆

فأما الفقراء فالأمر عليهم أسهل بل هم قريبون إلى الفضائل، قادرون عليها متمكنون من نيلها والإصابة منها. وحال المتوسطين من الناس متوسطة بين هاتين الحالتين.

(٢٨) وقد كان ملوك الفرس الفضلاء لا يربُّون أولادهم بين حشمهم وخواصهم خوفا عليهم من الأحوال التي ذكرناها، وكانوا ينفذونهم مع ثقاتهم إلى النواحي البعيدة منهم ومن سماع ما حذرت منه. وكان يتولى تربيتهم أهل الجفاء وخشونة العيش ومن لا يعرف التنعم ولا الترفه، وأخبارهم في ذلك مشهورة. وكثير من رؤساء الديلم في زماننا هذا ينقلون أولادهم عندما ينشأون الى بلادهم، ليتعودوا بها هذه الأخلاق ويبعدوا عن التفتح وعادات أهل البلدان الرديئة.

(٢٩) واذ قد عرفت هذه الطرق المحمودة في تأديب الأحداث، فقد عرفت أضدادها، أعني أن من نشأ على خلاف هذا المذهب والتأديب لم يُرجَ فلاحه، ولا ينبغي أن يُشتغل بصلاحه وتقديمه، فإنه قد صار بمنزلة الخنزير الوحشي الذي لا يطمع في رياضته، فإن نفسه العاقلة تصير خادمة لنفسه البهيمية ولنفسه الغضبية فهي منهمكة في مطالبها من النزوات. وكما لا سبيل الى رياضة سباع البهائم الوحشية التي لا تقبل التأديب، كذلك لا سبيل إلى رياضة من نشأ على هذه الطريقة واعتادها وأمعن قليلا في السن، اللّهم إلا أن يكون في جميع أحواله عالما بقبح سيرته، ذامًّا لها عاتبا على نفسه عازما على الإقلاع والإنابة، فإن مثل هذا الإنسان قد يرجى له النزوع عن أخلاقه بالتدريج، والرجوع إلى الطريقة المثلى بالتوبة ومصاحبة الأخيار وأهل الحكمة وبالإكباب على التفلسف.

al-Ghazālī

O Son!

TRANSLATED BY DAVID C. REISMAN

◆

Translator's Introduction

We have it on the authority of only one late source that this text was originally composed in Persian and later translated into Arabic (Murtaḍā al-Zabīdī, writing in the 18th century; see his *Sharh al-qāmūs,* 1:41). This information may be a conjecture based on the presence of a stanza of Persian poetry in *O Son!* (see paragraph 12 of the translation herein); there appear to be no extant Persian versions that do not derive from the Arabic.

The transmission of the Arabic text is very problematic. The manuscript evidence indicates centuries of additions to al-Ghazālī's original text in the nature of marginal additions, explanations, and glosses, some of which ultimately made their way into the text. The edition used here is that of Aḥmad Maṭlūb (Baghdad, 1986). There does not seem to have been any reason for Maṭlūb's choice of manuscripts beyond their availability, and they certainly do not offer any better readings than others that have been published. He has compared his text with two other unremarkable editions of the text, one of which was also collated with the edition of Jospeh Hammer-Purgstall (*O Kind! Die berühmte ethische Abhandlung Ghasali's* [Vienna: Gedruckt bey A. Strauss's sel. Witwe, 1838]. See Maṭlūb's introduction, 67–68). Furthermore, Maṭlūb's choices of readings do not appear to be based on any critical evaluation of the manuscripts. This produces a text which at times is at distinct odds with the manuscript readings from other editions. George H. Scherer examined thirty-two manuscripts for his translation (al-Ghazālī, *O Youth*) and presented his findings along with a facsimile of the entire text from MS Dresden 172 (which he judged the best), and variants from two other manuscripts. An important observation that Scherer made was that the earliest manuscripts of *O Son!* date to a period six centuries after the death of al-Ghazālī. This of course raises serious problems for editors seeking to reconstruct the original text. Another edition of the work was undertaken by Toufic Sabbagh (al-Ghazālī, *O Jeune Homme*). Sabbagh provides us with neither a critical apparatus nor even an indication of which manuscript or manuscripts he consulted, but his text may be based on Scherer's facsimile, since Scherer's own introduction is translated into French and Arabic in Sabbagh's publication. Additional bibliographical information concerning the work and the manuscripts can be had from Bouyges, *Essai de Chronologie*, and Badawī, *Muʾallafāt al-Ghazālī*.

The translation here follows Maṭlūb's edition, but occasionally departs from his readings. These departures are indicated in the notes with references to the variant readings recorded by Maṭlūb or, in some cases, to the publications of Scherer and Sabbagh. *O Son!* has not lacked for translations, but most are now dated; compare Hammer-Purgstall's German translation (1888), Scherer's English translation (1933), and Sabbagh's French translation (1951). To my knowledge, there is only one recent English version, by Tobias Mayer (al-Ghazālī, *Letter to a Disciple*). My translation, completed and submitted in full prior to the latter's publication date, does not reflect any knowledge of it, so it will not be compared in the notes below. I have added paragraph numbers which are not always consistent with Maṭlūb's paragraph divisions. Square brackets enclose my explanatory additions to the text.

Where possible, I have identified the prophetic hadiths by reference to Wensinck and Mensing, *Concordance*.

O Son! by al-Ghazālī

(may God provide us benefit through it!)

In the name of God, the Merciful and Compassionate

(1) Praise be to God, Lord of the Worlds, the Final Reward of the godfearing! And blessings and peace be upon His Prophet Muhammad and all his family!

(2) Know that a student in search of [spiritual] profit was regularly in the service of the Master and Imam, Ornament of the community and religion, the Proof of Islam, Abū Ḥāmid Muḥammad ibn Muḥammad al-Ghazālī (may God have mercy on him!),[1] and devoted himself to verifying and reading [the books of] knowledge to [his master], until he had gathered together the particular details of the sciences and perfected the virtues of his soul.

(3) Then one day he was reflecting on his condition and he thought to himself: "I have read the various types of sciences and spent the prime of my life learning and harmonizing them. Now I need to know which of them will benefit me in the future, bringing me solace in the tomb, and which will not, so that I might turn my back on it—as the Prophet said: 'Lord, I seek protection in You against any useless knowledge.'"[2] This thought stayed with him until he[3] wrote to the honorable

الغزالي

أيها الولد
نَفَعنا اللّٰهُ تعالى به

بسم الله الرحمن الرحيم

(١) الحمدُ لله ربِّ العالمين. والعاقبةُ للمتقين. والصلاةُ والسلام على نبيه محمدٍ وآله أجمعين.

(٢) واعلم أنَّ واحداً من الطلبة المستفيدين لازَمَ خدمةَ الشيخِ الامامِ زينِ المِلّةِ والدين حُجّةِ الاسلام أبي حامدٍ محمد بن محمدٍ الغزالي - رحمه الله وأرضاه وجعل الفردوسَ الأعلى مسكنَه ومثواه - واشتغل بالتحصيل وقراءةِ العلمِ عليه حتى جمع من دقائقِ العلوم واستكملَ فضائلَ النفس،

(٣) ثم إنَّه تفكَّرَ يوماً في حال نفسه وخَطَرعلى باله فقال: إنّي قرأتُ أنواعاً من العلوم وَصرَفْتُ ريعانَ عُمري على تعلّمها وجَمْعِها، والآنَ ينبغي أَنْ أعلَمَ أيُّ نوعها يَنْفَعني غداً ويُؤنِسُني في قبري، وأعلم الذي لا ينفع حتى أتركه كما قال رسولُ الله ﷺ «اللّٰهم إني أعوذ بك من علمٍ لا ينفع» فاستمرت مني هذه الفكرة حتى كتبت الى حضرة الشيخ

Master, the Proof of Islam, Muḥammad al-Ghazālī (may God have mercy on him!) in search of a formal opinion, asking him certain questions and calling upon him for advice and for a prayer of supplication.[4]

(4) He said [in his letter]: "Even though the books of the Master, such as the *Revival* [*of the Religious Sciences*][5] and others, may contain the answer to my questions, my hope is that the Master will write out my request on pages that I might keep with me throughout my life and that would survive my death, while I put into action what they contain in the course of my life, God willing."

(5) So the Master wrote this treatise as his response.

In the name of God, the Merciful and Compassionate

(6) O Son[6] and dear friend! May God lengthen your days of continued obedience to Him and guide you to the path of those He loves. Know that the advice commonly available is written down from the Source of Prophecy (peace be upon him!).[7] If any advice has reached you from him, then what need could you have for mine? And if it has not, then tell me, what have you achieved in these past years?

(7) O Son! The advice which the Prophet of God (blessings and peace upon him!) gave his community includes his statement: "One sign that God has turned away from His servant is [the servant's] preoccupation with anything that does not concern him. For any man who has spent so much as an hour of his life in anything unsuited to him deserves to long regret it, and anyone who has passed the age of forty and whose good works do not outweigh his bad, let him prepare for the fire."[8] This is advice enough for the knowledgeable.

(8) O Son! Giving advice is easy; the problem lies in taking it, because it can taste bitter to those who follow[9] their passions, since illicit things are in their hearts. This is especially true of anyone who pursues theoretical knowledge while being preocuppied with the soul's incitement and to worldly values, for he assumes that pure knowledge is a tool of his salvation[10] and deliverance, and that he need not put it into practice. This is the opinion of the philosophers. Praise be to God, the Almighty! A fool[11] such as this does not know that when he acquires

حجة الاسلام محمد الغزالي-رحمة الله عليه-استفتاءً وأسأل عنه مسائل والتمس منه نصيحةً ودعاء.

(٤) قال: وإن كان مصنفات الشيخ كالإحياء وغيره تشتمل على جواب مسائلي لكن مقصودي أن يكتب الشيخ حاجتي في ورقات تكون معي مدة حياتي وبعد مماتي وأعمل بما فيها مدة عمري إن شاء الله تعالى.

(٥) فكتب الشيخ هذه الرسالة في جوابه:

بسم الله الرحمن الرحيم

(٦) اعلم أيها الولد والمحب العزيز-أطال الله بقاك بطاعته وسلك بك سبيل أحبائه-أن منشور النصيحة يكتب من معدن الرسالة-عليه السلام-إن كان قد بلغك منه نصيحة فأي حاجة لك في نصيحتي، وإن لم يبلغك فقل لي. ماذا حصلت في هذه السنين الماضية؟

(٧) ايها الولد: من جملة ما نصح به رسول الله ﷺ أمته قوله: « علامة إعراض الله تعالى عن العبد اشتغاله بما لا يعنيه فإن امرءً ذهبت ساعة من عمره في غير ما خلق له لجدير أن تطول عليه حسرته، ومن جاوز الأربعين ولم يغلب خيره على شره فليتجهز إلى النار وفي هذه النصيحة كفاية لأهل العلم.

(٨) أَيُّها الولدُ: النصيحةُ سهلةٌ والمشكِلُ قبولها لأَنَّها في مذاق مُتَّبعي الهوى مُرَّة: إذ المناهي في قلوبهم، على الخصوص لمن كان طالب العلم الرسمي ويشتغل في حَظّ النفس ومناقب الدنيا فانه يحسب أن العلم المجرد له وسيلة ستكون نجاته وخلاصه فيه، وأَنَّهُ مُسْتَغْنٍ عن العمل. وهذا اعتقادُ الفلاسفة-سبحان الله العظيم-لا يعلم هذا

knowledge but does not put it into practice, the judgment against him is all the stronger—as the Prophet (blessings and peace upon him!) said: "The one who will suffer most on the Day of Resurrection is the one who has knowledge which God renders useless to him."[12]

(9) It was reported that Junayd[13] (may God sanctify his dear soul!) appeared in a dream after his death, and [the one dreaming] asked him: "What news, Abū al-Qāsim?"

(10) [Junayd responded]: "Explanations miss the mark and pointers come to nought. Nothing is of use to us [in the afterlife] but the prostrations we performed in the dead of night."

(11) O Son! Do not be bankrupt in actions, nor empty-handed in the states [of your soul]. You may be certain that theoretical knowledge will not stand you in good stead. For example, if a man in the wilderness had ten swords of Indian steel and yet more weapons, and he was a man of courage, experienced in battle, and if a ferocious lion leapt upon him, what say you? Would the weapons repel the menace from him without his using them and striking with them? It is common sense that they would not without his moving and striking with them. Likewise, if a man were to read a hundred thousand topics of science that he learned and studied but did not put into practice, they would be of no use to him except through action. For example, if a man had a fever or cholera, the cure for which is oxymel and barley water, recovery would not happen without using them.

(12) A poem:

Even if you pour out two thousand raṭls of wine,
If you do not drink it, you are not drunk

(13) Even if you had read in the sciences for a hundred years and summarized a thousand books, you would not have prepared for the mercy [of God] but through action. As God said: "[In the judgment of God] there is nought for man but his labors,"[14] and "whosoever hopes to meet God, let him do good works,"[15] and "[the houris in Paradise] will be recompense for what they have done,"[16] and "those that believe and do good deeds shall have the gardens of Paradise as their abode,"[17] and "those that repent and believe and do what is right [shall be admitted to Paradise]."[18]

المغرور أنه حين حصّل العلم إذا لم يعمل به تكون الحجة عليه آكَد، كما قال رسول الله ﷺ: « إنَّ أَشدَّ الناس عذابا يوم القيامة عالم لا ينفعه الله-تعالى-بعلمه ».

(٩) وروي أَنَّ الجنيد-قدس الله روحه العزيز-رُؤي في المنام بعد موته فقيل له: ما الخبر يا أبا القاسم؟

(١٠) قال: طاحت العبارات وفنيت الإشارات، ما نَفَعَتْنا إلاّ ركعات رَكَعناها في جوف الليل ».

(١١) أَيُّها الولد: لا تكن من الأعمال مفلسا ولا من الأَحوال خاليا، وتيقن أن العلم المجرد لا يأخذ اليد. مثاله لو كان على رجل في برية عشرةُ أسياف هنديةٍ مع أسلحة أخرى، ولو كان الرجل شجاعا وأهل حرب فحمل عليه أسد مهيب ما ظنك؟ هل تدفعُ الأَسلحة شره منه بلا استعمالها وضربها؟ من المعلوم أَنها لا تدفع إلا بالتحريك والضرب. وكذا لو قرأ رجلٌ مائة الفِ مسألةٍ علميةٍ علمها وتعلّمها ولم يعمل بها لا تفيده الاّ بالعمل. ومثاله لو كان لرجل حرارةٌ أو مرض صفراويٌ يكون علاجه بالسَّكَنْجَبين والكَشْكاب، فلا يحصل البرءُ إلا باستعمالها.

(١٢) شعر:

أگرمي دوهزار رطل پيمائي تامي نخوري نباشدت شيدائي

(١٣) ولو قرأت العلم مائة سنة وجمعت ألف كتاب لا تكون مستعدا للرحمة إلا بالعمل كما قال تعالى: ﴿وأن لَيسَ للإنسان إلا ما سعى﴾. ﴿فمن كان يرجو لقاء ربه فليعمل عملا صالحا﴾ ﴿جزاء بما كانوا يعملون﴾ ﴿جزاء بما كانوا يكسبون﴾ ﴿إن الذين آمنوا وعملوا الصالحات كانت لهم جنات الفردوس نزلا﴾ وآية ﴿إلا من تاب وآمن وعمل صالحا﴾

(14) And what do you say to this report from the Prophet: "Islam is built upon five [principles]: the testimony that there is no god but God and that Muḥammad is his prophet, the performance of prayer, the giving of alms, the fast of Ramaḍān, and the pilgrimage to the House[19] for those who are able."[20]

(15) Faith is spoken declaration, affirmation in the heart, performance of the basic requirements [of Islam], and proof of innumerable deeds. If the servant reaches Paradise through the bounty and munificence of God, that nonetheless comes only after he prepares himself through his obedience and worship, because "the mercy of God is within reach of the ones who do good deeds."[21] If someone were to say that [the believer] will reach Paradise through faith alone, we would say: "Yes, but when? How many precipitous paths await him before he arrives? The first of these is faith. Will he avoid being plundered and thus arriving empty-handed and destitute?"

(16) Al-Ḥasan [al-Bāṣrī][22] said: "On the Day of Resurrection God will say to his servants: 'enter the Garden by My mercy and divide it among yourselves according to your deeds.'"

(17) O Son! So long as you do not act, you will not be rewarded. It is told that a man of the Israelites worshipped God for seventy years, and then God designed to display him to the angels. So He sent to him an angel to tell him that despite his worship he remained unworthy [of Paradise]. When he heard this, the servant said: "We were created to worship God, so we should [continue to] worship Him." When the angel returned, he said: "Oh, God, You know better what he said." And God said: "Since he did not abandon worshipping us, We in Our beneficence will not abandon him. Bear witness, O angels, that I have pardoned his sins."

(18) The Prophet (blessings and peace upon him!) said: "Judge yourselves before you are judged; take measure of yourselves before you are measured."[23]

(19) ᶜAlī [ibn Abī Ṭālib][24] said: "The one who assumed he fell short in his efforts will reach [the afterlife] and be granted mercy, but the one who assumed he expended every effort will arrive and find himself challenged."

(20) Al-Ḥasan al-Bāṣrī (God have mercy on him!) said: "Expecting Paradise without having worked [for it] is one of the sins."

(21) And he said: "To know the true sense [of worship] is to stop thinking about the deed, but not to stop doing it."

(١٤) وماتقول في هذا الحديث: « بُنِيَ الاسلام على خمسٍ: شهادة أَنْ لا اله إلا الله وأنّ محمداً رسول الله، وإقامِ الصلاة، وإيتاء الزكاة، وصوم رمضان، وحجّ البيت من استطاع إليه سبيلا ».

(١٥) والإيمان قولٌ باللسان وتصديق بالجنان وعمل بالأركان ودليلُ الأعمال أكثرُ من أن يحصى، وإنْ كان العبد يبلغ الجنة بفضل الله تعالى وكرمه لكن بعد أن يستعد بطاعته وعبادته لأنّ « رحمة الله قريبٌ من المحسنين ». ولو قيل: يبلغ الجنة أيضا بمجرد الإيمان. قلنا: نعم، لكن متى يبلغ، وكم من عقبة كَؤودةٍ تستقبله إلى أن يصل؟ أوّلُ تلك العقباتِ عقبة الإيمان، هل يَسْلَمُ من السَّلْبِ أم لا؟ واذا وصل يكون خائبا مفلسا؟

(١٦) قال الحسن: « يقول الله تعالى لعباده يوم القيامة: ادخلوا الجنة برحمتي واقتسموها بأعمالكم ».

(١٧) أيها الولدُ: مالم تعمل لم تجد الأجر. حكي أنَّ رجلاً من بني إسرائيلَ عبدالله سبعين سنة فأراد الله أن يجلوه على الملائكة فأرسل إليه ملكا يخبره أنه مع تلك العبادة لا يليق به. فلما بلغه قال العابدُ: « نحن خُلقنا للعبادةِ فينبغي لنا أن نعبدهُ ». فلما رجع الملك قال: « إالهي أنت اعلمُ بما قال ». فقال الله تعالى: « إذا هو لم يُعرض عن عبادتنا فنحن مع الكرمِ لا نُعرِضُ عنه. اشهدوا يا ملائكتي أني قد غفرتُ له ».

(١٨) وقال رسول الله ﷺ: « حاسِبوا قبل ان تُحاسَبوا وزنوا قبل أن توزنوا ».

(١٩) وقال عليّ -رضي الله عنه-: « من ظنَّ أنه بدون الجهد يصل فهو متمنٍ، ومن ظنَّ أنه ببذل الجهد يصلُ فهو متعنت ».

(٢٠) وقال الحسن البصري -رحمه الله-: « طَلَب الجنَّة بلا عملٍ ذنبٌ من الذنوب ».

(٢١) وقال: « علمُ الحقيقة ترك ملاحظة العمل لا تركُ العمل ».

(22) The Prophet (blessings and peace upon him!) said: "The wise man constrains himself and works toward the afterlife; the fool indulges his appetites and pursues his desires in spite of God."[25]

(23) O Son! How many nights have you spent drilling yourself in knowledge and poring over books and denying yourself sleep? I do not know what is the motivation. If it is to gain worldly goods, to attract worldly ephemera, to acquire worldly appointments and compete with your peers and colleagues, then woe on you, and your judgment [in the hereafter]: woe on you! But if your aim in this is to reinvigorate the Prophet's law (blessings and peace upon him!), to rectify your moral principles, and to break the domination of your soul, then blessings upon you, and [in the hereafter]: blessings upon you! He spoke truly, the one who said:

Sleepless attention [to meet] another's standard makes for a wretch,
Crying over another's loss makes a hypocrite

(24) O Son! Live your life as you see fit, for you will surely die. Desire what you want, for you will surely depart. Do what you want, for you will surely pay for it. Gather up what you want, for you will surely leave it behind.

(25) O Son! What have you gained from studying theology, legal disputation, medicine, quotation books,[26] poetry, astrology, prosody, grammar, and morphology but a waste of your life? By God the Glorious! I have seen in the Gospel of Jesus[27] (peace upon him!) that he said: "From the time that the dead is readied for his funeral until he is placed at the lip of his grave, God in His glory asks him forty questions. In the first He says: 'My servant, you have appeared pure to your fellowman for years, but not to me for a single hour. Every day I look into your heart and say: 'Do you do not work for everyone but Me, though you be surrounded by *My* bounty?! Are you not deaf? Do you not hear?' "[28]

(26) O Son! Knowledge without action is sheer folly, but there is no action without knowledge. Know that any type of learning that does not distance you from sins and brings you back to obedience today will never remove you from the fire of hell tomorrow. When you do not act today, nor right your actions of past days, you will say tomorrow, on the Day of Resurrection: "Send us back to do good deeds!" and you will be told: "Oh, fool! You come now from there!"

(٢٢) وقال رسول الله ﷺ: «الكيّسُ مَنْ دان نفسه وعمل لما بعد الموتِ، والأحمقُ من أتبع نفسه هواها وتمنّى على الله تعالى».

(٢٣) أيها الولدُ: كم من ليالٍ أحييْتَها بتكرار العلم ومطالعة الكتب وحَرّمتَ على نفسك النومَ؟ لا أعلم ماكان الباعثُ فيه؟ إن كان نيل عرَض الدنيا وجذبَ حُطامها وتحصيل مناصبها والمباهاةَ على الاقرانِ والامثالِ فويلٌ لك، ثم حُكْمُكَ وَيلٌ لك، وإن كان قصدك فيه إحياءَ شريعة النبيّ ﷺ وتهذيب أخلاقك وكسر النفس الأمارةِ فطوبى لك ثم طوبى لك. ولقد صدق من قال شعراً:

سَهَرُ العيونِ لغير وجهكَ ضائعٌ   وبكا النفوسِ لغير فقدكَ باطلُ

(٢٤) أيها الولدُ: عِشْ ماشئتَ فإنكَ ميتٌ وأحببْ ماشئت فإنك مفارق. واعمل ماشِئْتَ فانك مجزيٌّ به، واجمع ماشئت فانك تاركه.

(٢٥) أيها الولدُ: أيُّ شيء حاصلكَ من تحصيل علم الكلام والخلاف والطب والدواوين والأشعار والنجومِ والعروضِ والنحو والتصريفِ غيرُ تضييع العمر. بجلال ذي الجلال اني رأيتُ في إنجيل عيسى-عليه السلام-قال: «من ساعة أن يوضع الميت على الجنازة إلى أن يوضع على شفير القبر يسألُ الله تعالى بعظمته منه أربعينَ سؤالاً. أوله يقول: عَبدي طهرت منظر الخلق في سنين وما طهرت منظري ساعة، كل يومٍ أنظر في قلبك. فيقول. ماتصنع لغيري فأنت محفوفٌ بخيري، أما أنت أصم لا تسمع.

(٢٦) أيها الولدُ: العلمُ بلا عملٍ جنونٌ، والعملُ بغير علمٍ لا يكونُ. واعلم أن علماً لا يبعدك اليوم عن المعاصي ولا يحملكَ على الطاعةِ لن يُبعدَك غدا عن نار جهنم. وإذا لم تعمل اليوم ولا تدارك الأيام الماضية تقولُ غداً، يوم القيامة: «فأرْجِعنا نعمل صالحًا» فيقال: «يا أحمق أنت من هناك تجيء».

(27) O Son! Put fervor in your spirit, resolution in your soul, and [the thought of] death in your body because your final resting place will be the cemetery, and those in their graves await you with every passing moment. Take care! Oh, take care not to arrive without provisions! Abū Bakr al-Ṣiddīq[29] (God be satisfied with him!) said: "These bodies are a cage for birds or[30] a stable for beasts of burden. Consider, which are you? If you are a high-flying bird, then when you hear the roll of drums, return, flying up until you come to rest on the highest tower of Paradise, as [the Prophet] (peace upon him!) said: 'The Throne of the Merciful rocked back and forth upon the death of Saᶜd ibn Muᶜādh.'[31] But God protect you if you are a beast of burden! As [God] said: 'Those are like cattle—indeed even more misguided; those are the careless.'[32] So do not feel so certain that you will not go from the asylum of Heaven to the abyss of Hell!"

(28) It is reported that al-Ḥasan al-Bāṣrī (God be satisfied with him!) was offered a drink of cool water, and when he took the cup he swooned and it fell from his hand. When he regained consciousness, he was asked: "What ails you, Abu Saᶜīd?" He responded: "I thought of the yearning of those in Hell when they ask those in Paradise to 'send down some water or anything else that God has provided you' and are told that God has forbidden both to those who disbelieved."

(29) O Son! If theoretical knowledge is enough for you and you have no need for action in addition, then would not [God's] summons, "Is there someone who asks? Is there someone seeking forgiveness? I forgive him. Is there someone repenting? I excuse him," be pointless and without benefit? It is reported that a group of Companions (God be satisfied with them all!) mentioned ᶜAbdallāh ibn ᶜUmar[33] in the presence of the Prophet (blessings and peace upon him!), who then said: "What an excellent man he would be if only he would pray at night!" And [the Prophet] (peace upon him!) said to one of his companions: "Oh, you! Do not sleep overmuch at night; for too much sleep at night makes one a pauper on the Day of Resurrection!"[34]

(30) O Son! "And pray during the night"[35] is a command. And "[the righteous] pray at dawn for God's forgiveness"[36] is a thanksgiving. And "those who ask God's forgiveness at dawn"[37] is a remembrance. He [peace be upon him!] said: "There are three voices that God loves: the voice of the rooster, the voice of the Quʾrān reciter, and the voices of those who seek God's forgiveness at dawn."

(٢٧) أيها الولدُ: اجعل الهمّة في الروح، والعزيمة في النفس، والموتَ في البدن، لأن منزلكَ المقبرةُ، وأهل القبور ينتظرونك في كل لحظةٍ متى تصل إليهم، إياك ثم إياك أن تصير بلا زاد. قال أبو بكر الصديق -رضي الله عنه-: «هذه الأجسادُ قَفَصُ الطيور واصطبل الدواب فتفكر في نفسك من أيهما أنت؟ إن كنت من الطيور العلوية فحين تسمع طنين طبل ارجعي، تطير صاعداً إلى أن تقعد في أعلى بروج الجنان كما قال -عليه السلام-: «اهتز عرش الرحمن من موت سعد بن معاذ». والعياذ بالله إن كنت من الدواب كما قال: «أولَئِكَ كَالْأَنعَامِ بَلْ هُم أَضَلُّ، أولَئِكِ هُمُ الْغَافِلُون». فلا تأمن من انتقالك من زاوية الدار إلى هاوية النار.

(٢٨) وروي أن الحسن البصري -رضي الله عنه- أُعطِيَ شربَةَ من ماءٍ باردٍ، فلما أخذ القدح غُشي عليه وسقط من يده. فلما أفاق قيل له: «مالك يا أبا سعيد؟». قال: ذكرت أُمنيَّةَ أهل النار حين يقولون لأهل الجنة: «أن أفِيضُوا عَلَيْنَا مِنَ الْمَاءِ أَوْ مِمَّا رَزَقَكُمُ اللهُ، قَالُوا إنَّ اللهَ حَرَّمَهُمَا عَلَى الْكَافِرِينَ».

(٢٩) أيُّها الولد: إن كان العلمُ المجرَّدُ كافياً لك ولا تحتاج إلى عملٍ سواه لكان نداء «هل من سائلٍ؟ وهل من مستغفرٍ فغفرت له؟ فهل من تائبٍ أتوب عليه؟» إلا ضائعاً بلا فائدة. وروي أن جماعة من الصحابة -رضوان الله عليهم أجمعين- ذكروا عبد الله بن عمر عند رسول الله ﷺ قال: «نعم الرجل هو لو كان يصلي بالليل». وقال -عليه السلام- لرجل من أصحابه: «يا فلان لا تكثر النوم بالليالي، فان كثرة النوم بالليل يدع صاحبه فقيراً يوم القيامة».

(٣٠) أيها الولد: «ومِنَ اللَّيْلِ فَتَهَجَّدْ بِهِ» أمرٌ، «وبِالْأَسحَارِ هُمْ يَسْتَغْفِرُون» شكر، «وَالْمُسْتَغْفِرِينَ بِالْأَسْحَارِ» ذكر. قال -عليه السلام-: «ثلاثة أصوات يحبها الله تعالى: صوت الديك، وصوتُ الذي يقرأ القرآن، وصوتُ المستغفرين بالأسحار».

(31) Sufyān al-Thawrī[38] (may God be satisfied with him!) said: "God causes the dawn wind to blow, carrying pious remembrances and appeals for forgiveness to Him, the King, the Mighty." He also said: "When someone calls out at the beginning of the night from under the throne [of God], 'Will not the believers arise?' they rise up and pray as long as God[39] wills. Then [when he] calls out in the middle of the night, 'Will not the pious arise?' they rise up and pray until dawn. When he calls out at dawn, 'Will not the repentant arise?' they rise up, seeking forgiveness. And when he calls out at daybreak 'Will not the negligent arise?' they rise up from their beds like the dead scattering from their graves."

(32) O Son! It is reported in the counsels of Luqmān[40] the Wise to his son that he said: "O my son! Do not let the rooster be more clever than yourself by crowing at dawn while you sleep on!" He certainly spoke well, the one who said:

Surely the pigeon in the tree had cooed
In the thick of night, while I slumbered on.

I lied [when I swore], 'By God's house! If I really love [Him]
The pigeons will not cry before me!'

I maintain that I am mad in love, possessed of passion for my Lord
But I do not cry when the beasts do!

(33) O Son! The sum total of learning is to know the meaning of obedience and service [to God].

(34) Know that to obey and serve is to follow in word and deed the commands and prohibitions of the Law-Giver. This means that everything you say and do and forswear in word and deed[41] is guided by the Law, just as though were you to fast on the day of the Feast of Sacrifice[42] and the last three days of the Hajj[43] you would be disobedient, or were you to pray in a stolen robe, albeit the outward form [of your prayers] would be worship, you would nonetheless have sinned.

(35) O Son! Your words and actions should be in accordance with the Law, since knowing and acting without observing the Law is to go astray and become lost. You should not let yourself be dazzled by the ecstatic locutions and outcries of the Sufis,[44] because following this path [that I outline here] requires you to strive, to cut short the passions of the soul and to slay its whims with the sword of discipline; [it is not earned] with pointless outcries and vain statements. Know that the

(٣١) قال سفيان الثوري -رضي الله عنه-: « إنَّ الله يهبّ الريح بالأسحار تحمل الأذكار والاستغفار الى الملك الجبار ». وقال أيضا: « إذا كان أول الليل ينادي منادٍ من تحت العَرْش: ألا لِيَقُم العابدون، فيقومون ويصلون إلى ما شاء الله. ثم ينادي منادٍ في شطر الليل. ألا ليقم القانتون، فيقومون ويصلون إلى السَّحَر. فإذا كان السحر نادى منادٍ: الا ليقم المستغفرون فيقيمون ويستغفرون. فإذا طلع الفجر نادى منادٍ: أَلا ليقم الغافلون فيقومون من فرشهم كالموتى نشروا من قبورهم.

(٣٢) أيها الولدُ: روي في وصايا لقمان الحكيم لابنه أنه قال: « يابني لا يكوننّ الديك أكيس منك فينادي بالأسحار وأنت نائم ». لقد أحسن مَنْ قال شعراً:

لقد هتفَت في جنح ليلٍ حمامةٌ   على فَنَنٍ وهْناً وإني لنائمُ
كَذَبْتُ وبيتِ اللهِ لوكنْتُ عاشقًا   لما سَبَقَتْني بالبكاءِ الحمائمُ
وأزعُمُ أَني هائمٌ ذو صبابةٍ   لربي، ولا أبكي وتبكي البهائمُ

(٣٣) أيّها الولد: خلاصة العلم أَن تعلم الطاعة والعبادة ماهي.

(٣٤) إعلم أن الطاعة والعبادةَ متابعةُ الشارع في الأوامر والنواهي بالقول والفعل يعني: كل ما تقول وتفعل وتترك قولا وفعلا يكون باقتداء الشرع كما لوصُمْتَ يوم العيد وأيام التشريق تكون عاصيا، أو صليت في ثوب مغصوبٍ وان كانت صورته عبادةً، تأثم.

(٣٥) أيها الولد: فينبغي لك أن يكون قولك وفعلك موافقا للشرع إذ العلم والعمل بلا اقتداء الشرع ضلالة وتياهة. وينبغي لك أن لا تغتر بشطح حُطاماتِ الدنيا وطامات الصوفية لأن سلوك هذه الطريق يكون بالمجاهدة وقطع شهوة النفس وقتل هواها بسيف الرياضة لا بالطامات والترهات واعلم أن اللسان المطلق

unrestrained tongue and the heart engulfed and filled with negligence and desire are marks of misery, so much so that unless you kill your soul by means of earnest endeavor, you will never revive your heart through the light of knowledge.

(36) Know that some of the questions which you asked me cannot be given a proper response in writing or speech. In fact, if you have already reached that state, then you know well what it is. Otherwise it cannot be understood; for it is a question of experience,[45] and no experience can be adequately described in words. The sweetness or bitterness of something cannot be known but through the experience of taste. [This is like] the story of the impotent man who wrote to a friend: "Tell me about the pleasure of sex." And the friend wrote in response: "Oh, you! I thought you were merely impotent; now I know that you are also a fool! This pleasure is a question of experience. If you get it, you know; if not, it cannot be described by speaking or writing [about it]."

(37) O Son! Some of your questions are like this. Others can be given a proper response. In fact, we have discussed [these issues] in *The Revival of the Religious Sciences* and elsewhere, but we will recount here some selections, directing attention to them by saying: First of all, a sound belief contains no innovation. Second, you do not slip up after *sincerely* repenting.[46] Third, [you should] seek reconciliation with your opponents so that none any longer has just cause against you. Fourth, [you should] acquire knowledge of the Divine Law in such a measure that you will be led to the commandments of God. Then [you should be acquiring] any other knowledge that [may provide you] with redemption.

(38) It is recounted that after al-Shiblī[47] (may God be pleased with him!) had served four hundred masters, he said: "I read four thousand reports of the Prophet, then selected one to put into practice and let the others go, because once I had reflected on it, I found that it contained my ultimate goal and salvation and that arrayed in it was the knowledge of all the early and later [believers], so it was sufficient for me. It is this: The Prophet (peace upon him!) said to one of his companions: 'Do as much in your world as befits your station in it; do as much for your afterlife as befits the time you [hope to] remain there; do as much for God as befits your need for him; and do as much for the fire of hell as befits your ability to endure it.'"

والقلب المطبق المملوءَ بالغفلة والشهوة علامات الشقاوة حتى لا تقتل نفسك بصدق المجاهدة، لن تحيي قلبك بأنوار المعرفة.

(٣٦) واعلم أن بعض مسائلك التي سألتني لا يستقيم جوابه بالكتابة والقول بل أن تبلغ تلك الحالة فتعرف ما هو وإلا فعلمه من المستحيلات لأنه ذوقي وكل ما يكون ذوقيا لا يستقيم وصفه بالقول كحلاوة الحلو ومرارة المرّ لا تعرف الا بالذوق كما حكي ان عنيناً كتب الى صاحب له: عرفني لذة المجامعة كيف تكون؟ فكتب في جوابه: يا فلانُ إني كنت حسبتك عنيناً فقط، الآن عرفت أنك عنين وأحمقُ. إنَّ هذه اللذة ذوقية إنْ تَصِلْ إليها تعرفْ وإلا لا يستقيم وصفُها بالقول والكتابة.

(٣٧) أيها الولدُ: بعض مسائلك من هذه القبيل، وأما البعض الذي يستقيم له الجواب فقد ذكرناه في «إحياء العلوم» وغيره، ونذكرهنا منه نبذاً ونشير إليه فنقول: أول ألامر: اعتقاد صحيحٌ لا تكون فيه بدعةٌ. والثاني: توبةٌ نصوح لا ترجع بعدها إلى الزلة. والثالث: استرضاء الخصوم حتى لا يبقى لاحد عليك حق. والرابع: تحصيل علم الشريعة قدر ما تؤدي به أَوامِرَ الله تعالى، ثم من العلوم الأُخَر ما يكون فيه النجاة.

(٣٨) حُكي أن الشبلي -رضي الله عنه- خدم أربعمائة استاذ وقال: قرأتُ أربعة آلاف حديثٍ ثم اخترتُ منها حديثا واحداً عملت به وخليت ما سواه لاني تأملته فوجدت خلاصي ونجاتي فيه، وكان علمُ الأولينَ والآخرين كلهُ مندرجاً فيه، فاكتفيتُ به. وذلك أن رسول الله ﷺ قال لبعض أصحابه: «اعمل لدنياك بقدر مُقامك فيها واعمل لآخرتك بقدر بقائك فيها، واعمل لله بقدر حاجتك اليه، واعمل للنار بقدر صبرك عليها».

(39) O Son! Once you act upon this report from the Prophet, you will no longer have need for so much learning. Consider another story. Ḥātim al-Asamm was a friend of Shaqīq al-Balkhī.[48] [Shaqīq] asked him one day: "You have kept my company for thirty years; what have you acquired in that time?" [Ḥātim] said: "I have acquired eight lessons in knowledge, and they are enough for me, because with them I look forward to my ultimate goal and salvation." Shaqīq said: "What are they?" And Ḥātim al-Asamm responded: "The first lesson is that I observed mankind and saw that every person has a beloved whom he loves and desires. Some of those beloved ones accompany him to the final illness, and some to the lip of the grave, but then all return and leave him alone; none enter with him into his grave. So I thought to myself and said: 'The best beloved of man is whatever will join him in his grave and give him comfort there.' And I found that [that] is good deeds alone, so I took them into my house as my beloved so that they might be a light in my grave, keeping me comfort, not leaving me alone.

(40) "The second lesson is that I saw that people worship their caprices and leap up to serve their souls' desires. So I reflected on God's word: 'He who fears to stand before his Lord and who denies his soul its whims shall have his refuge in Paradise,'[49] and I became convinced that the Quʾrān is true and sincere. I would regularly leap up to oppose my soul and hasten to fight it and refuse to cede to its whims until it had been curbed and trained to obey God.

(41) "The third lesson is that I saw everyone trying to gather up their ephemeral gains and then[50] hold them back in tight fists. So I reflected on God's word: 'What you have will dwindle away, while what God has will last forever,'[51] and then I gave away my earnings and distributed it to the poor so that it might be stored up for me with God.

(42) "The fourth lesson is that I saw that some people believe that their prestige and eminence lie in the large number of their relatives and kin, and they let themselves be dazzled by that, while others put stock in their great amount of wealth and children, and boast about that. According to some, eminence and prestige lie in extorting, oppressing, and slaughtering people, while another group believes that [eminence and prestige] lie in merging, dispersing, and distributing wealth. So I reflected on God's word, 'The noblest of you in God's judgment is the most devout,'[52] and I chose piety and determined that the Quʾrān is true and correct and all their convictions and beliefs utterly false.

(٣٩) أيها الولدُ: إذا عملت بهذا الحديث لا حاجة لك إلى العلم الكثير. وتأمل في حكاية أخرى وذلك أن حاتم الأصم كان من أصحاب شقيق البلخي فسأله يوما وقال: صاحبتني منذ ثلاثين سنة ما حصل لك فيها؟ قال: حصلت ثماني فوائد من العلم وهي تكفيني منه، لأني ارجو خلاصي ونجاتي فيها. فقال شقيق: ما هي؟ قال حاتم الأصم: الفائدة الاولى: أني نظرت إلى الخلق فرأيت لكل منهم محبوبا ومعشوقا يحبه ويعشقه، وبعض ذلك المحبوب يصاحبه إلى مرض الموت وبعضه يصاحبه الى شفير القبر ثم يرجع كله ويتركه فريدا وحيدا ولا يدخلُ معه في قبره منهم أحد فتفكرت وقلت: أفضل محبوب المرء ما يدخل معه في قبره ويؤنسه فيه، فما وجدته إلا الأعمال الصالحة فاتخذتها محبوبةً في بيتي لتكون سراجاً في قبري وتؤنسني فيه ولا تتركني فريدا.

(٤٠) الفائدة الثانية: أنّي رأيتُ الخَلْقَ يَعْبُدونَ أهواءَهم ويبادرون إلى مرادات أنفسهم فتأملت في قوله تعالى: ﴿وأمّا مَنْ خَافَ مَقَامَ رَبِّهِ وَنَهَى النَّفْسَ عَنِ الْهَوَى فإنَّ الجنَّةَ هِيَ الْمَأْوَىٰ﴾ وتيقنت أن القرآن حقٌّ صادق فبادرت إلى خلاف نفسي وتشمرت إلى مجاهدتها وما متعتها بهواها حتى ارتاضت لطاعة اللهِ وانقادت.

(٤١) الفائدة الثالثة: أني رأيت كل واحدٍ من الناس يسعى في جمع حطام الدنيا ثم كما يجمع يمسكه قابضا يده، فتأملت في قوله تعالى: ﴿مَا عِندَكُم يَنفَدُ وما عِندَ اللهِ بَاقٍ﴾ فبذلت محصولي ففرقته بين المساكين ليكون ذخرًا لي عند اللهِ تعالى.

(٤٢) الفائدة الرابعة: أني رأيت بعض الخلق يظن شَرَفَه وعِزَّه في كثرة الأقوام والعشائر فاغترّ بهم، وزعم آخرون في كثرة الأموال وكثرة الأولاد فافتخروا بها، وحسب بعضهم العز والشرف في غَصْبِ أموال الناس وظلمهم وسفك دمائهم، واعتقدت طائفة أنه في إتلاف المال وإسرافه وتبذيره فتأملت في قوله تعالى: ﴿إنّ أَكْرَمَكُم عِندَ الله أتقاكم﴾ فاخترت التقوى واعتقدت أن القرآن حقٌّ صادق فظنهم وحسابهم كلها باطل زائل.

(43) "The fifth lesson is that I saw people slandering and maligning one another, and I found the root of that to be envy over money, rank, and knowledge. So I reflected on God's word, 'It is We who portion out to them their livelihood in this world,'[53] and I knew that this apportionment was the pre-eternal determination of God. So I did not envy anyone, satisfied as I was with God's distribution.

(44) "The sixth lesson is that I saw people feuding with one another for one reason or another. So I reflected on God's word, 'Satan is your enemy, so treat him as an enemy,'[54] and I knew that fighting with anyone but Satan was unacceptable.

(45) "The seventh lesson is that I saw everyone striving assiduously and struggling excessively in pursuit of sustenance and livelihood, so much so that they would err and transgress [against the Law], debase themselves, and demean their worth. So I reflected on God's word, 'God provides for every single creature on earth,'[55] and I knew that God had vouchsafed for me my sustenance. Then I turned my attention to worshipping [Him] and stopped depending on anyone else.

(46) "The eighth lesson is that I saw everyone relying on something created, whether it be money, or possessions and property, or vocations and skills, or some such created thing. So I reflected on God's word, 'The one who relies on God completely knows that God attains His purpose; God has measured out the worth of everything,'[56] and I put all of my trust in God. He is sufficient for me—what an excellent trustee!"

(47) Shaqīq said: "God grant you success! I have pored over the Torah, the Gospel, the Psalms, and the Quʾrān and found that all four books revolve around these eight lessons. Whoever puts into practice these lessons puts into practice these books."

(48) O Son! You have learned from these two narratives that you do not need to increase your knowledge. Now I will explain to you what is required of the traveller in search of truth.

(٤٣) الفائدة الخامسة: أني رأيت الناس يذم بعضهم بعضا ويغتابه فوجدت ذلك من الحسد في المال والجاه والعلم فتأملت في قوله تعالى: ﴿نَحْنُ قَسَمْنَا بَيْنَهُم مَّعِيشَتَهُمْ فِي الْحَيَاةِ الدُّنْيَا﴾ فعلمت أن القسمة كانت من الله تعالى في الأزل فما حَسَدْتُ أحداً ورضيت بقسمة الله تعالى.

(٤٤) الفائدة السادسة: أني رأيت الناس يعادي بعضهم بعضا لغرضٍ وسبب فتأملت في قوله تعالى: ﴿إِنَّ الشَّيْطَانَ لَكُمْ عَدُوٌّ فَاتَّخِذُوه عَدُوًّا﴾ فعلمت أنه لا تجوز عداوة أحد غير الشيطان.

(٤٥) الفائدة السابعة: أني رأيت كل واحد يسعى بجد ويجتهد بمبالغة لطلبِ القوت والمعاش بحيث يقع في شبهة وحرام ويذل نفسه وينقص قدره، فتأملت في قوله تعالى: ﴿وَمَا مِن دَابَّةٍ فِي الْأَرْضِ إِلَّا عَلَى اللهِ رِزْقُها﴾ فعلمت أنَّ رزقي على الله وقد ضمنه فاشتغلت بعبادته وقطعت طمعي عمن سواه.

(٤٦) الفائدة الثامنة: أني رأيت كل أحد معتمدا إلى شيء مخلوقٍ بعضهم الى الدينار والدرهم وبعضهم إلى المال والملك، وبعضهم إلى الحرفة والصناعة، وبعضهم إلى مخلوق مثله، فتأملت في قوله تعالى: ﴿وَمَن يَتَوَكَّل عَلَى اللهِ فَهُوَ حَسْبُه إِنَّ اللهَ بَالِغُ أَمْرِه قَدْ جَعَلَ اللهُ لِكُلِّ شَيْءٍ قَدَرًا﴾، فتوكلت على الله فهو حسبي ونعم الوكيل.

(٤٧) فقال شقيق: وفقك الله تعالى، إني قد نظرت التوراة والانجيل والزبور والفرقان فوجدت الكتب الأربعة تدور على هذه الفوائد الثمانية، فمن عمل بها كان عاملا بهذه الكتب.

(٤٨) أيها الولدُ: قد علمتَ من هاتين الحكايتين أنَّك لا تحتاجُ إلى تكثيرِ العلم. والآن أُبينُ لك ما يجبُ على سالك سبيل الحق:

(49) Know that the traveller must have a master, a guide, a teacher to drive out his evil dispositions and replace them with good. Educating is akin to what the farmer does when he uproots the thorn bushes, and weeds out the coarse plants from around the crops to ensure that they will grow well and reach their fruition. The traveller must have a master to educate him and guide him to the path of God. A prerequisite of the master who is worthy to serve as the Prophet's proxy is that he be learned; but not just any learned person is worthy. Let me explain to you in a summary fashion some of [such a teacher's] characteristics, lest just anyone persuade [you] that he is a guide.

(50) Anyone who relinquishes love of this world and worldly status, having followed a wise master whose spiritual descent stretches back unbroken to the most eminent of creation, the Prophet (peace be upon him!), and who has trained his soul well through little food, speech, and sleep, and much prayer, almsgiving, and fasting, and who then, by following that wise master, has fashioned from his refined virtues a particular path, such as the path of patience, thanksgiving, trust in God, conviction, generosity, contentment, serenity, astuteness, modesty, learning, honesty, reserve, fidelity, sobriety, sedateness, deliberation, and other such qualities, then he is one of the Prophet's lights and worthy of emulation. However, such a one is rare, and more magnificent than gold. The one whose good fortune leads him to find and accept the master we describe should accord him due honor outwardly and inwardly.

(51) To honor him outwardly means to neither contest him nor distract him by arguing with him over any issue, even if [you] know he is wrong. [It means] not putting his prayer rug before him except at the call to prayer, and when he is finished, removing it. [It means] not overdoing the superogatory prayers in his presence. [It means] doing what he orders competently and obediently. To honor him inwardly means that everything [you] hear and accept from him externally [you] do not question inwardly, whether in deed or word, lest [you] be branded a hypocrite. If [you] cannot do this, leave his company, lest what [you] think comes to conform with what [you] do. [It means] guarding against the company of the wicked in order to drain the power of satanic jinn and men from the bowl of [your] heart, that it may be washed of malevolent pollution. [It means] that in every instance poverty is to be preferred over wealth.

(٤٩) واعلم أنه ينبغي للسالك شيخ مرشدٌ مُربٍ ليخرجَ الاخلاقَ السوءَ منه ويجعلَ مكانها خُلُقا حسنا. ومعنى التربية يُشبه فِعلَ الفلاح الذي يقلع الشوكَ ويخرجُ النباتاتِ الخشنةَ من بين الزرع ليحسنَ نباته ويكمَلَ ريعه. ولا بدَّ للسالك من شيخ يُربيه ويرشِدُه الى سبيل الله تعالى. وشرطُ الشيخ الذي يَصلح أن يكونَ نائبا للرسول ﷺ أن يكون عالمًا، لا أنَّ كل عالم يَصلحُ له. وإني لأُبين لك بعضَ علاماتهِ على سبيل الإجمالِ حتى لا يدَّعي كلُّ احدٍ أنه مرشده، فنقول:

(٥٠) من يُعرض عن حبّ الدنيا وحُبّ الجاه، وكان قد تابع لشيخٍ بصيرٍ تَتَسلسلُ متابعتهُ الى سيّد المرسلين ﷺ، وكان مُحسناً رياضةَ نفسه من قلةِ الأكلِ والقولِ والنَّومِ وكثرةِ الصلاةِ والصَّدقة والصَّوم، فكان بمتابعة الشيخ البصير جاعلاً محاسِنَ الاخلاق له سيرةً كالصَّبرِ والشُّكرِ والتوكُّلِ واليقين والسخاوةِ والقناعة وطُمأنينةِ النّفسِ والحِلْمِ والتواضع والعلم والصدق والحياء والوفاء والوقار والسكون والتأني وأمثالها، فهو نورٌ من أنوار النبي ﷺ يَصلحُ الاقتداءُ به لكن وجودَ مِثله نادرٌ أعزُّ من الكبريت الأحمر. ومَنْ ساعدتْه السعادةُ أنْ يجدَ الشيخَ كما ذكرناه، وقَبِله، ينبغي أنْ يحترمه ظاهرًا وباطنا.

(٥١) أمّا احترامُ الظاهرفأن لا يجادلهُ ولا يشغله بالاحتجاج معه في كلّ مسألةٍ وإن علم خطأه. ولا يُلقي بين يديه سجادَته الاَّ وقتَ أداء الصلاة فاذا فرغ يرفعُها. ولا يُكثرنوافلَ الصلاة بحضرته. ويعمل ما يأمُره الشيخُ من العمل بقدرِ وُسْعهِ وطاقته. اما احترام الباطن فهو أنْ كلَّ ما يسمع ويَقبلُ منه في الظاهر لا يُنكره في الباطن لا فِعلاً ولا قولاً لئلا يتَّسِمَ بالنفاق، وانْ لم يستطعْ يترُك صُحبته إلاّ أنْ يوافقَ باطنهُ ظاهره. ويحترز مجالسةَ الصاحب السّوء ليقصُرَ عن ولاية شياطين الجن والانس من صحن قلبه فيُصفّى عن لَوْثة الشيطانية وعلى كل حال يختارُ الفقرعلى الغنى.

(52) Next, know that being a Sufi requires two characteristics: rectitude[57] and forbearance with people. The one who seeks to be upright and virtuous with people and treats them with equanimity is a Sufi. Being upright is to sacrifice one's portion for someone else. Being virtuous with people [means] not imposing your wants upon others but rather imposing their wants upon yourself—as long as they do not contradict the Law.

(53) Then you asked me about how to serve God. There are three things. The first is to uphold the Law. The second is to be satisfied with the divine foreordination, decree, and apportionment. The third is to trust in God completely, which means that your belief in what God has promised is firmly grounded; in other words, you believe that what He has foreordained for you will assuredly come to you, even if anyone in the world were to try to divert it from you, and that whatever was not decreed for you, you will never obtain, even if the whole world were to aid you.

(54) You also asked me about sincere devotion to God. It is that all of your deeds are done for God and that your heart is not satisfied with what people deem praiseworthy or reprehensible. Know that hypocrisy is born of glorifying people and the cure for it is to see them as laughably incapable,[58] to judge them to be like inanimate objects in their lack of ability to attain to either contentment or misery, so that you may rid yourself of their hypocrisies. If you judge them to be possessed of power and will, hypocrisy will never be far from you.

(55) O Son! Some of your remaining questions are treated in my writings, so look [for the answers] there. Others it is unlawful to write. Do what you know so that what you do not know may become clear to you.

(56) O Son! In the future, do not ask me about what is obscure to you but through your heart,[59] because God says: "If they had waited until you went out to them, it would have been better for them."[60]

(57) Take the advice of Khiḍr[61] (peace upon him!): "Do not ask me about anything until I myself mention it to you."[62] Do not be impatient for [your questions] to be answered. Have you not seen [God's word]: "You will soon see My signs, so be not impatient"?[63] Do not ask before the appropriate time, and be certain that it is by the right paths that you arrive, for God said: "Did [the prophets] not travel the land and see the end of those who came before them?"[64]

(٥٢) ثم اعلم أنَّ التصوف له خصلتان: الاستقامةُ والسكونُ من الخَلق، فمن استقام وأحسن خُلُقَهَ بالناس وعاملهم بالحِلْمِ فهو صُوفي. والاستقامةُ أنْ يَفْدِي حَظَّ نفسه لنفسه. وحُسْنُ الخُلُقِ بالناس أنْ لا تَحْمِلَ الناسَ على مرادِ نفسك، بل تحمل نَفسك على مُرادِهم مالم يُخالفوا الشرع.

(٥٣) ثم إنك سألتني عن العُبودية وهي ثلاثةُ أشياء: أحَدُها: محافظةُ أمْرِ الشَّرْع. وثانيها: الرضاءُ بالقضاء والقدر وقسمةِ الله تعالى. وثالثُها: تَرْكُ رضاء نفسك في طلب رضاء الله تعالى. وسألتني عن التوكل: هو أن تستحكمَ اعتقادك بالله تعالى فيما وَعَدَ، يعني تعتقدُ أن ما قُدّر لك سَيصلُ اليك لا محالة، وإن اجتهدَ من في العالم على صَرْفِه عنك وما لم يُكتب لك لن تَصل اليه وإنْ ساعدك جميعُ العالم.

(٥٤) وسألتني عن الإخلاص وهو أنْ تكونَ أعمالك كُلُّها لله تعالى، ولا يرتاحُ قلبك بمحامدِ الناس ولا بمذامتهم واعلم أنَّ الرياءَ يتولدُ من تعظيم الخَلْق. وعلاجُه أنْ تراهم مسخّري القدرة وتحسبهم كالجمادات في عَدَم قُدرةٍ على إيصال الراحة والمشقة لتخلص من مراءاتهم. ولو تحسبُهم ذوي قُدرة وإرادة لن يَبْعُدَ عنك الرياء.

(٥٥) أيها الولدُ: الباقي من مسائلك بعضُها مسطور في مصنفاتي فاطلبه ثَمَّةَ، فكتابةُ بَعضِها حرام. اعمل أنت بما تعلم لينكشفَ لك مالم تَعلم.

(٥٦) أيها الولدُ: بعد اليوم لا تسألني ما أشكل عليك إلا بلسان الجنان لقوله تعالى: ﴿وَلَوْ أَنَّهُمْ صَبَرُوا حَتَّىٰ تَخْرُجَ إِلَيْهِمْ لَكَانَ خَيْرًا لَّهُمْ﴾.

(٥٧) واقبل نصيحة الخِضْرِ -عليه السلام-: « فلا تَسْأَلْني عن شيءٍ حتى أُحْدِثَ لك مِنْه ذكرا ». ولا تَستعجِلْ حتى تبلغ أوانه يُكشف لك. وأرأيتَ « سأريكُم آياتي فلا تَسْتَعجِلُون ». فلا تسأل قبل الوقت وتيقَّنْ أنَّك لا تَصِلُ إلاّ بالسير لقوله تعالى: ﴿أَفَلَمْ يَسِيرُوا فِي الْأَرْضِ فَيَنْظُرُوا كَيْفَ كَانَ عَاقِبَةُ الَّذِينَ مِنْ قَبْلِهِمْ؟﴾

(58) O Son! By God, if you journey, you will see the wonders at every station.[65] Expend your spirit; for the beginning [of this journey] is the surrender of the spirit, as Dhū al-Nūn al-Mīṣrī[66] (God have mercy on him!) said to one of his students: "If you are able to surrender your spirit, then off we go! Otherwise do not bother yourself with the barren deserts of the Sufis!"

(59) O Son! I will advise you of eight things. Accept them lest your deeds turn against you on the Day of Resurrection. Four you must do and four avoid.

(60) Among those to avoid, the first is that you not dispute with anyone on just any issue you are able, because there is much harm and a greater sin than benefit in that, since it is the source of all reprehensible qualities such as hypocrisy, envy, haughtiness, resentment, enmity, pride, and so on. In fact, if a question came up between you and an individual or group and you wanted the truth to be set forth and not missed, then discussion would be permissible, but two conditions are required: first, that it makes no difference whether the truth be explained by you or someone else; and second, that private discussion be more preferable to you than public discussion.

(61) Listen, and I will give you a useful pointer here. Know that asking about intricate problems evinces a sickness in the heart to the doctor, and the response is to try to remedy the illness. Know that the ignorant are the ones sick at heart and the learned are the doctors.[67] The scholar lacking in knowledge does not administer cures well, and the consummate scholar does not cure just every sick person; rather he cures only someone whom he hopes will be receptive to the cure and remedy. When the root cause is chronic or fatal, the cure will be ineffectual, so the acumen of the doctor then lies in saying that this is unresponsive to the remedy, so there is no point to administering medicines because that would be a waste of [the patient's remaining] life.

(62) Next, know that there are four types of illness due to ignorance, one alone is receptive to cure, the remainder incurable. The first incurable illness [is that of] someone whose questioning and challenging comes from his envy and hatred. The better, more clear, and more understandable the response he is given, the more enraged and resentful he becomes. The solution, then, is not to bother to respond, [as in the line of] poetry:

You may hope to dispel all enmity
Excepting that of the one who hates you out of envy.

(٥٨) أيها الولدُ: بالله أن تسيرَ ترالعجائبَ في كلِّ منزل. ابذُلْ روحك وإن رأسَ هذا الامر بذلُ الروح كما قال ذو النون المصري-رحمه الله-لأحد من تلامذتِهِ: «إن قدرتَ على بذل الروح فتعال والا فلا تشتغل بترّهات الصوفية».

(٥٩) أيها الولدُ: إنّي أنصحك بثمانيةِ أشياءَ، اقبلها مني لئلا يكونَ عملك خَصْماً عليك يومَ القيامة. تَعملُ منها أربعةً وَتدعُ منها أربعة.

(٦٠) أما اللواتي تَدع: أحدها: أنْ لا تناظرَ أحداً في مسألةٍ مااستطعتَ، لانَّ فيها آفةً كثيرةً، وإثمها أكبرُ من نفعها، إذ هي مَنبع كلِّ خُلُقٍ ذَميمٍ كالرياء والحسد والكِبر والحقدِ والعداوةِ والمباهاةِ وغيرها. نعم لو وَقع مسألة بينك وبين شخصٍ أو قومٍ وكان إرادتُك فيها أن يظهر الحقُّ ولا يضيع جازَ البحثُ لكن لتلك الإرادة علامتان: إحداهما: ان لا تُفرِّق بين أن يُكشف الحقُّ على لسانك أو على لسان غيرك. والثانية: أنْ يكونَ البحثُ في الخَلاء أحبَّ اليك من أنْ يكون في الملاء.

(٦١) واسمع أني أذكرلك هنا فائدة: اعلم أنَّ السؤال عن المشكلاتِ عَرْضُ مَرَضِ القَلْبِ إلى الطبيب والجواب فيه سَعْيٌ لإصلاح مَرضه. واعلم أنَّ الجاهلين المرضى قُلوبُهم، العلماءَ الأطباء. والعالِمَ الناقصَ لا يحسنُ المعالجةَ، والعالِمَ الكاملَ لا يُعالج كلَّ مريضٍ بل يُعالج مَنْ يرجو فيه قَبولَ المعالجة والصلاح. وإذا كانت العلة مزمنة أو عقيماً لا يقبل العلاج فحذاقةُ الطبيب فيه أن يقولَ: هذا لا يقبل العلاجَ فلا يَشتغل بمداواته لأن فيه تضييعَ العُمر.

(٦٢) ثم اعلم أنَّ مَرضَ الجهل على أربعة أنواع: أحدها يقبلُ العلاجَ والباقي لا يقبل العلاج، أما الذي لا يقبلُ: أحدُها: مَنْ كان سؤاله واعتراضه من حَسَدِه وبغضه، فكلما يُجيبه بأحسنِ الجواب وأفصحِه وأوضحِهِ لا يزيد له ذلك إلاَ غيظاً وحسداً. فالطريق لا تشتغل بجوابه. شعر:

كلُّ العداوةِ قَدْ تُرجى ازالتِها ... إلا عداوةَ من عَاداك عن حَسَدِ

You should turn away and leave him with his disease. God says: "Pay no heed to someone who ignores what We say and who wants only the life of this world."[68] The one who is envious in all he says and does kindles a fire in the field of his deeds, as the Prophet (peace be upon him!) said: "Envy devours the good the way fire eats through wood."[69]

(63) The second [type of illness due to ignorance] has its root cause in stupidity, and it also cannot be treated, as Jesus (peace upon him!) said: "Even though I managed to raise the dead, I have never been able to cure an idiot!"

(64) [The idiot] is someone who devotes himself to learning for a brief time and studies a little of the rational and religious sciences and then questions and contends, not knowing anything but what is difficult for him is also difficult for the great scholar. Whenever he does not take the time to reflect in this way, his questioning and challenging being the result of idiocy, one should not bother responding to him.

(65) The third [type of illness due to ignorance is that of] someone seeking guidance who, whenever he does not understand the words of the great leaders, lays the blame on his inability to understand. Although he asks in search of aid, he is too stupid to grasp the truths. One should not bother responding to him either, as the Prophet (peace be upon him!) said: "We, the companies of Prophets, are commanded to address people according to their level of understanding."

(66) As for the patient [sick with ignorance] who *is* receptive to cure, he is the one seeking guidance who is intelligent, who is not overcome with envy, anger, or the love of his desires and rank and money. He is searching for the righteous path, and his questioning and contention is not out of envy, or to annoy and try one. This one is receptive to cure, so you may take the time to respond to his question—in fact you must.

(67) The second thing you should avoid: Guard against being a preacher and sermonizer, because there is much harm in that unless you first do what you say, and only then preach it to people. Reflect on what was said to Jesus, Son of Mary (peace upon him!): "Admonish yourself, and if you take the warning, then admonish the people; otherwise, be shamed before your Lord!"

(68) If you have been put to the test in this work, then guard against two typical characteristics [of preaching]. The first is thoughtlessly repeating moral lessons, admonitions, Qur'anic verses and stanzas of poetry,

فينبغي ان تُعرض عنه وتتركه مع مرضه، قال الله تعالى: ﴿فأَعْرِضْ عَمَّنْ تولّى عَنْ ذِكْرِنا وَلَمْ يُرِدْ إلاّ الحَياةَ الدُّنيا﴾. والحسودُ بكل مايقولُ ويفعلُ يُوقِدُ النارَ في زَرْع عمله كما قال النبي ﷺ: «الحَسَدُ يأكلُ الحَسَناتِ كما تأكلُ النارُ الحَطَب».

(٦٣) والثاني: أنْ تكونَ عِلَّتُه من الحماقة وهو أيضاً لا يقبلُ العلاجَ كما قال عيسى - عليه السلام -: «إني ما عَجَزتُ عن إحياءِ الموتى وقد عَجَزتُ عن معالجةِ الاحمقِ».

(٦٤) وذلك رجلٌ يشتغلُ بطلبِ العلم زمانا قليلاً ويتعلم شيئاً من العلوم العقلية والشَّرعية فيسألُ فيتعرضُ لا يعلم شيئاً أنَّ ما أشكل عليه هو أيضاً مُشكلٌ للعالِم الكبيرِ فإذا لم يتفكرْ هذا القَدرَ ويكونُ سؤالهُ وإعراضه من الحماقة فينبغي أن لا تَشتغل بجوابه.

(٦٥) والثالثُ: أن يكون مُسترشدا وكلُّ مالا يَفهم من كلام الأكابرِ يَحمله على قُصور فَهْمه وكان سؤالهُ للاستفادة لكنْ يكونُ بليداً لا يدرِكُ الحقائقَ فلا ينبغي الاشتغالُ بجوابه أيضا كما قال النبي ﷺ: «نحن معاشِرُ الأنبياءِ، أُمِرنا ان نكلِّمَ الناس على قَدْرِ عقولهم».

(٦٦) وأمَا المرضُ الذي يقبلُ العلاجَ فهو أن يكون مُسترشِداً عاقلاً فهماً لا يكونُ مغلوبَ الحسدِ والغضب وحُبِّ الشَّهوة والجاهِ والمالِ. ويكونُ طالبَ الطريقِ المستقيم ولم يكنْ سؤاله واعتراضه عن حَسدٍ وتعنُّتٍ وامتحان. وهذا يقبلُ العلاجَ فيجوز أن تشتغلَ بجواب سؤاله بل يجب عليك إجابتُه.

(٦٧) والثاني: مما تدعُ، وهو أنْ تحترز من أن تكون واعظاً ومذكرًا لانَّ فيه آفةً كثيرةً إلاّ أن تعملَ بما تقولُ: أولاً، ثم تعِظُ به الناسَ فتفكر فيما قيل لعيسى بن مريم - عليه السلام -: «عِظ نفسك فان اتَّعظتَ فَعظ الناسَ والاّ فاستحي من ربك».

(٦٨) وإن ابتليت بهذا العمل فاحترز عن خصلتين: الأولى: عن التكلف في الكلام بالعباراتِ والإشاراتِ والطّاماتِ والأبياتِ والأشعار، لانَّ الله تعالى

because God loathes blind followers. The blind follower is the one who disregards the limit, signaling [his] interior barrenness and the negligence of [his] heart. The intention of recollecting is that the believer recall to himself the fire of the hereafter, constrain himself to the service of the Creator, reflect on his past life which consumed him with irrelevant things, reflect on the obstacles to the safety of faith that are before him at the end, and how he will be in the grasp of the King of death—will he be able to answer Munkar and Nakīr?[70]—and concern himself with his condition on the Day of Resurrection and its stages—will he cross the bridge safely or will he plunge into the abyss?[71]—and constantly recall these things in his heart so that it rouses him from his complacency. Fanning these flames and bewailing these calamities is called reminding and informing and telling people about these things and alerting them to their shortcomings and excesses and making them see their sins so that the assembly of people may sense the burning heat of these flames and grow anxious at those calamities and so that they may remind one another of their past deeds as best they can and become distressed [by the thought of] spending [their] remaining days disobeying God.

(69) This is the summary account of the path called preaching. It is as though you saw that a flood had swept down upon a house with the inhabitants inside and you [wanted to] say: "Beware! Beware! Flee from the path of the flood!" Would you in such circumstances really want to tell the owner of the house your news in hackneyed cliches, tired apothegms, and quick tips? No, you would not! That is the condition of the preacher. He should avoid it.

(70) The second characteristic [of preaching to guard against] is that it not be the goal of your sermon that the congregation bellow back their responses, exhibit excessive emotions, and rend their clothing in hysteria simply in order that it be said: "What a great assembly that was!" All of this leads to hypocrisy, born as it is of carelessness. Rather, your intention and aim should be to call people's attention away from this world to the next, from rebelliousness to compliance, from overindulgence to temperance, from stinginess to charity, from vanity to godliness. [Your intention should be] to extol the benefits that will accrue to them in the next world, to decry this world, and to teach them how to be worshipful and abstemious, because the dominating desire in their natures is to depart from the sure path of the Law, randomly to pursue things that displease God, and to divert themselves[72] immorally. So strike terror into their hearts, startle them, and warn them against the

يبغضُ المتكلفينَ، والمتكلفُ المتجاوزعن الحدّ يدلُّ على خراب الباطن وغفلة القلوب. ومعنى التذكرأن يذكرالعبدُ نارَالآخرة ويقتصرَنفسه في خدمةِ الخالق، ويتفكرُ في عُمره الماضي الذي أفناه فيما لا يعنيه، ويتفكر فيما بين يديه من العقبات من سلامة الإيمان في الخاتمة وكيفية حاله في قبض ملك الموت وهل يقدرعلى جواب منكر ونكير، ويهتم بحاله في القيامة ومواقفها وهل يعبرعلى الصراط سالما أو يقع في الهاوية ويستمرذكر هذه الأشياء في قلبه فيزعجه عن قراره. فغليان هذه النيران ونوحة هذه المصائب تسمى تذكيرا وإعلام الخَلق واطّلاعهم على هذه الأشياء وتنبيههم على تقصيرهم وتفريطهم وتبصيرهم بعيوب أنفُسهم لتمسَّ حرارة هذه النيران أهل المجالس وتجزِعهم تلك المصائب وليتداركوا العمرالماضي بقدرِ الطاقة ويتحسَّروا على الأيام الخالية في غير طاعة الله تعالى.

(٦٩) هذه الجملة على هذا الطريقِ تُسمى وَعْظاً، كما لو رأيتَ أنَّ السَّيلَ قد هجم على دارِ واحدٍ وكان هو مع أهله فيها فتقول: الحَذَرَ الحَذَرَ، فروا من سبيل السيل. وهل يشتهي قلبك في هذه الحالة أن تخبرصاحب الدار خَبرَكَ بتكليف العبارات والنكت والإشارات فلا تَشتهي البتَّة. فكذلك حالُ الواعظ، فينبغي أنْ يتجنبَ عنها.

(٧٠) والخصلةُ الثانيةُ: أن لا تكونَ همتُك في وَعْظك أنْ ينْعَرالخلقُ في مجلسك ويظهرالوجْدَ ويشقَ الثيابَ ليقال: نِعْمَ المجلسُ هذا. لأنَّ كله ميلٌ إلى الرياء وهو يتولدُ من الغفلة. بل ينبغي أن يكونَ عَزمُك وهمتك أن تدعوَ الناسَ من الدنيا الى الآخرة ومن المعصية إلى الطاعة ومن الحرص إلى الزهدِ ومن البخل إلى السَّخاوة، ومن الغرورِ إلى التَّقوى، وتحبِبْ المنفعةَ إليهم للآخرة وتُبغضَ عليهم الدنيا وتعلمهم عِلمَ العبادة والزهدِ لأن الغالبَ في طباعهم الزَّيغ عن نهج الشَّرع والسَّعي فيما لا يرضى اللهُ تعالى به، واشتغال بالأخلاق الرديَّة، فألقِ في قلوبهم الرُّعبَ ورَوّعهم وحذرهم عما

horrors they otherwise might face in the next world. And maybe their inner traits will change, their outward treatment of one another will alter, and the desire and wish to be obedient and give up rebelliousness will manifest itself.

(71) This is the way to preach and give advice. Any form of preaching that is not like this is a curse on the speaker and the listener. In fact, it is said to be a ghoul and a satan which leads people off the road and then destroys them. They must flee from it because not even Satan could do the damage to their piety that such a one [who preaches like this] would do. Anyone with the strength and will must drag [such a preacher][73] down from the pulpits of the believers[74] and prevent him from[75] his pursuit, for [such an act] is part of commanding the right and forbidding the wrong.[76]

(72) The third thing you should avoid: Neither associate with princes and kings nor even express an opinion about them, for thinking about them, attending their courts, and associating with them is very dangerous. If you have been tempted [to do this], immediately stop both censuring and praising them, because God grows angry when one praises the sinner and tyrant. Anyone who has prayed for the long life [of a ruler] has clearly deemed it acceptable to rebel against God in His world.

(73) The fourth thing to avoid: Do not accept presents and gifts from rulers, even if you know [that the gifts] are legally permissible, because to covet [anything] from them is to debase religion, since it leads one to sycophancy, compliance, and collusion in their acts of oppression. All of this is a corruptive force to religion. The least harmful element of this is that when you accept their gifts and benefit from their worldly possessions, you begin to love them. Now to love someone is necessarily to wish them long life both in this world and the next, but wishing for the continued existence of the tyrant is to seek the oppression of those who worship God and the ruination of the world. What could be more harmful to one's piety and final judgment than this! Beware of letting yourself be deceived by the wiles of Satan or by those who say to you that it is preferable and more appropriate to start taking money from out of the hands of the poor and indigent; for [the rulers] squander it in sin and sedition whereas your distribution of it to the poor would be better. For the Cursed One [i.e., Satan] has cut many a throat with such malicious susurration. The damage he causes is pervasive, as we recounted in *Revival of the Religious Sciences*. Look [for the discussion] there.[77]

يستقبلون من المخاوف. ولعلّ صفاتِ باطنهم تتغيرُ ومعاملةَ ظاهرهم تتبدل ويظهر الحرص والرغبة في الطاعة والرجوع عن المعصية.

(٧١) وهذا طريق الوعظ والنصيحةِ، وكلُّ وعظ لا يكونُ هكذا فهو وبالٌ على من قال وسمع بل انه غول وشيطانٌ يَذهب بالخلق عن الطريق فيهلِكهم، ويجب عليهم أن يَفرّوا منه لأن ما يفسدُ هذا القائلُ من دينهم لا يستطيعُ بمثله الشيطانُ. ومَنْ كانت له يدٌ وقدرةٌ يجبُ عليه أن ينزلهم من منابر المسلمين ويمنعهم عمّا باشرَ، فانه من جُملة الأمر بالمعروف والنهي عن المنكر.

(٧٢) والثالثُ مما تدَعُ: لا تخالط الأمراءَ والسلاطينَ ولا تراهم، لان رؤيتهم ومجالستهم ومخالطتهم آفةٌ عظيمةٌ. ولو ابتليت بها دَعْ عنك قدحهم وثناءَهم لأنَّ اللهَ تعالى يَغضَبُ اذا مُدحَ الفاسقُ والظالمُ؛ ومن دعا لطول بقائهم فقد أحبَّ أنْ يُعصى الله تعالى في أرضهِ.

(٧٣) والرابعُ: مما تدعُ: ان لا تَقبلْ شيئاً من عطاء الأمراءِ وهداياهم وإن علمتَ انها من الحلال؛ لأنَّ الطمعَ منهم يُفسدُ الدينَ؛ لأَنَّه يتولدُ منه المداهنةُ ومراعاةُ جانبهم والموافقةُ في ظلمهم وهذا كلُّه فسادٌ في الدين وأقلُّ مضرته أنّك اذا قبلتَ عطاياهم وانتفعتَ من دنياهم أحببتهم ومن أحبَّ أحداً يحبُّ طولَ عمره وبقائه بالضرورة وفي محبةِ بقاء الظالم إرادةُ الظلم على عباد الله تعالى وإرادة خراب العالم. فأيُّ شيءٍ يكونُ أضرَّ من هذا للدين والعاقبة؟ وإياك ان تخدع باستهواءِ الشيطان او بقول بعض الناس لك بأنَّ الافضل والاولى ان تأخذ الدينارَ والدرهمَ منهم وتفرقهما بين الفقراء والمساكين فانهم يُنفشونَ في الفسْقِ والمعصية، وانفاقُك على ضُعفاء الناس خيرٌ من إنفاقهم، فأنَّ اللعين قد قطعَ أعناقاً كثيراً من الناس بهذه الوَسوَسةِ وآفته فاشٍ كثير قد ذكرناه في «احياء علوم الدين» فاطلب ثمة.

(74) As for the four things that you should do, the first is that you make your conduct with God such that were your servant to deal with you in that manner, you would be pleased with him and not annoyed or angry with him, and anything that you do not find satisfactory about this theoretical servant of yours God as your true master would also not find satisfactory [about you].

(75) The second is that whatever you do to people should be what you would want done to you, because the faith of a believer is incomplete unless he wants for other people what he would want for himself.

(76) The third is that whenever you read and look into a field of learning, it should be something that improves your heart and cleanses your soul, as though you had learned that you had but one week to live—you certainly would not concern yourself with law, and legal disputation and theory, theology, and such things, because you would know that these sciences will not enrich you. Rather, you would pay attention to your heart, learn the characteristics of your soul, relinquish your ties to the world, purify your soul of its reprehensible traits, turn your attention to the love of God, to worshipping Him, and acquiring good traits. Not a day and night passes but that a man might not die in it.

(77) O Son! Hear another narrative from me and think about it until you arrive at a conclusion. If you were told that the Sultan was coming to visit you in a week, know that in the intervening time you would focus your attention on nothing but improving anything that you knew the Sultan's gaze would fall upon, such as your clothes, your body, the house and furniture, and so on. Now, reflect on the allusion, for you are intelligent and a single word suffices the wise. The Prophet (peace and blessing upon him!) said: "God looks at neither your manners nor your actions; He examines your hearts and intentions."[78] If you want to know the states of the heart, look in *The Revival*[79] and my other books. Such learning is an individual duty while others are collective. Excepting the measure of what the duties to God produce, may God grant you success in obtaining it!

(78) The fourth thing is that you do not accrue of worldly things more than is sufficient for a year, just as the Prophet (peace and blessing upon him!) would lay in provisions for one of the chambers [of his house] and say: "Oh, God, make the provisions of Muḥammad's family just enough!"[80] He would not store up provisions in all of the chambers,

(٧٤) وأما الأربعة التي ينبغي لك أن تفعلها: الأول: أن تجعلَ معاملتك مع الله-تعالى-بحيثُ لو عامل معك بها عبدُك ترضى بها منه ولا يضيقُ خاطرك عليه ولا تَغضب. وما لا ترضى لنفسك من عَبدك المجازي لا يُرضي الله تعالى، وهو سيدُك الحقيقي.

(٧٥) والثاني: كلما عملت بالناس أجعل كما ترضى لنفسك منهم، لأنه لا يكمل إيمانُ عبد حتى يحبَّ لسائر الناس مايُحبُّ لنفسه.

(٧٦) والثالث: إذا قرأتَ العلمَ وطالعته ينبغي أن يكونَ علماً يُصلحُ قلبك ويزَكّي نَفسك كما لو علمت أنَّ عُمرك ما بقي غير أسبوع فبالضرورة لا تشتغلَ فيها بعلم الفقه والخلاف والأصول والكلام وأمثالها لأنك تعلم أن هذه العلوم لا تُغنيك بل تشتغل بمراقبةِ القلب ومعرفةِ صفاتِ النَّفس والإعراض عن علائقِ الدنيا وتُزكي نَفسك عن الأخلاق الذميمة، وتشتغلُ بمحبة الله تعالى وعبادته والاتصاف بالأوصاف الحسنةِ. ولا يمرُّ على عبد يوم وليلة الاّ ويمكن انْ يكونَ موته فيها.

(٧٧) أيها الولدُ: اسمع مني كلاماً آخر وتفكرْ فيه حتى تجدَ خلاصاً، لوأُخبرت أن السلطان بعد أسبوع يجيئك زائرًا، اعلم أنك في تلك المدّةِ لا تشتغلَ إلا باصلاح ما علمت أنَّ نظرالسلطان سيقعُ عليه من الثياب والبدنِ والدار والفرش وغيرها. فالآن تفكرالى ما أشرتُ به فإنّك فَهِمٌ، والكلامُ الفردُ يكفي الكيّس. قال رسول الله ﷺ: «إن الله لا ينظرُ إلى صُورِكم ولا إلى أعمالكم ولكن ينظرُ إلى قلوبكم ونيّاتكم» وان أردتَ علم أحوال القَلب فانظرالى «الإحياء» وغيره من مصنفاتي وهذا العلم فرضُ عَينٍ، وغيرّه فرضُ كفاية الا مقدارَ ما يُؤدّى به فرائضُ الله تعالى، اللهُ يُوفّقك حتى تحصّله.

(٧٨) والرابع: أن لا تجمعَ من الدنيا أكثرمن كفايةِ سنة كما كان رسولُ اللهِ ﷺ يُعِدُّ لبعضِ حُجُراتِهِ وقال: «اللّهم اجْعل قُوتَ آلِ محمد كَفافا». ولم يكن يُعدّ ذلك لكل

but only for [whichever of his wives] he knew to be weak in faith. For any [whose faith] was certain, he would provide no more provisions than she needed for a day and a half.

(79) O Son! I have responded to your requests in this quire, so you should put them into practice. Do not forget me in your pious supplication. As for the supplication you requested from me,[81] look for it among the pious supplications [below]. Read this supplication in your times of prayer, especially in the remaining moments.

(80) O God! I ask of you perfect grace, abiding protection, encompassing mercy, and good health, the most bountiful means of subsistence, the happiest of lives, the most righteous behavior, the most comprehensive favors, the most pleasant bounty, and the most effective benevolence.

(81) O God! Be with us and not against us!

(82) O God! Seal the hour of our departure with happiness; fulfill our hopes in abundance; bind together our coming and going with forgiveness; make Your mercy our destination and return; pour out the bucket of Your absolution into the containers of our sins; bless us by rectifying our failings; make piety our provision—in Your religion lies effort and upon You lies our dependence and support. Set us firmly on the path of righteousness and protect us in this world from any cause for regret on the Day of Resurrection; lighten the load of our accountability, bless us with the life of the righteous, and save and steer us from the iniquity of the evil.[82] Hold back our necks and the necks of our ancestors from the hellfire through Your mercy, O Mighty, Forgiving, Generous, Concealing, Benevolent, Omnipotent God!

(83) O God! O God! By Your mercy! O Most Merciful! First of firsts and lasts! O Most Powerful! O You who bestow mercy on the weak! O Most Merciful! There is no god but You! Praise unto You, that I not be a wrongdoer! Praise unto God, the Lord of the Worlds!

◆

الحُجرات بل كان يُعده لمن علم أن في قلبها ضَعفا. وأمّا من كانت صاحبة يقينٍ ما كان يُعدُّ لها إلا قوتَ يومٍ ونصف.

(٧٩) أيها الولدُ: إني كتبت في هذا الفصل ملتمساتِكَ فينبغي لك أنْ تعمل بها ولا تنساني فيها من أن تذكرني في صالح دعائك. وأما الدعاءُ الذي سألتَ منّي فاطلُبه من الدعوات الصحاح واقرأ هذا الدعاءَ في أوقاتك خُصوصا أعقاب الصلاة.

(٨٠) «اللَّهم اني أسألك من النِعْمة تمامها، ومن العِصمةِ دوامها، ومن الرحمة شُمولَها، ومن العافية حُصولها، ومن العيش أرْغَده، ومن العُمر أسعَدَه، ومن الإحسان أتمه، ومن الإنعام أعمَّه، ومن الفضل أعذبه، ومن اللطف أنفَعه.

(٨١) اللَّهم كُنْ لنا ولا تكنْ علينا.

(٨٢) اللَّهم اختمْ بالسعادة آجالَنا وحققْ بالزيادة آمالَنا، واقرِنْ بالعافية غُدُوَّنا وآصالَنا، واجعلْ إلى رحمتك مصيرنا ومآلَنا اصْبُبْ سِجالَ عفوك على ذنوبنا، ومُنَّ علينا باصلاح عيوبنا، واجعل التقوى زادنا، وفي دينك اجتهادَنا، وعليك توكلنا واعتمادَنا، وثبتنا على نهج الاستقامة، وأعذنا في الدنيا من موجباتِ النَّدامةِ يومَ القيامة، وخَفّف عنّا ثِقَلَ الاوزار، وارزُقنا عيشة الابرار، واكفِنا واصرِفْ عنا شرَّ الاشرار، واعْتِقْ رقابنا ورقابَ آبائِنا وامهاتِنا من النار. برحمتك يا عزيزُ، يا غفّارُ يا كريمُ، يا ستارُ، يا حليمُ، يا جبار.

(٨٣) يا الله يا الله برحمتك ياأرحمَ الراحمين يا أوّلَ الأولين والآخرين، ياذا القوةِ المتين، يا راحمَ المساكين، ويا أرحمَ الراحمين لا إلهَ إلاّ انت سبحانك إني كُنتُ من الظالمين، والحمدُلله ربِّ العالمين.

تمّ.

al-Zarnūjī

Instruction of the Student: The Method of Learning

TRANSLATED BY
G. E. VON GRUNEBAUM & THEODORA M. ABEL*

◆

Author's Apology

In the name of God, the Merciful, the Compassionate.

(1) Praise is due God who favored the sons of Adam with knowledge and responsible action [*ᶜamal*] above all creation; blessings and peace upon Muḥammad, the Lord of the Arabs and non-Arabs, and upon his family and his companions from whom all knowledge and wisdom spring.

(2) During our times I have observed many students of science striving to attain knowledge but failing to do so, and debarred from its uses and benefits: [to wit] action in accordance with it and spreading it abroad, [and they reached this dead end] because they missed the [proper] methods of learning and abandoned the conditions [upon which science can be acquired]. Everyone who misses his way goes astray, and does not reach the goal, regardless of whether it is modest or glorious. [In view of this situation] I sought and desired to explain to them the ways of, studying that I had either read about in books or heard from my masters, the learned and wise, hoping that those sincerely interested in [my exposition] would pray for my deliverance and redemption on the Day of Judgment.

الإمام برهان الإسلام
الزرنوجي

تعليم المتعلم طريق التعلم
تلميذ صاحب الهداية

بِسْمِ اللهِ الرَّحْمَنِ الرَّحِيمِ

(١) الحمد لله الذي فضل بني آدم بالعلم والعمل على جميع العالم، والصلاة والسلام على محمد سيد العرب والعجم، وعلى آله وأصحابه ينابيع العلوم والحكم. « وبعد »

(٢) فلما رأيت كثيرا من طلاب العلم في زماننا يجدون إلى العلم ولا يصلون، ومن منافعه وثمراته يحرمون، لما أنهم أخطئوا طرائقه، وتركوا شرائطه، وكل من أخطا الطريق ضل، فلا ينال المقصود قل أو جل، أردت وأحببت أن أبين لهم طريق التعليم، على ما رأيت في الكتب وسمعت من أساتيذي أولي العلم والحكم، رجاء الدعاء من الراغبين فيه المخلصين، بالفوز والخلاص في يوم الدين.

(3) After I had asked God for guidance in the choice [of the material] I composed this tract and entitled it "Instruction of the Student—The Method of Learning," dividing it into [thirteen] chapters:

1. On the nature and merit of knowledge and learning.
2. On the purpose of study.
3. On the choosing of the subject matter of learning, the teachers, one's fellow students, and one's permanent affiliation.
4. On respecting knowledge and those who possess it.
5. On industriousness, perseverance, and assiduity (in the pursuit of learning).
6. On the beginning of study, its amount and its organization.
7. On placing one's faith in God.
8. On the time for the acquisition of knowledge.
9. On helpfulness and good advice.
10. On the means useful to the attainment of knowledge.
11. On abstinence from evil during the pursuit of learning.
12. What creates memory and what brings about forgetfulness.
13. Which things bring about and which prevent earning a livelihood, and which things augment or diminish the years of one's life.

(٣) بعد ما استخرت الله تعالى فيه، وسميته: تعليم المتعلم طريق التعلم، وجعلته فصولا:
فصل: في ماهية العلم والفقه وفضله.
فصل: في النية حال التعلم.
فصل: في اختيار العلم والأستاذ والشريك والثبات.
فصل: في تعظيم العلم وأهله.
فصل: في الجد والمواظبة والهمة.
فصل: في بداية النسبق وترتيبه وقدره.
فصل: في التوكل.
فصل: في وقت التحصيل.
فصل: في الشفقة والنصيحة.
فصل: في الاستفادة. فصل: في الورع حال التعلم.
فصل: فيما يورث الحفظ، وفيما يورث النسيان.
فصل: فيما يجلب الرزق، وما يمنعه، وما يزيد، في العمر، وما ينقص.

Chapter One

On the Nature and Merit of Knowledge and Learning

(4) The Messenger of God [i.e., Muḥammad] said: "The quest for knowledge is incumbent upon every Muslim man and Muslim woman." Know that it is not obligatory for every Muslim, man or woman, to seek all [aspects of] learning, but only that in keeping with his station in life. It is said: The most meritorious knowledge is that in keeping with one's station and the most meritorious action is to maintain one's station. It is necessary for the Muslim to strive for as much knowledge as he may need in his station whatever this is. Since he will have to perform his prayers he must needs know as much of the prayer ritual as will help him acquit himself of his duty to pray. [Furthermore], knowledge of his [other] religious obligations is incumbent upon him. For whatever leads to the ascertaining of duty is itself duty and what leads to the determining of obligation is itself obligation. This applies to fasting, and also to [the payment of the] poor-tax if [the believer] possesses wealth, and to the pilgrimage if one is under obligation to perform it. It also applies to trading if one is engaged in commerce.

(5) [Someone] said to Muḥammad b. al-Ḥasan:[1] "Will you not compose a book on asceticism?" He replied: "I composed a book on trading." [With this answer] he meant to say: "The [true] ascetic is he who is careful to protect himself against dubious and unsanctioned practices in commerce." The same thing [gathering of special knowledge] is required with respect to all the other occupations and professions. Everyone who works in one of them is in duty bound to learn how to guard against what is forbidden practice in it. Likewise, knowledge of the states of the heart [such as] complete reliance on God, repentance, fear, satisfaction [with His dispensation] is imperative, as it applies [to people] in every walk in life. And the nobility of learning is not hidden from anyone since it is peculiar to humankind. Exclusive of knowledge, men as well as all other animals are associated with every virtue, such as valor, courage, strength, generosity, compassion. Learning is the exception. Through it God revealed the preeminence of Adam over the angels whom He commanded to prostrate themselves before him.[2] Learning is noble for it leads to that fear of God which entitles [the believer] to God's benevolence and to eternal bliss. In this vein, Muḥammad b. al-Ḥasan Abū ʿAbdallāh[3] said:

فصل: في ماهية العلم والفقه وفضله

(٤) قال رسول الله ﷺ: «طلب العلم فريضة على كل مسلم ومسلمة». اعلم أنه لا يفترض على كل مسلم طلب كل علم، وإنما يفترض عليه طلب علم الحال. فإنه يقال: أفضل العلم علم الحال، وأفضل العمل حفظ الحال. ويفترض على المسلم طلب علم ما يقع له في حاله في أى حال كان، فإنه لا بد له من الصلاة فيفترض عليه علم ما يقع له في صلاته بقدر ما يؤدي به فرض الصلاة ويجب عليه بقدر ما يؤدي به الواجب، لأن ما يتوسل به إلى إقامة الفرض يكون فرضا، وما يتوسل به إلى إقامة الواجب يكون واجبا. وكذلك في الصوم والزكاة، إن كان له مال، والحج إن وجب عليه، وكذلك في البيوع إن كان يتجر.

(٥) قيل لمحمد بن الحسن رحمه الله: ألا تصنف كتابا في الزهد؟ قال: صنفت كتابا في البيوع! يعني الزاهد هو من يتحرز عن الشبهات والمكروهات في التجارات، وكذلك في سائر المعاملات والحرف. وكل من اشتغل بشيء منها يفترض عليه علم التحرز عن الحرام فيه، وكذلك يفترض عليه علم أحوال القلب: من التوكل، والإنابة، والخشية، والرضا، فإنه واقع في جميع الأحوال. وشرف العلم لا يخفى على أحد، إذ هو المختص بالإنسانية لأن جميع الخصال سوى العلم يشترك فيها الإنسان، وسائر الحيوانات كالشجاعة، والجراءة، والقوة، والجود، والشفقة وغيرها سوى العلم، وبه أظهر الله تعالى فضل آدم عليه السلام على الملائكة، وأمرهم بالسجود له، وإنما شرف العلم لكونه وسيلة إلى التقوى التي يستحق بها المرء الكرامة عند الله تعالى والسعادة الأبدية، كما قيل لمحمد ابن الحسن ابن عبد الله رحمة الله عليه:

Learn, for learning is an adornment for him who possesses it,
a virtue and a preface[4] *to every praiseworthy action.*

Profit each day by an increase of learning
and swim in the seas of beneficial knowledge.

Give yourself up to the study of jurisprudence, for the knowledge
of jurisprudence is the best guide to piety and fear of God,
and it is the straightest path to the goal.

It is the sign leading on to the ways of proper guidance;
it is the fortress which saves [one] from all hardships.

Verily, one godly person versed in jurisprudence
is more powerful against Satan than a thousand [ordinary] worshippers.

(6) Likewise, [knowledge has an important bearing] on all other qualities [of human character] such as generosity and avarice, cowardice and courage, arrogance and humility, chastity [and debauchery], prodigality and parsimony and so on. For arrogance, avarice, cowardice and prodigality are illicit. Only through knowledge of them and their opposites is protection against them possible. Thus learning is prescribed for all of us.

(7) The Most Illustrious Imām, the martyred Sayyid Nāṣir al-Dīn Abū al-Qāsim composed a book on Ethics [or: Moral Philosophy][5]—and praiseworthy is what he composed!—[a book] which is necessary for every Muslim to bear in mind! Keeping in mind [the prescriptions applying to] what comes up only upon certain occasions is a "collective duty."[6] [This means that] when some [people] fulfill it in a given place, others are excused from this [duty]; on the other hand, if no one fulfills it the sin resulting from such omission falls on the whole community. It is for the Imām to direct and for the community to submit with regard to this [obligation].

(8) It has been said that knowledge of matters affecting a person under all conditions holds a position equal to that of food; it cannot be dispensed with by anybody. Knowledge of matters affecting a person upon certain occasions holds a position equal to that of medicine which is needed at stipulated times only. Knowledge of the stars holds a position equal to that of disease; [but] its study is prohibited because it is both harmful and useless. Escape from the decree of God and his dispensation is impossible [so the study of the stars is both futile and sacrilegious].

تعلم فإن العلم زين لأهله وفضل وعنوان لكل المحامد
وكن مستفيدا كل يوم زيادة من العلم واسبح في بحور الفوائد
تفقه فإن الفقه أفضل قائد إلى البر والتقوى وأعدل قاصد
هو العلم الهادي إلى سنن الهدى هو الحصن ينجي من جميع الشدائد
فإن فقيها وحامدا متورعا أشد على الشيطان من ألف عابد

(٦) وكذلك في سائر الأخلاق نحو: الجود، والبخل، والجبن والجرأة، والتكبر، والتواضع، والعفة، والإسراف والتقتير وغيرها. فإن الكبر، والبخل، والجبن، والإسراف حرام، ولا يمكن التحرز عنها إلا بعلمها وعلم ما يضادها، فيفترض على كل إنسان علمها.

(٧) وقد صنف السيد الإمام الأجل الشهيد ناصر الدين أبو القاسم كتابا في الأخلاق، ونعم ما صنف، فيجب على كل مسلم حفظها. وأما حفظ ما يقع في بعض الأحايين ففرض على سبيل الكفاية، إذا قام به البعض في البلدة سقط عن الباقين، فإن لم يكن في البلدة من يقوم به اشتركوا جميعا في المأثم، فيجب على الإمام أن يأمرهم بذلك، ويجبر أهل البلدة عليه.

(٨) وقد قيل: إن علم ما يقع على نفسه في جميع الأحوال هو بمنزلة الطعام لا بد لكل واحد منه، وعلم ما يقع في بعض الأحايين بمنزلة الدواء يحتاج إليه حين المرض فقط، وعلم النجوم بمنزلة المرض فتعلمه حرام لأنه يضر، ولا ينفع، والهرب من قضاء الله تعالى وقدره غير ممكن.

(9) Every Muslim is expected to occupy himself at all times with the mention [of the name] of God and His invocation and supplication; with reading the Qurʾān, giving alms that ward off calamities, asking forgiveness and safety in this world and the next; so that God may defend him from trials and tribulations. For he who is granted [the gift of] invocation will not be denied a favorable response. If calamity is decreed to him, it will inevitably befall him, but God will make the [tribulation] easier for him to bear and will give him the patience [that is bestowed by] the invocation.

(10) [Astronomy is forbidden] with the qualification that one is permitted to study just enough of it to determine the *qiblah*[7] and the times of prayer. The study of the science of medicine is allowed because it deals with accidental [secondary] causes. Therefore its study is allowed just as is [that] of other accidental causes. The Prophet treated himself medically. It is related that al-Shafiᶜī[8] said that science has two branches: the science of legal doctrine which has to do with religious problems [*adyān*] and the science of medicine which has to do with [human] bodies [*abdān*]; any study that goes beyond [these sciences] is only a method of attracting an audience. As for commenting on matters of learning, it is a [secondary] means through which the nature of a propounded subject may become clear. *Al-fiqh* is the science of the fine points of knowledge.

(11) Abū Ḥanīfa[9] said: "Jurisprudence is a person's knowledge of his rights and duties." He said further:

(12) The purpose of learning is to act by it, while the purpose of action is the abandoning of the perishable for that which lasts forever. It is necessary for man neither to neglect his soul nor what helps or injures it in this life and in the next life. Hence man should try to provide what is useful while avoiding what is harmful to the [soul], lest his intelligence and his knowledge become weapons [arguments] against him and his punishment be increased. May God preserve us from His wrath and His punishment.

(13) On [the subject of] the virtues and excellences of learning there exist [a considerable number of] Qurʾānic verses and sound [i.e., well authenticated] and well-known traditions. We shall not bother to record these [here] lest this our book grow overly long.

(٩) فينبغي لكل مسلم أن يشتغل في جميع أوقاته بذكر الله تعالى والدعاء والتضرع وقراءة القرآن والصدقات الدافعة للبلاء، ويسأل الله تعالى العفو والعافية في الدنيا والآخرة، ليصونه الله تعالى عن البلاء والآفات، فإن من رزق الدعاء، لم يحرم الإجابة، فإن كان البلاء مقدرا يصبه لا محالة، لكن ييسره الله عليه، ويرزقه الصبر ببركة الدعاء.

(١٠) اللهم إلا إذا تعلم من النجوم قدر ما يعرف به القبلة وأوقات الصلاة فيجوز ذلك. وأما تعلم علم الطب، فيجوز لأنه سبب من الأسباب، فيجوز تعلمه كسائر الأسباب، وقد تداوى النبي عليه الصلاة والسلام. وقد حكى عن الشافعي رحمة الله عليه أنه قال: العلم علمان: علم الفقه للأديان، وعلم الطب للأبدان وما وراء ذلك بلغة مجلس. وأما تفسير العلم فهو صفة يتجلى بها لمن قامت هي به المذكور كما هو. والفقه: معرفة دقائق العلم مع نوع علاج.

(١١) قال أبو حنيفة رحمة الله عليه: الفقه معرفة النفس ما لها وما عليها.

(١٢) وقال: ما العلم إلا العمل به، والعمل به ترك العاجل للآجل. فينبغي للإنسان ألا يغفل عن نفسه، وما ينفعها وما يضرها في أولاها وأخراها. فيستجلب ما ينفعها ويجتنب ما يضرها كيلا يكون عقله وعلمه حجة عليه فيزداد عقوبة، نعوذ بالله من سخطه وعقابه.

(١٣) وقد ورد في مناقب العلم وفضائله آيات وأخبار صحيحة مشهورة لم نشتغل بذكرها كيلا يطول الكتاب.

Chapter Two

On the Purpose of Study

(14) Purpose is necessary in the study of science since it is the intention in which every deed is rooted, according to the words of the Prophet:

(15) "Deeds [or works] [are measured] by their intentions"—this is a genuine tradition—and, "How many are the deeds which bear the image of the deeds of this world and become, through their good intention, of the deeds of the next world! And how many again are the deeds which bear the image of the deeds of the next world, but then become, through their evil intention, of the deeds of this world!"

(16) And it is meet for the student in his quest for knowledge to strive for the good will of God, the future life, the removal of ignorance from himself and from the rest of the ignorant, the conservation[10] of religion, and the survival of Islam. For the survival of Islam depends on knowledge. And the ascetic life and piety are not perfect where there is ignorance.

(17) The professor, the venerable Sheikh, the Most Illustrious Imām, Burhān al-Dīn,[11] author of the *Hidāyah,*[12] recited a poem by an unnamed author:

An immoral man of learning is a great evil,
but a greater evil still is an ignoramus leading a godly life.

Both [these types of men] are a great trial everywhere
to him who clings to both [knowledge and godliness] in his religion.

(18) [The student should] aim [with his knowledge] at rendering thanks [to God] for a healthy mind and a sound body, not, however, at attracting people toward himself, or reining in the vanities of the world, or obtaining honors from the king [*sulṭān*], and the like.

(19) Muḥammad b. al-Ḥasan said: "If the people, all of them, were my slaves I would affranchise them and free myself from being their patron. And he who finds pleasure in knowledge and in acting according to it, only rarely does he desire man's [worldly] possessions."

فصل: في النية حال التعلم

(١٤) ثم لا بد له من النية في زمان تعلم العلم. إذ النية هي الأصل في جميع الأحوال. لقوله عليه الصلاة والسلام

(١٥) «إنما الأعمال بالنيات» حديث صحيح، وعن رسول الله ﷺ، «كم من عمل يتصور بصورة أعمال الدنيا ويصير بحسن النية من أعمال الآخرة، وكم من عمل يتصور بصورة أعمال الآخرة، ثم يصير من أعمال الدنيا بسوء النية»

(١٦) وينبغي أن ينوي المتعلم بطلب العلم: رضاء الله تعالى والدار الآخرة، وإزالة الجهل عن نفسه وعن سائر الجهال، وإحياء الدين، وإبقاء الإسلام، فإن بقاء الإسلام بالعلم، ولا يصح الزهد والتقوى مع الجهل.

(١٧) أنشدنى الأستاذ الشيخ الإمام الأجل برهان الدين صاحب الهداية لبعضهم:

فساد كبير عالم متهتك   وأكبر منه جاهل متنسك
هما فتنة في العالمين عظيمة   لمن بهما في دينه يتمسك

(١٨) وينوى به الشكر على نعمة العقل، وصحة البدن، ولا ينوى به إقبال الناس إليه، ولا استجلاب حطام الدنيا، والكرامة عند السلطان وغيره.

(١٩) قال محمد بن الحسن رحمه الله: لو كان الناس كلهم عبيدى لأعتقتهم، وتبرأت عن ولائهم؛ وذلك لأن من وجد لذة العلم والعمل به قلما يرغب فيما عند الناس.

(20) The Sheikh, the Most Illustrious Imām, the professor, Qiwām al-Dīn Ḥammād b. Ibrāhīm b. Ismāᶜīl al-Ṣaffār al-Anṣārī[13] recited a poem by Abū Ḥanīfa, dictating it to us:

Whoso strives for knowledge for the life to come
obtains an increase [or: surplus] in righteousness.

But woe to those that strive for it
to obtain an advantage over [or: from] their fellow-believers [ᶜibād]!

(21) [This is so] unless possibly he seeks position in order to command what is good and forbid what is evil, and in order to promote the truth and strengthen religion, and not in order to satisfy his ego and his desires. And that [i.e., the repression of selfish aims] becomes more and more possible in proportion as [the learned in a worldly position] undertakes to command the good and forbid the evil.

(22) And it is meet that he who strives for knowledge should reflect thereon. For, verily, one should study science with great assiduity and not apply it [this science] to this base, small and perishable world. A poem:

This world is more worthless than the worthless,
and its lover is baser than the base.

It renders people deaf by its magic
and makes them blind so they become perplexed, with no guide.

(23) And it behooves him who seeks knowledge not to debase himself by desiring what should not be desired, and abstain from those things which degrade science and its bearers. One should also be modest, for modesty lies between arrogance and humility. Chastity, too, is like that [i.e., the golden means between two extremes]. This can be learnt from the *Kitāb al-akhlāq.*[14]

(٢٠) أنشدنا الشيخ الإمام الأجل الأستاذ قوام الدين حماد بن إبراهيم بن إسماعيل الصفار الأنصاري إملاء لأبى حنيفة رحمه الله تعالى شعرا:

من العلم للمعاد فاز بفضل من الرشاد
في الخسران طالبيه لنيل فضل من العباد

(٢١) اللّهم إلا إذا طلب الجاه للأمر بالمعروف والنهى عن المنكر، وتنفيذ الحق، وإعزاز الدين لا لنفسه وهواه، فيجوز ذلك بقدر ما يقيم به الأمر بالمعروف، والنهى عن المنكر.

(٢٢) وينبغي لطالب العلم أن يتفكر في ذلك فإنه يتعلم العلم بجهد كثير فلا يصرفه إلى الدنيا الحقيرة القليلة الفانية:

هي الدنيا أقل من القليل وعاشقها أذل من الذليل
تصم بسحرها قوما وتعمي فهم متحيرون بلا دليل

(٢٣) وينبغي لأهل العلم ألا يذل نفسه بالطمع في غير مطمع، ويتحرز عما فيه مذلة العلم وأهله، ويكون متواضعا، والتواضع بين التكبر والمذلة والعفة، ويعرف ذلك في كتاب الأخلاق.

(24) The Sheikh, the Most Illustrious Imām, the late professor Rukn al-Islām,[15] who is known as al-Adīb al-Mukhtār, recited for me a poem composed by himself:

Verily, modesty is a quality of the god-fearing,
and by its means the pious mounts to the heights of Paradise.

A wondrous thing is the wondering of the ignorant
whether he is [or: is to be] happy or wretched.

Or [his wondering] in what way his life will end, or whether his soul
on the day of his death will descend to inferior regions
or be raised to a sublime place.

Truly, pride belongs to our Lord, an attribute peculiar to Him—
therefore avoid it and fear God.

(25) Abū Ḥanīfa spoke to his companions thus: "Make your turbans ample and enlarge your sleeves." Verily, he spoke thus in order not to cause science and its bearers to be disdained.

(26) And it is compulsory for him who seeks knowledge to acquire the *Kitāb al-waṣiyyah* [the Bequest] which Abū Ḥanīfa wrote to Yūsuf b. Khālid al-Samtī[16] when he returned to his people. He who seeks [to obtain this book] will find it. Our late teacher, the Sheikh al-Islām, the proof of the imāms, ᶜAlī b. Abī Bakr [al-Marghīnānī] commanded me to write it[17] out on returning to my country, which I did. Both he who teaches the higher knowledge, [*mudarris,* teacher in a madrasa], and he who gives legal opinions [*muftī*] cannot dispense with it in their dealings with people.

(٢٤) أنشدني الشيخ الامام الأجل الأستاذ ركن الإسلام المعروف بالأديب المختار، رحمه الله شعرا لنفسه:

إن التواضع من خصال المتقي وبه التقي إلى المعالى يرتقي
ومن العجائب عجب من هو جاهل في حاله أهو السعيد
أم الشقي أم كيف يختم عمره أو روحه يوم التوى متسفل أو مرتقي
والكبرياء لربنا صفة به مخصوصة فتجنبنها واتقي

(٢٥) قال أبو حنيفة رحمه الله لأصحابه: عظموا عمائمكم، و وسعوا أكمامكم، وإنما قال ذلك لئلا يستخف بالعلم وأهله.

(٢٦) وينبغي لطالب العلم أن يحصل كتاب الوصية التي كتبها أبو حنيفة ليونس بن خالد السمتي رحمة الله عليه عند الرجوع إلى أهله: يجده من يطلبه، وقد كان أستاذنا شيخ الإسلام برهان الأئمة علي بن أبي بكر قدس الله روحه العزيز أمرني بكتابته عند الرجوع إلى بلدي وكتبته. ولا بد للمدرس والمفتي في معاملات الناس منه.

Chapter Three

On Choosing the Subject Matter of Learning, One's Teacher, One's Fellow Students, and One's Permanent Connection

(27) When undertaking the study of knowledge it is necessary to choose among all the branches of learning the one most beneficial to oneself.[18] One should [also] select what is essential according to the stage reached in one's religious development and finally [one should] choose what will be necessary for one in the future. And thus [the individual] perfects himself in the knowledge of the unity of God and learns about Almighty God through logical evidence. For the faith of him who blindly follows authority, even though it may be correct in our[19] view, still is defective because of his failure to ask for proofs.

(28) It is essential to choose ancient before new things. It is said: Stick to ancient things while avoiding new things. Beware of becoming engrossed in those disputes which come about after one has cut loose from the ancient authorities. For [such dispute] keeps the student away from knowledge, wastes away his life and leaves him with [nothing but] solitude and hostility. [A dispute] is one of the indications of the Hour[20] and the annihilation of both knowledge and doctrine. Thus is it stated by Tradition.

(29) Regarding the choice of a teacher, it is important to select the most learned, the most pious, and the most advanced in years. In this way [after due deliberation and reflection] Abū Ḥanīfa chose Ḥammād b. Abī Sulaimān[21] saying: "I found him venerable, with a serious mien, gentle, and patient." He [also said]: "I was on safe ground with Ḥammād b. Abī Sulaimān and I grew." Then he stated: "I heard a sage from Samarqand say: 'Verily, one of the students of knowledge consulted me about the inquiry into "science" and [after the consultation] he decided to take a journey to Bukhārā in order to acquire learning [there]'."

(30) Thus is it necessary to ask advice in all matters. Verily, God Almighty commanded [even] His messenger to seek counsel about all of his affairs. Although [in reality] there was no one more intelligent than [Muḥammad], nevertheless he was instructed to consult with others. So he sought advice from his friends in all affairs including domestic matters.

فصل: في اختيار العلم والأستاذ والشريك والثبات

(٢٧) ينبغي لطالب العلم أن يختار من كل علم أحسنه، مما يحتاج إليه في أمر دينه في الحال، ثم ما يحتاج إليه في المآل، فيقدم علم التوحيد والمعرفة، ويعرف الله تعالى بالدليل، فإن إيمان المقلد؛ وإن كان صحيحا عندنا لكن يكون آثما بترك الأستدلال.

(٢٨) ويختار العتيق دون المحدثات. قالوا: عليكم بالعتيق، وإياكم والمحدثات، وإياك أن تشتغل بهذا الجدل الذي ظهر بعد انقراض الأكابر من العلماء فإنه يبعد الطالب عن الفقه، ويضيع العمر، ويورث الوحشة والعداوة، وهو من أشراط الساعة، وارتفاع العلم والفقه، كذا ورد في الحديث.

(٢٩) وأما اختيار الأستاذ فينبغي أن يختار الأعلم والأورع والأسن، كما اختار أبو حنيفة حماد بن سليمان رحمه الله بعد التأمل والتفكر، وقال: وجدته شيخا وقورا حليما صبورا، وقال: ثبت عند حماد بن سليمان فنميت. قال رحمه الله: سمعت حكيما من حكماء سمرقند يقول: إن واحدا من طلبة العلم شاورني في طلب العلم، وكان عازما على الذهاب إلى بخارى لطلب العلم.

(٣٠) وهكذا ينبغي أن يشاور في كل أمر، فإن الله تعالى أمر رسوله ﷺ بالمشاورة في كل الأمور، ولم يكن أحد أفطن منه، ومع ذلك أمر بالمشاورة وكان يشاور أصحابه في جميع الأمور حتى حوائج البيت.

(31) ᶜAlī b. Abī Ṭālib[22] stated: "No man ever perished from seeking advice." It is said: A man, half a man, and nothing. A man is the one who is intelligent in his judgment and consults [others]. A half-man is he who is intelligent in his judgment but does not seek advice or seeks advice but is not intelligent, while one who is nothing is he who is neither intelligent nor seeks advice. Jaᶜfar al-Ṣadiq[23] said to Sufyān al-Thaurī:[24] "Seek advice in your affairs of those who are god-fearing. The quest of knowledge is among the most exalted and difficult tasks;[24a] consequently seeking advice in study of this kind is most important and most urgent."

(32) Al-Ḥakīm [al-Samarqandī][25] stated: "If you come to Bukhārā do not hasten hither and thither from one master to another. Rather, be patient a couple of months until you reflect concerning the choice of a teacher.[26] For, if you come to a learned man and begin to study with him right away, his teaching may often not be to your liking. [If this is the case] you leave him and come to another teacher. But no blessing will come to you by taking up your studies in this manner. Hence reflect two months about the [right] choice of a teacher and seek advice in order that it will not be necessary to leave him and withdraw from him. [It is better] that you remain with him until your studies have prospered and you have come to profit a great deal from the knowledge you have attained. Know that patience and perseverance form a large core in all affairs but [nevertheless] they are rare, as it is said in a verse:

The effort in the attainment of glory wearies,
but persistence is rare among men.

(33) It is said: Courage is the endurance of one hour. Hence it is necessary for the pursuer of knowledge to be firm and exert patience with his teacher and his book so as not to leave [his studies] incomplete.[27] [Also exert patience] with one discipline in order not to be distracted by another discipline before the first is perfected. [Likewise have patience] with a country so as not to migrate to another land unnecessarily. For all these changes[28] disturb one's affairs, preoccupy the heart, lose time and injure the teacher. It is essential to be strong in abstaining from what one's soul and one's desire wish one to do. A poet said:

Verily, desire is baseness in its essence,
and the victim of any desire is the victim of baseness.

(٣١) قال علي كرم الله وجهه: ما هلك امرؤ عن مشورة. قيل: الناس رجل، ونصف رجل، ولا شيء، فالرجل من له رأى صائب ويشاور، ونصف الرجل من له رأي صائب، ولكن لا يشاور، أو يشاور ولكن لا رأى له، ولا شيء من لا رأي له ولا يشاور. قال: جعفر الصادق رضي الله عنه لسفيان الثورى: شاور في أمرك الذين يخشون الله تعالى. وطلب العلم من أعلى الأمور، وأصعبها فكانت المشاورة فيه أهم وأوجب.

(٣٢) قال الحكيم: إذا ذهبت إلى بخارى لا تعجل في الاختلاف إلى الأئمة، وامكث شهرين حتى تتأمل وتختار أستاذا، فإنك إذا ذهبت إلى عالم وبدأت بالسبق عنده ربما لا يعجبك درسه فتتركه وتذهب إلى آخر فلا يبارك لك في التعلم، فتأمل شهرين في اختيار الأستاذ وشاور حتى لا تحتاج إلى تركه والإعراض عنه فتثبت عنده حتى يكون تعلمك مباركا وتنتفع بعلمك كثيرا. واعلم أن الصبر والثبات أصل كبير في جميع الأمور، ولكنه عزيز كما قيل:

لكل إلى شأو العلا حركات ولكن عزيز في الرجال ثبات

(٣٣) قيل: الشجاعة، صبر ساعة، فينبغي لطالب العلم أن يثبت ويصبر على أستاذ، وعلى كتاب حتى لا يتركه أبتر، وعلى فن حتى لا يشتغل بفن آخر قبل أن يتقن الأول، وعلى بلد حتى لا ينتقل إلى بلد آخر من غير ضرورة، فإن ذلك كله يفرق الامور ويشغل القلب، ويضيع الأوقات، ويؤذي المعلم، وينبغي أن يصبر عما تريده نفسه وهواه. قال الشاعر:

إن الهوى لهو الهوان بعينه وصريع كل هوى صريع هوان

(34) And [it is necessary] to be patient in calamity and affliction. It is said: The treasure of benefits lies on the arches of calamities. I recited a poem which is said to be by ᶜAlī b. Abī Ṭālib:

The pursuit of knowledge is not carried on without six things
which I shall indicate to you through words that are clear:

Ingenious acumen, fervent desire, patience, sufficient sustenance,
guidance of a teacher, and length of time.

(35) As to the selection of one's companions, it is necessary to choose the one who is diligent, religious, gifted with a good character, and understanding; [on the other hand, it is essential] to escape from the one who is indolent and negligent, loquacious, corrupt, and a trouble maker. It is said in a verse:

Do not inquire concerning a man but observe his companion,
for verily one companion imitates the other companion;

And if the companion is evil, then quickly shun him,
but if [the companion] is good, associate with him.
In this way you will be led in the right direction.

(36) Another poem was recited to me:

Do not associate yourself with a companion indolent in his ways.
How often through the corruption of another man is a pious man corrupted.

Contagion spreads quickly from the lazy to the [lively] one,
just as when one places a [burning] coal in ashes, the fire is allayed.

(37) The Prophet said: "Everyone born is born a Muslim unless his parents make him a Jew, a Christian, or a Magian." This is the Tradition.[29] And it is said according to the Wisdom of the Persians:

A bad friend is worse than an evil snake;
[swear] by the pure essence of the Eternal God!

A bad companion leads you toward Hell;
take a good companion in order to secure success.[29a]

(٣٤) ويصبر على المحن والبليات، فقد قيل: خزائن المنن على قناطر المحن، وأنشدت، وقيل إنه لعلي بن أبي طالب رضي الله تعالى عنه:

ألا لا تنال العلم إلا بستة سأنبيك عن مجموعها ببيان
ذكاء وحرص واصطبار وبلغة وإرشاد أستاذ، وطول زمان

(٣٥) وأما اختيار الشريك فينبغي أن يختار المجد والورع وصاحب الطبع المستقيم، ويفر من الكسلان، والمعطل، والمكثار، والمفسد، والفتان. قال الشاعر:

عن المرء لا تسأل وأبصر قرينه فكل قرين بالمقارن يقتدي
فإن كان ذا شر فجانبه سرعة وإن كان ذا خير فقارنه تهتدي

(٣٦) وأنشدت:

لا تصحب الكسلان في حالاته كم صالح بفساد آخر يفسد
عدوى البليد إلى الجليد سريعة كالجمر يوضع في الرماد فتخمد

(٣٧) وقال ﷺ: « كل مولود يولد على فطرة الإسلام إلا أن أبويه يهودانه، أو ينصرانه، أو يمجسانه » الحديث، ويقال في الحكمة بالفارسية:

يار بد بدتر بود از مار بد حق ذات بالك الله الصمد
يار بد آرد ترا سوى جحيم يار نيكو كير تا يابى نعيم

(38) And it is said:

If you seek knowledge from those who possess it
or from a witness who tells you about what you know not;

Appraise the country from its reputation
and the companion by his companion.

Chapter Four

On Respecting Knowledge and Those Who Possess It

(39) Know that in the study of science one does not acquire learning nor profit from it unless one holds in esteem knowledge and those who possess it. One [must also] glorify and venerate the teacher. It is said: He who attains knowledge does not do so except through respect, while he who fails [in this goal] does so by ceasing to respect and venerate learning and its bearers. [In addition] it is stated: "Respect is preferable to obedience, for do you not perceive that man does not become an unbeliever through rebellion [against divine law] but rather by making light of [his rebellion] and by discarding reverence." One aspect of glorifying knowledge consists in holding the teacher in esteem. ᶜAli said: "I am the slave of him who taught me one letter of the alphabet. If he wishes he may sell me; if he so desires he may set me free; and if he cares to he may make use of me as a slave."

(40) On this subject I [al-Zarnūjī] have composed these lines:

It seems to me the greatest duty is that which is due the teacher,
and that which is the most necessary thing for each Moslem to observe.

Indeed it is a duty to offer him a thousand drachmae as a sign of honor
for his instruction in one single letter of the alphabet.

(41) Verily, he who teaches you one letter of those you need for your religious instruction is your father in religion. Our teacher, the venerable Imām, Sadīd al-Dīn al-Shīrāzī,[30] used to say: "Our elders stated: whoever wishes his son to become learned will have to cultivate traveling scholars,[31] esteem them, venerate them as well as offer them remuneration." Verily, if [in the case of such comportment] one's son does not become learned, one's grandson does. In venerating the teacher [among

(٣٨) وقيل:

إن كنت تبغي العلم من أهله ... أو شاهدا يخبر عن غائب
فاعتبر الأرض بأسمائها ... واعتبر الصاحب بالصاحب

فصل: في تعظيم العلم وأهله

(٣٩) اعلم أن طالب العلم لا ينال العلم، ولا ينتفع به إلا بتعظيم العلم وأهله، وتعظيم الأستاذ وتوقيره، فقد قيل: ما وصل من وصل إلا بالحرمة، وما سقط من سقط إلا بترك الحرمة، وقيل: الحرمة خير من الطاعة. ألا ترى أن الإنسان لا يكفر بالمعصية، وإنما يكفر باستخفافها، وبترك الحرمة، ومن تعظيم العلم تعظيم المعلم. قال علي كرم الله وجهه: أنا عبد من علمني حرفا واحدا، إن شاء باع، وإن شاء أعتق، وإن شاء استرق.

(٤٠) وقد أنشدت في ذلك شعرا:

وأيت أحق الحق حق المعلم ... وأوجبه حفظا على كل مسلم
لقد حق أن يهدى إليه كرامة ... لتعليم حرف واحد ألف درهم

(٤١) فإن من علمك حرفا مما تحتاج إليه في الدين فهو أبوك في الدين، وكان أستاذنا الشيخ الإمام سديد الدين الشيرازي رحمه الله تعالى يقول: قال مشايخنا رحمهم الله: من أراد أن يكون ابنه عالما فينبغي أن يراعي الغرباء من الفقهاء،

other things it is necessary to avoid] walking in front of him or sitting in his place. Also, one should not begin speaking in his presence without his permission, and then one should not speak to any great extent before him. One should not ask him any [question] when he is weary. One should observe the correct time [i.e., not intrude at the wrong moment] and not knock on the door but have patience until [the teacher] comes out. In short, one should seek his approval, avoid his resentment, and obey his commands in those things which are not sinful in the eyes of God—but never is created man to be obeyed in rebellion against the creator. The Prophet spoke thus: Verily, the most evil man is he who relinquishes his religion for the religion of other men. In this, he is sinning against God.[32]

(42) Revering the teacher includes respecting the teacher's children and those who belong to him. Our instructor, the venerable Imām, Burhān al-Dīn, author of the *Ḥidāyah,* used to narrate that one of the greatest imāms of Bukhārā [at one time] had sat lecturing and had sometimes risen in the middle of his discourse. When asked the reason [for this] he explained: "Verily, the son of my teacher played with boys on the street and came sometimes to the gate of the Mosque. As often as I saw him I arose for him in order to honor my teacher."

(43) The judge, the Imām Fakhr al-Dīn al-Arsābandī,[33] was the chief imām in Marw; the Sultan held him in the highest regard. Fakhr al-Dīn frequently said: "Verily, I have reached this rank only by serving my teacher, for I have served my teacher, the judge, the Imām Abū Yazīd al-Dabūsī.[34] I both waited on him and prepared his food for thirty years but I never ate anything thereof." The venerable Imām, the most glorious sun among the imāms, al-Ḥulwānī,[35] left Bukhārā and settled for some time in a certain town because of an incident which befell him. His students visited him with the exception of the venerable Imām, the Judge, Abū Bakr al-Zaranjī.[36] When he met him al-Ḥulwānī asked him: "Why did you not come to visit me?" Abū Bakr replied: "I was occupied serving my mother." Al- Ḥulwānī answered: "You will obtain a livelihood but you will not attain the glamour of teaching." And this is just what happened for [Abū Bakr] lived most of his life in villages and was unable to carry on lectures. Thus is deprived of the fruits of learning who has slighted his teacher, and only in a small way does he profit from his knowledge.

ويكرمهم، ويطعمهم، ويعظمهم ويعطيهم شيئا، فإن لم يكن ابنه عالما يكون حفيده عالما، ومن توقير المعلم ألا يمشى أمامه، ولا يجلس مكانه، ولا يبتدىء بالكلام عنده إلا بإذنه، ولا يكثر الكلام عنده إلا باذنه، ولا يسأل شيئا عند ملالته، ويراعى الوقت، ولا يدق الباب بل يصبر حتى يخرج. وفى الجملة يطلب رضاه، ويجتنب سخطه، ويمتثل أمره في غير معصية الله تعالى، فإنه لا طاعة لمخلوق في معصية الخالق كما قال النبى عليه الصلاة والسلام: «إن شر الناس من يذهب دينه لدنيا غيره».

(٤٢) ومن توقيره توقير أولاده، ومن يتعلق به، وكان أستاذنا شيخ الإسلام برهان الدين صاحب الهداية رحمة الله عليه يحكي أن واحدا من كبار أئمة بخارى كان يجلس مجلس الدرس، وكان يقوم في خلال الدرس أحيانا، فسألوه عن ذلك فقال: إن ابن أستاذى يلعب مع الصبيان في السكة، ويجيء أحيانا إلى باب المسجد، فإذا رأيته أقوم له تعظيما لأستاذي.

(٤٣) وكان القاضي الإمام فخر الدين الأرسابندى رئيس الأئمة في مرو، وكان السلطان يحترمه غاية الاحترام، ويقول: إنما وجدت في هذا المنصب بخدمة الأستاذ فإني كنت أخدم الأستاذ القاضي الإمام أبا يزيد الدبوسي، وكنت أخدمه، وأطبخ طعامه ثلاثين سنة، ولا آكل منه شيئا، وكان الشيخ الإمام الأجل شمس الأئمة الحلواني رحمه الله قد خرج من بخارى وسكن في بعض القرى أياما لحادثة وقعت له، وقد زاره تلاميذه غير الشيخ الإمام القاضي شمس الأئمة أبي بكر الزرنجي رحمه الله تعالى، فقال له حين لقيه: لم لم تزرني؟ فقال له: كنت مشغولا بخدمة الوالدة، فقال: ترزق العمر، ولا ترزق رونق الدرس وكان كذلك، فإنه كان يسكن في أكثر أوقاته القرى ولم ينتظم له الدرس، فمن تأذى منه أستاذه يحرم بركة العلم، ولا ينتفع به إلا قليلا.

Neither the teacher nor the physician advise you
unless they are honored.

So bear your disease patiently if you have wronged its healer
and be satisfied with your ignorance if you have wronged a teacher.

(44) It is reported that the Caliph, Hārūn al-Rashīd,[37] sent his son to al-Aṣmaᶜī[38] to take up the study of science [i.e., in this context, grammar] and *adab.*[38a] One day [the Caliph] saw [al-Aṣmaᶜī] purifying himself and washing his feet while the son of the Caliph poured water over his feet. So [the Caliph] reprimanded al-Aṣmaᶜī in this manner saying: "Indeed, I sent him [my son] to you to learn grammar and be instructed in *adab,* so why is it that you don't ask him to pour water with one hand and wash your foot with the other hand?"

(45) One way of holding knowledge in esteem is through Veneration of the Book [the Qurᵓān]. Hence it behooves the student not to take up the Book unless he is in a state of [ritual] purity. It has been told concerning the venerable Imām, the sun of the imāms, al-Ḥulwānī, that he said: "Verily, I obtained this learning by means of veneration for I never took up paper unless I was pure." And the venerable Imām, the sun of the imāms, al-Sarakhsi,[39] had a stomach ache. It was his wont to repeat the Qurᵓān at night. So he purified himself seventeen times [each time after he had been compelled to relieve nature] in order not to resume recitation without being pure. He did this since learning is light and purification is light; thus the light of learning is increased by [purification].

(46) The required veneration [of the Book] includes the obligation not to stretch out one's foot toward the Book, to place books of [Qurᵓān] interpretation above other Books, and not to place anything else above the Book. Our teacher, the venerable Imām, Burhān al-Dīn often told about when a certain Sheikh [saw] a scholar putting an inkwell on the Book; he said to him in Persian, "*bar na-yābī*"—"You will reap no fruit" [from your labors owing to this act of disrespect].

إن المعلم والطبيب كلاهما لا ينصحان إذا هما لم يكرما
فاصبر لدائك إن جفوت طبيبه واقنع بجهلك إن جفوت معلما

(٤٤) وحكي أن الخليفة هارون الرشيد: بعث ابنه إلى الأصمعي ليعلمه العلم والأدب، فرآه يوما يتوضأ ويغسل رجله، وابن الخليفة يصب الماء على رجله، فعاتب الأصمعي في ذلك بقوله: إنما بعثته إليك لتعلمه وتؤدبه، فلماذا لم تأمره بأن يصب الماء بإحدى يديه، ويغسل بالأخرى رجلك؟

(٤٥) ومن تعظيم المعلم تعظيم الكتاب، فينبغى لطالب العلم ألا يأخذ الكتاب إلا بالطهارة. وحكي عن الشيخ شمس الأئمة الحلواني رحمة الله عليه أنه قال: إنما نلت هذا العلم بالتعظيم، فإني ما أخذت الكاغد إلا بالطهارة، والشيخ الإمام شمس الأئمة السرخسي رحمه الله تعالى كان مبطونا، وكان يكرر في ليلة فتوضأ في تلك الليلة سبع عشرة مرة، لأنه كان لا يكرر إلا بالطهارة وهذا لأن العلم نور، والوضوء نور، فيزداد نور العلم به.

(٤٦) ومن التعظيم الواجب ألا يمد رجله إلى الكتاب، ويضع كتب التفسير فوق سائر الكتب تعظيما، ولا يضع على الكتاب شيئا آخر. وكان أستاذنا شيخ الإسلام برهان الدين رحمه الله تعالى يحكي عن شيخ من المشايخ أن فقيها كان وضع المحبرة على الكتاب، فقال له بالفارسية: « برنيابى ».

(47) It was our teacher, the judge, the most illustrious glory of Islam, known as Qādīkhān,[40] who used to say: "If one does not [break the rules for handling the Qur'ān] from a wish to treat the Book with disdain there is no harm in so doing, but it is better to guard oneself against [the possibility of such a breach of rules]".

(48) The required veneration implies the duty to write the Book beautifully and not in a cramped style, and not to leave notes in the margin except when it cannot be helped. When Abū Ḥanīfa saw someone writing the Book in a cramped style, he said: "Do not cramp your handwriting. If you live you will regret it and if you die you will be taken to task [for so doing, on Judgment Day]." It is told of the venerable Imām, Majd al-Dīn al-Sarakhsī,[41] that he stated: "Let us not write in a cramped style lest we regret it and let us not make selections [abridgments] lest we regret it; and let us not omit to collate [what we have written] lest we regret it." And the form of the Book must be square. For this is the form [employed by] Abū Ḥanīfa. It is the easiest for lifting, placing, and reading. And it is necessary not to have any red color in the Book for thus was the usage of the philosophers but not the usage of our ancestors; to our Sheikhs[42] the use of red mixture [for writing] is abhorrent.

(49) Veneration of learning includes veneration of one's companions in the quest of knowledge and our fellows in the lecture room. Adulation is blameworthy except in the quest of knowledge; for it will be necessary to praise one's teacher and one's fellow students in order that one can profit from their learning.

(50) And it is essential in seeking knowledge to listen to knowledge and wisdom with reverence and veneration even if one hears one question and one word a thousand times. It is said: He whose respect after a thousand times is not equal to his respect the first time [he hears these things] is not worthy of knowledge. In seeking knowledge it is necessary not to choose oneself the kind of learning to pursue, but to entrust the matter to the teacher. For indeed experience has come to the teacher in these matters so that he has more knowledge of what is needed for each person and what is suitable to the nature [of each student]. The venerable Imām, the most glorious teacher, Burhān [al-Ḥaqq] wa'l-Dīn[43] used to

(٤٧) وكان أستاذنا القاضي الإمام الأجل فخر الإسلام المعروف بقاضيخان رحمه الله تعالى يقول: إن لم يرد بذلك الاستخفاف فلا بأس به، والأولى أن يتحرز عنه.

(٤٨) ومن التعظيم الواجب أن يجود كتابة الكتاب، ولا يقرمط، ويترك الحاشية إلا عند الضرورة، ورأى أبو حنيفة رحمه الله تعالى كاتبا يقرمط في الكتابة، فقال: لم تقرمط خطك، إن عشت تندم، وإن مت تشتم، يعنى إذا كبرت وضعف بصرك ندمت على ذلك. وحكي عن الشيخ الإمام مجد الدين السرجكي أنه قال: ما قرمطنا إلا ندمنا، وما انتخبنا إلا ندمنا، وما لم نقابل إلا ندمنا. وينبغي أن يكون تقطيع الكتاب مربعا فإنه تقطيع أبي حنيفة وحمه الله، وهو أيسر إلى الرفع والوضع والمطالعة. وينبغي ألا يكون في الكتاب شيء من الحمرة، فإنها صنيع الفلاسفة لا صنيع السلف. ومن مشايخنا من كره استعمال المركب الأحمر.

(٤٩) ومن تعظيم العلم تعظيم الشركاء في طلب العلم والدرس، ومن يتعلم منه. والتملق مذموم إلا في طلب العلم، فإنه ينبغي أن يتملق لأستاذه وشركائه ليستفيد منهم.

(٥٠) وينبغي لطالب العلم أن يستمع العلم بالتعظيم والحرمة، وإن سمع المسئلة الواحدة أو الكلمة الواحدة ألف مرة. قيل: من لم يكن تعظيمه بعد ألف مرة كتعظيمه في أول مرة، فليس بأهل للعلم. وينبغي لطالب العلم ألا يختار نوع علم بنفسه، بل يفوض أمره إلى الأستاذ؛ فإن الأستاذ قد حصل له التجارب في ذلك، فكان أعرف بما ينبغي لكل أحد، وما يليق بطبيعته. وكان الشيخ الإمام الأجل الأستاذ برهان الدين

say: "In the quest for learning in early times the students entrusted their problems of instruction to their teacher and in this manner their goal and their aim; but now they make their own choice and they do not reach their proposed goal [in religious and legal knowledge]." It is related that Muḥammad b. Ismāʿīl al-Bukhārī[44] came to Muḥammad b. al-Ḥasan with the Book of Prayer [probably a Law Book]. And Muḥammad b. al-Ḥasan said to him: "Go out and learn the science of Tradition," since indeed he estimated that this [kind of] knowledge was better suited to his nature. So [this student] investigated the science of Tradition and finally became superior to all the other imāms of Tradition.

(51) It further behooves the student not to sit near the teacher during the lecture except under necessity, rather is it essential that the pupils sit in a semi-circle at a certain distance from the teacher, for indeed this is more appropriate to the respect due [the teacher]. And it is necessary in the quest of knowledge to be on one's guard against shameful traits of character, for verily these are the howling dogs of the spirit. The Messenger of God has said: "The angels do not enter a home in which is a dog or a picture." Verily, man only learns through the medium of the angel, and certain shameful traits are known from the *Kitāb al-akhlāq*—and this book of ours cannot offer a discussion of these traits—particularly pride; for as long as pride is harbored, knowledge cannot be attained.

(52) It is said:

Knowledge is hostile to the haughty youth
just as the torrent is hostile to the highest place.

(53) It is also said:

All glory is attained by exertion, not by luck—
for is luck without exertion glorious?

How many a slave ranks with the free,
and how many a free-born man ranks with the slave!

يقول: كان طلبة العلم في الزمان الأول يفوضون أمورهم في التعلم إلى أستاذهم، فكانوا يصلون إلى مقاصدهم ومرادهم، والآن يختارون بأنفسهم فلا يحصل مقصودهم من العلم والفقه. وكان يحكى أن محمد بن إسماعيل البخاري رحمه الله تعالى كان بدأ بكتاب الصلاة على محمد بن الحسن، فقال له محمد رحمه الله تعالى: اذهب وتعلم علم الحديث؛ لما رأى أن ذلك العلم أليق بطبعه، فطلب علم الحديث فصار فيه مقدما على جميع أئمة الحديث.

(٥١) وينبغي لطالب العلم ألا يجلس قريبا من الأستاذ عند السبق بغير ضرورة، بل ينبغي أن يكون بينه وبين الأستاذ قدر القوس، فإنه أقرب إلى التعظيم. وينبغي لطالب العلم أن يحترز عن الأخلاق الذميمة، فإنها كلاب معنوية، وقد قال رسول الله ﷺ «لا تدخل الملائكة بيتا فيه كلب أو صورة»؛ وإنما يتعلم الإنسان بواسطة الملائكة. والأخلاق الذميمة تعرف في كتاب الأخلاق، وكتابنا هذا لا يحتمل بيانها، وليحترز خصوصا عن التكبر، فمع التكبر لا يحصل العلم.

(٥٢) قيل:

العلم حرب للفتى المتعالي كالسيل حرب للمكان العالي

(٥٣) وقيل:

بجدي لا بجد كل مجد فهل جد بلا جد بمجدي

فكم عبد يقوم مقام حر وكم حر يقوم مقام عبد

Chapter Five

In Industriousness, Perseverance, and Assiduity [in the pursuit of learning]

(54) Furthermore, earnestness, perseverance, and assiduity are indispensable in the quest for knowledge. This is indicated in the Qurʾān in the words of the Exalted One:[45] "Those who have earnestly striven in our cause, we shall surely lead them along our ways"; and "Yaḥya, take the Book with power."[46] It is said: He who seeks something and is industrious [in so doing] finds it, and he who knocks at the door and is persistent [succeeds in] entering. And it is said: To the extent to which you pursue something you will reach what you desire. It is said: Industriousness of three kinds of people is essential in [the pursuit of] science and learning. These people are the student, the teacher, and the father, if he is among the living.

(55) The venerable Imām, the most glorious professor, Sadīd al-Dīn al-Shirāzī, recited to me a poem composed by al-Shafiᶜī:

Earnest application makes accessible every remote affair
and industriousness opens every locked door.

The creature of God most worthy to excite grief is a man of high aspirations
who is worn out by a life of straightened circumstances.

The afflictions of the wise and the easy life of the fool
point up the wisdom of destiny.

Lack of wealth will nourish intellectual power:
[wealth and intellect are] opposites, how far apart!

(56) A poem by another author was recited to me:

Do you desire to become learned and skilled in argument except by labor?
There are various kinds of stupidity.

No gain of riches is possible without difficulties
which you must take upon yourself.
And hence, how is it possible for learning [to be acquired without difficulty]?

فصل: في الجد والمواظبة والهمة

(٥٤) ثم لا بد من الجد والمواظبة والملازمة لطالب العلم، وإليه الإشارة في القرآن بقوله تعالى: ﴿والذين جاهدوا فينا لنهدينهم سبلنا﴾. وقوله تعالى: ﴿يا يحيى خذ الكتاب بقوة﴾. وقد قيل: من طلب شيئا وجد وجد. ومن قرع الباب ولج ولج، وقيل: بقدر ما تتعنى تنال ما تمنى. قيل: يحتاج في التعلم والتفقه إلى الجد ثلاثة: المتعلم والأستاذ والأب إن كان في الأحياء.

(٥٥) أنشدني الشيخ الإمام الأستاذ سديد الدين الشيرازي رحمة الله عليه للإمام الشافعي:

الجد يدني كل أمر شاسع ... والجد يفتح كل باب مغلق
وأحق خلق الله بالهم امرؤ ... ذو همة يبلى بعيش ضيق
ومن الدليل على القضاء وحكمه ... بؤس اللبيب وطيب عيش الأحمق
لكن من رزق الحجى حرم الغنى ... ضدان يفترقان أي تفرق

(٥٦) وأنشدت لغيره:

تمنيت أن تمسى فقيها مناظرا ... بغير عناء والجنون فنون
وليس اكتساب المال دون مشقة ... تحملها، فالعلم كيف يكون

(57) Abū al-Ṭayyib [al-Mutanabbī][47] said:

I do not see a fault among the faults of men
like the imperfection of those able to reach perfection.

(58) And it is essential in the seeking of knowledge to maintain a vigil throughout the nights, as the poet says:

By means of a large amount of hard work you gain the highest distinction.
So he who seeks learning keeps awake during the night.

You strive after glory but then you sleep at night.
He who seeks pearls immerses himself in the sea.

The height of [the builder's] blocks depends on the height of his aspirations;
a man's dignity rests on his nightly vigils.

Whoso desires elevation without fatigue
wastes his life in the quest for the absurd.

I have forsaken sleep at night
to win your satisfaction, O Lord of Lords.

So let me attain the winning of knowledge
and let me reach the utmost degree of accomplishment.

(59) It is said: Take night as your camel, with it you will attain your hope. The writer [of this book] said: "I made up a poem on this theme:"

He who desires to carry out all his aspirations
should use his nights as camel on his road to reach them.

Diminish your food in order to maintain a vigil
if you wish, O my friend, to attain perfection.

(٥٧) قال أبو الطيب:

ولم أر في عيوب الناس عيبا   كنقص القادرين على التمام

(٥٨) ولا بد للطالب من سهر الليالي، كما قال الشاعر:

بقدر الكد تكتسب المعالي   ومن طلب العلا سهر الليالي
تروم العز ثم تنام ليلا   يغوص البحر من طلب اللآلي
علو الكعب بالهمم العوالي   وعز المرء في سهر الليالي
ومن رام العلا من غير كد   أضاع العمر في طلب المحال
تركت النوم ربي في الليالي   لأجل رضاك يامولى الموالي
فوفقني إلى تحصيل علم   وبلغني إلى أقصى المعالي

(٥٩) وقيل: اتخذ الليل جملا، تدرك به أملا. قال المصنف رحمه الله تعالى: وقد اتفق لى نظم في هذا المعنى:

من شاء أن يحتوى آماله جملا   فليتخذ ليله في دركها جملا
أقلل طعامك كى تحظى به سهرا   إن شئت يا صاحبي أن تبلغ الكملا

(60) And it is said: He who keeps watch at night will rejoice in his heart during the day.

(61) In the search for knowledge it behooves one to persevere in study and repetition both at the beginning of the night and at its end. For verily the time between dusk and the hour of dawn is a blessed time. On this subject verses have been composed:

O student of knowledge, occupy yourself with reverence for God;
avoid sleep and leave off satisfying your hunger.

And persevere in study. Do not cease from this,
for learning exists and grows through study.

(62) [And in the quest for learning] one must make use of the days of early youth and adolescence. And it is said:

By the amount of work [you do] you will obtain what you strive for.
So he who strives for a goal stays up by night.

Make use of the days of early youth
for verily the period of youth does not remain with you.

(63) But [in order to pursue knowledge] one should not exhaust nor weaken oneself so that one cuts oneself off from work. On the contrary, one should practice temperance in this respect for moderation is one great source of all success. The Messenger of God said: "Indeed, this religion of mine is solidly grounded, so enter into it with moderation." Do not make hateful to yourself the service of God. Verily, he who makes plants grow does not cut up the ground nor does he neglect it entirely. The Prophet also said: "Your mind is your riding-beast, hence use it with moderation."

(64) It is obligatory in seeking knowledge to have the highest aspiration level for learning, since verily man flies by his aspirations like the bird flies with his wings.

(٦٠) وقيل: من أسهر نفسه بالليل، فقد فرح قلبه بالنهار.

(٦١) ولا بد لطالب العلم من المواظبة على الدرس، والتكرار في أول الليل وآخره، فإن ما بين العشاءين و وقت السحر وقت مبارك. قيل في المعنى شعر:

يا طالب العلم باشر الورعا وجنب النوم واترك الشبعا
داوم على الدرس لا تفارقه فالعلم بالدرس قام وارتفعا

(٦٢) فيغتنم أيام الحداثة وعنفوان الشباب كما قيل:

بقدر الكد تعطى ما تروم فمن رام المنى ليلا يقوم
وأيام الحداثة فاغتنمها ألا إن الحداثة لا تدوم

(٦٣) ولا يجهد نفسه جهدا، ولا يضعف النفس حتى ينقطع عن العمل، بل يستعمل الرفق في ذلك، والرفق أصل عظيم في جميع الأشياء. قال عليه الصلاة والسلام: «ألا إن هذا الدين متين، فأوغلوا فيه برفق، ولا تبغض على نفسك عبادة الله تعالى، فإن المنبت لا أرضا قطع ولا ظهرا أبقى» وقال عليه الصلاة والسلام: «نفسك مطيتك فارفق بها».

(٦٤) ولا بد لطالب العلم من الهمة العالية في العلم، فإن المرء يطير بهمته، كالطير يطير بجناحيه.

(65) Abū al-Ṭayyib [al-Mutanabbī][48] said:

Decisions are arrived at according to the statute of those who decide,
generous deeds according to the open-handedness of the generous.

And small things are great in the eyes of the small person
and great things are small in the eyes of the great.

(66) Aids to the acquisition of anything are industriousness and an ambition that aims high. He who aspires to memorizing all of the books of Muḥammad b. al-Ḥasan and adds [to this ambition] industriousness and perseverance, will clearly remember the greater part of these books or at least a half. But if one has the most extreme aspiration but does not have industriousness, or has industriousness but does not aspire high, knowledge comes to one only in a small amount.

(67) The venerable Imām, the most glorious Professor, Raḍī al-Dīn al-Naisābūrī[49] recalled in the book *Makārim al-akhlāq* [Ethics] that when Dhū al-Qarnain [Alexander the Great] wished to make an expedition in order to become master of the East and the West, he consulted learned men and asked: "Why do I make an expedition for such an amount of empire? For verily, the world is small and perishable and rule of the world is a contemptible affair. So this [expedition] is not a noble way to exert oneself." But the learned men said: "Make the expedition in order that you may have possession of the present and the future world." So he said: "This is good." And the Messenger of God said: "Surely, God, the Exalted One, loves noble undertakings and abhors contemptible ones." It is said:

Do not make haste in your affairs but proceed slowly with them.
For nothing will straighten your stick like a slow fire.

(٦٥) قال أبو الطيب:

على قدر أهل العزم تأتي العزائم وتأتي على قدر الكرام المكارم
وتعظم في عين الصغير صغارها وتصغر في عين العظيم العظائم

(٦٦) والرأس في تحصيل الأشياء: الجد والهمة العالية، فمن كانت همته حفظ جميع كتب محمد بن الحسن رحمه الله تعالى، واقترن بذلك الجد والمواظبة، فالظاهر أنه يحفظ أكثرها أو نصفها، فأما إذا كانت له همة عالية، ولم يكن له جد، أو كان له جد ولم يكن له همة عالية، فلا يحصل له علم إلا القليل.

(٦٧) وذكر الشيخ الأجل الإمام الأستاذ رضي الدين النيسابوري رحمه الله في كتاب مكارم الأخلاق: أن ذا القرنين لما أراد أن يسافر ليستولي على المشرق والمغرب شاور الحكماء في ذلك، وقال: كيف أسافر لهذا القدر من الملك؟ فإن الدنيا قليلة فانية وملك الدنيا أمر حقير، فليس هذا من علو الهمة، فقال الحكماء: سافر ليحصل لك ملك الدنيا والآخرة، قال: هذا أحسن، وقال رسول الله ﷺ: «إن الله تعالى يحب معالي الأمور، ويكره سفسافها»، وقيل:

فلا تعجل بأمرك واستدمه فما صلى عصاك كمستديم

(68) It is reported that Abū Ḥanīfa said to Abū Yūsuf:[50] "You were a hick but assiduity in your studies made you emerge [from your ignorance]. But beware of laziness, for, verily, it is impropitious and a great calamity." The venerable Imām Abū Naṣr al-Ṣaffār al-Anṣarī[50a] stated:

O my soul, my soul, do not become lax in your work
of piety and justice and good works [carried on] in calmness.

For each one who does good deeds experiences happiness
while each one who acts in a lazy manner has afflictions and unhappiness.

(69) The writer [of this book] said: There came to me a poem in the same vein:

Let go of laziness and slovenliness, O my soul—
otherwise you will bring on you contempt.

For I do not see that the lazy have a share in anything,
but contrition and frustration of hopes.

(70) And it is said:

How much shame and weakness and contrition
is born to men from laziness.

Beware of laziness in investigating the doubtful
and the exceptional that come to your knowledge.

(71) It is said further: Laziness comes from paucity of meditation on the virtues of knowledge and its merits. Hence it is necessary when embarking on study to bestir oneself for the acquisition [of knowledge] and [prod oneself] to industriousness and perseverance in the meditation of the merits of learning. For truly, knowledge remains while riches disappear, just as the Prince of Believers, ʿAlī b. Abī Ṭālib, said:

We are satisfied with the allotment made by the All-Powerful;
to us, knowledge; to the enemies, wealth.

For wealth will soon perish
while knowledge will remain forever.

(٦٨) قال أبو حنيفة لأبي يوسف رحمهما الله تعالى: كنت بليدا فأخرجتك المواظبة، وإياك والكسل فإنه شؤم، وآفة عظيمة. قال الشيخ الإمام أبو نصر الصفار الأنصارى رحمه الله تعالى:

يا نفس يا نفس لاترخي عن العمل في البر والعدل والإحسان في مهل
فكل ذي عمل في الخير مغتبط وفي بلاء وشؤم كل ذي كسل

(٦٩) قال المصنف: وقد اتفق لي في هذا المعنى:

دعي نفسى التكاسل والتوانى وإلا فاثبتى في ذا الهوان
فلم أر للكسالى الحظ يعطي سوى ندم وحرمان الأماني

(٧٠) وقيل:

كم من حياء وكم عجز وكم ندم جم تولد للإنسان من كسل
إياك عن كسل في البحث عن شبه فيما علمت، وما قد شذ عنك سل

(٧١) وقد قيل: الكسل من قلة التأمل في مناقب العلم وفضائله، فينبغي للمتعلم أن يبعث نفسه على التحصيل والجد والمواظبة بالتأمل في فضائل العلم، فإن العلم يبقى ببقاء. المعلومات، والمال يفنى، كما قال أمير المؤمنين على بن أبى طالب كرم الله وجهه:

رضينا قسمة الجبار فينا لنا علم وللأعداء مال
فإن المال يفنى عن قريب وإن العلم يبقى لا يزال

(72) From useful knowledge good fame derives and remains after one's death. Indeed, this is life everlasting. The venerable Imām, the most glorious Ẓahīr al-Dīn, Muftī of the imāms, al-Ḥasan b. ʿAlī, known as al-Marghīnānī,[51] recited to us:

The ignorant are dead before their death
while the learned live even though they are dead.

(73) The Sheikh al-Islām, Burhān al-Dīn recited to us:

Ignorance is a death before the death to those that harbor it,
and their bodies are graves before the graves.

Verily, a man who does not live by knowledge is dead
nor will there be a resurrection for him at the time of resurrection.

(74) Somebody else said:

The master of knowledge stays alive forever after his death
while his bones rot under the dust.

But the ignorant is dead while still he walks on the ground,
thought to be alive but actually non-existent.

(75) Another poet said:

The life of the heart is knowledge, so go after it,
and the death of the heart is ignorance, so shun it.

(٧٢) والعلم النافع يحصل به حسن الذكر ويبقى ذلك بعد وفاته، فإنه حياة أبدية. أنشدنا الشيخ الإمام الأجل ظهير الدين مفتى الأئمة حسن بن على المعروف بالمر غينانى رحمه الله تعالى:

الجاهلون فموتى قبل موتهم والعالمون وإن ماتوا فأحياء

(٧٣) وأنشدنا شيخ الإسلام برهان الدين:

وفى الجهل قبل الموت موت لأهله فأجسامهم قبل القبور قبور
وإن امرأ لم يحيى بالعلم ميت وليس له حين النشور نشور

(٧٤) وقال غيره:

أخو العلم حى خالد بعد موته وأوصاله تحت التراب رميم
وذو الجهل ميت وهو يمشي على الثرى يظن من الأحياء وهو عديم

(٧٥) وقال آخر:

حياة القلب علم فاغتنمه وموت القلب جهل فاجتنبه

(76) The venerable Imām, the Professor Burhān al-Dīn recited for us:

Behold learning occupies the highest rank
while inferior to it is the grandeur of the greatest in a princely procession.

For the man of learning, his splendor continues to increase after his death
while the stupid man just lies below the ground after his death.

No one who ascends the ladder of empire and of generalship[52]
can at all hope for the heights [reached by the man of learning].

I shall dictate to you some of the things of which [knowledge] consists.
So listen, for it is not possible for me to tell about all the virtues of learning.

[Knowledge] is the most perfect light which leads men along the right path
away from blindness while the ignorant man passes his life
among the shades [in darkness].

[Knowledge] is the most extreme height which protects him
who seeks refuge with it
and by means of it one goes along secure against adversity.

Through it one is taken into the [divine] confidence
while [ordinary] men remain unconcerned.
Through it one has hope [for eternal life] even while the soul remains still
within the breast [i.e., while still alive].

By means of it man intercedes for the one who descends in rebellion
[against God]
to the very bottom of Hell, the most terrible of punishments.

So he who aspires to learning aspires to all necessary things.
And he who possesses it possesses all those things that are worthy of quest.

This is the honor of honors, O possessor of intelligence!
So when you have won it, you make light of the [worldly] honors
you fail to attain.

And if the world seems to escape you as well as its voluptuous pleasures,
then blink your eyes at them, for verily knowledge is the best of gifts.

(٧٦) وأنشدنا الشيخ الأستاذ شيخ الإسلام برهان الدين رحمه الله:

ذا العلم أعلى رتبة في المراتب ... ومن دونه عز العلى في المواكب
فذو العلم يبقى عزه متضاعفا ... وذو الجهل بعد الموت تحت التيارب
فهيهات لا يرجو مداه من ارتقى ... رقي ولي الملك والي الكتائب
سأملي عليكم بعض ما فيه فاسمعوا ... فبي حصر عن ذكر كل المناقب
هو النور كل النور يهدي عن العمى ... وذو الجهل مر الدهر بين الغياهب
هو الذروة الشماء تحمي من التجا ... إليها ويمشي آمنا في النوائب
به ينتجي والناس في غفلاتهم ... به يرتجى والروح بين الترايب
به يشفع الإنسان من راح عاصيا ... إلى درك النيران شر العواقب
فمن رامه رام المآرب كلها ... ومن حازه قد حاز كل المطالب
هو المنصب العالي فيا صاحب الحجا ... إذا نلته هون بفوت المناصب
فإن فاتك الدنيا وطيب نعيمها ... فغمض فإن العلم خير المواهب

(77) There was recited to me a poem by some other poet:

Since the learned man is held in honor through his knowledge,
knowledge of the Law is the most worthy of honors.

How much fragrance does it exhale, but not perishable like musk!
And how high does it soar, but not full of greed like the hawk!

(78) There was also recited to me another poem by another poet:

Learning is the most precious thing which you could store.
He who takes up learning will never have his glory effaced.

So acquire for yourself those matters of which you previously were ignorant.
For the beginning and the end of knowledge is happiness.

(79) The pleasures of knowledge, learning and insight are sufficient incentive for intelligent men to acquire knowledge. Laziness is often derived from a great deal of phlegm and "humor," so the way to diminish [laziness] is by a reduction of food.

(80) It is said that seventy prophets agreed that forgetfulness comes from a great deal of phlegm, while a great deal of phlegm comes from a great deal of drinking of water, and a great deal of drinking of water comes from a great deal of eating. Dry bread cuts out phlegm and so does the eating of dried figs with unseasoned bread to the extent of eliminating any necessity for drinking water and thereby increasing phlegm. Using the toothpick reduces phlegm and increases memory and talent for speaking. It is also a practice prescribed by the Sunna [the tradition of the Prophet], for it increases the efficacy of prayer and the reading of the Qurʾān, and likewise vomiting reduces phlegm and humor. The way of reducing eating is to reflect on the advantages of eating a small amount; [these advantages] are health, chastity, and honor.

(81) On this subject it is said:

Disgrace and again disgrace and disgrace once more
is man's affliction on account of food.

(٧٧) وأنشدت لبعضهم:

إذا ما اعتز ذو علم بعلم فعلم الفقه أولى باعتزاز
فكم طيب يفوح ولا كمسك وكم طير يطير ولا كبازى

(٧٨) وأنشدت أيضا:

الفقه أنفس شيء أنت ذاخره من يدرس العلم لم تدرس مفاخره
فاكسب لنفسك ما أصبحت تجهله فأول العلم إقبال وآخره

(٧٩) وكفى بلذة العلم والفقه والفهم داعيا وباعثا للعاقل على تحصيل العلم، وقد يتولد الكسل من كثرة البلغم والرطوبات، وطريق تقليله تقليل الطعام.

(٨٠) قيل: اتفق سبعون نبيا عليهم الصلاة والسلام على أن أكثر النسيان من كثرة البلغم، وكثرة البلغم من كثرة شرب الماء، وكثرة شرب الماء من كثرة الأكل. والخبز اليابس يقطع البلغم، وكذلك أكل الزبيب على الريق، ولا يكثر منه حتى لا يحتاج إلى شرب الماء فيزيد البلغم. والسواك يقلل البلغم، ويزيد في الحفظ والفصاحة، فإنه سنة سنية، ويزيد في ثواب الصلاة، وقراءة القرآن. وكذلك القيء يقلل البلغم والرطوبات. وطريق تقليل الأكل التأمل في منافع قلة الأكل، وهى الصحة والعفة والإيثار.

(٨١) وقد قيل:

فعار ثم عار ثم عار شقاء المرء من أجل الطعام

(82) The Prophet is reported to have said: "Three kinds of people are beyond doubt hateful to God: the glutton, the miser and the arrogant. Reflection reveals the ill effects of excessive eating for this is unhealthy and dulling to the character. It is said: The [full] stomach destroys intelligence. It is reported that Jālīnūs (Galenos)[53] stated: "The pomegranate is useful, all of it, while fish is harmful, all of it." Nevertheless a little fish is better than a great deal of pomegranate. Through [excessive eating] there is also loss of wealth and eating beyond satiety is entirely harmful. By [eating too much] punishment is merited in the next world and the glutton is detestable to [righteous] souls. The correct way of reducing food is to eat oily dishes as well as the most delicate and most desirable[54] food, and not eat with a terrible appetite. However, if one has an honest objective in eating a great deal, [an objective] such as that of becoming strong by this means in order to fast, pray and do difficult work, then this [practice] is permissible.

Chapter Six

On the Beginning of Study, Its Amount and Its Organization

(83) Our teacher, the venerable Sheikh al-Islām, Burhān al-Dīn, used to begin his studies on Wednesday. In so doing he had the backing of tradition, for he quoted the Prophet who said: "Nothing is begun on Wednesday but will be perfected." Abū Ḥanifa used to do likewise.

(84) Burhān al-Dīn was wont to relate [the following tradition] which he [heard] from his teacher, the venerable Imām, the most glorious Qiwām al-Dīn Aḥmad b. ᶜAbdarrashīd:[55] "I heard from a certain man, in whom I have confidence, that the venerable Imām Yūsuf al-Hamadāni[56] undertook all his best work on Wednesday. [He did] this because Wednesday is the day in which light was created and it is a day injurious to the ways of the infidel at the same time being a day propitious for the believer."

(85) On the subject of the amount of study to be undertaken in the initial stages [of learning], Abū Ḥanifa quoted the venerable Judge, the Imām ᶜUmar, son of the Imām Abū Bakr al-Zaranjī, who said: "Our elders stated: 'It is necessary that the amount of study for the beginner

(٨٢) وعن النبى عليه الصلاة والسلام أنه قال: «ثلاثة نفر يبعضهم الله تعالى من غير جرم: الأكول والبخيل والمتكبر» والتأمل في مضار كثرة الأكل، وهي الأمراض وكلالة الطبع. قيل: البطنة تذهب الفطنة. حكي عن جالينوس أنه قال: الرمان نفع كله، والسمك ضرر كله. وقليل السمك خير من كثير الرمان. وفيه أيضا إتلاف المال. والأكل فوق الشبع ضرر محض، ويستحق به العقاب في الدار الآخرة، والأكول بغيض في القلوب. وطريق تقليل الأكل أن يأكل الأطعمة الدسمة، ويقدم في الأكل الألطف والأشهى، ولا يأكل مع الجيعان، إلا إذا كان له غرض صحيح في كثرة الأكل، بأن يتقوى به على الصيام والصلاة والأعمال الشاقة فله ذلك.

فصل: في بداية السبق وقدره وترتيبه

(٨٣) كان أستاذنا شيخ الإسلام برهان الدين رحمه الله تعالى يوقف بداءاة السبق على يوم الأربعاء، وكان يروى في ذلك حديثا، ويستدل به ويقول: قال رسول الله ﷺ «ما من شيء بدئ في يوم الأربعاء إلا وقد تم» وهكذا كان يفعل أبو حنيفة رحمه الله تعالى.

(٨٤) وكان يروي هذا الحديث عن أستاذه الشيخ الإمام الأجل قوام الدين أحمد بن عبد الرشيد رحمه الله تعالى، وسمعت ممن أثق به أن الشيخ أبا يوسف الهمداني رحمه الله تعالى كان يوقف كل عمل من أعمال الخير على يوم الأربعاء، وهذا لأن يوم الأربعاء يوم خلق فيه النور، وهو يوم نحس في حق الكفار فيكون مباركا للمؤمنين.

(٨٥) وأما قدر السبق في الابتداء، فقدكان أبو حنيفة رحمه الله تعالى يحكى عن الشيخ القاضى الإمام عمر بن الإمام أبي بكر الزرنجي رحمه الله تعالى أنه قال: قال

be an amount he can retain in his memory after two repetitions.'" Every day he should increase [the span of] his memorial recall by one word so that even if the duration and quantity of his study become large, it would [still] remain possible for him to recall it [by repeating it] two times, and thus increase [his retention] gently and gradually. But if study in the beginning is [to be] long so that it is necessary to make ten repetitions [of the material], then in the end [the learner] is also able to proceed in this fashion [i.e., to become proficient gently and gradually]. [He can do this] because he becomes accustomed to this [amount] and does not break this habit without great effort. It is said: Learning is [worth] one letter while repetition is [worth] a thousand letters.

(86) It is necessary to begin [one's study] with matters that are more readily understood. The venerable Imām, Professor Sharaf al-Dīn al-ᶜUqailī,[57] used to say: "In my opinion the right procedure [in study] is what our elders practiced, for verily they chose to begin with a few subjects of broad content because these are more readily understood and retained, are less fatiguing and occur frequently among men." It is [also] essential to write down an extract [of the material] after memorizing and [to practice] a great deal of repetition, since indeed this [method] is most profitable. Nor should the student write anything unless it is fully understood, for verily [writing down of undigested matter] blunts the character, destroys intelligence and wastes time. It is important that the student exert himself strenuously to understand what he is offered by the teacher, applying both intelligence and meditation as well as a great deal of repetition. For if reading is limited but repetition and reflection are extensive then [the student] will attain a firm grasp and understanding. It is stated: Holding in memory two letters is better than listening to two loads [of books] while the comprehension of two letters is better than the retention in memory of two loads [of books]. But if there is lack of comprehension and one does not exert oneself [at least] one or two times, one becomes used to this [negligence] so that even an easy proposition will not be comprehended. And it is necessary not to neglect understanding [one's subject matter] and to do one's work diligently while praying to Almighty God and beseeching Him humbly. Verily He hearkens to those who call upon Him and does not disappoint those who have hope in Him.

مشايخنا رحمهم الله تعالى. ينبغي أن يكون قدر السبق للمبتدىء قدر ما يمكن ضبطه بالإعادة مرتين بالرفق، ويزيد كل يوم كلمة حتى إنه وإن طال السبق وكثر يمكن ضبطه بالإعادة مرتين، ويزيد بالرفق والتدريج، فأما إذا طال السبق في الابتداء واحتاج إلى الإعادة عشر مرات، فهو في الانتهاء أيضا يكون كذلك لأنه يعتاد ذلك، ولا يترك تلك العادة إلا بجهد كثير، وقد قيل: السبق حرف، والتكرار ألف.

(٨٦) وينبغي أن يبتديء بشيء يكون أقرب إلى فهمه، وكان الشيخ الإمام الأستاذ شرف الدين العقيلي رحمه الله تعالى يقول: الصواب عندي في هذا ما فعله مشايخنا رحمهم الله فإنهم كانوا يختارون للمبتدئ صغارات المبسوط، لأنه أقرب إلى الفهم والضبط، وأبعد عن الملالة وأكثر وقوعا بين الناس، وينبغي أن يعلق السبق بعد الضبط والإعادة كثيرا، فإنه نافع جدا، ولا يكتب المتعلم شيئا لا يفهمه، فإنه يورث كلالة الطبع، ويذهب الفطنة، ويضيع أوقاته، وينبغي أن يجتهد في الفهم عن الأستاذ، أو بالتأمل والتفكر وكثرة التكرار، فإنه إذا قل السبق وكثر التكرار والتأمل يدرك ويفهم، فقد قيل حفظ حرفين خير من سماع وقرين، وفهم حرفين خير من حفظ وقرين، وإذا تهاون في الفهم ولم يجتهد مرة أو مرتين يعتاد ذلك، فلا يفهم الكلام اليسير، فينبغي ألا يتهاون في الفهم بل يجتهد، ويدعو الله تعالى، ويتضرع إليه، فإنه يجيب من دعاه، ولا يخيب من رجاه.

(87) The venerable Imām, the most glorious Qiwām al-Dīn Ḥammād b. Ibrāhīm b. Ismāᶜīl al-Ṣaffār al-Anṣāri recited a poem to us composed by the Judge al-Khalīl b. Aḥmad al-Sarahsī[58] who had it dictated to him:

Serve knowledge in a way that it becomes a useful thing [to you],
and keep its lesson alive by praiseworthy action.

And if you do not retain anything, repeat it,
then affirm it in a most energetic manner [i.e., hammer it into your head].

Then make notes about it in order that you
may return to it and its study always.

Then when you are sure it will not slip from your grasp,
go on after it to something new;

But at the same time repeat what preceded [this new knowledge];
and establish firmly [in your mind] the import of this increase [in knowledge].

Discuss with people subjects of learning in order that you may live.
Do not keep yourself away from the enlightened.

If you conceal knowledge you will be forgotten
so that you see no one but the ignorant and the boorish.

Then you will be bridled with a fire on the Day of Resurrection
and will be made to burn with a vehement chastisement.

(88) And it is necessary to pursue knowledge by means of discussion, argument and questioning. It is [also] essential that [one does these things] with fairness, circumspection and deliberation, and by fortifying oneself against altercation and anger. For discussion and argument are [a kind of] consultation. Consultation again aims at establishing the truth. This result is only attained through circumspection, the avoidance of violent dispute, and fairness [in general], not however through hostility and anger.[58a] For verily [argument and discussion] aiming at forcing and crushing the adversary are illicit. They are permissible only when they seek to bring out the truth. Feints and tricks are not admissible [in discussion] except when the opponent is quibbling and does not seek the truth. Muḥammad b. Yaḥya used to say when perplexity [in an

(٨٧) أنشدنا الشيخ الإمام الأجل قوام الدين حماد بن إبراهيم بن إسماعيل الصفار رحمه الله تعالى إملاء للقاضي الخليل بن أحمد السجزري في ذلك:

اخدم العلم خدمة المستفيد وأدم درسه بعقل حميد
وإذا ما حفظت شيئا أعده ثم أكده غاية التأكيد
ثم علقه كي تعود إليه وإلى درسه على التأبيد
وإذا ما أمنت منه فواتا فانتدب بعده لشيء جديد
مع تكرار ما تقدم منه اعتناء بشأن هذا المزيد
ذاكر الناس بالعلوم لتحيا لا تكن من أولى النهى ببعيد
إن كتمت العلوم أنسيت حتى لا ترى غير جاهل وبليد
ثم ألجمت في القيامة نارا وتلهبت في العذاب الشديد

(٨٨) ولا بد لطالب العلم من المذاكرة والمناظرة والمطارحه، فينبغي أن يكون بالإنصاف والتأني والتأمل، ويتحرز عن الشغب والغضب، فإن المناظرة والمذاكرة مشاورة، والمشاورة إنما تكون لاستخراج الصواب، وذلك إنما يحصل بالتأمل والتأني والإنصاف، ولا يحصل بالغضب والشغب. فإن كانت نيته إلزام الخصم فلا تحل المناظرة، وإنما تحل لإظهار الحق والتمويه، والحيلة فيها لا تجوز إلا إذا كان الخصم متعنتا لا طالبا للحق. وكان محمد بن يحيى رحمه الله تعالى: إذا توجه عليه

argument] assailed him and the answer did not present itself to him: "That which you have forced me to admit [appears] indeed to be necessarily so, and I shall go into it further; 'above every knowing [man] is a Knower [i.e., God']."[59] The usefulness of posing questions and discussing is greater than the usefulness of sheer repetition since in this there is repetition and one more element. And it is said: Posing questions for an hour is better than a month of repetition; but this holds good only when the discussion is carried on with someone who has a just and candid nature. Beware of an argument with an adversary who is a quibbler of perverse nature, for indeed [undesirable traits of] character creep in stealthily, habits are contagious and proximity [to those of perverse habits] leaves its traces. In the poem which Khalil b. Aḥmad quoted, there were many useful points.

(89) It is further said:

Knowledge has this condition for the one who serves it,
that he should make all men the servants of knowledge.

(90) It is incumbent [upon the student] in the quest for knowledge that he meditate at all times on the more subtle matters [or, the fine points] of knowledge and that he accustom himself thereto; for only by reflection can subtle problems be solved. For this reason it is said: Reflect and you will reach a solution. And it is essential to reflect before speaking in order to speak correctly [or, the truth]. For verily, a speech is like an arrow, [so that] it is necessary to "aim" by means of reflection before speaking so that one gets directly to the point. [The author of this book] said regarding the principles of jurisprudence [*uṣūl al-fiqh*]: This is an important principle, namely, that the discourse of the arguing jurist be based on reflection. It is said that the first principle of intelligence is to discourse with consideration and circumspection.

(91) Somebody said:

I commend to you in the composing of your speech five things,
that is, if you are obedient to him who makes recommendations
to you meaning you well.

Do not neglect the purpose of the discourse,
its time, its quality and quantity, and its place.

الإشكال ولم يحضره الجواب يقول. ما ألزمته لازم وأنا فيه ناظر، وفوق كل ذي علم عليم، وفائدة المطارحة والمناظرة أقوى من فائدة مجرد التكرار، لأن فيها تكررا، وزيادة فقد قيل: مطارحة ساعة خير من تكرار شهر، ولكن إذا كان مع منصف سليم الطبيعة. وإياك والمذاكرة مع متعنت غير مستقيم الطبع فإن الطبيعة متسربة، والأخلاق متعدية، والمجاورة مؤثرة، وفي الشعر الذي ذكره الخليل بن أحمد رحمه الله فوائد كثيرة.

(٨٩) وقد قيل:

العلم من شرطه لمن خدمه   أن يجعل الناس كلهم خدمه

(٩٠) وينبغي لطالب العلم أن يكون متأملا في جميع الأوقات في دقائق العلوم ويعتاد ذلك؛ فإنما تدرك الدقائق بالتأمل، ولهذا قيل: تأمل تدرك. ولا بد من التأمل قبل الكلام حتى يكون صوابا، فإن الكلام كالسهم فلا بد من تقويمه بالتأمل قبل الرمي حتى يكون مصيبا. قال في أصول الفقه: هذا أصل كبير وهو أن يكون كلام الفقيه المناظر بالتأمل. وقيل: رأس العقل أن يكون الكلام بالتثبت والتأمل.

(٩١) قال القائل:

أوصيك في نظم الكلام بخمسة   إن كنت للموصي الشفيق مطيعا
لا تغفلن سبب الكلام ووقته   والكيف والكم والمكان جميعا

(92) [And the student should also] under all circumstances and at all times endeavor to profit from everybody present. The Messenger of God said: "Wisdom is an aberrant beast of the believer—wherever he finds it, he seizes it." It is said: Seize whatever is clear and discard whatever is turbid. I heard the venerable Imām, the most glorious Professor Fakhr al-Dīn al-Kisāʾī[60] say: "Abū Yūsuf had a female slave who [for a time] was given as a surety [or, in trust] to Muḥammad [b. al-Ḥasan] who said to her 'Do you remember anything learned which Abū Yūsuf said?' She said: 'Nothing except that he used to repeat frequently: "A share in tribal [clan] holdings is not transmissible by will."' So Muḥammad remembered this [which he heard] from her. This question had been perplexing to Muḥammad and now his doubt was removed by the statement. He then realized that knowledge could be attained from everyone. Therefore Abū Yūsuf said when he was asked, 'By what means did you attain your knowledge?' 'I never scorned to profit [by anyone] nor was I stingy in profiting [others].'"

(93) It was said to Ibn ʿAbbās:[61] "In what way did you pursue knowledge?" He answered: "With the aid of a tongue fond of asking and a heart full of good sense." Verily, the student of knowledge is called a "what-do-you-say" only because very often they used to say in the early days, "What do you say?" concerning this or that question. And indeed Abū Ḥanifa used to study [or: study law] by propounding questions often and discussing them in his shop when he was a cloth-merchant. By this example one recognizes that the acquisition of knowledge and learning can be linked to the earning of a livelihood. Abū Ḥafṣ al-Kabīr[62] used to work for a living and at the same time repeat assiduously [what he was learning]. For if it is obligatory for the student of learning to make a living so as to be able to keep his family and other [dependents], let [him] work for his livelihood and [at the same time] repeat assiduously and discuss rather than let him be idle [or lazy]. For him who is of sane mind and body, there is no excuse for omitting the study of knowledge and learning [on the pretext of poverty], for no one was poorer than Abū Yūsuf and this did not prevent him from learning. But whoever possesses a great deal of wealth, then his honest[ly acquired] property will be beneficial to the honest man who plods on in the path of learning. It was said to a learned man: "By what means did you acquire knowledge?" He said: "Through a rich father. Because by means of his [riches] he supported virtuous and learned men and so was the cause of an augmentation of learning."[63]

(٩٢) ويكون مستفيدا في جميع الأحوال والأوقات من جميع الأشخاص. قال رسول الله ﷺ. «الحكمة ضاله المؤمن، أينما وجدها أخذها». وقيل: خذ ما صفا ودع ما كدر. وسمعت الشيخ الإمام الأستاذ فخر الدين الكاشانى رحمه الله تعالى يقول: كانت جارية أبي يوسف رحمه الله أمانة عند محمد رحمة الله عليه، فقال لها محمد: هل تحفظين في هذا الوقت من أبي يوسف في الفقه شيئا. قالت: لا، إلا أنه كان يكرر ويقول: سهم الدور ساقط. فحفظ ذلك منها، وكانت المسئلة مشكلة على محمد رحمه الله تعالى. فارتفع إشكاله بهذه الكلمة، فعلم أن الاستفادة ممكنة من كل أحد، ولهذا قال أبويوسف رحمه الله حين قيل له: بم أدركت العلم؟ قال: ما استنكفت من الاستفادة، وما بخلت بالإفادة.

(٩٣) قيل: لابن عباس رضى الله تعالى عنهما: بم أدركت العلم؟ قال: بلسان سئول، وقلب عقول، وإنما سمي طالب العلم: «ما تقول،» لكثرة ما كانوا يقولون في الزمان الأول. «ما تقول في هذه المسألة؟». وإنما تفقه أبو حنيفة رحمه الله تعالى بكثرة المطارحة، والمذاكرة في دكانه حين كان بزازا. وبهذا يعلم أن تحصيل العلم والفقه يجتمع مع الكسب. وكان أبو حفص الكبير رحمه الله يكتسب ويكرر. فإن كان لا بد لطالب العلم من الكسب لنفقة عياله وغيرهم. فليكتسب وليكرر وليذاكر، ولا يكسل. وليس لصحيح البدن والعقل عذر في ترك التعلم والتفقه، فإنه لا يكون أفقر من أبي يوسف رحمه الله تعالى، ولم يمنعه ذلك من التفقه. فمن كان له مال كثير فنعم المال الصالح للرجل الصالح المنصرف في طريق العلم. قيل لعالم: بم أدركت العلم؟ قال: بأب غنى، لأنه كان يصطنع به أهل العلم والفضل، فإنه سبب زيادة العلم لأنه شكر على نعمة العقل والعلم، وهو سبب الزيادة.

(94) Abū Ḥanifa is quoted as saying: "Verily, I acquired knowledge by praising God and thanking Him. As often as I understood an item of learning and gained grasp of a point of law or a piece of wisdom, I said: Praise be to God. Thus my knowledge was augmented." In the same manner [as did Abū Ḥanīfa], is it necessary in the quest for learning to occupy oneself with giving thanks by means of the tongue, the heart, the hands, and one's wealth. [It is important] to realize that knowledge, learning and guidance come from God Almighty, and to ask for the assistance of God by praying to him and beseeching Him. For indeed, the Almighty One is the leader of those who seek His guidance. So they who follow the truth—the followers of the Prophet's tradition and of the common opinion [the consensus] of the community[64]—seek the truth from God Almighty who is the highest truth, the elucidator, the leader [along the right path], the defender [against error]. So God the Almighty leads them and defends them from error. Those, however, who err [from the religion of God], admire their own intelligence and their own opinions, seeking the truth from man who is weak and has only his reasoning [for a tool]. For reasoning does not reach everything in all respects just as vision does not reveal all things to the sight. Hence they [the people who seek truth from man alone] are excluded from and incapable [of the highest truth]. Consequently, they err and cause others to deviate [from the path of God].

(95) The Messenger of God said: "It is prudent for a person to act by using his intellect, so the first thing to do is to act with the mind in order to recognize one's own limitations."[65] The Prophet further said: "He who knows himself knows his Lord. But if he knows his own limitations, he knows the power of God, and he does not lean [depend entirely] on himself and his own intellect but rather puts his trust in God and seeks the truth from Him; and those who put their faith in God, God will be their sufficiency and assistance. He will lead them along the right way."

(96) He who possesses wealth should not be avaricious, hence it is necessary to seek refuge in God so as to avoid avarice. The Prophet said: "What affliction is worse than avarice?" The father of the venerable Imām, the Sun of the imāms, al-Ḥulwānī was poor and sold sweets. He used to get learned men to accept his sweets and he said [to them]: "Pray for my son." Thus, through the lavishness of his liberality, his trust, his compassion, and his supplication, his son attained what he did, [i.e., eminence as a scholar]. With wealth one can buy books as well as

(٩٤) قال أبو حنيفة رحمه الله تعالى: إنما أدركت العلم بالحمد والشكر فكلما فهمت شيئا من العلوم و وقفت على فقه وحكمة قلت الحمد لله تعالى، فازداد علمي. وهكذا ينبغي لطالب العلم أن يشتغل بالشكر باللسان والجنان والأركان والمال، ويرى الفهم والعلم والتوفيق من الله تعالى، ويطلب الهداية من الله تعالى بالدعاء منه والتضرع إليه، فإنه تعالى هاد من استهداه؛ فأهل الحق، وهم أهل السنة والجماعة، طلبوا الحق من الله تعالى الحق المبين الهادى العاصم، فهداهم الله تعالى وعصمهم عن الضلالة. وأهل الضلالة أعجبوا برأيهم وعقلهم وطلبوا الحق من المخلوق العاجز وهو العقل لأن العقل، لا يدرك جميع الأشياء، كالبصر لا يبصر جميع الأشياء، فحجبوا وعجزوا وضلوا وأضلوا.

(٩٥) قال صلى الله عليه وآله وسلم: «من عرف نفسه عرف ربه»، فإذا عرف عجز نفسه عرف قدرة الله تعالى عزوجل، ولا يعتمد على نفسه وعقله بل يتوكل على الله تعالى ويطلب الحق منه، ومن يتوكل على الله فهو حسبه، ويهديه إلى صراط مستقيم.

(٩٦) ومن كان له مال فلا يبخل، وينبغي أن يتعوذ بالله تعالى من البخل. قال النبي عليه الصلاة والسلام: «أي داء أدوأ من البخل؟» وكان أبو الشيخ الامام الأجل شمس الأئمة الحلوانى رحمه الله تعالى فقيرا يبيع الحلواء، وكان يعطى الفقهاء من الحلواء ويقول: ادعوا لابني فببركة جوده واعتقاده وتضرعه نال ابنه ما نال. ويشترى

concern oneself with having books written. For this is a help in [attaining] knowledge and learning. Muḥammad b. al-Ḥasan had so much wealth that he [hired] 300 curators to look after his riches, but he paid out all of his wealth for [attaining] knowledge and learning. [In fact], he did not retain a single valuable garment. So when Abū Yūsuf saw him [dressed] in shabby garments he sent him some luxurious clothes, but he did not accept them saying: "To you [good] things are given in advance but to us [good] things are put off [until the future life]." Although the acceptance of a gift is in accordance with the Prophet's tradition, he perhaps did not accept these [clothes] because [in receiving these particular gifts] he saw an abasement of himself. The Prophet said: "Believers are not allowed to vilify themselves."

(97) It is reported that the venerable Fakhr al-Islām al-Arsābandī [after] collecting the rinds of melons discarded in a desolate place washed them and ate them. A female slave saw him and told her master about it [this performance]. He had her prepare a supper for him [al-Arsābandī] and summoned him to it but he did not accept the invitation for this reason [i.e., so as not to abase himself].

(98) Thus it is essential in the quest for knowledge to nurse the highest aspiration as well as no craving for the wealth of men. The Prophet said: "Beware of cupidity for it is poverty ever present nor [let anyone] be avaricious with what wealth he has, but spend it on himself or on others." The Prophet said: "All the people are poor for fear of poverty." In ancient times people learned handicrafts, then they pursued the study of knowledge so that they did not desire the possessions of men. In the book of Wisdom[66] it is said: He who wants to grow rich with the wealth of men, becomes poor. If the scholar is covetous he no longer preserves the integrity of knowledge nor does he speak the truth. And for this reason the founder of the Law [of the Muḥammad an religion] took refuge with God to avoid [covetousness] and he said: "I take refuge in God to escape from cupidity which leads to disgrace." It is essential for believers not to hope [for anything] unless it comes from God and not to fear anything except from God, and this is evident that [unless one has hope in and fear of God alone] one violates the ordinances of the Law. So he who sins against God Almighty for fear of human beings, fears another than God Almighty, [which, in itself, is sinful]. But if he does not sin against God Almighty for fear of his fellow men, and keeps within the ordinances of the law, then he does not fear anyone other than God, but only fears God Almighty. The same thing takes place with respect to hope.

بالمال الكتب ويستكتب فيكون عونا على التعلم والتفقه. وقد كان لمحمد بن الحسن رحمه الله تعالى مال كثير، حتى كان له ثلاثمائة من الوكلاء على ماله، فأنفقه كله في العلم والفقه ولم يبق له ثوب نفيس، فرآه أبو يوسف رحمه الله تعالى في ثوب خلق، فأرسل ثيابا نفيسة فلم يقبلها وقال: عجل لكم وأجل لنا. ولعله إنما لم يقبلها، وإن كان قبول الهدية سنة، لما رأى أن في ذلك مذلة لنفسه، وقد قال النبي عليه الصلاة والسلام: «ليس للمؤمن أن يذل نفسه».

(٩٧) وحكى أن الشيخ فخر الإسلام الأرسابندى رحمه الله جمع قشور البطيخ الملقاة في مكان خال فغسلها وأكلها، فرأته جارية، فأخبرت بذلك مولاها، فاتخذ له دعوة ودعاه إليها فلم يقبل لهذا. وهكذا ينبغي لطالب العلم أن يكون ذا همة عالية لا يطمع في أموال الناس. قال رسول الله ﷺ: «إياك والطمع فإنه فقر حاضر».

(٩٨) ولا يبخل بما عنده من المال، بل ينفق على نفسه وعلى غيره، وقال النبى عليه الصلاة والسلام: «الناس من خوف الفقر في فقر». وكانوا في الزمان الأول يتعلمون الحرفة، ثم يتعلمون العلم حتى لا يطمعوا في أموال الناس، وفى الحكمة: من استغنى بمال الناس افتقر، والعالم إذا كان طماعا لم تبق له حرمة العلم، ولا يقول بالحق، ولهذا كان يتعوذ صاحب الشرع عليه السلام منه ويقول: «أعوذ بالله من طمع يدني إلى طبع». وينبغي للمؤمن ألا يرجو إلا من الله تعالى، ولا يخاف إلا منه تعالى، ويظهر ذلك بمجاوزة حد الشرع وعدمها، فمن عصى الله تعالى خوفا من المخلوق فقد خاف غير الله تعالى، فإذا لم يعص الله تعالى لخوف المخلوق، وراقب حدود الشرع، فلم يخف غير الله تعالى، بل خاف الله تعالى، وكذا في جانب الرجاء.

(99) It is obligatory in seeking knowledge that one count and measure for oneself the amount of repetition [needed], for verily one's mind is not at ease until it attains this [correct] amount. It is further necessary to repeat the lesson of yesterday five times, and the lesson of the preceding day four times, and the lesson of the day previous to that, three times, and the one which comes before, two times, and that of the day before that, one time. For this [method] is the most stimulating for holding [subject matter] in the memory. And it is essential not to become accustomed to repeating silently since it is necessary that learning and repetition be carried on with vim and alacrity, lest one break the habit of repetition. It is not necessary to speak in a loud voice when talking to oneself for this impedes repetition. The best conditions [for learning in general] are the middle ones [those in which a moderate course is pursued]. It is reported that Abū Yūsuf discussed jurisprudence with learned men vigorously and with alacrity and his son-in-law who was among these men of learning, marveled at his performance and said: "I know that he has been hungry for five days and in spite of this hunger, he discusses vigorously and with zeal."

(100) It is essential that there be no break and no intermission in the pursuit of learning, for this is indeed harmful. It was our teacher, the venerable Imām Burhān al-Dīn who said: "Verily, I became superior to my companions since neither relaxation nor perturbance interfered with my study of knowledge."

(101) It was reported by the venerable Imām, Sheikh al-Islām ᶜAlī al-Asbījābī[67] that there occurred during the time of his learning of knowledge a break [in his formal schooling] during a period of twelve years because of the overthrow of the government. So he left the country with his companion, with whom he was wont to debate matters, and did not cease his discussions. The two of them used to sit [together] in order to hold a discussion each day and they did not leave off getting together for the purpose of argumentation back and forth during this period of twelve years. Later his companion became the venerable Sheikh al-Islām for the Shafiᶜites since he had [always] been a Shafiᶜite [and thus was not to be influenced by the Ḥanafite ᶜAlī].

(102) And it was our teacher, the venerable Judge Fakhr al-Islām Qāḍī Khān who said: "It is necessary in making a study of legal knowledge to memorize one particular law book constantly so that after this it will be easy for one to retain whatever legal information one hears."

(٩٩) وينبغي لطالب العلم أن يعد ويقدر لنفسه تقديرا في التكرار، فإنه لا يستقر قلبه حتى يبلغ ذلك المبلغ. وينبغي لطالب العلم أن يكرر سبق الأمس خمس مرات، وسبق اليوم الذي قبل الأمس أربع مرات، والسبق الذي قبله ثلاث مرات، والذي قبله اثنين، والذي قبله مرة واحدة، فهذا أدعى إلى الحفظ. وينبغي ألا يعتاد المخافتة في التكرار، لأن الدرس والتكرار ينبغي أن يكونا بقوة ونشاط، ولا يجهر جهرا يجهد نفسه كيلا ينقطع عن التكرار، فخير الأمور أوسطها. حكي أن أبا يوسف رحمه الله تعالى كان يذاكر الفقه مع الفقهاء بقوة ونشاط، وكان صهره عنده يتعجب من أمره ويقول: أنا أعلم أنه جائع منذ خمسة أيام، ومع ذلك يناظر بقوة ونشاط.

(١٠٠) وينبغي ألا يكون لطالب العلم فترة فإنها آفته، وكان أستاذنا شيخ الإسلام برهان الدين رحمه الله تعالى يقول: إنما فقت على شركائي بأني لم تقع لي الفترة في التحصيل.

(١٠١) وكان يحكي عن شيخ الإسلام الإسبيجابي أنه وقع له في زمان تحصيله وتعلمه فترة اثنتي عشرة سنة بانقلاب الملك، فخرج مع شريكه في المناظرة إلى حيث يمكنهما الاستمرار في طلب العلم، وظلا يدرسانه معا اثنتي عشرة سنة فصار شريكه شيخ الإسلام للشافعيين، وكان هو شافعيا.

(١٠٢) وكان أستاذنا الشيخ القاضي الإمام فخر الإسلام قاضيخان يقول: ينبغي للمتفقه أن يحفظ كتابا واحدا من كتب الفقه دائما ليتيسر له بعد ذلك حفظ ما يسمع من الفقه.

Chapter Seven

On Placing One's Faith in God

(103) It is necessary in the quest for knowledge to put one's trust in God while one pursues learning and not be concerned with matters pertaining to the sustenance of life [food] nor occupy one's mind therewith. Abū Ḥanīfa told about what he heard from ᶜAbdallāh b. al-Ḥasan al-Zabīdī,[68] the companion of the Messenger of God: "A man who devotes all he has to [the study of] the religion of God—God Almighty gives him sufficient care and nourishes him in unexpected ways." So verily, he who occupies himself with matters of sustenance, such as food and clothing, is not yet free for the acquisition of noble traits and elevated matters [i.e., acquiring a scholarly bent and religious knowledge].

(104) It is said:

Renounce noble matters, do not make a journey to seek them,
but remain where you are for verily you are zealous for food and clothes.

(105) A man said to Manṣūr al-Ḥallāj:[69] "Give me sound advice." So he said: "[My advice] has to do with your own soul. If you do not keep it occupied and work it hard, it will keep you occupied." So it is necessary for everyone to occupy himself with good deeds so that the soul does not concern itself with [mundane] desires. The intelligent man should not be eager for the affairs of this world since this kind of solicitude and sad concern does not avert calamity nor is of use, but rather is harmful to the spirit, the mind and the body. These [concerns with worldly matters] cause a cessation of good works. One [should rather] attend to matters pertaining to the future life since these prove useful. And, as for his [i.e., the Prophet's] saying: "Verily, there are sins whose only excuse is [man's unavoidable] concern with his [earthly] life," this means that there should be only as much concern [for affairs of this world] as does not interfere with doing good deeds or as would not keep the heart from complete concentration in prayer. For indeed this [minimum] amount of solicitude and effort [of the mind for this life] belongs to the deeds of [i.e., is conducive to] the future life.

فصل: في التوكل

(١٠٣) ثم لا بد لطالب العلم من التوكل في طلب العلم، ولا يهتم لأمر الرزق، ولا يشغل قلبه بذلك. روى أبو حنيفة رحمه الله عن عبد الله بن الحسن الزبيدي رضي الله عنه صاحب رسول الله ﷺ: «من تفقه في دين الله كفاه الله تعالى همه ورزقه من حيث لا يحتسب» فإن من اشتغل قلبه بأمر الرزق من القوت والكسوة، قلما يتفرغ لتحصيل مكارم الأخلاق، ومعالي الأمور.

(١٠٤) قيل:

دع المكارم لا ترحل لبغيتها واقعد فإنك أنت الطاعم الكاسي

(١٠٥) قال رجل لمنصور الحلاج: أوصني، فقال: هي نفسك إن لم تشغلها شغلتك؛ فينبغي لكل أحد أن يشغل نفسه بأعمال الخير حتى لا تشتغل بهواها. ولا يهتم العاقل لأمر الدنيا لأن الهم والحزن لا يرد المصيبة ولا ينفع. بل يضر بالقلب والعقل والبدن، ويخل بأعمال الخير، ويهتم لأمر الآخرة لأنه ينفع، وأما قوله عليه السلام «إن من الذنوب ذنوبا لا يكفرها إلا هم المعيشة»، فالمراد منه قدر هم لا يخل بأعمال الخير، ولا يشغل القلب شغلا يخل بإحضار القلب في الصلاة، فإن ذلك القدر من الهم والقصد من أعمال الآخرة.

(106) It is further essential in the search for knowledge to reduce one's attachment to worldly affairs as much as one can. Therefore [the students] elect to go abroad [in order to acquire knowledge]. And it is necessary to bear patiently one's labors and hardships in the journey of learning [i.e., in a journey undertaken for the sake of study]. Just as Mūsá[70] said about the journey of knowledge—and this saying was not related of him with reference to any other kind of journey—"Indeed, we experienced fatigue from this journey of ours,"[71] so that it should be known that the journey of acquiring knowledge is a very serious affair; according to most learned men it is more excellent than a holy war against the infidels. The [divine] recompense is determined by the amount of toil and labor [exerted], so he who perseveres in this [toil and labor] will encounter such delight in knowledge as to overcome all other delights of this world. On this matter Muḥammad b. al-Ḥasan used to say when he spent nights awake and solved his difficult problems: "How far removed are the sons of kings from these [unspeakable] delights!"

(107) It is obligatory for the student not to be occupied with anything else but knowledge and never turn away from learning. Muḥammad b. al-Ḥasan said: "Indeed, this trade of ours[72] goes on from the cradle to the grave; so he who wishes to refrain from this pursuit of knowledge for even one hour, might as well leave it entirely this very hour."

(108) A learned jurist, Ibrāhīm b. al-Jarrāḥ,[73] came to Abū Yūsuf to visit him during his mortal illness, when he was very close to his death. Abū Yūsuf asked him: "Is the throwing of stones [during the *ḥajj*] on horseback superior to the throwing of stones on foot?"[74] Then when the other did not know the answer, Abū Yūsuf gave the answer himself, namely, that the early authorities preferred the throwing of stones on foot.

(109) Thus is it important for the learned one to concern himself with study at all times. In this way then one attains great delight in this [pursuit]. And it was said that after his death Muḥammad [b. al-Ḥasan] appeared to someone in a dream and was asked: "How was the moment in which you actually passed away?" So he answered: "I was meditating on a certain question regarding the slave buying his freedom. In this way I did not notice the departure of my soul [from my body]." And it is said, that he told in the last [days] of his life: "Questions pertaining to the slave buying his freedom have drawn me away from preparing for the day [of my death]." Verily, he said this because of his humility.

(١٠٦) ولا بد لطالب العلم من تقليل العلائق الدنيوية بقدر الوسع، ولهذا اختاروا الغربة. ولا بد من تحمل النصب والمشقة في سفر التعلم كما قال موسى، صلوات الله وسلامه على نبينا وعليه، في سفر التعلم، ولم ينقل عنه ذلك في غيره من الأسفار: « لقد لقينا من سفرنا هذا نصبا ». ليعلم أن سفر العلم لا يخلو من التعب، لأن العلم أمر عظيم، وهو أفضل من الجهاد عند أكثر العلماء، والأجر على قدر التعب والنصب، فمن صبر على ذلك وجد لذة تفوق سائر لذات الدنيا؛ ولهذا كان محمد بن الحسن إذا سهر الليالي وانحلت له المشكلات يقول: أين أبناء الملوك من هذه اللذات؟

(١٠٧) وينبغي لطالب العلم ألا يشتغل بشيء آخر غير العلم، ولا يعرض عن الفقه، قال محمد بن الحسن رحمه الله: إن صناعتنا هذه من المهد إلى اللحد، فمن أراد أن يترك علمنا هذا ساعة فليتركه الساعة.

(١٠٨) ودخل فقيه على أبي يوسف يعوده في مرض موته، وهو يجود بنفسه، فقال أبو يوسف له: رمي الجمار راكبا أفضل أم راجلا؟ فلم يعرف الجواب، فأجاب بنفسه.

(١٠٩) وهكذا ينبغي للفقيه أن يشتغل به في جميع أوقاته، فحينئذ يجد لذة عظيمة في ذلك. وقيل: رؤي محمد في المنام بعد وفاته، فقيل له: كيف كنت في حال النزع؟ فقال: كنت متأملا في مسئلة من مسائل المكاتب فلم أشعر بخروج روحي، وقيل: إنه قال في آخر عمره: شغلتني مسائل المكاتب عن الاستعداد لهذا اليوم، وإنما قال ذلك تواضعا.

Chapter Eight

On the Time for the Acquisition of Knowledge

(110) It is said the time for learning [extends] from the cradle to the grave. Ḥasan b. Ziyād,[75] who reached the age of eighty years, had taken up the study of theology. Over a period of forty years he never spent the night stretched out on a couch. Then for the next forty years he gave legal opinions.

(111) The best periods [for study] are at the beginning of adolescence as well as the hour of dawn and that between the setting of the sun and the first vigil of the night. And it is necessary to put all one's energy into the study of knowledge at all times. But if one becomes irked by one discipline one occupies oneself with some other subject. When he became tired of scholastic theology, Ibn ᶜAbbās used to say: "Let me have the collections of the poets." Muḥammad b. al-Ḥasan did not sleep in the night but placed codices before him and when he got tired of one kind of book, looked for another. And he drove away sleep with (cold) water for he used to say: "Verily, sleep is induced by heat so it must be driven off with cold water."

Chapter Nine

On Helpfulness and Good Advice

(112) It is obligatory that the possessor of knowledge be sympathetic and helpful rather than jealous. For envy is injurious to him and of no use. Our teacher, the venerable Sheikh al-Islām Burhān al-Dīn, used to say: "They said: 'The son of the learned man will be learned himself because the man of knowledge wishes that his disciples in learning the Qurʾān become scholars. So through the blessing that comes from his faith and compassion, his son will become learned'." And it is reported that al-Ṣadr al-Ajall Burhān al-Aʾimma[76] fixed the time for study with his sons, al-Ṣadr al-Shahīd Ḥusām al-Dīn[77] and al-Ṣadr al-Saᶜīd Tāj al-Dīn,[78] as the height of the morning [late morning] after [the completion] of all his [other] lessons. But they [the sons] said: "Our natural faculties are tired and worn out at that time." So their father replied [and said]: "Foreigners and the sons of the great come to me from various regions of the earth. Hence, I have to take up their instruction first [i.e., before I

فصل: في وقت التحصيل

(١١٠) قيل: وقت التعلم من المهد إلى اللحد.

(١١١) وأفضل الأوقات شرخ الشباب، ووقت السحر، وما بين العشاءين. وينبغي لطالب العلم أن يستغرق جميع أوقاته، فإذا مل من علم يشتغل بعلم آخر. وكان ابن عباس رضي الله تعالى عنه إذا مل من علم الكلام يقول: هاتوا ديوان الشعراء. وكان محمد بن الحسن لا ينام الليل، وكان يضع عنده الدفاتر، وكان إذا مل من نوع ينظر في نوع آخر.

فصل: في الشفقة والنصيحة

(١١٢) ينبغي أن يكون صاحب العلم مشفقا ناصحا غير حاسد؛ فالحسد يضر ولا ينفع. وكان أستاذنا شيخ الإسلام برهان الدين رحمه الله يقول: إن ابن المعلم يكون عالما، لأن المعلم يريد أن تكون تلاميذه علماء، فببركة اعتقاده وشفقته يكون ابنه عالما. وكان يحكى أن الصدر الأجل برهان الأئمة رحمه الله جعل وقت السبق لابنيه الصدر الشهيد حسام الدين، والصدر السعيد تاج الدين رحمهما الله تعالى وقت الضحوة الكبرى، بعد جميع الأسباق، وكانا يقولان: طبيعتنا تكل وتمل في ذلك الوقت، فقال أبوهما: إن الغرباء وأولاد الكبراء يأتونني من أقطار الأرض، فلا بد

teach you].” Thus, through the blessing [resulting from] his benevolence, his sons became superior [in legal knowledge] to most jurisconsults of the world at that time.

(113) And it is necessary not to enter into a litigation with anyone nor have an altercation with him because this is time-consuming. It is said: He who does good to others is rewarded because of his beneficence, while he who does evil, his evil deeds suffice him.

(114) The venerable Imām al-Zāhid Rukn al-Islām Muḥammad b. Abī Bakr, known as Imām Khwāhar-Zāda al-Muftī,[79] told me: “Sultan al-Sharīᶜa [the Prince of the Canon Law] Yūsuf al-Hamadānī recited this verse to me:

Send the man away. Do not punish him for the misdeeds he committed.
His character and his deed will be sufficient [punishment] for him.”

(115) It is said: He who wishes to humiliate his enemy by showing his superiority to him[80] let him repeat these verses:

If you wish to see your enemy prostrated
and to kill him with grief and inflame him with worry,

Then strive for the noblest [attainments] and increase your knowledge
more and more.
Verily, he who adds to his knowledge continuously increases
the sorrow of the man who envies him.

(116) It is stated: You should apply yourself to things useful to your soul, not to conquer your enemy. Nevertheless, if you concern yourself with things that are valuable to your soul, you guarantee [this] conquest over your enemy. But beware of hostile action for this will cover you with shame and waste your time. Furthermore, you must bear injustice patiently, especially if it comes from the fools. ᶜĪsa b. Maryam[81] said: “Bear once with a fool so you may gain tenfold [reward from God].”

من أن أقدم أسباقهم. فببركة شفقته تفوق ابناه على أكثر فقهاء أهل الأرض في ذلك العصر في الفقه.

(١١٣) وينبغي ألا ينازع أحدا، ولا يخاصمه لأنه يضيع أوقاته. قيل: المحسن سيجزى بإحسانه، والمسيء ستكفيه مساويه.

(١١٤) أنشدني الشيخ الإمام ركن الإسلام محمد بن أبي بكر المعروف بإمام خواهر زاده المفتي رحمه الله. قال: أنشدني سلطان الشريعة يوسف الهمداني رحمه الله تعالى:

ولا تجز إنسانا على سوء فعله سيكفيه ما فيه وما هو فاعله

(١١٥) وقيل: من أراد أن يرغم أنف عدوه فليكرر هذا الشعر. وأنشدت:

إذا شئت أن تلقى عدوك راغما وتقتله غما وتحرقه غما
فرم للعلا وازدد من العلم إنه من ازداد علما زاد حاسده غما

(١١٦) وعليك أن تشتغل بمصالح نفسك لا بقهر عدوك، فإذا قمت بمصالح نفسك تضمن ذلك قهر عدوك. وإياك والمعاداة فإنها تفضحك وتضيع أوقاتك. وعليك بالتحمل، لا سيما من السفهاء. قال عيسى ابن مريم صلوات الله على نبينا وعليه: احتملوا من السفيه واحدة كي تربحوا عشرا.

(117) A poem of unknown authorship was recited to me:

I put men to the test one generation after another
and I did not see anything but trickery and prattle.

Nor did I find of any trials anything more hurtful
and harder to bear than the mutual hostility of men.

And I tasted the bitterness of things everywhere
and there was nothing more bitter than begging.

(118) Beware lest you think evil of the believer for, verily, to do this produces hostility. This is not allowed according to [the Prophet's] word: "Think only good things of believers." Indeed, this [evil thinking] springs from malignity of intent and wickedness of the character. It is just as Abū al-Ṭayyib [al-Mutanabbī] said:[82]

If the deeds of a man are evil, then his thoughts are evil.
And he believes whatever suspicion haunts him.

He makes enemies of his friends on the basis of what their enemies say;
and he plunges into a dark night of doubt.

(119) Another poem of unknown authorship was recited to me:

Draw away from the vile and do not seek him out;
but to whom you have already dispensed good, increase this
[do him even more good].

You may protect yourself against every guile of your enemy;
but when the enemy plots [against you] do not plot against him.

(120) A poem by the Sheikh al-ᶜAmīd Abū al-Fatḥ al-Bustī[83] was recited to me:

The intelligent man is not safe from a fool
who besets him with tribulation and causes him annoyance.

Let him choose peace in preference to war
and remain silent even if someone shout at him.

(١١٧) وأنشدت لبعضهم:

بلوت الناس قرنا بعد قرن فلم أر غير ختال وقالي
ولم أر في الخطوب أشد وقعا وأصعب من معاداة الرجال
وذقت مرارة الأشياء طرا فما شيء أمر من السؤال

(١١٨) وإياك أن تظن شرا بالمؤمنين فإنه منشأ العداوة، ولا يحل ذلك لقوله عليه الصلاة والسلام: «ظنوا بالمؤمنين خيرا». وإنما ينشأ ذلك من خبث النية، وسوء السريرة كما قال أبو الطيب:

إذا ساء فعل المرء ساءت ظنونه وصدق ما يعتاده من توهم
وعادى محبيه بقول عداته وأصبح في ليل من الشك مظلم

(١١٩) وأنشدت لبعضهم:

تنح عن القبيح ولا ترده ومن أوليته حسنا فزده
ستكفى من عدوك كل كيد إذا كاد العدو فلا تكده

(١٢٠) وأنشدت للشيخ العميد أبي الفتح البستي رحمه الله:

ذو العقل لا يسلم من جاهل يسومه ظلما وإعناتا
فليختر السلم على حربه وليلزم الإنصات إن صاتا

Chapter Ten

On the Means Useful to the Attainment of Knowledge

(121) It is necessary to him who is engaged in the pursuit of knowledge to seek it at all times, so that he may attain excellence. And the way to attain knowledge is to have ink[84] on hand on every occasion so that one can jot down items of scientific interest. It is said: He who commits to memory is [uncertain as if] in flight; but he who writes down a matter stands firm. It is [also] said: Knowledge is that which is taken from the lips of men since they recall only the best things they hear and mention only the best things they recall.

(122) I heard the Sheikh, the Imām al-Adīb, the professor Rukn al-Islām,[85] known as al-Adīb al-Mukhtār, say: "Hilāl b. Yasār[86] said: 'I saw the Prophet telling his companions some items of knowledge and wisdom; so I said: "O Messenger of God, repeat to me what you said to those people." The Prophet replied: "Do you have any ink with you?" Whereupon I said: "I do not have ink with me." So he said: "O Hilāl, do not separate yourself from ink for it is good in itself and it is good for those who have it in their possession till the Day of Resurrection."'"

(123) Al-Ṣadr al-Shahīd Ḥusām al-Dīn[87] made the recommendation to his son Shams al-Dīn that he commit to memory some slight amount of knowledge and wisdom every day for [the reason that] it will grow and, in a brief space of time, it will amount to a great deal.

(124) And ᶜIṣām b. Yūsuf[88] purchased for himself a reed-pen for one dinar in order to write down at once matters which he heard. For verily life is short while knowledge is extensive.

(125) It is necessary not to waste time nor hours but make use of nights as well as periods of retirement.

(126) Yaḥya b. Muᶜādh al-Rāzī[89] is reported to have said: "The night is long, so do not shorten it by sleeping, and the day is brilliant, so do not obscure it with your sins."

فصل: في الاستفادة

(١٢١) وينبغي أن يكون طالب العلم مستفيدا في كل وقت حتى يحصل له الفضل. وطريق الاستفادة أن يكون معه في كل وقت محبرة، حتى يكتب ما يسمع من الفوائد. فقد قيل: من حفظ فر، ومن كتب شيئا قر. وقيل: العلم ما يؤخذ من أفواه الرجال، لأنهم يحفظون أحسن ما يسمعون، ويقولون أحسن ما يحفظون.

(١٢٢) وسمعت الشيخ الإمام الأديب الأستاذ زين الإسلام، المعروف بالأديب المختار، يقول: قال هلال بن يسار: رأيت النبي ﷺ يقول لأصحابه شيئا من العلم والحكمة، فقلت: يا رسول الله أعد لي ما قلت لهم. فقال لى هل معك محبرة؟ فقلت ما معي محبرة. فقال: يا هلال، لا تفارق المحبرة، فإن الخير فيها وفى أهلها إلى يوم القيامة.

(١٢٣) ووصى الصدر الشهيد حسام الدين ابنه شمس الدين أن يحفظ كل يوم شيئا يسيرا من العلم والحكمة، فإنه عن قريب يكون كثيرا.

(١٢٤) واشترى عصام بن يوسف قلما بدينار ليكتب ما سمعه في الحال؛ فالعمر قصير، والعلم كثير.

(١٢٥) فينبغي ألا يضيع الأوقات والساعات، ويغتنم الليالى والخلوات.

(١٢٦) عن يحيى بن معاذ الرازى أنه قال: الليل طويل فلا تقصره بمنامك، والنهار مضيء فلا تكدره بآثامك.

(127) It is necessary to question venerable men and acquire information from them for it is not possible ever more to attain what has escaped [us]. Just as our teacher, the Sheikh al-Islām, said with respect to his venerable colleagues and teachers [*fī mashyahatihi*]: "How many a Sheikh, great in knowledge and excellence, did I reach without consulting him sufficiently." And I say this kind of missed opportunity is the source of the verse:

Alas for a meeting missed, alas!
Nothing that has passed by and vanished can be obtained [again].

(128) ʿAlī said: "If you are occupied with [learning] something then concentrate on it wholeheartedly. To withdraw from [the study of] the knowledge of God makes for a full measure of shame and loss; so seek refuge in God from this [distraction] both night and day."

(129) It is essential for the student of knowledge to bear miseries and baseness patiently while seeking learning. Flattery is blameworthy except in the quest of knowledge. In order to attain information, flattery of the professor and one's associates cannot be helped.

(130) It is said: Knowledge is nobility without debasement. But no one reaches it except through debasement in which there is no nobility.

(131) Someone said:

I see that you desire to ennoble your heart;
but you will not attain nobility ere you have humbled it.

Chapter Eleven

On Abstinence during the Pursuit of Learning

(132) A certain author related a tradition on the subject-heading [of this chapter] as coming from the Messenger of God, who said: "He who does not exert abstinence while learning, God the Almighty chastises in one of three ways: either he deprives him of life in his youth or exiles him into [far-off] country districts, or punishes him [forcing him to enter] the service of the Sultan." Thus, the more continent the seeker of knowledge, the more useful his knowledge, the easier [his] learning and the more extensive [his] acquisition of useful matters. It is part of perfect continence to guard against satiety and a large amount of sleep as well as

(١٢٧) وينبغي أن يغتنم الشيوخ ويستفيد منهم، وليس كل ما فات يدرك، كما قال استاذنا شيخ الإسلام رحمة الله عليه: « كم من شيخ كبير أدركته وما استخبرته ».
وأقول على هذا الفوت منشئا هذا البيت:

لهفى على فوت التلاقي لهفا ما كل ما فات ويفنى يلفى

(١٢٨) قال علي كرم الله وجهه: إذا كنت في أمر فكن فيه، وكفى بالإعراض عن علم الله خزيا وخسارا، واستعذ بالله منه ليلا ونهارا.

(١٢٩) ولا بد لطالب العلم من تحمل المشقة والمذلة في طلب العلم، والتملق مذموم إلا في طلب العلم؛ فإنه لا بد له من التملق للأستاذ والشركاء وغيرهم للاستفادة منهم.

(١٣٠) قيل: العلم عز لا ذل فيه، ولا يدرك إلا بذل لا عز فيه.

(١٣١) وقال القائل:

أرى لك نفسا تشتهي أن تعزها فلست تنال العز حتى تذلها

فصل في الورع في حالة التعلم

(١٣٢) روى بعضهم حديثا في هذا الباب عن رسول الله صلى الله عليه وآله وسلم أنه قال: « من لم يتورع في تعلمه ابتلاه الله تعالى بأحد ثلاثة أشياء: إما أن يميته في شبابه، أو يوقعه في الرساتيق، أو يبتليه بخدمة السلطان »؛ فهما كان طالب العلم أورع، كان علمه أنفع، والتعلم له أيسر، وفوائده أكثر. ومن الورع

a great deal of conversation about useless matters. Also, one must beware of eating food in the market place if possible, because food of the market is more apt to be impure and contaminated. Eating in the market [is also] more remote from the contemplation of God and nearer neglect of Him. And [one should not eat in the market place] since there the eyes of the poor fall on the food, the poor who are not able to purchase anything. Thereby they are harmed and the blessing of the food vanishes.

(133) It is related by the venerable Imām al-Jalīl Muḥammad b. al-Faḍ[190] that, when he was in the process of acquiring knowledge, he did not eat food of the market place. Once when his father, who used to live in the country, prepared his [son's] food and brought it to him on Friday, saw bread from the market place in the house of [his] son, he did not address him since he was [so] displeased with him. So his son made excuses by saying: "I myself did not bring it nor did I get satisfaction out of it, but my friend brought it." His father replied: "If you were on your guard and abstemious in matters of this kind then your associate would not venture to do this."

(134) Thus the [students] used to be abstemious. Hence they attained knowledge and spread it to such an extent that their names will remain known up to the Day of Resurrection.

(135) A certain educated man among the learned ascetics admonished a student of knowledge by saying: "It is your duty to be on your guard against slander and keeping company with the loquacious." He went on to say: "He who talks a great deal robs you of your life and wastes your time."

(136) In being abstinent, one must avoid [associating with] corrupt people and those who are sinful and negligent [of their religious duties; or: and who strip God of his attributes]. [One must also] choose the upright as one's neighbors. For without doubt proximity leaves its traces. [Furthermore], one should sit facing Mecca and be a follower of the usage [*sunna*] of the Prophet, and one should enlist the prayer of good people while avoiding that of the trespassers.

(137) It is reported that two men went abroad in quest for knowledge and they were companions in learning. After some years they returned to their native land. One of them had become a legist but the other had not. So the jurists of the land pondered [this matter] and enquired after their condition, their method of reciting their subject and how they had sat when studying. They were then informed that the one who mastered Muslim law had sat in such a way, while he repeated what he had learned,

الكامل أن يحترز عن الشبع وكثرة النوم، وكثرة الكلام فيما لا ينفع. وأن يتحرز عن أكل طعام السوق إن أمكن؛ لأن طعام السوق أقرب للنخاسة والخيانة، وأبعد عن ذكر الله، وأقرب إلى الغفلة، ولأن أبصار الفقراء تقع عليه ولا يقدرون على الشراء منه، فيتأذون بذلك فتذهب بركته.

(١٣٣) حكي أن الشيخ الإمام الجليل محمد بن الفضل رحمه الله كان في حال تعلمه لا يأكل من طعام السوق، وكان أبوه يسكن في الرستاق ويهيئ له طعامه ويدخل إليه يوم الجمعة. فرأى في بيت ابنه خبز السوق يوما فلم يكلمه ساخطا عليه، فاعتذر ابنه وقال: ما اشتريته ولم أرض به، ولكن أحضره شريكي، فقال له أبوه: لو كنت تحتاط وتتورع عن مثله لم يجترئ شريكك على ذلك.

(١٣٤) وهكذا كانوا يتورعون، فلذلك وفقوا للعلم والنشر حتى بقي اسمهم إلى يوم القيامة.

(١٣٥) ووصى فقيه من زهاد الفقهاء طالب علم، فقال له: عليك أن تتحرز عن الغيبة وعن مجالسة المكثار. وقال إن من يكثر الكلام يسرق عمرك، ويضيع أوقاتك.

(١٣٦) ومن الورع أن يجتنب أهل الفساد والمعاصي والتعطيل ويجاور الصلحاء، فإن المجاورة مؤثرة لا محالة، وأن يجلس مستقبلا القبلة، ويكون مستنا بسنة النبي عليه الصلاة والسلام، ويغتنم دعاء أهل الخير ويحترز عن دعاء المظلومين.

(١٣٧) حكي أن رجلين خرجا في طلب العلم للغربة، وكانا شريكين في العلم، فرجعا بعد سنين إلى بلدهما، وقد فقه أحدهما ولم يفقه الآخر، فتأمل فقهاء البلدة وسألوا عن حالهما وتكرارهما وجلوسهما فأخبروا أن جلوس الذي تفقه في حال

that he faced the *qiblah* [Mecca] and the city in which he had gathered his knowledge. On the other hand, the other one had turned his back to the *qiblah* [Mecca] and his face away from this city. So these theologians and legists agreed that the jurist masters the law through the blessing of turning in the direction of the *qiblah,* since this is the traditional way of sitting except under compulsion to do otherwise, and through the blessing of the prayer of the Muslims. For the city of his studies is not devoid of pious men and good people, and it is clear that some pious man prays for him in the night.

(138) It is necessary in the quest for learning not to neglect the proprieties [*adab*] and the usage of the Prophet, for verily he who is negligent of proprieties is deprived of the usage of the Prophet, and he who neglects the usage of the Prophet is deprived of the fulfillment of his legal obligations. He who is deprived of the fulfillment of his legal obligations is denied the future life. [Some say: This tradition comes from the Messenger of God.]

(139) It is essential that there be many prayers and that the prayers be said in humility for indeed this is a help to the study and the acquisition of knowledge:

(140) A poem was recited to me by Sheikh al-Jalīl al-Zāhid al-Ḥajj Najm al-Dīn ᶜUmar b. Muḥammad an-Nasafī:[91]

Be observant of commands and prohibitions
and be assiduous and observant of prayer.

Seek knowledge of the divine law and be diligent and procure help
through good deeds;
then you will become a legist, guardian of the law.

Ask God that He preserve your memory for you who desire its excellence,
for God is supreme in remembering.

(141) He further said:

Be obedient and work diligently and do not become lazy:
Thus will you return to your Lord.

And do not sleep at night for the best of mankind
only sleep a little part of the night.

التكرار كان مستقبلا القبلة والمصر الذي حصل العلم فيه، والآخر كان مستدبرا القبلة ووجهه إلى غير المصر، فاتفق العلماء والفقهاء أن الفقيه فقه ببركة استقبال القبلة إذ هو السنة في الجلوس، إلا عند الضرورة، وببركة دعاء المسلمين؛ فإن المصر لا يخلو عن العباد وأهل الخير، فالظاهر أن عابدا من العباد دعا له في الليل.

(١٣٨) فينبغي لطالب العلم ألا يتهاون بالآداب والسنن، فإن من يتهاون بالآداب يحرم السنن، ومن تهاون بالسنن حرم الفرائض، ومن تهاون بالفرائض حرم الآخرة.

(١٣٩) وينبغي أن يكثر الصلاة ويصلي صلاة الخاشعين، فإن ذلك عون له على التحصيل والتعلم.

(١٤٠) أنشدت للشيخ الجليل الزاهد الحاج نجم الدين عمر ابن محمد النسفي:

كن للأوامر والنواهي حافظا ... وعلى الصلاة مواظبا ومحافظا
واطلب علوم الشرع واجهد واستعن ... بالطيبات تصر فقيها حافظا
واسأل إلهك حفظ حفظك راغبا ... في فضله فالله خير حافظا

(١٤١) وقال أيضا رحمه الله:

أطيعوا وجدوا ولا تكسلوا ... وأنتم إلى ربكم ترجعون
ولا تهجعوا فخيار الورى ... قليلا من الليل ما يهجعون

(142) And it is necessary to have a book with one under every condition, in order to read it. It is said: He who does not have a book in his sleeve, wisdom is not well established in his heart. It is also obligatory that in the book there be some blank pages and that one carry ink in order to write down what one hears. We have already recalled the tradition of Hilāl b. Yasār [concerning this].

Chapter Twelve

What Creates Memory and What Brings about Forgetfulness

(143) The most forceful factors in [strengthening] memory are industriousness and assiduousness. [Also] a reduction of eating as well as praying at night and reading of the Qurʾān are among the causes of remembering. It is said: There is nothing that increases memory more than reading the Qurʾān silently,[92] and reading the Qurʾān silently is the most excellent thing because of the word [of the Prophet]: "And the most excellent among the works of my community is the reading of the Qurʾān silently."

(144) Shaddād b. Ḥakīm[93] saw one of his deceased brothers in his sleep and said to him: "What thing did you find the most useful [in procuring for yourself admission to Paradise]?" He replied: "Reading the Qurʾān silently."

(145) And one should say while lifting the Qurʾān: "In the name of God, and Glory be to God, and Praise be to God, and There is no God but God, and God is greatest, and There is no power or strength except in God, the Exalted, the Mighty, Who knows the number of all the letters that ever were and that ever shall be written throughout the centuries and ages." And let it be said after every written section [of the text]: "I believe in one unique God, the sole truth, Who has no companion; and I do not believe in any [deity] besides Him." There also should be considerable praying to the Prophet since he is a mercy for the worlds.

(146) It is said in a poem:

I complained to Wakīʿ[94] of my bad memory.
So he directed me to cease from evil doing;

For verily memory is a benefit of God
and a benefit of God is not given to him who sins.

(١٤٢) وينبغي أن يستصحب دفترا على كل حال ليطالعه، وقيل: من لم يكن له دفتر في كمه، لم تثبت الحكمة في قلبه. وينبغي أن يكون في الدفتر بياض ليكتب فيه ما سمعه من أفواه الرجال، ويستصحب المحبرة ليكتب ما يستمع، وقد ذكرنا حديث هلال ابن يسار.

فصل: فيما يورث الحفظ

(١٤٣) وأقوى أسباب الحفظ: الجد والمواظبة وتقليل الغذاء وصلاة الليل. وقراءة القرآن من أسباب الحفظ. قيل: ليس شيء أزيد للحفظ من قراءة القرآن نظرا. وقراءة القرآن نظرا أفضل.

(١٤٤) ورأى شداد بن حكيم بعض إخوانه في المنام بعد وفاته فقال: أي شيء وجدته أنفع؟ قال قراءة القرآن نظرا.

(١٤٥) ويقول عند رفع الكتاب: بسم الله وسبحان الله والحمد لله ولا إله إلا الله والله أكبر ولا حول ولا قوة إلا بالله العلي العظيم العزيز العليم عدد كل حرف كتب ويكتب أبد الآبدين ودهر الداهرين. ويقول بعد كل مكتوبة آمنت، بالله الواحد الأحد الحق وحده لا شريك له، وكفرت بما سواه. ويكثر الصلاة على النبي ﷺ فإنه رحمة للعالمين.

(١٤٦) قال الشافعي رضي الله عنه:

شكوت إلى وكيع سوء حفظي ... فأرشدني إلى ترك المعاصي
فإن الحفظ فضل من إلهي ... وفضل الله لا يهدى لعاصي

(147) Rubbing the teeth, drinking honey and eating the incense plant[95] with sugar as well as eating 21 raisins,[96] red ones, each day on an empty stomach, create memory, since [these things] cure one of a great many sicknesses and illnesses. For everything that diminishes phlegm and "humor" increases memory and everything that augments phlegm creates forgetfulness. Moreover amongst those things which create forgetfulness are sinful deeds, the commission of many perfidies as well as concern and worry over worldly affairs and being distracted by many occupations and attachments. We have mentioned earlier in this book that it is not befitting the wise man to concern himself with worldly matters since these are harmful and useless. Worldly solicitudes of necessity create darkness in the heart, but concern over the future life of necessity brings light into the heart. One trace [sign of this light] becomes apparent through prayer, Care for worldly affairs impedes one from doing good, while concern for the future life gives one impetus to do good as does occupying oneself with prayer in a spirit of humility.

(148) The acquisition of learning drives out concern and sorrow just as the venerable Imām Naṣr b. al-Ḥasan al-Marghīnānī[97] said in one of his poems:

Find your wealth, O Naṣr b. al-Ḥasan,
in all [branches of] learning which can be amassed.

These will keep sorrow away.
Nothing else can be relied on [to do so].

(149) The Sheikh, the glorious Imām Najm al-Dīn ᶜUmar b. Muḥammad al-Nasafī said in one of his poems:

Farewell greetings to her who enslaved me through her elegance,
the splendor of her cheeks, and the furtive glances of her eyes.

A charming young maiden captivated me and filled me with love.
Imagination is baffled by the attempt to describe her [charms].

But I said [to her]: "Leave me alone and excuse me,
for indeed I have become enamored of the study of the fields of knowledge and their unveiling.

And for me seeking science and learning and reverence for God
suffice to keep me from the song of singing maidens and their perfume."

(١٤٧) والسواك وشرب العسل وأكل الكندر مع السكر، وأكل إحدى وعشرين زبيبة حمراء كل يوم على الريق، يورث الحفظ ويشفي من كثير من الأمراض والأسقام. وأكل ما يقلل البلغم والرطوبات يزيد في الحفظ. وأما ما يورث النسيان فالمعاصي وكثرة الذنوب والهموم والأحزان في أمور الدنيا، وكثرة الأشغال والعلائق؛ وكل ما يزيد في البلغم يورث النسيان. وقد ذكرنا أنه لا ينبغي للعاقل أن يهتم لأمر الدنيا لأنه يضر ولا ينفع، وهموم الدنيا لا تخلو عن الظلمة في القلب وهموم الآخرة لا تخلو عن النور في القلب، ويظهر أثره في الصلاة. وهم الدنيا يمنعه عن الخير، وهم الآخرة يحمله عليه، والاشتغال بالصلاة على الخشوع.

(١٤٨) وتحصيل العلم ينفي الهم والحزن، كما قال الشيخ الإمام نصر بن الحسن المرغيناني في قصيدة له:

اعتن نصر بن حسن — بكل علم يختزن
ذاك الذي ينفي الحزن — وغيره لا يؤتمن

(١٤٩) وقال الشيخ الإمام الأجل نجم الدين عمر بن محمد النسفي في أم ولد له:

سلام على من تيمتني بظرفها — ولمعة خديها ولمحة طرفها
سبتني وأصبتني فتاة مليحة — تحيرت الأوهام في كنه وصفها
فقلت ذريني واعذريني فإنني — شغفت بتحصيل العلوم وكشفها
ولي في طلاب العلم والفضل والتقى — غنى عن غناء الغانيات وعرفها

(150) And the eating of fresh coriander, acid apples and beholding a man crucified, and reading the inscriptions on tombs, as well as passing through a train of camels and throwing live fleas on the ground, and the application of the cupping glass to the nape of the neck, all of these things create forgetfulness.

Chapter Thirteen

Which Things Bring, and Which Prevent Earning a Livelihood, and Which Things Augment, or Diminish, the Years of One's Life

(151) It is essential for the student of learning that he have sustenance, and knowledge of those things which increase it as well as the duration of life and health in order to be free from [all other] occupations so as to [devote his time to] the pursuit of knowledge only. Books have been written describing all of these matters, so I shall only cite from some of them briefly.

(152) The Messenger of God said: "The decrees of God are not averted except by prayer, and your span of life is not augmented except through piety. For verily man is deprived of sustenance because of a crime he has committed." This tradition establishes for certain that the perpetration of a crime is the cause of deprivations of sustenance especially in the case of the crime of telling lies which entails poverty. There is a special tradition which establishes this [i.e., with regard to the effect of lying].

(153) So does sleep in the morning cut off sustenance and a great deal of sleep is the factor that brings about poverty and the poverty of learning also.

(154) Somebody said:

The joy of man lies in putting on [fine] clothes
[whereas] the collecting of knowledge is [achieved] through leaving off sleeping.

(155) Another one said:

Is it not a great loss [shame] that the nights pass without use
and yet are considered as part of my life?

(١٥٠) أما أسباب نسيان العلم فأكل الكزبرة الرطبة، وأكل التفاح الحامض، والنظر إلى المصلوب، وقراءة لوح القبور، والمرور بين قطار الجمال، وإلقاء القمل الحي على الأرض، والحجامة على نقرة القفا، كلها تورث النسيان.

فصل: فيما يجلب الرزق وما يمنعه وما يزيد في العمر وما ينقص

(١٥١) ثم لا بد لطالب العلم من القوت ومعرفة ما يزيد فيه وما يزيد في العمر والصحة، ليتفرغ طالب العلم للسعي إلى غرضه، وفي كل ذلك صنفوا كتبا فأوردت ههنا بعضها على سبيل الاختصار.

(١٥٢) قال رسول الله ﷺ: «لا يرد القدر إلا الدعاء، ولا يزيد في العمر إلا البر، فإن الرجل ليحرم الرزق بالذنب يصيبه». ثبت بهذا الحديث أن ارتكاب الذنب سبب حرمان الرزق، خصوصا الكذب فإنه يورث الفقر، وقد ورد فيه حديث خاص.

(١٥٣) وكذا نوم الصبحة يمنع الرزق، وكثرة النوم تورث الفقر وفقد العلم أيضا.

(١٥٤) قال القائل:

سرور الناس في لبس اللباس وجمع العلم في ترك النعاس

(١٥٥) وقال بعضهم:

أليس من الخسران أن لياليا تمر بلا نفع وتحسب من عمري

(156) Again another said:

You there, get up this night! Perhaps you will be well guided.
Until when will you sleep through your night while your life is consumed [wasted]?

(157) To sleep naked and urinate naked, to eat in a state of impurity and to eat lying down on one's side on a couch and to disdain [neglect] the remnants of the table, to burn up the skins of onion and garlic, to sweep the house in the night and leave sweepings in the house, to go ahead of venerable old people [or: of learned men], to call one's parents by their given names; the using of toothpicks made of every kind of wood [while only bitter wood should be used], washing the hand with mud and earth and sitting on the doorstep, lying on one's side against one of the doorposts, making sacred ablutions in the latrine, sewing clothes on one's body, drying one's face with clothes, leaving spiderwebs in the house; to neglect prayers, to make a hasty exit from the mosque after the morning prayers, to be very early in going to the market and to be late in returning from it, to buy pieces of bread from poor people, to beg, to invoke evil on one's children, to leave off covering vessels and extinguishing the lantern by blowing at it [with one's breath]—all of these [activities] bring about poverty. This is known through traditions going back to Muḥammad.

(158) Likewise to write with a knotted reed-pen,[98] to comb oneself with a broken comb, to keep from praying for one's parents, to be seated while winding one's turban around the head, to put on one's trousers standing up, [to show] avarice and miserliness, extravagance, laziness, sluggishness and neglect in one's affairs—all lead to poverty.

(159) The Messenger of God said: "By almsgiving bring down [from God] your sustenance." Early rising is blessed since it increases all kinds of good things, especially sustenance. [Also] beauty of handwriting is among the keys to securing sustenance and a merry expression on the face and good speech increase sustenance.[99]

(160) According to al-Ḥasan b. ʿAlī,[100] sweeping the courtyard and washing the pots and pans[101] lead to riches. The strongest factor in bringing about the means for sustaining life is the performance of prayer with reverence and humility and modesty and right position of the body, the rest of the obligatory things, traditional rites and accepted practices pertaining to it [prayer].

(١٥٦) وقال آخر:

قم الليل يا هذا لعلك ترشد إلى كم تنام الليل والعمر ينفد

(١٥٧) والنوم عريانا، والبول عريانا، والأكل جنبا، والأكل متكئا على جنب، والتهاون بسقاطة المائدة، وحرق قشر البصل والثوم، وكنس البيت بالمنديل، وكنس البيت في الليل، وترك القمامة في البيت، والمشي قدام المشايخ ونداء الأبوين باسمهما، والخلال بكل خشبة، وغسل اليد بالطين والتراب، والجلوس على العتبة، والاتكاء على أحد مصراعي الباب، والتوضؤ في البرز، وخياطة الثوب على بدنه، وتجفيف الوجه بالثوب، وترك بيت العنكبوت في البيت، والتهاون بالصلاة، وإسراع الخروج من المسجد بعد صلاة الفجر، والابتكار بالذهاب إلى السوق، والإبطاء في الرجوع منه، وشراء كسيرات الخبز من الفقراء السوال، ودعاء الشر على الولد، وترك تخمير الأواني، وإطفاء السراج بالنفس؛ كل ذلك يورث الفقر، عرف ذلك بالآثار.

(١٥٨) وكذا الكتابة بالقلم المعقود، والامتشاط بمشط منكسر، وترك الدعاء بالخير للوالدين، والتعمم قاعدا، والتسرول قائما، والبخل والتقتير والإسراف والكسل والتواني، والتهاون في الأمور.

(١٥٩) قال رسول الله ﷺ: «استنزلوا الرزق بالصدقة». والبكور مبارك يزيد في جميع النعم خصوصا في الرزق. وحسن الخط من مفاتيح الرزق، وبسط الوجه، وطيب الكلام يزيد في الحفظ والرزق.

(١٦٠) وعن الحسن بن علي رضي الله عنهما: «كنس الفناء، وغسل الإناء مجلبة الغنى». وأقوى الأسباب الجالبة للرزق: إقامة الصلاة بالتعظيم والخشوع وتعديل الأركان وسائر واجباتها وسننها وآدابها.

(161) The forenoon prayer is a known, nay, a famed [procedure] in [assuring sustenance]; [equally effective are] reading of the *Sūra al-Wāqiᶜa,*[102] particularly at night at the time [one usually] sleeps, and reading the *Sūra al-Mulk,*[103] the *Sūra al-Muzammil,*[104] and "By the night when it veils,"[105] and "Have we not expanded for thee thy breast."[106] And [to attain sustenance one should] be in the place of worship before the call to public prayer, prolong purification and carry out the ritual of the morning prayer as well as private prayers in the house. [Furthermore], one should not speak of mundane [profane] matters after the private prayers nor sit too frequently with women unless it is necessary. One should not engage in vain discourse benefiting neither one's worldly nor one's religious station.

(162) It is said: Whoever occupies himself with those things which are not significant for him, those things which are important to him will escape him.

(163) Buzurjmihr[107] said: "When you see a man who speaks a good deal be persuaded he is insane." And ᶜAlī said: "When intelligence is complete speech becomes rare."

(164) The writer [of this book] said: "On this subject there occurred to me the following verse:"

When the intelligence of a man is perfect, his speech becomes rare.
Contrarily, you can be sure of the stupidity of a man if he speaks a great deal.

(165) Somebody else said:

Speech is a necessary evil, but silence is salvation.
So when you have to talk do not be prolific.

You will never once repent of your silence,
but oftentimes you will repent of your speech.

(166) Also sustenance is increased if one recites each day from the moment of daybreak to the time when the prayer starts a hundred times: Praise be to God, the Exalted, Praise be to God; and: In praising Him [I am asking] God to forgive me my sins, and: I turn to him penitently. And by saying every day in the morning and evening one hundred times: There is no God but He, the King, the Truth, the Elucidator.

(١٦١) وصلاة الضحى في ذلك معروفة مشهورة، وقراءة سورة الواقعة خصوصا بالليل وقت النوم، وقراءة سورة «الملك» و«المزمل»، و«الليل إذا يغشى»، و«ألم نشرح لك»، وحضور المسجد قبل الآذان، والمداومة على الطهارة، وأداء سنة الفجر والوتر في البيت، وألا يتكلم بكلام الدنيا بعد الوتر، ولا يكثر مجالسة النساء إلا عند الحاجة، وألا يتكلم بكلام لغو غير مفيد لدينه ودنياه.

(١٦٢) قيل: من اشتغل بما لا يعنيه يفوته ما يعنيه.

(١٦٣) قال بزرجمهر: إذا رأيت الرجل يكثر الكلام فاستيقين بجنونه. وقال علي كرم الله وجهه: إذا تم العقل نقص الكلام.

(١٦٤) وقال المصنف. اتفق لي في هذا المعنى:

إذا تم عقل المرء قل كلامه ... وأيقن بحمق المرء إن كان مكثرا

(١٦٥) وقال آخر:

النطق زين والسكوت سلامة ... فإذا نطقت فلا تكن مكثارا
ما إن ندمت على سكوتي مرة ... ولقد ندمت على الكلام مرارا

(١٦٦) ومما يزيد في الرزق أن يقول كل يوم بعد انشقاق الفجر إلى وقت الصلاة: «سبحان الله العظيم، سبحان الله وبحمده أستغفر الله وأتوب إليه» مائة مرة؛ وأن يقول: «لا إله إلا الله الملك الحق المبين». كل يوم صباحا ومساء مائة مرة، وأن

And one should say after both morning and evening prayer each day thirty-three times: Praise be to God and Glory, there is no God but He. Also [repeat]: God is the greatest one, four times three hundred times.[108] And one should seek pardon from sins from God, the Exalted, seventy times after the morning prayer and one should repeat frequently the words: There is no strength nor power except in God the Most High, the Greatest; and: Benediction and peace on the Prophet. And one should say every Friday seventy times: O God! make me content with those things which are allowed by you rather than those things which are prohibited by you. And make me satisfied with your favor to the exclusion of anybody else's. And let one say this in praise of Him every day and night: You are God the most glorious, the wise one; you are God the king, the most sanctified; you are God the forbearing, the generous; you are God the creator of good and evil; you are God the creator of Paradise and Hell, the one who knows the hidden and the manifest, and the one who is cognizant of secret things and those out in the open. You are the greatest, the most exalted; you are God the creator of everything and to you everything reverts. You are God the Judge on the Day of Judgment. You never did cease nor will you ever cease.

(167) [Say also]: You are God, there is no God but you, the unique, the eternal. "He brought not forth, nor hath He been brought forth; coequal with Him, there hath never been any one."[109] You are God. There is no God but you, the Compassionate, the Merciful. You are God. There is no God but you, the King, the Most Sanctified, the Preserver of Peace, the one who is trusted, the tutor, the glorious, the omnipotent, the magnificent. There is no one who is God but you, the creator, the founder, the fashioner, whose are the most beautiful names. Whatever there is in the heaven and the earth praises him, for he is glorious and wise.

(168) Increase of the span of life is further owed to piety and that one leave off doing harmful things and venerate the elders and stand by one's kin; and that one say both at dawn and at dusk every day three times: Praise be to God who fills the scales of judgment, the ultimate limit of knowledge, the highest measure of satisfaction and the weighty occupant of the Throne.

يقول بعد صلاة الفجر كل يوم: الحمد لله وسبحان الله، ولا إله إلا الله، ثلاثا وثلاثين مرة، وبعد صلاة المغرب أيضا. ويستغفر الله أربعين مرة بعد صلاة الفجر، ويكثر من قول: لا حول ولا قوة إلا بالله العلى العظيم، والصلاة على النبي صلى الله عليه وآله وسلم، ويقول يوم الجمعة سبعين مرة: اللّهم أغنني بحلالك عن حرامك، واكفني بفضلك عمن سواك. ويقول هذا الثناء كل يوم وليلة: أنت الله العزيز الحكيم، أنت الله الملك القدوس، أنت الله الحكيم الكريم، أنت الله خالق الخير والشر، أنت الله خالق الجنة والنار عالم السر وأخفي، أنت الله الكبير المتعال، أنت الله خالق كل شيء، أنت الله يا ديان يوم الدين لم تزل ولا نزال.

(١٦٧) أنت الله لا إله إلا أنت الاحمد الصمد الذي لم يلد ولم يولد ولم يكن له كفوا أحد، أنت الله لا إله إلا أنت الرحمن الرحيم، أنت الله لا إله إلا أنت الملك القدوس السلام المؤمن المهيمن العزيز الجبار المتكبر لا إله إلا هو الخالق الباريء المصور له الأسماء الحسني يسبح له ما في السموات والأرض وهو العزيز الحكيم.

(١٦٨) ومما يزيد في ثلث مرات سبحان الله ملأ الميزان ومنتهي العلم ومبلغ الرضى وزنة العرش.

(169) And one should beware of cutting down green trees unless it is necessary. And [there should be] carrying out purification completely and praying with glorification [of God] and reading the Qurʾān and [going on] both the ḥajj and informal visits to the sacred places [*ᶜumra*].[110] One should [also] preserve good relations to one's fellowmen.

(170) And it is necessary that one learn something of medicine and obtain the blessings of traditions of Muḥammad handed down to us concerning medicine which the venerable Imām Abū al-ᶜAbbās al-Mustaghfirī has collected in his book called "The Medicine of the Prophet" [*Ṭibb al-nabī*].[111] Whoever looks for this book will find it.

(171) May the blessing of God rest on our lord Muḥammad, the seal of the noble envoys, and on his kin and his companions, the outstanding leaders of the community, forever and ever. Amen.

(١٦٩) وأن يتحرز عن قطع الأشجار الرطبة إلا عند الضرورة وإسباغ الوضوء والصلاة بالتعظيم وقراءة القرآن وحفظ الصحة.

(١٧٠) ولا بد من أن يتعلم شيئا من الطب و يتبرك بالأثار الواردة في الطب الذي جمعه الإمام أبو العباس المستغفري رحمه الله تعالى في كتابه المسمى بطب النبي ﷺ يجده من يطلبه

(١٧١) والحمد لله أولا وآخرا.

Ibn Jamāʿah

A Memorandum for Listeners and Lecturers: Rules of Conduct for the Learned and the Learning

(ABRIDGED)

TRANSLATED BY MICHAEL FISHBEIN

◆

[Introduction]

In the name of God, the Merciful, the Compassionate,
in Whom is my succor.

(1) Praise be to God the Benevolent and Compassionate, the All-embracing and All-knowing, the Possessor of great bounty. And the greatest blessing and most perfect peace be upon our master, Muḥammad the noble prophet, to whom was revealed in the Wise Remembrance that, "Surely thou art of an excellent character."[1] And upon his family and companions may there be proximity to him in the Abode of Bliss.

(2) To proceed: One of the most important things that a person of intelligence seeks in the prime of his youth and exerts himself to obtain and acquire is good education.[2] Both the religious law and reason attest to its value, and opinions and tongues agree in praising its possessors. The people worthiest of this excellent quality and likeliest to possess this exalted station are the people of learning, who by means of learning have encamped at the summit of glory and splendor and finished first

ابن جماعة

تذكرة السامع والمتكلم في أدب العالم والمتعلم

بسم الله الرحمن الرحيم

وبه توفيقي

(١) الحمد لله البر الرحيم، الواسع العليم، ذي الفضل العظيم، وأفضل الصلاة وأتم التسليم على سيدنا محمد النبي الكريم، المنزل عليه في الذكر الحكيم ﴿وَإِنَّكَ لَعَلَىٰ خُلُقٍ عَظِيمٍ﴾، وعلى آله وأصحابه الكرام جواره في دار النعيم.

(٢) أما بعد؛ فإن من أهم ما يبادر به اللبيب شرخ شبابه، ويدئب نفسه في تحصيله واكتسابه حسن الأدب الذي شهد الشرع والعقل بفضله، واتفقت الآراء والألسنة على شكر أهله، وإن أحق الناس بهذه الخصلة الجميلة وأولاهم بحيازة هذه المرتبة الجليلة أهل العلم الذين جلوا به ذروة المجد والسناء وأحرزوا به قصبات

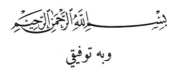

in the race for the legacy of the prophets. This they could do because of their knowledge of the Prophet's noble traits and rules of conduct and of the good example set by the pure guides among his family and companions—knowledge of what our earliest leading scholars professed and what the elders of succeeding generations took as a model to emulate. . . .

(3) Because the dignity of education is so great and the ways of attaining its benefits are hidden, I was moved by what I have seen of students' need for it and the inconvenience of repeatedly acquainting them with it, either due to shyness that prevents them from attendance or harshness that causes aversion, to compile this brief work to remind the teacher of what has been entrusted to him, to apprise the student of what is incumbent upon him, and to present the rules of conduct common to both, the rules to be followed in using books, and the rules of behavior for those who live in colleges [*madrasahs*][3] either as graduates or as students, as such colleges are usually the residences of seekers of learning nowadays.

(4) I have compiled the book from accepted reports, things I have heard from leading masters, things I have encountered in my readings, or things learned from studies. I have suppressed the chains of authorities and proof-texts, lest the book become lengthy or tedious to the reader.

(5) I have gathered in it—praise God—a variety of rules of conduct on these subjects that I have never yet seen gathered together in one book. I have prefaced to it a short chapter on the excellence of learning and scholars in order to seek blessing and follow their example.

(6) I have organized the book into five chapters that cover its subject: chapter one, on the excellence of learning and its practitioners, and the eminence of the scholar and his nobility; chapter two, rules of conduct for the teacher himself and for him in relation to his students and in his class; chapter three, rules of conduct for the student himself and in relation to his master, colleagues, and class; chapter four, how to use books and the rules relating to them; chapter five, rules of conduct for residence in colleges and the benefits of such residence.

(7) I have entitled the book, *A Memorandum for Listeners and Lecturers: Rules of Conduct for the Learned and the Learning.* May God guide us to knowledge and good works, and by His favor bring us to the end we hope for.

السبق إلى وراثة الأنبياء لعلمهم بمكارم أخلاق النبي صلى الله عليه وسلم وآدابه وحسن سيرة الأئمة الأطهار من أهل بيته وأصحابه وبما كان عليه أئمة علماء السلف واقتدى بهديهم فيه مشايخ الخلف. . . .

(٣) ولما بلغت رتبة الأدب هذه المزية وكانت مدارك مفضلاته خفية دعاني ما رأيت من احتياج الطلبة إليه وعسر تكرار توقفهم عليه إما لحياء فيمنعهم الحضور أو لجفاء فيورثهم النفور، إلى جمع هذا المختصر مذكرا للعالم ما جعل إليه ومنبها للطالب على ما يتعين عليه وما يشتركان فيه من الأدب وما ينبغي سلوكه في مصاحبة الكتب ثم أدب من سكن المدارس منتهيا أو طالبا لأنها مساكن طلبة العلم في هذه الأزمنة غالبا.

(٤) وجمعت ذلك مما اتفق في المسوعات أو سمعته من المشايخ السادات أو مررت به في المطالعات او استفدته في المذاكرات وذكرته محذوف الأسانيد والأدلة كيلا يطول على مطالعه أو يمله.

(٥) وقد جمعت فيه بحمد الله تعالى من تفاريق آداب هذه الأبواب ما لم أره مجموعا في كتاب، وقدمت على ذلك بابا مختصرا في فضل العلم والعلماء على وجه التبرك والاقتداء.

(٦) وقد رتبته على خمسة أبواب تحيط بمقصود الكتاب. الباب الأول في فضل العلم وأهله وشرف العالم ونسله. الباب الثاني في آداب العالم في نفسه ومع طلبته ودرسه. الباب الثالث في أدب المتعلم في نفسه ومع شيخه ورفقته ودرسه. الباب الرابع في مصاحبة الكتب وما يتعلق بها من الأدب. الباب الخامس في آداب سكنى المدارس وما يتعلق به من النفائس.

(٧) وقد سميته «تذكرة السامع والمتكلم في أدب العالم والمتعلم» والله تعالى يوفقنا للعلم والعمل، ويبلغنا من رضوانه نهاية الأمل.

Chapter One

On the Excellence of Knowledge and Scholars, and the Excellence of Imparting Knowledge and Acquiring It

(8) God has said: "God will raise up in rank those of you who believe and have been given knowledge."[4] Ibn ʿAbbās[5] said: "Scholars are a hundred ranks above believers, with a hundred years between each two ranks."

(9) God has said: "God bears witness that there is no god but He—and the angels, and men possessed of knowledge—upholding justice."[6] God mentions Himself first, His angels second, and men of knowledge third. What greater honor, excellence, augustness, and nobility could they have?

(10) God has said: "Say: 'Are they equal—those who know and those who know not?' "[7] God has said: "Question the people of the Remembrance, if it should be that you do not know."[8] God has said: "[And those similitudes—We strike them for the people,] but none understands them save those who know."[9] God has said: "Nay; rather it is signs, clear signs in the breasts of those who have been given knowledge."[10] God has said: "Only those of His servants fear God who have knowledge."[11] God has said: "[But those who believe, and do righteous deeds,] those are the best of creatures; [their recompense is with their Lord—Gardens of Eden, underneath which rivers flow, therein dwelling for ever and ever. God is well-pleased with them, and they are well-pleased with Him;] that is for him who fears his Lord."[12]

(11) The last two verses imply that those who have knowledge, the ulama, are those who fear God, and those who fear God are the best of creatures. It follows that those who have knowledge, the ulama, are the best of creatures.

(12) The Messenger of God said: "When God wishes a person well, He instructs him in religion." He also said: "Scholars are the heirs of the prophets." What greater degree of glory and pride could there be, and what greater rank of honor and renown. For as there is no rank above prophethood, so there is no honor above the honor of the heir of that rank.

(13) The Prophet, when two men were mentioned in his presence, one of them a worshiper, the other a scholar, said, "The superiority of the scholar to the worshiper is as my superiority to the least of you."

الباب الاول

في فضل العلم والعلماء وفضل تعليمه وتعلمه

(٨) قال الله تعالى ﴿يَرْفَعِ اللّٰهُ الَّذِينَ آمَنُوا مِنكُم والَّذِينَ أوتُوا العِلْمَ دَرَجاتٍ﴾. قال ابن عباس في فضل العلم العلماء فوق المؤمنين مائة درجة ما بين الدرجتين مائة عام.

(٩) قال تعالى: ﴿شَهِدَ اللّٰهُ أَنَّهُ لَا إِلٰهَ إِلاَّ هُوَ وَالْمَلَائِكَةُ وأُولُوا الْعِلْمِ قَائِمًا بِالْقِسْطِ . . . ﴾ الآية بدأ سبحانه بنفسه وثنى بملائكته وثلّث بأهل العلم، وكفاهم ذلك شرفا وفضلا وجلالة ونُبلا.

(١٠) وقال تعالى: ﴿قُلْ هَلْ يَسْتَوِي الَّذِينَ يَعْلَمُونَ والَّذِينَ لَا يَعْلَمُون﴾ وقال تعالى: ﴿فَسْئَلُوا أَهْلَ الذِكْرِ إِنْ كُنتُمْ لَا تَعْلَمُون﴾-وقال تعالى: ﴿وَمَا يَعْقِلُها إلا الْعَالِمون﴾ وقال تعالى: ﴿بَلْ هُوَ آياتٌ بَيِّنَاتٌ فِي صُدُورِ الَّذِينَ أُوتُوا الْعِلْمَ﴾ وقال تعالى: ﴿إِنَّمَا يَخْشَى اللهَ مِنْ عِبادِهِ الْعُلَمَاءُ﴾، وقال تعالى: ﴿أُولٰئِكَ هُمْ خَيْرُ الْبَرِيَّةِ﴾ إلى قوله ﴿ذَلِكَ لِمَنْ خَشِيَ رَبَّهُ﴾.

(١١) فاقتضت الآيتان أن العلماء هم الذين يخشون الله تعالى، وأنَّ الذين يخشون الله تعالى هم خير البرية فينتج أنّ العلماء هم خير البرية.

(١٢) وقال رسول الله ﷺ: « مَن يرد الله به خيرا يفقهه في الدين » وعنه ﷺ: « العلماء ورثة الانبياء ». وحسبك هذه الدرجة مجدا وفخرا، وبهذه الرتبة شرفا وذكرا؛ فكما لا رتبة فوق رتبة النبوة، فلا شرف فوق شرف وارث تلك الرتبة.

(١٣) وعنه ﷺ لما ذكر عنده رجلان أحدهما عابد والآخر عالم فقال: « فضل العالم على العابد كفضلي على أدناكم ».

(14) The Prophet said: "Whoever travels a road seeking knowledge travels one of the roads to Paradise. The angels lower their wings for the seeker of knowledge because God is well-pleased with him. All in heaven and all on earth, even whales deep in the water, pray that the scholar may receive God's forgiveness. The scholar's superiority to the worshiper is as the superiority of the full moon over all other heavenly bodies. Scholars are the heirs of the prophets: the prophets have bequeathed neither dinars nor dirhams, but only knowledge; and whoever acquires it acquires a great fortune. . . ."

(15) Abū al-Aswad al-Duʾalī[13] said: "Nothing is more powerful than knowledge: kings are rulers over people, but scholars are rulers over kings. . . ."

(16) According to Muᶜādh:[14] "Acquire knowledge, for acquiring it is a good deed, pursuing it is worship, studying it is praise of God, seeking it is combat for the sake of God, imparting it is closeness to God, and teaching it to those who do not know is charity. . . ."

(17) From what we have mentioned it is apparent that dedication to knowledge for the sake of God is more excellent than supererogatory bodily devotions, such as worship, fasting, praise, and prayer; for knowledge benefits the knower and all people, while supererogatory bodily devotions benefit only the performer. Knowledge corrects other devotions; they require it and depend on it, but it does not depend on them. Scholars are the heirs of the prophets, a status that does not belong to the devout. Obedience to scholars in what they know is incumbent upon others. The effect of knowledge remains after the knower's death, while other works of supererogation cease with the death of the doer. In the survival of knowledge lies the vitality of the religious law and the preservation of the signposts of the community.

SECTION

(18) Know, however, that everything we have said about the excellence of knowledge and scholars applies only to scholars who practice what they know, who are reverent and God-fearing, who by their knowledge seek the Face of God and proximity to Him in the gardens of Paradise. It does not apply to those who seek knowledge with evil intent, malicious designs, or worldly purposes such as fame, wealth, or vying in number of disciples and students.

(١٤) وعنه ﷺ: «من سلك طريقا يطلب فيه علما سلك به طريقا من طرق الجنة. وإن الملائكة لَتَضَعُ أجنحتها لطالب العلم رضى الله عنه، وإن العالم ليستغفر له من في السماوات ومن في الأرض حتى الحيتان في جوف الماء، وإن فضل العالم على العابد كفضل القمر ليلة البدر على سائر الكواكب، وإن العلماء ورثة الأنبياء، وإن الأنبياء لم يورثوا دينارا ولا درهما، وإنّما ورثوا العلم؛ فمن أخذه أخذ بحظ وافٍ» . . . .

(١٥) وقال أبو الأسود الدؤلي: ليس شيء أعز من العلم؛ الملوك حكام على الناس، والعلماء حكام على الملوك . . . .

(١٦) وعن معاذ (رضي الله عنه): تعلموا العلم فإن تعلمه حسنة، وطلبه عبادة، ومذاكرته تسبيح، والبحث عنه جهاد، وبذله قربة، وتعليمه من لا يعلمه صدقة . . . .

(١٧) وقد ظهر بما ذكرناه أن الاشتغال بالعلم لله أفضل من نوافل العبادات البدنية من صلاة وصيام وتسبيح ودعاء ونحو ذلك؛ لأن نفع العلم يعم صاحبه والناس، والنوافل البدنية مقصورة على صاحبها، ولأن العلم مصحح لغيره من العبادات فهي تفتقر إليه وتتوقف عليه ولا يتوقف هو عليها، ولأن العلماء ورثة الأنبياء عليهم الصلاة والتسليم وليس ذلك للمتعبدين، ولأن طاعة العالم واجبة على غيره فيه، ولأن العلم يبقى أثره بعد موت صاحبه، وغيره من النوافل تنقطع بموت صاحبها، ولأن في بقاء العلم إحياء الشريعة وحفظ معالم الملة.

فصل

(١٨) واعلم أن جميع ما ذكر من فضيلة العلم والعلماء إنما هو في حق العلماء العاملين الأبرار المتقين، الذين قصدوا به وجه الله الكريم، والزلفى لديه في جنات النعيم، لا مَنْ طلبه لسوء نية، أو خبث طوية، أو لأغراض دنيوية من جاه أو مال أو مكاثرة في الأتباع والطلاب.

(19) It is related that the Prophet said: "Whoever seeks knowledge in order to argue with fools, vie with other scholars, or attract attention to himself, God will cause him to enter the Fire." (The hadith was authenticated by al-Tirmidhī.[15])

(20) The Prophet said: "Anyone who acquires any knowledge for other than God's sake or who thereby seeks anything but the Face of God, let him take his seat in the Fire." (The hadith was transmitted by al-Tirmidhī. . . .)

Chapter Two

Rules of Conduct for the Teacher Himself and on How He Should Supervise His Students and Class—Containing Three Sections

SECTION ONE

Rules of Conduct for the Teacher Himself—Consisting of Twelve Rules

(21) **Rule One:** He should be mindful of God constantly in his secret heart and outward actions. He should maintain the fear of God in all his movements and thoughts, words and deeds. For he is the guardian of the knowledge committed to him and of the senses and intelligence with which he has been endowed. God has said: "O believers, betray not God and the Messenger, and betray not your trusts while you know."[16] God has said: ". . . following such portion of God's book as they were given to keep and were witnesses to. So fear not men, but fear Me. . . ."[17]

(22) **Rule Two:** He should preserve knowledge as the earliest Muslim scholars preserved it. He should champion it with all the honor and dignity that God has given it. He should not disgrace it by paying court without need or necessity to worldly folk who are unworthy of it or to those of them who would acquire knowledge from him, though they be great and powerful. . . .

(23) However, if need or necessity call for it, or a religious benefit outweighing the harm of the alternative requires it, and his intent is good, there is no harm in it, if God wills. That is how one should interpret the reports that such leading early scholars as al-Zuhrī[18] and al-Shāfiʿī[19] paid court to rulers and governors, not that they were interested in vain worldly goals. Similarly, if the person visited has a large amount of

(١٩) فقد روي عن النبي ﷺ: « من طلب العلم ليماري به السفهاء، أو يكاثر به العلماء، أو يصرف به وجوه الناس إليه، أدخله الله النار » . أخرجه الترمذي.

(٢٠) وعنه ﷺ: « من تعلم عِلْما لغير الله، أو أراد به غير وجه الله، فليتبوأ مقعده من النار » . رواه الترمذي . . . .

الباب الثاني

في أدب العالم في نفسه ومراعاة طالبه ودرسه. وفيه ثلاثة فصول

الفصل الأول في آدابه في نفسه وهو اثنا عشر نوعا

(٢١) النوع الأول: دوام مراقبة الله تعالى في السر والعلن والمحافظة على خوفه في جميع حركاته وسكناته وأقواله وأفعاله؛ فإنه أمين على ما أودع من العلوم، وما منح من الحواس والفهوم. قال الله تعالى: ﴿لَا تَخُونُوا ٱللَّهَ وَٱلرَّسُولَ وَتَخُونُوا أَمَانَاتِكُمْ وَأَنتُمْ تَعْلَمُونَ﴾ وقال تعالى: ﴿بِمَا ٱسْتُحْفِظُوا مِن كِتَابِ ٱللَّهِ وَكَانُوا عَلَيْهِ شُهَدَاءَ فَلَا تَخْشَوُا ٱلنَّاسَ وَٱخْشَوْنِ﴾ . . . .

(٢٢) الثاني: أن يصون العلم كما صانه علماء السلف، ويقوم له بما جعله الله تعالى له من العزة والشرف؛ فلا يذله بذهابه ومشيه إلى غير أهله من أبناء الدنيا من غير ضرورة أو حاجة، أو إلى من يتعلمه منه منهم وإن عظم شانه وكبر قدره . . . .

(٢٣) فان دعت حاجة إلى ذلك أو ضرورة أو اقتضته مصلحة دينية راجحة على مفسدة بدله وحسنت فيه نية صالحة، فلا بأس به إن شاء الله تعالى. وعلى هذا يحمل ما جاء عن بعض أئمة السلف من المشي إلى الملوك وولاة الأمر كالزهري والشافعي وغيرهما؛ لا على أنهم قصدوا بذلك فضول الأغراض الدنيوية. وكذلك إذا كان

knowledge and a high degree of asceticism, there is no harm in frequenting him to teach him. Sufyān al-Thawrī used to go to Ibrāhīm ibn Adham[20] and teach him.

(24) **Rule Three:** He should cultivate asceticism and abstemiousness with regard to this world to the extent that it does not harm himself or his dependents. Therefore, what he needs for this purpose for a moderate degree of contentment is not considered worldly. But as a minimum, a scholar should eschew attachment to this world, for he, of all people, is most aware of the world's meanness, allure, transience, and its great toil and weariness. Thus he ought not to fix his eyes on it or busy himself with its concerns.

(25) Al-Shāfiᶜī said: "If it were bequeathed to the most reasonable of men, it would be delivered to the ascetics, for I know of no one more likely among the learned to increase and perfect the intellect. . . ."

(26) **Rule Four:** He should keep his knowledge pure so that he does not make it a ladder for reaching worldly goals such as prestige, wealth, reputation, fame, office, or advancement over his colleagues.

(27) The Imām al-Shāfiᶜī said: "I wish that all mankind had acquired this learning with not a word of it ascribed to me."

(28) Likewise he should keep his knowledge pure from the hope of gaining money or service from his students because of their studying with him and association with him. Manṣūr[21] never asked assistance in any affair from anyone who frequented him. . . .

(29) **Rule Five:** He should shun low employments of vile nature or discountenanced by custom and religious law, such as cupping, tanning, money changing, and goldsmithery. He should avoid places likely to arouse suspicions however remote. He should do nothing that implies lack of manliness or that appears to be reprehensible, even if it really is allowable, because he will expose himself to suspicion and his honor to slander, raising odious suspicions in people and leading them to commit the sin of slander. If perchance any such thing occurs out of need or similar reason, he should inform the person who saw him of the legal status of his action, his justification, and his intention, lest the person offend because of him, or, avoiding him, not benefit from his knowledge, and so that the ignorant one may learn from him. . . .

المأتي إليه من العلم والزهد في المنزلة العلية والمحل الرفيع، فلا بأس بالتردد إليه لإفادته؛ فقد كان سفيان الثوري يمشي إلى إبراهيم بن أدهم ويفيده.

(٢٤) الثالث: أن يتخلق بالزهد في الدنيا، والتقلل منها بقدر الإمكان الذي لا يضر بنفسه أو بعياله فإن ما يحتاج إليه لذلك على الوجه المعتدل من القناعة ليس يعد من الدنيا. وأقل درجات العالم أن يستقذر التعلق بالدنيا، لأنه أعلم الناس بخستها وفتنتها وسرعة زوالها وكثرة تعبها ونصبها؛ فهو أحق بعدم الالتفات إليها والاشتغال بهمومها.

(٢٥) وعن الشافعي (رضي الله عنه): لو أوصي إلى أعقل الناس صرف إلى الزهاد، فليت شعري من أحق من العلماء بزيادة العقل وكماله . . . .

(٢٦) الرابع: أن ينزه علمه عن جعله سُلّما يتوصل به إلى الأغراض الدنيوية من جاه أو مال أو سمعة أو شهرة أو خدمة أو تقدم على أقرانه.

(٢٧) قال الامام الشافعي (رضي الله عنه): وددت أن الخلق تعلموا هذا العلم، على أن لا ينسب إليّ حرف منه.

(٢٨) وكذلك ينزهه عن الطمع في رفق من طلبته بمال أو خدمة أو غيرهما بسبب اشتغالهم عليه وترددهم إليه. كان منصور لا يستعين بأحد يختلف إليه في حاجة . . . .

(٢٩) الخامس: أن يتنزه عن دني المكاسب ورذيلها طبعا، وعن مكروهها عادة وشرعا، كالحجامة والدباغة والصرف والصياغة. وكذلك يتجنب مواضع التهم وإن بعدت، ولا يفعل شيئا يتضمن نقص مروءته أو ما يستنكر ظاهرا وإن كان جائزا باطنا؛ فإنه يعرض نفسه للتهمة، وعرضه للوقيعة، ويوقع الناس في الظنون المكروهة، وتأثيم الوقيعة؛ فإن اتفق وقوع شيء من ذلك لحاجة أو نحوها، أخبر من شاهده بحكمه وبعذره ومقصوده كيلا يأثم بسببه أو ينفر عنه، فلا ينتفع بعلمه وليستفيد ذلك الجاهل به.

(30) Therefore the Prophet said to two men who saw him with [his wife] Ṣafīyah and turned away, "At your ease! it is Ṣafīyah." Then he said, "Satan runs in a man's veins like the blood. I was afraid that he might cast something into your hearts and that you might perish."

(31) **Rule Six:** He should diligently observe the rituals and outward ordinances of Islam, such as performing the congregational prayers in mosque, greeting dignitaries and commoners with "peace be upon you," promoting virtue and forbidding vice, being patient when wronged for this, pronouncing the truth in the presence of rulers, and devoting himself to God without fearing the reproach of anyone. He should remember God's words: "And bear patiently whatever may befall thee; surely that is true constancy."[22] He should remember the patience of Our Master, the Messenger of God, and the other prophets in the face of wrong and what they bore for the sake of God until they received their reward. He should promote the traditions of the Prophet and combat innovations. He should perform for God's sake the affairs of religion and the things that entail the welfare of Muslims in the prescribed way and established path diligently. In his outward and inward acts he should not be satisfied with what is merely acceptable; he should oblige himself to do what is best and most perfect, for scholars are the model. They are the authorities to whom people refer in matters of religion and God's convincing argument for the common people. . . .

(32) **Rule Seven:** He should be diligent in the performance of recommended religious observances of word and deed, constantly reciting the Qurʾān, remembering God in his heart and on his tongue, offering traditional prayers and litanies by night and by day, and performing supererogatory prayers, fastings, and pilgrimages. He should bless the Prophet; for love, reverence, and praise of him are a duty, and courtesy is required and traditional whenever one hears his name and mention of his traditions. . . .

(33) Whenever he recites the Qurʾān, he should ponder its meaning, its commands and prohibitions, and its promises and threats. He should understand its injunctions. Let him beware of forgetting it after memorizing it, for prophetic tradition rebukes those who do so. . . .

(٣٠) ولذلك قال النبي ﷺ للرجلين لما رأياه يتحدث مع صفية فوليا: على رسلكما إنها صفية. ثم قال: إن الشيطان يجري من ابن آدم مجرى الدم، فخفت أن يقذف في قلوبكما شيئا، أو قال فتهلكا.

(٣١) السادس: أن يحافظ على القيام بشعائر الإسلام وظواهر الأحكام، كإقامة الصلاة في المساجد للجماعات، وإفشاء السلام للخواص والعوام، والأمر بالمعروف والنهي عن المنكر، والصبر على الأذى بسبب ذلك، صادعا بالحق عند السلاطين، باذلا نفسه لله، لا يخاف فيه لومة لائم، ذاكرا قوله تعالى: ﴿واصْبِرْ عَلَى مَا أَصَابَكَ إنَّ ذَلِكَ مِنْ عَزْمِ الأُمُورِ﴾. وما كان سيدنا رسول الله ﷺ وغيره من الأنبياء عليه من الصبر على الأذى، وما كانوا يتحملونه في الله تعالى حتى كانت لهم العقبى وكذلك القيام بإظهار السنن وإخماد البدع والقيام لله في أمور الدين وما فيه مصالح المسلمين على الطريق المشروع والمسلك المطبوع، ولا يرضى من أفعاله الظاهرة والباطنة بالجائز منها، بل يأخذ نفسه بأحسنها وأكملها فإن العلماء هم القدوة وإليهم المرجع في الأحكام وهم حجة الله تعالى على العوام. . . .

(٣٢) السابع: أن يحافظ على المندوبات الشرعية القولية والفعلية؛ فيلازم تلاوة القرآن وذكر الله تعالى بالقلب واللسان. وكذلك ما ورد من الدعوات والأذكار في آناء الليل والنهار؛ ومن نوافل العبادات من الصلاة والصيام وحج البيت الحرام والصلاة على النبي ﷺ؛ فإن محبته وإجلاله وتعظيمه واجب، والأدب عند سماع اسمه وذكر سنته مطلوب وسنة. . . .

(٣٣) وينبغي له إذا تلا القرآن أن يتفكر في معانيه، وأوامره ونواهيه، ووعده ووعيده؛ والوقوف عند حدوده. وليحذر من نسيانه بعد حفظه، فقد ورد في الأخبار النبوية ما يزجر عن ذلك. . . .

(34) **Rule Eight:** His treatment of people should be marked by generous traits of character: a cheerful countenance, effusive greetings, offering food, controlling his anger, averting harm from people, and bearing it from them. He should be beyond provocation; he should avoid selfishness; he should be equitable and not demand his due; he should be thankful for favors; he should create ease; he should strive to fulfill requests; he should use his prestige for intercession; he should be kind to the poor; he should show love to neighbors and relatives; and he should be gentle to students, helping and nurturing them as will be discussed below.

(35) If he sees anyone who does not observe the prescribed prayers, the rules of purity, or any other duties, he will guide him gently and kindly, as the Messenger of God did with the Bedouin who urinated in the mosque or with Muʿāwiyah ibn al-Ḥakam when he spoke during prayers.

(36) **Rule Nine:** He should cleanse himself inwardly and outwardly from mean traits of character and fill himself with agreeable traits. Mean traits include rancor, envy, wrongdoing, anger other than for the sake of God, deceit, arrogance, hypocrisy, vanity, concern with fame, stinginess, malice, wantonness, avarice, pride, conceit, vying for the things of this world and boasting of them, flattery and adorning oneself for people, love of being praised for what one has not done, blindness to one's own faults and preoccupation with the faults of others, zeal and fanaticism not for the sake of God, making entreaty to and fearing anyone but God, slandering, backbiting, defaming, lying, using foul language, and despising people even if they be beneath him. Beware, beware of these noxious traits and defects of character! They are the gate of every evil; nay, they are evil entire! Some wicked spirits among the scholars of this age have been afflicted with many of these traits—except those whom God has protected—especially envy, vanity, hypocrisy, and contempt for people. The remedies for this affliction are discussed at length in the books of spiritual exhortation. Whoever wants to purify himself should read them. One of the most useful is *Kitāb al-riʿāyah* by al-Muḥāsibī. . . .[23]

(٣٤) الثامن: معاملة الناس بمكارم الأخلاق من طلاقة الوجه، وإفشاء السلام، وإطعام الطعام، وكظم الغيظ، وكف الأذى عن الناس، واحتماله منهم، والإيثار، وترك الاستئثار، والإنصاف، وترك الاستنصاف، وشكر التفضل، وإيجاد الراحة، والسعي في قضاء الحاجات، وبذل الجاه في الشفاعات، والتلطف بالفقراء، والتحبب إلى الجيران والأقرباء، والرفق بالطلبة، وإعانتهم وبرّهم، كما سيأتي إن شاء الله تعالى.

(٣٥) وإذا رأى من لا يقيم صلاته أو طهارته أو شيئا من الواجبات عليه، أرشده بتلطف و رفق، كما فعل رسول الله ﷺ مع الأعرابي الذي بال في المسجد، ومع معاوية بن الحكم لما تكلم في الصلاة.

(٣٦) التاسع: أن يطهّر باطنه وظاهره من الأخلاق الرديئة، ويعمره بالأخلاق المرضية؛ فمن الأخلاق الرديئة الغل والحسد والبغي والغضب لغير الله تعالى، والغش والكبر، والرئاء والعجب، والسمعة، والبخل، والخبث، والبطر، والطمع، والفخر، والخيلاء، والتنافس في الدنيا، والمباهاة بها، والمداهنة، والتزين للناس، وحب المدح بمالم يفعل، والعمى عن عيوب النفس، والاشتغال عنها بعيوب الخلق، والحمية، والعصبية لغير الله، والرغبة والرهبة لغير الله، والغيبة، والنميمة، والبهتان، والكذب، والفحش في القول، واحتقار الناس ولو كانوا دونه. فالحذر الحذر من هذه الصفات الخبيثة والأخلاق الرذيلة، فإنها باب كل شر، بل هي الشر كله، وقد بلي بعض أصحاب النفوس الخبيثة من فقهاء الزمان بكثير من هذه الصفات، إلا من عصم الله تعالى، ولا سيما الحسد والعجب والرئاء واحتقار الناس. وأدوية هذه البلية مستوفى في كتب الرقائق فمن أراد تطهير نفسه منها فعليه بتلك الكتب، ومن أنفعها كتاب «الرعاية» للمحاسبي رحمه الله . . . .

(37) **Rule Ten:** He should constantly desire to grow by practicing seriousness and effort and should be diligent in the offices of prayer with regard to religious observances and in study. He should busy himself reciting the Qurʾān, teaching others to recite it, reading, meditating, commenting, memorizing, writing, and researching.

(38) He should waste none of his time with things unrelated to his purpose of knowledge and good works, except to the extent that such matters as eating, drinking, sleeping, relief of weariness, performing one's duty to a wife or guest, and obtaining one's sustenance are necessary, or because of some illness that renders study impossible, for the rest of a believer's life is without value. Anyone two days of whose life are equal has been defrauded. . . .

(39) **Rule Eleven:** He should not be too proud to learn what he does not know from someone beneath him in rank, lineage, or age. Rather, he should be eager to obtain benefit wherever it may be. Wisdom is the believer's lost treasure: he snatches it up wherever he finds it.

(40) Saʿīd ibn Jubayr[24] said: "A man remains a scholar as long as he learns. When he stops learning, thinks he needs no more, and is satisfied with what he has, he is the most ignorant of men. . . ."

(41) **Rule Twelve:** He should busy himself compiling, collecting, and composing, though with full excellence and perfect qualification. For he will become acquainted with the most worthy arts and most subtle branches of knowledge due to the need for much investigation, reading, exploration, and review. As al-Khaṭīb al-Baghdādī[25] said, "It strengthens the memory, sharpens the mind, hones the nature, improves eloquence, brings good remembrance and abundant reward, and immortalizes one for all times."

(42) It is best that he attend to what is of general benefit and much needed. Let him attend to what has not been previously written about, taking care to use clear language in what he writes, avoiding tedious prolixity or undue brevity, and giving each composition what befits it. His composition should not leave his hand before he has polished, reviewed, and arranged it. Some people disapprove of the writing and composing of books nowadays by people who are evidently qualified and known for their knowledge. The only reason for such disapproval is the

(٣٧) العاشر: دوام الحرص على الازدياد بملازمة الجد والاجتهاد، والمواظبة على وظائف الأوراد من العبادة، والاشتغال والإشغال قراءة وإقراء، ومطالعة وفكرا، وتعليقا وحفظا، وتصنيفا وبحثا.

(٣٨) ولا يُضيع شيئا من أوقات عمره في غير ما هو بصدده من العلم والعمل، إلا بقدر الضرورة من أكل أوشرب أونوم أواستراحة لملل، أو أداء حق زوجة أو زائر، أوتحصيل قوت، وغيره مما يحتاج إليه، أولألم أوغيره مما يتعذر معه الاشتغال، فإن بقية عمر المؤمن لا قيمة له. ومن استوى يوماه، فهو مغبون. . . .

(٣٩) الحادي عشر: أن لا يستنكف أن يستفيد ما لا يعلمه ممن هو دونه منصبا أونسبا أو سنا، بل يكون حريصا على الفائدة حيث كانت. والحكمة ضالة المؤمن، يلتقطها حيث وجدها.

(٤٠) قال سعيد بن جبير: لا يزال الرجل عالما ما تعلم، فإذا ترك التعلم وظن أنه قد استغنى واكتفى بما عنده، فهو أجهل ما يكون. . . .

(٤١) الثاني عشر: الاشتغال بالتصنيف والجمع والتأليف، لكن مع تمام الفضيلة وكمال الأهلية؛ فإنه يطلع على حقائق الفنون ودقائق العلوم للاحتياج إلى كثرة التفتيش والمطالعة، والتنقيب والمراجعة. وهو كما قال الخطيب البغدادي: يثبت الحفظ ويذكي القلب ويشحذ الطبع، ويجيد البيان، ويكسب جميل الذكر، وجزيل الأجر، ويخلده إلى آخر الدهر.

(٤٢) والأولى أن يعتني بما يعم نفعه، وتكثر الحاجة إليه؛ وليكن اعتناؤه بما لم يسبق إلى تصنيفه، متحريا إيضاح العبارة في تأليفه، معرضا عن التطويل الممل، والإيجاز المخل، مع إعطاء كل مصنف ما يليق به. ولا يخرج تصنيفه من يده قبل تهذيبه وتكرير النظر فيه وترتيبه. ومن الناس من ينكر التصنيف والتأليف في هذا الزمان على من ظهرت أهليته وعرفت معرفته، ولا وجه لهذا الإنكار إلا التنافس

rivalry between people of different ages. Anyone who uses his paper and ink to write poems, decent stories, and such things does not become an object of disapproval; why, then, when one turns paper and ink to writing on beneficial religious subjects does one receive disapproval and disparagement? However, when a person is unqualified to write, the disapproval results from the ignorance that the book contains and the misleading of the book's reader by it and from the fact that the author has wasted his time on something at which he has no skill and has not given the work the perfection that it deserves.

SECTION TWO

Rules of Conduct for the Teacher in His Class—Consisting of Twelve Rules

(43) **Rule One:** Before he goes to the lecture hall, he should purify himself from pollution and filth, cleanse and perfume himself, and dress in some of his best clothes, as befits him among the people of his time, in order to honor learning and exalt the religious law.

(44) Whenever people came to Mālik[26] to study hadith, he would wash, perfume himself, put on new clothes, and put his cloak over his head. He would sit on a raised platform and burn aloes wood as incense until he had finished. He used to say, "I wish to honor the hadith of the Messenger of God, may God bless him and grant him peace. . . ."

(45) **Rule Two:** When he leaves his house, he should pray the prayer handed down from the Prophet: "O God, I take refuge in Thee from straying or leading astray, from slipping or causing to slip, from wrongdoing or being wronged, from acting ignorantly or being treated ignorantly. He who seeks Thy protection is strong, and Thy praise is exalted. There is no god but Thee." Then he should say: "In the name of God and by God: God is enough for me; in Him have I put my trust. There is no strength nor power save in God, the High, the Mighty. O God, make firm my heart and put the truth onto my tongue."

بين أهل الأعصار، وإلا فمن إذا تصرف في مداده وورقه بكتابة ما شاء من أشعار وحكايات مباحة أو غير ذلك، لا ينكر عليه؟ فَلِمَ إذا تصرف فيه بتسويد ما ينتفع به من علوم الشريعة ينكر ويستهجن؟ أما من لم يتأهل لذلك، فالإنكار عليه نتيجة لما يتضمنه من الجهل، وتغرير من يقف على ذلك التصنيف به، ولكونه يضيع زمانه فيما لم يتقنه، ويدع الإتقان الذي هو أحرى به منه.

الفصل الثاني

في آداب العالم في درسه وفيه اثنا عشر نوعا

(٤٣) الأول: إذا عزم على مجلس التدريس، تطهر من الحدث والخبث، وتنظف وتطيب، ولبس من أحسن ثيابه اللائقة به بين أهل زمانه، قاصدا بذلك تعظيم العلم، وتبجيل الشريعة.

(٤٤) كان مالك (رضي الله عنه) إذا جاءه الناس لطلب الحديث، اغتسل وتطيب ولبس ثيابا جددا، ووضع رداءه على رأسه، ثم يجلس على منصة، ولا يزال يبخر بالعود حتى يفرغ. وقال: أحب أن أعظم حديث رسول الله ﷺ . . . .

(٤٥) الثاني: إذا خرج من بيته دعا بالدعاء الصحيح عن النبى ﷺ وهو: « اللّٰهم إني أعوذ بك أن أَضِل أو أُضل، أو أَزل أو أُزل، أو أَظلم أو أُظلم، أو أَجهل أو يُجهل علي، عز جارك، وجل ثناؤك، ولا إله غيرك » . ثم يقول: « بسم الله وبالله، حسبي الله، توكلت على الله، لا حول ولا قوة إلا بالله العلي العظيم، اللّٰهم أثبت جناني وأدر الحق على لساني » .

(46) He should meditate on God constantly until he arrives at the lecture hall. When he arrives, he should greet the class and pray two prostrations, unless it is a time when prayer is disapproved; however, if the place is a mosque, prayer is recommended with no restrictions. Then he should beseech God for success, help, and protection. . . .

(47) **Rule Three:** He should sit visible to all in attendance. He should reverence those who are superior in knowledge, age, righteousness, and honor, raising them up according to their precedence in leadership. He should be kind to the others and honor them with a fine greeting, cheerful countenance, and great respect. He should not hesitate to stand up to honor the leaders of Islam, for many texts have come down concerning how one should honor scholars and students.

(48) He should directly face those in attendance as necessary, but should single out for greater attention and concern anyone who addresses him, questions him, or enters into discussion with him as is proper, even if the person is young or humble. Not doing so is to act like the proud and haughty.

(49) **Rule Four:** Before beginning to discuss or lecture, he should, as is customary, recite something from the Qur᾿ān as a blessing and auspicious beginning. If this is taking place in a college where there is a specific provision about this, he should follow that provision. After the recitation he should beseech God for himself, for those in attendance, and for all Muslims.

(50) Then he should take refuge in God from Satan the Accursed One. He should mention God's name and praise Him. He should bless the Prophet, the Prophet's family, and the Prophet's companions, and pray for God's favor upon the imams of the Muslims and upon his elders. He should pray for himself, for those present, and for all their parents. If he is in a college or similar institution, he should pray that its founder[27] may be rewarded for his good deed and achieve his objective. . . .

(51) **Rule Five:** If there are a number of lectures to be given, he should give them in order of honor and importance. He should give preference to Qur᾿ānic exegesis, then hadith, then the fundamentals of religion, then the fundamentals of jurisprudence, then the doctrine of his legal school, then disagreements [among schools], then grammar or dialectic.

(٤٦) ويُديم ذكر الله تعالى إلى أن يصل إلى مجلس التدريس، فإذا وصل إليه سلم على من حضر، وصلى ركعتين، إن لم يكن وقت كراهة، فإن كان مسجدا، تأكدت الصلاة مطلقا، ثم يدعو الله تعالى بالتوفيق والإعانة والعصمة. . . .

(٤٧) الثالث: أن يجلس بارزا لجميع الحاضرين ويوقر أفاضلهم بالعلم والسن والصلاح والشرف ويرفعهم على حسب تقديمهم في الإمامة، ويتلطف بالباقين، ويكرمهم بحسن السلام، وطلاقة الوجه، ومزيد الاحترام، ولا يكره القيام لأكابر أهل الإسلام على سبيل الإكرام. وقد ورد في إكرام العلماء وإكرام طلبة العلم نصوص كثيرة.

(٤٨) ويلتفت إلى الحاضرين التفاتا قصدا بحسب الحاجة، ويخص من يكلمه أو يسأله أو يبحث معه على الوجه عند ذلك بمزيد التفات إليه، وإقبال عليه وإن كان صغيرا أو وضيعا، فان ترك ذلك من أفعال المتجبرين المتكبرين.

(٤٩) الرابع: أن يقدّم على الشروع في البحث والتدريس قراءة شيء من كتاب الله تعالى تبركا وتيمنا، أو كما هو العادة فإن كان ذلك في مدرسة شرط فيها ذلك، اتبع الشرط، ويدعو عقيب القراءة لنفسه وللحاضرين وسائر المسلمين.

(٥٠) ثم يستعيذ بالله من الشيطان الرجيم، ويسمي الله تعالى ويحمده، ويصلي على النبي ﷺ وعلى آله وأصحابه. ويترضى عن أئمة المسلمين ومشايخه، ويدعو لنفسه وللحاضرين ولوالديهم أجمعين، وعن واقف مكانه إن كان ذلك في مدرسة أو نحوها جزاء لحسن فعله، وتحصيلا لقصده. . . .

(٥١) الخامس: إذا تعددت الدروس قدم الأشرف فالأشرف، والأهم فالأهم؛ فيقدم تفسير القرآن، ثم الحديث، ثم أصول الدين، ثم أصول الفقه، ثم المذهب، ثم الخلاف، أو النحو، أو الجدل.

(52) Some learned ascetics used to conclude the lectures with a lecture on spiritual exhortations, from which those in attendance would derive the benefit of inward purification, or with similar matters such as homilies and texts to foster tender-heartedness, asceticism, and patience.

(53) If he is in a college whose founder has made specific provision about the lectures, he should follow that provision and not violate the main purpose for which the building was constructed and endowed.

(54) In his lecture he should join together the things that ought to be joined, and he should pause at the stopping points where there is a break in the argument.

(55) Having raised an obscure or doubtful question of religion, he should not postpone the answer to it until another lecture. He should discuss both the question and its answer or omit them both. Because of the potential harm, he should not in this case bind himself to a book whereby he would have to postpone the answer to the obscure point, especially if the lecture is being attended both by specialists and by nonspecialists. . . .

(56) **Rule Six:** He should neither raise his voice more than is necessary nor lower it so much that it is not fully understandable. . . .

(57) It is best that his voice neither go beyond his class nor fail to reach the hearing of those in attendance. If someone hard of hearing is present in the class, there is no harm in his raising his voice enough to allow him to hear. There is a hadith about the merit of doing so. He should not speak rapidly and without pauses; he should make his speech distinct, orderly, and leisurely, so that he and his audience may ponder it. . . .

(58) When he finishes a topic or section, he should be silent for a time, so that anyone who wishes may speak. For as we shall mention later, a teacher should not be interrupted while he is speaking; and so, if he does not make such a pause, a useful point might escape notice.

(59) **Rule Seven:** He should protect his class from clamor, for error is married to clamor,[28] as well as from the raising of voices and diverse directions of discussion.

(60) Al-Rabīᶜ[29] says that whenever anyone debating a point with al-Shāfiᶜī would pass to another point, al-Shāfiᶜī would say, "Let us finish this point, and then go on to what you want."

(٥٢) وكان بعض العلماء الزهاد يختم الدروس بدرس دقائق يفيد به الحاضرين تطهير الباطن، ونحو ذلك من عظة ورقة وزهد وصبر.

(٥٣) فإن كان في مدرسة ولواقفها في الدروس شرط اتبعه، ولا يخل بما هو أهم ما بنيت له تلك البناية ووقفت لأجله.

(٥٤) ويصل في درسه ما ينبغي وصله، ويقف في مواضع الوقف ومنقطع الكلام.

(٥٥) ولا يذكر شبهة في الدين في درس، ويؤخر الجواب عنها إلى درس آخر، بل يذكرهما جميعا، أو يدعهما جميعا. ولا يتقيد في ذلك لمصنف يلزم منه تأخير جواب الشبهة عنها، لما فيه من المسألة، لا سيما إذا كان الدرس يجمع الخواص والعوام . . . .

(٥٦) السادس: أن لا يرفع صوته زائدا على قدر الحاجة، ولا يخفضه خفضا لا يحصل معه كمال الفائدة . . . .

(٥٧) والأولى أن لا يجاوز صوته مجلسه، ولا يقصر عن سماع الحاضرين، فإن حضر فيهم ثقيل السمع فلا بأس بعلو صوته بقدر ما يسمعه؛ فقد روي في فضيلة ذلك حديث. ولا يسرد الكلام سردا، بل يرتله ويرتبه، ويتمهل فيه ليفكر فيه هو وسامعه . . . .

(٥٨) وإذا فرغ من مسألة أو فصل سكت قليلا حتى يتكلم من في نفسه، لأنا سنذكر، إن شاء الله، أنه لا يقطع على العالم كلامه، فإذا لم يسكت هذه السكتة ربما فاتت الفائدة.

(٥٩) السابع: أن يصون مجلسه عن اللغط، فإن الغلط تحت اللغط؛ وعن رفع الأصوات، واختلاف جهات البحث.

(٦٠) قال الربيع: كان الشافعي إذا ناظره إنسان في مسألة، فعدا إلى غيرها، يقول: نفرغ من هذه المسألة، ثم نصير إلى ما تريد.

(61) He should gently dispel clamor at the start, before it spreads and spirits become agitated. He should remind the class of the traditions concerning the hatefulness of wrangling, especially after the truth has emerged. . . .

(62) **Rule Eight:** He should rebuke anyone who behaves aggressively in discussion or who shows quarrelsomeness, bad manners, or unfairness after the truth has emerged; anyone who uselessly continues shouting or who insults others who are present or absent; anyone in the class who exalts himself over someone worthier than he, or sleeps, or talks with others, or laughs, or ridicules a member of the class, or violates the rules of behavior for students in a class. We shall mention the details of this later. But this should be done only if no greater evil ensues.

(63) He should have an intelligent, astute, and trained monitor (*naqīb*) to seat by rank those in attendance and anyone who enters, to waken the sleeper, to point out anyone who fails to do what he ought to do or who does what he ought not to do, and to command that they listen and attend to the lectures.

(64) **Rule Nine:** He should always be equitable in discussing and speaking. He should listen carefully to the student's question, even if the student is young. He should not disdain listening to him, thereby depriving the student of benefit.

(65) If the questioner, from shyness or inability, cannot formulate or phrase the question properly, but manages to express the meaning, he should state what the student meant to say, explain the reason for posing the question, and answer the questioner. He should answer with what he thinks or ask someone else for an answer. He should ponder his response when he replies. If he is asked about what he does not know, he should say that he does not know, for it is part of knowledge to say that one does not know. Someone once said that "I do not know" is half of knowledge. Ibn ʿAbbās said, "If a scholar fails to hit 'I do not know,' his own vitals will be hit."[30] It has been said that a scholar should instill in his companions the habit of saying "I do not know" by saying it frequently himself. Muḥammad ibn ʿAbd al-Ḥakam[31] said: "I asked al-Shāfiʿī whether in a temporary marriage there can be divorce, inheritance, obligatory support, or testimony. He answered, 'By God, I do not know!' "

(٦١) ويتلطف في دفع ذلك من مباديه قبل انتشاره وثوران النفوس، ويذكر الحاضرين بما جاء في كراهية المماراة، لا سيما بعد ظهور الحق . . . .

(٦٢) الثامن: أن يزجر من تعدى في بحثه، أو ظهر منه لدد في بحثه، أو سوء أدب، أو ترك الإنصاف بعد ظهور الحق، أو أكثر الصياح بغير فائدة، أو أساء أدبه على غيره من الحاضرين أو الغائبين، أو ترفع في المجلس على من هو أولى منه، أو نام، أو تحدث مع غيره، أو ضحك، أو استهزأ بأحد من الحاضرين أو فعل ما يخل بأدب الطالب في الحلقة. وسيأتي تفصيله إن شاء الله تعالى. هذا كله بشرط أن لا يترتب على ذلك مفسدة تربو عليه.

(٦٣) وينبغي أن يكون له نقيب فطن كيس درب، يرتب الحاضرين، ومن يدخل عليهم على قدر منازلهم، ويوقظ النائم، ويشير إلى من ترك ما ينبغي فعله، أو فعل ما ينبغي تركه، ويأمر بسماع الدروس والإنصات لها.

(٦٤) التاسع: أن يلازم الإنصاف في بحثه وخطابه، ويسمع السؤال من مورده على وجهه، وإن كان صغيرا، ولا يترفع على سماعه فيحرم الفائدة.

(٦٥) وإذا عجز السائل عن تقرير ما أورده أو تحرير العبارة فيه لحياء أو قصور، ووقع على المعنى، عبّر عن مراده وبيّن وجه إيراده، ورد على من عليه، ثم يجيب بما عنده، أو يطلب ذلك من غيره، ويتروى فيما يجيب به رده. وإذا سئل عن ما لم يعلمه، قال: لا أعلمه، أولا أدرى؛ فمن العلم أن يقول لا أعلم. وعن بعضهم: لا أدرى نصف العلم. وعن ابن عباس (رضي الله عنهما): إذا أخطأ العالم لا أدرى، اصيبت مقاتله. وقيل ينبغي للعالم أن يورث أصحابه لا أدرى؛ لكثرة ما يقولها. قال محمد بن عبد الحكم: سألت الشافعي (رضي الله عنه) عن المتعة: أكان فيها طلاق أو ميراث أو نفقة تجب أو شهادة؟ فقال: والله ما أدري.

(66) Know that saying "I do not know" does not lower the esteem in which the person asked is held, as some ignorant people suppose; it raises his esteem because it is a great sign of his great rank, the strength of his religion, his fear of God, the purity of his heart, and the perfection of his knowledge. . . .

(67) **Rule Ten:** He should be friendly to any stranger who comes to him, receiving him cheerfully to set him at ease, for it is normal for a newcomer to be perplexed. He should not turn toward him or look at him frequently out of curiosity, for that would embarrass him.

(68) If an eminent scholar comes in when he has begun a question, he should stop until the man sits down. If he arrives when he is discussing a question, he should repeat it or the gist of it for him.

(69) If a jurist comes into class at the moment he is finishing and the class is about to rise, he should delay what remains. He should occupy himself with discussing something else until the jurist takes his seat. Then he should repeat or finish what remained, so as not to embarrass the newcomer by the class's rising to leave just as he was taking his seat.

(70) In setting an early or late hour for his lecture he should consider the welfare of the class as a whole if he is under no necessity or great inconvenience. One of the greatest scholars ruled that if the professor delivers his lecture at a college before sunrise or delays it until the afternoon, he does not deserve the salary for teaching unless the founder's stipulation requires such a time, given that he has violated customary usage in the matter.

(71) **Rule Eleven:** It is customary at the conclusion of each lecture for the professor to say, "But God knows best." A mufti[32] writes the same words at the end of his responsum. However, before these words it is best to say something to signal the conclusion of the lecture, such as "This is the end of the matter," or, "The sequel to this will come, God willing," or similar words. Thus his saying, "But God knows best," will be a sincere remembrance of God and fully intended. He should also begin every lecture with the words, "In the name of God, the Merciful, the Compassionate," so that he mentions God at the beginning and end of the lecture.

(72) It is best for the professor to linger a bit after the class rises to leave, and this for the sake of benefit and out of courtesy for them and for himself. For example, they will not jostle him; or if anyone has any question left, he can ask it; or if he is riding, he will not ride among them.

(٦٦) واعلم أن قول المسئول لا أدرى لا يَضع مِن قدره، كما يظنه بعض الجهلة، بل يرفعه لأنه دليل عظيم على عظم محله، وقوة دينه، وتقوى ربه، وطهارة قلبه، وكمال معرفته. . . .

(٦٧) العاشر: أن يتودد لغريب حضر عنده، وينبسط له لينشرح صدره؛ فإن للقادم دهشة، ولا يكثر الالتفات والنظر إليه استغرابا له، فإن ذلك يخجله.

(٦٨) وإذا أقبل بعض الفضلاء، وقد شرع في مسألة، أمسك عنها حتى يجلس، وإذا جاء وهو يبحث في مسألة، أعادها له أو مقصودها.

(٦٩) وإذا أقبل فقيه، وقد بقي لفراغه وقيام الجماعة بقدر ما يصل الفقيه الى المجلس، فليؤخر تلك البقية، ويشتغل عنها ببحث أو غيره إلى أن يجلس الفقيه، ثم يعيدها أو يتم تلك البقية، كيلا يخجل المقبل بقيامهم عند جلوسه.

(٧٠) وينبغي مراعاة مصلحة الجماعة في تقديم وقت الحضور وتأخيره، إذا لم يكن عليه فيه ضرورة، ولا مزيد كلفة. وأفتى بعض أكابر العلماء أن المدرس إذا ذكر الدرس في مدرسة قبل طلوع الشمس، أو أخره إلى بعد الظهر، لم يستحق معلوم التدريس، إلا أن يقتضيه شرط الواقف لمخالفة العرف المعتاد في ذلك.

(٧١) الحادي عشر: جرت العادة أن يقول المدرس عند ختم كل درس: والله اعلم، وكذلك يكتب المفتي بعد كتابة الجواب. لكن الأولى أن يُقال قبل ذلك كلام يشعر بختم الدرس، كقوله: وهذا آخره، أو ما بعده يأتي إن شاء الله تعالى ونحو ذلك، ليكون قوله: والله اعلم خالصا لذكر الله تعالى، ولقصد معناه. ولهذا ينبغي أن يستفتح كل درس ببسم الله الرحمن الرحيم، ليكون ذاكرا لله تعالى في بدايته وخاتمته.

(٧٢) والأولى للمدرس أن يمكث قليلا بعد قيام الجماعة، فإن فيه فوائد وآدابا له ولهم، منها عدم مزاحمتهم، ومنها إن كان في نفس أحد بقايا سؤال سأله له، ومنها

It is desirable that when he rises to leave he should pray the prayer handed down in hadith: "Praised and extolled art Thou, O God. There is no god but Thou. I ask for Thy forgiveness and turn to Thee in repentance."

(73) **Rule Twelve:** He should not accept a teaching position if he is not qualified for it. He should not deliver a lecture on a subject he does not know, regardless of whether or not the founder has stipulated it, for by doing so he trifles with religion and shows contempt among people.

(74) The Prophet said: "He who boasts of abundance which he has not received is like the wearer of two garments of falsity." Al-Shiblī[33] said: "He who claims a professor's chair before his time, seeks his own humiliation."

(75) Abū Ḥanīfah[34] said: "He who seeks preeminence when it is not his time for it will continue in humiliation as long as he lives." The wise man is he who protects himself from involvement with something in which he will be judged to be deficient, unjust for undertaking it, or immoral for insisting on it. For when he is unqualified for what the founder stipulated in his endowment or for what custom demands in such a case, he, by insisting on holding what he is not entitled to hold, is acting immorally. . . .

SECTION THREE

Universal Rules of Conduct for the Teacher with His Students in His Class— Consisting of Fourteen Rules

(76) **Rule One:** His intention in instructing and educating his students should be to do so for the sake of God; for the spread of learning; for the revival of the religious law; for the constant manifestation of truth and the oblivion of falsehood; for the constant welfare of the community through the multitude and merit of its scholars; for the acquisition of the merit, prayers, and pleas for God's mercy on his behalf of those to whom his learning descends; for his own entry into the chain of learning between the Prophet and his students; and that he may be numbered among the transmitters of God's revelation and ordinances, for the teaching of knowledge is one of the most important matters of religion and one of the highest ranks of believers. . . .

عدم ركوبه بينهم إن كان يركب، وغير ذلك. ويستحب إذا قام أن يدعو بما ورد به الحديث: سبحانك اللهم وبحمدك، لا إله إلا أنت، أستغفرك وأتوب إليك.

(٧٣) الثاني عشر: أن لا ينتصب للتدريس إذا لم يكن أهلا له، ولا يذكر الدرس من علم لا يعرفه، سواء أشرطه الواقف أو لم يشرطه؛ فإن ذلك لعب في الدين وازدراء بين الناس.

(٧٤) قال النبي ﷺ: المتشبع بما لم يعط كلابس ثوبي زور. وعن الشبلي: من تصدر قبل أوانه، فقد تصدى لهوانه.

(٧٥) وعن أبي حنيفة: من طلب الرياسة في غير حينه، لم يزل في ذل ما بقي. واللبيب من صان نفسه عن تعرضها لما يُعد فيه ناقصا، وبتعاطيه ظالما، وبإصراره عليه فاسقا، فإنه متى لم يكن أهلا لما شرطه الواقف في وقفه، أو لما يقتضيه عرف مثله، كان بإصراره على تناول ما لا يستحقه فاسقا. . . .

الفصل الثالث

في أدب العالم مع طلبته مطلقا في حلقته
وهو أربعة عشر نوعا

(٧٦) الأول: أن يقصد بتعليمهم وتهذيبهم وجه الله تعالى، ونشر العلم، وإحياء الشرع، ودوام ظهور الحق، وخمول الباطل، ودوام خير الأمة بكثرة علمائها، واغتنام ثوابهم، وتحصيل ثواب من ينتهي إليه علمه من بعضهم، وبركة دعائهم له، وترحمهم عليه، ودخوله في سلسلة العلم بين رسول الله ﷺ وبينهم، وعداده في جملة مبلغي وحي الله تعالى وأحكامه؛ فإن تعليم العلم من أهم أمور الدين وأعلى درجات المؤمنين. . . .

(77) **Rule Two:** He should not refrain from teaching a student because of the impurity of the latter's intention, for one can hope that the student will acquire good intention through the blessing of knowledge. An early Muslim said, "We sought knowledge not for God's sake, but God willed that it should be for His sake." This is said to mean that the outcome was that it came to be for God's sake. Furthermore, if pure intention were made a prerequisite for the teaching of beginners despite its difficulty for many of them, the effect would be to deprive many people of the opportunity to learn. Rather, the master should gradually spur the beginner to good intention by word and deed. Having befriended him, he should teach him that through the blessing of good intention one attains high rank in learning and in works. . . .

(78) **Rule Three:** He should frequently awaken the student's desire for knowledge and its pursuit by mentioning the noble dwelling places that God has prepared for scholars, how they stand on pulpits of light as the prophets' heirs, that the prophets and martyrs call them blessed, and similar things about the excellence of learning and scholars found in Qurʾānic verses, Prophetic traditions, historical reports, and poems.

(79) Also, he should gradually awaken the student's desire for the things that will help him in his education: restricting oneself to such worldly goods as are within easy reach and adequate, and being satisfied with this so that one's heart is not preoccupied with attachment to this world, overwhelming anxiety, and scattered interests. For it is most strengthening to the student's heart, most salutary to his body, most ennobling to his soul, most exalting to his rank, most diminishing to his enviers, and most conducive to his acquiring and increasing knowledge that his heart should turn from attachment to and desire for this world, from seeking ever more of it, and from sorrowing over what escapes of it. Therefore few acquire a goodly share of knowledge except those who at the beginning of their education were in the condition I have described of poverty, contentment, and aversion to the pursuit of this world and its transitory goods. Our chapter on rules of conduct for the student will contain more on this subject.

(80) **Rule Four:** He should love for the student what he loves for himself, as stated in a Prophetic tradition, and loathe for the student what he loathes for himself. Ibn ᶜAbbās said: "The most precious of men to me is my companion with whom I sit,[35] who steps over the necks of the people to reach me. If I could keep the flies from landing on him, I would." Another version reads, "The flies land on him and it pains me."

(٧٧) الثاني: أن لا يمتنع من تعليم الطالب لعدم خلوص نيته، فإن حسن النية مرجوله ببركة العلم. قال بعض السلف: طلبنا العلم لغير الله، فأبى أن يكون إلا لله. قيل معناه فكان عاقبته أن صار لله. ولأن إخلاص النية لو شرط في تعليم المبتدئين فيه مع عسره على كثير منهم لأدى ذلك إلى تفويت العلم كثيرا من الناس، لكن الشيخ يحرض المبتدئ على حسن النية بتدريج قولا وفعلا، ويعلمه بعد أنسه به أنه ببركة حسن النية ينال الرتبة العلية من العلم والعمل . . . .

(٧٨) الثالث: أن يرغبه في العلم وطلبه في أكثر الأوقات، بذكر ما أعد الله تعالى للعلماء من منازل الكرامات، وأنهم ورثة الأنبياء، وعلى منابر من نور يغبطهم الأنبياء والشهداء، أو نحو ذلك مما ورد في فضل العلم والعلماء من الآيات والآثار والأخبار والأشعار.

(٧٩) ويرغبه مع ذلك بتدريج على ما يعين على تحصيله، من الاقتصار على الميسور وقدر الكفاية من الدنيا، والقناعة بذلك عن شغل القلب بالتعلق بها، وغلبة الفكر، وتفريق الهم بسببها؛ فإن انصراف القلب عن تعلق الأطماع بالدنيا، والإكثار منها، والتأسف على فائتها؛ أجمع لقلبه، وأروح لبدنه، وأشرف لنفسه، وأعلى لمكانته، وأقل لحساده، وأجدر لحفظ العلم وازدياده. ولذلك قلّ من نال من العلم نصيبا وافرا إلا من كان في مبادئ تحصيله على ما ذكرت من الفقر والقناعة، والإعراض عن طلب الدنيا وعرضها الفاني. وسيأتي في هذا النوع أكثر من هذا في أدب المتعلم إن شاء الله تعالى.

(٨٠) الرابع: أن يحب لطالبه ما يحب لنفسه، كما جاء في الحديث، ويكره له ما يكره لنفسه. قال ابن عباس: أكرم الناس عليّ جليسي الذي يتخطى رقاب الناس إليّ، لو استطعت أن لا يقع الذباب عليه لفعلت. وفي رواية: إن الذباب ليقع عليه فيؤذيني.

(81) He should look out for the student's welfare and treat him with the same affection, compassion, charity, and patience toward misbehavior that he shows toward the dearest of his children. If the student ever falls short, as scarcely anyone fails to do, or at times behaves badly, he should accept his excuse as much as possible; yet he should alert him to what he has done with good advice and polite words, not with severity and oppressiveness. His intention should be to raise the student well, improve his character, and make him better. If the student is intelligent enough to take a hint, there will be no need for an explicit statement; if he can understand only from an explicit statement, the teacher should make such a statement and try to lead him on gradually by kindness. He should educate the student to good conduct, incite him to a pleasing character, and by means of matters of custom entrust to him the statutes of the religious law.

(82) **Rule Five:** He should be generous to the student with smoothness of delivery in his teaching of him and with the use of polite words in making him understand, especially if the student is apt for this because of his good manners and liberal pursuit of knowledge. He should encourage the student to seek useful knowledge and to master what is rare and unusual. He should not withhold from the student any branch of learning that he asks for, provided that the student is ready for it, for withholding often oppresses the mind, alienates the heart, and breeds estrangement.

(83) On the other hand, he should not deliver to the student anything for which he is not ready, for this will scatter his mind and confuse his understanding. If the student asks him something of this sort, he should not answer him, but should tell him that this will harm him, not benefit him. He should tell him that he has withheld it out of concern and kindness, not because he begrudges him it. Then he should urge him to apply himself and study so as to become ready for such—and for other branches of knowledge. Some people explain the word *rabbānī* as meaning one who nourishes, rears, or raises (*yurabbī*) people with the smaller branches of knowledge before the greater ones.[36]

(84) **Rule Six:** He should eagerly teach the student and make him understand by exerting himself and by bringing the meaning home to him without excess that the student's mind cannot tolerate or extensiveness that his memory cannot grasp. He should express himself clearly to the student of modest intelligence and consider repeating and reiterating the explanation to him.

(٨١) وينبغي أن يعتني بمصالح الطالب، ويعامله بما يعامل به أعز أولاده، من الحنو والشفقة عليه، والإحسان إليه، والصبر على جفاء، ربما وقع منه نقص لا يكاد يخلو الإنسان عنه، وسوء أدب في بعض الأحيان، ويبسط عذره بحسب الإمكان، ويوقفه مع ذلك على ما صدر منه بنصح وتلطف، لا بتعنيف وتعسف، قاصدا بذلك حسن تربيته، وتحسين خلقه، وإصلاح شأنه. فإن عرف ذلك لذكائه بالإشارة، فلا حاجة إلى صريح العبارة، وإن لم يفهم ذلك إلا بصريحها، أتى بها، وراعى التدريج في التلطف. ويؤدبه بالآداب السنية، ويحرّضه على الأخلاق المرضية، ويوصيه بالأمور العُرفية على الأوضاع الشرعية.

(٨٢) الخامس: أن يسمح له بسهولة الإلقاء في تعليمه، وحسن التلطف في تفهيمه، لا سيما إذا كان أهلا لذلك، لحسن أدبه، وجودة طلبه. ويحرضه على طلب الفوائد، وحفظ النوادر الفرائد، ولا يدخر عنه من أنواع العلوم ما يسأله عنه وهو أهل له؛ لأن ذلك ربما يوحش الصدر، وينفر القلب، ويورث الوحشة.

(٨٣) وكذلك لا يلقي إليه ما لم يتأهل له، لأن ذلك يبدد ذهنه، ويفرق فهمه. فإن سأله الطالب شيئا من ذلك، لم يجبه، ويعرفه أن ذلك يضره ولا ينفعه، وإن مَنْعه إياه منه لشفقة عليه ولُطف به، لا بخلا عليه، ثم يرغبه عند ذلك في الاجتهاد والتحصيل، ليتأهل لذلك وغيره. وقد روي في تفسير الرباني: أنه الذي يربي الناس بصغار العلم قبل كباره.

(٨٤) السادس: أن يحرص على تعليمه وتفهيمه ببذل جهده، وتقريب المعنى له من غير إكثار لا يحتمله ذهنه، أو بسط لا يضبطه حفظه. ويوضح لمتوقف الذهن العبارة، ويحتسب إعادة الشرح له وتكراره.

(85) He should begin by sketching out the problems. Then he should clarify them with examples and mention the proofs. However, for those who are not ready to understand the sources and proofs, he should limit himself to sketching out the problem and giving examples. He should mention the proofs and sources to anyone capable of understanding them, explaining to him the meanings, legal consequence, and causes of any obscurities. To him he may explain all the theoretical and practical sides of the question and the errors that have occurred in judgment, publication of traditions, or transmission, but in well-rendered language that avoids detracting from any scholar. His purpose in calling attention to such errors should be to give good advice and make known the sound channels of transmission. He should mention similar problems, both those that are like the one at hand and those that differ. He should clarify the reason for the two different judgments and the difference between the two questions. . . .

(86) **Rule Seven:** When the teacher finishes presenting a lesson, it will not be amiss for him to ask the students questions about to it to test their understanding and grasp of what he has expounded to them. He should praise those who demonstrate to him their solid understanding by repeatedly answering these questions correctly. He should repeat courteously for those who have not understood him. The reason for asking questions is that the student sometimes is ashamed to say that he has not understood, either to spare the teacher the trouble of repeating, or due to lack of time, or from embarrassment before those present, or so that their recitation does not fall behind because of him.

(87) Some people therefore have said that the teacher should not ask the student whether he has understood unless he is sure that the student will not say yes before he has understood. If he fears that the student may lie from embarrassment or some other reason, he should not ask him whether he has understood since the student may fall into lying by saying yes for the aforementioned reasons. Rather, he should ask him questions as we have mentioned. If the teacher asks the student whether he has understood and he says yes, the teacher should ask him no more questions unless the student requires this because of his possible bashfulness that the opposite of his reply may become apparent.

(88) The teacher should command the students to accompany each other in studying, as we shall explain, and to repeat the explanation among themselves after his departure so that it becomes fixed in their minds and fast in their understanding, for this will spur them to reflect and to hold themselves responsible to seek certitude.

(٨٥) ويبدأ بتصوير المسائل، ثم يوضحها بالأمثلة وذكر الدلائل، ويقتصر على تصوير المسألة وتمثيلها لمن لم يتأهل لفهم مأخذها ودليلها، ويذكر الأدلة والمأخذ لمحتملها، ويبين له معاني أسرار حكمها وعللها، وما يتعلق بتلك المسألة من فرع وأصل، ومن وَهَم فيها في حكم أو تخريج أو نقل، بعبارة حسنة الأداء، بعيدة عن تنقيص أحد من العلماء، ويقصد ببيان ذلك الوهم طريق النصيحة، وتعريف النقول الصحيحة، ويذكر ما يشابه تلك المسألة ويناسبها، وما يفارقها ويقاربها، ويبين مأخذ الحكمين، والفرق بين المسألتين . . . .

(٨٦) السابع: إذا فرغ الشيخ من شرح درس، فلا بأس بطرح مسائل تتعلق به على الطلبة؛ يمتحن بها فهمهم وضبطهم لما شرح لهم؛ فمن ظهر استحكام فهمه له بتكرار الإصابة في جوابه، شكره؛ ومن لم يفهمه، تلطف في إعادته له. والمعنى بطرح المسائل أن الطالب ربما استحيا من قوله لم أفهم، إما لرفع كلفة الإعادة على الشيخ، أو لضيق الوقت، أو حياء من الحاضرين، أو كيلا تتأخر قراءتهم بسببه.

(٨٧) ولذلك قيل لا ينبغي للشيخ أن يقول للطالب: هل فهمت؟ إلا إذا أمن من قوله نعم قبل أن يفهم؛ فإن لم يأمن من كذبه لحياء أو غيره، فلا يسأله عن فهمه؛ لأنه ربما وقع في الكذب بقوله نعم، لما قدمناه من الأسباب، بل يطرح عليه مسائل كما ذكرناه، فإن سأله الشيخ عن فهمه فقال نعم، فلا يطرح عليه المسائل بعد ذلك إلا أن يستدعي الطالب ذلك لاحتمال خجله بظهور خلاف ما أجاب به.

(٨٨) وينبغي للشيخ أن يأمر الطلبة بالمرافقة في الدروس كما سيأتي إن شاء الله تعالى، وبإعادة الشرح بعد فراغه فيما بينهم، ليثبت في أذهانهم ويرسخ في أفهامهم، ولأنه يحثهم على استعمال الفكر، ومواخذة النفس بطلب التحقيق.

(89) **Rule Eight:** At certain times he should ask the students to repeat what they have memorized and should test their grasp of the important principles and unusual cases he has presented to them. He should test them with problems based on a general principle he has established or on a proof he has mentioned.

(90) He should praise and commend among the class members anyone whom he deems to be correct in his answer and who he is sure will not become conceited. He should do this to spur the student and the others to diligence in the pursuit of more knowledge. Anyone whom he deems deficient, but who he is sure will not turn away, he should rebuke for his deficiency and spur him to be more ambitious and to acquire eminence in the quest for knowledge—especially if he is the sort of student whose spirit is increased by rebuke and whose joy by praise. He should repeat whatever needs repetition so that the student may have a firm understanding of it.

(91) **Rule Nine:** If a student pursues his studies beyond what his condition demands or his ability will tolerate, and the teacher fears that he will become distressed, the teacher should counsel him to be gentle with himself. He should remind him of the words of the Prophet, "He who journeys to the point of exhaustion fails to cover the distance and ruins his camel," and similar sayings that will lead him to deliberateness and moderation in his effort. Similarly, if any kind of weariness or distress or the beginnings of such feelings in the student become apparent to the teacher, he should command him to rest and to moderate his studies. He should not advise a student to learn what his understanding and age cannot bear or recommend to him a book that his mind cannot understand. . . .

(92) **Rule Ten:** He should mention to the students such maxims of art as are not to be disturbed: either universally, such as giving precedence to *mubāsharah* over *sabab* in cases of *ḍamān*;[37] or in most instances, such as that the oath is to be sworn by the defendant if there is no clear evidence, except in cases of *qasāmah*.[38] He should mention the matters that are exceptions to the rules, such as the dictum about following the newer of two judgments, one old and one new, except in fourteen cases, and he should mention them. He should mention that every oath denying the act of someone else is an oath denying knowledge, except that someone whose slave is alleged to have committed a crime swears categorically. He should mention that every act of worship is terminated by performing what is incompatible with it or invalidates it, except the pilgrimage or lesser pilgrimage. He should mention that every ablution

(٨٩) الثامن: أن يطالب الطلبة في بعض الأوقات بإعادة المحفوظات، ويمتحن ضبطهم لما قدم لهم من القواعد المهمة والمسائل الغريبة، ويختبرهم بمسائل تبنى على أصل قرره أو دليل ذكره.

(٩٠) فمن رآه مصيبا في الجواب، ولم يخف عليه شدة الإعجاب، شكره وأثنى عليه بين أصحابه، ليبعثه وإياهم على الاجتهاد في طلب الازدياد؛ ومن رآه مقصرا ولم يخف نفوره، عنفه على قصوره، وحرضه على علو الهمة، ونيل المنزلة في طلب العلم، لا سيما إن كان ممن يزيده التعنيف نشاطا، والشكر انبساطا؛ ويعيد ما يقتضي الحال إعادته ليفهمه الطالب فهما راسخا.

(٩١) التاسع: إذا سلك الطالب في التحصيل فوق ما يقتضيه حاله أو تحمله طاقته، وخاف الشيخ ضجره، أوصاه بالرفق بنفسه، وذكّره بقول النبي ﷺ: «إن المُنْبَتّ لا أرضا قطع، ولا ظهرا أبقى». ونحو ذلك مما يحمله على الأناة والاقتصاد في الاجتهاد. وكذلك إذا ظهر له منه نوع سآمة أو ضجر أو مبادي ذلك، أمره بالراحة وتخفيف الاشتغال، ولا يشير على الطالب بتعليم ما لا يحتمله فهمه أو سنه، ولا بكتاب يقصر ذهنه عن فهمه . . . .

(٩٢) العاشر: أن يذكر للطلبة قواعد الفن التي لا تنخرم، إما مطلقا كتقديم المباشرة على السبب في الضمان؛ أو غالبا كاليمين على المدعى عليه إذا لم تكن بينة، إلا في القسامة، والمسائل المستثناة من القواعد، كقوله: العمل بالجديد من كل قولين قديم وجديد إلا في أربع عشرة مسألة، ويذكرها. وكل يمين على نفي فعل للغير فهي على نفي العلم إلا من ادعي عليه أن عبده جنى، فيحلف على البتّ على الأصح. وكل عبادة

before prayer is to be performed in a required sequence, except when the obligation of ablution is fulfilled by full washing of the body because of major ritual impurity—and similar matters. . . .

(93) **Rule Eleven:** He should not show the students any preference of one over another in his affection or attention when they are alike in the attributes of age, merit, education, or religion, for such preference often oppresses the mind and alienates the heart. If any student learns more, applies himself more diligently, or deports himself better, the teacher should show him honor and preference, but he should make it clear that the student's receiving greater honor was for these reasons. There is no harm in this as it will stimulate and motivate the students to acquire these qualities.

(94) Similarly, he should not give one student preference when it is another's turn, nor should he postpone a student's turn unless he sees some benefit in this that is greater than the benefit of maintaining turns. However, if one student allows another to take his turn, there is no harm. We shall discuss this at length later, God willing.

(95) He should be affectionate to those who are present, and he should speak well of those who are absent and praise them. He should inquire about their names, genealogies, places of birth, and circumstances. He should pray often for their welfare.

(96) **Rule Twelve:** He should monitor the state of the students with regard to their manners, deportment, and morals inwardly and outwardly. Anyone from whom something improper in this regard originates—such as committing something forbidden, reprehensible, or leading to corruption; ceasing to study; disrespecting the teacher or someone else; talking much without direction or sense; associating with someone unsuitable; or anything else that we shall mention below in the chapter on rules of conduct for students—the teacher should allude to the prohibition against such things in the presence of the perpetrator, but he should not allude to him or identify him. If the student takes no heed, the teacher should forbid him in secret. He should content himself with a hint with those for whom a hint suffices, but if the student takes no heed, he should forbid him publicly. If the situation demands it, he should speak bluntly to him, so that he and others will restrain themselves and so that everyone who hears will be disciplined. If the student still does not heed, he may expel him and shun him until he repents, especially if he fears that some fellow students and friends may imitate him.

يخرج منها بفعل منا فيها ومبطلها، إلا الحج والعمرة. وكل وضوء يجب فيه الترتيب إلا وضوءا تحلله غسل الجنابة وأشباه ذلك. . . .

(٩٣) الحادي عشر: أن لا يظهر للطلبة تفضيل بعضهم على بعض عنده في مودة أو اعتناء، مع تساويهم في الصفات من سن أو فضيلة أو تحصيل أو ديانة؛ فإن ذلك ربما يوحش منه الصدر وينفر القلب. فإن كان بعضهم أكثر تحصيلا وأشد اجتهادا، أو أبلغ اجتهادا، أو أحسن أدبا؛ فأظهر إكرامه وتفضيله، وبيّن أن زيادة إكرامه لتلك الأسباب، فلا بأس بذلك لأنه ينشط ويبعث على الاتصاف بتلك الصفات.

(٩٤) وكذلك لا يقدم أحدا في نوبة غيره، أو يؤخره عن نوبته، إلا إذا رأى في ذلك مصلحة تزيد على مصلحة مراعاة النوبة؛ فان سمح بعضهم لغيره في نوبته فلا بأس، وسنذكر ذلك مفصلا إن شاء الله تعالى.

(٩٥) وينبغي أن يتودد لحاضرهم، ويذكر غائبهم بخير وحسن ثناء؛ وينبغي أن يستعلم أسماءهم وأنسابهم ومواطنهم وأحوالهم، ويكثر الدعاء لهم بالصلاح.

(٩٦) الثاني عشر: أن يراقب أحوال الطلبة في آدابهم وهديهم وأخلاقهم، باطنا وظاهرا؛ فمن صدر منه من ذلك مالا يليق من ارتكاب محرّم أو مكروه، أو ما يؤدي إلى فساد حال أو ترك اشتغال، أو إساءة أدب في حق الشيخ أو غيره، أو كثرة كلام بغير توجيه ولا فائدة، أو حرص على كثرة الكلام، أو معاشرة من لا تليق عشرته، أو غير ذلك مما سيأتي ذكره إن شاء الله تعالى في آداب المتعلم، عرّض الشيخ بالنهي عن ذلك بحضور من صدر منه، غير معرض به ولا معيّن له؛ فان لم ينته، نهاه عن ذلك سرا، ويكتفي بالإشارة مع من يكتفي بها؛ فان لم ينته نهاه عن ذلك جهرا، ويغلظ القول عليه إن اقتضاه الحال، لينزجر هو وغيره، ويتأدب به كل سامع؛ فإن لم ينته فلا بأس حينئذ بطرده والإعراض عنه إلى أن يرجع، ولا سيما إذا خاف على بعض رفقائه وأصحابه من الطلبة موافقته.

(97) He should likewise observe how the students behave toward each other in such matters as greeting each other with the salutation of peace, addressing each other politely in conversation, showing affection toward each other, and helping each other in good deeds, piety, and their own endeavors. In short, as he teaches them the things that benefit their religion and their relations with God, so he should teach them the things that benefit their life in this world and relations with people, so that they may excel in both respects.

(98) **Rule Thirteen:** He should work for the welfare of the students, encouraging them and helping them with whatever influence and wealth he has, whenever he can do so without harming his religion or impoverishing himself. For God helps men as long as men help their brothers; He attends to the needs of those who attend to the needs of their brothers; and He eases the reckoning on Judgment Day for those who give ease to the impoverished, especially if they do so to help in the quest for knowledge, which is one of the best ways of drawing near to God.

(99) If any student or regular in the class is absent more than usual, he should inquire about him, his condition, and the condition of those connected to him. If he can learn nothing about him, he should send a message to him, or, better, he should go to his home himself.

(100) If the student is sick, he should visit him; if in distress, he should comfort him; if departed on a journey, he should visit his family and those connected to him, inquire about them, address himself to their needs, and give them what he can. If he can relieve the student, he should do so; if he cannot, he should be affectionate to him and pray for him.

(101) Know that a righteous student brings the teacher more good in this world and the next than his dearest friends and closest family members. . . .

(102) **Rule Fourteen:** He should be humble with the student and with anyone who seeks guidance and asks for help, if the latter performs his duties toward God and toward him. He should take him under his wing and be gracious to him. God has said: "Lower thy wing to those who follow thee, being believers."[39] It is a sound tradition that the Prophet said: "God has revealed to me that you should be humble, and that if anyone humbles himself to God, God will raise him up." This refers to men generally; how much more so with regard to anyone who has the right of companionship, the sanctity of intimacy, the sincerity of friendship, and the honor of being a student! There is a hadith that says:

(٩٧) وكذلك يتعاهد ما يعامل به بعضهم بعضا من إفشاء السلام، وحسن التخاطب في الكلام والتحابب والتعاون على البر والتقوى، وعلى ما هم بصدده. وبالجملة فكما يعلمهم مصالح دينهم لمعاملة الله تعالى، يعلمهم مصالح دنياهم لمعاملة الناس لتكمل لهم فضيلة الحالتين.

(٩٨) الثالث عشر: أن يسعى في مصالح الطلبة وجمع قلوبهم، ومساعدتهم بما تيسر عليه من جاه ومال عند قدرته على ذلك وسلامة دينه وعدم ضرورته؛ فإن الله تعالى في عون العبد، ما دام العبد في عون أخيه؛ ومن كان في حاجة أخيه، كان الله تعالى في حاجته؛ ومن يسر على معسر، يسر الله عليه حسابه يوم القيامة، ولا سيما إذا كان ذلك إعانة على طلب العلم الذي هو من أفضل القربات.

(٩٩) وإذا غاب بعض الطلبة أو ملازمي الحلقة زائدا عن العادة، سأل عنه؛ وعن أحواله وعن من يتعلق به، فإن لم يخبر عنه بشيء أرسل إليه أو قصد منزله بنفسه وهو أفضل.

(١٠٠) فإن كان مريضا عاده، وإن كان في غَمّ خفض عليه، وإن كان مسافرا تفقد أهله ومن يتعلق به وسأل عنهم وتعرض لحوائجهم ووصلهم بما أمكن، وإن كان فيما يحتاج إليه فيه أعانه، وإن لم يكن شيء من ذلك تودد عليه ودعا له.

(١٠١) واعلم أن الطالب الصالح أَعْوَدُ على العالِم بخير الدنيا والآخرة من أعز الناس عليه وأقرب أهله إليه . . . .

(١٠٢) الرابع عشر: أن يتواضع مع الطالب وكل مسترشد سائل إذا قام بما يجب عليه من حقوق الله تعالى وحقوقه، ويخفض له جناحه، ويلين له جانبه. قال الله تعالى لنبيه: ﴿واخْفِضْ جَنَاحَكَ لِمَنِ اتَّبَعَكَ مِنَ الْمُؤْمِنِين.﴾ وصحّ عن النبي ﷺ إن الله تعالى أوحى إليّ أن تواضعوا، وما تواضع أحد لله إلا رفعه الله، وهذا لمطلق الناس، فكيف بمن له حق الصحبة، وحرمة التردد، وصدق التودد، وشرف

"Be gentle to those you teach and to those from whom you learn." And it has been related on the authority of al-Fuḍayl[40] that "whoever humbles himself to God, God will bestow wisdom on him."

(103) He should address each of them, and especially the outstanding and distinguished, by his *kunyah*[41] or some similar name that the person prefers, one that exalts and respects the person. The following hadith is transmitted on the authority of the Prophet's wife ʿĀʾishah: "The Messenger of God used to refer to his companions by *kunyah* to honor them." He should likewise welcome the students when he meets them or when they approach him. He should treat them politely and set them at ease when they take their seats before him, asking how they and their family are, after returning their greeting. . . .

Chapter Three

Containing Three Sections
On Rules of Conduct for the Student

SECTION ONE

Rules of Conduct for the Student Himself—
Containing Ten Rules

(104) **Rule One:** He should cleanse his heart of every dishonesty, impurity, rancor, envy, misbelief, and vice, that he may become fit to receive and retain knowledge and to become acquainted with its subtle meanings and abstruse truths. For as a certain scholar has said, knowledge is the prayer of the secret thought, the worship of the heart, and the drawing near to God of the inward being. As the canonical prayer, which is the worship of the visible members, is valid only when what is visible is clean of pollution and filth, knowledge, which is the worship of the heart, is valid only when the heart is clean of filthy traits and of the pollution of base and evil manners. If the heart is made fragrant for knowledge, the blessing of knowledge will emerge and grow, just as when the soil is made fragrant for the plant, the plant grows and thrives. There is a hadith that says: "In the body there is a morsel of flesh which, if it be whole, all the body is whole and which, if it be diseased, all the body is diseased; and that, truly, is the heart."[42] Sahl[43] said: "Light is forbidden to enter a heart while it contains anything that God dislikes."

الطلب! وفي الحديث: «لينوا لمن تُعلّمون، ولمن تتعلّمون منه». وعن الفُضيل: «من تواضع لله ورّثه الله الحكمة».

(١٠٣) وينبغي أن يخاطب كلا منهم، لا سيما الفاضل المتميز، بكنية ونحوها من أحب الأسماء إليه وما فيه تعظيم له وتوقير؛ فعن عائشة (رضي الله عنها): كان رسول الله ﷺ يكني أصحابه إكراما لهم. وكذلك ينبغي أن يترحب بالطلبة إذا لقيهم وعند إقبالهم عليه ويكرمهم إذا جلسوا إليه ويؤنسهم بسؤاله عن أحوالهم وأحوال من يتعلق بهم بعد رد سلامهم. . . .

الباب الثالث

وفيه ثلاثة فصول في آداب المتعلم

الفصل الأول في آدابه في نفسه وفيه عشرة أنواع

(١٠٤) الأول: أن يطهر قلبه من كل غش ودنس وغل وحسد وسوء عقيدة وخلق، ليصلح بذلك لقبول العلم وحفظه، والاطلاع على دقائق معانيه وحقائق غوامضه. فإن العلم كما قال بعضهم: صلاة السر وعبادة القلب وقربة الباطن، وكما لا تصح الصلاة -التي هي عبادة الجوارح الظاهرة- إلا بطهارة الظاهر من الحدث والخبث، فكذلك لا يصح العلم، الذي هو عبادة القلب، إلا بطهارته عن خبث الصفات، وحَدَث مساوئ الأخلاق ورديئها. وإذا طيب القلب للعلم، ظهرت بركته ونما، كالأرض إذا طيبت للزرع نما زرعها وزكا. وفي الحديث: إن في الجسد مضغة، إذا صلحت صلح الجسد كله، وإذا فسدت فسد الجسد كله، ألا وهي القلب. وقال سهل: حرام على قلب أن يدخله النور وفيه شيء مما يكره الله عز وجل.

(105) **Rule Two:** He should have a sincere intention in pursuing knowledge, meaning that he should seek it for God's sake, to put it into practice, to revive the religious law, to illuminate his heart, to adorn his inward being, to draw near to God on the Day of Resurrection, and to apply himself to the things that God of His favor and great grace has prepared for its people. . . .

(106) Knowledge is a form of worship and of drawing close to God: if its intention is sincere, it is accepted, declared righteous, and its blessing grows; however, if it is sought for some other purpose than for the sake of God, it fails, is lost, and brings no profit. These purposes having eluded the seeker and he having failed to achieve them, his endeavor will be disappointed and his effort wasted.

(107) **Rule Three:** He should hasten to acquire an education in his youth and time of inexperience. Let him not be taken in by the deceptions of procrastination and hope, for no hour of his life that passes has a replacement or compensation. Let him cut as many as possible of the attachments that distract and obstacles that hinder the completion of the quest, the exertion of effort, and the strength of diligence in obtaining an education, for these things are like roadblocks. That is why the earliest Muslims recommended leaving one's family and departing from one's homeland, because the mind, if distracted, cannot attain to truths and abstruse subtleties. "God has given no man two hearts in his body."[44] It is also said, "Knowledge will not give part of itself to you until you give all of yourself to it. . . ."

(108) **Rule Four:** He should be content with whatever food is available, even if it is little, and with whatever clothing covers him, even if it is threadbare, for by patiently enduring straitened circumstances one attains abundance of knowledge and recollects the heart from the distractions of ambition, so that springs of wisdom well up in it. . . .

(109) Al-Khaṭīb said, "It is preferable for the student to be a bachelor as long as he can, so as not to be distracted from the completion of his quest by marital obligations and earning a living."

(110) Sufyān al-Thawrī[45] said, "Anyone who marries has set out to sail the sea, and when a child is born to him, his ship is wrecked." In short, avoiding marriage is preferable for anyone who does not need it or cannot support it, especially for the student, whose capital is a collected mind, a concentrated heart, and a busy intellect.

(١٠٥) الثاني: حسن النية في طلب العلم بأن يقصد به وجه الله تعالى والعمل به وإحياء الشريعة وتنوير قلبه وتحلية باطنه والقرب من الله تعالى يوم القيامة، والتعرض لما أعد لأهله من رضوانه وعظيم فضله. . . .

(١٠٦) والعلم عبادة من العبادات وقربة من القرب. فإن خلصت فيه النية، قبل وزكي ونمت بركته، وإن قصد به غير وجه الله تعالى، حبط وضاع وخسرت صفقته وبما تفوته تلك المقاصد ولا ينالها فيخيب قصده ويضيع سعيه.

(١٠٧) الثالث: أن يبادر شبابه وأوقات عمره إلى التحصيل، ولا يغتر بخدع التسويف والتأميل؛ فإن كل ساعة تمضي من عمره لا بدل لها ولا عوض عنها، ويقطع ما يقدر عليه من العلائق الشاغلة والعوائق المانعة عن تمام الطلب وبذل الاجتهاد وقوة الجد في التحصيل، فإنها كقواطع الطريق؛ ولذلك استحب السلف التغرّب عن الأهل والبعد عن الوطن، لأن الفكرة إذا توزعت قصرت عن درك الحقائق وغموض الدقائق، « وَمَا جَعَلَ اللّٰهُ لِرَجُلٍ مِنْ قَلْبَيْنِ فِي جَوْفِهِ » وكذلك يقال: العلم لا يعطيك بعضه حتى تعطيه كلك. . . .

(١٠٨) الرابع: أن يقنع من القوت بما تيسر وإن كان يسيرا، ومن اللباس بما يستر مثله وإن كان خلقا. فبالصبر على ضيق العيش ينال سعة العلم، ويجمع شمل القلب عن مفترقات الآمال فتجر فيه ينابيع الحكم. . . .

(١٠٩) قال الخطيب: ويستحب للطالب أن يكون عزبا ما أمكنه لئلا يقطعه الاشتغال بحقوق الزوجية وطلب المعيشة عن إكمال الطلب.

(١١٠) وقال سفيان الثوري: من تزوج فقد ركب البحر، فإن ولد له ولد فقد كسر به. وبالجملة فترك التزويج لغير المحتاج إليه أو غير القادر عليه أولى، لا سيما للطالب الذي رأس ماله جمع الخاطر وإجمام القلب واشتغال الفكر.

(111) **Rule Five:** He should apportion the hours of his night and day and make use of what remains of his life, for the rest of life has no value.

(112) The best time for memorizing is the predawn, for research the morning, for writing the midday, and for reading and reviewing the night. . . .

(113) Al-Khaṭīb said, "The best place for memorizing is an upstairs room or any place far from distractions." He also said, "It is not advisable to memorize one's lessons in the presence of plants, greenery, rivers, busy streets, or noisy voices because these things usually prevent the mind from being alone with itself."

(114) **Rule Six:** One of the greatest helps to study, understanding, and avoidance of weariness is to eat permitted foods and in small amounts. . . .

(115) It is preferable that the maximum amount of food he takes should be what has come down in the saying of the Prophet: "No son of Adam ever filled a worse vessel than his belly. Sufficient for the son of Adam are a few mouthfuls to maintain his strength. If filling the belly is unavoidable, let it be one-third for his food, one-third for his drink, and one-third for his breath." (The hadith was transmitted by al-Tirmidhī.) If he eats more than that, the excess is extravagance that violates the tradition of the Prophet. God has said: "Eat and drink, but be you not prodigal."[46] One scholar has said that God summed up all medicine in these words.

(116) **Rule Seven:** He should hold himself to abstinence in all his affairs. He should seek what is religiously permissible in his food, drink, clothing, and dwelling and in everything that he and his dependents need, that his heart may be illuminated and ready to obtain and benefit from knowledge and its light. As long as abstinence is possible for him and need does not force him, he should not be content with what is outwardly permissible according to religious law or make the allowable his standard; rather, he should seek the highest rank.

(117) He should follow the example of the pious early scholars who abstained from many things they pronounced permissible. The most worthy person for him to imitate in this regard is our master, the Messenger of God, who did not eat the date he found in the street for fear that it might have been given out in charity, unlikely as that was. Furthermore, people imitate scholars and follow their practice, so if scholars do not practice abstinence, who will?

(١١١) الخامس: أن يقسم أوقات ليله ونهاره، ويغتنم ما بقي من عمره؛ فإن بقية العمر لا قيمة له.

(١١٢) وأجود الأوقات للحفظ الأسحار، وللبحث الأبكار، وللكتابة وسط النهار، وللمطالعة والمذاكرة الليل . . . .

(١١٣) قال: وأجود أماكن الحفظ الغرف، وكل موضع بعيد عن الملهيات. قال: وليس بمحمود الحفظ بخضرة النبات والخضرة والأنهار وقوارع الطرق وضجيج الأصوات لأنها تمنع من خلو القلب غالبا.

(١١٤) السادس: من أعظم الأسباب المعينة على الاشتغال والفهم وعدم الملال أكل القدر اليسير من الحلال . . . .

(١١٥) والأولى أن يكون أكثر ما يأخذ من الطعام ما ورد في الحديث عن النبي ﷺ: « ما ملأ ابن آدم وعاءً شرا من بطنه، بحسب ابن آدم لقيمات يقمن صلبه، فإن كان لا محالة فثلث لطعامه وثلث لشرابه وثلث لنفسه ». رواه الترمذي. فإن زاد على ذلك، فالزيادة إسراف خارج عن السنة. وقد قال الله تعالى: ﴿وَكُلُوا وَٱشْرَبُوا وَلَا تُسْرِفُوا﴾. قال بعض العلماء: جمع الله بهذه الكلمات الطب كله.

(١١٦) السابع: أن يأخذ نفسه بالورع في جميع شأنه، ويتحرى الحلال في طعامه وشرابه ولباسه ومسكنه، وفي جميع ما يحتاج إليه هو وعياله؛ ليستنير قلبه، ويصلح لقبول العلم ونوره والنفع به، ولا يقنع لنفسه بظاهر الحل شرعا مهما أمكنه التورع ولم تلجئه حاجة أو يجعل حظه الجواز، بل يطلب الرتبة العالية.

(١١٧) ويقتدي بمن سلف من العلماء الصالحين في التورع عن كثير مما كانوا يفتون بجوازه، وأحق من اقتدي به في ذلك سيدنا رسول الله ﷺ، حيث لم يأكل التمرة التي وجدها في الطريق خشية أن تكون من الصدقة، مع بُعدكونها منها؛ ولأن أهل العلم يقتدى بهم ويؤخذ عنهم، فإذا لم يستعملوا الورع فمن يستعمله؟

(118) On the other hand, he should practice leniency in its place when it is needed and there is reason for it, likewise following their example in this, for God wants His ordinances of indulgence to be observed, just as He wants His obligatory ordinances to be observed.

(119) **Rule Eight:** He should make sparing use of the foods that cause dullness and weakness of the senses, such as sour apples and fava beans, or drinking vinegar, as well as anything whose use increases the phlegm that dulls the mind and makes the body sluggish, such as much dairy food, fish, and the like.

(120) He should make use of the things that God has given as means to sharpen the intelligence, such as chewing gum and mastic, as is customary, and eating raisins in the morning and rose-water, and other things that need not be explained here. . . .

(121) **Rule Nine:** He should sleep little, as long as this does not harm him in body or mind. He should sleep no more than eight hours, which is one-third of the day. If his constitution will bear it, he should sleep less.

(122) There is no harm in his resting himself, his heart, his mind, or his eyes, if any of them become tired, by walking or strolling in a park, so that he restores himself and does not waste his time.

(123) There is no harm in the habit of walking to exercise the body, for it is said to stimulate the vital heat, eliminate excess humors, and refresh the body.

(124) There is no harm in licit sexual intercourse if one needs it. Physicians say that it dries up excess secretions and that it animates and clears the mind when it is done in moderation when needed. But he should guard against too much of it as he would guard against a foe, for, as has been said, "The fluid of life is spilled into wombs," and it weakens hearing, sight, nerves, bodily heat, and digestion, and it causes other vile diseases. . . .

(125) A certain eminent scholar used to gather his friends in a place of recreation on certain days of the year, and they would joke with each other without harming their religion or honor.

(126) **Rule Ten:** He should avoid socializing, for avoiding it is one of the most desirable things for a seeker of knowledge, especially with those who are not of his sort, and particularly those who jest much and think little. For character is a great thief, and the bane of socializing is that

(١١٨) وينبغي له أن يستعمل الرخص في مواضعها عند الحاجة إليها و وجود سببها ليقتدى بهم فيه، فإن الله تعالى يحب أن تؤتى رخصه كما يحب أن تؤتى عزائمه.

(١١٩) الثامن: أن يقلل استعمال المطاعم التي هي من أسباب البلادة وضعف الحواس، كالتفاح الحامض والباقلا وشرب الخل، وكذلك ما يُكثِر استعماله البلغم المبلد للذهن المثقل للبدن ككثرة الألبان والسمك وأشباه ذلك.

(١٢٠) وينبغي أن يستعمل ما جعله الله تعالى سببا لجودة الذهن كضغ اللبان والمصطكى على حسب العادة، وأكل الزبيب بكرة، والجلاّب ونحو ذلك مما ليس هذا موضع شرحه . . . .

(١٢١) التاسع: أن يقلل نومه ما لم يلحقه ضرر في بدنه وذهنه، ولا يزيد في نومه في اليوم والليلة على ثمان ساعات، وهو ثلث الزمان، فإن احتمل حاله أقل منها فعل.

(١٢٢) ولا بأس أن يريح نفسه وقلبه وذهنه وبصره إذا كلَّ شيء من ذلك أو ضعف بتنزه وتفرج في المستنزهات بحيث يعود إلى حاله ولا يضيع عليه زمانه.

(١٢٣) ولا بأس بمعاناة المشي و رياضة البدن به، فقد قيل إنه ينعش الحرارة، ويذيب فضول الأخلاط وينشط البدن.

(١٢٤) ولا بأس بالوطى الحلال إذا احتاج إليه، فقد قال الأطباء بأنه يجفف الفضول وينشط ويصفي الذهن، إذا كان عند الحاجة باعتدال، ويحذر كثرته حذر العدو؛ فانه- كما قيل: ماء الحياة يصب في الأرحام- يُضعف السمع والبصر والعصب والحرارة والهضم وغير ذلك من الأمراض الرديئة . . . .

(١٢٥) وكان بعض أكابر العلماء يجمع أصحابه في بعض أماكن التنزه في بعض أيام السنة ويتمازحون بما لا ضرر عليهم في دين ولا عرض.

(١٢٦) العاشر: أن يترك العشرة فإن تركها من أهم ما ينبغي لطالب العلم، ولا سيما لغير الجنس وخصوصا لمن كثر لعبه وقلت فكرته؛ فإن الطباع سراقة. وآفة العشرة

one wastes one's life without benefit and loses one's wealth, honor, and religion if one associates with those who are unworthy.

(127) A seeker of knowledge should mix only with those who will benefit him or benefit from him, as has been transmitted from the Prophet: "Become a scholar or a student, but do not be a third thing lest you perish."

(128) If he enters into or is exposed to the companionship of someone with whom he will waste his life, who will not benefit him, from whom he will learn nothing, and who will not help him in his endeavors, let him gently break off the association at the beginning, before it becomes firmly established. For once things become firmly established, they are difficult to remove. Jurists have a maxim: "Warding off is easier than removing."

(129) If he needs to be his companion, let him be a righteous, pious, God-fearing, abstinent, and intelligent companion, given to much good and little evil, amiable and unargumentative—who, if he forgets, reminds him; who, if he remembers, helps him; who, if he needs, shares with him; and who, if he is troubled, comforts him. . . .

SECTION TWO

Rules for the Student's Conduct with His Teacher and Model and the Great Reverence in Which He Should Hold the Teacher—Consisting of Thirteen Rules

(130) **Rule One:** A seeker of knowledge should consider carefully and ask God's guidance regarding the person with whom he would study and from whom he would acquire good character and manners. If it is possible, let him be a person whose qualifications have become complete, whose kindliness has been confirmed, whose manliness has become apparent, whose continence has become known, and whose reputation has become renowned; someone who excels at teaching and is very good at imparting understanding. The student should not desire great learning accompanied by lack of reserve or religion or by the absence of good character.

(131) One early scholar said: "This knowledge is religion, so be careful about the person from whom you receive your religion. . . ."

ضياع العمر بغير فائدة، وذهاب المال والعرض إن كان لغير أهل وذهاب الدين إن كانت لغير أهله.

(١٢٧) والذي ينبغي لطالب العلم أن لا يخالط إلا من يفيده أو يستفيد منه لما روي عن النبي ﷺ: «اغد عالما أو متعلما ولا تكن الثالث فتهلك».

(١٢٨) فإن شرع أو تعرض لصحبة من يضيع عمره معه ولا يفيده ولا يستفيد منه ولا يعينه على ما هو بصدده، فليتلطف في قطع عشرته من أول الأمر قبل تمكنها، فإن الأمور إذا تمكنت عسرت إزالتها. ومن الجاري على ألسنة الفقهاء: «الدفع أسهل من الرفع».

(١٢٩) فإن احتاج إلى أن يصحبه، فليكن صاحبا صالحا دينا تقيا ورعا ذكيا، كثير الخير قليل الشر، حسن المداراة قليل المماراة، إن نسي ذكره وإن ذكر أعانه، وإن احتاج واساه، وإن ضجر صبّره. . . .

الفصل الثاني

في آدابه مع شيخه وقدوته وما يجب عليه من عظيم حرمته وهو ثلاثة عشر نوعا

(١٣٠) الأول: أنه ينبغي للطالب أن يقدم النظر ويستخير الله فيمن يأخذ العلم عنه، ويكتسب حسن الأخلاق والآداب منه. وليكن، إن أمكن، ممن كملت أهليته وتحققت شفقته وظهرت مرؤته وعرفت عفته واشتهرت صيانته، وكان أحسن تعليما وأجود تفهيما. ولا يرغب الطالب في زيادة العلم مع نقص في ورع أو دين أو عدم خلق جميل.

(١٣١) فعن بعض السلف: هذا العلم دين فانظروا عمن تأخذون دينكم. . . .

(132) He should be diligent that the teacher be someone fully acquainted with the religious sciences, someone who has studied much with and listened long to the trusted teachers of his age, not someone who has learned from amidst the leaves of books and is unacquainted with the companionship of skilled teachers.

(133) Al-Shāfiʿī said: "Anyone who acquires his knowledge from amidst books will fail to gain mastery." Another scholar used to say, referring to those who learned from books, "One of the greatest misfortunes is making a sheet of paper your teacher."

(134) **Rule Two:** He should obey his teacher in his affairs. He should not depart from the teacher's opinion and direction, but should be with him like a patient with a skilled doctor. He should ask his advice regarding what he proposes and seek his approval in what he intends. He should show him great reverence and draw close to God by serving him. He should know that his abasement to his teacher is a source of honor, his submissiveness to him a source of pride, and his humility to him a source of exaltation. . . .

(135) **Rule Three:** He should regard his teacher with the eye of esteem and focus on his degree of accomplishment, for that will be most conducive to his profiting from him. An early scholar used to give alms when he was on his way to his teacher and would say, "O God, hide my teacher's faults from me, and may the blessing of his knowledge not depart from me."

(136) Al-Shāfiʿī said: "I used to turn the page very gently in front of Mālik out of respect for him, lest he hear its fall." Al-Rabīʿ said, "By God, I never dared to drink water while al-Shāfiʿī was looking at me out of respect for him. . . ."

(137) **Rule Four:** He should acknowledge the teacher's right and not forget his favor. Shuʿbah[47] said: "Whenever I heard a Prophetic tradition from anyone, I became his servant as long as he lived." He also said: "I never heard anything from anyone except that I frequented him more on account of what I heard from him."

(138) Part of this is that the student should hold the teacher in great reverence. He should be angered by any slander of him and refute it. If he cannot, he should get up and leave the gathering. . . .

(139) **Rule Five:** He should endure any harshness or bad manners on the teacher's part; it should not discourage him from studying with him or thinking well of him. He should give the best possible interpretation to any of the teacher's acts that seem wrong. When the teacher is

(١٣٢) وليجتهد على أن يكون الشيخ ممن له على العلوم الشرعية تمام الاطلاع، وله مع من يوثق به من مشايخ عصره كثرة بحث وطول اجتماع، لا ممن أخذ عن بطون الأوراق ولم يعرف بصحبة المشايخ الحذاق.

(١٣٣) قال الشافعي (رضي الله عنه): من تفقه من بطون الكتب ضيّع الإحكام. وكان بعضهم يقول: من أعظم البلية تشيخ الصحيفة، أي الذين تعلموا من الصحف.

(١٣٤) الثاني: أن ينقاد لشيخه في أموره، ولا يخرج عن رأيه وتدبيره، بل يكون معه كالمريض مع الطبيب الماهر، فيشاوره فيما يقصده، ويتحرى رضاه فيما يعتمده، ويبالغ في حرمته ويتقرب إلى الله تعالى بخدمته؛ ويعلم أن ذُلّه لشيخه عز، وخضوعه له فخر، وتواضعه له رفعة. . . .

(١٣٥) الثالث: أن ينظره بعين الإجلال ويعتقد فيه درجة الكمال، فإن ذلك أقرب إلى نفعه به. وكان بعض السلف إذا ذهب إلى شيخه تصدق بشيء وقال: اللّهم استر عيب شيخي عني ولا تُذهب بركة علمه مني.

(١٣٦) وقال الشافعي (رضي الله عنه): كنت أصفح الورقة بين يدي مالك صفحا رفيقا هيبة له لئلا يسمع وقعها. وقال الربيع: والله ما اجترأت أن أشرب الماء والشافعي ينظر إليّ هيبة له. . . .

(١٣٧) الرابع: أن يعرف له حقه ولا ينسى له فضله، قال شعبة كنت إذا سمعت من الرجل الحديث كنت له عبدا ما يحيا، وقال ما سمعت من أحد شيئا إلا واختلفت إليه أكثر مما سمعت منه.

(١٣٨) ومن ذلك أن يعظم حرمته ويرد غيبته ويغضب لها، فإن عجز عن ذلك قام وفارق ذلك المجلس. . . .

(١٣٩) الخامس: أن يصبر على جفوة تصدر من شيخه أو سوء خلق ولا يصده ذلك عن ملازمته وحسن عقيدته، ويتأول أفعاله التي يظهر أن الصواب خلافها

harsh, the student should be the first to apologize and repent for what happened and ask his forgiveness. He should attribute to his teacher a reason for such behavior and put the blame on himself, for this will better serve to preserve the teacher's affection and sustain his heart, and it will be more beneficial to the student in this world and the next.

(140) An early scholar said: "Whoever does not endure the humiliation of being instructed remains forever in the blindness of ignorance; whoever endures it comes to honor in this world and the next."

(141) **Rule Six:** He should thank his teacher for alerting him to the things wherein lies excellence and censuring him for the things wherein lies deficiency, any indolence that overcomes him, any shortcoming that he sees, or anything else where alerting him or censuring him involve his guidance and welfare. He should consider this from his teacher to be an instance of God's grace toward him through the teacher's concern and regard for him, for such an attitude is more likely to make the teacher's heart incline toward him and to motivate the teacher to be concerned for his welfare.

(142) If the teacher alerts the student to a point of manners or a shortcoming on the student's part and the student already knew it, the student should not reveal that he knew it and neglected it; rather, he should thank the teacher for informing him and being concerned about him. However, if he has an excuse for his behavior and informing the teacher about it is more beneficial, there is no harm in doing so; otherwise, he should not do so, unless not explaining the excuse involves detriment, so that it becomes his duty to inform the teacher of it.

(143) **Rule Seven:** The student should not come into the teacher's presence outside of class without asking permission, regardless of whether the teacher is alone or with somebody. If he asks permission to enter in such a way that the teacher is aware but does not give permission, the student should leave and not ask a second time. If he is not sure the teacher knows, he should not ask permission to enter more than three times or rap more than three times on the door or with the knocker. Out of politeness he should rap lightly on the door with his fingernails, then with his fingers, then with the knocker little by little. If the teacher's place is far from the door and the knocker, there is no harm in making the rapping loud enough to be heard, but no more. If the people seeking entry are a group, the student should give the most excellent and oldest of them precedence in entering and greeting the teacher; then they should greet the teacher in order of excellence.

على أحسن تأويل ويبدأ هو عند جفوة الشيخ بالاعتذار والتوبة مما وقع والاستغفار وينسب الموجب إليه ويجعل العتب عليه، فإن ذلك أبقى لمودة شيخه وأحفظ لقلبه وأنفع للطالب في دنياه وآخرته.

(١٤٠) وعن السلف: من لم يصبر على ذل التعليم بقي عمره في عماية الجهالة، ومن صبر عليه آل أمره إلى عز الدنيا والآخرة . . . .

(١٤١) السادس: أن يشكر الشيخ على توقيفه على ما فيه فضيلة وعلى توبيخه على ما فيه نقيصة، أو على كسل يعتريه أو قصور يعاينه، أو غير ذلك مما في إيقافه عليه وتوبيخه إرشادُه وصلاحُه، وَيَعُدّ ذلك من الشيخ من نعم الله تعالى عليه باعتناء الشيخ به ونظره إليه؛ فإن ذلك أمثل إلى قلب الشيخ وأبعث على الاعتناء بمصالحه.

(١٤٢) وإذا أوقفه الشيخ على دقيقة من أدب أو نقيصة صدرت منه وكان يعرفه من قبل، فلا يظهر أنه كان عارفا به وغفل عنه، بل يشكر الشيخ على إفادته ذلك واعتنائه بأمره؛ فإن كان له في ذلك عذر، وكان إعلام الشيخ به أصلح، فلا بأس به، وإلا تركه؛ إلا أن يترتب على ترك بيان العذر مفسدة فيتعين إعلامه به.

(١٤٣) السابع: أن لا يدخل على الشيخ في غير المجلس العام إلا باستئذان، سواء كان الشيخ وحده أو كان معه غيره؛ فإن استأذن بحيث يعلم الشيخ ولم يأذن له انصرف، ولا يكرر الاستئذان، وإن شك في علم الشيخ به فلا يزيد في الاستئذان فوق ثلاث مرات أو ثلاث طرقات بالباب أو الحلقة، وليكن طرق الباب خفيا بأدب بأظفار الأصابع ثم بالأصابع ثم بالحلقة قليلا قليلا؛ فإن كان الموضع بعيدا عن الباب والحلقة فلا بأس برفع ذلك بقدر ما يسمع لا غير. وإذا أذن وكانوا جماعة يقدم أفضلهم وأسنهم بالدخول والسلام عليه ثم سلم عليه الأفضل فالأفضل.

(144) He should come before the teacher looking his best, with purified and clean garments, having pared his nails, cut his hair, and eliminated any unpleasant odors as necessary, especially if he is coming into a class, for it is an assembly for the remembrance of God and a gathering for worship.

(145) If he visits the teacher outside of class and the teacher has someone talking to him but they stop talking, or if he enters when the teacher is alone praying, studying, writing, or reading and stops or falls silent and does not speak to him first or engage him in conversation, he should greet the teacher and leave quickly unless the teacher urges him to stay. If he stays, he should not stay long, unless the teacher tells him to. . . .

(146) **Rule Eight:** He should sit politely before the teacher as a boy sits before a Qurʾān teacher or sit cross-legged in humility, obedience, silence, and submissiveness. He should listen to the teacher, looking at him, completely attentive to him, and grasping his words so that he does not compel the teacher to repeat his words a second time. He should not turn around unnecessarily; he should look neither right nor left, neither up nor down, without need, especially when the teacher is discussing something with him or speaking to him.

(147) He should look only at the teacher. He should not become restless because of some noise that he hears or turn toward it, especially when the teacher is discussing something with him. He should not shake his sleeves, bare his forearms, or play with his hands, feet, or other part of his body. He should not put his hand on his chin or mouth or pick his nose or extract something from it. He should not open his mouth, grind his teeth, strike the ground with his palm, or draw on it with his fingers. He should not fold his hands or play with his buttons.

(148) He should not lean in the teacher's presence against a wall, pillow, or railing or put his hand on them. He should not turn his side or back to the teacher or lean on his hand toward his back or side. He should not speak at length without need, relate things that provoke laughter, contain obscenity, or include improper or impolite language. He should not laugh at something not amazing, nor should he marvel before the teacher. If he is overcome, he should smile without making a sound. . . .

(١٤٤) وينبغي أن يدخل على الشيخ كامل الهيئة متطهر البدن والثياب نظيفهما بعد ما يحتاج إليه من أخذ ظفر وشعر وقطع رائحة كريهة، لا سيما إن كان يقصد مجلس العلم فإنه مجلس ذكر واجتماع في عبادة.

(١٤٥) ومتى دخل على الشيخ في غير المجلس العام، وعنده من يتحدث معه فسكتوا عن الحديث، أو دخل والشيخ وحده يصلي أو يذكر أو يكتب أو يطالع، فترك ذلك أو سكت ولم يبدأه بكلام أو بسط حديث، فليسلم ويخرج سريعا، إلا أن يحثه الشيخ على المكث، وإذا مكث فلا يطيل إلا أن يأمره بذلك . . . .

(١٤٦) الثامن: أن يجلس بين يدي الشيخ جلسة الأدب كما يجلس الصبي بين يدي المقرئ، أو متربعا بتواضع وخضوع وسكون وخشوع، ويصغي إلى الشيخ ناظرا إليه ويقبل بكليته عليه متعقلا لقوله بحيث لا يحوجه إلى إعادة الكلام مرة ثانية، ولا يلتفت من غير ضرورة ولا ينظر إلى يمينه أو شماله أو فوقه أو قدامه بغير حاجة، ولا سيما عند بحثه له أو عند كلامه معه.

(١٤٧) فلا ينبغي أن ينظر إلا إليه، ولا يضطرب لضجة يسمعها أو يلتفت إليها، ولا سيما عند بحث له، ولا ينفض كُمَّه ولا يحسر عن ذراعيه ولا يعبث بيديه أو رجليه أو غيرهما من أعضائه، ولا يضع يده على لحيته أو فمه أو يعبث بها في أنفه أو يستخرج منها شيئا، ولا يفتح فاه ولا يقرع سنه ولا يضرب الأرض براحته أو يخط عليها بأصابعه، ولا يشبك بيديه أو يعبث بأزراره.

(١٤٨) ولا يسند بحضرة الشيخ إلى حائط أو مخدة أو درابزين أو يجعل يده عليها، ولا يعطي الشيخ جنبه أو ظهره، ولا يعتمد على يده إلى ورائه أو جنبه. ولا يكثر كلامه من غير حاجة، ولا يحكي ما يضحك منه أو ما فيه بذاءة أو يتضمن سوء مخاطبة أو سوء أدب، ولا يضحك لغير عجب، ولا يعجب دون الشيخ؛ فإن غلبه تبسم تبسما بغير صوت البتة . . . .

(149) **Rule Nine:** He should address the teacher in the best possible manner. He should not say to him, "Why?" or "We do not accept!" or "Who transmitted that?" or "Where is it to be found?" If he wants to learn these things, he should find out politely or when he is in a different class where such things are more likely to be taught. . . .

(150) If the teacher insists on a statement or proof that does not seem correct to him or misspeaks inadvertently, the student should not alter his face or eyes or gesture to anyone as if he were disputing what the teacher said. He should maintain a pleasant countenance even if the teacher is wrong due to negligence, inadvertence, or insufficient reflection on the subject, for infallibility among men belongs to the prophets. . . .

(151) **Rule Ten:** If he hears the teacher mention the solution to a legal problem, or an unusual idea, or relate a story, or recite a poem that he has already committed to memory, he should listen to him like one learning it for the first time, eager and joyful as if he had never heard it. . . .

(152) If the teacher asks him at the start whether he has committed it to memory, he should neither say yes, for that would imply his having no need of the teacher in the matter, nor say no, for that would be a lie; rather he should say that he would like to hear it from the teacher, or would like to learn it from him, or that he heard it long ago, or that the teacher will transmit it more accurately. If he knows that the teacher, out of joy for him, would prefer to know about his having already committed the matter to memory, or if the teacher has indicated that he is testing the accuracy of his memory or wants to demonstrate that he has learned it, there is no harm in falling in with the teacher's purpose in order to gain the teacher's pleasure and increase his approval.

(153) The student should not ask again about what he already knows or seek an explanation of what he already understands, for this wastes time and could annoy the teacher. Al-Zuhrī said: "Repeating an account is worse than moving a stone." The student should not be remiss in listening and understanding, nor, having occupied his mind with thoughts or conversation, should he then ask the teacher to repeat what he said, for that is bad manners; rather he should listen to what the teacher is saying and focus his mind on what he is hearing the first time it is said. . . .

(١٤٩) التاسع: أن يحسن خطابه مع الشيخ بقدر الإمكان. ولا يقول له لم؟ ولا لا نسلم، ولا من نقل هذا، ولا أين موضعه وشبه ذلك؛ فان أراد استفادته تلطف في الوصول إلى ذلك، ثم هو في مجلس آخر أولى على سبيل الإفادة . . . .

(١٥٠) وإذا أصر الشيخ على قول أو دليل ولم يظهر له، أو على خلاف صواب سهواً فلا يغيّر وجهه أو عينيه أو يشير إلى غيره كالمنكر لما قاله؛ بل يأخذه ببشر ظاهر وإن لم يكن الشيخ مصيبا لغفلة أو سهو أو قصور نظر في تلك الحال، فإن العصمة في البشر للأنبياء صلى الله عليهم وسلم . . . .

(١٥١) العاشر: إذا سمع الشيخ يذكر حكما في مسألة أو فائدة مستغربة، أو يحكي حكاية أو ينشد شعرا وهو يحفظ ذلك أصغى إليه إصغاء مستفيد له في الحال متعطش إليه فرح به كأنه لم يسمعه قط . . . .

(١٥٢) فان سأله الشيخ عند الشروع في ذلك عن حفظه له فلا يجيب بنعم، لما فيه من الاستغناء عن الشيخ فيه، ولا يقل لا، لما فيه من الكذب؛ بل يقول: أحب أن أسمعه من الشيخ أو أن أستفيده منه أو بعد عهدي أو هو من جهتكم أصح. فإن علم من حال الشيخ أنه يؤثر العلم بحفظه له مسرة به، أو أشار إليه بإتمامه امتحانا لضبطه وحفظه أو لإظهار تحصيله، فلا بأس باتباع غرض الشيخ ابتغاء مرضاته وازدياد الرغبة فيه.

(١٥٣) ولا ينبغي للطالب أن يكرر سؤال ما يعلمه، ولا استفهام ما يفهمه؛ فإنه يضيع الزمان وربما أضجر الشيخ. قال الزهري: إعادة الحديث أشد من نقل الصخر. وينبغي أن لا يقصر في الإصغاء والتفهم، أو يشتغل ذهنه بفكر أو حديث ثم يستعيد الشيخَ ما قاله، لأن ذلك إساءة أدب، بل يكون مصغيا لكلامه حاضر الذهن لما يسمعه من أول مرة . . . .

(154) **Rule Eleven:** He should not anticipate the teacher in explaining a problem or answering a question raised by the teacher or someone else; he should not compete with him to answer it or demonstrate his knowledge or understanding of it before the teacher. However, if the teacher initially suggests it or asks him to, there is no harm in it.

(155) He should not interrupt the teacher, whatever he is saying. He should not vie or compete with him, but should wait patiently until the teacher finishes what he is saying, and then he should speak. He should not talk to anyone else while the teacher is talking to him or to the entire class.

(156) His mind should be present at all times, so that if the teacher commands him to do something, asks him for something, or makes a request, he will not force the teacher to repeat it a second time, but will hasten to do it. He should not talk back to the teacher or oppose him by saying, "What if it isn't so? . . ."

(157) **Rule Twelve:** If the teacher hands him something, he should take it with his right hand. If he hands the teacher something, he should hand it to him with his right hand. If it is a sheet of paper for him to read, such as a legal opinion, narrative, or legal document, he should unfold it and then give it to him; he should not give it to him folded unless he knows or thinks that the teacher prefers it. If he takes a sheet of paper from the teacher, he should make haste to take it unfolded, before he folds it or sprinkles it with dust to dry the ink.

(158) If he hands the teacher a book, he should hand it to him ready for him to open it and read it without having to turn it around. If the discussion concerns a certain point, let the book be open to it and let him point out the place to him. He should not throw anything to the teacher, be it book, sheet of paper, or anything else. He should not stretch out his hands to the teacher if he is far away, nor should he force the teacher to extend his hand also to take something from him or give him something; rather, he should get up and go to him, standing up and not crawling toward him. If he sits down before him for that purpose, he should not get so close to him that it might be attributed to bad manners on his part. . . .

(159) If he hands the teacher a pen with which to write, let him fill it with ink before he gives it to him. If he sets an inkwell before him, let it have its cover open and be ready for writing. If he hands him a knife, he should not point its blade or handle toward him while his hand grasps

(١٥٤) الحادي عشر: أن لا يسبق الشيخ إلى شرح مسألة أو جواب سؤال منه أو من غيره. ولا يساوقه فيه، ولا يظهر معرفته به أو إدراكه له قبل الشيخ، فإن عرض الشيخ عليه ذلك ابتداء والتمسه منه فلا بأس.

(١٥٥) وينبغي أن لا يقطع على الشيخ كلامه، أي كلام كان، ولا يسابقه فيه ولا يساوقه؛ بل يصبر حتى يفرغ الشيخ كلامه ثم يتكلم ولا يتحدث مع غيره والشيخ يتحدث معه أو مع جماعة المجلس.

(١٥٦) وليكن ذهنه حاضرا في كل وقت بحيث إذا أمره بشيء أو سأله عن شيء أو أشار إليه لم يحوجه إلى إعادته ثانيا؛ بل يبادر إليه مسرعا ولم يعاوده فيه أو يعترض عليه بقوله: فإن لم يكن الأمر كذا؟ . . .

(١٥٧) الثاني عشر: إذا ناوله الشيخ شيئا تناوله باليمين، وإن ناوله شيئا ناوله باليمين؛ فإن كان ورقة يقرؤها كفتيا أو قصة أو مكتوب شرعي ونحو ذلك نشرها ثم دفعها إليه ولا يدفعها إليه مطوية إلا إذا علم أو ظن إيثار الشيخ لذلك، وإذا أخذ من الشيخ ورقة بادر إلى أخذها منشورة قبل أن يطويها أو يتربها.

(١٥٨) وإذا ناول الشيخ كتابا ناوله إياه مهيئا لفتحه والقراءة فيه من غير احتياج إلى إدارته، فإن كان النظر في موضع معين فليكن مفتوحا كذلك، ويعين له المكان، ولا يحذف إليه الشيء حذفا من كتاب أو ورقة أو غير ذلك. ولا يمد يديه إليه إذا كان بعيدا، ولا يحوج الشيخ إلى مد يده أيضا لأخذ منه أو عطاء؛ بل يقوم إليه قائما ولا يزحف إليه زحفا. وإذا جلس بين يديه لذلك فلا يقرب منه قربا كثيرا يُنْسَب فيه إلى سوء أدب . . . .

(١٥٩) وإذا ناوله قلما ليمد به فليمده قبل إعطائه إياه، وإن وضع بين يديه دواة فلتكن مفتوحة الأغطية مهيأة للكتابة منها، وإن ناوله سكينا فلا يصوب إليه شفرتها

the blade; rather, let it be sideways, with the edge of its blade pointing toward him, while he grasps the part of handle next to the blade, placing the handle to the taker's right.

(160) If he hands the teacher a carpet to pray on, he should unroll it first. It is good manners for him to spread it when the teacher means for him to do so. When he spreads it out, he should fold over the back of the left side as is the Sufi custom. If the carpet is folded, he should put its sides to the worshipper's right. If the carpet has the design of a prayer niche on it, he should try to set it facing Mecca if he can. . . .

(161) **Rule Thirteen:** When he walks with the teacher, let him be ahead of him by night and behind him by day unless the situation dictates otherwise due to crowding or some other reason. He should go ahead of the teacher in places where the footing is uncertain, such as mud or puddles, or in dangerous places. He should take care that the teacher's clothes do not get splattered. When he is in a crowd, he should protect the teacher from it with his hands either from in front or from behind.

(162) When he walks ahead of the teacher, he should turn to look at him frequently. If he is alone and the teacher is talking to him as they walk, the two of them being in the shade, let him be to the teacher's right (some say to his left), a little ahead of him, and turning to look at him. Let him acquaint the teacher with any distinguished person who approaches him or seeks him and whom the teacher does not know. . . .

(163) When he meets his teacher in the street by chance, he should be the first to pronounce a greeting. He should go toward the teacher to greet him if he is far away. He should not call out to the teacher or greet him from a distance or from behind; rather, he should approach him, go before him, and then greet him. He should not volunteer advice to the teacher about taking a certain road until the teacher asks for his advice. When the teacher asks his advice, he should be polite in responding to his opinion.

(164) Regarding what the teacher thinks is right but is wrong, he should not say, "That is wrong," or "That is not right." He should address the teacher politely in correcting him. He should say, for example, "It appears that such and such would be advantageous." He should not say, "I think the right opinion is such and such."

ولا نصابها ويده قابضة على الشفرة بل يكون عرضا وحد شفرتها إلى جهته قابضا على طرف النصاب مما يلي النصل جاعلا نصابها على يمين الآخذ.

(١٦٠) وإن ناوله سجادة ليصلي عليها نشرها أولا، والأدب أن يفرشها هو عند قصد ذلك، وإذا فرشها ثنى مؤخر طرفها الأيسر كعادة الصوفية، فإن كانت مثنية جعل طرفيها إلى يسار المصلي، وإن كانت فيه صورة محراب تحرى به جهة القبلة إن أمكن . . . .

(١٦١) الثالث عشر: إذا مشى مع الشيخ فليكن أمامه بالليل وخلفه بالنهار إلا أن يقتضي الحال خلاف ذلك لزحمة أو غيرها، ويتقدم عليه في المواطئ المجهولة الحال كوحل أو حوض، أو المواطئ الخطرة، ويحترز من ترشيش ثياب الشيخ، وإذا كان في زحمة صانه عنها بيديه إما من قدامه أو من ورائه.

(١٦٢) وإذا مشى أمامه التفت إليه بعد كل قليل، فإن كان وحده والشيخ يكلمه حالة المشي وهما في ظل فليكن في يمينه - وقيل عن يساره - متقدما عليه قليلا ملتفتا إليه، ويعرف الشيخ بمن قرب منه أو قصده من الأعيان إن لم يعلم الشيخ به . . . .

(١٦٣) وإذا صادف الشيخَ في طريقه بدأه بالسلام، ويقصده بالسلام إن كان بعيدا، ولا يناديه ولا يسلم عليه من بعيد ولا من ورائه؛ بل يقرب منه ويتقدم عليه ثم يسلم، ولا يشير عليه ابتداء بالأخذ في طريق حتى يستشيره ويتأدب فيما يستشيره الشيخ بالرد إلى رأيه.

(١٦٤) ولا يقول لما رآه الشيخ، وكان خطأ: « هذا خطأ » ولا « هذا ليس برأي »، بل يحسن خطابه في الرد إلى الصواب كقوله: « يظهر أن المصلحة في كذا »، ولا يقول « الرأي عندي كذا » وشبه ذلك.

SECTION THREE

Rules for the Student's Conduct in His Studying and Reading in Class and How He Should Behave There with the Teacher and Colleagues—Consisting of Thirteen Rules

(165) **Rule One:** He should begin first with God's mighty book, the Qurᵓān. He should memorize it thoroughly. He should strive to master its interpretation and its other ancillary sciences, for the Qurᵓān is the root and source of all the sciences and the most important of them.

(166) Then in each subject he should memorize a short compendium that sums up Prophetic traditions, their ancillary sciences, the fundamentals of religion and law, and Arabic syntax and morphology. However, none of this should distract him from studying and renewing his acquaintance with the Qurᵓān. He should continue to recite a portion[48] of it every day, or days, or week, as has been mentioned already. Let him beware of forgetting it after memorizing it, for Prophetic traditions rebuking this have been handed down.

(167) He should study with teachers the explanation of the things he has committed to memory. Let him beware of always relying on books in this; rather, in each subject he should rely on someone proficient at teaching it, thoroughly acquainted with it, and more learned than he—a scholar expert with the book that he has read. However, he should first attend to the attributes of character we have discussed above: piety, uprightness, compassion, and so forth. . . .

(168) **Rule Two:** At the beginning of his education the student should beware of immersing himself in disagreements between scholars or among people generally in matters of reason or revelation, for this perplexes the mind and confounds the intellect. Let him first master one book on one subject, or several books on several subjects if he is able, on a single path approved for him by his teacher. If the teacher's method is to transmit the opinions of different schools and their disagreements and he has no single view, al-Ghazālī has said that such a teacher can do more harm than good.

الفصل الثالث

في آدابه في دروسه وقراءته في الحلقة وما يعتمده فيها مع الشيخ والرفقة وهو ثلاثة عشر نوعا

(١٦٥) النوع الأول: أن يبتدئ أولا بكتاب الله العزيز فيتقنه حفظا ويجتهد على إتقان بتفسيره وسائر علومه فإنه أصل العلوم وأمها وأهمها.

(١٦٦) ثم يحفظ من كل فن مختصرا يجمع فيه بين طرفيه من الحديث وعلومه والأصولين والنحو والتصريف، ولا يشتغل بذلك كله عن دراسة القرآن وتعهده وملازمة ورده منه في كل يوم أو أيام أو جمعة كما تقدم، وليحذر من نسيانه بعد حفظه فقد ورد فيه أحاديث تزجر عنه.

(١٦٧) ويشتغل بشرح تلك المحفوظات على المشايخ، وليحذر من الاعتماد في ذلك على الكتب أبدا، بل يعتمد في كل فن من هو أحسن تعليما له وأكثر تحقيقا فيه وتحصيلا منه، وأخبرهم بالكتاب الذي قرأه، وذلك بعد مراعاة الصفات المقدمة من الدين والصلاح والشفقة وغيرهما . . . .

(١٦٨) الثاني: أن يحذر في ابتداء أمره من الاشتغال في الاختلاف بين العلماء أو بين الناس مطلقا في العقليات والسمعيات، فإنه يحير الذهن ويدهش العقل؛ بل يتقن أولا كتابا واحدا في فن واحد أو كتبا في فنون إن كان يحتمل ذلك على طريقة واحدة يرتضيها له شيخه. فإن كانت طريقة شيخه نقل المذاهب والاختلاف ولم يكن له رأي واحد، قال الغزالي: فليحذر منه فإن ضرره أكثر من النفع به.

(169) At the beginning of his quest the student should also beware of readings in detached sections of different works. This will waste his time and scatter his mind. Rather, he should give the book he is reading or subject he is studying his all until he masters it. He should also beware of needlessly shifting from book to book, for that is a sign of discontent and lack of progress. . . .

(170) **Rule Three:** Before he memorizes anything, he should carefully verify[49] the text he is reading either with his teacher or with someone whom the latter appoints. Afterward, he should thoroughly memorize it and then repeat it well to him. He should review the text at times that he sets for repeating his past lessons. He should not memorize anything before verifying it, because he will fall into misreadings and textual corruption. We have already said that knowledge cannot be gotten from books, for that is one of the worst sources of harm.

(171) He should bring his inkwell, pen, and penknife with him so that he can correct words and indicate vowels.

(172) If the teacher rejects the student's reading of a word and the student thinks or knows that the teacher's rejection of it is wrong, the student should repeat the word along with what went before it, so that the teacher becomes aware of it, or he should say the correct word in a questioning tone, for what happened may have been inadvertent or the teacher's tongue may have slipped accidentally. He should not say, "No! this is how it is." He should politely draw the teacher's attention. If the teacher does not notice, he should say, "Might one read it this way?" If the teacher corrects himself, nothing should be said; if not, the student should politely leave the matter till another class for resolution, for the teacher may have been right. . . .

(173) **Rule Four:** He should listen to Prophetic hadiths early in the day. He should not neglect to study them and their ancillary sciences and to examine their chains of transmission, the men who transmitted them, their meanings, their degrees of soundness, their legal implications, their language, and their dates. He should study the *Ṣaḥīḥ* of al-Bukhārī and the *Ṣaḥīḥ* of Muslim,[50] then the remaining recognized major books in the field, such as the *Muwaṭṭa*ʾ of Mālik, the *Sunan* of Abū Dāwūd, the *Sunan* of al-Nasāʾī, the *Sunan* of Ibn Mājah, the *Jāmi*ᶜ of al-Tirmidhī, and the *Musnad* of al-Shāfiᶜī. He should not limit himself to less than this. A great aid to the student of law is the *Kitāb al-sunan al-kabīr* by Abū Bakr al-Bayhaqī,[51] as well as the *musnad* books,[52] such as the *Musnad* of Ibn Ḥanbal,[53] that of Ibn Ḥumayd,[54] and that of al-Bazzār.[55]

(١٦٩) وكذلك يحذر في ابتداء طلبه من المطالعات في تفاريق المصنفات، فإنه يضيع زمانه ويفرق ذهنه، بل يعطي الكتاب الذي يقرؤه أو الفن الذي يأخذه كليته حتى يتقنه، وكذلك يحذر من التنقل من كتاب إلى كتاب من غير موجب فإنه علامة الضجر وعدم الإفلاح . . . .

(١٧٠) الثالث: أن يصحح ما يقرؤه قبل حفظه تصحيحا متقنا، إما على الشيخ أو على غيره مما يعينه، ثم يحفظه بعد ذلك حفظا محكما، ثم يكرر عليه بعد حفظه تكرارا جيدا، ثم يتعاهده في أوقات يقررها لتكرار مواضيه، ولا يحفظ شيئا قبل تصحيحه لأنه يقع في التحريف والتصحيف، وقد تقدم أن العلم لا يؤخذ من الكتب فإنه من أضر المفاسد.

(١٧١) وينبغي أن يحضر معه الدواة والقلم والسكين للتصحيح ولضبط ما يصححه لغة وإعرابا.

(١٧٢) وإذا رد الشيخ عليه لفظة وظن أن رده خلاف الصواب أو علمه، كرر اللفظة مع ما قبلها لينتبه لها الشيخ أو يأتي بلفظ الصواب على سبيل الاستفهام فربما وقع ذلك سهوا أو سبق لسان لغفلة، ولا يقل: «بل هي كذا»، بل يتلطف في تنبيه الشيخ لها، فإن لم يتنبه قال: «فهل يجوز فيها كذا؟» فإن رجع الشيخ إلى الصواب فلا كلام، وإلا ترك تحقيقها إلى مجلس آخر بتلطف لاحتمال أن يكون الصواب مع الشيخ . . . .

(١٧٣) الرابع: أن يبكر بسماع الحديث ولا يهمل الاشتغال به وبعلومه والنظر في إسناده ورجاله ومعانيه وأحكامه وفوائده ولغته وتواريخه. ويعتني أولا بصحيحي البخاري ومسلم ثم ببقية الكتب الأعلام والأصول المعتمدة في هذا الشأن كموطأ مالك وسنن أبي داود والنسائي وابن ماجه وجامع الترمذي ومسند الشافعي ولا ينبغي أن يقتصر على أقل من ذلك. ونعم المعين للفقيه كتاب السنن الكبير لأبي بكر البيهقي ومن ذلك المسانيد كمسند أحمد بن حنبل وابن حميد والبزار.

(174) He should learn to distinguish "sound" (*ṣaḥīḥ*), "good" (*ḥasan*), and "weak" (*ḍaʿīf*) hadiths, hadiths with an uninterrupted chain of transmitters (*musnad*), ones with an incomplete chain of transmitters (*mursal*), and the other kinds of hadith, for this is one of the two wings that support the scholar of the religious law, and it clarifies many things in the other wing, namely the Qurʾān.

(175) He should not be satisfied with merely hearing,[56] like most of the hadith transmitters of this age; he should be more interested in understanding than in reciting. Al-Shāfiʿī said: "A person's authority becomes stronger if he has examined the hadith, because understanding is the objective of transmitting and communicating hadith."

(176) **Rule Five:** When he has explicated the short compendia that he has memorized and has mastered the problems and important ideas they contain, he can move on to studying extensive works. Along with this goes constant reading, taking notes on valuable ideas, subtle questions, and unusual applications he encounters or hears, and resolving the problems and differences between decisions regarding obscure matters in all branches of learning. He should consider no lesson he hears inconsequential or be careless about any rule he masters; rather, he should hasten to write notes on them and memorize them. Let his zeal in the pursuit of knowledge be high. Let him not be satisfied with little learning when great learning is possible. Let him not be content with a small portion of the legacy of the prophets. Let him not postpone the acquisition of a lesson he can learn. Let hope and procrastination not distract him, for procrastination is a great source of evil, and, if he learns something at the present time, he can learn something else at a future time.

(177) He should make use of his hours of leisure and energy, the time of his health, youthful prime, mental alertness, and lack of distractions, before the symptoms of fatigue set in or the obstacles of preeminence. ʿUmar said, "Become learned before you become a ruler." Al-Shāfiʿī said, "Become learned before you become a leader, for once you become a leader there is no way to become learned." He should beware of seeing himself with an eye of kindness. He should not dispense with teachers, for that is utter ignorance and lack of knowledge, and what he loses will be greater than what he attains. We have already cited the words of Saʿīd ibn Jubayr: "A man remains a scholar as long as he learns. The opinion that one has no further need is the worst kind of ignorance."

(١٧٤) ويعتني بمعرفة صحيح الحديث وحسنه وضعيفه ومسنده ومرسله وسائر أنواعه فإنه أحد جناحي العالم بالشريعة المبين لكثير من الجناح الآخر وهو القرآن.

(١٧٥) ولا يقنع بمجرد السماع كغالب محدثي هذا الزمان، بل يعتني بالدراية أشد من اعتنائه بالرواية. قال الشافعي (رضي الله عنه): من نظر في الحديث قويت حجته لأن الدراية هي المقصود بنقل الحديث وتبليغه.

(١٧٦) الخامس: إذا شرح محفوظاته المختصرات، وضبط ما فيها من الإشكالات والفوائد المهمات، انتقل إلى بحث المبسوطات مع المطالعة الدائمة وتعليق ما يمر به أو يسمعه من الفوائد النفيسة والمسائل الدقيقة والفروع الغريبة وحل المشكلات والفروق بين أحكام المتشابهات من جميع أنواع العلوم. ولا يستقل بفائدة يسمعها أو يتهاون بقاعدة يضبطها، بل يبادر إلى تعليقها وحفظها. ولتكن همته في طلب العلم عالية فلا يكتفي بقليل العلم مع إمكان كثيره، ولا يقنع من إرث الأنبياء صلوات الله عليهم بيسيره، ولا يؤخر تحصيل فائدة تمكن منها أو يشغله الأمل والتسويف عنها فإن للتأخير آفات ولأنه إذا حصلها في الزمن الحاضر حصل في الزمن الثاني غيرها.

(١٧٧) ويغتنم وقت فراغه ونشاطه و زمن عافيته وشرخ شبابه ونباهة خاطره وقلة شواغله قبل عوارض البطالة أو موانع الرياسة. قال عمر (رضي الله عنه): تفقهوا قبل أن تسودوا. وقال الشافعي (رضي الله عنه): تفقه قبل أن ترأس فإذا رأست فلا سبيل إلى التفقه. وليحذر من نظر نفسه بعين الجمال والاستغناء عن المشايخ فإن ذلك عين الجهل وقلة المعرفة وما يفوته أكثر مما حصله، وقد تقدم قول سعيد بن جبير: لا يزال الرجل عالما ما تعلم، فإذا ترك التعلم وظن أنه قد استغنى أسوأ جهل ما يكون.

(178) When his competence has become complete, his preeminence apparent, and he has gone through most of the books on a subject or the best-known of them, having studied, reviewed, and perused them, he can devote himself to writing and to examining the different schools of scholars, following the path of fairness with regard to the disagreements he encounters, as we have already mentioned in the chapter on rules of conduct for the teacher.

(179) **Rule Six:** He should stick to his teacher's circle for lectures and recitation, and, indeed, all his classes if possible, for this will but increase him in good and attainment and in manners and excellence, as ᶜAlī said in the saying we have cited above. He should not become sated from the length of his discipleship, for the teacher is like a date palm: you wait for something to fall on you from it. He should strive to be diligent and prompt in serving him, for that will gain him honor and respect.

(180) If possible, he should not limit himself in the class to reciting his lesson, for that is a sign of insufficient interest, lack of progress, and slowness of understanding. He should concern himself with all the lessons that are being explained, to learn them accurately, take notes on them, and transmit them, if his mind is up to it. He should participate with the reciter of each lesson, so that it is as if each lesson belonged to him. This, by my life, is what an eager student should do. If he cannot master all the lessons, he should attend to them in order of importance. . . .

(181) **Rule Seven:** When he comes to the teacher's class, he should salute those present with a voice that everybody can hear, and he should bestow additional greetings and respect on the teacher. He should make his salutation in the same way when he leaves.

(182) Some have held that classes in progress are among the places where one does not pronounce a greeting. This goes against custom and practice, but it applies to a single person busy memorizing and repeating his lesson. Having pronounced a greeting, one whose rank does not entitle him to do so should not step over the necks of those present to get close to the teacher; he should sit in the last row, as mentioned in a Prophetic tradition. If the teacher and those present tell him to move forward, or it is his place, or he knows that the teacher and the group would prefer it, there is no harm in doing so.

(١٧٨) وإذا كملت أهليته وظهرت فضيلته ومر على اكثر كتب الفن أو المشهورة منها بحثا ومراجعة ومطالعة، اشتغل بالتصنيف وبالنظر في مذاهب العلماء سالكا طريق الإنصاف فيما يقع له من الخلاف كما تقدم في أدب العالم.

(١٧٩) السادس: أن يلزم حلقة شيخه في التدريس والإقراء بل وجميع مجالسه إذا أمكن، فانه لا يزيده إلا خيرا وتحصيلا وأدبا وتفضيلا كما قال علي (رضي الله عنه) في حديثه المتقدم. ولا تشبع من طول صحبته فإنما هو كالنخلة تنتظر متى يسقط عليك منها شيء، ويجتهد على مواظبته في خدمته والمسارعة إليها فإن ذلك يكسبه شرفا وتبجيلا.

(١٨٠) ولا يقتصر في الحلقة على سماع درسه فقط إذا أمكنه، فإن ذلك علامة قصور الهمة وعدم الفلاح وبطء التنبه، بل يعتني بسائر الدروس المشروحة ضبطا وتعليقا ونقلا. وإن احتمل ذهنه ذلك ويشارك أصحابها حتى كأن كل درس منها له، ولعمرى إن الامر كذلك للحريص، فإن عجز عن ضبط جمعها اعتنى بالأهم فالأهم منها . . . .

(١٨١) السابع: إذا حضر مجلس الشيخ سلم على الحاضرين بصوت يسمع جميعهم، ويخص الشيخ بزيادة تحية وإكرام وكذلك يسلم إذا انصرف.

(١٨٢) وعد بعضهم حلق العلم في حال أخذهم فيه من المواضع التي لا يسلم فيها، وهذا خلاف ما عليه العرف والعمل، لكن يتجه ذلك في شخص واحد مشتغل بحفظ درسه وتكراره، وإذا سلم فلا يتخطى رقاب الحاضرين إلى قرب الشيخ من لم يكن منزلته كذلك، بل يجلس حيث انتهى به المجلس كما ورد في الحديث، فإن صرح له الشيخ والحاضرون بالتقدم، أو كانت منزلته أو كان يعلم إيثار الشيخ والجماعة لذلك، فلا بأس.

(183) He should not cause anyone to get up from his seat or crowd anyone intentionally. If another student offers to give up his seat to him, he should not accept it unless there is some benefit known to everyone in doing so and unless the students will benefit from his discussions with the teacher because of his closeness to him or because he is old and of great virtue and piety. . . .

(184) **Rule Eight:** He should be polite to those who attend the teacher's class, for this is a matter of good manners toward the teacher and respect for his class, and they are his companions. He should respect his companions and honor his elders and peers. He should not sit down in the middle of the circle or in front of anyone, except from necessity, as in gatherings to impart hadith.[57] He should not separate two companions or friends except with the permission of both. He should not sit higher than someone worthier than he.

(185) When a newcomer arrives, those present should greet him, make room for him in the gathering, make space for him, and honor him appropriately. When room has been made for him, even if it is narrow, he should join the group.

(186) He should not spread out or turn his side or back to anyone. He should refrain from doing so and be especially careful when the teacher is discussing something with him. He should not lean on his neighbor, set his elbow to his side, or violate the symmetry of the circle by coming forward or lagging behind.

(187) During his or someone else's lesson, he should not speak about something unrelated or that interrupts the discussion. When someone begins a lesson, he should not speak about what relates to a completed lesson or to another one not completed except with the permission of the teacher and of the person reciting that lesson. . . .

(188) **Rule Nine:** He should not be ashamed to ask about what is unclear to him and seek to comprehend what he has not understood. He should do this courteously, with polite address, good manners, and a well-formulated question. ᶜUmar[58] said, "He who is bashful,[59] his knowledge will be weak." It has also been said, "He who is bashful when asking, his deficiency will become apparent when men gather together." Mujāhid[60] said, "Neither the bashful nor the proud become learned." The Prophet's wife ᶜĀʾishah said, "God bless the wives of the Muslims of Medina, for bashfulness did not prevent them from becoming learned

(١٨٣) ولا يقيم أحدا من مجلسه أو يزاحمه قصدا، فإن آثره الغير بمجلسه لم يقبله إلا أن تكون في ذلك مصلحة يعرفها القوم وينتفعون بها من بحثه مع الشيخ لقربه منه أو لكونه كبير السن أو كثير الفضيلة والصلاح . . . .

(١٨٤) الثامن: أن يتأدب مع حاضري مجلس الشيخ، فإنه أدب معه واحترام لمجلسه وهم رفقاؤه فيوقر أصحابه ويحترم كبراءه وأقرانه، ولا يجلس وسط الحلقة ولا قدام أحد الإلضرورة، كما في مجالس التحديث، ولا يفرق بين رفيقين ولا بين متصاحبين إلا بإذنهما معا، ولا فوق من هو أولى منه.

(١٨٥) وينبغي للحاضرين إذا جاء القادم أن يرحبوا به ويوسعوا له في المجلس وإن كان حرجا ضم نفسه.

(١٨٦) ولا يتوسع ولا يعطي أحدا منهم جنبه ولا ظهره ويتحفظ من ذلك ويتعهده عند بحث الشيخ له، ولا يجنح على جاره أو يجعل مرفقه قائما في جنبه أو يخرج عن نسق الحلقة بتقدم أو تأخر.

(١٨٧) ولا يتكلم في أثناء درس غيره أو درسه بما لا يتعلق به أو بما يقطع عليه بحثه، وإذا شرع بعضهم في درس فلا يتكلم بكلام يتعلق بدرس فرغ ولا بغيره مما لا تفوت فائدة إلا بإذن من الشيخ وصاحب الدرس . . . .

(١٨٨) التاسع: أن لا يستحيي من سؤال ما أشكل عليه وتفهم ما لم يتعقل بتلطف وحسن خطاب وأدب وسؤال. قال عمر (رضي الله عنه): من رق وجهه رق علمه. وقد قيل: من رق وجهه عند السؤال. ظهر نقصه عند اجتماع الرجال. وقال مجاهد: لا يتعلم العلم مستحي ولا مستكبر. وقالت عائشة (رضي الله عنها): رحم الله نساء الأنصار، لم يكن الحياء يمنعهن أن يتفقهن في الدين. وقالت أم سليم

in religion." Umm Sulaym[61] once said to the Prophet: "God is not bashful about the truth. Does a woman have to bathe herself fully if she dreams about sexual intercourse? . . ."

(189) **Rule Ten:** He should take his turn and not precede someone else whose turn it is. It is reported that a Medinese Muslim came to the Prophet to ask him for something. Then a man from the tribe of Thaqīf came, to whom the Prophet said: "O brother of Thaqīf, this Medinese Muslim came to ask before you. Sit down, so that we can start with the Medinese Muslim's need before your need. . . ."

(190) If the person whose turn comes later has a pressing need that the person whose turn comes first knows, and the teacher indicates that he should go first, it is desirable that the person whose turn comes first give up his turn. However, if that or something similar is not the case, some people have held it undesirable to give up one's turn, because the recitation of knowledge and hastening to acquire it are a means of drawing near [to God], and giving up the means of drawing near [to God] is undesirable. Priority of turn comes from priority of arrival at the teacher's class or its location. One's right to one's turn does not lapse because one has to go to answer a call of nature and then renew one's ablutions, if one returns afterward.

(191) It two students arrive simultaneously and argue with each other, they should draw lots, or the teacher should give one of them precedence if the person volunteers; but if it is the teacher's duty to have both of them recite, then it should be by lot. If it has been stipulated that the school assistant is to have the students of the school recite at a certain time, he should not give strangers priority over them at that time without their permission. . . .

(192) **Rule Eleven:** His sitting before the teacher should be in accordance with the details and appearance mentioned above in [the section on] his manner of behavior with his teacher. He should bring with him the book from which he is to read. He should carry it himself. He should not put it open on the ground during his reading, but hold it in his hands and read from it. He should not read until he asks the teacher permission. Al-Khaṭīb mentions this on the authority of a number of early authorities and says, "He should not recite until the teacher gives him permission."

(193) He should not recite while the teacher's mind is occupied, or when he is weary, distressed, angry, hungry, thirsty, sleepy, excited, or tired.

(رضي الله عنها) لرسول الله ﷺ: إن الله لا يستحيي من الحق، هل على امرأة من الغسل إذا احتلمت . . . .

(١٨٩) العاشر: مراعاة نوبته، فلا يتقدم عليه بغير رضا من هي له. روي أن أنصاريا جاء إلى النبي ﷺ يسأله، وجاء رجل من ثقيف، فقال النبي ﷺ: يا أخا ثقيف إن الأنصاري قد سبقك بالمسألة، فاجلس كيما نبدأ بحاجة الأنصاري قبل حاجتك . . . .

(١٩٠) وكذلك إذا كان للمتأخر حاجة ضرورية وعلمها المتقدم أو أشار الشيخ بتقدمه فيستحب إيثاره، فإن لم يكن شيء من ذلك ونحوه فقد كره قوم الإيثار بالنوبة لأن قراءة العلم والمسارعة إليه قربة، والإيثار بالقرب مكروه. ويحصل تقدم النوبة بتقدم الحضور في مجلس الشيخ أو إلى مكانه، ولا يسقط حقه بذهابه إلى ما يضطر إليه من قضاء حاجة وتجديد وضوء إذا عاد بعده.

(١٩١) وإذا تساوى اثنان وتنازعا أقرع بينهما، أو يقدم الشيخ أحدهما إن كان متبرعا، وإن كان عليه إقراؤهما فالقرعة. ومعيد المدرسة إذا شرط عليه إقراء أهلها فيها في وقت فلا يقدم عليهم الغرباء فيه بغير إذنهم . . . .

(١٩٢) الحادي عشر: أن يكون جلوسه بين يدي الشيخ على ما تقدم تفصيله وهيأته في أدبه مع شيخه، ويحضر كتابه الذي يقرأ منه معه، ويحمله بنفسه ولا يضعه حال القراءة على الأرض مفتوحا، بل يحمله بيديه ويقرأ منه. ولا يقرأ حتى يستأذن الشيخ. ذكره الخطيب عن جماعة من السلف وقال: يجب أن لا يقرأ حتى يأذن له الشيخ.

(١٩٣) ولا يقرأ عند شغل قلب الشيخ أو ملله أو غمه أو غضبه أو جوعه أو عطشه أو نعاسه أو استيفازه أو تعبه.

(194) If he sees that the teacher would rather stop, he should cut things short and not force the teacher to tell him to be brief. If the teacher's preference has not become apparent to the student, so that the teacher has commanded him to be brief, he should halt wherever the teacher commanded him; he should not ask permission to recite more. If a certain amount has been assigned to him, he should not go beyond it. No student should tell another to shorten his recitation, except with the teacher's permission or when it is apparent that the teacher would prefer it.

(195) **Rule Twelve:** When his turn comes, he should ask the teacher permission, as we have mentioned. When the teacher gives it to him, the student should say, "I take refuge in God from Satan the accursed one." Then, having invoked God and praised Him, he should bless the Prophet, his family, and his companions. Finally, he should pray for his teacher, his parents, his elders, himself, and the rest of the Muslims. Thus should he do whenever he begins to recite a lesson, repeat it, read it, or collate [the readings of his book with those of another] in the teacher's presence or absence. However, he should specifically mention the teacher in his prayer when he is about read to him.

(196) He should ask God's mercy on the author of the book when he reads it. When the student prays for the teacher, he should say, "May God be pleased with you," or, "with our teacher and imam," or something similar referring to the teacher. Having finished the lesson, he should again pray for the teacher. The teacher also should pray for the student whenever the latter prays for him. If the student from ignorance or forgetfulness neglects to begin as we have described, the teacher should alert him, teach him how, and remind him, for this is one of the most important rules of conduct. A Prophetic tradition has been transmitted about beginning important matters with praise of God, and this is one of them.

(197) **Rule Thirteen:** He should encourage the other students to acquire knowledge and guide them to where it may be found. He should dispel from them the anxieties that distract from its acquisition and should lighten its burden for them. He should discuss with them the ideas, rules, and unusual things he has learned and give them good advice about religion, for in this way his heart will be illuminated and his deeds righteous. He who gives to others grudgingly, his knowledge will not hold firm; even if it holds firm, it will not bear fruit. Many of the early Muslims put this to the test. He should not exalt himself over them or become conceited about the excellence of his mind; he should rather praise God for his learning and seek more of it from Him by constantly thanking Him.

(١٩٤) وإذا رأى الشيخ قد آثر الوقوف اقتصر، ولا يحوجه إلى قوله «اقتصر»، وإن لم يظهر له ذلك فأمره بالاقتصار اقتصر حيث أمره ولا يستزيده. وإذا عين له قدرا فلا يتعداه، ولا يقول طالب لغيره «اقتصر» إلا بإذن الشيخ أو ظهور إيثاره ذلك.

(١٩٥) الثاني عشر: إذا حضرت نوبته استأذن الشيخ كما ذكرناه، فإذا أذن له استعاذ بالله من الشيطان الرجيم ثم يسمي الله تعالى ويحمده ويصلي على النبي ﷺ وعلى آله وصحبه، ثم يدعو للشيخ ولوالديه ولمشايخه ولنفسه ولسائر المسلمين. وكذلك يفعل كلما شرع في قراءة درس أو تكراره أو مطالعته أو مقابلته في حضور الشيخ أو في غيبته، إلا أنه يخص الشيخ بذكره في الدعاء عند قراءته عليه.

(١٩٦) ويترحم على مصنف الكتاب عند قراءته، وإذا دعا الطالب للشيخ قال: ورضي الله عنكم أو عن شيخنا وإمامنا ونحو ذلك، ويقصد به الشيخ، وإذا فرغ من الدرس دعا للشيخ أيضا، ويدعو الشيخ أيضا للطالب كلما دعا له، فإن ترك الطالب الاستفتاح بما ذكرناه جهلا أو نسيانا نبهه عليه وعلمه إياه وذكره به فإنه من أهم الآداب، وقد ورد الحديث في ابتداء الأمور المهمة بحمد الله تعالى وهذا منها.

(١٩٧) الثالث عشر: أن يرغب بقية الطلبة في التحصيل ويدلهم على مظانه ويصرف عنهم الهموم المشغلة عنه ويهون عليهم مؤنته، ويذاكرهم بما حصله من الفوائد والقواعد والغرائب وينصحهم بالدين، فبذلك يستنير قلبه ويزكو عمله. ومن بخل عليهم لم يثبت علمه، وإن ثبت لم يثمر، وقد جرب ذلك جماعة من السلف. ولا يفخر عليهم أو يعجب بجودة ذهنه، بل يحمد الله تعالى على ذلك ويستزيده منه بدوام شكره.

Chapter Four

Rules of Conduct to Be Observed with Books, Which Are the Tool of Knowledge: How They Should Be Corrected and Pointed, Carried and Set Down, Bought, Borrowed or Copied, and Other Matters—Containing Eleven Rules

(198) **Rule One:** The seeker of knowledge should set his mind to acquiring the books he requires by purchase, to the extent that it is possible; if that is not possible, then by renting or borrowing them, for books are the tool of education. But he should not make acquiring a multitude of books his share of knowledge, and collecting them his portion of understanding, as do many claimants to knowledge of law and hadith. How well the poet spoke!

If you are not one who has memorized and can recall,
your book-collecting is useless.

(199) If the student can purchase books, he should not occupy himself with copying them. He should not occupy himself with constant copying, except insofar as he cannot buy the book because he does not have its price or the fee for having it copied. A student should not be overly concerned with the beauty of the book's writing, only with its being correct or with correcting it. He should not borrow a book when he can buy it or rent it.

(200) **Rule Two:** It is commendable to lend books to people to whom no harm will come from the books and from whom no harm will come to the books. Some authorities disapproved of lending books, but the first opinion is preferable inasmuch as lending books promotes knowledge and lending itself brings merit and reward. . . .

(201) The borrower should thank the lender and reward him well. The borrower should not needlessly prolong the book's stay with him. He should return it when he is done with it. He should not withhold it if the owner asks for it or he no longer needs it. He must not make corrections in the book without the owner's permission; he must not make notes in the margin or write in the blank space before or after the text unless he knows that the owner approves. It is like what the hadith scholar writes on a portion he has heard or has written down. He should

الباب الرابع

في الآداب مع الكتب التي هي آلة العلم وما يتعلق بتصحيحها وضبطها وحملها و وضعها وشرائها وعاريتها ونسخها وغير ذلك وفيه أحد عشر نوعا.

(١٩٨) الأول: ينبغي لطالب العلم أن يعتني بتحصيل الكتب المحتاج إليها ما أمكنه شراء وإلا فإجارة أو عارية، لأنها آلة التحصيل. ولا يجعل تحصيلها وكثرتها حظه من العلم وجمعها نصيبه من الفهم كما يفعله كثير من المنتحلين للفقه والحديث. وقد أحسن القائل.

إذا لم تكن حافظا واعيا   فجمعك للكتب لا ينفع

(١٩٩) وإذا أمكن تحصيلها شراء، لم يشتغل بنسخها. ولا ينبغي أن يشتغل بدوام النسخ إلا فيما يتعذر عليه تحصيله لعدم ثمنه أو أجرة استنساخه. ولا يهتم المشتغل بالمبالغة في تحسين الخط وإنما يهتم بتصحيحه وتصحيحه، ولا يستعير كتابا مع إمكان شرائه أو إجارته.

(٢٠٠) الثاني: يستحب إعارة الكتب لمن لا ضرر عليه فيها ممن لا ضرر منه بها، وكره قوم عاريتها، والأول أولى لما فيه من الإعانة على العلم مع ما في مطلق العارية من الفضل والأجر . . . .

(٢٠١) وينبغي للمستعير أن يشكر للمعير ذلك ويجزيه خيرا. ولا يطيل مقامه عنده من غير حاجة، بل يرده إذا قضى حاجته ولا يحبسه إذا طلبه المالك أو استغنى عنه. ولا يجوز أن يصلحه بغير إذن صاحبه. ولا يحشيه ولا يكتب شيئا في بياض فواتحه أو خواتمه إلا إذا علم رضا صاحبه، وهو كما يكتبه المحدث على جزء

not make a rough copy of it, lend it to someone else, or entrust it to someone else unnecessarily where it is legally permissible. He should not copy from it without the owner's permission.

(202) If the book has been donated as an endowment for anyone who can benefit from it, not a specific person, there is no harm in his copying from it with caution nor in his correcting it if he is qualified. But it is good for him to ask permission from the administrator of the endowment. If he copies from the book with the permission of the owner or administrator, he should not write from it with the sheet of paper inside the book or on its writing. He should not place the inkwell on the book or move the inked pen over the book's writing. . . .

(203) **Rule Three:** When he copies from the book or reads it, he should not put it on the floor spread out and unfolded; he should put it between two books, two things, or on the customary bookstand so as not to hasten the tearing of its cord. When he puts books in a place in a row, let them be on a bookstand, a wooden shelf, or the like. It is best that there be a space between it and the floor; he should not put books on the floor, lest they become damp or decay.

(204) When he puts books onto a wooden shelf or the like, he should put something over them or under them to prevent their bindings from becoming worn, and he should do likewise between the books and any wall or other object that touches them or supports them. . . .

(205) He should not use a book as a place for storing unbound fascicles or anything else, nor should he use it as a pillow, fan, press, cushion, backrest, insect swatter, or the like, particularly if it is of paper, for these things are more damaging to paper.

(206) He should not fold over the edge or corner of the page or use a stick or something rough as a bookmark: he should use a paper or the like. If he uses his fingernail [to mark his place as he reads], he should not press hard with it. . . .

(207) **Rule Four:** When he borrows a book, he should examine it when he is about to take it and when he returns it. When he buys a book, he should look at its beginning, end, middle, and the sequence of its chapters and fascicles. He should flip through its leaves and weigh the book's correctness. Something that will render it probable that the book is correct if there is not enough time to examine it is what al-Shāfiᶜī said: "If you see that the book contains additions or corrections, judge that it is correct." One authority said, "A book does not give light until it becomes darkened," by which he meant that it receives corrections.

سمعه أو كتبه، ولا يسوده ولا يعيره غيره ولا يودعه لغير ضرورة حيث يجوز شرعا ولا ينسخ منه بغير إذن صاحبه.

(٢٠٢) فإن كان الكتاب وَقْفا على من ينتفع به غير معيّن، فلا بأس بالنسخ منه مع الاحتياط ولا بإصلاحه ممن هو أهل لذلك، وحسن أن يستأذن الناظر فيه. وإذا نسخ منه بإذن صاحبه أو ناظره فلا يكتب منه والقرطاس في بطنه أو على كتابته، ولا يضع المحبرة عليه ولا يمر بالقلم الممدود فوق كتابته. . . .

(٢٠٣) الثالث: إذا نسخ من الكتاب أو طالعه فلا يضعه على الأرض مفروشا منشورا، بل يجعله بين كتابين أو شيئين أو كرسي الكتب المعروف، يكلا يسرع تقطيع حبله. وإذا وضعها في مكان مصفوفة، فلتكن على كرسي أو تخت خشب أو نحوه، والأولى أن يكون بينه وبين الأرض خلو، ولا يضعها على الأرض يكلا تتندى أو تَبْلى.

(٢٠٤) وإذا وضعها على خشب ونحوه، جعل فوقها أو تحتها ما يمنع تأكل جلودها به، وكذلك يجعل بينها وبين ما يصادفها أو يسندها من حائط أو غيره. . . .

(٢٠٥) ولا يجعل الكتاب خزانة للكراريس أو غيرها، ولا مخدة ولا مروحة ولا مكبسا ولا مسندا ولا متكأ ولا مقتلة للبق وغيره، ولا سيما في الورق فهو على الورق أشد.

(٢٠٦) ولا يطوي حاشية الورقة أو زاويتها، ولا يعلم بعود أو شيء جاف بل بورقة أو نحوها. وإذا ظفر فلا يكبس ظفره قويا. . . .

(٢٠٧) الرابع: إذا استعار كتابا فينبغي له أن يتفقده عند إرادة أخذه ورده. وإذا اشترى كتابا تعهد أوله وآخره ووسطه وترتيب أبوابه وكراريسه وتصفح أوراقه واعتبر صحته. ومما يغلب على الظن صحته إذا ضاق الزمان عن تفتيشه كما قاله الشافعي (رضي الله عنه) قال: إذا رأيت الكتاب فيه إلحاق وإصلاح، فاشهد له بالصحة. وقال بعضهم: لا يضيء الكتاب حتى يظلم. يريد إصلاحه.

(208) **Rule Five:** Whenever he copies something from books of religious learning he should be in a state of ritual purity, facing the direction of Mecca, clean of body and clothes, and using clean ink. He should begin each book by writing, "In the name of God, the Merciful, the Compassionate." If the book begins with an opening discourse including praise of God and a blessing on His Messenger, he should write that discourse after the words, "In the name of God, the Merciful, the Compassionate." If there is no such preface, he himself should write the praise of God and a blessing on His Messenger after the words, "In the name of God, the Merciful, the Compassionate."

(209) Then he should write what is in the book. He should do likewise at the conclusion of the book or at the end of each volume after he writes, "End of Volume One," or, "End of Volume Two," for example, and, "There Follows Volume . . . " if the book is not finished. If the book is complete, he should write, "The Book *N.* Is Complete." These things are very useful.

(210) Whenever he writes the name of God, he should follow it with a declaration of God's greatness, such as "the Exalted" or "the Highly Praised," or "the Mighty and Lofty," or "the Holy."

(211) Whenever he writes the name of the Prophet, he should follow it with the words, "May God bless him and grant him peace." He should also pronounce this blessing with his tongue. . . .

(212) Whenever he comes to the name of a companion of the Prophet, especially the major ones, he should write, "May God be pleased with him." He should not write the words of blessing and peace for anyone but the prophets and the angels, only following them. Whenever he comes to the name of a pious early Muslim (*salaf*), he should do likewise or write, "May God have mercy on him," especially the imams, dignitaries, and guides of Islam.

(213) **Rule Six:** He should avoid writing small in copying. Handwriting is a sign, and the clearest kind is the best. Whenever a certain early Muslim saw a small handwriting, he used to say, "This is the handwriting of someone who is not sure of having a follower from God." One scholar has said, "Write what will be of use to you when you need it; do not write what you will be unable to use when you need it." He meant when you are old and weak-sighted. Some itinerant scholars intentionally write small to lighten their load. Although this is a good intention, the benefit lost in the end is greater than the benefit gained by having a light load.

(٢٠٨) الخامس: إذا نسخ شيئا من كتب العلوم الشرعية، فينبغي أن يكون على طهارة مستقبل القبلة طاهر البدن والثياب بحبر طاهر، ويبتدئ كل كتاب بكتابة « بسم الله الرحمن الرحيم » فإن كان الكتاب مبدوءاً فيه بخطبة تتضمن حمد الله تعالى والصلاة على رسوله، كتبها بعد البسملة؛ وإلا كتب هو ذلك بعدها، ثم كتب ما في الكتاب.

(٢٠٩) وكذلك يفعل في ختم الكتاب أو آخر كل جزء منه بعد ما يكتب آخر الجزء الأول أو الثاني مثلا، ويتلوه كذا وكذا إن لم يكن تم الكتاب، ويكتب إذا كمل تم الكتاب الفلاني، ففي ذلك فوائد كثيرة.

(٢١٠) وكلما كتب اسم الله تعالى، أتبعه بالتعظيم، مثل: تعالى أو سبحانه أو عز وجل أو تقدس ونحو ذلك.

(٢١١) وكلما كتب اسم النبي ﷺ كتب بعد: الصلاة عليه والسلام عليه، ويصلي هو عليه بلسانه أيضا . . . .

(٢١٢) وإذا مر بذكر الصحابي، لا سيما الأكابر منهم، كتب « رضي الله عنه » ولا يكتب « الصلاة والسلام » لأحد غير الأنبياء والملائكة إلا تبعا لهم. وكلما مر بذكر أحد من السلف فعل ذلك أو كتب « رحمه الله » ولا سيما الأئمة الأعلام وهداة الإسلام.

(٢١٣) السادس: ينبغي أن يجتنب الكتابة الدقيقة في النسخ، فإن الخط علامة فأبينه أحسنه. وكان بعض السلف إذا رأى خطا دقيقا قال: هذا خط من لا يوقن بالخلف من الله تعالى. وقال بعضهم: اكتب ما ينفعك وقت حاجتك إليه، ولا تكتب ما لا تنتفع به وقت الحاجة. والمراد وقت الكبر وضعف البصر. وقد يقصد بعض السفارة بالكتابة الدقيقة خفة المحمل، فهذا وإن كان قصدا صحيحا إلا أن المصلحة الفائتة به في آخر الأمر أعظم من المصلحة الحاصلة بخفة الحمل.

(214) Writing with tannate ink is preferable to writing with lamp-black ink because it is more permanent.[62]

(215) It has also been said that the pen should not be so stiff as to hinder the flow, nor so soft that it quickly becomes worn.

(216) Someone[63] once said: "If you want your handwriting to be good, lengthen your pen's paring and make it fat; cut your nib obliquely, inclining it to the right."

(217) Let the knife be very sharp and specifically for sharpening pens and scraping paper; let it not be used for anything else. Let the thing on which the pen's nib is cut be very hard. The experts recommend very dry Persian reeds and hard, polished ebony.

(218) **Rule Seven:** When the student corrects a book by collating it with a sound original or with a teacher, the student should add vowel points to anything confusing, dot ambiguous letters, indicate the correct reading of whatever is uncertain, and look for places that need correction. If something in the text of the book needs correction or explanation in the margin, he should do so and write a sign over it, and similarly if a word needs to be spelled out at length or given a detailed explanation. For example, if the name Ḥarīz occurs in the text, he can say in the margin, "It is spelled with a *ḥāʾ* that has no dots, then a *rāʾ*, then a *yāʾ* (the last letter of the alphabet), then a *zāy.*" Or, [if the correct reading is Jarīr, he can say,] "It is with a *jīm,* then a *yāʾ* (the final letter of the alphabet) between two undotted *rāʾ*s. . . ."[64]

(219) **Rule Eight:** If he wants to add a marginal reference to another text or correct an omission (this is called *laḥq*), he should make a sign at its place turned slightly in the direction of the correction (the right is preferable if possible). Then he should write the addition starting opposite the sign, writing upwards on the page, not downwards, since there might be another addition to write in the margin after it. He should make the tops of the letters point to the right, regardless of whether the marginal note is to the right of the text or to the left of it.

(220) He should determine the number of lines that have fallen out before he writes them. If there are two or more lines, he should make the last line be adjacent the text, if the addition is in the right margin. If it is on the left, he should make the first line adjacent to it.

(٢١٤) والكتابة بالحبر أولى من المداد لأنه أثبت.

(٢١٥) قالوا: ولا يكون القلم صلبا جدا فيمنع سرعة الجري، ولا رخوا فيسرع إليه الجفا.

(٢١٦) وقال بعضهم: إذا أردت أن يجود خطك فأطل جلفتك وأسمنها، وحرف قَطّتك وأيمنها.

(٢١٧) ولتكن السكين حادة جدا لبراية الأقلام وكشط الورق خاصة، ولا تستعمل في غير ذلك. وليكن ما يُقَطّ عليه القلم صلبا جدا، وهم يحمدون القصب الفارسي اليابس جدا والآبنوس الصلب الصقل.

(٢١٨) السابع: إذا صحح الكتاب بالمقابلة على أصله الصحيح أو على شيخ فينبغي له أن يشكل المشكل ويعجم المستعجم ويضبط الملتبس ويتفقد مواضع التصحيح. إذا احتاج ضبطه ما في متن الكتاب إلى ضبطه في الحاشية وبيانه فعل وكتب عليه بيانا، وكذا إن احتاج إلى ضبطه مبسوطا في الحاشية وبيان تفصيله مثل أن يكون في المتن اسم حريز فيقول في الحاشية هو بالحاء المهملة وراء بعدها وبالياء الخاتمة بعدها زاي، أو هو بالجيم والياء الخاتمة بين رائين مهملتين وشبه ذلك. . . .

(٢١٩) الثامن: إذا أراد تخريج شيء في الحاشية، ويسمى اللحق بفتح الحاء، علّم له في موضعه بخط منعطف قليلا إلى جهة التخريج وجهة اليمين أولى إن أمكن، ثم يكتب التخريج من محاذاة العلامة صاعدا إلى أعلى الورقة لا نازلا إلى أسفلها لاحتمال تخريج آخر بعده؛ ويجعل رؤوس الحروف إلى جهة اليمين سواء كان في جهة يمين الكتابة أم يسارها.

(٢٢٠) وينبغي أن يحسب الساقط وما يجيء منه من الأسطر قبل أن يكتبها، فإن كان سطرين أو أكثر جعل آخر سطر منها يلي الكتابة إن كان التخريج عن يمينها، وإن كان التخريج عن يسارها جعل أول الأسطر مما يليها.

(221) He should not allow the book's text and any marginal lines to come into contact; he should leave a space so that erasure is possible several times if necessary. At the end of the marginal correction he should write "correct." After "correct," some people write the word in the text that follows the words in the margin, as a guide to how the paragraph continues.

(222) **Rule Nine:** There is no harm in the student's writing marginalia, useful information, or important notes in the margins of a book that he owns; however, to distinguish this from a correction to the text of the book, he should not write "correct" at the end. Some people write the word "marginal note" or "useful information" over it; others write it at the end. He should only write important information relevant to that book, such as a note about an obscure point, a reservation, an allusion, an error, or the like.

(223) He should not blacken the book by citing unusual cases and applications. He should not so multiply marginalia that they darken the book and obscure its passages to the student.

(224) He should not write between the lines. Some people do this between lines set off by red ink or the like; however, in general, it is best not to do it.

(225) **Rule Ten:** There is no harm in writing chapter, section, and subsection titles in red, for it sets them off more clearly—and likewise the marks separating sections. There is no harm in signaling names, legal schools, dicta, chains of witnesses, types, words, numbers, or the like in red. If he does so, he should explain his conventions at the beginning of the book in order to clarify their meaning to anyone who takes up the book. Many scholars of hadith law, theology and others have marked text in red with the intention of abridgment.

(226) If the chapter, section, and subsection titles we have mentioned are not in red, he should distinguish them from other text by using a thick pen, one with a long slit in the nib, by setting them apart on a line, or the like, so that it is easier to find them when desired.

(227) He should separate paragraphs[65] by a circular mark, a heading, or a thick pen. He should not make the entire text continuous in a single style because of the difficulty this causes in extracting what one wants and the waste of time involved. Only a very foolish person would do so.

(٢٢١) ولا يوصل الكتابة والأسطر بحاشية الورقة، بل يدع مقدارا يحتمل الحك عند حاجته مرات، ثم يكتب في آخر التخريج «صح» وبعضهم يكتب بعد «صح» الكلمة التي تلي آخر الكلام في متن الكتاب علامة على اتصال الكلام.

(٢٢٢) التاسع: لا بأس بكتابة الحواشي والفوائد والتنبيهات المهمة على حواشي كتاب يملكه ولا يكتب في آخره «صح»، فرقا بينه وبين التخريج، وبعضهم يكتب عليه «حاشية» أو «فائدة» وبعضهم يكتبه في آخرها ولا يكتب إلا الفوائد المهمة المتعلقة بذلك الكتاب مثل تنبيه على إشكال أو احتراز أو رمز أو خطأ ونحو ذلك.

(٢٢٣) ولا يسوّده بنقل المسائل والفروع الغريبة، ولا يكثر الحواشي كثرة تظلم الكتاب أو يضيع مواضعها على طالبها.

(٢٢٤) ولا ينبغي الكتابة بين الأسطر وقد فعله بعضهم بين الأسطر المفرقة بالحمرة وغيرها وترك ذلك أولى مطلقا.

(٢٢٥) العاشر: لا بأس بكتابة الأبواب والتراجم والفصول بالحمرة، فانه أظهر في البيان وفي فواصل الكلام، وكذلك لا بأس به على أسماء ومذاهب أو أقوال أو طرق أو أنواع أو لغات أو أعداد ونحو ذلك، ومتى فعل ذلك بيّن اصطلاحه في فاتحة الكتاب ليفهم الخائض فيه معانيها. وقد رمز بالأحمر جماعة من المحدثين والفقهاء والأصوليين وغيرهم لقصد الاختصار.

(٢٢٦) فإن لم يكن ما ذكرناه من الأبواب والفصول والتراجم بالحمرة، أتى بما يميزه عن غيره من تغليظ القلم وطول المشق واتحاده في السطر ونحو ذلك ليسهل الوقوف عليه عند قصده.

(٢٢٧) وينبغي أن يفصل بين كل كلامين بدائرة أو بترجمة أو قلم غليظ، ولا يوصل الكتابة كلها على طريق واحدة لما فيه من عسر استخراج المقصود يضيع الزمان فيه، ولا يفعل ذلك إلا غبي جدا.

(228) **Section Eleven:** People have said that striking out is better than rubbing out, especially in books of hadith. Rubbing out creates suspicion and ignorance of what was there or was written, and, because it takes longer, it wastes time. Also it is more dangerous, because sometimes one pierces the paper and spoils what one penetrates to, so that one weakens it. However, if it is just a matter of removing a dot or vowel point, rubbing out is better.

(229) When the student corrects a book by reading it to the teacher or collating it, he should mark the stopping point with words such as *balagha* ("he has reached"), *balaghtu* ("I have reached)", *balagha al-ʿarḍ* ("the review has reached"), or words of similar meaning. If it is a matter of listening to hadith, he should write, "This is where he reached on the first date," or "second," and so forth, specifying the number. Al-Khaṭīb says that when a corrector corrects something, he should spread shavings of teak or another wood. He disapproves of sprinkling dust [to dry the ink].

Chapter Five

Rules of Conduct for Residing in Colleges for Students and Those Who Have Completed Their Studies, Colleges Being Their Usual Places of Residence—Consisting of Eleven Rules

(230) **Rule One:** As far as possible, he should choose for himself a college (*madrasah*) whose founder was closest to piety and farthest from undesirable religious innovations, so that he can be reasonably sure that the college and its endowment are from a licit source of income and that any stipend he receives is from untainted funds. The need for caution about one's residence is as great as the need for caution about one's food, clothing, and other things.

(231) It is preferable to avoid as far as possible anything established by rulers whose state when building and endowing is unknown. As for those whose state is known, one can judge their affairs by the evidence. However, it is rare for all of their aides to be free from wrongdoing and oppression.

(٢٢٨) الحادي عشر: قالوا الضرب أولى من الحك لا سيما في كتب الحديث، لأن فيه تهمة وجهالة فيما كان أوكتب، ولأن زمانه أكثر فيضيع، وفعله أخطر فربما ثقب الورقة وأفسد ما ينفذ إليه فأضعفها، فإن كان إزالة نقطة أو شكلة ونحو ذلك فالحك أولى.

(٢٢٩) وإذا صحح الكاتب على الشيخ أو في المقابلة، عَلّم على موضع وقوفه «بلغ أو بلغت» أو «بلغ العرض» أو غير ذلك مما يفيد معناه. فإن كان ذلك في سماع الحديث كتب: «بلغ في الميعاد الأول أو الثاني» إلى آخرها فيُعيّن عَدَده. قال الخطيب فيما إذا أصلح شيئا ينشر المصلح بنحاتة الساج أو غيره من الخشب وينفي الشريب.

الباب الخامس

في آداب سكنى المدارس للمنتهي والطالب لأنها مساكنهم في الغالب وهو أحد عشر نوعا

(٢٣٠) الأول: أن ينتخب لنفسه من المدارس بقدر الإمكان ما كان واقفه أقرب إلى الورع وأبعد عن البدع بحيث يغلب على ظنه أن المدرسة ووقفها من جهة حلال، وأن معلومها، إن تناوله، من طيب المال؛ لأن الحاجة إلى الاحتياط في المسكن كالحاجة إليه في المأكل والملبس وغيره.

(٢٣١) ومهما أمكن التنزه عما أنشأه الملوك الذين لم يعلم حالهم في بنائها ووقفها، فهو أولى، وأما من علم حاله فالإنسان على بينة من أمره مع أنه قل أن يخلو جميع أعوانهم عن ظلم وعسف.

(232) **Rule Two:** The professor at the college should possess pre-eminence, merit, piety, intellect, dignity, loftiness, honor, and uprightness. He should possess love toward the eminent and affection for the weak. He should attract pupils, encourage diligent students, dismiss triflers, and act equitably toward researchers. He should be eager to benefit others and assiduous in teaching. The rest of the rules for his behavior have already been given.

(233) If he has an assistant, let him be chosen from among the most upright of the outstanding and the most outstanding of the upright, patient with students' characters, eager for them to benefit and learn from him, and diligent in the task of tutoring them. . . .

(234) The assistant at the college should give priority to tutoring its students over any others at the regular time specified, especially if he is receiving a stipend for his assistantship, for this is what he has been appointed to do as long as he is an assistant. Tutoring others is beyond the call of duty, or it is a collective duty.[66] He should inform the professor or administrator of any student who gives promise of success, so that he can be given more aid and encouragement. The assistant should require the students to recite what they have memorized, if no one else has been appointed for this, and he should repeat to them the parts of the professor's lectures that are difficult for them to understand—that is why he is called a "repeater."

(235) If the founder stipulated that what has been memorized should be subjected to examination every month or every season in front of everyone, he should reduce the amount to be presented by those who have a talent for research, reflection, reading, and disputation, because rigid adherence to the same writ distracts from thinking, which is the mother of education and understanding.[67]

(236) Beginners and finished scholars should each be asked to do what suits their condition and mind. The rest of the rules of conduct for the teacher with the student have been discussed above.

(٢٣٢) الثاني: أن يكون المدرس بهاذا رياسة وفضل وديانة وعقل ومهابة وجلالة وناموس وعدالة ومحبة في الفضلاء وعطف على الضعفاء، يقرب المحصلين ويرغب المشتغلين ويبعد اللغائين وينصف الباحثين، حريصا على النفع مواظبا على الإفادة، وقد تقدم سائرآدابه.

(٢٣٣) فإن كان له معيد فليكن من صلحاء الفضلاء وفضلاء الصلحاء، صبورا على أخلاق الطلبة، حريصا على فائدتهم وانتفاعهم به، قائما على وظيفة أشغالهم. . . .

(٢٣٤) وينبغي للمعيد بالمدرسة أن يقدم أشغال أهلها على غيرهم في الوقت المعتاد أو المشروط إن كان يتناول معلوم الإعادة، لأنه معين عليه ما دام معيدا، أو أشغال غيرهم نفل أو فرض كفاية، وأن يعلم المدرس أو الناظر بمن يرجى فلاحه ليزاد ما يستعين به ويشرح صدره، وأن يطالبهم بعرض محفوظاتهم إن لم يعين لذلك غيره ويعيد لهم ما توقف فهمه عليهم من دروس المدرس ولهذا يسمى معيدا.

(٢٣٥) وإذا شرط الواقف استعراض المحفوظ كل شهر أو كل فصل على الجميع، خفف قدر العرض على من له أهلية البحث والفكر والمطالعة والمناظرة لأن الجمود على نفس المسطور يشغل عن الفكر الذي هو أم التحصيل والتفقه.

(٢٣٦) وأما المبتدئون والمنتهون فَيُطالَب كل منهم على ما يليق بحاله وذهنه وقد تقدم سائرآداب العالم مع الطلبة.

(237) **Rule Three:** He should acquaint himself with the stipulations [of the school's endowment] so that he can fulfill them. The more he can keep aloof from the school stipend the better, especially in schools whose provisions have been made narrow and whose salaries have been made strait—most scholars of our day have suffered from this. We pray to God for contentment with His kindness and generosity in prosperity and health! If obtaining his daily bread makes him lose time and prevents him from attending fully to his studies, or if he has no other craft to sustain himself and his dependents, there is no harm in his thus seeking aid, with the intention of devoting himself completely to acquiring knowledge so that people may benefit from it, but he should be careful to fulfill all of the school's stipulations.

(238) He should call himself to account for this. Yet he should not feel distressed[68] if he seeks [remuneration] from him or is criticized for it; he should consider it a blessing from God and should thank God for having granted him someone whom He has charged with performing that which saves him from the snare of the forbidden and sin.[69] The smart man is one who has high aspirations and a lofty soul.

(239) **Rule Four:** If the founder has restricted residence in the school to stipendiaries[70] only, no one else may live there; if anyone else does so, he is being disobedient and unjust. If the founder made no such restriction, there is no harm in it if the resident is worthy.

(240) If a nonstipendiary resides in the school, he should be courteous to its people and give them priority over himself in what they need from the school. He should attend the school's teaching, that being the greatest of the religious purposes for which it was built and endowed; for in the course of this teaching the Qurʾān is recited, prayers are offered for the founder, and gatherings are held for the remembrance of God and the transmission of knowledge. If the resident abandons this, he has abandoned the purpose for which his residence was built, and this obviously violates the founder's intent. . . .

(241) **Rule Five:** He should not busy himself there with socializing and companionship. The resident should be content with the coinage[71] and the Friday sermon; indeed, he should devote himself to his affairs and education and the purpose for which the college was built. He should completely avoid socializing there because, as we have already said, it spoils the atmosphere and wastes money.

(٢٣٧) الثالث: أن يتعرف بشروطها ليقوم بحقوقها، ومهما أمكنه التنزه عن معلوم المدارس فهو أولى، لا سيما في المدارس التي ضيق في شروطها وشدد في وظائفها كما قد بلي أكثر فقهاء الزمان به نسأل الله تعالى القناعة بمنه وكرمه في خير وعافية. فإن كان تحصيله البلغة يضيع زمانه ويعطله عن تمام الأشغال، أو لم يكن له حرفة أخرى تحصل بلغته وبلغة عياله فلا بأس بالاستعانة بذلك بنية التفرغ لأخذ العلم ونفع الناس به ولكن يتحرى القيام بجميع شروطها.

(٢٣٨) ويحاسب نفسه على ذلك ولا يجد في نفسه إذا طلب منه أو وبخ عليه بل يعد ذلك نعمة من الله تعالى ويشكره عليه إذ وفق له من يكلفه القيام بما يخلصه من ربقة الحرام والإثم، واللبيب من كان ذا همة عالية ونفس سامية.

(٢٣٩) الرابع: إذا حصر الواقف سكنى المدرسة على المرتبين بها دون غيرهم لم يسكن فيها غيرهم، فإن فعل كان عاصيا ظالما بذلك. وإن لم يحصر الواقف ذلك فلا بأس إذا كان الساكن أهلا لها.

(٢٤٠) واذا سكن في المدرسة غير مرتب بها فليكرم أهلها ويقدمهم على نفسه فيما يحتاجون إليه منها، ويحضر درسها لأنه أعظم الشعائر المقصودة ببنائها ووقفها لما فيه من القراءة والدعاء للواقف والاجتماع على مجلس الذكر وتذاكر العلم، فإذا ترك الساكن فيها ذلك فقد ترك المقصود ببناء مسكنه الذى هو فيه وذلك يخالف مقصود الواقف ظاهرا. . . .

(٢٤١) الخامس: أن لا يشتغل فيها بالمعاشرة والصحبة، ويرضى من سكنها بالسكة والخطبة، بل يقبل على شأنه وتحصيله. وما بنيت المدرسة له يقطع العشرة فيها جملة لأنها تفسد الحال وتضيع المال كما تقدم.

(242) The smart student makes the college a way station where he fulfills his objective and then leaves. If he befriends someone who aids him to achieve his goals, helps him complete his studies, encourages him to inquire more, and lessens his grief and fatigue—someone of whose piety, trustworthiness, and good character as a companion he can be confident—there is no harm in it; nay, it is good thing, if he gives him good advice for God's sake and is not shallow and frivolous. . . .

(243) Colleges and their endowments were not established merely for residence and socializing or merely for devotion to prayer and fasting like Sufi hostels. They were established to help people acquire learning, devote themselves to it, and isolate themselves from distractions in the dwellings of their family and kin. The man of intellect knows that his most blessed day is the day in which he increases in virtue and knowledge, to the annoyance and dismay of his enemies among the jinn and mankind.

(244) **Rule Six:** He should honor the college's residents by greeting each of them and showing affection and respect. He should respect their claim to neighborliness, companionship, and brotherhood in religion and calling, for they are the practitioners of learning, its transmitters, and its seekers.

(245) He should disregard their shortcomings, forgive their lapses, veil their imperfections, thank those who are charitable, and forgive those who offend.

(246) If they are such bad neighbors and evildoers that he cannot concentrate, he should leave the college in order to calm his heart and concentrate his mind. Once his heart has become calm, he should not move about needlessly, for that is very undesirable for beginning students. It is even more undesirable, as we have already said, for them to shift from book to book, for it is a sign of discontent, trifling, and lack of promise.

(247) **Rule Seven:** He should, if possible, choose for his neighbor the most upright, diligent, generous natured, and honorable of people, so that his neighbor may be an aide in his enterprise. As the proverbs say: "Neighbor before house, and companion before road." And, "Character is a great thief." And, "Like imitates like."

(٢٤٢) واللبيب المحصل يجعل المدرسة منزلا يقضي وطره منه ثم يرتحل عنه، فإن صاحب من يعينه على تحصيل مقاصده ويساعده على تكميل فوائده وينشطه على زيادة الطلب ويخفض عنه ما يجد من الضجر والنصب ممن يوثق بدينه وأمانته ومكارم أخلاقه في مصاحبته، فلا بأس بذلك بل هو حسن إذا كان ناصحا له في الله غير لاعب ولا لاه. . . .

(٢٤٣) فإن المدارس وأوقافها لم تجعل لمجرد المقام والعشرة ولا لمجرد التعبد بالصلاة والصيام كالخوانك، بل لتكون معينة على تحصيل العلم والتفرغ له والتجرد عن الشواغل في أوطان الأهل والأقارب. والعاقل يعلم أن أبرك الأيام عليه يوم يزداد فيه فضيلة وعلما ويكسب عدوه من الجن والأنس كربا وغما.

(٢٤٤) السادس: أن يكرم أهل المدرسة التي يسكنها بإفشاء السلام وإظهار المودة والاحترام، ويرعى لهم حق الجيرة والصحبة والأخوة في الدين والحرفة لأنهم أهل العلم وحملته وطلابه.

(٢٤٥) ويتغافل عن تقصيرهم ويغفر زللهم ويستر عوراتهم ويشكر محسنهم ويتجاوز عن مسيئهم.

(٢٤٦) فإن لم يستقر خاطره لسوء جيرتهم وخبث صفاتهم أو لغير ذلك، فليرتحل عنها ساعيا في جمع قلبه واستقرار خاطره. وإذا اجتمع قلبه فلا ينتقل من غير حاجة، فإن ذلك مكروه للمبتدئين جدا، وأشد منه كراهية تنقلهم من كتاب إلى كتاب كما تقدم فإنه علامة على الضجر واللعب وعدم الفلاح.

(٢٤٧) السابع: أن يختار لجواره إن أمكن أصلحهم حالا وأكثرهم اشتغالا وأجودهم طبعا وأصونهم عرضا ليكون معينا له على ما هو بصدده. ومن الأمثال: «الجار قبل الدار، والرفيق قبل الطريق»، و«الطباع سراقة»، و«من دأب الجنس التشبه بجنسه».

(248) High lodgings, for anyone not too weak to climb up to them, are better for the student and his concentration, if the neighbors are sound. We have already cited the words of al-Khaṭīb: "The best place for memorizing is an upstairs room."

(249) As for the weak, the untrustworthy, and those to whom people come for legal opinions and tuition, lower apartments are more appropriate for them.

(250) The stairs close to the door or to the entrance hall are appropriate for the trustworthy. The interior stairs that require one to pass through the grounds of the college are appropriate for unknown or untrustworthy persons.

(251) It is best that no fair-faced person or boy reside in the college without an alert guardian and that no women live in areas where men pass by the doors or that have windows overlooking the courtyard of the college. . . .

(252) **Rule Eight:** If the student's lodging is in the college mosque or in the assembly room and he passes over its mats and carpets, let him take care when he goes up to it that nothing fall from his shoes. He should not allow the soles of his shoes to point in the direction of Mecca, people's faces, or his clothing. Instead, after shaking out his shoes, he should put the sole of one shoe toward the sole of the other. He should not throw his shoes on the floor with force, nor should he leave them where people and visitors are likely to sit, such as the ends of the stone bench.[72] Instead, he should leave them, when he leaves them, under the middle part of it; he should not place them under the mats in the mosque so that they become broken.

(253) If he lodges in the upper rooms, he should walk lightly, lie down lightly, and set heavy objects down carefully, so that he does not disturb anyone below. . . .

(254) **Rule Nine:** He should not make the door of the college his sitting-place. In fact, if it is possible, he should sit down only for some need or rarely because of dejection or worry. He should not sit in the college's entrance hall that is uncovered to the street. Sitting in the street has been forbidden, and this pertains to it or falls under the same heading, especially if he is someone before whom people might feel embarrassed, an object of suspicion, or a frivolous person. It is a place where

(٢٤٨) والمساكن العالية لمن لا يضعف عن الصعود إليها أولى بالمشتغل وأجمع لخاطره إذا كان الجيران صالحين، وقد تقدم قول الخطيب أن الغرف أولى بالحفظ.

(٢٤٩) وأما الضعيف والمتهم ومن يقصد للفتيا والاشتغال عليه، فالمساكن السفلية أولى بهم.

(٢٥٠) والمراقي التي تقرب من الباب أو من الدهليز أولى بالموثوق بهم، والمراقي الداخلة التي يحتاج فيها إلى المرور بأرض المدرسة أولى بالمجهولين والمتهمين.

(٢٥١) والأولى أن لا يسكن المدرسة وسيم الوجه أو صبي ليس له فيها ولي فطن، وأن لا يسكنها نساء في أمكنة تمر الرجال على أبوابها، أو لها كوى تشرف على ساحة المدرسة. . . .

(٢٥٢) الثامن: إذا كان مسكنه في مسجد المدرسة أو في مكان الاجتماع ومروره على حصيره وفرشه، فليتحفظ عند صعوده إليه من سقوط شيء من نعليه، ولا يقابل بأسفلهما القبلة ولا وجوه الناس ولا ثيابه، بل يجعل أسفل أحدهما إلى أسفل الأخرى بعد نفضهما، ولا يلقيهما إلى الأرض بعنف، ولا يتركهما في مظنة مجالس الناس والواردين إليها غالبا كطرف الصفة بل يتركهما إذا تركهما في أسفل الوسط ونحوه، ولا يضعهما تحت الحصير في المسجد بحيث تنكسر.

(٢٥٣) وإذا سكن في البيوت العليا خفف المشي والاستلقاء عليها ووضع ما يثقل كيلا يؤذي من تحته. . . .

(٢٥٤) التاسع: أن لا يتخذ باب المدرسة مجلسا، بل لا يجلس إذا أمكن إلا لحاجة أو في ندرة لقبض أو ضيق صدر، ولا في دهليزها المهتوك إلى الطريق؛ فقد نهي عن الجلوس على الطرقات وهذا منها أو في معناها، لا سيما إن كان ممن

a scholar is likely to enter with his food or effects; he might be embarrassed before the sitter, or he might be put to the trouble of greeting them.[73] It is also a place where the womenfolk of someone attached to the college might enter, and it might trouble and annoy the person. Finally, it involves idleness and vulgarity.

(255) He should not make it a practice to walk around idly in the courtyard of the college when he does not need rest or exercise or is waiting for someone. He should minimize his entries and exits as much as possible, and he should greet whoever is at the door when he passes him.

(256) He should not enter the public ablution room when it is crowded with common folk, except from necessity, for there is an element of vulgarity in doing so. He should wait patiently there and knock on the door lightly three times if it is shut and then open it slowly. He should not use the wall as a stone to purify himself, thereby polluting it, nor should he wipe his filthy hand on the wall.

(257) **Rule Ten:** He should not in passing look into anyone's room through cracks in the door or the like, nor should he turn toward him if the door is open. If he pronounces a greeting, he should pronounce it as he passes, without turning. He should not point frequently at windows, especially if there are women in them.

(258) He should not raise his voice excessively in repeating, calling someone, or discussion, so as not to disturb others. In general, he should lower his voice as much as possible, especially in the presence of worshippers or teachers giving lectures. He should be on guard against treading heavily with clogs, slamming doors, disturbing people when he enters, leaves, goes up, or comes down, knocking unnecessarily hard on the door of the college, or calling from below to someone upstairs unless it is necessary and done in a moderate voice.

(259) If the college is open to the public thoroughfare through a door or window, he should be on guard against taking off his clothes there or uncovering the top of his head unnecessarily.

يستحيا منه أو ممن هو في محل تهمة أو لعب، ولأنها في مظنة دخول فقيه بطعامه وحاجته فربما استحيا من الجالس أو يكلف سلامه عليهم، وفي مظنة دخول نساء من يتعلق بالمدرسة ويشق عليه ذلك ويؤذيه ولأن في ذلك بطالة وتبذلا.

(٢٥٥) ولا يكثر التمشي في ساحة المدرسة بطالا من غير حاجة إلى راحة أو رياضة أو انتظار أحد، ويقلل الدخول والخروج ما أمكنه، ويسلم على من بالباب إذا مر به.

(٢٥٦) ولا يدخل ميضأتها العامة عند الزحام من العامة إلا لضرورة لما فيه من التبذل، ويتأنى عنده ويطرق الباب إن كان مردودا طرقا خفيا ثلاثا ثم يفتحه بتأن، ولا يستجمر بالحائط فينجسه ولا يمسح يده المتنجسة بالحائط أيضا.

(٢٥٧) العاشر: أن لا ينظر في بيت أحد في مروره من شقوق الباب ونحوه، ولا يلتفت إليه إذا كان مفتوحا، وإن سلم سلم وهو مار من غير التفات، ولا يكثر الإشارة إلى الطاقات لا سيما إن كان فيهن نساء.

(٢٥٨) ولا يرفع صوته جدا في تكرار أو نداء أحد أو بحث كيلا يشوش على غيره، بل يخفضه ما أمكنه مطلقا، لا سيما بحضور المصلين أو حضور أهل الدرس. ويتحفظ من شدة وقع القبقاب والعنف في إغلاق الباب وإزعاج المشي في الدخول والخروج والصعود والنزول، وطرق باب المدرسة بشدة لا يحتاج إليها ونداء من بأعلى المدرسة من أسفلها إلا أن يكون بصوت معتدل عند الحاجة.

(٢٥٩) وإذا كانت المدرسة مكشوفة إلى الطريق السالك من باب أو شباك تحفظ فيها عن التجرد عن الثياب وكشف الرأس الطويل من غير حاجة.

(260) He should avoid anything held shameful, such as eating while walking, jesting frequently, extending the sole of his shoe [toward someone], stretching out excessively and leaning on the side and the back of the head, and unseemly laughter and guffawing. He should not climb to the overlooking roof of the college without need or necessity.

(261) **Rule Eleven:** He should arrive at the place of the lecture before the professor. He should not delay until the professor and the class have sat down, so as to oblige them to stand up to return his greeting as is customary. Among them there might be someone with a justifiable reason [for not standing], and he, not knowing his reason, might become angry with him.

(262) The early authorities said that the rule of good conduct with a professor is that the jurists should wait for him, not he for them. Part of the etiquette to be observed in attending a lecture is that one come looking one's best and as clean as possible. Shaykh Abū ʿAmr[74] would exclude any jurist who came to the lecture casually dressed without a turban or with his gown unbuttoned. One should sit, listen, cite passages, respond to questions, discuss, and address people in the proper manner.

(263) The student should not precede the professor in reciting the Qurʾān or in saying "I take refuge in God." If, as is customary, the professor prays at the start of the lecture for those present, those present should respond by praying for the teacher. One of my greatest teachers, a distinguished ascetic, would severely rebuke anyone who neglected to do so.

(264) He should guard himself against sleep, drowsiness, talking, laughter, and such other things as have been discussed previously in the chapter on rules to be observed by the student. The student should not speak between two lectures if the professor concludes the first one with the words, "And God is most knowing," except with the professor's permission. He should not speak about a topic when the professor has begun to speak about another. He should not speak about anything until he considers whether there is any benefit or point to it. He should beware of wrangling and exaggerating in debate. If he becomes excited, he should bridle his ardor with the bridle of silence and patience, obeying the words of the Prophet: "He who avoids wrangling, even when he is right, God will build for him a house in the highest part of paradise." This is

(٢٦٠) ويتجنب ما يعاب كالأكل ماشيا وكلام الهزل غالبا، والبسط بالنعل وفرط التمطي والتمايل على الجنب والقفا، والضحك الفاحش بالقهقهة، ولا يصعد إلى سطحها المشرف من غير حاجة أو ضرورة.

(٢٦١) الحادي عشر: إن يتقدم على المدرس في حضور موضع الدرس ولا يتأخر إلى بعد جلوسه وجلوس الجماعة فيكلفهم المعتاد من القيام ورد السلام وربما فيهم معذور فيجد في نفسه منه ولا يعرف عذره.

(٢٦٢) وقد قال السلف: من الأدب مع المدرس أن ينتظره الفقهاء ولا ينتظرهم. وينبغي أن يتأدب في حضور الدرس بأن يحضره على أحسن الهيئات وأكمل الطهارات. وكان الشيخ أبو عمرو يقطع من يحضر من الفقهاء الدرس مخففا بغير عمامة أو مفكك أزرار الفرجية. ويحسن جلوسه واستماعه وإيراده وجوابه وكلامه وخطابه.

(٢٦٣) ولا يستفتح القراءة والتعوذ قبل المدرس، وإذا دعا المدرس في أول الدرس للحاضرين على العادة أجابه الحاضرون بالدعاء له أيضا، وكان بعض أكابر مشايخي الزهاد الأعلام يزبر تارك ذلك ويغلظ عليه.

(٢٦٤) ويتحفظ من النوم والنعاس والحديث والضحك وغير ذلك مما تقدم في أدب المتعلم، ولا يتكلم بين الدرسين إذا ختم المدرس الأول بقوله «والله اعلم» إلا بإذن منه، ولا يتكلم في مسأله أخذ المدرس الكلام في غيرها، ولا يتكلم بشيء حتى ينظر فيه فائدة وموضعا، ويحذر المماراة في البحث والمغالبة فيه، فإن ثارت نفسه ألجمها بلجام الصمت والصبر والانقياد؛ لما روي عنه ﷺ: من تَرَكَ المراء وهو مُحِقّ بنى

the best way to prevent anger from spreading and hearts from becoming estranged. Each person in attendance should strive for purity of heart toward his companion and freedom from hatred. He should not rise from the lecture with any anger in his soul toward his companion. And when he leaves the lecture, let him say what has been transmitted in a hadith:

(265) "We praise and extol Thee, O God. There is no god but Thee. I ask Thee for forgiveness and repent to Thee. Forgive me my sin, for there is none who forgives sins but Thou."

(266) Here ends, with praise and thanks to God, the *Book of Rules of Conduct.*

Praise Be to God,
First and Last, Outwardly and Inwardly.

May God Bless and Grant Peace to
Our Master Muḥammad and His Family.

الله له بيتا في أعلى الجنة. فإن ذلك أقطع لا نتشار الغضب وأبعد عن منافرة القلوب، ويجتهد كل من الحاضرين على طهارة القلب لصاحبه وخلوه عن الحقد، وأن لا يقوم وفي نفسه منه شيء، وإذا قام من الدرس فليقل ما جاء في الحديث:

(٢٦٥) سبحانك اللّهم وبحمدك ولا إله إلا أنت، أستغفرك وأتوب اليك، فاغفر لي ذنبي، إنه لا يغفر الذنوب إلا أنت.

(٢٦٦) تم كتاب الآدب بحمد لله تعالى ومنه

والحمد لله أولا وآخرا وظاهرا وباطنا

وصلى الله على سيدنا محمد وآله وسلم

Ibn Khaldūn

Selections from *The Muqaddimah*

TRANSLATED FROM THE ARABIC BY

FRANZ ROSENTHAL

◆

Note

This chapter reproduces selected portions of Franz Rosenthal's three-volume annotated translation of Ibn Khaldūn's *Muqaddimah*[1] (hereafter referred to as *Muqaddimah,* Rosenthal trans.). The selections are 2.411–13 (paragraphs 1–5 herein), 2.419–33 (paragraphs 6–49 herein); and 3.288–315 (paragraphs 50–119 herein).

The following minor modifications have been made to the text as first published in the Bollingen series: Section numbers have been eliminated while paragraph numbers running consecutively throughout the selected material have been added in parentheses; annotations have been renumbered; cross-references to other portions of the Rosenthal translation of *Muqaddimah,* along with a few other bibliographical details, have been edited for clarity; and the transliteration style has been brought into conformity with that employed throughout the rest of this volume.

Rosenthal used parentheses throughout his translation to indicate language he added in order to smooth or clarify the reading ("contextual sense supplied"). These parentheses have been retained, though in other pieces included in this volume such interpolations by the translator are indicated by square brackets. References to the Qur'ān in Rosenthal's notes feature additional numbers in parentheses. These refer to the alternate versification found in some editions of the Qur'ān. Note also that A, B, C, etc. in Rosenthal's annotations are sigla used to denote various manuscripts of the *Muqadimah,* described by Rosenthal in his preface (1.xc ff.). In addition, the following abbreviations are used in Rosenthal's notes:

Autobiography = Muḥammad Tāwīt al-Ṭanjī, ed., *al-Taʿrīf bi-Ibn Khaldūn wa-riḥlatuhū gharban wa-sharqan.* Cairo, 1951.

Bombaci = A. Bombaci, "Ostille alla traduzione De Slane della Muqaddimah di Ibn Ḫaldūn," *Annali dell' Istituto Universitario Orientale di Napoli,* N.S. III (1949): 439–72.

Bulaq = Naṣr al-Hūrīnī, ed., *Ibn Khaldūn: Muqaddimah.* Bulaq, 1857.

GAL = C. Brockelmann, *Geschichte der arabischen Literatur.* Weimar, 1898; Berlin, 1902.

GAL, Suppl. = C. Brockelmann, *Geschichte der arabischen Literatur. Supplementbände.* Leiden, 1937–42.

Issawi = C. Issawi, tr., *An Arab Philosophy of History: Selections from the Prolegomena of Ibn Khaldūn of Tunis* (1332–1406). London, 1950.

Paris edition = E. Quatremère, ed., *Prolégomènes d'Ebn-Khaldoun.* Vols. 16–18 of the Notices et Extraits des manuscrits de la Bibliothèque Impériale (Académie des Inscriptions et Belles-Lettres). Paris, 1858.

Prefatory Discussion[2]

On man's ability to think, which distinguishes human beings from animals and which enables them to obtain their livelihood, to co-operate to this end with their fellow men, and to study the Master whom they worship, and the revelations that the Messengers transmitted from Him. God thus caused[3] all animals to obey man and to be in the grasp[4] of his power. Through his ability to think, God gave man superiority over many of His creatures.

Man's ability to think.

(1) It[5] should be known that God distinguished man from all the other animals by an ability to think which He made the beginning of human perfection and the end of man's noble superiority over existing things.

(2) This comes about as follows: Perception—that is, consciousness, on the part of the person who perceives, in his essence of things that are outside his essence—is something peculiar to living beings to the exclusion of all other being[6] and existent things. Living beings may obtain consciousness of things that are outside their essence through the external senses God has given them, that is, the senses of hearing, vision, smell, taste, and touch. Man has this advantage over the other beings that he may perceive things outside his essence through his ability to think, which is something beyond his senses. It is the result of (special) powers placed in the cavities of his brain.[7] With the help of these powers, man takes the pictures of the *sensibilia,* applies his mind to them, and thus abstracts from them other pictures. The ability to think is the occupation with pictures that are beyond sense perception, and the application of the mind to them for analysis and synthesis. This is what is meant by the word *af'idah* "hearts" in the Qur'ān: "He gave you hearing and vision and hearts."[8] *Af'idah* "hearts" is the plural of *fu'ad*. It means here the ability to think.

ابن خلدون

من المقدمة

فصل في الفكر الإنسانى

(١) اعلم أن الله سبحانه وتعالى ميّز البشر عن سائر الحيوانات بالفكر الذي جعله مبأ كماله ونهاية فضله على الكائنات وشرفه.

(٢) وذلك أن الإدراك وهو شعور المدرك في ذاته بما هو خارج عن ذاته هو خاص بالحيوان فقط من بين سائر الكائنات والموجودات. فالحيوانات تشعر بما هو خارج عن ذاتها، بما ركّب الله فيها من الحواس الظاهرة: السمع والبصر والشم والذوق واللمس. ويزيد الإنسان من بينها أنه يدرك الخارج عن ذاته بالفكر الذى وراء حسّه، وذلك بقوى جعلت له في بطون دماغه، ينتزع بها صور المحسوسات، ويجول بذهنه فيها، فيجرد منها صورا أخرى. والفكر هو التصرف في تلك الصور وراء الحسّ وجولان الذهن فيها بالانتزاع والتركيب، وهو معنى الأفئدة في قوله تعالى: ﴿وجَعلَ لكُم السَّمْعَ والأبْصَارَ والأفئِدَةَ﴾ (٢٣:٦٧). والأفئدة جمع فؤاد، وهو هنا الفكر.

(3) The ability to think has several degrees. The first degree is man's intellectual understanding of the things that exist in the outside world in a natural or arbitrary order, so that he may try to arrange them with the help of his own power. This kind of thinking mostly consists of perceptions. It is the discerning intellect,[9] with the help of which man obtains the things that are useful for him and his livelihood, and repels the things that are harmful to him.

(4) The second degree is the ability to think which provides man with the ideas and the behavior needed in dealing with his fellow men and in leading them. It mostly conveys apperceptions, which are obtained one by one through experience, until they have become really useful. This is called the experimental intellect.

(5) The third degree is the ability to think which provides the knowledge, or hypothetical knowledge, of an object beyond sense perception without any practical activity (going with it). This is the speculative intellect. It consists of both perceptions and apperceptions. They are arranged according to a special order, following special conditions, and thus provide some other knowledge of the same kind, that is, either perceptive or apperceptive. Then, they are again combined with something else, and again provide some other knowledge. The end of the process is to be provided with the perception of existence as it is, with its various genera, differences, reasons, and causes. By thinking about these things, (man) achieves perfection in his reality and becomes pure intellect and perceptive soul. This is the meaning of human reality.

. . . .

The sciences (knowledge) of human beings and the sciences (knowledge) of angels.

(6) We observe in ourselves through sound intuition[10] the existence of three worlds.

(7) The first of them is the world of sensual perception. We become aware of it by means of the perception of the senses, which the animals share with us.

(8) Then, we become aware of the ability to think which is a special quality of human beings. We learn from it that the human soul exists. This knowledge is necessitated by the fact that we have in us scientific perceptions which are above the perceptions of the senses. They must thus be considered as another world, above the world of the senses.

(٣) وهو على مراتب: (الأولى) تعقل الأمور المرتبة في الخارج ترتيباً طبيعياً أو وضعياً ليقصد إيقاعها بقدرته. وهذا الفكر أكثره تصورات. وهو العقل التمييزى الذى يحصّل منافعه ومعاشه ويدفع مضاره.

(٤) (الثانية) الفكر الذي يفيد الآراء والآداب في معاملة أبناء جنسه وسياستهم. وأكثرها تصديقات تحصل بالتجربة شيئاً فشيئاً إلى أن تتم الفائدة منها. وهذا هو المسمى بالعقل التجريبى.

(٥) (الثالثة) الفكر الذى يفيد العلم أو الظن بمطلوب وراء الحسّ لا يتعلق به عمل. فهذا هو العقل النظري. وهو تصورات وتصديقات تنتظم انتظاماً خاصاً على شروط خاصة، فتفيد معلوما آخر من جنسها في التصور أو التصديق، ثم ينتظم مع غيره فيفيد علوماً أُخَر كذلك. وغاية إفادته تصور الوجود على ما هو عليه بأجناسه وفصوله وأسبابه وعلله، فيكمل الفكر بذلك في حقيقته ويصير عقلاً محضا ونفسا مدركة، وهو معنى الحقيقة الإنسانية.

. . . .

فصل في علوم البشر وعلوم الملائكة

(٦) إنا نشهد في أنفسنا بالوجدان الصحيح وجود ثلاثة عوالم:

(٧) أولها عالم الحس، ونعتبره بمدارك الحس الذي شاركنا فيه الحيوانات بالإدراك.

(٨) ثم نعتبر الفكر الذي اختص به البشر فنعلم عنه وجود النفس الإنسانية علما ضروريا بما بين جنبينا من مداركها العلمية التي هي فوق مدارك الحس، فنراه عالماً آخر فوق عالم الحس.

(9) Then, we deduce (the existence of) a third world, above us, from the influences that we find it leaves in our hearts, such as volition and an inclination toward active motions. Thus, we know that there exists an agent there who directs us toward those things from a world above our world. That world is the world of spirits and angels. It contains essences that can be perceived because of the existence of influences they exercise upon us, despite the gap between us and them.

(10) Often, we may deduce (the existence of) that high spiritual world and the essences it contains, from visions and things we had not been aware of while awake but which we find in our sleep and which are brought to our attention in it and which, if they are true (dreams), conform with actuality. We thus know that they are true and come from the world of truth. "Confused dreams," on the other hand, are pictures of the imagination that are stored inside by perception and to which the ability to think is applied, after (man) has retired from sense perception.[11]

(11) We do not find any clearer proof than this for (the existence) of the spiritual world. Thus, we have a general knowledge of it, but no particulars. The metaphysicians make conjectures about details concerning the essences of the spiritual world and their order. They call these essences "intellects:" However, none of it is certain, because the conditions of logical argumentation as established in logic do not apply to it. One of these conditions is that the propositions of the argument must be primary and essential, but the spiritual essences are of an unknown essentiality. Thus, logical argumentation cannot be applied to them. Our only means of perceiving something of the details of these worlds are what we may glean from matters of religious law, as explained and established by religious faith.

(12) Of the (three) worlds, the one we can perceive best is the world of human beings, since it is existential and attested by our corporeal and spiritual perceptions. The world of the senses is shared by us with the animals, but the world of the intellect and the spirits is shared by us with the angels, whose essences are of the same kind as the essences of that world. They are essences free from corporeality and matter, and they are pure intellect in which intellect, thinker, and the object of thinking are one. It is, in a way, an essence the reality of which is perception and intellect.

(13) The sciences (knowledge) of the (angels), thus, always agree by nature with the things to be known. They can never have any defect. The knowledge of human beings, on the other hand, is the attainment of the form of the thing to be known in their essences, after it had not

(٩) ثم نستدل على عالم ثالث فوقنا بما نجد فينا من آثاره التي تلقى في أفئدتنا كالإرادات والوجهات نحو الحركات الفعلية، فنعلم أن هناك فاعلا يبعثنا عليها من عالم فوق عالمنا، وهو عالم الأرواح والملائكة، وفيه ذوات مدركة، لوجود آثارها فينا، مع ما بيننا وبينها من المغايرة.

(١٠) وربما يستدل على هذا العالم الأعلى الروحاني وذواته بالرؤيا وما نجد في النوم ويلقى إلينا فيه من الأمور التي نحن في غفلة عنها في اليقظة، وتطابق الواقع في الصحيحة منها؛ فنعلم أنها حق، ومن عالم الحق. وأما أضغاث الأحلام فصور خيالية يخزنها الإدراك في الباطن، ويجول فيها الفكر بعد الغيبة عن الحس.

(١١) ولا نجد على هذا العالم الروحاني برهانا أوضح من هذا؛ فنعلمه كذلك على الجملة ولا ندرك له تفصيلا. وما يزعمه الحكماء الإلاهيون في تفصيل ذواته وترتيبها المسماة عندهم بالعقول فليس شيء من ذلك بيقيني، لاختلال شرط البرهان النظري فيه، كما هو مقرر في كلامهم في المنطق؛ لأن من شرطه أن تكون قضاياه أولية ذاتية، وهذه الذوات الروحانية مجهولة الذاتيات؛ فلا سبيل للبرهان فيها، ولا يبقى لنا مدرك في تفاصيل هذه العوالم إلا ما نقتبسه من الشرعيات التي يوضحها الإيمان ويحكمها.

(١٢) وأقعد هذه العوالم في مدركنا عالم البشر؛ لأنه وجداني مشهود في مداركنا الجسمانية والروحانية، ويشترك في عالم الحس مع الحيوانات، وفي عالم العقل والأرواح مع الملائكة الذين ذواتهم من جنس ذواته، وهي ذوات مجردة عن الجسمانية والمادة، وعقل صرف يتحد فيه العقل والعاقل والمعقول، وكأنه ذات حقيقتها الإدراك والعقل.

(١٣) فعلومهم حاصلة دائما مطابقة بالطبع لمعلوماتهم لا يقع فيها خلل ألبتة. وعلم البشر هو حصول صورة المعلوم في ذواتهم بعد ألا تكون حاصلة. فهو كله

been there. It is all acquired. The essence in which the forms of the things to be known are obtained, namely, the soul, is a material substance[12] that gradually takes over the forms of existence with the help of the forms of the things to be known that it obtains. Eventually, it reaches perfection, and, through death, its existence fulfills itself as regards both its matter and its form.

(14) The objects in the soul are subject to constant vacillation between negation and assertion. One of the two is sought by means of some middle (term) to connect the two extremes. When that is achieved and the object has become known, it must be explained that there exists agreement (between knowledge and the thing known). Such agreement may often be clarified by technical logical argumentation, but that is from "behind the veil," and it is not like the direct vision[13] that is found in connection with the sciences (knowledge) of the angels.

(15) The "veil" may be removed, and the agreement may, thus, be effected through direct perceptive vision. It has been explained that human beings are ignorant by nature, because vacillation affects their knowledge. They learn through acquisition (of knowledge) and technique, because they obtain the objects they seek by applying their ability to think according to technical rules. The removal of the veil to which we have referred is achieved only through training in *dhikr* exercises[14]—which the best is prayer, which forbids sinful and evil actions—through abstinence from all distracting food of consumption—of which the most important part[15] is fasting—and through devoting oneself to God with all one's powers.

(16) "God taught man what he did not know."[16]

The sciences (knowledge) of the prophets.

(17) We find that this kind of human being is in a divine condition that is different from (ordinary) human ambitions and conditions. In prophets, the trend toward the divine is more powerful than their humanity, as far as the powers of perception, the powers of desire—that is, concupiscence and wrath—and the other conditions of the body are concerned. (Prophets) keep away from things human, except in as much as they are necessary for life. They turn toward divine matters, such as worship and the remembrance (*dhikr*) of God, as their knowledge of Him requires. They give information about Him and (transmit) the revelation for the guidance of the nation (of believers) which they received in

مكتسب. والذات التي تحصل فيها صور المعلومات وهي النفس مادة هيولانية تلبس صور الوجود بصور المعلومات الحاصلة فيها شيئا شيئا حتى تستكمل ويصح وجودها بالموت في مادتها وصورتها.

(١٤) فالمطلوبات فيها مترددة بين النفي والإثبات دائما بطلب أحدهما بالوسط الرابط بين الطرفين. فإذا حصل وصار معلوما افتقر إلى بيان المطابقة، وربما أوضحها البرهان الصناعي، لكن من وراء الحجاب وليس كالمعاينة التي في علوم الملائكة.

(١٥) وقد ينكشف ذلك الحجاب فيصير إلى المطابقة بالعِيان الإدراكي. فقد تبين أن البشر جاهل بالطبع، للتردد الذي في علمه، وعالم بالكسب والصناعة، لتحصيله المطلوب بفكره بالشروط الصناعية. وكشف الحجاب الذي أشرنا إليه إنما هو بالرياضة بالأذكار التي أفضلها صلاة تنهى عن الفحشاء والمنكر، وبالتنزه عن المتناولات المهمة، ورأسها الصور، وبالوجهة إلى الله بجميع قواه.

(١٦) والله ﴿عَلَّمَ الإِنْسَانَ مَا لَمْ يَعْلَمْ﴾.

فصل في علوم الأنبياء عليهم الصلاة والسلام

(١٧) إنا نجد هذا الصنف من البشر تعتريهم حالة إلهية خارجة عن منازع البشر وأحوالهم؛ فتغلب الوجهة الربانية فيهم على البشرية في القوى الإدراكية والنزوعية من الشهوة والغضب وسائر الأحوال البدنية. فتجدهم متنزهين عن الأحوال البشرية إلا في الضرورات منها، مقبلين على الأحوال الربانية من العبادة والذكر لله بما تقتضي

(their divine) condition. They do that according to one particular method and in a manner known to be peculiar to them. It undergoes no change in them and is like a natural disposition which God has given them.

(18) Revelation has already been discussed by us at the beginning of the book, in the chapter dealing with people who possess supernatural perception.[17] We explained there that the whole of existence in (all) its simple and composite worlds is arranged in a natural order of ascent and descent, so that everything constitutes an uninterrupted continuum. The essences at the end of each particular stage of the worlds are by nature prepared to be transformed into the essence adjacent to them, either above or below them. This is the case with the simple material elements; it is the case with palms and vines, (which constitute) the last stage of plants, in their relation to snails and shellfish, (which constitute) the (lowest) stage of animals. It is also the case with monkeys, creatures combining in themselves cleverness and perception, in their relation to man, the being who has the ability to think and to reflect. The preparedness (for transformation) that exists on either side, at each stage of the worlds, is meant when (we speak about) their connection.[18]

(19) Above the human world, there is a spiritual world. It is known to us by its influence upon us, in that it gives us the powers of perception and volition. The essences of that spirit-world are pure perception and absolute intellection. It is the world of the angels.

(20) It follows from all this that the human soul must be prepared to exchange humanity for angelicality, in order actually to become part of the angelic species at any time, in a single instant. It will afterwards resume its humanity. But in the world of angelicality, it has meanwhile accepted (ideas) that it is charged to transmit to its fellow human beings. That is the meaning of revelation and being addressed by the angels.

(21) All prophets possess this predisposition. It is like a natural disposition for them. In exchanging (their humanity for angelicality), they experience strain and sensations of choking, as is known in this connection.[19]

(22) Their (supernatural) knowledge is one of direct observation and vision. No mistake or slip attaches itself to it, and it is not affected by errors or unfounded assumptions. The agreement in it is an essential one, because the veil of the supernatural is gone, and clear and direct observation has been attained. When[20] (the prophets) quit that state and reassume their humanity, this clarity does not quit the knowledge they have, for it has become attached to it in the former condition. And because they possess the virtue that brings them to that condition, their

معرفتهم به، مخبرين عنه بما يوحى إليهم في تلك الحالة من هداية الأمة على طريقة واحدة وسَنَنٍ معهود منهم لا يتبدل فيهم كأنه جِبِلَّة فطرهم الله عليها.

(١٨) وقد تقدم لنا الكلام في الوحى أول الكتاب في فصل المدركين للغيب، وبينا هنالك أن الوجود كله في عوالمه البسيطة والمركبة على ترتيب طبيعى من أعلاها وأسفلها متصلة كلها اتصالا لا ينخرم، وأن الذوات التي في آخر كل أفق من العوالم مستعدة لأن تنقلب إلى الذات التي تجاورها من الأسفل والأعلى استعداداً طبيعياً كما في العناصر الجسمانية البسيطة، وكما هو في النخل والكرم من آخر أفق النبات مع الحلزون والصدف من أفق الحيوان، وكما في القردة التي استجمع فيها الكيس والإدراك مع الإنسان صاحب الفكر والروية. وهذا الاستعداد الذي في جانبي كل أفق من العوالم هو معنى الإتصال فيها.

(١٩) وفوق العالم البشري عالم روحاني شهدت لنا به الآثار التي فينا منه، بما يعطينا من قوى الإدراك والإرادة. فذوات ذلك العالم إدراك صرف وتعقل محض؛ وهو عالم الملائكة.

(٢٠) فوجب من ذلك كله أن يكون للنفس الإنسانية إستعداد للانسلاخ من البشرية إلى المَلَكِيَّة لتصير بالفعل من جنس الملائكة وقتا من الأوقات وفي لمحة من اللمحات، ثم تراجع بشريتها وقد تلقت في عالم الملكية ما كُلِّفت بتبليغه إلى أبناء جنسها من البشر. وهذا هو معنى الوحي وخطاب الملائكة.

(٢١) والأنبياء كلهم مفطورون عليه كأنه جِبِلَّة لهم.

(٢٢) ويعالجون في ذلك الانسلاخ من الشدة والغطيط ما هو معروف عنهم. وعلمهم في تلك الحالة علم شهادة وعيان لا يلحقه الخطأ والزلل، ولا يقع فيه الغلط والوهم؛ بل المطابقة فيه ذاتية، لزوال حجاب الغيب وحصول الشهادة الواضحة عند مفارقة هذه الحالة إلى البشرية. لا يفارق علمهم الوضوح استصحابا له من تلك الحالة

(experience) constantly repeats itself, until their guidance of the nation (of believers), which was the purpose for which they were sent, is accomplished. Thus, it is said in the Qur'ān: "I am merely a human being like you, to whom it has been revealed that your God is one God. Thus, be straightforward with Him and ask Him for forgiveness."[21]

(23) This should be understood. One should compare what we said earlier at the beginning of the book, about the different kinds of people possessing supernatural perception. It will constitute clear comment and explanation. There, we have explained the matter at sufficient length.

(24) God gives success.

Man is essentially ignorant, and becomes learned through acquiring (knowledge).

(25) We have already explained at the beginning of these sections[22] that man belongs to the genus of animals and that God distinguished him from them by the ability to think, which He gave man and through which man is able to arrange his actions in an orderly manner. This is the discerning intellect. Or, when it helps him to acquire from his fellow men a knowledge of ideas and of the things that are useful or detrimental to him, it is the experimental intellect. Or, when it helps him to obtain perception of the existent things as they are, whether they are absent or present,[23] it is the speculative intellect.

(26) Man's ability to think comes to him (only) after the animality in him has reached perfection. It starts from discernment. Before man has discernment, he has no knowledge whatever, and is counted one of the animals. His origin, the way in which he was created from a drop of sperm, a clot of blood, and a lump of flesh,[24] still determines his (mental make-up). Whatever he attains subsequently is the result of sensual perception and the "hearts"—that is, the ability to think—God has given him. In recounting the favor He bestowed upon us, God said: "And He gave you hearing and vision and hearts."[25]

(27) In his first condition, before he has attained discernment, man is simply matter, in as much as he is ignorant of all knowledge. He reaches perfection of his form through knowledge, which he acquires through his own organs. Thus, his human essence reaches perfection of existence.

الأولى، ولما هم عليه من الذكاء المفضي بهم إليها؛ يتردد ذلك فيهم دائماً إلى أن تكمل هداية الأمة التي بعثوا لها، كما في قوله تعالى: ﴿إِنَّمَا أَنَا بَشَر مِثْلُكُم يُوحى إِلَيَّ أَنَّما إِلا هُكُم إِلَاهٌ وَاحِدٌ فَاسْتَقِيمُوا إِلَيْهِ وَاسْتَغْفِرُوه﴾.

(٢٣) فافهم ذلك وراجع ما قدمناه لك في أول الكتاب في أصناف المدركين للغيب، يتضح لك شرحه وبيانه، فقد بسطناه هنالك بسطاً شافيا.

(٢٤) والله الموفق.

فصل في أن الإنسان جاهل بالذات عالم بالكسب

(٢٥) قد بينا أول هذه الفصول أن الإنسان من جنس الحيوانات، وأن الله تعالى ميزه عنها بالفكر الذي جعل له، يوقع به أفعاله على انتظام، وهو العقل التمييزى، أو يقتنص به العلم بالآراء والمصالح والمفاسد من أبناء جنسه وهو العقل التجريبى، أو يحصل به في تصور الموجودات غائباً وشاهداً على ما هي عليه وهو العقل النظري.

(٢٦) وهذا الفكر إنما يحصل له بعد كمال الحيوانية فيه. ويبدأ من التمييز. فهو قبل التمييز خلو من العلم بالجملة، معدود من الحيوانات، لاحق بمبدئه في التكوين من النطفة والعلقة والمضغة، وما حصل له بعد ذلك فهو بما جعل الله له من مدارك الحس والأفئدة التي هي الفكر. قال تعالى في الامتنان علينا: ﴿وجَعَلَ لَكُمُ السَّمْعَ والْأَبْصَارَ والْأَفْئِدَةَ﴾.

(٢٧) فهو في الحالة الأولى قبل التمييز هيولي فقط لجهله بجميع المعارف، ثم تستكمل صورته بالعلم الذي يكتسبه بآلاته، فتكمل ذاته الإنسانية في وجودها.

(28) One may compare the word of God when His Prophet began to receive the revelation. "Recite: In the name of your Lord who created, created man out of a clot of blood. Recite: And your Lord the most noble who taught with the calamus, taught man what he did not know."[26] That is, He let him acquire knowledge he did not yet possess, after he had been a clot of blood and a lump of flesh.

(29) Man's nature and essence reveal to us the essential ignorance and acquired (character of the) knowledge that man possesses, and the noble verse of the Qur'ān refers to it at the very beginning and opening of the revelation, and establishes through it the fact that (man) has received (from God) as a favor the first of the stages of his existence, which is humanity and its two conditions, the innate one and the acquired one.

(30) "God has been knowing and wise."[27]

Scientific instruction is a craft.[28]

(31) This is because skill in a science, knowledge of its diverse aspects, and mastery of it are the result of a habit which enables its possessor to comprehend all the basic principles of that particular science, to become acquainted with its problems, and to evolve the details of it from its principles. As long as such a habit has not been obtained, skill in a particular discipline is not forthcoming.

(32) Habit is different from understanding and knowing by memory. Understanding of a single problem in a single discipline may be found equally in someone well versed in the particular discipline and in the beginner, in the common man who has no scientific knowledge whatever, and in the accomplished scholar. Habit, on the other hand, belongs solely and exclusively to the scholar or the person well versed in scientific disciplines. This shows that (scientific) habit is different from understanding.

(33) All habits are corporeal, whether they are of the body, or, like arithmetic, of the brain and resulting from man's ability to think and so on. All corporeal things are *sensibilia*. Thus, they require instruction. Therefore, a tradition of famous teachers with regard to instruction in any science or craft, is acknowledged (to be necessary) by the people of every region and generation (race).

(٢٨) وانظر إلى قوله تعالى مبدأ الوحى على نبيه: ﴿اقْرَأْ بِاسْمِ رَبِّكَ الَّذِي خَلَقَ؛ خَلَقَ الإِنْسَانَ مِنْ عَلَقٍ؛ اقْرَأْ وَ رَبُّكَ الأَكْرَمُ؛ الَّذِي عَلَّمَ بِالْقَلَمِ؛ عَلَّمَ الإِنْسَانَ مَا لَمْ يَعْلَمْ﴾، أى أكسبه من العلم ما لم يكن حاصلاً له بعد أن كان عَلَقَة ومُضْغَة.

(٢٩) فقد كشفت لنا طبيعتُه وذاتُه ما هو عليه من الجهل الذاتي والعلم الكسبي، وأشارت إليه الآية الكريمة تقرر فيه الامتنان عليه بأول مراتب وجوده وهي الإنسانية وحالتاها الفطرية والكسبية في أول التنزيل ومبدأ الوحى.

(٣٠) وكان الله عليماً حكيماً.

فصل في أن التعليم للعلم من جملة الصنائع

(٣١) وذلك أن الحذق في العلم والتفنن فيه والاستيلاء عليه إنما هو بحصول مَلَكة في الإحاطة بمبادئه وقواعده والوقوف على مسائله واستنباط فروعه من أصوله. وما لم تحصل هذه الملكة لم يكن الحذق في ذلك الفن المتناول حاصلاً.

(٣٢) وهذه الملكة هي غير الفهم والوعي. لأنا نجد فهم المسألة الواحدة من الفن الواحد و وعيها مشتركاً بين من شدا في ذلك الفن وبين من هو مبتدئ فيه وبين العامي الذي لم يحصل علماً وبين العالم النحرير. والملكة إنما هي للعالم أو الشادي في الفنون دون من سواهما. فدل على أن هذه الملكة غير الفهم والوعي.

(٣٣) والملكات كلها جسمانية سواء كانت في البدن أو في الدماغ من الفكر وغيره كالحساب. والجسمانيات كلها محسوسة؛ فتفتقر إلى التعليم. ولهذا كان السند في التعليم في كل علم أو صناعة إلى مشاهير المعلمين فيها معتبراً عند كل أهل أفق وجيل.

(34) The fact that scientific instruction is a craft is also shown by the differences in technical terminologies. Every famous authority has his own technical terminology for scientific instruction, as is the case with all crafts. This shows that technical terminology is not a part of science itself. If it were, it would be one and the same with all scholars. One knows how much the technical terminology used in the teaching of speculative theology differs between the ancients and the moderns. The same applies to the principles of jurisprudence as well as to Arabic (philology) and to jurisprudence. It applies to any science one undertakes to study. The technical terminologies used in teaching it are always found to be different. This shows that the (terminologies) are crafts used for instruction, while each individual science as such is one and the same.

(35) If[29] this has been established, it should be known that the tradition of scientific instruction at this time has practically ceased (to be cultivated) among the inhabitants of the Maghrib, because the civilization of the Maghrib has disintegrated and its dynasties have lost their importance, and this has resulted in the deterioration and disappearance of the crafts, as was mentioned before.[30] Al-Qayrawān and Córdoba were centers of sedentary culture in the Maghrib and in Spain, respectively. Their civilization was highly developed, and the sciences and crafts were greatly cultivated and very much in demand in them. Since these two cities lasted a long time and possessed a sedentary culture, scientific instruction became firmly rooted in them. But when they fell into ruins, scientific instruction ceased (to be cultivated) in the West. Only a little of it, derived from (al-Qayrawān and Córdoba), continued to exist during the Almohad dynasty in Marrakech. Sedentary culture, however, was not firmly rooted in Marrakech because of the original Bedouin attitude of the Almohad dynasty and because of the shortness of time between its beginning and its destruction. Sedentary culture enjoyed only a very minor continuity there.

(36) After the destruction of the dynasty in Marrakech,[31] in the middle of the seventh [thirteenth] century, Judge Abū l-Qāsim b. Zaytūn[32] traveled from Ifrīqiyah to the East. He entered into contact with the pupils of the imam Ibn al-Khaṭīb.[33] He studied with them and learned their (method of) instruction. He became skilled in intellectual and traditional matters. Then, he returned to Tunis with a great deal of knowledge and a good (method of) instruction. He was followed back from the East by Abū ʿAbdallāh b. Shuʿayb al-Dukkālī,[34] who had traveled from the Maghrib to (Ibn Zaytūn). He studied with Egyptian professors and

(٣٤) ويدل أيضاً على أن تعليم العلم صناعة اختلاف الاصطلاحات فيه. فلكل إمام من الأئمة المشاهير اصطلاح في التعليم يختص به شأن الصنائع كلها فدل على أن ذلك الاصطلاح ليس من العلم، وإذ لو كان من العلم لكان واحداً عند جميعهم. ألا ترى إلى علم الكلام كيف تخالف في تعليمه اصطلاح المتقدمين والمتأخرين، وكذا أصول الفقه، وكذا العربية، وكذا كل علم يتوجه إلى مطالعته تجد الاصطلاحات في تعليمه متخالفة. فدل على أنها صناعات في التعليم، والعلم واحد في نفسه.

(٣٥) وإذا تقرر ذلك فاعلم أن سند تعليم العلم لهذا العهد قد كاد ينقطع عن أهل المغرب باختلال عمرانه. وتناقص الدول فيه، وما يحدث عن ذلك من نقص الصنائع وفقدانها كما مر. وذلك أن القيروان وقرطبة كانتا حاضرتي المغرب والأندلس، واستبحر عمرانهما وكان فيهما للعلوم والصنائع أسواق نافقة وبحور زاخرة. ورسخ فيهما التعليم لامتداد عصورهما وما كان فيهما من الحضارة. فلما خربتا انقطع التعليم من المغرب إلا قليلاً كان في دولة الموحدين بمراكش مستفاداً منها؛ ولم ترسخ الحضارة بمراكش لبداوة الدولة المُوَحِّدِية في أولها وقرب عهد انقراضها بمبدئها فلم تتصل أحوال الحضارة فيها إلا في الأقل.

(٣٦) وبعد انقراض الدولة بمراكش ارتحل إلى المشرق من أفريقية القاضي أبو القاسم بن زيتون لعهد أواسط المائة السابعة، فأدرك تلميذ الإمام ابن الخطيب فأخذ عنهم ولقن تعليمهم وحذق في العقليات والنقليات، ورجع إلى تونس بعلم كثير وتعليم حسن. وجاء على أثره من المشرق أبو عبد الله بن شعيب الدكالي كان ارتحل إليه من المغرب فأخذ عن مشيخة مصر ورجع إلى تونس واستقرَّ بها وكان تعليمه مفيداً.

returned to Tunis, where he remained. His (method of) instruction was effective. The inhabitants of Tunis studied with both Ibn Zaytūn and Ibn Shuᶜayb. Their tradition of scientific instruction was steadily continued by their pupils, generation after generation. Eventually, it reached Judge Muḥammad b. ᶜAbd-al-Salām,[35] the commentator and pupil of Ibn al-Ḥājib,[36] and was transplanted from Tunis to Tlemcen through Ibn al-Imām and his pupils. Ibn al-Imām[37] had studied with Ibn ᶜAbd-al-Salām under the same professors in the same classes. Pupils of Ibn ᶜAbd-al-Salām can be found at this time in Tunis, and pupils of Ibn al-Imām in Tlemcen. However, they are so few that it is to be feared that the tradition may come to an end.

(37) At the end of the seventh [thirteenth] century, Abū ᶜAlī Nāṣir-al-dīn al-Mashaddālī[38] traveled eastward[39] from Zawāwah and got in touch with the pupils of Abū ᶜAmr b. al-Ḥājib. He studied with them and learned their (method of) instruction. He studied with Shihāb-al-dīn al-Qarāfī[40] in the same classes. He became skilled in intellectual and traditional matters. He returned to the Maghrib with much knowledge and an effective (method of) instruction. He settled in Bougie. His tradition of scientific instruction was steadily continued among the students of Bougie. ᶜImrān al-Mashaddālī,[41] one of his pupils, frequently went to Tlemcen. He settled in Tlemcen and propagated his method there. At this time, in Tlemcen and Bougie, his pupils are few, very few.

(38) Fez and the other cities of the Maghrib have been without good instruction since the destruction of scientific instruction in Córdoba and al-Qayrawān. There has been no continuous tradition of scientific instruction in Fez. Therefore, it has been difficult for the people of Fez to obtain the scientific habit and skill.

(39) The easiest method of acquiring the scientific habit is through acquiring the ability to express oneself clearly in discussing and disputing scientific problems. This is what clarifies their import and makes them understandable. Some students spend most of their lives attending scholarly sessions. Still, one finds them silent. They do not talk and do not discuss matters. More than is necessary, they are concerned with memorizing. Thus, they do not obtain much of a habit in the practice of science and scientific instruction. Some of them think that they have obtained (the habit). But when they enter into a discussion or disputation, or do some teaching, their scientific habit is found to be defective. The only reason for their deficiency is (lack of) instruction, together with the break in the tradition of scientific instruction (that affects them).

فأخذ عنهما أهل تونس واتصل سند تعليمهما في تلاميذهما جيلاً بعد جيل حتى انتهى إلى القاضي محمد بن عبد السلام. شارح ابن الحاجب وتلميذه، وانتقل من تونس إلى تلمسان في ابن الإمام وتلميذه، فإنه قرأ مع ابن عبد السلام على مشيخة واحدة في مجالس بأعيانها. وتلميذه ابن عبد السلام بتونس وابن الإمام بتلمسان لهذا العهد. إلا أنهم من القلة بحُيث يخشى انقطاعُ سندهم.

(٣٧) ثم ارتحل من زواوة في آخر المائة السابعة أبو علي ناصر الدين المشدالي وأدرك تلميذ أبي عمرو ابن الحاجب، وأخذ عنهم ولقن تعليمهم وقرأ مع شهاب الدين القرافي في مجالس واحدة، وحذق في العقليات والنقليات ورجع إلى المغرب بعلم كثير وتعليم مفيد، ونزل ببجاية واتصل سندُ تعليمه في طلبتها. وربما انتقل إلى تِلْمسان عمرانُ المشدالي من تلميذه وأوطنها وبث طريقته فيها؛ وتِلْميذه لهذا العهد ببجاية وتلمسان قليل أو أقل من القليل.

(٣٨) وبقيت فاس وسائر أقطار المغرب خلواً من حسن التعليم من لدن انقراض تعليم قرطبة والقيروان، ولم يتصل سند التعليم فيهم فعسر عليهم حصول الملكة والحذق في العلوم.

(٣٩) وأيسر طرق هذه الملكة فتق اللسان بالمحاورة والمناظرة في المسائل العلمية؛ فهو الذي يقرب شأنها ويحصل مرامها. فتجد طالب العلم منهم بعد ذهاب الكثير من أعمارهم في ملازمة المجالس العلمية سكوتاً لا ينطقون ولا يفاوضون. وعنايتهم بالحفظ أكثر من الحاجة. فلا يحصلون على طائل من ملكة التصرف في العلم والتعليم؛ ثم بعد تحصيل من يرى منهم أنه قد حصل تجد ملكته قاصرة في علمه إن فاوض

Apart from that, their memorized knowledge may be more extensive than that of other scholars, because they are so much concerned with memorizing. They think that scientific habit is identical with memorized knowledge. But that is not so.

(40) This is attested in the Maghrib (in Morocco) by the fact that the period specified for the residence of students in college there is sixteen years, while in Tunis it is five years. Such a (fixed) period of attendance is recognized as the shortest in which a student can obtain the scientific habit he de-sires, or can realize that he will never be able to obtain it. In the Maghrib (in Morocco), the period is so long at the present day for the very reason that the poor quality of scientific instruction there makes it difficult (for the student to acquire the scientific habit), and not for any other reason.

(41) The institution of scientific instruction has disappeared among the inhabitants of Spain. Their (former) concern with the sciences is gone, because Muslim civilization in Spain has been decreasing for hundreds of years. The only scholarly discipline remaining there is Arabic (philology) and literature, to which the (Spanish Muslims) restrict themselves. The tradition of teaching these disciplines is preserved among them, and thus the disciplines as such are preserved. Jurisprudence is an empty institution among them and a mere shadow of its real self. Of the intellectual disciplines, not even a shadow remains. The only reason for that is that the tradition of scientific instruction has ceased (to be cultivated) in Spain, because civilization there has deteriorated and the enemy has gained control over most of it, except for a few people along the coast who are more concerned with making a living than with the things that come after it.

(42) "God has the power to execute His commands."[42]

(43) In[43] the East, the tradition of scientific instruction has not ceased (to be cultivated). Scientific instruction is very much in demand and greatly cultivated in the East, because of the continuity of an abundant civilization and the continuity of the tradition (of scientific instruction) there. It is true that the old cities, such as Baghdad, al-Baṣrah, and al-Kūfah, which were the (original) mines of scholarship, are in ruins. However, God has replaced them with cities even greater than they were. Science was transplanted from the (early centers) to the non-Arab ʿIrāq of Khurāsān, to Transoxania in the East, and to Cairo and adjacent

أو ناظر أو علم، وما أتاهم القصور إلا من قبل التعليم وانقطاع سنده، وإلا فحفظهم أبلغ من حفظ سواهم لشدة عنايتهم به، وظنهم أنه المقصود من الملكة العلمية، وليس كذلك.

(٤٠) ومما يشهد بذلك في المغرب أن المدة المعينة لسكنى طلبة العلم بالمدارس عندهم ست عشرة سنة، وهي بتونس خمس سنين، وهذه المدة بالمدارس على المتعارف هو أقل ما يأتى فيها لطالب العلم حصول مبتغاه من الملكة العلمية أو اليأس من تحصيلها، فطال أمدها في المغرب لهذه المدة لأجل عسرها من قلة الجودة في التعليم خاصة، لا مما سوى ذلك.

(٤١) وأما أهل الأندلس فذهب رسم التعليم من بينهم وذهبت عنايتهم بالعلوم لتناقص عمران المسلمين بها منذ مئين من السنين. ولم يبق من رسم العلم فيهم إلا فن العربية والأدب اقتصروا عليه والحفظ سند تعليمه بينهم، فانحفظ بحفظه. وأما الفقه بينهم فرسم خلو وأثر بعد عين. وأما العقليات فلا أثر ولا عين. وما ذاك إلا لانقطاع سند التعليم فيها بتناقص العمران وتغلب العدو على عامتها إلا قليل بسيف البحر، شغلهم بمعايشهم أكثر من شغلهم بما بعدها.

(٤٢) «والله غالب على أمره.»

(٤٣) وأما المشرق فلم ينقطع سند التعليم فيه بل أسواقه نافقة وبحوره زاخرة لاتصال العمران الموفور واتصال السند فيه. وإن كانت الأمصار العظيمة التي كانت معادن العلم قد خربت مثل بغداد والبصرة والكوفة إلا أن الله تعالى قد أدال منها بأمصار أعظم من تلك وانتقل العلم منها إلى عراق العجم بخراسان وما وراء النهر

regions in the West. These cities have never ceased to have an abundant and continuous civilization, and the tradition of scientific instruction has always persisted in them.

(44) The inhabitants of the East are, in general, more firmly rooted in the craft of scientific instruction and, indeed, in all the other crafts (than Maghribīs). In fact, many Maghribīs who have traveled to the East in quest of knowledge, have been of the opinion that[44] the intellect of the people of the East is, in general, more perfect than that of the Maghribīs. They have supposed the rational souls (of the people of the East) to be by nature more perfect than those of the Maghribīs. They have claimed that there exists a difference in the reality of humanity between ourselves (the Maghribīs) and them,[45] because their cleverness in the sciences and crafts seemed remarkable to them. This is not so. There is no difference between the East and the West great enough (to be considered) a difference in the reality (of human nature), which is one (and the same everywhere).

(45) (Such a difference) does in fact exist in the intemperate zones, such as the first and the seventh zones. The tempers there are intemperate, and the souls are correspondingly intemperate, as has been mentioned before.[46] The superiority of the inhabitants of the East over those of the West lies in the additional intelligence that accrues to the soul from the influences of sedentary culture, as has been stated before in connection with the crafts.[47] We are now going to comment on that and to verify it. It is as follows:

(46) Sedentary people observe (a) particular (code of) manners in everything they undertake and do or do not do, and they thus acquire certain ways of making a living, finding dwellings, building houses, and handling their religious and worldly matters, including their customary affairs, their dealings with others, and all the rest of their activities.[48] These manners constitute a kind of limitation which may not be transgressed, and, at the same time, they are crafts that (later) generations take over from the earlier ones. No doubt, each craft that has its proper place within the arrangement of the crafts, influences the soul and causes it to acquire an additional intelligence, which prepares the soul for accepting still other crafts. The intellect is thus conditioned for a quick reception of knowledge.

من المشرق ثم إلى القاهرة وما إليها من المغرب. فلم تزل موفورة وعمرانها متصلاً وسند التعليم بها قائماً.

(٤٤) فأهل المشرق على الجملة أرسخ في صناعة تعليم العلم بل وفي سائر الصنائع، حتى أنه ليظن كثير من رحَّالة أهل المغرب إلى المشرق في طلب العلم أن عقولهم على الجملة أكمل من عقول أهل المغرب، وأنهم أشد نباهة وأعظم كَيْساً بفطرتهم الأولى، وأن نفوسهم الناطقة أكمل بفطرتها من نفوس أهل المغرب؛ ويعتقدون التفاوت بيننا وبينهم في حقيقة الإنسانية ويتشيعون لذلك، ويولعون به، لما يرون من كيسهم في العلوم والصنائع، وليس كذلك. وليس بين قطر المشرق والمغرب تفاوت بهذا المقدار الذي هو تفاوت في الحقيقة الواحدة.

(٤٥) اللّهم إلا الأقاليم المنحرفة مثل الأول والسابع فإن الأمزجة فيها منحرفة والنفوس على نسبتها كما مر. وإنما الذي فضل به أهل المشرق أهل المغرب هو ما يحصل في النفس من آثار الحضارة من العقل المزيد كما تقدم في الصنائع، ونزيده الآن شرحاً وتحقيقاً.

(٤٦) وذلك أن الحضر لهم آداب في أحوالهم في المعاش والمسكن والبناء وأمور الدين والدنيا، وكذا سائر أعمالهم وعاداتهم ومعاملاتهم، وجميع تصرفاتهم، فلهم في ذلك كله آداب يوقف عندها في جميع ما يتناولونه ويتلبسون به من أخذ وترك، حتى كأنها حدود لا تتعدى. وهي مع ذلك صنائع يتلقاها الآخر عن الأول منهم. ولا شك أن كل صناعة مرتبة يرجع منها إلى النفس أثر يكسبها عقلاً جديداً تستعد به لقبول صناعة أخرى، ويتهيأ بها العقل لسرعة الإدراك للمعارف.

(47) We hear that the Egyptians have achieved things hardly possible in the teaching of the crafts. For instance, they teach domestic donkeys and (other) dumb animals, quadrupeds and birds, to speak words and to do things that are remarkable for their rarity and that the inhabitants of the Maghrib would not be capable of understanding, let alone teaching.[49]

(48) Good habits in scientific instruction, in the crafts, and in all the other customary activities, add insight to the intellect of a man and enlightenment to his thinking, since the soul thus obtains a great number of habits. We have stated before[50] that the soul grows under the influence of the perceptions it receives and the habits accruing to it. Thus, (the people of the East) become more clever, because their souls are influenced by scientific activity. The common people then suppose that it is a difference in the reality of humanity. This is not so. If one compares sedentary people with Bedouins, one notices how much more insight and cleverness sedentary people have. One might, thus, come to think that they really differ from the Bedouins in the reality of humanity and in intelligence. This is not so. The only reason for the difference is that sedentary people have refined technical habits and manners as far as customary activities and sedentary conditions are concerned, all of them things that are unknown to the Bedouins. Sedentary people possess numerous crafts, as well as the habits that go with them, and good (methods of) teaching the crafts. Therefore, those who do not have such habits think that they indicate an intellectual perfection possessed (exclusively) by sedentary people, and that the natural qualifications of the Bedouins are inferior to those of sedentary people. This is not so. We find Bedouins whose under-standing, intellectual perfection, and natural qualifications are of the highest rank. The seeming (superiority of) sedentary people is merely the result of a certain polish the crafts and scientific instruction give them. It influences the soul, as we have stated before.[51] Now, the inhabitants of the East are more firmly grounded and more advanced in scientific instruction and the crafts (than the Maghribīs), and the Maghribīs are closer to desert life, as we have stated before in the preceding section.[52] This leads superficial people to think that the inhabitants of the East are distinguished from the Maghribīs by a certain perfection (of theirs) touching the reality of humanity. That is not correct, as one should be able to understand.

(49) God "gives in addition to the creatures whatever He wishes to give to them."[53]

. . . .

(٤٧) ولقد بلغنا في تعليم الصنائع عن أهل مصر غايات لا تدرك مثل أنهم يعلمون الحُمُرَ الأنسية والحيوانات العجم من الماشي والطائر مفردات من الكلام والأفعال يستغرب ندورها، ويعجز أهل المغرب عن فهمها فضلاً عن تعليمها.

(٤٨) وحسن الملكات في التعليم والصنائع وسائر الأحوال العادية يزيد الإنسان ذكاء في عقله وإضاءة في فكره بكثرة الملكات الحاصلة للنفس، إذ قدمنا أن النفس إنما تنشأ بالإدراكات وما يرجع إليها من الملكات، فيزدادون بذلك كَيْساً لما يرجع إلى النفس من الآثار العلمية، فيظنه العامي تفاوتاً في الحقيقة الإنسانية وليس كذلك. ألا ترى إلى أهل الحضر مع أهل البدو كيف تجد الحضري متحلياً بالذكاء ممتلئاً من الكيس، حتى أن البدوي ليظنه أنه قد فاته في حقيقة إنسانيته وعقله وليس كذلك. وما ذاك إلا لإجادته في ملكات الصنائع والآداب في العوائد والأحوال الحضرية ما لا يعرفه البدوي. فلما امتلأ الحضري من الصنائع وملكاتها وحسن تعليمها ظن كل من قصر عن تلك الملكات أنها لكمالٍ في عقله، وأن نفوس أهل البدو قاصرة بفطرتها وجبلّتها عن فطرته، وليس كذلك. فإنا نجد من أهل البدو من هو في أعلى رتبة من الفهم والكمال في عقله وفطرته. إنما الذي ظهر على أهل الحضر من ذلك هو رونق الصنائع والتعليم فإن لهما آثاراً ترجع إلى النفس كما قدمناه. وكذا أهل المشرق لما كانوا في التعليم والصنائع أرسخ رتبة وأعلى قدماً، وكان أهل المغرب أقرب إلى البداوة لما قدمناه في الفصل قبل هذا، ظن المغفلون في بادئ الرأي أنه لكمال في حقيقة الإنسانية اختصوا به عن أهل المغرب، وليس ذلك بصحيح فتفهمه.

(٤٩) والله «يزيد في الخلق ما يشاء»، وهو إله السموات والأرض.

. . . .

The great number of scholarly works (available) is an obstacle on the path to attaining scholarship.

(50) It should be known that among the things that are harmful to the human quest for knowledge and to the attainment of a thorough scholarship are the great number of works (available), the large variety in technical terminology (needed for purposes) of instruction, and the numerous (different), methods (used in those works).[54] The student is required to have a ready knowledge of (all) that. Only then is he considered an accomplished scholar.

(51) Thus, the student must know all the (works), or most of them, and observe the methods used in them.[55] His whole lifetime would not suffice to know all the literature that exists in a single discipline, (even) if he were to devote himself entirely to it. Thus, he must of necessity fall short of attaining scholarship.

(52) For the Mālikite school of jurisprudence, this (situation) may be exemplified, for instance, by the *Mudawwanah,* its legal commentaries, such as the books of Ibn Yūnus, al-Lakhmī, and Ibn Bashīr, and the notes and introductions (to it).[56] Or (one may take) the sister work of the *Mudawwanah,* the *ᶜUtbīyah* and the work written on it (by Ibn Rushd under the title of) *al-Bayīn wa-t-taḥṣīl*;[57] or the book of Ibn al-Ḥājib and the works written on it. Furthermore, the student must be able to distinguish between the Qayrawānī method (of the Mālikite school) and the methods of Cordovan, Baghdādī, and Egyptian (Mālikites) and those of their more recent successors. He must know all that. Only then is a person considered able to give juridical decisions.

(53) All of (these things) are variations of one and the same subject. The student is required to have a ready knowledge of all of them and to be able to distinguish between them. (Yet,) a whole lifetime could be spent on (but) one of them. If teachers and students were to restrict themselves to the school problems, (the task) would be much easier and (scholarly) instruction would be simple and easily accessible. However, this is an evil that cannot be cured, because it has become firmly ingrained through custom. In a way, it has become something natural, which cannot be moved or transformed.

(54) Another example is Arabic philology.[58] There is the *Book* of Sībawayh and all the literature on it; (there are) the methods of the Baṣrians, the Kūfians, the Baghdādīs, and, later on, the Spaniards; and (there are) the methods of the ancient and modem philologists, such as

(فصل) في أن كثرة التآليف في العلوم عائقة عن التحصيل

(٥٠) اعلم أنه مما أضر بالناس في تحصيل العلم والوقوف على غاياته كثرة التآليف واختلاف الاصطلاحات في التعليم، وتعدد طرقها، ثم مطالبة المتعلم والتلميذ باستحضار ذلك، وحينئذ يسلم له منصب التحصيل.

(٥١) فيحتاج المتعلم إلى حفظها كلها أو أكثرها ومراعاة طرقها، ولا يفي عمره بما كتب في صناعة واحدة إذا تجرد لها، فيقع القصور، ولا بد، دون رتبة التحصيل.

(٥٢) ويمثل ذلك من شأن الفقه في المذهب المالكي بكتاب المدونة مثلا، وما كتب عليها من الشروحات الفقهية مثل كتاب ابن يونس واللخمي وابن بشير والتنبيهات والمقدمات والبيان والتحصيل على العُتْبِيَّة وكذلك كتاب ابن الحاجب وما كتب عليه. ثم إنه يحتاج إلى تمييز الطريقة القيروانية من القرطبية والبغدادية والمصرية وطرق المتأخرين عنهم، والإحاطه بذلك كله، وحينئذ يسلم له منصب الفُتْيا.

(٥٣) وهي كلها متكررة والمعنى واحد، والمتعلم مطالب باستحضار جميعها وتمييز ما بينها، والعمر ينقضي في واحد منها. ولو اقتصر المعلمون المتعلمين على المسائل المذهبية فقط لكان الأمر دون ذلك بكثير، وكان التعليم سهلا، ومأخذه قريباً. ولكنه داء لا يرتفع لاستقرار العوائد عليه. فصارت كالطبيعة التي لا يمكن نقلها ولا تحويلها.

(٥٤) ويمثل أيضاً علم العربية من كتاب سيبويه، وجميع ما كتب عليه، وطرق البصريين والكوفيين والبغداديين والأندلسيين من بعدهم، وطرق المتقدمين والمتأخرين مثل

Ibn al-Ḥājib and Ibn Mālik, and all the literature on that. This (wealth of material) requires a great deal from the student. He could spend his (whole) life on less (material). No one would aspire to complete knowledge of it, though there are a few, rare exceptions (of men who have a complete knowledge of philology). For instance, we modern Maghribīs have received the works of an Egyptian philologist whose name is Ibn Hishām. The contents show that Ibn Hishām has completely mastered the habit of philology as it had not been mastered (before) save by Sībawayh, Ibn Jinnī, and people of their class, so greatly developed is his philological habit and so comprehensive is his knowledge and experience as regards the principles and details of philology. This proves that excellence (in scholarship) is not restricted to the ancients,[59] especially if (one considers) our remarks about the many obstacles (on the path to mastery of a science in modern times), which the great number of schools, methods, and works presents. No! "His excellence God bestows upon whomever He wants to."[60] (Ibn Hishām) is one of the rare wonders of the world. Otherwise, it is obvious that were the student to spend his entire lifetime on all these things, it would not be long enough for him to acquire, for instance, (a complete knowledge of) Arabic philology, which is (but) an instrument and means (for further studies). How, then, is it with the intended fruit (of study, the acquisition of thorough and comprehensive scholarship)? But "God guides whomever He wants to guide."[61]

The great number of brief handbooks (available) on scholarly subjects is detrimental to (the process of) instruction.

(55) Many[62] recent scholars have turned to brief presentations of the methods and contents of the sciences. They want to know (the methods and contents), and they present them systematically in the form of brief programs for each science. (These) brief handbooks express all the problems of a given discipline and the evidence for them in a few brief words that are full of meaning. This (procedure) is detrimental to good style and makes difficulties for the understanding.

(56) (Scholars) often approach the main scholarly works on the various disciplines, which are very lengthy, intending to interpret[63] and explain (them). They abridge them, in order to make it easier (for students) to acquire expert knowledge of them. Such, for instance, was done by Ibn al-Ḥājib in jurisprudence and the principles of jurisprudence,[64] by Ibn Mālik in Arabic philology,[65] by al-Khūlnajī in logic,[66] and so on. This (procedure)

ابن الحاجب وابن مالك وجميع ما كتب في ذلك، وكيف يطالب به المتعلم وينقضي عمره دونه ولا يطمع أحد في الغاية منه إلا في القليل النادر؛ مثل ما وصل إلينا بالمغرب لهذا العهد من تآليف رجل من أهل صناعة العربية من أهل مصر يعرف بابن هشام، ظهر من كلامه فيها أنه استولى على غاية من مَلَكَة تلك الصناعة لم تحصل إلا لسيبويه وابن جني وأهل طبقتهما لعظم ملكته وما أحاط به من أصول ذلك الفن وتفاريعه وحسن تصرفه فيه، ودل ذلك على أن الفضل ليس منحصراً في المتقدمين سيما مع ما قدمناه من كثرة الشواغب بتعدد المذاهب والطرق والتآليف؛ ولكن فضل الله يؤتيه من يشاء؛ وهذا نادر من نوادر الوجود. وإلا فالظاهر أن المتعلم ولو قطع عمره في هذا كله فلا يفي له بتحصيل علم العربية مثلا الذى هو آلة من الآلات ووسيلة؛ فكيف يكون في المقصود الذي هو الثمرة؛ «وَلَكِنَّ اللهَ يَهْدِي مَنْ يَشَاءُ».

(فصل) في أن كثرة الاختصارات المؤلفة في العلوم مخلة بالتعليم

(٥٥) ذهب كثير من المتأخرين إلى اختصار الطرق والأنحاء في العلوم، يولعون بها ويدونون منها برنامجاً مختصراً في كل علم يشتمل على حصر مسائله وأدلتها باختصار في الألفاظ وحشو القليل منها بالمعانى الكثيرة من ذلك الفن. وصار ذلك مخلا بالبلاغة وَعِسراً على الفهم.

(٥٦) وربما عمدوا إلى الكتب الأمهات المطولة في الفنون للتفسير والبيان فاختصروها تقريبا للحفظ كما فعله ابن الحاجب في الفقه وأصول الفقه، وابن مالك في العربية، والخونجى في المنطق وأمثالهم. وهو فساد في التعليم وفيه إخلال بالتحصيل.

has a corrupting influence upon the process of instruction and is detrimental to the attainment of scholarship. For it confuses the beginner by presenting the final results of a discipline to him before he is prepared for them. This is a bad method of instruction, as will be mentioned.[67]

(57) (The procedure) also involves a great deal of work for the student. He must study carefully the words of the abridgment, which are complicated to understand because they are crowded with ideas, and[68] try to find out from them what the problems of (the given discipline) are. Thus, the texts of such brief handbooks are found to be difficult and complicated (to understand). A good deal of time must be spent on (the attempt to) understand them.

(58) Moreover, after all these (difficulties), the (scholarly) habit that results from receiving instruction from brief handbooks, (even) when (such instruction) is at its best and is not accompanied by any flaw, is inferior to the habits resulting from (the study of) more extensive and lengthy works. The latter contain a great amount of repetition and lengthiness, but both are useful for the acquisition of a perfect habit. When there is little repetition, an inferior habit is the result. This is the case with the abridgments. The intention was to make it easy for students to acquire expert knowledge (of scholarly subjects), but the result is that it has become (more) difficult for them, because they are prevented from acquiring useful and firmly established habits.

(59) Those whom God guides, no one can lead astray, and "those whom God leads astray have no one to guide them."[69]

The right attitude in scientific instruction and toward the method of giving such instruction.[70]

(60) It[71] should be known that the teaching of scientific subjects to students is effective only when it proceeds gradually and little by little. At first, (the teacher) presents (the student) with the principal problems within each chapter of a given discipline. He acquaints him with them by commenting on them in a summary fashion. In the course of doing so, he observes the student's intellectual potential and his preparedness for understanding the material that will come his way until the end of the discipline under consideration (is reached). In the process, (the student) acquires the habit of the science (he studies). However, that habit will be an approximate[72] and weak one. The most it can do is to enable the student to understand the discipline (he studies) and to know its problems.

وذلك لأن فيه تخليطا على المبتدىء بإلقاء الغايات من العلم عليه، وهو لم يستعد لقبولها بعد؛ وهو من سوء التعليم كما سيأتى.

(٥٧) ثم فيه مع ذلك شغل كبير على المتعلم بتتبع ألفاظ الاختصار العويصة للفهم بتزاحم المعانى عليها وصعوبة استخراج المسائل من بينها. لأن ألفاظ المختصرات تجدها لأجل ذلك صعبة عويصة، فينقطع في فهمها حظ صالح من الوقت.

(٥٨) ثم بعد ذلك فالملكة الحاصلة من التعليم في تلك المختصرات إذا تم على سداده ولم تعقبه آفة فهى ملكة قاصرة عن الملكات التي تحصل من الموضوعات البسيطة المطولة بكثرة ما يقع في تلك من التكرار والإحالة المفيدين لحصول الملكة التامة. وإذا اقتُصِرَ عن التكرار قصرت الملكة لقلته كشأن هذه الموضوعات المختصرة. فقصدوا إلى تسهيل الحفظ على المتعلمين فأركبوهم صعباً يقطعهم عن تحصيل الملكات النافعة وتمكنها.

(٥٩) ومن يهد الله فلا مضل له ومن يضلل فلا هادى له. والله سبحانه وتعالى أعلم.

(فصل) في وجه الصواب في تعليم العلوم وطريق إفادته

(٦٠) اعلم أن تلقين العلوم للمتعلمين إنما يكون مفيداً إذا كان على التدريج شيئاً فشيئاً وقليلاً قليلا. يلقى عليه أولاً مسائل من كل باب من الفن هي أصول ذلك الباب، ويقرب له في شرحها على سبيل الإجمال، ويراعى في ذلك قوة عقله واستعداده لقبول ما يرد عليه، حتى ينتهى إلى آخر الفن، وعند ذلك يحصل له ملكة في ذلك العلم؛ إلا أنها جزئية وضعيفة، وغايتها أنها هيأته لفهم الفن وتحصيل مسائله.

(61) (The teacher,) then, leads (the student) back over the discipline a second time. He gives him instruction in it on a higher level. He no longer gives a summary but full commentaries and explanations. He mentions to him the existing differences of opinion and the form these differences take all the way through to the end of the discipline under consideration. Thus, the student's (scholarly) habit is improved. Then, (the teacher) leads (the student) back again, now that he is solidly grounded. He leaves nothing (that is) complicated, vague, or obscure, unexplained. He bares all the secrets (of the discipline) to him. As a result, the student, when he finishes with the discipline, has acquired the habit of it.

(62) This is the effective method of instruction. As one can see, it requires a threefold repetition. Some students can get through it with less than that, depending on their natural dispositions. and qualifications.

(63) We have observed that many teachers[73] of the time in which we are living are ignorant of this effective method of instruction. They begin their instruction by confronting the student with obscure scientific problems. They require him to concentrate on solving them. They think that that is experienced and correct teaching, and they make it the task of the student to comprehend and know such things. In actual fact, they (merely) confuse him by exposing him to the final results of a discipline at the beginning (of his studies) and before he is prepared to understand them. Preparedness for and receptivity to scientific knowledge and understanding grow gradually. At the beginning, the student is completely unable to understand any but a very few (points). (His understanding is) only approximate and general and (can be achieved only) with the help of pictures (*muthul*) derived from sensual perception. His preparedness, then, keeps growing gradually and little by little when he faces the problems of the discipline under consideration and has them repeated (to him) and advances from approximate understanding of them to a complete, higher knowledge. Thus the habit of preparedness and, eventually, that of attainment materialize in the student, until he has a comprehensive knowledge of the problems of the discipline (he studies). But if a student is exposed to the final results at the beginning, while he is still unable to understand and comprehend (anything) and is still far from being prepared to (understand), his mind is not acute enough to (grasp them). He gets the impression that scholarship is difficult and becomes loath to occupy himself with it. He constantly dodges and avoids it. That is the result of poor instruction, and nothing else.

(٦١) ثم يرجع به إلى الفن ثانية فيرفعه في التلقين عن تلك الرتبة إلى أعلى منها، ويستوفى الشرح والبيان، ويخرج عن الإجمال، ويذكر له ما هنالك من الخلاف ووجهه إلى أنْ ينتهى إلى آخر الفن فتجود ملكته. ثم يرجع به وقد شدا فلا يترك عويصاً ولا مبهما ولا مغلقاً إلا وضحه وفتح له مقفله؛ فيخلص من الفن وقد استولى على ملكته.

(٦٢) هذا وجه التعليم المفيد. وهو كما رأيت إنما يحصل في ثلاث تكرارات. وقد يحصل للبعض في أقل من ذلك بحسب ما يخلق له ويتيسر عليه.

(٦٣) وقد شاهدنا كثيراً من المعلمين لهذا العهد الذي أدركنا يجهلون طرق التعليم وإفادته ويحضرون للمتعلم في أول تعليمه المسائل المقفلة من العلم ويطالبونه بإحضار ذهنه في حلها، ويحسبون ذلك مراناً على التعليم وصواباً فيه، ويكلفونه وعي ذلك وتحصيله، ويخلطون عليه بما يلقون له من غايات الفنون في مبادئها، وقبل أن يستعد لفهمها. فإن قبول العلم والاستعدادات لفهمه تنشأ تدريجاً، ويكون المتعلم أول الأمر عاجزاً عن الفهم بالجملة إلا في الأقل وعلى سبيل التقريب والإجمال وبالأمثال الحسية. ثم لا يزال الاستعداد فيه يتدرج قليلاً قليلا بمخالفة مسائل ذلك الفن وتكرارها عليه، والانتقال فيها من التقريب إلى الاستيعاب الذى فوقه، حتى تتم الملكة في الاستعداد ثم في التحصيل، ويحيط هو بمسائل الفن. وإذا ألقيت عليه الغايات في البدايات وهو حينئذ عاجز عن الفهم والوعي وبعيد عن الاستعداد له، كلَّ ذهنه عنها، وحسب ذلك من صعوبة العلم في نفسه فتكاسل عنه وانحرف عن قبوله وتمادى في هِجْرَانِه. وإنما أتى ذلك من سوء التعليم.

(64) The teacher should not ask more from a student than that he understand the book he is engaged in studying, in accordance with his class (age group)[74] and his receptivity to instruction, whether he is at the start or at the end (of his studies). (The teacher) should not bring in problems other than those found in that particular book, until the student knows the whole (book) from beginning to end, is acquainted with its purpose, and has gained a habit from it, which he then can apply to other (books). When the student has acquired (the scholarly) habit in one discipline, he is prepared for learning all the others. He also has become interested in looking for more and in advancing to higher (learning). Thus, he eventually acquires a complete mastery of scholarship. But if one confuses a student, he will be unable to understand (anything). He becomes indolent. He stops thinking. He despairs of becoming a scholar and avoids scholarship and instruction.

(65) "God guides whomever He wants to guide."[75]

(66) It is also necessary (for the teacher) to avoid prolonging the period of instruction in a single discipline or book, by breaks in the sessions and long intervals between them. This causes (the student) to forget and disrupts the nexus between the different problems (of the discipline being studied). The result of such interruptions is that attainment of the (scholarly) habit becomes difficult. If the first and last things of a discipline are present in the mind and prevent the effects of forgetfulness, the (scholarly) habit is more easily acquired, more firmly established, and closer to becoming a (true) coloring. For habits are acquired by continuous and repeated activity. When one forgets to act, one forgets the habit that results from that particular action.

(67) God "taught you what you did not know."[76]

(68) A good and necessary method and approach in instruction is not to expose the student to two disciplines at the same time.[77] Otherwise, he will rarely master one of them, since he has to divide his attention and is diverted from each of them by his attempt to understand the other. Thus, he will consider both of them obscure and difficult, and be unsuccessful in both. But if the (student's) mind is free to study the subject that he is out (to study) and can restrict himself to it, that (fact) often makes it simpler (for the student) to learn (the subject in question).

(69) God gives success to that which is correct.

(٦٤) ولا ينبغي للمعلم أن يزيد متعلمه على فهم كتابه الذى أكب على التعليم منه بحسب طاقته، وعلى نسبة قبوله للتعليم مبتدئاً كان أو منتهياً، ولا يخلط مسائل الكتاب بغيرها حتى يعيه من أوله إلى آخره ويحصل أغراضه ويستولي منه على ملكة بها ينفذ في غيره. لأن المتعلم إذا حصَّل ملكة ما في علم من العلوم، استعد بها لقبول ما بقي، وحصل له نشاط في طلب المزيد والنهوض إلى ما فوق، حتى يستولي على غايات العلم. وإذا خلط عليه الأمر عجز عن الفهم، وأدركه الكلال، وانطمس فكره، ويئس من التحصيل. وهجر العلم والتعليم.

(٦٥) والله يهدى من يشاء.

(٦٦) وكذلك ينبغي لك أن لا تُطوِّل على المتعلم في الفن الواحد بتفريق المجالس وتقطيع ما بينها، لأنه ذريعة إلى النسيان وانقطاع مسائل الفن بعضها من بعض، فيعسر حصول الملكة بتفريقها. وإذا كانت أوائل العلم وأواخره حاضرة عند الفكرة، مجانبة للنسيان، كانت الملكة أيسر حصولا وأحكم ارتباطاً وأقرب صبغة. لأن الملكات إنما تحصل بتتابع الفعل وتكراره، وإذا تنوسى الفعل تنوسيت الملكة الناشئة عنه.

(٦٧) والله علمكم ما لم تكونوا تعلمون.

(٦٨) ومن المذاهب الجميلة والطرق الواجبة في التعليم أن لا يُخلَط على المتعلم علمان معاً فإنه حينئذ قل أن يظفر بواحد منهما لما فيه من تقسيم البال وانصرافه عن كل واحد منهما إلى تفهم الآخر، فيستغلقان معاً ويستصعبان، ويعود منهما بالخيبة. وإذا تفرغ الفكر لتعليم ما هو بسبيله مقتصراً عليه، فربما كان ذلك أجدر بتحصيله.

(٦٩) والله سبحانه وتعالى الموفق للصواب.

(70) You,[78] student, should realize that I am here giving you useful (hints) for your study. If you accept them and follow them assiduously, you will find a great and noble treasure. As an introduction that will help you to understand these (hints), I shall tell you the following:

(71) Man's ability to think is a special natural gift which God created exactly as He created all His other creations. It is an action and motion[79] in the soul by means of a power (located) in the middle cavity of the brain.[80] At times, (thinking) means the beginning of orderly and well-arranged human actions. At other times, it means the beginning of the knowledge of something that had not been available (before). The (ability to think) is directed toward some objective whose two extremes[81] it has perceived (*taṣawwur*), and (now) it desires to affirm or deny it. In almost no time, it recognizes the middle term which combines the two (extremes), if (the objective) is uniform. Or, it goes on to obtain another middle term, if (the objective) is manifold. It thus finds its objective. It is in this way that the ability to think, by which man is distinguished from all the other animals, works.

(72) Now, the craft of logic is (knowledge of the) way in which the natural ability to think and speculate operates. Logic describes it, so that correct operation can be distinguished from erroneous. To be right, though, is in the essence of the ability to think. However, in very rare cases, it is affected by error. This comes from perceiving (*taṣawwur*) the two extremes in forms other than are properly theirs, as the result of confusion in the order and arrangement of the propositions from which the conclusion is drawn. Logic helps to avoid such traps. Thus,[82] it is a technical procedure which parallels (man's) natural ability to think and conforms to the way in which it functions. Since it is a technical procedure, it can be dispensed with in most cases. Therefore, one finds that many of the world's most excellent thinkers have achieved scholarly results without employing the craft of logic, especially when their intention was sincere and they entrusted themselves to the mercy of God, which is the greatest help (anyone may hope to find). They proceeded with the aid of the natural ability to think at its best, and this (ability), as it was created by God, permitted them by (its very) nature to find the middle term and knowledge of their objective.

(٧٠) واعلم أيها المتعلم أني أتحفك بفائدة في تعلمك فإن تَلَقَّيْتَهَا بالقبول وأمسكتها بيد الصناعة ظفرت بكنز عظيم وذخيرة شريفة. وأقدم لك مقدمة تعينك في فهمها.

(٧١) وذلك أن الفكر الإنساني طبيعة مخصوصة فطرها الله كما فطر سائر مبتدعاته، وهو وجدان حركة للنفس في البطن الأوسط من الدماغ، تارة يكون مبدأً للأفعال الإنسانية على نظام وترتيب، وتارة يكون مبدأ لعلم ما لم يكن حاصلا بأن يتوجه إلى المطلوب. وقد يصور طرفيه ويروم نفيه أو إثباته فيلوح له الوسط الذي يجمع بينهما أسرع من لمح البصر إن كان واحداً، وينتقل إلى تحصيل آخر إن كان متعدداً، ويصير إلى الظفر بمطلوبه. هذا شأن هذه الطبيعة الفكرية التي تميز بها البشر من بين سائر الحيوانات.

(٧٢) ثم الصناعة المنطقية هي كيفية فعل هذه الطبيعة الفكرية النظرية تصفه لتعلم سداده من خطئه، لأنها، وإن كان الصواب لها ذاتياً إلا أنه، قد يعرض لها الخطأ في الأقل من تصور الطرفين على غير صورتهما من اشتباه الهيآت في نظم القضايا وترتيبها للنتاج. فَتَعَيَّنَ المنطق للتخلص من ورطة هذا الفساد إذا عرض. فالمنطق إذاً أَمرٌ صناعي مساوق للطبيعة الفكرية ومنطبق على صورة فعلها. ولكونه أمرًا صناعيًا استغنى عنه في الأكثر. ولذلك تجد كثيرًا من فحول النُظَّارِ في الخليقة يحصلون على المطالب في العلوم دون صناعة المنطق، ولا سيما مع صدق النية والتعرض لرحمة الله، فإن ذلك أعظم معنى، ويسلكون بالطبيعة الفكرية على سدادها، فيفضي بالطبع إلى حصول الوسط والعلم المطلوب كما فطرها الله عليه.

(73) Besides the technical procedure called logic, the (process of) study involves another introductory (discipline), namely, the knowledge of words and the way in which they indicate ideas in the mind by deriving them from what the forms (of the letters) say, in the case of writing, and from what the tongue—speech—says in the case of spoken utterances.[83] You, the student, must pass through all these veils, in order to reach (the state where you can) think about your objective.

(74) First, there is the way in which writing indicates spoken words.[84] This is the easiest part of it. Then, there is the way in which the spoken words indicate the ideas one is seeking. Further, there are the rules for arranging the ideas in their proper molds, as they are known from the craft of logic, in order to (be able to) make deductions. Then, there are those ideas in the mind that are abstract and (used) as nets with which one goes hunting for the (desired) objective with the help of one's natural ability to think (and) entrusting oneself to the mercy and generosity of God.[85]

(75) Not everyone is able to pass through all these stages quickly and to cut through all these veils easily during the (process of) instruction.[86] Disputes often cause the mind to stop at the veils of words. Disturbing quarrels and doubts cause it to fall into the nets of argument, so that the mind is prevented from attaining its objective. Rarely do more than a few (individuals), who are guided by God, succeed in extricating themselves from this abyss.

(76) If you are afflicted by such (difficulties) and hampered in your understanding (of the problems) by misgivings or disturbing doubts in your mind, cast them off! Discard the veils of words and the obstacles of doubt! Leave all the technical procedures and take refuge in the realm of the natural ability to think given to you by nature! Let your speculation roam in it and let your mind freely delve in it, according to whatever you desire (to obtain) from it! Set foot in the places where the greatest thinkers before you did! Entrust yourself to God's aid, as in His mercy He aided them and taught them what they did not know![87] If you do that, God's helpful light will shine upon you and show you your objective. Inspiration will indicate (to you) the middle term which God made a natural requirement of the (process of) thinking, as we have stated.[88] At that particular moment, return with (the middle term) to the molds and forms (to be used) for the arguments, dip it into them, and give it its due of the technical norm (of logic)! Then, clothe it with the forms of words and bring it forth into the world of spoken utterances, firmly girt and soundly constructed!

(٧٣) ثم من دون هذا الأمر الصناعي، الذي هو المنطق، مقدمة أخرى من التعلم وهي معرفة الألفاظ ودلالتها على المعاني الذهنية تردها من مشافهة الرسوم بالكتاب ومشافهة اللسان بالخطاب. فلابد أيها المتعلم من مجاوزتك هذه الحجب كلها إلى الفكر في مطلوبك.

(٧٤) فأولا دلالة الكتابة المرسومة على الألفاظ المقولة وهي أخفها، ثم دلالة الألفاظ المقولة على المعاني المطلوبة، ثم القوانين في ترتيب المعانى للاستدلال في قوالبها المعروفة في صناعة المنطق، ثم تلك المعاني مجردة في الفكر أشراكا يقتنص بها المطلوب بالطبيعة الفكرية بالتعرض لرحمة الله ومواهبه.

(٧٥) وليس كل أحد يتجاوز هذه المراتب بسرعة، ولا يقطع هذه الحجب في التعليم بسهولة؛ بل ربما وقف الذهن في حجب الألفاظ بالمناقشات، أو عثر في أشراك الأدلة بشغب الجدال والشبهات، وقعد عن تحصيل المطلوب. ولم يكد يتخلص من تلك الغمرة إلا قليل ممن هداه الله.

(٧٦) فإذا ابتليت بمثل ذلك وعرض لك ارتباك في فهمك أو تشغيب بالشبهات في ذهنك، فاطِّرِحْ ذلك وانتبذ حجب الألفاظ وعوائق الشبهات، واترك الأمر الصناعي جملة، واخلص إلى فضاء الفكر الطبيعي الذي فطرت عليه، وسرِّح نظرك فيه، فرِّغ ذهنك له للغوص على مرامك منه، واضعا لها حيث وضعها أكابر النُّظَّار قبلك، مستعرضا للفتح من الله كما فتح عليهم من ذهنهم من رحمته وعلمهم ما لم يكونوا يعلمون. فإذا فعلت ذلك أشرقت عليك أنوار الفتح من الله بالظفر بمطلوبك وحصل الإلهام الوسط الذي جعله الله من مقتضيات ذاتيات هذا الفكر وفطره عليه كما قلنا. وحينئذ فارجع به إلى قوالب الأدلة وصورها فأفرغه فيها، ووفه حقه من القانون الصناعي، ثم اكسه صور الألفاظ، وابرزه إلى عالم الخطاب والمشافهة وثيق العرى صحيح البنيان.

(77) Verbal disputes and doubts concerning the distinction between right and wrong logical evidence are all technical and conventional matters. Their numerous aspects are all alike or similar, because of their conventional and technical character. If they stop you, (you[89] will not be able) to distinguish the truth in them, for the truth becomes distinguishable only if it exists by nature. All the doubts and uncertainties will remain. The veils will cover the objective sought and prevent the thinker from attaining it. That has been the case with most recent thinkers, especially with those who formerly spoke a language other than Arabic, which was a mental handicap,[90] or those who were enamored with logic and partial to it.[91] They believe that logic is a natural means for the perception of the truth. They become confused when doubts and misgivings arise concerning the evidence, and they are scarcely able to free themselves from (such doubts).

(78) As a matter of fact, the natural means for the perception of the truth is, as we have stated, (man's) natural ability to think, when it is free from all imaginings and when the thinker entrusts himself to the mercy of God. Logic merely describes the process of thinking and mostly parallels it. Take that into consideration and ask for God's mercy when you have difficulty in understanding problems! Then, the divine light will shine upon you and give you the right inspiration.

(79) God guides in His mercy. Knowledge comes only from God.

Study of the auxiliary sciences should not be prolonged, and their problems should not be treated in detail.[92]

(80) It[93] should be known that the sciences customarily known among civilized people are of two kinds. There are the sciences that are wanted *per se,* such as the religious sciences of Qurʾān interpretation, Prophetic traditions, jurisprudence, and speculative theology, and the physical and metaphysical sciences of philosophy. In addition, there are sciences that are instrumental and auxiliary to the sciences mentioned. Among such auxiliary sciences are Arabic philology, arithmetic, and others, which are auxiliary to the religious sciences, and logic which is auxiliary to philosophy and often also to speculative theology and the science of the principles of jurisprudence (when treated) according to the method of recent scholars.[94]

(٧٧) وأما إن وقفت عند المناقشة والشبهة في الأدلة الصناعية وتمحيص صوابها من خطئها-وهذه أمور صناعية وضعية تستوى جهاتها المتعددة وتتشابه لأجل الوضع والاصطلاح فلا تتميز جهة الحق، إنما تستبين إذا كانت بالطبع-فيستمر ما حصل من الشك والارتياب، وتسدل الحجب على المطلوب، وتقعد بالناظر عن تحصيله. وهذا شأن الأكثرين من النُظَّار والمتأخرين، سيما من سبقت له عجمة في لسانه فربطت عن ذهنه، ومن حصل له شغب بالقانون المنطقي، تعصب له فاعتقد أنه الذريعة إلى إدراك الحق بالطبع، فيقع في الحيرة بين شبه الأدلة وشكوكها، ولا يكاد يخلص منها.

(٧٨) والذريعة إلى دَرْكِ الحق بالطبع إنما هو الفكر الطبيعي كما قلناه، إذا جرد عن جميع الأوهام وتعرض الناظر فيه إلى رحمة الله تعالى. وأما المنطق فإنما هو واصف لفعل هذا الفكر، فيساوقه لذلك في الأكثر. فاعْتَبِر ذلك، واستمطر رحمة الله تعالى متى أعوزك فهم المسائل، تشْرِقْ عليك أنواره بالإلهام إلى الصواب.

(٧٩) والله الهادى إلى رحمته. وما العلم إلا من عند الله.

(فصل) في أن العلوم الآلية لا تُوَسَّع فيها الأنظار ولا تُفَرَّع المسائل

(٨٠) اعلم أن العلوم المتعارفة بين أهل العمران على صنفين: علوم مقصودة بالذات، كالشرعيات من التفسير والحديث والفقه وعلم الكلام، وكالطبيعيات والإلهيات من الفلسفة؛ وعلوم هي آلية وسيلة لهذه العلوم كالعربية والحساب وغيرهما للشرعيات، وكالمنطق للفلسفة، وربما كان آلة لعلم الكلام ولأصول الفقه على طريقة المتأخرين.

(81) In the case of the sciences that are wanted (*per se*), it does no harm to extend their discussion, to treat their problems in detail, and to present all the evidence and (all the different) views (which exist concerning them). It gives the student of them a firmer habit and clarifies the ideas they contain which one wants to know. But the sciences that are auxiliary to other sciences, such as Arabic philology, logic, and the like, should be studied only in so far as they are aids to the other (sciences). Discussion of them should not be prolonged, and the problems should not be treated in detail, as this would lead away from their purpose, and their purpose is (to facilitate understanding of) the sciences to which they are auxiliary, nothing else. Whenever the (auxiliary sciences) cease to be (auxiliary to other sciences), they abandon their purpose, and occupation with them becomes an idle pastime.

(82) Moreover,[95] it is (also) difficult to acquire the habit of them, because they are large subjects with many details. Their (difficulty) is often an obstacle to acquiring the sciences wanted *per se,* because it takes so long to get to them. However, they are more important, and life is too short to acquire a knowledge of everything in this (thorough) form. Thus, occupation with the auxiliary sciences constitutes a waste of one's life, occupation with something that is of no concern.[96]

(83) Recent scholars have done this with grammar and logic and even with the principles of jurisprudence. They have prolonged the discussion of these disciplines both[97] by transmitting (more material) and (by adding to the material) through deductive reasoning. They have increased the number of details and problems,[98] causing them to be no longer auxiliary sciences, but disciplines that are wanted *per se.* In consequence, (the auxiliary sciences) often deal with views and problems for which there is no need in the disciplines that are wanted *per se* (and are the sole *raison d'être* of the auxiliary sciences). Thus, they are a sort of idle pastime and also do outright harm to students, because the sciences that are wanted (*per se*) are more important for them than the auxiliary and instrumental sciences. (Now,) if they spend all their lives on the auxiliary (sciences), when will they get around to (the sciences) that are wanted (*per se*)? Therefore, teachers of the auxiliary sciences ought not to delve too deeply in them[99] and increase the number of their problems. They must advise the student concerning their purpose and have him stop there. Those who have the mind to go more deeply (into them) and consider themselves capable and able to do so, may choose (such a course) for themselves. Everyone is successful at the things for which he was created.[100]

(٨١) فأما العلوم التي هي مقاصد، فلا حرج في توسعة الكلام فيها، وتفريع المسائل واستكشاف الأدلة والأنظار؛ فإن ذلك يزيد طالبها تمكناً في ملكته وإيضاحاً لمعانيها المقصودة. وأما العلوم التي هي آلة لغيرها مثل العربيه والمنطق وأمثالها فلا ينبغي أن ينظر فيها إلا من حيث هي آلة لذلك الغير فقط، ولا يوسع فيها الكلام ولا تفرع المسائل، لأن ذلك مخرج لها عن المقصود، إذ المقصود منها ما هي آلة له لا غير، فكلما خرجت عن ذلك خرجت عن المقصود وصار الاشتغال بها.

(٨٢) لغواً مع ما فيه من صعوبة الحصول على ملكتها لطولها وكثرة فروعها. وربما يكون ذلك عائقاً عن تحصيل العلوم المقصودة بالذات لطول وسائلها؛ مع أن شأنها أهم والعمر يقصر عن تحصيل الجميع على هذه الصورة، فيكون الاشتغال بهذه العلوم الآلية تضييعاً للعمر وشغلا بما لا يعني.

(٨٣) وهذا كما فعل المتأخرون في صناعة النحو وصناعة المنطق وأصول الفقه، لأنهم أوسعوا دائرة الكلام فيها وأكثروا من التفاريع والاستدلالات بما أخرجها من كونها آلة وصيرها من المقاصد. وربما يقع فيها أنظار لا حاجة بها في العلوم المقصودة فهي من نوع اللغو. وهي أيضاً مضرة بالمتعلمين على الإطلاق؛ لأن المتعلمين اهتمامهم بالعلوم المقصودة أكثر من اهتمامهم بوسائلها؛ فإذا قطعوا العمر في تحصيل الوسائل فمتى يظفرون بالمقاصد؟! فلهذا يجب على المعلمين لهذه العلوم الآلية أن لا يستبحروا في شأنها، وينبهوا المتعلم على الغرض منها، ويقفوا به عنده. فمن نزعت به همته بعد ذلك إلى شيء من التوغل فليَرْقَ له ما شاء من المراقي صعباً أو سَهلا. وكلٌّ ميسَّرٌ لما خُلِقَ له.

The instruction of children and the different methods employed in the Muslim cities.

(84) It should be known that instructing children in the Qurʾān is a symbol of Islam. Muslims have, and practice, such instruction in all their cities, because it imbues hearts with a firm belief (in Islam) and its articles of faith, which are (derived) from the verses of the Qurʾān and certain Prophetic traditions. The Qurʾān has become the basis of instruction, the foundation for all habits that may be acquired later on. The reason for this is that the things one is taught in one's youth take root more deeply (than anything else). They are the basis of all later (knowledge). The first impression the heart receives is, in a way, the foundation of (all scholarly) habits. The character of the foundation determines the condition of the building. The methods of instructing children in the Qurʾān differ according to differences of opinion as to the habits that are to result from that instruction.

(85) The Maghribī method is to restrict the education of children to instruction in the Qurʾān and to practice, during the course (of instruction), in Qurʾān orthography and its problems and the differences among Qurʾān experts on this score. The (Maghribīs) do not bring up any other subjects in their classes, such as traditions, jurisprudence, poetry, or Arabic philology, until the pupil is skilled in (the Qurʾān), or drops out before becoming skilled in it. In the latter case, it means, as a rule, that he will not learn anything. This is the method the urban population in the Maghrib and the native Berber Qurʾān teachers who follow their (urban compatriots), use in educating their children up to the age of manhood. They use it also with old people who study the Qurʾān after part of their life has passed. Consequently, (Maghribīs) know the orthography of the Qurʾān, and know it by heart, better than any other (Muslim group).

(86) The Spanish method is instruction in reading and writing as such. That is what they pay attention to in the instruction (of children). However, since the Qurʾān is the basis and foundation of (all) that and the source of Islam and (all) the sciences, they make it the basis of instruction, but they do not restrict their instruction of children exclusively to (the Qurʾān). They also bring in (other subjects), mainly poetry and composition, and they give the children an expert knowledge of Arabic and teach them a good handwriting. They do not stress teaching of the Qurʾān more than the other subjects. In fact, they are more concerned with teaching handwriting than any other subject, until the child

(فصل) في تعليم الوِلْدان

(٨٤) اعلم أن تعليم الوِلْدان للقرآن شعار من شعائر الدين، أخذ به أهل الملة، ودرجوا عليه في جميع أمصارهم، لما يسبق فيه إلى القلوب من رسوخ الإيمان وعقائده من آيات القرآن وبعض متون الأحاديث. وصار القرآن أصل التعليم الذي ينبني عليه ما يحصل بعد من الملكات. وسبب ذلك أن تعليم الصغر أشد رسوخاً وهو أصل لما بعده، لأن السابق الأول للقلوب كالأساس للملكات، وعلى حسب الأساس وأساليبه يكون حال ما ينبني عليه. واختلفت طرقهم في تعليم القرآن للولدان باختلافهم باعتبار ما ينشأ عن ذلك التعليم من الملكات.

(٨٥) فأما أهل المغرب فمذهبهم في الولْدان الاقتصار على تعليم القرآن فقط، وأخذهم أثناء المدارسة بالرسم ومسائله واختلاف حَمَلة القرآن فيه، لا يخلطون ذلك بسواه في شيء من مجالس تعليمهم، لا من حديث ولا من فقه ولا من شعر ولا من كلام العرب، إلى أن يحذق فيه أو ينقطع دونه، فيكون انقطاعه في الغالب انقطاعاً عن العلم بالجملة. وهذا مذهب أهل الأمصار بالمغرب ومن تبعهم من قرى البربر أمم المغرب في وِلْدانِهم إلى أن يجاوزوا حد البلوغ إلى الشبيبة. وكذا في الكبير إذا راجع مدارسة القرآن بعد طائفة من عمره. فهم لذلك أقوم على رسم القرآن وحفظه من سواهم.

(٨٦) وأما أهل الأندلس فمذهبهم تعليم القرآن والكتاب من حيث هو، وهذا هو الذي يراعونه في التعليم. إلا أنه لما كان القرآن أصل ذلك وأسه، ومنبع الدين والعلوم، جعلوه أصلا في التعليم. فلا يقتصرون لذلك عليه فقط بل يخلطون في تعليمهم لِلوِلْدان روايةَ الشعر في الغالب والترسل وأخذهم بقوانين العربية وحفظها وتجويد الخط والكتاب. ولا تختص عنايتهم في التعليم بالقرآن دون هذه، بل عنايتهم

reaches manhood. He then has some experience and knowledge of the Arabic language and poetry. He has an excellent knowledge of handwriting, and he would have a thorough acquaintance with scholarship in general, if the tradition of scholarly instruction (still) existed in (Spain), but he does not, because the tradition no longer exists there.[101] Thus, (present-day Spanish children) obtain no further (knowledge) than what their Primary instruction provides. It is enough for those whom God guides. It prepares (them for further studies), in the event that a teacher (of them) can be found.

(87) The people of Ifrīqiyah combine the instruction of children in the Qurʾān, usually, with the teaching of traditions. They also teach basic scientific norms and certain scientific problems. However, they stress giving their children a good knowledge of the Qurʾān and acquainting them with its various recensions and readings more than anything else. Next they stress handwriting. In general, their method of instruction in the Qurʾān is closer to the Spanish method (than to Maghribī or Eastern methods), because their (educational tradition) derives from the Spanish *shaykhs* who crossed over when the Christians conquered Spain, and asked for hospitality in Tunis.[102] From that time on, they were the teachers of (Tunisian) children.

(88) The People of the East, as far as we know, likewise have a mixed curriculum. I do not know what (subjects) they stress (primarily). We have been told that they are concerned with teaching the Qurʾān and the works and basic norms of (religious) scholarship once (the children) are grown up. They do not combine (instruction in the Qurʾān) with instruction in handwriting. They have (special) rule(s) for teaching it, and there are special teachers for it,[103] just like any other craft which is taught (separately) and not included in the school curriculum for children. The children's slates (on which they practice) exhibit an inferior form of handwriting. Those who want to learn a (good) handwriting may do so later on (in their lives) from professional (calligraphers), to the extent of their interest in it and desire.

(89) The fact that the people of Ifrīqiyah and the Maghrib restrict themselves to the Qurʾān makes them altogether incapable of mastering the linguistic habit. For as a rule, no (scholarly) habit can originate from the (study of the) Qurʾān, because no human being can produce anything like it. Thus, human beings are unable to employ or imitate its ways (*uslūb*), and they also can form no habit in any other respect. Consequently, a person who knows (the Qurʾān) does not acquire the

فيه بالخط أكثر من جميعها، إلى أن يخرج الولد من عمر البلوغ إلى الشبيبة وقد شدا بعض الشيء في العربية والشعر والبَصَر بهما، وبرَّز في الخط والكِتاب وتعلق بأذيال العلم على الجملة لو كان فيها سند لتعليم العلوم. لكنهم ينقطعون عند ذلك لانقطاع سند التعليم في آفاقهم، ولا يحصل بأيديهم إلا ما حصل من ذلك التعليم الأول، وفيه كفاية لمن أرشده الله تعالى، واستعداد إذا وجد المعلم.

(٨٧) وأما أهل إفْرِيقيَة فيخلطون في تعليمهم للولدان القرآن بالحديث في الغالب، ومدارسة قوانين العلوم وتلقين بعض مسائلها. إلا أن عنايتهم بالقرآن، واستظهار الوِلدان إياه، ووقوفهم على اختلاف رواياته وقراءاته، أكثر مما سواه، وعنايتهم بالخط تبع لذلك. وبالجملة فطريقتهم في تعليم القرآن أقرب إلى طريقة أهل الأندلس؛ لأن سند طريقتهم في ذلك متصل بمشيخة الأندلس الذين أجازوا عند تغلب النصارى على شرق الأندلس، واستقروا بتونس، وعنهم أخذ وِلْدانُهُم بعد ذلك.

(٨٨) وأما أهل المشرق فيخلطون في التعليم كذلك على ما يبلغنا؛ ولا أدرى بم عنايتهم منها. والذى ينقل لنا أن عنايتهم بدراسة القرآن وصحف العلم وقوانينه في زمن الشبيبة ولا يخلطون بتعليم الخط؛ بل لتعليم الخط عندهم قانون ومعلمون له على انفراده، كما تتعلم سائر الصنائع، ولا يتداولونها في مكاتب الصبيان. وإذا كتبوا لهم الألواح فبخط قاصر عن الإجادة. ومن أراد تعلم الخط فعلى قدر ما يسنح له بعد ذلك من الهمة في طلبه، ويبتغيه من أهل صنعته.

(٨٩) فأما أهل إفريقية والمغرب فأفادهم الاقتصار على القرآن القصور عن ملكة اللسان جملة، وذلك أن القرآن لا ينشأ عنه في الغالب ملكة، لما أن البشر مصروفون عن الإتيان بمثله، فهم مصروفون لذلك عن الاستعمال على أساليبه والاحتذاء بها، وليس لهم ملكة في غير أساليبه، فلا يحصل لصاحبه ملكة في اللسان العربى،

habit of the Arabic language. It will be his lot to be awkward in expression and to have little fluency in speaking. This situation is not quite so pronounced among the people of Ifrīqiyah as among the Maghribīs, because, as we have stated, the former combine instruction in the Qur'ān with instruction in the terminology of scientific norms. Thus, they get some practice and have some examples to imitate. However, their habit in this respect does not amount to a good style (eloquence), because their knowledge mostly consists of scholarly terminology which falls short of good style, as will be mentioned in the proper section.[104]

(90) As for the Spaniards, their varied curriculum with its great amount of instruction in poetry, composition, and Arabic philology gave them, from their early years on, a habit providing for a better acquaintance with the Arabic language. They were less proficient in all the other (religious) sciences, because they were little familiar with study of the Qur'ān and the traditions that are the basis and foundation of the (religious) sciences. Thus, they were people who knew how to write and who had a literary education that was either excellent or deficient, depending on the secondary education they received after their childhood education.

(91) In his *Riḥlah,* Judge Abū Bakr b. al-ᶜArabī[105] made a remarkable statement about instruction, which retains (the best of) the old, and presents (some good) new features.[106] He placed instruction in Arabic and poetry ahead of all the other sciences, as in the Spanish method, since, he said, "poetry is the archive of the Arabs.[107] Poetry and Arabic philology should be taught first because of the (existing) corruption of the language.[108] From there, the (student) should go on to arithmetic and study it assiduously, until he knows its basic norms. He should then go on to the study of the Qur'ān, because with his (previous) preparation, it will be easy for him." (Ibn al-ᶜArabī) continued: "How thoughtless are our compatriots in that they teach children the Qur'ān when they are first starting out. They read things they do not understand and work hard at something that is not as important for them as other matters." He concluded: "The student should study successively the principles of Islam, the principles of jurisprudence, disputation, and then the Prophetic traditions and the sciences connected with them." He also forbade teaching two disciplines at the same time, save to the student with a good mind and sufficient energy.[109]

وحظه الجمود في العبارات وقلة التصرف في الكلام. وربما كان أهل افريقية في ذلك أخف من أهل المغرب لما يخلطون في تعليمهم القرآن بعبارات العلوم في قوانينها كما قلناه، فيقتدرون على شيء من التصرف ومحاذاة المثل بالمثل، إلا أن ملكتهم في ذلك قاصرة عن البلاغة، لما أن أكثر محفوظهم عبارات العلوم النازلة عن البلاغة كما سيأتي في فصله.

(٩٠) وأما أهل الأندلس فأفادهم التفنن في التعليم وكثرة رواية الشعر والترسل ومدارسة العربية من أول العمر حصولَ ملكة صاروا بها أعرف في اللسان العربي، وقصروا في سائر العلوم لبعدهم عن مدارسة القرآن والحديث الذي هو أصل العلوم وأساسها فكانوا لذلك أهل خط وأدب بارع أو مقصر على حسب ما يكون التعليم الثاني من بعد تعليم الصبا.

(٩١) ولقد ذهب القاضي أبو بكر بن العربي في كتاب رحلته إلى طريقة غريبة في وجه التعليم، وأعاد في ذلك وأبدأ، وقدم تعليم العربية والشعر على سائر العلوم كما هو مذهب أهل الأندلس قال: «لأن الشعر ديوان العرب ويدعو إلى تقديمه وتعليم العربية في التعليم ضرورَةُ فساد اللغة. ثم يُنْتَقَلُ منه إلى الحساب فيتمرن فيه حتى يرى القوانين. ثم ينتقل إلى درس القرآن فإنه يتيسر عليه بهذه المقدمة». ثم قال: «ويا غفلة أهل بلادنا في أن يؤخذ الصبي بكتاب الله في أول أمره، يقرأ ما لا يفهم ويَنْصَب في أمرٍ غَيْرُه أَهمُّ عليه» ثم قال: «ينظر في أصول الدين ثم أصول الفقه ثم الجدل ثم الحديث وعلومه». -ونهى مع ذلك أن يخلط في التعليم علمان إلا أن يكون المتعلم قابلا لذلك بجودة الفهم والنشاط.

(92) This is Judge Abū Bakr's advice. It is a good method indeed. However, accepted custom is not favorable to it, and custom has greater power over conditions (than anything else). Accepted custom gives preference to the teaching of the Qur'ān. The reason is the desire for the blessing and reward (in the other world resulting from knowledge of the Qur'ān) and a fear of the things that might affect children in "the folly of youth"[110] and harm them and keep them from acquiring knowledge. They might miss the chance to learn the Qur'ān. As long as they remain at home, they are amenable to authority. When they have grown up and shaken off the yoke of authority, the tempests of young manhood often cast them upon the shores of wrongdoing. Therefore, while the children are still at home and under the yoke of authority, one seizes the opportunity to teach them the Qur'ān, so that they will not remain without knowledge of it. If one could be certain that a child would continue to study and accept instruction (when he has grown up), the method mentioned by the judge would be the most suitable one ever devised in East or West.

(93) "God decides, and no one can change His decision."[111]

Severity to students does them harm.

(94) This comes about as follows. Severe punishment in the course of instruction does harm to the student, especially to little children, because it belongs among (the things that make for a) bad habit. Students,[112] slaves, and servants who are brought up with injustice and (tyrannical) force are overcome by it. It makes them feel oppressed and causes them to lose their energy. It makes them lazy and induces them to lie and be insincere. That is, their outward behavior differs from what they are thinking, because they are afraid that they will have to suffer tyrannical treatment (if they tell the truth). Thus, they are taught deceit and trickery. This becomes their custom and character. They lose the quality that goes with social and political organization and makes people human, namely, (the desire to) protect and defend themselves and their homes, and they become dependent on others.[113] Indeed, their souls become too indolent to (attempt to) acquire the virtues and good character qualities. Thus, they fall short of their potentialities and do not reach the limit of their humanity. As a result, they revert to the stage of "the lowest of the low."[114]

(٩٢) هذا ما أشار إليه القاضي أبو بكر رحمه الله. وهو لعمري مذهب حسن. إلا أن العوائد لا تساعد عليه، وهي أَمْلَكُ بالأحوال. ووجه ما اختُصَّت به العوائد من تقدم دراسة القرآن إيثاراً للتبرك والثواب، وخشية ما يعرض للولد في جنون الصبا من الآفات والقواطع عن العلم، فيفوته القرآن؛ لأنه ما دام في الحِجْر منقاد للحكم، فإذا تجاوز البلوغ وانحل من رِبْقَةِ القهر، فربما عصفت به رياح الشبيبة فألقته بساحل البَطالة. فيغتنمون في زمان الحِجْر ورِبقَةَ الحكم تحصيلَ القرآن لئلا يذهب خلواً منه. ولو حصل التيقن باستمراره في طلب العلم وقبوله التعليم لكان هذا المذهب الذى ذكره القاضي أولى مما أخذ به أهل المغرب والمشرق.

(٩٣) ولكن الله يحكم ما يشاء، لا مُعَقِّبَ لحكمه، سبحانه.

(فصل) في أن الشدة على المتعلمين مضرة بهم

(٩٤) وذلك أن إرهاف الحد في التعليم مضر بالمتعلم، سيما في أصاغر الوُلد لأنه من سوء المَلَكَةِ. ومن كان مرباه بالعسف والقهر من المتعلمين أو المماليك أو الخدم سطا به القهر، وضيق على النفس في انبساطها، وذهب بنشاطها، ودعاه إلى الكسل، وحُمِل على الكذب والخبث، وهو التظاهر بغير ما في ضميره خوفاً من انبساط الأيدي بالقهر عليه، وعلّمه المكر والخديعة لذلك، وصارت له هذه عادة وخلقاً، وفسدت معاني الإنسانية التي له من حيث الاجتماع والتمرن، وهي الحَمِيَّة والمدافعة عن نفسه ومنزله، وصار عيالاً على غيره في ذلك، بل وكسلت النفس عن اكتساب الفضائل والخلق الجميل، فانقبضت عن غايتها ومدى إنسانيتها، فارتكس وعاد في أسفل السافلين.

(95) That[115] is what happened to every nation that fell under the yoke of tyranny and learned through it the meaning of injustice. One may check this by (observing) any person who is not in control of his own affairs and has no authority on his side to guarantee his (safety). One will thus be able to infer (from the observable facts) that things are (as I have stated). One may look at the Jews and the bad character they have acquired,[116] such that they are described in every region and period as having the quality of *khurj*,[117] which, according to well-known technical terminology, means "insincerity and trickery." The reason is what we have (just) said.

(96) Thus, a teacher must not be too severe toward his pupil, nor a father toward his son, in educating them. In the book that Abū Muḥammad b. Abī Zayd wrote on the laws governing teachers and pupils, he said: "If children must be beaten, their educator must not strike them more than three times."[118] ᶜUmar said: "Those who are not educated (disciplined) by the religious law are not educated (disciplined) by God."[119] He spoke out of a desire to preserve the souls from the humiliation of disciplinary punishment and in the knowledge that the amount (of disciplinary punishment) that the religious law has stipulated is fully adequate to keep (a person) under control, because the (religious law) knows best what is good for him.

(97) One of the best methods of education was suggested by al-Rashīd to Khalaf b. Aḥmar, the teacher of his son Muḥammad al-Amīn. Khalaf b. Aḥmar[120] said: "Al-Rashīd told me to come and educate his son Muḥammad al-Amīn, and he said to me: 'O Aḥmar, the Commander of the Faithful is entrusting (his son) to you, the life of his soul and the fruit of his heart. Take firm hold of him and make him obey you. Occupy in relation to him the place that the Commander of the Faithful has given you. Teach him to read the Qurʾān. Instruct him in history. Let him transmit poems and teach him the Sunnah of the Prophet. Give him insight into the proper occasions for speech and how to begin a (speech). Forbid him to laugh, save at times when it is proper. Accustom him to honor the Hāshimite dignitaries[121] when they come to him, and to give the military leaders places of honor when they come to his salon. Let no hour pass in which you do not seize he opportunity to teach him something useful. But do so without vexing him, which would kill his mind. Do not always be too lenient with him, or he will get to like leisure and become used to it. As much as possible, correct him kindly and gently. If he does not want it that way, you must then use severity and harshness.'"

(٩٥) وهكذا وقع لكل أمة حصلت في قبضة القهر ونال منها العسف. واعتبره في كل من يُمْلَكُ أمره عليه، ولا تكون المَلَكَة الكافلة له رفيقة به، وتجد ذلك فيهم استقراء. وانظره في اليهود وما حصل بذلك فيهم من خلق السوء، حتى إنهم يوصفون في كل أفق وعصر بالحرج ومعناه في الاصطلاح المشهور التخابث والكيد، وسببه ما قلناه.

(٩٦) فينبغي للمعلم في مُتَعلِّمه، والوالد في وُلْدِه، أن لا يستبد عليهم في التأديب. وقد قال محمد بن أبي زيد في كتابه الذي ألفه في حكم المعلمين والمتعلمين لا ينبغي لمؤدب الصبيان أن يزيد في ضربهم، إذا احتاجوا إليه، على ثلاثة أسواط شيئا. ومن كلام عمر (رضي الله عنه): « من لم يؤدبه الشرع لا أدَّبهُ الله »، حرصا على صون النفوس عن مذلة التأديب، وعلماً بأن المقدار الذى عينه الشرع لذلك أملك له، فإنه أعلم بمصلحته.

(٩٧) ومن أحسن مذاهب التعليم ما تقدم به الرشيد لمعلم وُلْده محمد الأمين فقال: « يا أحمر! إن أمير المؤمنين قد دفع إليك مهجة نفسه وثمرة قلبه، فصيِّر يدك عليه مبسوطة، وطاعتَه لك واجبة. فكن له بحيث وضعك أمير المؤمنين. أقرئه القرآن وعرفه الأخبار، وروه الأشعار، وعلمه السنن، وبصره بمواقع الكلام وبدئه، وامنعه من الضحك إلا في أوقاته، وخذه بتعظيم مشايخ بني هاشم إذا دخلوا عليه، ورفع مجالس القواد إذا حضروا مجلسه. ولا تَمُرَّن بك ساعة إلا وأنت مغتنم فائدة تفيده إياها، من غير أن تحزنه فتميت ذهنه. ولا تمعن في مسامحته فيستحلي الفراغ ويألفه، وقوِّمه ما استطعت بالقرب والملاينة؛ فإنْ أباهُما فعليك بالشدة والغلظة » انتهى.

A scholar's education is greatly improved by traveling in quest of knowledge and meeting the authoritative teachers (of his time).

(98) The reason[122] for this is that human beings obtain their knowledge and character qualities and all their opinions and virtues either through study, instruction, and lectures, or through imitation of a teacher and personal contact with him. The only difference here is that habits acquired through personal contact with a teacher are more strongly and firmly rooted. Thus, the greater the number of authoritative teachers (*shaykhs*), the more deeply rooted is the habit one acquires.

(99) Furthermore, the technical terminologies used in scientific instruction are confusing to the student. Many students even suppose them to be part of a given science. The only way to deliver them from that (wrong notion) is by personal contact with teachers, for different teachers employ different terminologies. Thus, meeting scholars and having many authoritative teachers (*shaykhs*) enables the student to notice the difference in the terminologies used by different teachers and to distinguish among them. He will thus be able to recognize the science itself behind the (technical terminology it uses). He will realize that (terminologies) are (merely) means and methods for imparting (knowledge). His powers will work toward acquiring strongly and firmly rooted habits. He will improve the knowledge he has and be able to distinguish it from other (knowledge). In addition, his habits will be strengthened through his intensive personal contact with teachers, when they are many and of various types. This is for those for whom God facilitated the ways of scholarship and right guidance. Thus, traveling in quest of knowledge is absolutely necessary for the acquisition of useful knowledge and perfection through meeting authoritative teachers (*shaykhs*) and having contact with (scholarly) personalities.

(100) God "guides whomever He wants to guide to a straight path."[123]

Scholars are, of all people, those least familiar with the ways of politics.

(101) The[124] reason for this is that (scholars) are used to mental speculation and to a searching study of ideas which they abstract from the *sensibilia* and conceive in their minds as general universals, so that they may be applicable to some matter in general but not to any particular

فصل في أن الرحلة في طلب العلوم ولقاء المشيخة مزيد كمال في التعلم

(٩٨) والسبب في ذلك أن البشر يأخذون معارفهم وأخلاقهم وما ينتحلون به من المذاهب والفضائل تارة علماً وتعليماً وإلقاء، وتارة محاكاة وتلقيناً بالمباشرة. إلا أن حصول الملكات عن المباشرة والتلقين أشدا ستحكاماً وأقوى رسوخاً. فعلى قدر كثرة الشيوخ يكون حصول الملكات و رسوخها.

(٩٩) والاصطلاحات أيضاً في تعليم العلوم مخلِّطةٌ على المتعلم. حتى لقد يظن كثير منهم أنها جزء من العلم. ولا يدفع عنه ذلك إلا مباشرته لاختلاف الطرق فيها من المعلمين. فلقاء أهل العلوم، وتعدد المشايخ يفيده تمييز الاصطلاحات بما يراه من اختلاف طرقهم فيها، فيجرد العلم عنها، ويَعْلَمُ أنها انحاء تعليم وطرق توصيل، وتنهض قواه إلى الرسوخ والاستحكام في الملكات، ويصحح معارفه ويميزها عن سواها، مع تقوية ملكته بالمباشرة والتلقين وكثرتهما من المشيخة عند تعددهم وتنوعهم. وهذا لمن يسر الله عليه طرق العلم والهداية. فالرِّحْلَةُ لا بد منها في طلب العلم لاكتساب الفوائد والكمال بلقاء المشايخ ومباشرة الرجال.

(١٠٠) « وَاللهُ يَهْدِي مَنْ يَشَاءُ إِلَىٰ صِرَاطٍ مُسْتَقِيمٍ ».

فصل في أن العلماء من بين البشر أبعد عن السياسة ومذاهبها

(١٠١) والسبب في ذلك أنهم معتادون النظر الفكري والغوص على المَعاني وانتزاعها من المحسوسات وتجريدها في الذهن أموراً كلية عامة ليحكم عليها بأمر العموم

matter, individual, race, nation, or group of people. (Scholars,) then, make such universal ideas conform (in their minds) to facts of the outside world. They also compare things with others that are similar to or like them, with the help of analogical reasoning as used in jurisprudence, which is something familiar to them. All their conclusions and views continue to be something in the mind. They come to conform (to the facts of the outside world) only after research and speculation has come to an end, or they may never come to conform (to them). The facts of the outside world are merely special cases of the (ideas) that are in the mind. For instance, the religious laws are special cases derived from the well-known (texts) of the Qurʾān and the Sunnah. In their case, one expects the facts of the outside world to conform to them, in contrast with the intellectual sciences, where, in order to (prove) the soundness of views, one expects those views to conform to the facts of the outside world.

(102) Thus, in all their intellectual activity, scholars are accustomed to dealing with matters of the mind and with thoughts. They do not know anything else. Politicians, an the other hand, must pay attention to the facts of the outside world and the conditions attaching to and depending on (politics). (These facts and conditions) are obscure. They may contain some (element) making it impossible to refer them to something like and similar, or contradicting the universal (idea) to which one would like them to conform. The conditions existing in civilization cannot (always) be compared with each other. They may be alike in one respect, but they may differ in other respects.

(103) (Now,) scholars are accustomed to generalizations and analogical conclusions. When they look at politics, they press (their observations) into the mold of their views their way of making deductions. Thus, they commit many errors, or (at least) they cannot be trusted (not to commit errors). The intelligent and alert (segment) of civilized people falls into the same category as (scholars). Their penetrating minds drive them toward a searching occupation with ideas, analogy, and comparison, as is the case with jurists. Thus, they (too) commit errors.

(104) The average person of a healthy disposition and a mediocre intelligence has not got the mind for (such speculation) and does not think of it. Therefore, he restricts himself to considering every matter as it is, and to judging every kind of situation and every type of individual by its

لا بخصوص مادة ولا شخص ولا جيل ولا أمة ولا صنف من الناس، ويطبقون من بعد ذلك الكلي على الخارجيات. وأيضاً يقيسون الأمور على أشباهها وأمثالها بما اعتادوه من القياس الفقهي. فلا تزال أحكامهم وأنظارهم كلها في الذهن ولا تصير إلى المطابقة إلا بعد الفراغ من البحث والنظر. ولا تصير بالجملة إلى مطابقة، وإنما يتفرع ما في الخارج عما في الذهن من ذلك، كالأحكام الشرعية فإنها فروع عما في المحفوظ من أدلة الكتاب والسنة، فتُطْلَبُ مطابقةُ ما في الخارج لها، عكس الأنظار في العلوم العقلية التي تُطْلَبُ في صحتها مطابقَتُها لما في الخارج.

(١٠٢) فهم متعودون في سائر أنظارهم الأمور الذهنية والأنظار الفكرية لا يعرفون سواها. والسياسة يحتاج صاحبها إلى مراعاة ما في الخارج وما يلحقها من الأحوال ويتبعها فإنها خفية، ولعل أن يكون فيها ما يمنع من إلحاقها بشبه أو مثال وينافي الكلي الذي يحاول تطبيقه عليها. ولا يقاس شيء من أحوال العمران على الآخر؛ إذ كما اشتبها في أمر واحد، فلعلهما اختلفا في أمور.

(١٠٣) فتكون العلماء، لأجل ما تعودوه من تعميم الأحكام وقياس الأمور بعضها على بعض، إذا نظروا في السياسة أفرغوا ذلك في قالب أنظارهم ونوع استدلالاتهم، فيقعون في الغلط كثيراً ولا يؤمن عليهم. ويلحق بهم أهل الذكاء والكَيْسِ من أهل العمران لأنهم ينزِعون بثقوب أذهانهم إلى مثل شأن الفقهاء من الغوص على المعاني والقياس والمحاكاة، فيقعون في الغلط.

(١٠٤) والعامي السليم الطبع المتوسط الكيس، لقصور فكره عن ذلك وعدم اعتياده إياه، يقتصر لكل مادة على حكمها، وفي كل صنف من الأحوال والأشخاص

particular (circumstances). His judgment is not infected with analogy and generalization. Most of his speculation stops at matters perceivable by the senses, and he does not go beyond them in his mind, like a swimmer who stays in the water near the shore, as the poet says:

Do not go out too deep when swimming.
Safety lies near the shore.

(105) Such a man, therefore, can be trusted when he reflects upon his political activities. He has the right outlook in dealing with his fellow men. Thus, he makes a good living and suffers no damage or harm in the (process of making a living), because he has the right outlook.

(106) "And He knows more than any scholar."[125]

(107) This (situation) makes one realize that logic cannot be trusted to prevent the commission of errors, because it is too abstract and remote from the *sensibilia.* (Logic) considers the secondary *intelligibilia.* It is possible that material things contain something that does not admit of (logical) conclusions and contradicts them, when one looks for unequivocal conformity (between them and the facts of the outside world). It is different with speculation about the primary *intelligibilia,* which are less abstract. They are matters of the imagination and pictures of the *sensibilia.* They retain (certain features of the *sensibilia*) and permit verification of the conformity of (the *sensibilia* to the primary *intelligibilia*).[126]

Most of the scholars in Islam have been non-Arabs (Persians).[127]

(108) It[128] is a remarkable fact that, with few exceptions, most Muslim scholars both in the religious and in the intellectual sciences have been non-Arabs. When a scholar is of Arab origin, he is non-Arab in language and upbringing and has non-Arab teachers. This is so in spite of the fact that Islam is an Arabic religion, and its founder was an Arab.

(109) The reason for it is that at the beginning Islam had no sciences or crafts. That was due to the simple conditions (that prevailed) and the desert attitude. The religious laws, which are the commands and prohibitions of God, were in the breasts of the authorities. They knew their sources, the Qur'ān and the Sunnah, from information they bad received directly from the Lawgiver (Muḥammad) himself and from the men

على ما اختص به، ولا يُعدّى الحكم بقياس ولا تعميم، ولا يفارق في أكثر نظره المواد المحسوسة ولا يجاوزها في ذهنه، كالسابح لا يفارق البر عند الموج. قال الشاعر:

فلا تُوغِلَنَّ إذا ما سبحت فإن السلامة في الساحل

(١٠٥) فيكون مأموناً من النظر في سياسته مستقيم النظر في معاملة أبناء جنسه؛ فيحسن معاشه وتندفع آفاته ومضاره باستقامة نظره:

(١٠٦) «وَفَوْقَ كُلِّ ذِي عِلْمٍ عَلِيمٌ».

(١٠٧) ومن هنا يتبين أن صناعة المنطق غير مأمونة الغلط لكثرة ما فيها من الانتزاع وبعدها عن المحسوس، فإنها تنظر في المعقولات الثواني، ولعل المواد فيها ما يمانع تلك الأحكام وينافيها عند مراعاة التطبيق اليقيني. وأما النظر في المعقولات الأَوَل وهي التي تجريدها قريب فليس كذلك، لأنها خيالية وصور المحسوسات حافظة مؤذنة بتصديق انطباقه. والله سبحانه وتعالى أعلم، وبه التوفيق.

فصل في أن حملة العلم في الإسلام أكثرهم العجم

(١٠٨) من الغريب الواقع أن حملة العلم في الملة الإسلامية أكثرهم العجم لا من العلوم الشرعية ولا من العلوم العقلية إلا في القليل النادر، وإن كان منهم العربي في نسبته فهو عجمي في لغته ومرباه ومشيخته، مع أن الملة عربية، وصاحب شريعتها عربي.

(١٠٩) والسبب في ذلك أن الملة في أولها لم يكن فيها علم ولا صناعة لمقتضى أحوال السذاجة والبداوة، وإنما أحكام الشريعة التي هي أوامر الله ونواهيه كان الرجال ينقلونها في صدورهم وقد عرفوا مأخذها من الكتاب والسنة بما تلقوه

around him. The people at that time were Arabs. They did not know anything about scientific instruction or the writing of books and systematic works. There was no incentive or need for that. This was the situation during the time of the men around Muḥammad and the men of the second generation. The persons who were concerned with knowing and transmitting the (religious laws) were called "Qurʾān readers," that is, people who were able to read the Qurʾān and were not illiterate. Illiteracy was general at that time among the men around Muḥammad, since they were (Arab) Bedouins.[129] People who knew the Qurʾān were at that time called "Qurʾān readers" with reference to the fact (that they were literate). They read the Qurʾān and the Sunnah, which were transmitted from God, (in order to know the religious laws,) because the religious laws were known only from the (Qurʾān) and from the traditions which are mostly explanations of and commentaries upon, the (Qurʾān). Muḥammad said: "I left among you two things. You will not go astray as long as you hold on to them: the Qurʾān and my Sunnah."[130]

(110) By the time of the reign of al-Rashīd, (oral) tradition had become far removed (from its starting point). It was thus necessary to write commentaries on the Qurʾān and to fix the traditions in writing, because it was feared that they might be lost.[131] It was also necessary to know the chains of transmitters and to assess their reliability, in order to be able to distinguish sound chains of transmitters from inferior ones.[132] Then, more and more laws concerning actual cases were moved from the Qurʾān and the Sunnah. Moreover, the (Arabic) language became corrupt,[133] and it was necessary to lay down grammatical rules.

(111) All the religious sciences had (thus) become habits connected with producing and deriving (laws and norms) and with comparison and analogical reasoning. Other, auxiliary sciences became necessary, such as knowledge of the rules of the Arabic language, (knowledge of) the rules that govern the derivation (of laws) and analogical reasoning, and defense of the articles of faith by means of arguments, because a great number of innovations and heresies (had come into existence). All these things developed into sciences with their own habits, requiring instruction (for their acquisition). Thus, they case to fall under the category of crafts.

(112) We have mentioned before that the crafts are cultivated by sedentary people and that of all peoples the Arab (Bedouins) are least familiar with the crafts.[134] Thus, the sciences came to belong to sedentary culture, and the Arabs were not familiar with them or with their cultivation. Now, the (only) sedentary people at that time were non-Arabs

من صاحب الشرع وأصحابه. والقوم يومئذ عرب لم يعرفوا أمر التعليم والتأليف والتدوين، ولا دُفِعوا اليه، ولا دعتهم إليه حاجة. وجرى الأمر على ذلك زمن الصحابة والتابعين. وكانوا يسمون المختصين بحَمْلِ ذلك ونَقْلِه «القراءَ» أى الذين يقرأون الكتاب وليسوا أميين، لأن الأمية يومئذ صفة عامة في الصحابة بما كانوا عرباً، فقيل لحملة القرآن يومئذ قراء إشارة إلى هذا؛ فهم قراء لكتاب الله والسنة المأثورة عن رسول الله، لأنهم لم يعرفوا الأحكام الشرعية إلا منه ومن الحديث، الذي هو في غالب موارده تفسير له وشرح؛ قال ﷺ: «تَرَكْتُ فيكم أمرين لن تضلوا ما تمسكتم بهما: كتابَ الله وسُنَّتي».

(١١٠) فلما بَعُدَ النقل من لدن دولة الرشيد فما بعد احتيج إلى وضع التفاسير القرآنية وتقييد الحديث مخافة ضياعه. ثم احتيج إلى معرفة الأسانيد وتعديل الناقلين للتمييز بين الصحيح من الأسانيد وما دونه. ثم كثر استخراج أحكام الواقعات من الكتاب والسنة وفسد مع ذلك اللسان فاحتيج إلى وضع القوانين النحوية.

(١١١) وصارت العلوم الشرعية كلها ملكات في الاستنباطات والاستخراج والتنظير والقياس. واحتاجت إلى علوم أخرى وهي وسائل لها من معرفة قوانين العربية وقوانين ذلك الاستنباط والقياس والذب عن العقائد الإيمانية بالأدلة لكثرة البدع والإلحاد. فصارت هذه العلوم كلها علوماً ذات ملكات محتاجة إلى التعليم فاندرجت في جملة الصنائع.

(١١٢) وقد كنا قدمنا أن الصنائع من منتحل الحضر وأن العرب أبعد الناس عنها. فصارت العلوم لذلك حضرية، وبعد عنها العرب وعن سوقها. والحضر لذلك العهد

and, what amounts to the same thing, the clients and sedentary people who followed the non-Arabs at that time in all matters of sedentary culture, including the crafts and professions. They were most versed in those things, because sedentary culture had been firmly rooted among them from the time of the Persian Empire.

(113) Thus, the founders of grammar were Sībawayh and, after him, al-Fārisī and al-Zajjāj.[135] All of them were of non-Arab (Persian) descent. They were brought up in the Arabic language and acquired the knowledge of it through their upbringing and through contact with Arabs. They invented the rules of (grammar) and made (grammar) into a discipline (in its own right) for later (generations to use).

(114) Most of the scholars of Hadith who preserved traditions for the Muslims also were non-Arabs (Persians), or Persian in language and upbringing, because[136] the discipline was widely cultivated in the ᶜIrāq and the regions beyond. (Furthermore,) all the scholars who worked in the science of the principles of jurisprudence were non-Arabs (Persians), as is well known. The same applies to speculative theologians and to most Qurᵓān commentators. Only the non-Arabs (Persians) engaged in the task of preserving knowledge and writing systematic scholarly works. Thus, the truth of the following statement by the Prophet becomes apparent: "If scholarship hung suspended at the highest parts of heaven, the Persians[137] would (reach it and) take it."

(115) The Arabs who came into contact with that flourishing sedentary culture and exchanged their Bedouin attitude for it, were diverted from occupying themselves with scholarship and study by their leading position in the ᶜAbbāsid dynasty and the tasks that confronted them in government. They were the men of the dynasty, at once its protectors and the executors of its policy. In addition, at that time, they considered it a contemptible thing to be a scholar, because scholarship is a craft, and political leaders are always contemptuous of the crafts and professions and everything that leads to them.[138] Thus, they left such things to non-Arabs and persons of mixed Arab and non-Arab parentage (*muwallad*). The latter cultivated them, and (the Arabs) always considered it their right to cultivate them, as they were their custom (*dīn*) and their sciences, and never felt complete contempt for the men learned in them. The final result, (however,) was that when the Arabs lost power and the non-Arabs took over, the religious sciences had no place with the men in power, because the latter had no relations with (scholarship). Scholars were viewed with contempt,[139] because the (men in power) saw

هم العجم أو من في معناهم من الموالى وأهل الحواضر الذين هم يومئذ تبع للعجم في الحضارة وأحوالها من الصنائع والحرف، لأنهم أقوم على ذلك للحضارة الراسخة فيهم منذ دولة الفرس.

(١١٣) فكان صاحب صناعة النحو سيبويه والفارسي من بعده والزجاج من بعدهما وكلهم عجم في أنسابهم، وانما ربوا في اللسان العربى فاكتسبوه بالمَرْبَى ومخالطة العرب وصيَّروه قوانين وفنا لمن بعدهم.

(١١٤) وكذا حملة الحديث الذين حفظوه عن أهل الإسلام أكثرهم عجم أو مستعجمون باللغة والمربى. وكان علماء أصول الفقه كلهم عجماً كما يعرف؛ وكذا حملة علم الكلام؛ وكذا أكثر المفسرين. ولم يقم بحفظ العلم وتدوينه إلا الأعاجم. وظهر مصداق قوله ﷺ: «لو تعلق العلم بأكناف السماء لناله قوم من أهل فارس».

(١١٥) وأما العرب الذين أدركوا هذه الحضارة وسُوقَها وخرجوا إليها عن البداوة فشغلتهم الرياسة في الدولة العباسية وما دفعوا إليه من القيام بالملك عن القيام بالعلم، والنظر فيه، فإنهم كانوا أهل الدولة وحاميتها وأولي سياستها، مع ما يلحقهم من الأنفة عن انتحال العلم حينئذ بما صار من جملة الصنائع، والرؤساء أبداً يستنكفون عن الصنائع والمهن وما يجر إليها، ودفعوا ذلك إلى من قام به من العجم والمولدين. وما زالوا يرون لهم حق القيام به، فإنه دينهم وعلومهم، ولا يحتقرون حَمَلتها كل الاحتقار. حتى إذا خرج الأمر من العرب جملة وصار للعجم، صارت العلوم الشرعية غريبة النسبة عند أهل الملك، بما هم عليه من البعد عن نسبتها، وامتُهن

that (scholars) had no contact with them and were occupying themselves with things that were of no interest to the (men in power) in governmental and political matters, as we mentioned in connection with the religious ranks.[140] The fact established here is the reason why (all) scholars in the religious sciences, or most of them, are non-Arabs.

(116) The intellectual sciences, as well, made their appearance in Islam only after scholars and authors had become a distinct group of people and all scholarship had become a craft. (The intellectual sciences) were then the special preserve of non-Arabs, left alone by the Arabs, who did not cultivate them. They were cultivated only by Arabicized non-Arabs (Persians)[141] as was the case with all the crafts, as we stated at the beginning.

(117) This situation continued in the cities as long as the Persians and the Persian countries, the ᶜIrāq, Khurāsān, and Transoxania, retained their sedentary culture. But when those cities fell into ruins, sedentary culture, which God has devised for the attainment of sciences and crafts, disappeared from them. Along with it, scholarship altogether disappeared from among the non-Arabs (Persians), who were (now) engulfed by the desert attitude. Scholarship was restricted to cities with an abundant sedentary culture. Today, no (city) has a more abundant sedentary culture than Cairo (Egypt). It is the mother of the world, the great center (*īwān*) of Islam, and the mainspring of the sciences and the crafts.[142]

(118) Some sedentary culture has also survived in Transoxania, because the dynasty there provides some sedentary culture. Therefore, they have there a certain number of the sciences and the crafts, which cannot be denied. Our attention was called to this fact by the contents of the writings of a (Transoxanian) scholar, which have reached us in this country. He is Saᶜd-al-dīn al-Taftazānī.[143] As far as the other non-Arabs (Persians) are concerned, we have not seen, since[144] the imam Ibn al-Khaṭīb and Naṣīr-al-dīn al-Ṭūsī, any discussions that could be referred to as indicating their ultimate excellence.

(119) When one considers and ponders this fact, one will observe (in it) one of the wondrous circumstances of this world. "God creates whatever He wishes." "There is no God but Him."[145]

◆

حَمَلَتُها بما يرون أنهم بعداء عنهم، مشتغلون بما لا يغني ولا يجدي عنهم في الملك والسياسة كما ذكرناه في فصل المراتب الدينية.

فهذا الذي قررناه هو السبب في أن حملة الشريعة أو عامتهم من العجم.

(١١٦) وأما العلوم العقلية أيضاً فلم تظهر في الملة إلا بعد أن تميز حملة العلم ومؤلفوه واستقر العلم كله صناعة فاختصت بالعجم وتركتها العرب، وانصرفوا عن انتحالها، فلم يحملها إلا المعربون من العجم شأن الصنائع كما قلناه أولا.

(١١٧) فلم يزل ذلك في الأمصار ما دامت الحضارة في العجم وبلادهم من العراق وخراسان وما وراء النهر. فلما خربت تلك الأمصار وذهبت منها الحضارة التي هي سر الله في حصول العلم والصنائع، ذهب العلم من العجم جملة لما شملهم من البداوة، واختص العلم بالأمصار الموفورة الحضارة. ولا أوفر اليوم في الحضارة من مصر فهي أم العالم وإيوان الإسلام وينبوع العلم والصنائع.

(١١٨) وبقي بعض الحضارة فيما وراء النهر لما هناك من الحضارة بالدولة التي فيها، فلهم بذلك حصة من العلوم والصنائع لا تنكر. وقد دلنا على ذلك كلام بعض علمائهم في تآليف وصلت إلينا إلى هذه البلاد، وهو سعد الدين التفتازاني. وأما غيره من العجم فلم نر لهم من بعد الإمام ابن الخطيب ونصير الدين الطوسى كلاماً يعول على نهايته في الإصابة.

(١١٩) فاعتبر ذلك وتأمله ترجعباً في أحوال الخليقة. والله يخلق ما يشاء، لا إله إلا هو وحده لا شريك له، له الملك وله الحمد، وهو على كل شيء قدير، وحسبنا الله ونعم الوكيل، والحمد لله.

Notes to the English Text

Introduction

1. For an interesting and controversial anomaly in this tradition, see Rashid, "Was Muḥammad Literate?" and Goldziher, "Muslim Education," 198. Both authors go against the widely accepted notion that Muḥammad was illiterate, arguing that Muḥammad, as a prominent Meccan merchant, could scarcely manage his trade without at least the rudiments of reading and writing. Most Muslims, however, would interpret Qur'ān 29:48 as literal evidence that the Prophet could neither read nor write: "And thou wast not able to recite a Book before this, nor art thou able to transcribe it with thy right hand."

2. Qur'ān 96:1–5. Elements in this section have drawn on Bradley J. Cook's article "Islam" in *Encyclopedia of Education*. Reprinted by permission of The Gale Group.

3. Qur'ān 58:11, 20:114, and 2:282.

4. Narrated by Ibn Mājah. See al-Mundhirī, *Targhīb*, 54. Also see Qaraḍāwī, *Muntaqā*, 120.

5. Narrated by Imam Muslim. See al-Mundhirī, *Targhīb*, 656.

6. Narrated by Ibn Mājah. See al-Mundhirī, *Targhīb*, 54. Also see Qaraḍāwī, *Muntaqā*, 120.

7. Sakkākī, *Miftāḥ al-ʿulūm*, 1.

8. Shawkānī, *Fawāʾid*, 272.

9. Narrated by Ibn Qayyin al-Jawzīyah, *Miftāḥ*, 251.

10. Ibn Jamāʿah, *Tadhkirat al-sāmiʿ*, 4.10 herein.

11. Some of the most prominent works in English on Islamic education include Makdisi, *Rise of Colleges*; Leiser, "The *Madrasa*"; Tibawi, *Islamic Education*; Khan, "Theories of Education"; Dodge, *Muslim Education*; Nakosteen, *Islamic Origins of Western Education*; Shalabi, *History of Muslim Education*; Goldziher, "Muslim Education"; Berkey, *Transmission of Knowledge*; *EI*^{2} s.v. "Masdjid"; Nasr, "Islamic Philosophers' Views"; Tritton, *Materials on Muslim Education*; Rosenthal, *Knowledge Triumphant*; MacDonald, "Moral Education"; Totah, *Contribution of the Arabs to Education*; Stanton, *Higher Learning in Islam*; and Rahman, *Islam and Modernity*.

A series on Islamic education was published by Hodder and Stoughton, London; and King ʿAbd al-Aziz University, Jeddah: al-Attas, ed., *Aims and Objectives of Islamic Education*; Husain and Ashraf, eds., *Crisis in Muslim Education*; Wasiullah, ed., *Education and Society in the Muslim World*; al-Faruqi and Nasseef, *Social and Natural Sciences*; Nasr, *Philosophy, Literature and Fine Arts*; and Afandi and Balocu, *Curriculum and Teacher Education.* The *Muslim Education Quarterly,* a journal published by the Islamic Academy, Cambridge, UK since 1983, is another good source on various dimensions of Islamic education.

12. Ibn ʿAbd al-Barr (d. 1070), *Jāmiʿ bayān al-ʿilm*; al-ʿAskarī (d. 1009), *Al-haththʿalá ṭalab*; Khaṭīb al-Baghdādī (d. 1070), *Jāmiʿ li-akhlāq*; Samaʿānī (d. 1166), *Adab al-imlāʾ*; Shawkānī and Sarīḥī (d. 1839), *Adab al-ṭalab*; Haythamī (d. 1566), *Taḥrīr al-maqāl*; al-ʿAlmawī (d. 1573), *Al-muʿīd fī adab*; Ibn al-Ṣalāḥ al-Shahrazūrī (d. 1245), *Adab al-muftī.*

13. Material from Cook, "Islamic Versus Western Conceptions of Education," has been drawn on here with the kind permission of Kluwer Academic Publishers and Springer Science and Business Media.

14. Hamidullah, "Educational System in the Time of the Prophet," 54.

15. Nakosteen identifies six types of teachers in classical Islam: The *muʿallim, mudarris, muʾaddib, ustādh, shaykh,* and *imām,* with each title having a slightly different connotation. See Nakosteen, *History,* 56.

16. Both *kuttāb* and *maktab* are derived from the same Arabic root *K-T-B*, meaning to write. Early textual sources indicate that the two terms were synonymous, meaning a place where younger students were taught the Qurʿān and the rudiments of reading and writing. In contemporary nomenclature, *kuttāb* has all but replaced the term *maktab.* See EI^2 s.v. "Maktab."

17. Aḥmad Shalabi argues that the mosques were seldom used for the education of young children because they were too messy and noisy. See Shalabi, *History of Muslim Education,* 25.

18. EI^2 s.v. "kuttāb."

19. Al-Qābisī, *Risāla al-mufaṣṣila,* 143–44.

20. Tirmidhī, *Sunan,* 338.

21. Ibn Sīnā, *Kitāb al-sīyasa,* 103–4.

22. See 1.61 and 3.68 herein.

23. See 3.32–33 herein. Al-Qābisī quotes a hadith in which the Prophet encouraged the education of even slave girls. Muslims who gave slave girls a good education and then freed them would be rewarded twice in the hereafter. See 3.21 herein.

24. See 6.6 herein, or Zarnūjī, *Taʿlīm,* 22.

25. See 5.33 herein. Certain historical records identify five schools established in Cairo during the Mamluk period by women for educating women. Seven similar schools were also established in Damascus. Education for women was not limited to young girls; the thirteenth century witnessed several institutions for elderly, divorced, or widowed women. See Bewley, *Islam: The Empowering of Women,* 19–20.

26. Al-Ghazālī, *On Disciplining the Soul,* 75.

27. Ibid., 81. Also see al-Qābisī at 3.28 herein.

28. Nakosteen, *History,* 93.

29. Miskawayh, *Tahdhīb al-akhlāq,* 67. See also his detailed discussions of the views of Galan, Aristotle, the Stoics, and other philosophers on this issue (41–45).

30. Al-Attas, *Prolegomena,* 14.

31. Ibn Jamāᶜah, *Tadhkirat,* 2.

32. Al-Sakhāwī in Berkey, *Transmission,* 29.

33. See 6.99 herein or Zarnūjī, *Taᶜlīm,* 54. See also note 24 above.

34. Williamson, *Education and Social Change,* 26.

35. See Shahi, "Educational Cross-Currents," 80–91 for more on modes of instruction and memorization.

36. Al-Jāḥiẓ, *Collection,* 29–30.

37. The discussion on positives and negatives of memorization of the Qurᶜān by young children has been ongoing in many Muslim countries for generations. Several studies have been published in this regard. See, for example Yūnus, et al., *Tarbīya,* 229–303.

38. In an amusing anecdote, Radwan comments on a young prince, who, when speaking about his educational experience, "reminisced about receiving a flogging about as regularly as he received his lunch." See Radwan, *Old and New Forces,* 62.

39. See 1.62 (Ibn Saḥnūn), 3.71 (Qābisī), and 8.96 (Ibn Khaldūn) herein.

40. See 3.71 herein.

41. See 3.71 herein.

42. See 4.19 herein or Miskawayh, *Tahdhīb,* 52.

43. See 6.61, 111 (Zarnūjī) and 7.112 (Ibn Jamāᶜah) herein.

44. See 4.27 herein or Miskawayh, *Tahdhīb,* 56. See also 7.123 (Ibn Jamāᶜah) and al-Ghazālī, *On Disciplining the Soul,* 78.

45. Shalabi, *History,* 57.

46. Ibid., 55.

47. Tibawi, *Islamic Education,* 30.

48. Leiser, "Notes on the Madrasa," 18.

49. Tibawi, *Islamic Education,* 31.

50. Pederson, "History of the Madrasa," 528.

51. Makdisi, "Madrasa and the University," 260.

52. *EI*[2] s.v. "Madrasa."

53. Leiser, "Notes," 16. Leiser goes on to say that *madrasa* "has lost its meaning in Arabic to simply mean 'school.' "

54. Talbani claims that the curriculum of the madrasa was confined solely to religious and linguistic studies and other ancillary subjects were considered "dangerous" and "unnecessary." (See Talbani, "Pedagogy, Power, and Discourse," 68.) Other contemporary Islamic apologists, such as Badawi and Peer, stridently defend traditional Islamic education as being much less insular, saying that "other disciplines not bearing directly on Islamic studies were not neglected or excluded from the system," (Badawi, "Traditional Islamic Education" in al-Attas, *Aims,* 114–15.) Undoubtedly, both camps of thought are correct depending on the region and the substantive variations of personalities and qualitative differences in religious interpretation of the *muᶜallimīn.*

55. Talbani, "Pedagogy, Power, and Discourse," 69.

56. See Meyerhof, "Science and Medicine," 311–55 for an excellent summary of other achievements made by the Islamic world.
57. Kâtip Çelebi, *Kashf al-ẓunūn.*
58. Al-Ghazālī in Radwan, *Old and New,* 43.
59. Tibawi, *Islamic Education,* 31.
60. Ibid., 70.
61. Certain contemporary Islamicists, such as Taha Alwani, isolate *taqlīd* as the single most deleterious factor in the decline of the Islamic intellectual tradition and call it "an illness which entered the Muslim mind." See Alwani, "*Taqlīd.*"
62. See 6.28 herein or Zarnūjī, *Taᶜlīm al-mutaᶜallim,* 28, 58.
63. El-Shayyal, "Intellectual and Social Life," 119.
64. Dodge, *Muslim Education,* 24.
65. International Institute of Islamic Thought, *Islamization of Knowledge,* 29.
66. Esposito, *Oxford History of Islam,* 337–41, 602.
67. Williamson, *Education,* 19.
68. Hitti, *History of the Arabs*; and Peer, "Muslim Approach to Education," 166.
69. Peer, "Muslim Approach to Education," 166.
70. Khalīl, *Madkhal ilá al-tārīkh,* 84–85.
71. Ali, "Conflict," 54.
72. Mohamed, "Islamization," 17.
73. Ali, "Conflict," 51.
74. Al-Faruqi, *Islamization of Knowledge,* x.
75. Husain, *Crisis,* 16–17.
76. Sulaiman, "Education," 32.
77. Al-Attas, *Islam,* 13.
78. Sulaiman, "Education," 32.
79. Rahman, *Islam and Modernity,* 130.
80. Al-Attas, *Aims and Objectives,* 157.
81. Ibid., 158.
82. ᶜAbd al-Raḥmān, *Educational Theory,* 116.
83. Qurʾān 51:56.
84. ᶜAbd al-Raḥmān, *Educational Theory,* 116.
85. Nasr, "The Islamic Philosophers' Views," 7.
86. Al-Saud, "Glorious Qurʾān," 126–27.
87. Ibid., 127.
88. Al-Attas, *Islam,* 200.
89. Quṭb, M., *Manhāj al-tarbīyya,* 8.
90. Nasr, "Islamic Philosophers' Views," 13.
91. Halstead, "Toward a Unified View," 30.
92. Ashraf, "Editorial," 2.
93. Ibid.
94. Ali, "Conflict," 52.
95. Ibid.
96. Ibid.
97. As defined by the Dutch theologian Cornelius van Peursen as cited in al-Attas, *Islam,* 15.
98. Ibid.

99. Ashraf, "Education and Values," 4.
100. Hobson and Edwards, *Religious Education,* 15.
101. Qurʾān 2:164.
102. Al-Attas, *Islam,* xix. Al-Attas uses an interesting analogy to underscore this idea. He has one imagine that he arrives at an intersection in a road with a signpost pointing to various roads leading from that point. The signpost is "made of marble finely wrought, and the pointing arms were sculptured into forms wondrous and beautiful, the place names and their relative distances from the spot chiseled into letters of pure gold and embellished with rare gems." Rather than following the sign post to its final destination—that of the knowledge of God—secular science has become preoccupied with the marvelous sign itself.
103. El-Nejjar, "Limitations of Science," 59–63.
104. Ibid., 61–62.
105. Badawi in al-Attas, *Aims,* 114–15.
106. Quṭb, *Mustaqbal,* 10. Yūsuf al-Qaraḍāwī, an influential figure in contemporary Islamic thought, argues that there is no struggle between science and faith as Europeans witnessed in their medieval period, because both science and faith can be in a state of harmony and integration. Science, he argues, confirms faith, and faith blesses science, because truth does not negate truth. See Qaraḍāwī, *Reason and Science,* 96.
107. Moussalli, "View of Knowledge," 324.
108. Ibid., 322.
109. Quṭb, *ʿAdala,* 30, cited in Moussalli, "View of Knowledge," 323.
110. Hirst, *Moral Education,* 4.
111. *History and Social Sciences,* 48, quoted in Watson, *Education,* 28.
112. Watson, *Education,* 29.
113. Nasr, "Views on Education," 13.
114. Ashraf, "Education," 11.
115. Ibid., 7.
116. Bailey, *Beyond the Present,* 20.
117. White, "Reply," 119. Also see White's larger work, *Aims of Education Restated,* for an elaboration on this general theme.
118. Bailey, *Beyond the Present,* 21.
119. Ashraf, "Education," 10.
120. Halstead, "Unified View," 40.
121. White, *Aims,* 50; cited in Halstead, "Unified View," 40.
122. Barrow, *Plato, Utilitarianism and Education,* 188; quoted in Halstead, "Unified View," 40.
123. Ali, "Conflict," 53.
124. Ibid., 51.
125. Ibid., 53.
126. Ritter, "Reign of al-Muʿtaṣim," 157.
127. Stanton, *Higher Learning in Islam,* 185.
128. Muʿnis, *Riyāḍ al-nufūs,* 35.
129. Mahfuẓ, *Tarājim,* 19–20.
130. EI^2 s.v. "Muḥammad Ibn Saḥnūn."

131. See 2.24 herein.
132. See 2.8 herein.
133. See 2.1 herein.
134. See 3.62 herein.
135. *EI*^{2} s.v. "Miskawayh."
136. Donaldson, *Muslim Ethics,* 122.
137. See 4.13 herein, or Miskawayh, *Refinement of Character,* 50. Also see T. J. Winter's translation of al-Ghazālī, *On Disciplining the Soul,* lxiv.
138. Denny, *Introduction to Islam,* 240.
139. See 5.33.
140. See 5.76.
141. See 5.11.
142. Tibawi, *Islamic Education,* 39.
143. See 6.16 herein.
144. See the introduction of Grunebaum and Abel to al-Zarnūjī, *Ta*ᶜ*līm,* 1.
145. See 6.151 ff. herein.
146. See 6.53 herein.
147. See 6.29 herein.
148. See 6.37.
149. See the introduction of Grunenbaum and Abel to al-Zarnūjī, *Ta*ᶜ*līm,* 17.
150. *EI*^{2} s.v. "Ibn Khaldūn."
151. See Ibn Khaldūn, *Muqaddimah* (ed. Dawood), 338.
152. See 8.78 herein.
153. Nasr, *Science and Civilization,* 62.
154. See 8.60 ff. herein.
155. See 8.68 herein.
156. See 8.94 herein.
157. See 8.97 herein.

Ibn Saḥnūn

1. For details of Ibn Saḥnūn's biography, see the introduction to this volume, pp. xxxv–vi; the introduction to the French translation of the present work: Ibn Saḥnūn, "Livre des règles"; *GAS,* 1.472–73; and the introduction by Dr. Maḥmūd ᶜAbd al-Mawlā to his edition of this work in Ibn Saḥnūn, *Kitāb adab al-mu*ᶜ*allimīn.* For an Arabic biography, see Ibn Mūsá, *Tartīb,* vol. 3–4, pp. 104–18.

2. Abū Saᶜīd ᶜAbd al-Salām ibn Saᶜīd al-Tanūkhī (nicknamed Saḥnūn on account of his shrewdness or from the name of a bird) was born in 160/777 and died in 240/855. His father, a native of Syria, had come to North Africa as a soldier in the army that brought the province into the Abbasid orbit and received an allocation of land for his service. After his initial education in Qayrawān, Saḥnūn went to the East, where he studied with disciples of Mālik ibn Anas in Medina and then with the Egyptian Ibn al-Qāsim al-ᶜAtakī, with whom he produced two legal works, the *Asadiyyah* and the *Mudawwanah.* The latter, together with Mālik's own work, the *Muwaṭṭa*ʾ, formed the basis of Saḥnūn's teaching in Qayrawān. Saḥnūn thus contributed to the ultimate

triumph of the Mālikī school in North Africa. See *EI^2*, s.v. "Saḥnūn"; *GAS,* 1.468–71; and Ibn Mūsá, *Tartīb,* vol. 1–2, pp. 585–626.

3. Abū Muḥammad ʿAbdallāh ibn Wahb ibn Muslim al-Fihrī al-Qurashī was born in Egypt in 125/743 and died in 197/812. He was a student of the jurist Mālik ibn Anas, and Saḥnūn studied with him in Egypt. See *GAS,* 1.466.

4. Abū ʿAbdallāh Sufyān ibn Saʿīd ibn Masrūq al-Thawrī (d. 161/778) was a traditionist, theologian, and ascetic active in al-Kūfah. See *GAS,* 1.518–19; and Ibn Ḥajar, *Tahdhīb,* 4.111–15.

5. Abū al-Ḥārith ʿAlqamah ibn Marthad al-Ḥaḍramī, a traditionist, died ca. 120/738. See Ibn Ḥajar, *Tahdhīb,* 7.278–79.

6. Abū ʿAbd al-Raḥmān ʿAbdallāh ibn Ḥabīb al-Sulamī was a *tābiʿī* (son of a Companion of the Prophet) and lived in al-Kūfah as a traditionist and Qurʾān reader. See Ibn Ḥajar, *Tahdhīb,* 5.183–84.

7. ʿUthmān ibn ʿAffān, the third of the caliphs, succeeded ʿUmar ibn al-Khaṭṭāb in 23/644 and was assassinated in 35/656.

8. ʿAbd al-Mawlá (Ibn Saḥnūn, *Adab,* 69) identifies him as Abū Ṭāhir Aḥmad ibn ʿAbdallāh ibn ʿUmar ibn al-Sarḥ (d. 250/864), an Egyptian legal scholar, transmitter of hadith, and commentator on Mālik's *Muwaṭṭaʾ,* with whom Ibn Saḥnūn is known to have studied. Another possibility is Abū Ṭāhir Aḥmad ibn ʿAmr al-Umawī (d. 255/869), another Egyptian traditionist and commentator on Mālik's *Muwaṭṭaʾ.* Both men studied with Ibn Wahb. See Ibn Ḥajar, *Tahdhīb,* 1.64.

9. Yaḥyá ibn Ḥassān ibn Ḥabbān (d. 208/823) was a traditionist who lived in Tinnīs in Egypt. See Ibn Ḥajar, *Tahdhīb,* 11.197.

10. ʿAbd al-Wāḥid ibn Ziyād al-ʿAbdī was a traditionist of al-Baṣrah who died in 176/792. See Ibn Ḥajar, *Tahdhīb,* 6.434–35.

11. Abū Shaybah ʿAbd al-Raḥmān ibn Isḥāq ibn Saʿd passed on traditions from his uncle, al-Nuʿmān ibn Saʿd. See Ibn Ḥajar, *Tahdhīb,* 6.136–37.

12. Al-Nuʿmān ibn Saʿd ibn Ḥabtah al-Anṣārī was active in al-Kūfah. See Ibn Ḥajar, *Tahdhīb,* 10.453.

13. ʿAlī ibn Abī Ṭālib, the Prophet's cousin and son-in-law, was the fourth of the caliphs by Sunni reckoning and first of the imams in Shiʿi doctrine. He succeeded ʿUthmān ibn ʿAffān in 35/656 and was assassinated in 40/660–61. See *EI^2*, s.v. "ʿAlī b. Abī Ṭālib."

14. Yaʿqūb ibn Ḥumayd ibn Kāsib, sometimes called Yaʿqūb ibn Ḥumayd after his grandfather, of Medinese origins, lived in Mecca, where he died in 240/854 or 241/855. See Ibn Ḥajar, *Tahdhīb*, 11.383–85. Ibn Mūsá, *Tartīb,* vol. 3–4, p. 104, reports that Ibn Saḥnūn studied with him in Medina.

15. Abū Salamah ibn ʿAbd al-Raḥmān ibn ʿAwf al-Zuhrī was a prolific Medinese traditionist who died in 94/712 or 104/722. See Ibn Ḥajar, *Tahdhīb,* 12.115–18.

16. Abū Dāwūd ʿAbd al-Raḥmān ibn Hurmuz al-Aʿraj was a Medinese scholar who migrated to Alexandria, where he died in 117/735 CE. See Ibn Ḥajar, *Tahdhīb,* 6.290–91.

17. ʿUbaydallāh ibn Abī Rāfiʿ was the son of the Prophet's freedman and served as ʿAlī's secretary. See Ibn Ḥajar, *Tahdhīb,* 7.10–11.

18. Correcting the dittography in ed. Tunis and Cairo (ᶜAbdallāh ibn ᶜAbdallāh . . .) on the basis of Dr. ᶜAbd al-Mawlā's note in Ibn Saḥnūn, *Adab,* 70. ᶜAbdallāh ibn Nāfiᶜ al-Ṣāʾigh (d. 206/822), was a Medinese jurist and student of Mālik. He is mentioned below as having transmitted an opinion of Mālik's directly to Saḥnūn. See Melchert, *Sunni Schools of Law,* 166.

19. Correcting ed. Cairo's "Ḥusayn transmitted to me from ᶜAbdallāh ibn Ḥamzah." See Ibn Saḥnūn, *Adab,* 71.

20. I.e., Abū Jaᶜfar Mūsá ibn Muᶜāwiyah al-Ṣumādiḥī (d. late in 225/840), mentioned by his full name two paragraphs below. He was a Mālikī legal scholar of Qayrawān who, according to one biographer, accompanied Saḥnūn to Medina and then went on to Damascus. See the biography in Ibn Mūsá, *Tartīb,* vol. 4–5, p. 5.

21. ᶜAbd al-Raḥmān ibn Mahdī (d. 198/813) was a leading Iraqi traditionist. He is said to have become upset at the way Mālik's legal opinions were being interpreted in al-Baṣrah to favor the use of personal opinion (*raʾy*) and to have written to the scholar Muḥammad ibn Idrīs al-Shāfiᶜī asking for a statement in support of the authoritative sources of the law. Shāfiᶜī is said to have written his *Risālah* in response to Ibn Mahdī. See Shāfiᶜī, *Risāla,* 19–21.

22. The reading is uncertain. Ed. Cairo reads ᶜAbd al-Raḥmān ibn *Nawfal* al-Ashjaᶜī. He was the son of a Companion of the Prophet and settled in al-Kūfah where he transmitted hadith. See Ibn Ḥajar, *Tahdhīb,* 10.493.

23. If one reads "ibn Nawfal," then Nawfal al-Ashjaᶜī was a Companion of the Prophet. He later settled in al-Kūfah. See Ibn Ḥajar, *Tahdhīb,* 10.493.

24. Anas ibn Mālik became the Prophet's servant at age ten. He died in ca. 93/711 at an advanced age at al-Baṣrah, where he was a prolific traditionist. See *EI²,* s.v. "Anas b. Mālik"; and see Ibn Ḥajar, *Tahdhīb,* 1.376–79.

25. Mālik ibn Anas (d. 179/796), a Medinese jurist and traditionist, was the author of the *Muwaṭṭaʾ,* one of the earliest surviving Muslim law books, and the eponymous founder of what became North Africa's dominant legal school (*madhhab*), to which Saḥnūn and his son Ibn Saḥnūn adhered. See *EI²,* s.vv. "Mālik b. Anas" and "Mālikiyya."

26. Ibn Shihāb al-Zuhrī (d. 124/742) was a major early traditionist and historian. See *GAS,* 1.280–83; and Duri, *Rise,* 95–121.

27. ᶜUrwah ibn al-Zubayr b. al-ᶜAwwām (d. 94/712–13) was the son of a prominent Companion of the Prophet and the younger brother of ᶜAbdallāh ibn al-Zubayr, who unsuccessfully challenged the rule of the Umayyads. ᶜUrwah became one of the most respected Medinese authorities on prophetic traditions and early Islamic history. See *GAS,* 1.278–79; and Duri, *Rise,* 76–95.

28. That is, ᶜAbd al-Raḥmān ibn ᶜAbd, of the tribe of al-Qārah (a group famous as archers). They were allies (*ḥulafāʾ*) of the Banū Zuhrah clan of Quraysh. See Dhahabī, *Al-moschtabih,* 392–93; and Ibn Manẓūr, *Lisān al-ᶜArab,* s.v. *Q-W-R.*

29. ᶜUmar ibn al-Khaṭṭāb, the second caliph, succeeded Abū Bakr and ruled from 13/634 to 23/644.

30. Literally, "The Qurʾān was revealed according to seven *ḥarf*s (letters, manners or modes of reciting, dialects)." Because the first written texts of the Qurʾān lacked vowel points and the dots differentiating otherwise identical

letters of the Arabic alphabet, many words could be read in two or more ways. When vowel points and dots were added later, they did not suppress the memory that different Companions of the Prophet had read certain passages differently. The belief arose that a certain number of variant manners of reciting the Qurʾān (usually seven) were equally valid, as the differing vocalizations of the same consonantal text rarely affected the meaning. About two generations after Ibn Saḥnūn, these *qirāʾāt* or "readings" were codified by Ibn Mujāhid (d. 324/936), the chief Qurʾān reader of Baghdad, and each was ascribed to a famous early reader. The two that are most common today are that of ʿĀṣim of Kūfah (d. 128/745) and Nāfiʿ of Medina (d. 169/785)—ʿĀṣim's reading dominating the east and center of the Islamic world, Nāfiʿ dominating North Africa. See *EI²*, s.v. "Ḳirāʾa."

31. According to Ibn Mūsá, *Tartīb,* vol. 3–4, p. 8, this is not Sufyān al-Thawrī, who has been mentioned above, but Sufyān ibn ʿUyaynah (d. 196/811), who also transmitted hadith from al-Aʿmash. See also Ibn Ḥajar, *Tahdhīb,* 4.117–22.

32. Sulaymān ibn Mihrān al-Asadī al-Aʿmash (d. 148/765) was a Qurʾān reader at Kūfah. See Ibn Ḥajar, *Tahdhīb,* 4.222–26, and *EI²*, s.v. "al-Aʿmash."

33. Tamīm ibn Salamah al-Sulamī (d. 100/718) was active in al-Kūfah. See Ibn Ḥajar, *Tahdhīb,* 1.512–13.

34. Two Companions of the Prophet had the name Ḥudhayfah, but because of the Kūfan *isnād* this is probably Ḥudhayfah ibn al-Yamān (d. 36/656), who emigrated to al-Kūfah. See Ibn Ḥajar, *Tahdhīb* 2.219–20, and al-Ṭabarī, *Taʾrīkh* 1.1483.

35. Literally, "Whoever recites the Qurʾān with *iʿrāb*..." This might mean simply reciting it clearly and without mistakes; however, *iʿrāb* later became a technical term in grammar for the endings marking the cases of Arabic nouns and the moods of some verbs, endings that were becoming obsolete in the Arabic of sedentary populations, but survived longer in the language of the nomads (the true *ʿArab,* from whom the verb *aʿraba,* to speak clearly or like a true Arab, and its associated noun *iʿrāb* were derived). The Prophet would therefore be urging reciters to maintain the pure Arabic language and not allow colloquial corruptions to creep into their recitations. This interpretation (that *iʿrāb* refers to grammar, not clarity of pronunciation) is on the face of it anachronistic, since Arabic grammar had not been formalized in the days of Muḥammad, but it is probably how the tradition was understood in Ibn Saḥnūn's day.

36. Abū Muṣʿab Aḥmad ibn Abī Bakr al-Zuhrī (d. 242/857) was a Medinese scholar who studied with Mālik ibn Anas and transmitted Mālik's major work, the *Muwaṭṭaʾ*. See Ibn Ḥajar, *Tahdhīb,* 1.20–21; and *GAS,* 1.471–72.

37. Perhaps this is Muḥammad ibn Ṭalḥah ibn Yazīd ibn Rukānah, who appears twice in al-Ṭabarī's *History* as an immediate informant of the historian Muḥammad ibn Isḥāq (d. 150/767 or 151/768).

38. Ed. Cairo reads "Saʿīd ibn Saʿīd *al-Maghribī*" (*gh* and *q* are easily confused in Arabic script): Saʿīd ibn Abī Saʿīd al-Maqrubī (d. ca. 117/735) was a Medinese traditionist who transmitted hadith from Abū Hurayrah. See Ibn Ḥajar, *Tahdhīb,* 4.38–40. Ed. Algiers reads "al-Muqriʾ."

39. Abū Hurayrah, a Companion of the Prophet, acquired his nickname ("the man with the kitten") from the kitten he kept to play with while he herded goats. He came to Medina in 7/628 and later became a prolific narrator of traditions. He died between 57/676 and 59/678. See *EI^2*, s.v. "Abū Hurayra"; and Ibn Ḥajar, *Tahdhīb*, 12.262–67.

40. Ed. Cairo, "Abū Mūsá."

41. Muʿāwiyah ibn Ṣāliḥ died in 158/774. See *GAS*, 1.27.

42. Correcting the manuscript reading, "al-ʿAlāʾ": ʿAṭāʾ ibn al-Sāʾib was a Kūfan transmitter of traditions. Ibn Khallikān (*Wafayāt al-aʿyān*, 5.379) mentions him as a teacher of the judge Abū Yūsuf (b. 113/731, d. 182/798), the companion of Abū Ḥanīfah, the famous Iraqi jurist.

43. Ibn Masʿūd (ʿAbdallāh ibn Ghāfil ibn Ḥabīb) was a very early Meccan convert to Islam who emigrated to Abyssinia and then returned to follow the Prophet to Medina. After Muḥammad's death, he settled in al-Kūfah, where he was a reader of the Qurʾān and transmitter of traditions. He died in 32/652–53. See *EI^2*, s.v. "Ibn Masʿūd."

44. The reference to the time of Muʿāwiyah and the evidence of al-Qābisī ("Risālah," 297) point to Abū Muḥammad ʿAṭāʾ ibn Abī Rabāḥ Aslam (b. 27/647, d. 114/732), an early Qurʾān commentator and jurist. He was a student of ʿAbdallāh ibn al-ʿAbbās. See *GAS*, 1.31.

45. Ed. Algiers, *al-katb* (writing). The sense, I think, demands the reading of ed. Cairo, *al-kitāb*, usually "the Qurʾān," but sometimes "writing."

46. Muʿāwiyah ibn Abī Sufyān, the founder of the Umayyad dynasty of caliphs, succeeded ʿAlī in 41/661 and ruled from Damascus until his death in 60/680. See *EI^2*, s.v. "Muʿāwiya I."

47. ʿAbd al-Malik ibn ʿAbd a-ʿAzīz ibn Jurayj (born 80/699, died 150/767) was a Meccan traditionist and jurist who composed a Qurʾān commentary based in part on the work of ʿAṭāʾ ibn Abī Rabāḥ. See *GAS*, 1.91.

48. Abū ʿUmar Ḥafṣ ibn ʿUmārah al-Dūrī (b. ca. 150/767, d. 240/854), lived in Samarra in Iraq and was a transmitter of hadith and authority on Qurʾān readings. See *GAS*, 1.13. Ed. Cairo reads ". . . ibn Maysarah," i.e., Abū ʿUmar Ḥafṣ ibn Maysarah al-ʿUqaylī (d. 181/797), who lived in ʿAsqalān. See Ibn Ḥajar, *Tahdhīb*, 2.419–20. The parallel text in al-Qābisī's "Risālah" agrees with ed. Algiers in reading "Ḥafṣ ibn ʿUmar."

49. Abū Yazīd Yūnus ibn Yazīd al-Aylī was a *mawlā* (freedman or client) of Muʿāwiyah ibn Abī Sufyān. He wrote down and transmitted traditions from Ibn Shihāb al-Zuhrī. See Ibn Ḥajar, *Tahdhīb*, 11.450–52.

50. Ed. Cairo reads "Saʿd ibn Mālik," i.e., Abū Saʿīd ibn Sinān al-Khudrī (d. ca. 63/682), a Companion of the Prophet who gave legal opinions in Medina. See Ibn Hajar, *Iṣābah* 3.78–80. But this misses the point of the Iraqi connection. Saʿd ibn Abī Waqqāṣ was the great general who conquered Iraq and founded the city of al-Kūfah. He died near Medina in 50/670 or 55/675. (The parallel text in al-Qābisī, "Risālah," 307, also reads "Saʿd ibn Abī Waqqāṣ.")

51. In older Arabic *al-kitāb* is ambiguous and may mean either the Book (the Qurʾān) or simply "writing" (i.e., *al-kitābah* in later Arabic). Al-Qābisī, "Risālah," 307, notes that the report has come down in at least three versions, one of which is "to teach . . . writing (*al-kitāb*) and the Qurʾān (*al-Qurʾān*)." Al-Qābisī says that he is not sure which reading is correct.

52. See the section below on the question of special remuneration (*khitmah*) to be paid to the teacher when the student finishes learning one of the major divisions of the Qurʾān or the whole Qurʾān.

53. This could be Muḥammad ibn [ʿAbdallāh ibn] ʿAbd al-Raḥīm (scribal error?) al-Barqī (d. 249/863), the best-known member of an Egyptian family of Mālikī legal scholars. See Ibn Mūsá, *Tartīb,* vol. 3–4, p. 83.

54. Abū ʿAlī al-Fuḍayl ibn ʿIyāḍ b. Masʿūd al-Tamīmī was born in 105/723 in Samarqand. He was a highway robber during his youth, but later led an ascetic life and devoted himself to studying hadith. He lived for a time in Baghdād, and later went to Mecca, where he died in 187/802. See *GAS,* 1.636; and Ibn Ḥajar, *Tahdhīb,* 8.294–96.

55. Possibly al-Layth ibn Saʿd (b. 94/713, d. 175/791), who was a famous Egyptian legal scholar. See *GAS,* 1.520; and Ibn Ḥajar, *Tahdhīb,* 8.463.

56. Perhaps to be identified as Ḥasan al-Baṣrī (b. Medina 21/642, d. al-Baṣrah 110/728), one of the most respected of the *tābiʿī* generation who followed that of the Companions of the Prophet. He transmitted traditions, was interested in theological questions, and was renowned for his piety. See *GAS,* 1.591–94.

57. Ed. Cairo, "ibn Masʿūd," but the position of this ʿAbdallāh in the *isnād* makes the famous Companion of the Prophet (d. 32/652) an unlikely candidate.

58. The *isnād* up to Anas ibn Mālik consists of unknown men. Al-Qābisī, "Risālah," 317, mentions this: "Ibn Saḥnūn mentioned on the authority of Anas ibn Mālik, with an *isnād* that is not of Saḥnūn's transmission."

59. I.e., a text from the Qurʾān (cf. Qurʾān 56:80 and 69:43, where the Qurʾān is described in these words).

60. The parallel in al-Qābisī, "Risālah," 318, makes it clear that "I" refers to Muḥammad ibn Saḥnūn, who is addressing the question to his father.

61. The manuscripts read a verb form from the root *l-ʿ-ṭ,* which the dictionaries gloss as "to brand (a beast) on the neck, to tattoo (a person); to wound someone (with an arrow); to pasture near dwellings (of an animal); to go along a wall." However, in the hadith that closes the section, the word *yalʿaṭ* is glossed as *yalʿaq,* he licks, which is clearly the meaning intended here.

62. *Masāʾil* usually are hypothetical legal questions with their answers, such as would be studied by more advanced students. As the text discusses only primary education in the *kuttāb* (Qurʾānic school), the reference must be to the brief maxims in which legal doctrines were often formulated at an early date. See Schacht, *Introduction,* 39.

63. *Min dhikr Allāh*: literally, "from God's memorial," i.e., the Qurʾān.

64. Abū ʿImrān Ibrāhīm ibn Yazīd al-Nakhaʿī (b. 50/670, d. 96/715) was an important Kūfan legal scholar. See *GAS,* 1.403–4, and Ibn Ḥajar, *Tahdhīb,* 1.177–79.

65. Probably ʿAbd al-Raḥmān ibn al-Qāsim al-ʿAtaqī (or al-ʿUtaqī, referred to as Ibn al-Qāsim below), the disciple of Mālik with whom Saḥnūn studied in Egypt. See *GAS,* 1.465.

66. Ed. Cairo: Yūsuf.

67. The name means Saʿd the Bootmaker.

68. ʿIkrimah, a freedman (*mawlā*) of Ibn ʿAbbās and one of the most distinguished transmitters, is said to have died around 104–7/722–25 at the age of eighty. See Ibn Ḥajar, *Tahdhīb,* 7.263–73, and *EI*[2], s.v. "ʿIkrima."

69. ʿAbdallāh ibn ʿAbbās, a cousin of the Prophet, was born three years before the Hijrah. He spent much of his life at al-Ṭāʾif as a scholar and authority on Qurʾān interpretation. He died ca. 68/687. See *GAS,* 1.25–28, and EI^2, s.v. "ʿAbd Allāh b. al-ʿAbbās."

70. The manuscripts and editions indicate no change of speaker, but the context demands it.

71. The *ḥadd* punishments (the term means "limit") are corporal punishments defined in the Qurʾān for certain crimes. For wine drinking, for example, the punishment was 80 lashes. See Schacht, *Introduction,* 178–81.

72. Wakīʿ ibn al-Jarrāḥ was born in al-Kūfah in 129/746, where he became a famous scholar of traditions. He died on pilgrimage in 197/812. See *GAS,* 1.96–97, and Ibn Ḥajar, *Tahdhīb,* 9.126.

73. This may be Hishām ibn Abī ʿAbdallāh al-Dastawāʾī al-Bakrī, a traditionist of al-Baṣrah, who died in 152/769. See Ibn Ḥajar, *Tahdhīb,* 9.43–45. The *isnād* in the Tunis manuscript seems to have been truncated. The Rabat manuscript reads (addition in italics): "from Hishām ibn Abī ʿAbdallāh, *from Yaḥyá ibn Abī Kathīr, from al-Muhājir, from ʿIkrimah, from ʿAbdallāh* ibn Abī Bakr." See ed. Algiers, p. 76. For Yaḥyá b. Abī Kathīr (d. 129/746) see Ibn Ḥajar, *Tahdhīb,* 9.268–70.

74. Identified by the Algiers editor as probably Rabāḥ ibn Thābit al-Azdī (d. 237/851–52); see Ibn Saḥnūn, *Adab,* 77. Ed. Cairo reads: "Rabāḥ *from* Thābit."

75. Abū Ayyūb ʿAbd al-Raḥmān ibn Ziyād (d. ca. 156/772–73) was a judge in North Africa. Saḥnūn is said to have pronounced him "trustworthy" (*thiqah*) as a transmitter of traditions. See Ibn Ḥajar, *Tahdhīb,* 6.173–76.

76. Abū ʿAbd al-Raḥmān ʿAbdallah ibn Yazīd al-Maʿāfirī al-Ḥublī (d. ca. 100/718–19), of Egyptian origin, was a member of the *tābiʿī* generation. He is said to have been sent by the caliph ʿUmar II to teach the people of Ifrīqiyā. He is said to have accompanied the expedition of Mūsá ibn Nuṣayr to Spain, but then returned and died in North Africa. See Ibn Saḥnūn, *Adab* (ed. Algiers), 77; Ibn Ḥajar, *Tahdhīb,* 6.81–82. Note that the *isnād* is obviously incomplete, as Abū ʿAbd al-Raḥmān (who never met the Prophet) simply says that "it was reported to me that the Messenger of God said," without giving details of who transmitted the tradition to him.

77. I have translated the text of ed. Algiers. The text is uncertain.

78. I.e., ʿAbdallāh ibn ʿUmar ibn al-Khaṭṭāb (son of the caliph ʿUmar), who died in 73/692. See EI^2, s.v. ʿAbd Allāh b. ʿUmar.

79. Lecomte understands the sentence quite differently: that the disciplinary punishment should be proportional to the fault, and may at times surpass the legally defined *ḥadd* punishment. He takes *ḥadd*, which I have translated in its general sense as "limit," to have its technical sense here.

80. Abū Muḥammad Saʿīd ibn al-Musayyab ibn Ḥazn al-Makhzūmī (b. 13/634, d. 94/713) was an early genealogist, historian, traditionist, and legal scholar. He is particularly important for having transmitted the legal decisions of the caliph ʿUmar. See *GAS,* 1.276.

81. Islamic jurisprudence conditions the weight given to testimony on the witness's ethical status (*ʿadālah*), persons of loose morals being assumed to be

ready to lie in court. Saḥnūn is saying that since most teachers do not fulfill their professional obligations, their testimony in court is of dubious validity.

82. For *yaḍribuhum* (strike them), al-Qābisī, "Risālah," 320, reads *yaḍurruhum* (harm them).

83. I.e., the ᶜĪd al-Fiṭr that marks the conclusion of the month-long fast of Ramaḍān. It is marked by special public prayers and feasting. See *EI²*, s.vv. "ᶜĪd" and "ᶜĪd al-Fiṭr."

84. I.e., the ᶜĪd al-Aḍḥā, on the tenth day of the month of Dhū al-Ḥijjah. On this day pilgrims to Mecca sacrifice an animal (usually a sheep) to commemorate the animal that God sent to Abraham to sacrifice instead of his son. Muslims outside Mecca also celebrate the day with special public prayers and by slaughtering a sheep and feasting. See *EI²*, s.v. "ᶜĪd al-Aḍḥā."

85. Ed. Cairo has an abbreviated text. I have translated according to ed. Algiers and the parallel text in al-Qābisī, "Risālah," 321.

86. There is a textual problem. The Tunis manuscript reads *aflām* (an unattested word); the Rabat manuscript has a lacuna. "Banners" (*aᶜlām*) is an emendation proposed by Lecomte, "Le Livre," 90. ᶜAbd al-Mawlā, in Ibn Saḥnūn, *Adab,* 81, suggests reading *īlām,* "giving banquets," which makes sense and fits the context of throwing fruit. Al-Ahwānī, in al-Qābisī, *Al-tarbiyah,* 359, guessed that *aflām* might be an acronym made up from the opening "mystical letters" of the second sura of the Qurᵓān (*alif-lām-mīm*). The meaning would be, "What people customarily do regarding the *alif-lām-mīm* [sura], at the time of conclusion, and the fruit, etc." Since students began their study of the Qurᵓān with the short concluding suras and worked back to the beginning (the first sura having already been memorized as being necessary for use in prayer), completion of the long second sura would signal completion of the entire Qurᵓān. But this seems forced. Saḥnūn's answer, which speaks only to the second part of the question, throws no light on the correct reading.

87. Translating ed. Algiers, *al-katb.* Ed. Cairo has *al-kitāb,* which could also mean "the Book," i.e., the Qurᵓān, but the context implies "writing" in the general sense. It would be superfluous to say that the Qurᵓān is something "that will improve them and educate them." Furthermore, the next paragraphs deal with the teacher's copying out books for his own use and the use of others.

88. Reading *yatakhāyarūn,* with ed. Algiers and al-Ahwānī's suggestion in al-Qābisī, *Al-tarbiyah,* 359, on the basis of al-Qābisī's "Risālah." Ed. Cairo reads *yatajāwazūn* ("go beyond").

89. Translating ed. Algiers, *li-aḥad.* Ed. Cairo has *ilá aḥad,* "to someone," which seems less likely. In a community where literacy was limited, one can imagine the teacher's receiving commissions to compose letters. He might be tempted to have the students assist him.

90. Arabic *gharīb* refers to rare and unusual words that occur in the Qurᵓān and hadith.

91. Arabic *iᶜrāb* refers to the endings that mark the cases of Arabic nouns and moods of Arabic verbs. Since most of these endings had fallen away from the colloquial dialects, correct production of them would be difficult for the student.

92. The next paragraph can be taken to imply that "good reading" (*qirāʾah ḥasanah*) has a technical sense: that the teacher should choose the most respected of the variant readings of the text (in the Mālikī school this meant the reading of Nāfiʿ of Medina), although some reference to other readings was not out of place. But the parallel text in al-Qābisī's "Risālah," 304, has "good reading with pausing and clear articulation," implying a more general sense.

93. Because early Qurʾāns had little punctuation, the teacher passed on oral tradition about where to pause (*tawqīf*) and where not to pause in order to convey the meaning clearly. In time a system of marks was developed to indicate where a pause is mandatory, optional, or prohibited.

94. Poetry (*shiʿr*) was valued for its intrinsic beauty and its value as providing training in the classical Arabic language. Verses of early poetry were often cited to illustrate the meaning of an obscure word in the Qurʾān.

95. The whip (*dirrah*) was made of twisted cords or thongs. The discussion below implies that these were attached to a wooden handle that the teacher was not permitted to allow to come in contact with the child. The *falaqah* was a board with two holes (like the stocks) or a rod with loops of rope at either end to hold the feet of the pupil being beaten on the soles of his feet.

96. A homily (*khuṭbah*) formed part of the congregational prayer on Friday. Collections of homilies by famous figures in Islamic history existed and could be used as texts to be taught and memorized.

97. Reading with ed. Cairo, *al-kuttāb*. Ed. Algiers has *al-katb,* "writing."

98. I.e., if he starts with the second teacher at a point where he still has more than one-third of the text to recite. "Yūnus" is the twelfth sura of the Qurʾān; "Hūd" the eleventh. "Hūd" comes in the middle of the eleventh of the thirty "parts" (*juzʾ*, pl. *ajzāʾ*) into which the text of the Qurʾān is divided. If the student begins his study with the second teacher with either of these suras, bearing in mind that the suras of the Qurʾān are first studied in reverse order, he still has more than one-third of the text left to learn.

99. Literally, it is not something that can be derived by analogical reasoning (*qiyās*), but only something that can be considered commendable (*mustaḥsan*).

100. Correcting the printed text's *yaqūlu* (he says) to *taqūlu* (you say). The text as printed would translate: "What should he [i.e., the teacher] say if he [the parent] says . . . ?"

101. I.e., Ibn al-Qāsim, the scholar with whom Saḥnūn studied in Egypt. He is mentioned below as Ibn al-Qāsim.

102. In the *rukūʿ* (bowing) the worshipper leans at a right angle, with his hands placed on his knees. See *EI*², s.v. "Ṣalāt."

103. In the *sujūd* (prostration) the worshipper prostrates himself, the body resting on the forehead, the palms of both hands, both knees, and both feet. Standing upright, bowing, prostration, and sitting (*julūs*) (along with the words associated with each) are the main constituents of each *rakʿah* ("an invariable series of attitudes and formulas which constitute an element to be repeated a set number of times in the course of a completed ritual prayer"). Ibid.

104. This formula is said at the very beginning of each ritual prayer to signal the worshipper's entry into a state of sacralization (*takbīrat al-iḥrām*)

before the bowing (*rukūᶜ*) in each *rakᶜah,* before each prostration (*sujūd*), and while the worshipper is seated (*julūs*) between prostrations. Ibid.

105. Between the two prostrations that occur in each *rakᶜah,* the worshipper sits on his heels, knees on the ground, hands placed on the thighs. Ibid.

106. At the very beginning of each ritual prayer, the worshipper raises his hands above his shoulders, to the level of the ears, and recites the *takbīr*: *Allāhu akbar* (God is most great!). The hands are then placed on the base of the chest, right hand over the left, and a short opening prayer is recited. Ibid.

107. At the end of the final *rakᶜah* of each ritual prayer, the worshipper, still seated, turns to the right, saying *al-salāmu ᶜalaykum wa-rāḥmatu Llāhi wa-barakātuhu* (Peace be upon you and God's mercy and blessings!); then he turns to the left, repeating the same words. These actions terminate the ritual prayer. Ibid.

108. While the worshipper sits at the end of the prostrations of the second and fourth *rakᶜah* of each ritual prayer (or at the end of the second and third *rakᶜah* of the sunset prayer, which has only three *rakᶜah*s), an affirmation of faith (*tashahhud*) is added. The formula includes a salutation to God, a blessing on the Prophet, and recitation of the creedal statement (*shahādah,* literally "testimony"): There is no god but God, and Muḥammad is the messenger of God. Ibid.

109. On the Supplication of Standing (this is the mostly likely meaning of *duᶜāᵓ al-qunūt,* so called because it is recited standing, but other interpretations are given), see *EI*², s.v. "Ḳunūt." The evidence of the various hadith collections implies that the *qunūt* consisted of supplications for various needs of the community inserted in the morning worship and sometimes in the evening worship.

110. Sunna is a usage sanctioned by tradition, usually authenticated by reference to an action or saying of the Prophet. See *EI*², s.v. "Sunna."

111. Abū Bakr, the first caliph, succeeded to the leadership of the Islamic community at the death of Muḥammad in 11/632 and ruled until his death in 13/634.

112. I.e., supplications on various occasions that are not part of the five obligatory ritual prayers (*ṣalāh*).

113. I.e., performs the *ṣalāt al-istisqāᵓ* (also mentioned in the next paragraph), a special communal prayer for rain in times of drought. See *EI*², s.v. "Ṣalāt," 931.

114. Addition from al-Qābisī, "Risālah," 305.

115. Arabic *sunan,* plural of *sunna.*

116. See note 103 above.

117. *Witr* means "consisting of an odd number." It became customary (*sunnah*) to pray a prayer of an odd number of *rakᶜah*s (usually one plus two, to give three) between the evening prayer and the dawn prayer. See *EI*², s.v. "Ṣalāt," 930.

118. The time and ritual of communal prayer on the Feast of Breaking the Fast (*Īd al-Fiṭr*) and the Feast of Sacrificing (*Īd al-Aḍḥā*) differ from other communal prayers. Ibid., 930.

119. "In the case of eclipse of the sun or of the moon, a communal prayer of two *rakᶜah*s is held in the mosque. Its time is the same as that of the two

feasts [i.e., approximately half an hour after the rising of the sun]. There is neither call to prayer nor *iqāma* nor sermon. The Qurʾānic recitations are spoken in a whisper. The peculiarity of this prayer is that each *rakʿah* contains, after the inclination and the standing upright, which are very prolonged, a second long inclination and a second standing upright before the prostration." Ibid., 931.

120. The *ṣalāt al-janāzah* is unique in that it involves no *rakʿah,* but is performed standing. Ibid., 931.

121. A *sajdah* is a place in the Qurʾānic text at which it is customary for the reciter to make a prostration, for example, 32:15: "Only those believe in Our signs who, when they are reminded of them, fall down prostrate and proclaim the praise of their Lord, not waxing proud." Tradition (there are some variations) specifies fourteen such passages. See *EI*^{2}, s.v. "Sadjdah."

122. I.e., the young pupil is not yet qualified to act as a prayer-leader (*imām*).

123. I.e., for the boys (the Arabic pronoun is masculine plural). Al-Qābisī's quotation of the sentence uses the feminine plural pronoun, changing the meaning to "because that is corruption for the *girls.*" (al-Qābisī, "Risālah," 315.)

124. *Allāhu aʿlam* (God knows best) is a way of saying that the speaker is not sure of the correct answer to the question.

125. Shajarah ibn ʿĪsā al-Maʿāfirī (d. 232/846–47) was a judge in Tunis in the time of Saḥnūn. See Ibn Mūsá, *Tartīb,* vol. 3–4, 12.

126. Reading with ed. Algiers, *tubaʿʿaḍu,* as against ed. Tunis and Cairo, *tuqḍā* (it is decided [legally]).

127. The sentence is obscure. The Arabic word *muʾnah* means provision or maintenance. What seems to be implied is that wealthier parents might offer the teacher an allowance of food in addition to monetary remuneration, and this allowance should not be stopped suddenly.

128. Abū ʿAmr Ashhab ibn ʿAbd al-ʿAzīz ibn Dāwūd al-Qaysī was born in Egypt in 145/762. He was a pupil of Ibn Wahb, whom he also served as secretary. He died in 204/819. See *GAS,* 1.466–67.

129. Abū ʿAbdallāh Muḥammad ibn Ibrāhīm ibn Dīnār (d. 182/798–99) was a famous Meccan jurist. See Ibn Ḥajar, *Tahdhīb,* 9.7ff.

130. I.e., I, Muḥammad ibn Saḥnūn, heard my father, Saḥnūn, say.

131. The manuscripts and printed editions add: "ibn Shuʿbah," which is impossible. Al-Mughīrah ibn Shuʿbah (d. 49/669 or 50/670) was a Companion of the Prophet who served as governor of al-Baṣrah and then of al-Kūfah. He was not a contemporary of the jurist Ibn Dīnār. The parallel in al-Qābisī ("Risālah," 331) omits "ibn Shuʿbah." Toward the end of this section, Ibn Saḥnūn quotes his father as having referred to Mālik and al-Mughīrah as "our colleagues" (*aṣḥābunā*). This makes it clear that "ibn Shuʿbah" has been added here by mistake and that the person in question is the Medinese jurist al-Mughīrah ibn ʿAbd al-Raḥmān ʿAyyāsh, died 186/802. See Ibn Ḥajar, *Tahdhīb,* 10.264–65.

132. Literally, those in charge of oversight for the Muslims (*ulū al-naẓar li-l-muslimīn*). The phrase is ambiguous.

133. Because study of the Qurʾān customarily began with the short suras at the end of the book and worked back by sections, *Sūrat al-Baqarah* (the

Qurʾān's longest sura) would also be the last sura to be studied (the first sura, *al-Fātiḥah,* having been studied earlier, as it is necessary for prayer). The meaning is that special remuneration is due if the child has studied the last third, including the final sura to be learned. The parallel text in al-Qābisī (*Risālah,* 331) reads "*from* the one-third to *Sūrat al-Baqarah.*"

134. Reading with ed. Algiers, *sannah,* as against eds. Tunis and Cairo, *al-ṣibyān* (the children).

135. Abū ᶜAbdallāh ᶜAbd al-Raḥmān ibn al-Qāsim al-ᶜAtakī (d. 191/807) was a disciple of Mālik with whom Saḥnūn studied in Fusṭāṭ (Egypt), composing the *Mudawwanah,* a legal text based on the teachings of Mālik that Saḥnūn took back to his native Qayrawān and that became "decisive in the crystallization and diffusion of the *madhhab* of Mālik throughout the Muslim West." See *EI*², s.v. "Saḥnūn," and *GAS,* 1.465–66 (where the name is given as al-ᶜUtakī).

136. Abū ᶜAbd al-Raḥmān ᶜAbdallāh ibn Lahīᶜah b. ᶜUqbah (b. 97/715) was appointed by the Caliph al-Manṣūr to be chief judge of Egypt in 154/770. He transmitted historical reports and hadith and died in 174/790. See *GAS,* 1.94, 354; and *EI*², s.v. "Ibn Lahīᶜa."

137. Abū al-ᶜAbbās Yaḥyá ibn Ayyūb al-Ghāfiqī (d. 168/784) was a traditionist who also transmitted historical reports about Egypt. See *GAS,* 1.354.

138. The Tunis manuscript and the printed editions have "ᶜUmārah ibn ᶜArafah," who is otherwise unknown. Dr. ᶜAbd il-Mawlā, in his edition, 93, corrects on the basis of a similar *isnād* in Saḥnūn's *Mudawwanah.* ᶜUmārah ibn Ghaziyyah also occurs in an *isnād* in al-Ṭabarī's *History,* 1.2134, as transmitting to Ibn Lahīᶜah.

139. In cases of unintentional homicide, Islamic law provides two remedies. On the one hand, the slayer must perform a religious expiation (*kaffārah*) for the act, preferably by manumitting a Muslim slave, or, if he cannot perform this, by fasting the daylight hours of two consecutive months. On the other hand, the victim's kin must be indemnified by the payment of blood money (*diyah*). Originally, those responsible for paying the blood money were the paternal kin of the slayer. The term for these persons (*ᶜāqilah*) could be extended to mean the man's entire clan or tribe; it could also be taken to mean those who served in the same military unit or in the same trade. It is derived from a verb meaning to restrain a camel by binding its folded foreleg with a rope to prevent the camel from rising, as the *diyah* originally consisted of a hundred camels to be paid by the kin of the slayer to the kin of the victim, if the victim was an adult male, or a lesser number for women, children, slaves, etc.—this was the full blood money (*diyah mughallaẓah*) assessed for homicide. Equivalent cash payments were later fixed. A lesser blood money was assessed for bodily injury and, as implied here, where the death resulted from action within the rights of the slayer. See Schacht, *Introduction,* 181–87.

140. This is said to have taken place after the Battle of Badr (Ramaḍān 2/ March 624). Some of the captured Meccans were too poor to ransom themselves, so Muḥammad allowed them to teach writing to the children of Medina in lieu of a cash ransom. Ibn ᶜAbbās's report of the incident is as follows: "Some of the prisoners from the Battle of Badr had no ransom, so the Messenger of God set as their ransom that they should teach writing to the children of the

Medinese Muslims. One day a boy came crying to his father, who asked him what was wrong. The boy said that his teacher had struck him. So the father said, 'The wicked fellow is seeking vengeance for Badr. By God, you shall never go to him'" (Ibn Ḥanbal, *Musnad,* 1.247). Similar reports, attributed to ᶜĀmir and ᶜIkrimah, are found in Ibn Saᶜd, *Ṭabaqāt*: "The Messenger of God captured seventy prisoners at the Battle of Badr. He set their ransom according to their wealth. The people of Mecca used to write, but the people of Medina did not write. So anyone who had no ransom money was given ten boys from Medina and taught them. When they became proficient, that was his ransom" (2.1.14).

141. The translation follows what I take to be the better reading in al-Qābisī, "Risālah," 343: "*wa-in jāwaza, ḍamina l-diyata min mālihi maᶜa al-adab.*" The text as printed begins, "*wa-in jāwaza al-adab,*" i.e., "If he goes beyond the rule." But this destroys the logical progression of hypotheses.

142. The addition is from the parallel passage in al-Qābisī, "Risālah," 343.

143. The addition is from the parallel passage in al-Qābisī, "Risālah," 344.

144. *Abū jād* refers to the eight nonsense words used as a mnemonic device to memorize the numerical value of each letter of the Arabic alphabet. (The first of these words was pronounced *abjad* or *abujad.*) Since regular arithmetical operations soon came to be done using the numerals borrowed from India (what the Arabs called Indian and we call Arabic numerals), the letters of the alphabet used as numbers came to be relegated to subordinate uses, much as Roman numerals in the West. One of these uses was in various divinatory procedures and in composing certain talismans. This association of the *abjad* with magic rendered it suspect to some jurists. See *EI*[2], s.v. "Abdjad."

145. Ḥafṣ ibn Ghiyāth al-Nakhaᶜī (b. 117/735, d. 194/810) of Kūfan origin, studied with Abū Ḥanīfah and served as judge in Baghdad and al-Kūfah under Hārūn al-Rashīd. See Kaḥḥālah, *Muᶜjam,* 1.649.

146. It is not clear which Sābūr (Shapur) is meant. Shapur I reigned 240–70 AD; Shapur II reigned 309–79. Of the two, Shapur II is more likely, as he conducted extensive military campaigns against the Arabs. See al-Ṭabarī, *History,* 5.50–66.

147. The words [in the world to come] are added from Qur'ān 3:77, which the words *lā khalāqa lahum* (they have no share) echo.

148. I.e., the kin of the slain child may slay the teacher in retaliation.

149. Ed. Cairo, "our."

Ikhwān al-Ṣafā'

1. The preceding chapter or epistle deals with numerical proportions and their significance for arithmetic, music (especially harmony), and prosody.

2. Similarly to Aristotle, the Ikhwān al-Ṣafā' divide the arts into two classes: (1) the practical arts (*al-ṣanā'iᶜ al-ᶜamaliyyah*) aiming at utility or pleasure and making use of bodily organs or artificial tools (i.e., the Aristotelian τέχναι within the meaning of *Metaphysica* 1 (1.981b17ff.), and (2) the scientific arts (*al-ṣanā'iᶜ al-ᶜilmiyyah*), which are subdivided into various classes of science (*ᶜulūm*) and whose primary aim is to gain knowledge. Since the latter comprise not

only theoretical but also practical sciences such as politics and economics, the term "scientific arts" seems to be preferable over "theoretical arts" proposed elsewhere. For the sciences included under the scientific arts, see "Chapter on the Genera of the Sciences," below. Details concerning the practical arts, which play no more than a minor part in the *Rasāᵓil Ikhwān al-Ṣafāᵓ* are provided in the eighth epistle (*Rasāᵓil*, 1.276–95). It is worth noticing that the *Rasāᵓil* on the whole do not keep to the threefold classification of the scientific arts outlined in this chapter.

3. According to the Ikhwān al-Ṣafāᵓ, knowledge is a spiritual accident that adheres to spiritual substances as its substratum. These are exemplified here through the souls of the students. However, the Ikhwān al-Ṣafāᵓ do not generally equate spiritual substances with human souls, as the somewhat ambiguous diction seems to suggest here.

4. This remark obviously refers to a later work—specifically, the tenth epistle of the Ikhwān al-Ṣafāᵓ. For the conclusions which can be drawn from this and many other internal references with respect to the chronology and the original and revised orders of single sections of the work, see EI^2 s.v. "Ikhwān al-Ṣafāᵓ" (Y. Marquet).

5. Reading *wa-ḥarakatin wa-sukūn* instead of *wa-khiffatin wa-sukūn.*

6. The black and the yellow bile (χολὴ μέλαινα, χ. ξανθή). For ancient theories of the two biles and their reception in Arabic medical sciences and philosophy, see Hans Hinrich Biesterfeldt and Dimitri Gutas, "The Malady of Love," *Journal of the American Oriental Society* 104, no. 1 (1984): 21–55.

7. The Arabic term *ḥayawānī* denotes, like Latin *animal,* both human and animal life to the exclusion of plant life. The idea of plants and animals as being provided with a specific soul was set forth in Plato's *Timaeus* and later taken up and modified by Aristotle. For its reception in the psychology of the Ikhwān al-Ṣafāᵓ see the ninth epistle of the *Rasāᵓil* (in particular, *Rasāᵓil,* 1.311–14).

8. See below, note 69.

9. For the expression *ᶜaraḍ al-dunyā,* see Ibn Manẓūr, *Lisān,* 2887a.

10. The Qurᵓān makes mention of different levels or ranks (*darajāt*) in Paradise which are assigned to the faithful according to their deeds and piety (see Qurᵓān 4:96, 6:132, 8:4, etc.). On the highest level there is a kind of upper story chamber (*ghuraf*).

11. The terms *knowledge, object of knowledge, teaching,* and *learning* (as well as *teacher, student, scholar,* and *the knowledgeable,* below) all derive from the same Arabic root (*ᶜ-l-m*). It is not possible to mirror this etymological relationship in the English translation.

12. This paragraph is based on the Aristotelian theory of act and potency and its application to the process of learning and knowing; see Aristotle, *De Anima* 2.1–2 (412a1ff.), and the relevant commentaries.

13. See the fourth epistle of the section "On Psychical and Intellectual Matters" in *Rasāᵓil,* 3.231–48, on being and not-being, especially p. 232.18ff.

14. The Arabic terms *ḥadd* and *rasm* correspond to the Aristotelian terms ὁρισμός, the essential definition in the strict sense of the word, and ὑπογραφή, the rough outline or approximate description, which is used for things of

which there is no precise definition. For examples see Aristotle, *Topica* 4.4 (141b15ff.). However, the subsequent explanation of the terms has not much in common with Aristotle's theory of definition.

15. See the first epistle of the section "On Bodies and Physical Matters" in *Rasāʾil,* 2.5–23; on matter and form, see especially 6–9.

16. This is the definition of man given and explained by Porphyry in his *Isagoge* (*CAG* 4.1, pp. 8–12). For a more detailed account in the *Rasāʾil Ikhwān al-Ṣafāʾ,* see the tenth epistle (*Rasāʾil,* 1.392).

17. For this subdivision of the quantity and the following examples, see Aristotle, *Metaphysica* 5.13 (1020a7ff.).

18. See Epistle 1 in *Rasāʾil,* 1.48.

19. See note 15, above; note especially *Rasāʾil,* 2.12–20.

20. See *Rasāʾil,* 1.2.

21. See *Rasāʾil,* 1.11.

22. From the subsequent explanations it appears that the Ikhwān differentiate between three sorts of "where": two corporeal and one spiritual. The second sort, the position (*maḥall*) of accidents in relation to certain substances, is omitted here. Accordingly, *baynahumā* in the following sentence is to be replaced by *baynahā.*

23. The assignment of different capacities of the soul and dispositions of character to specific parts of the body is rooted in Plato's *Timaeus.* The idea was elaborated and refined by Galen (c. 129–c. 199 AD) and had, through Arabic translations of Plato's and Galen's works, an immense influence on Islamic thinkers.

24. See the ninth epistle of the section "On Bodies and Physical Matters" in *Rasāʾil,* 2.378–95, especially 383–85.

25. See the second epistle of the section "On Bodies and Physical Matters" in *Rasāʾil,* 2.199–211.

26. See above, note 15; especially *Rasāʾil,* 2.17.

27. The famous division by Aristotle, who differentiated between four classes of the cause, known as *causa materialis, causa formalis, causa efficiens,* and *causa finalis.* The preceding expression "caused by production" (*maʿlūl ṣināʿī*) excludes two further kinds of causation: by accident (*biʾl-bakht*), and spontaneously (*min tilqāʾ nafsihī*).

28. For the controversy on whether the interrogative pronoun *man* (*who?*) is only applicable to human beings or to animals as well, see Carter, *Arab Linguistics,* §§ 11.754, 11.755, and notes, p. 268f.; and the literature mentioned in Simon, *Mittelalterliche arabische Sprachbetrachtung,* 217, note 427. From the following examples it appears that the Ikhwān al-Ṣafāʾ opt for the position adopted by the grammarians.

29. The *Isagoge* was composed by the Neoplatonic philosopher Porphyry (c. 234–c. 305) as an introduction into Aristotelian logic. It was widely used in the curriculum of the philosophical school of Alexandria and in philosophical circles in the Islamic world. Several medieval Arabic commentaries are extant.

30. Reading *ʿulūm* instead of *ʿilm* as required by the following pronouns, which refer to a word in the plural.

31. The following subdivision comprises various *termini technici* of specifically Islamic disciplines that require more explanation than a footnote will afford. For a general introduction, see *EI*² s.v. "Sharīᶜa" (N. Calder), and the literature referred to in the subsequent notes.

32. See *EI*² s.vv. "Ḥadīth" (J. Robson) and "Riwāya" (S. Leder).

33. For a brief survey, see Muranyi, "Fiqh"; and *EI*² s.v. "Sunna" (G. H. A. Juynboll).

34. For these terms see Chapter 1 in Schimmel, *Mystical Dimensions.*

35. The Arabic word translated here as *successors* has also the meaning "deputy, vicar" and served as a sovereign title (i.e., *caliph*).

36. The Arabic text gives a transliteration of the Greek γεωμετρία, explained by the Persian loanword *handasa,* both of which comprise theoretical geometry and practical geodesy.

37. This kind of astronomy, i.e., theoretical or mathematical astronomy and astrology, has to be distinguished from physical astronomy, which is ranked among the physical sciences under the name *science of the heavens and the cosmos,* see below.

38. The five species are named by transliterations of the Aristotelian nomenclature. These transliterations were confused by the scribe of the manuscript that the Arabic edition is based on. In the case in hand here the text should read *būyiṭīqī* (for ποιητική) instead of *anūlūṭīqiyā.*

39. Reading *rīṭūrīqī* (for ῥητορική) instead of *rīṭūrīqiyā,* i.e., Aristotle's *Ars rhetorica.* On the inclusion of Poetics and Rhetoric within the scope of the logical sciences, which is rooted in the philosophical school of Alexandria, see Black, *Logic and Aristotle's Rhetoric and Poetics,* especially the introduction.

40. Reading *ṭūbīqā* instead of *ṭūsīqā,* i.e., Aristotle's *Topica.*

41. Reading *anūlūṭīqā* instead of *yūlūṭīqā* (ed. Ziriklī, Cairo 1347/1928), or *būlūṭīqā* (*Rasā'il,* 1.268). This term refers to Aristotle's *Analytica priora* and *Analytica posteriora.*

42. The Arabic *sūfisṭīqā* is a transliteration based on the title of Aristotle's work Περὶ τῶν σοφιστικῶν ἐλέγχων (*On Sophistical Refutations*).

43. Literally, "of those who deceive [through tricky or misleading questions and statements]."

44. That is, in addition to those whose titles served as nomenclature for the preceding subdivision of the logical sciences.

45. This is the common Arabic title of Aristotle's *Posterior Analytics.* Both because of its eminent importance for the theory of science and cognition and because of the fact that it was translated into Arabic much later than most of the other books of the so-called Aristotelian *Organon,* this book had an outstanding and autonomous position (hence a separate title) among the medieval Islamic scholars.

46. Again, all three titles are given in transliterations of the Greek (the works referred to are Aristotle's *Categoriae, Liber de interpretatione,* and *Analytica priora*). They are rendered here by their common English translations.

47. Literally *ells.*

48. The Arabic text has a technical term of Arabic prosody which stands for one of the poetic licenses, i.e., the alteration of a metrical foot by suppression

of a letter; see Stoetzer, *Theory and Practice in Arabic Metrics,* 40. (For the use of the seventh verb stem instead of the more common form *ziḥāf,* see Dihkhudā, *Lughat-nāma,* s.v. *inziḥāf.*)

49. Reading *Furfūriyūs* with *Rasā'il,* 1.269.1, instead of *Qurqūriyūs,* as given in the edition of al-Ziriklī, Cairo 1347/1928.

50. As a matter of fact, the *Rasā'il Ikhwān al-Ṣafā'* comprise separate epistles on Porphyry's *Isagoge* (1.10), Aristotle's *Categories* (1.11), *On Interpretation* (1.12), *Prior Analytics* (1.13), and *Posterior Analytics* (1.14), but none on Aristotle's *Poetics, Rhetoric,* or *Topics.*

51. The Arabic *nukat mā yuḥtāju ilayhā* is not quite clear. In the concrete sense *nukta,* the singular of *nukat,* means *point, spot*; in the figurative sense *witticism* or *point of a joke.* It probably refers to the main points of the logical arts here.

52. Porphyry's *Isagoge* tells us about five such concepts (the well-known *quinque voces* of medieval philosophy), while the Ikhwān al-Ṣafā' distinguish between six simple concepts (*al-alfāẓ al-sitta*), as do other Syriac and Arabic philosophers of the 8th–10th centuries AD. See, for example, the anonymous author of a Syriac commentary on the *Isagoge* (H. Hugonnard-Roche's edition is available in *Revue d'histoire des textes* 24, 1994), Ya'qūb b. Isḥaq al-Kindī, or Abū Naṣr al-Fārābī. For a more detailed account, see R. Arnzen, Review of "Frammenti e testimonianze," 363.

53. For *rasm* meaning "outline," see above, note 14.

54. Instead of "syllogism" the edited Arabic text has "something perceptible" (*shay'un maḥsūsun*), which makes no sense here. It is most probably a corruption in the manuscript used for the edition, caused by a copyist who was not familiar with Hellenistic philosophy. In Arabic handwriting the two words, written closely together, look quite similar to the Arabic transliteration of Greek συλλογισμός, i.e., *sulūjismūs.* As a matter of fact, this transliteration is employed by the Ikhwān al-Ṣafā' in the epistle on Aristotle's *Prior Analytics*; see *Rasā'il,* 1.421.3.

55. The Arabic term *yāqūt* is a collective name for various minerals that serve to prepare gems, most of which belong to the class of oxides and hydroxides (as corundum, ruby, sapphire, or amethyst), very few to that of silicates (as topaz). For the Arabic terminology in this paragraph and medieval Islamic mineralogy in general see the section "Mining Technology" in *EI*[2] s.v. "Ma'din."

56. Reading *bādzahrāt* instead of *bānzahrāt*; in Tīfāshī, *Azhār al-afkār,* 117–41 and also Ibn al-Bayṭār, *Jāmi' li-mufradāt,* 1.81.

57. Literally, "scatter themselves"; *tafarruq* might be a corruption for *tafarru'.*

58. Reading *ghilaẓ,* with the edition of al-Ziriklī, instead of *ghalaṭ,* as in *Rasā'il,* 1.371.10.

59. A doubtful passage; literally, "their enemies and whom they know."

60. In all probability, this last paragraph of the chapter is a later addition. The introduction of new facts in the closing lines of a chapter does not correspond to the usual style of the *Rasā'il Ikhwān al-Ṣafā'.* Contradictory to what is explained here, both the science of crop and stock farming and the science of the handicrafts were classified as species of the propaedeutical sciences at the beginning of this chapter. As in al-Fārābī's classification of the sciences,

medicine is not included among the theoretical or scientific arts in the *Rasāʾil Ikhwān al-Ṣafāʾ*.

61. Reading *wa-ʿālimu al-ghaybi waʾl-shahādati.* Another vocalization—i.e., *wa-ʿālami al-ghaybi waʾl-shahādati* ("and [the director] of the invisible and the visible worlds") is equally possible.

62. This chapter is influenced by the Neoplatonic theory of hierarchically structured hypostases, the members of which are generated by emanation of the lower level of being from the next higher and finally from The One. For the origins of this doctrine and its transformation in the *Rasāʾil Ikhwān al-Ṣafāʾ*, see Netton, *Muslim Neoplatonists,* 33–52.

63. The Arabic term *siyāsah,* usually translated as "politics," has many different meanings, most of which belong to the semantic field of statecraft-government-power. The translation, "exercise of sovereignty" seems to be the most appropriate for the subsequent subdivision. For a survey of the different meanings and connotations of *siyāsah* see Lewis, "Siyāsa." A thorough analysis of the present section of the *Rasāʾil Ikhwān al-Ṣafāʾ* is found in C. Baffioni, "The 'General Policy' of the Ikhwān al-Ṣafāʾ."

64. For the role of prophecy in Islamic political philosophy, see Rahman, *Prophecy in Islam.* For a general account of medieval political theory in Islam, see Rosenthal, *Political Thought in Medieval Islam.*

65. See below, note 69.

66. Reading *biʾl-idhkār* instead of *waʾl-idhkār.*

67. This is a well-known Qurʾānic catch phrase, of which both the internal interpretation and the external question of who in the Islamic community is competent or responsible for performing this duty or office were constantly disputed. For an introduction (including further reading), see Ess, *Theologie und Gesellschaft,* 387–90. For a detailed survey, see Cook, *Commanding Right and Forbidding Wrong.*

68. See above, note 35.

69. Both terms, *al-maʿād* ("the returning") and *al-nashʾah al-ukhrá* ("the other coming into being"), are of Qurʾānic origin. The life to come begins, according to the Qurʾān, with a second creation that is called "the other" or "the last coming into existence" (*al-nashʾah al-ukhrá* or *al-nashʾah al-ākhirah*); see Qurʾān 28:85, 29:20, 53:47, 56:6, and some of the Qurʾānic passages quoted above.

70. The Arabic passage bears many allusions to the Qurʾān which are lost in the translation, e.g., the word translated here as "stand" (*qiyām*) is very similar to the term meaning "resurrection" (*qiyāmah*); "the right road" (*al-ṣirāṭ al-mustaqīm*) is a frequently repeated simile for the right, God-guided faith. Standing in a straight line is a common Qurʾānic image for the Day of Resurrection on which risen human beings shall stand in a single line in front of God in order to receive His judgment.

71. Vocalizing *ṭarafan min tilka al-maʿānī,* as in *Rasāʾil,* 1.274.21. Another vocalization, i.e., *ṭurfan min . . .* ("[even] remote aspects of those concepts") is equally possible.

72. The terminology employed here is borrowed from Islamic mysticism. One of the central ideas of Islamic mysticism is that of the path of mystical

education with various stations of ascetic and moral perfection. Those who are willing to enter this path, the novices or disciples, are called *murīdūn*. In order to make progress on their path, they need constant control and guidance (*irshād*) by a master. For details see Schimmel, *Mystical Dimensions,* 98–108.

73. See above, note 10.

74. See Wensinck and Mensing, *Concordance,* 98, s.n. *khayr.*

al-Qābisī

1. Ellipses indicate where the text has been abridged.

2. Correcting the ms. *al-Maᶜrūf al-Qābisī,* which is grammatically unlikely, to *al-Maᶜāfirī al-Qābisī,* as proposed in a note of the printed edition. Our author's father, Muḥammad ibn Khalaf, was a native of al-Maᶜāfiriyyīn in the neighborhood of Qābis (Gabès). See EI^2 s.v. "al-Ḳābisī."

3. I.e., the compilation of "sound" (*ṣaḥīḥ*) traditions by al-Bukhārī, usually known simply as the *Ṣaḥīḥ* of Bukharī. It is one of the six canonical collections of traditions. Al-Qābisī is known to have studied al-Bukhārī's work and to have spread his edition of it in North Africa. Ibid., 341.

4. Abū ᶜAbd al-Raḥmān Aḥmad ibn ᶜAlī ibn Shuᶜayb ibn Baḥr ibn Sinān al-Nasāʾī (d. 303/915) was the author of one of the six canonical collections of traditions.

5. The literal meaning of *muḥkam* is "made firm." Hence, the word is applied to any passage or portion of the Qurʾān whose the meaning is clear and not liable to misinterpretation, or which has not been abrogated by a subsequent passage. See Qurʾān 3:5. *Mufaṣṣal* in this context means "made distinct." The latter term is sometimes interpreted as referring to the short suras at the end of the Qurʾān because of the many separations between them.

6. Abū ᶜAbdallāh Muḥammad ibn Saḥnūn ibn Ḥabīb al-Tanūkhī, one of al-Qābisī's predecessors as a Mālikī scholar, was born at Qayrawān in 202/817. He was educated mostly in his home country, where his father (referred to by al-Qābisī as Saḥnūn) was a renowned scholar, but also travelled to the east. He succeeded to his father's position as head of the incipient Mālikī school upon the latter's death, and died in 256/870.

7. Arabic *kuttāb* refers to a primary school where young children learn basic reading and writing and memorize the Qurʾān.

8. The reference is to the notches in the ear that were used as brands to identify camels. No camel is born with such a notch. They are born *jamᶜāʾ,* i.e., whole and intact.

9. Arabic *ḥākim* is a general term. It can refer to anyone from the ruler of a country to a judge or community official.

10. Adolescent girls (*ᶜawātiq*) are defined as a girl that has attained to the commencement of the state of puberty, and has been kept behind the curtain in the tent of her family, but has not been married yet.

11. The Qurʾān is called "God's argument (*ḥujjah*) against His servants" in the sense that at the Last Judgment the revelation to mankind of the Qurʾān, summoning all to submit to God's will for righteousness, will make it impossible for individuals to plead ignorance when they are judged.

12. The Arabic *aʾimmah,* the plural of *imām,* is used here in the general sense of a leading religious scholar, especially the founder of a legal school.

13. Arabic *katātīb,* plural of *kuttāb,* a school in which children learn to read the Qurʾān.

14. Since the Mālikī jurist al-Ḥārith ibn Miskīn lived from 154/771 to 250/864, one must read 173 (789–90).

15. Abū Muḥammad ʿAbdallāh ibn Wahb ibn Muslim al-Fihrī al-Qurashī was born in Egypt in 125/743 and died there in 197/812. He was a student of the jurist Mālik ibn Anas, and Saḥnūn studied with him in Egypt. His presence in the chain of transmitters linked al-Qābisī to Mālik ibn Anas, the founder of the legal school to which al-Qābisī belonged. See J. David-Weill in *EI^2,* vol. 3, 963, and *GAS,* 466.

16. Mālik ibn Anas (d. 179/796), a Medinese jurist and traditionist, was the author of the *Muwaṭṭaʾ,* one of the earliest surviving Muslim law books, and the eponymous founder of what became North Africa's dominant legal school (*madhhab*), to which Ibn Wahb, Saḥnūn, his son Ibn Saḥnūn, and al-Qābisī belonged. See *EI^2* s.vv. "Mālik b. Anas;" and "Mālikiyya."

17. Abū ʿAbdallāh Sufyān ibn Saʿīd ibn Masrūq al-Thawrī (d. 161/778) was a traditionist, theologian, and ascetic active in Kūfah. See *GAS,* 518–19; and Aḥmad ibn ʿAlī Ibn Ḥajar al-ʿAsqalānī, *Tahdhīb al-tahdhīb* (Hyderabad al-Dakkan: Maṭbaʿat Majlis Dāʾirat al-Maʿārif al-Niẓāmīyah, 1325–27/1907–9, vol. 4, 111–15.

18. Correcting the manuscript reading, "al-ʿAlāʾ": ʿAṭāʾ ibn al-Sāʾib was a Kūfan transmitter of traditions. Ibn Khallikān, *Wafayāt al-aʿyān,* ed. Iḥsān ʿAbbās (Beirut: Dār Ṣādir, 1968), vol. 6, 379, mentions him as a teacher of the judge Abū Yūsuf (b. 113/731, d. 182/798), the companion of Abū Ḥanīfah, the famous Iraqi jurist.

19. Ibn Masʿūd (ʿAbdallāh ibn Ghāfil ibn Ḥabīb) was a very early Meccan convert to Islam who emigrated to Abyssinia and then returned to follow the Prophet to Medina. After Muḥammad's death, he settled in al-Kūfah, where he was a reader of the Qurʾān and transmitter of traditions. He died in 32/652–53. See *EI^2* s.v. "Ibn Masʿūd."

20. "People" renders Arabic *al-nās.*

21. Abū Muḥammad ʿAṭāʾ ibn Abī Rabāḥ Aslam (b. 27/647, d. 114/732) was an early Qurʾan commentator and jurist. He was a student of ʿAbdallāh ibn al-ʿAbbās. See *GAS,* 31.

22. Ḥasan al-Baṣrī (b. Medina 21/642, d. al-Baṣrah 110/728). One of the most respected of the *tābiʿī* generation that followed that of the Companions of the Prophet. He transmitted traditions, was interested in theological questions, and was renowned for his piety. See *EI^2,* s.v. "Ḥasan al-Baṣrī"; *GAS,* 591–94.

23. Qurʾān 1:1.

24. The word *farāʾiḍ* has both the general sense of "religious obligations, religious ordinances," and the particular sense of the division of inheritances according to the system of shares laid down in the Qurʾān. Since the context here suggests more advanced studies, I have opted for the more specific sense in my translation, although the more general sense is also possible. Teaching the division of inheritances would require teaching arithmetic.

25. Abū ᶜAbdallāh ᶜAbd al-Raḥmān ibn al-Qāsim al-ᶜAtakī (d. 191/807) was a disciple of Mālik with whom Saḥnūn studied in Fusṭāṭ (Egypt), composing the *Mudawwanah,* a legal text based on the teachings of Mālik that Saḥnūn took back to his native Qayrawān and that became "decisive in the crystallization and diffusion of the *madhhab* of Mālik throughout the Muslim West." See EI^2 s.v. "Saḥnūn," and *GAS,* 465–66 (where the name is given as al-ᶜUtakī).

26. Mālik's objection can be understood better in light of the distinction between *ᶜilm* and *fiqh* in older usage. As J. Schacht explains in his article "Fiḳh," in EI^2, vol. 2, 886–91: "In older theological language the word [*fiḳh*] did not have this comprehensive meaning [of 'jurisprudence']; it was rather used in opposition to *ᶜilm.* While the latter denotes, beside the Ḳurʾān and its interpretation, the accurate knowledge of the legal decisions handed down from the Prophet and his Companions . . . , the term *fiḳh* is applied to the independent exercise of the intelligence, the decision of legal points by one's own judgment in the absence or ignorance of a traditional ruling bearing on the case in question. The result of such independent consideration is *raʾy* (opinion, *opinio prudentium*), with which it is also sometimes used synonymously."

27. Arabic *iᶜrāb* refers to the endings that mark the cases of Arabic nouns and moods of Arabic verbs. Since most of these endings had fallen away from the colloquial dialects, correct production of them would be difficult for the student.

28. The next sentence can be taken to imply that "good reading" (*qirāʾah ḥasanah*) has a technical sense: that the teacher should choose the most respected of the variant readings of the text (in the Mālikī school this meant the reading of Nāfiᶜ of Medina), although some reference to other readings was not out of place. But the context of "good reading with pausing and clear articulation," implies a more general sense.

29. Because early Qurʾāns had little punctuation, the teacher passed on oral tradition about where to pause (*tawqīf*) and where not to pause in order to convey the meaning clearly. In time a system of marks was developed to indicate where a pause is mandatory, optional, or prohibited.

30. A homily (*khuṭbah*) formed part of the congregational prayer on Friday. Collections of homilies by famous figures in Islamic history existed and could be used as texts to be taught and memorized.

31. I.e., Ibn al-Qāsim, the scholar with whom Saḥnūn studied in Egypt.

32. In the *rukūᶜ* (bowing) the worshipper leans at a right angle, with his hands placed on his knees. See EI^2 s.v. "Ṣalāt."

33. In the *sujūd* (prostration) the worshipper prostrates himself, the body resting on the forehead, the palms of both hands, both knees, and both feet. Standing upright, bowing, prostration, and sitting (*julūs*) are the main constituents of each *rakᶜah* ("an invariable series of attitudes and formulas which constitute an element to be repeated a set number of times in the course of a completed ritual prayer"). Ibid.

34. This formula is said at the very beginning of each ritual prayer to signal the worshipper's entry into a state of sacralization (*takbīrat al-iḥrām*), before the bowing (*rukūᶜ*) in each *rakᶜah,* before each prostration (*sujūd*), and while the worshipper is seated (*julūs*) between prostrations. Ibid.

35. Between the two prostrations that occur in each *rakᶜah,* the worshipper sits on his heels, knees on the ground, hands placed on the thighs. Ibid.

36. At the very beginning of each ritual prayer, the worshipper raises his hands above his shoulders, to the level of the ears, and recites the *takbīr*: *Allāhu akbar* (God is most great!). The hands are then placed on the base of the chest, right hand over the left, and a short opening prayer is recited. Ibid.

37. At the end of the final *rakᶜah* of each ritual prayer, the worshipper, still seated, turns to the right, saying *al-salāmu ᶜalaykum wa-raḥmatu Allāhi wa-barakātuhu* (Peace be upon you and God's mercy and blessings!); then he turns to the left, repeating the same words. These actions terminate the ritual prayer. Ibid.

38. While the worshipper sits at the end of the prostrations of the second and fourth *rakᶜah* of each ritual prayer (or at the end of the second and third *rakᶜah* of the sunset prayer, which has only three *rakᶜah*s), an affirmation of faith (*tashahhud*) is added. The formula includes a salutation to God, a blessing on the Prophet, and a recitation of the creedal statement (*shahādah,* literally "testimony"): There is no god but God, and Muḥammad is the messenger of God. Ibid.

39. On the Supplication of Standing (this is the most likely meaning of *duᶜāʾ al-qunūt,* so called because it is recited standing; but other interpretations are given), see *EI*² s.v. "Ḳunūt." The evidence of the various hadith collections implies that the *qunūt* consisted of supplications for various needs of the community inserted in the morning worship and sometimes in the evening worship.

40. Sunna is a usage sanctioned by tradition, usually authenticated by reference to an action or saying of the Prophet. See *EI*² s.v. "Sunna."

41. The *ṣalāt al-janāzah* is unique in that it involves no *rakᶜah,* but is performed standing. See *EI*² s.v. "Ṣalāt," 931.

42. Arabic *sunan,* plural of *sunnah.*

43. *Witr* means "consisting of an odd number." It became customary (*sunnah*) to pray a prayer of an odd number of *rakᶜah*s (usually one plus two, to give three) between the evening prayer and the dawn prayer. Ibid., 930.

44. The time and ritual of communal prayer on the Feast of Breaking the Fast (*ᶜĪd al-fiṭr*) and the Feast of Sacrificing (*ᶜĪd al-aḍḥā*) differ from other communal prayers. Ibid.

45. "In the case of eclipse of the sun or of the moon, a communal prayer of two *rakᶜah*s is held in the mosque. Its time is the same as that of the two feasts [i.e., approximately half an hour after the rising of the sun]. There is neither call to prayer, nor *iqāma,* nor sermon. The Qurʾānic recitations are spoken in a whisper. The peculiarity of this prayer is that each *rakᶜah* contains, after the inclination and the standing upright, which are very prolonged, a second long inclination and a second standing upright before the prostration." (Ibid., 931).

46. I.e., supplications on various occasions that are not part of the five obligatory ritual prayers (*ṣalāh*).

47. I.e., performs the *ṣalāt al-istisqāʾ* (also mentioned in the next paragraph), a special communal prayer for rain in times of drought. Ibid.

48. Arabic *gharīb* refers to rare and unusual words that occur in the Qur'ān and hadith.

49. Poetry (*shi'r*) was valued for its intrinsic beauty and its value as providing training in the classical Arabic language. Verses of early poetry were often cited to illustrate the meaning of an obscure word in the Qur'ān.

50. The Days of the Arabs (*Ayyām al-'Arab*) were traditional accounts in prose and verse of the famous battles of pre-Islamic times.

51. The subjects mentioned here were seen by Muslims as particularly characteristic of pagan Arab culture and opposed to Islam. *Ḥamīyah,* which I have translated as "unbridled violence," was the unbounded attachment of the pre-Islamic Arab to his tribe. In later usage it came to mean something like "chauvinism." Satire (*hijā'*), which was often characterized by obscenity, was condemned by Islam.

52. 'Umar ibn 'Abd al-'Azīz was an Umayyad caliph who reigned from 99/717 to 101/720. Unlike most of the caliphs of the Umayyad dynasty, he had a reputation for piety and is often cited with approval by legal writers.

53. I.e., for the girls (the Arabic pronoun is feminine plural in al-Qābisī's quotation). The text preserved by Ibn Saḥnūn (1.61 herein) uses the masculine plural pronoun, changing the meaning to "because that is corruption for them [all]"—i.e., both boys and girls.

54. I.e., a text from the Qur'ān (cf. Qur'ān 56:80 and 69:43, where the Qur'ān is described in these words).

55. The manuscripts read a verb form from the root *l-'-ṭ,* which the dictionaries gloss as "to brand (a beast) on the neck, to tattoo (a person); to wound someone (with an arrow); to pasture near dwellings (of an animal); to go along a wall." However, in the hadith that closes the section, the word *yal'aṭ* is glossed as *yal'aq,* he licks, which is clearly the meaning intended here.

56. Instead of *rasā'il* (messages, letters), the printed edition of Ibn Saḥnūn reads *mas'āil*, which usually refers to hypothetical legal questions with their answers, such as would be studied by more advanced students. As the text discusses only primary education in the *kuttāb* (Qur'ānic school), the reference must be to the brief maxims in which legal doctrines were often formulated at an early date. See J. Schacht, *An Introduction to Islamic Law* (Oxford: Clarendon Press, 1964), 39.

57. *Min dhikr Allāh*: literally, "from God's memorial," i.e., the Qur'ān.

58. The plain sense of the Arabic, *ilá waqt al-kitābah,* is clear, but the meaning is not. Does it mean that a new section of the Qur'ān would be written for them on Thursday morning and that they would then be allowed to leave for the rest of the day and Friday morning? I am not sure.

59. Islamic jurisprudence conditions the weight given to testimony on the witness's ethical status (*'adālah*), persons of loose morals being assumed to be ready to lie in court. Saḥnūn is saying that since most teachers do not fulfill their professional obligations, their testimony in court is of dubious validity.

60. The Arabic idiom, *akl al-suḥt,* has the general sense of consuming food or property that is unlawfully obtained, but it can refer more particularly to taking bribes.

61. According to Lane's dictionary, the whip (*dirrah*) was made of twisted cords or thongs, and I have retained the translation here, although Qābisī's comment below that the *dirrah* should be fresh or green (*raṭbah*) seems to point to something like a hickory switch. The *falaqah* was a board with two holes (like the stocks) or a rod with loops of rope at either end to hold the feet of the pupil being beaten on the soles of his feet.

62. The Arabic, *yuḥsinu al-taqwīm,* here translated as "pronounces well," is ambiguous. The general meaning is clear: one of the teachers is a native Arabic speaker whose pronunciation and grammar are good, while the other is a non-Arab Muslim (of Berber or other origin) who may know Arabic grammar, but not have perfect pronunciation. Dozy records the idiom, *aqāmah al-iʿrāb,* meaning "he pronounced the desinential endings of classical Arabic," this being a criterion of the true Arab in early times. *Taqwīm* in this passage seems to be related in meaning.

63. Literally, "and knows *al-ʿarabiyyah.*" Qābisī probably intends the term to be understood in the wider sense of Arabic philology: the study of pre-Islamic and early Islamic Arabic literature, valued insofar as it shed light on the use of archaic and rare words in the Qurʾān.

64. Correcting *ijārah* (wage, hire) in the printed edition to *ijādah.* The word *ijādah,* which I have translated in its general sense of "doing well, being proficient," may be an unattested synonym of the technical term *tajwīd,* meaning chanting the Qurʾān in a clear voice and simple melody, so that all the words are clearly distinguishable.

65. Although *al-Baqarah* is the second sura of the Qurʾān, in the traditional order of instruction, which begins with the last section of the Qurʾān and works backward by sections, it would be the last section studied.

66. Literally, it is not something that can be derived by analogical reasoning (*qiyās*), but only something that can be considered commendable (*mustaḥsan*).

67. Arabic *qawm* usually refers to a tribal group, although it can be more general.

68. For the rules governing such contracts, termed *salam,* see Schacht, *Introduction,* 153.

69. Arabic *raṭibah* seems to imply that the *dirrah* is a switch taken from the branch of a tree, rather than a whip, as Lane's dictionary states.

70. I.e., the kin of the slain child may slay the teacher in retaliation.

Miskawayh

1. Originally published in Miskawayh, *Refinement of Character,* 44–57 and notes. Used by permission of the American University of Beirut.

2. This is an interesting allusion to Miskawayh's own personal experience, which was no doubt affected by his ethical study and reflection. Cf., the equally interesting "*waṣīyah*" (testament) cited by Yāqūt in the *Irshād* (ed. Margoliouth, II, 95–96), which Miskawayh took upon himself as an engagement: "*muʿāhadah*" and a reminder: "*tadhkirah.*" The same "*waṣīyah*" is quoted by Tawḥīdi, *Muqābasāt* (ed. Ḥasan al-Sandūbi, Cairo, 1929, pp. 323–26), where Miskawayh's name does not appear, and the author is given merely as

"*baʿḍ aṣḥābina*" (one of our friends), and in the text "*fulān ibn fulān*" (so-and-so). Cf. another "*waṣīyah*" published by Mohammed Arkoun from *Ṣīwān al-Ḥikmah* in "Textes inédits de Miskawayh," *Annales Islamologiques* 5 (1963): 191–94 and the preceding introduction by Arkoun.

3. In the original: "*Ḥayawānāt*" (animals), which raises a question about "*malik*" translated as "king." Cf, the designation of the three faculties of the soul as "*malikīyah*" (kingly), "*sabʿīyah*" (leonine), and "*bahīmīyah*" (beastly); Miskawayh, *Refinement of Character,* p. 15, ll. 16–20.

4. A Greek author, probably of the Neo-Pythagorean School and of the 1st century AD. See, regarding his name, identity, work, and influence, Martin Plessner, *Der OIKONOMIKOC des Neupythagoreers 'Bryson' und sein Einfluss auf die islamische Wissenschaft* (Heidelberg, 1928). Regarding the relation of this work to the *Tahdhīb*: pp. 49–52, 139–141, *et passim.* The text of this work had been published by Louis Cheikho, but with no definite identification of the author, *Machreq,* XIX (1921), pp. 161–81; and *Majmūʿat Arbaʿat Rasāʾil . . .* (Beirut, 1920–23), pp. 13–33.

5. The Arabic original of this word is not clear in the Mss., or in the texts used by Plessner (p. 192, l.12; p. 194, l.3; and p. 196, l.11) or by Cheikho (p. 178, l.2). See my edition of the *Tahdhīb*, p. 60, n.l. The reading adopted here: "*yufattiḥuhu,*" (and below: "*al-tafattuḥ*") agrees with Plessner's reading in the first two references in his text. Plessner renders this word as "ihn öffnet (d.h. schlaff macht)" (Ibid., p. 250, l.24; p. 251, l.19), and mentions (p. 285 §133) Bergsträsser's derivation of this word from the root *ftḥ* 'im Sinne von "die فتح المسام Poren des Körpers öffnen", d.h. "verweichlichen."'

al-Ghazālī

1. Two additional clauses, "and met with [his master's] satisfaction, and made the loftiest garden his residence and dwelling [i.e., he sat closest to his master in class]" appear in three of the MSS used by the editor but do not figure in any of the other extant MSS (cf. Scherer in ibid.).

2. Wensinck, *Condordance,* 6.511.

3. The readings of the various MSS combined indicate that this passage should be read in the third person, consistent with the narrative structure of the introduction and not in the first person, as understood by the editor.

4. The supplication (*duʿāʾ*) is usually made after the believer completes the prescribed prayers; the performance of the supplication is of considerable importance in the Sufi tradition and al-Ghazālī devotes a chapter to it in his *Revival of the Religious Sciences*; see now the translation by Kojiro Nakamura in al-Ghazālī, *Invocations and Supplications.* The supplication requested of al-Ghazālī here is found below in the concluding paragraphs.

5. There are multiple editions of the *Iḥyāʾ ʿulūm al-dīn*; the edition used for references here is Būlāq, 1872, along with relevant translations.

6. The term *walad,* translated here as "son," is to be understood metaphorically as an element of the topos of older man advising the younger man. Al-Ghazālī is clearly addressing a man, if of indeterminate age, certainly younger than himself, but nonetheless of considerable learning. The textual transmission of this treatise is not without problems. The introduction, in

which we are given an explanation for the reason al-Ghazālī wrote his letter, may be a later addition, but this does not warrant the conclusion of some scholars that al-Ghazālī's use of the term *walad* for his correspondent is to be taken literally (see, for example, Hourani, "Revised Chronology," 297), since occasional allusions by al-Ghazālī in the letter itself indicate that his correspondent has a long history of study (e.g., paragraph 25 below). The evidence from MS Paris 4932, which provides us with the name ᶜAbdallāh ibn al-Ḥājj Khalīl as al-Ghazālī's correspondent, is singular and should therefore be treated with caution; at any rate, it has been impossible to discover any additional information about this individual (cf. Scherer's note in al-Ghazālī, *O Youth,* 51, note 6).

7. I.e. the Prophet Muḥammad, through the Qurʾān.

8. Wensinck, *Condordance,* 4.398.

9. Reading the plural *muttabiᶜī* with one of the MSS, instead of the singular (cf. the text in Sabbagh).

10. Al-Ghazālī is making implicit reference to *al-Najāt,* or *The Salvation,* by the philosopher Ibn Sīnā (Avicenna), which earlier in his life he summarized (see al-Ghazālī, *Maqāṣid al-falāsifa*) and later refuted (Ghazālī, *Incoherence*).

11. Reading *al-maghrūr* with one MS for *al-Q-D-R* (cf. the text in Sabbagh).

12. Wensinck, *Condordance,* 4.169.

13. Abū l-Qāsim Junayd (d. 298/910) was the master of the Sufis in Baghdad in the 3rd/9th century. See A. J. Arberry's article in *EI²,* 2.600, and Schimmel, *Mystical Dimensions,* 57–59.

14. Qurʾān 53:39.

15. Qurʾān 18:110.

16. Qurʾān 56:24.

17. Qurʾān 18:107.

18. Qurʾān 19:60.

19. I.e., the Kaaba in Mecca.

20. Wensinck, *Condordance,* 1.221.

21. Qurʾān 7:56.

22. Ḥasan al-Bāṣrī (d. 110/728) is one of those pivotal figures in early Islam to whom is traced so many of the later intellectual and spiritual currents. See H. Ritter's article in *EI²*, 3.247–48.

23. Wensinck, *Condordance,* 1.463.

24. The cousin and son-in-law of the Prophet; see L. Veccia Vaglieri's article in *EI²,* 1.381–86.

25. Wensinck, *Condordance,* 2.163.

26. For this sense of *dīwān* as a collection of religious and historical reports, philological explanations of the Qurʾān, and sundry other material, see R. Dozy, *Supplément,* s.v. "*dīwān.*"

27. For the figure of Jesus in the Islamic tradition see the introductory remarks by G. C. Anawati in *EI²*, 4.81–7.

28. The editor has badly mangled the text here; compare the manuscript variants and the facsimile in Scherer, *O Youth,* 36.

29. The first caliph in Islam, d. 13/634; see W. M. Watt's article in *EI²*, 1.109–11.

30. Reading *aw,* "or" with the majority of MSS for *wa-*, "and."

31. The chief of one of the most important tribal clans in Medina and a supporter of the Prophet, he died shortly after the siege of Medina in 5/627; see W. M. Watt's article in *EI*², 8.697–8. For the hadith, see Wensinck, *Condordance,* 7.87.

32. Qur'ān 7:179.

33. The son of the second caliph; see L. Veccia Vaglieri's article in *EI*², 1.53–4.

34. Wensinck, *Condordance,* 7.49.

35. Qur'ān 17:79.

36. Qur'ān 51:18.

37. Qur'ān 3:17.

38. This is the Kūfan expert in Qu'rān and hadith who died in 611/778. See H. P. Raddatz's article in *EI*², 10.770–72.

39. Reading *allāh* with three of the MSS for *li-llāh.*

40. For the figure of Luqmān the Sage in Islamic tradition, see Heller and Stillman's article in *EI*², 5.811–13.

41. Reading *qawlan wa-fiʿlan* with one MS for *qawluhū.*

42. The Feast of Sacrifice, occurring at the end of the Pilgrimage, is one of the most important Muslim festivals. See E. Mittwoch's article in *EI*², 3.1007–8.

43. These are the so-called *ayyām al-tashrīq,* the name for which has been variously interpreted in the Islamic tradition. During these final days of the pilgrimage, after the Feast of Sacrifice, the pilgrims are allowed to eat and drink. See the article by Paret and Graham in *EI*², 10.356–57.

44. Omitting "the vanities of the world" (*ḥuṭāmāt al-dunyā*), following the majority of MSS. For the practice of ecstatic locution (*shaṭh*) in Sufism, see C. Ernst's article in *EI*², 9.361–62.

45. *dhawq,* lit. "taste."

46. Or, following another reading in the MSS, "after sincere repentance, you do not return to immorality."

47. This is Abū Bakr Dulaf ibn Jahdar (d. 334/945), the "sober" mystic who rebuked Junayd for the excesses of his Sufism and who denounced the mystic Hallāj during the latter's heresy trial; see F. Sobieroj's article in *EI*², 9.432–33, and Schimmel, *Mystical Dimensions,* 77–79.

48. Abū ʿAlī Shaqīq ibn Ibrāhīm al-Azdī (d. 193/809) was a Khurasanian mystic recognized by the later Sufi tradition as an early expert on *tawakkul* (complete dependence on God). Ḥātim al-Asamm was his foremost disciple; see Schimmel, *Mystical Dimensions,* 38.

49. Qur'ān 79:40–41.

50. Omitting *ka-mā yajmaʿu* "just as he gathers" with the majority of MSS.

51. Qur'ān 16:96.

52. Qur'ān 49:13.

53. Qur'ān 43:32.

54. Qur'ān 35:6.

55. Qur'ān 11:6.

56. Qur'ān 65:3.

57. Other manuscripts add "rectitude *with God,*" but the explanation that follows in the paragraph does not allude to this.

58. Reading *musakhkharī* with the majority of MSS.
59. Reading *lā tasʾalnī... illá bi-lisāni al-jinān* with the majority of MSS.
60. Qurʾān 49:5.
61. For the Quʾrānic figure of Khiḍr or Khaḍir in Islamic tradition, see A. J. Wensinck's article in *EI²*, 4.903–35. In the Sufi tradition he represents the spiritual guide *par excellence*; see Schimmel, *Mystical Dimensions, passim.*
62. Qurʾān 18:70.
63. Qurʾān 21:37.
64. Qurʾān 12:109.
65. Reading *in tasir tara al-ʿajāʾib* with half of the MSS.
66. Abū al-Fayḍ Thawbān ibn Ibrāhīm, known as Dhū al-Nūn al-Miṣrī, was an early Egyptian Sufi whose name is associated with alchemy and magic; see M. Smith's article in *EI²*, 1.242.
67. Omitting *wa-* "and" with the MSS.
68. Qurʾān 53:29.
69. Wensinck, *Condordance,* 1.465.
70. The two angels who, according to Islamic tradition, interrogate the dead in their graves; see A. J. Wensinck, "Munkar wa-Nakīr," in *EI²*, 7.138–42.
71. In Islamic eschatology, believers must pass over a bridge between heaven and hell; those whose faith is pure will pass safely; unbelievers will plunge into hell.
72. Reading *ishtighāl bi-* with the majority of the MSS.
73. Reading the masculine singular attached pronouns with the majority of the MSS.
74. Or "the preachers' pulpits" as in other MSS.
75. Reading *ʿammā* with the majority of the MSS.
76. Al-Ghazālī treats this subject in the *Iḥyāʾ*, 2.9. For a historical evaluation of this religious duty, see Michael Cook, *Commanding the Right.*
77. See *Iḥyāʾ*, 1.3.
78. Wensinck, *Condordance,* 3.49.
79. See *Iḥyāʾ*, 3.1; and the translation by Scherer in al-Ghazālī, *O Youth,* 84–89.
80. Wensinck, *Condordance,* 5.478.
81. See above, paragraph 3.
82. Omitting with the majority of MSS the phrase "and the deceit of the debauched, and anything that contests the cycle of day and night [i.e., anything unnatural]."

al-Zarnūjī

*Reprinted from Grunebaum and Abel's translation in al-Zarnūjī, *Taʿlīm,* with some minor adjustments to punctuation and transliteration style for consistency with other selections in this volume. There is no authoritative version of the Arabic text, and as the translators note in their original introduction (al-Zarnūjī, *Taʿlīm,* Introduction I, footnote 1), the two versions from which they worked (Cairo, Maḥmūdiyya, n.d., 32 pp. [= Maḥ. in the notes]; and Leipzig, Baumgaertner, 1838, 48 pp. [= Leip. in the notes]) were both flawed.

There are, therefore, occasional discrepancies between the translation and the Arabic text presented here, many of which are indicated in the notes.

1. Abu ʿAbdallāh Muḥammad b. al-Ḥasan b. Farqad al-Shaibānī, legist, student of Abū Ḥanīfa, d. 804. (All the jurists mentioned in this text, with two exceptions, follow the Ḥanafite rite; so their school affiliation need not be mentioned.)
2. See Qurʾān 7:10.
3. The text erroneously has Ibn ʿAbdallāh for Abū ʿAbdallāh.
4. Lit: title page.
5. The *Kitāb al-akhlāq* referred to cannot be identified with certainty. Abū al-Qāsim al-Ḥasan al-Rāghib al-Iṣfahānī's (d. 1108) book of this title may be meant. Haji Khalifah, *Lexicon bibliographicum et encyclopaedicum, ad codicum Vindobonensium, Parisiensium et Berolinensis fidem primum edidit,* vol. 1, ed. G. L. Flügel (Leipzig: Oriental translation fund of Great Britain and Ireland, 1835–1858), 200–205, where the *akhlāq* works are listed, does not help.
6. *Farḍ ʿalá sabīl al-kifāyah.*
7. *Qiblah*: the direction toward Mecca or, more accurately, toward the central Muslim sanctuary of the Kaaba in this city. This direction has to be observed during the *ṣalāt,* the ritual prayer.
8. Shafiʿī, founder of the Shafiʿite school of Muslim law, d. 819.
9. Abū Ḥanīfa, founder of the Ḥanafite school of Muslim law, to which Zarnūjī adhered. He died in 767.
10. Lit: revival.
11. ʿAlī b. Abī Bakr al-Farghānī al-Marghīnānī, famous Ḥanafite lawyer, ob. 1197.
12. *Hidāyah fī furūʿ al-fiqh,* a renowned work on Muslim law.
13. Qiwām al-Dīn Ḥammād. . . : probably the son of the juris-consult, Ibrāhīm b. Ismāʿīl al-Ṣaffār, d. 1139/40.
14. Cf. the book cited at note 5.
15. Rukn al-Islām al-Adīb al-Mukhtār: al-Zarnūjī seems to refer to Rukn al-Islām Muḥammad b. Abī Bakr Imāmzāda, Muftī of Bukhārā, d. 1177/8.
16. Died 795.
17. Abū Ḥanīfa's booklet.
18. Lit: of all the branches of learning the best part.
19. I.e., the Muslims'.
20. I.e., the Last Day.
21. Ḥammād b. Abī Sulaimān (text omits *Abī*), a teacher of Abū Ḥanīfa, d. 738.
22. ʿAlī b. Abī Ṭālib, the 4th caliph, 656–661.
23. See al-Zarnūjī, *Taʿlīm,* Introduction I, footnote 12.
24. Sufyān al-Thaurī, outstanding theologian, traditionist and jurist, d. 778.
24a. Lit: things.
25. Abū al-Qāsim Isḥāq b. Muḥammad, known as al-Ḥakīm al-Samarqandī—a judge in Samarqand, d. 953.
26. Lit: reflect and choose.
27. Lit: mutilated.

28. Lit: things.

29. Tradition, Hadith. Technically, the word is used for "a communication or narrative . . . of a record of action or sayings of the Prophet and his companions." (Th. W. Juynboll, *Encyclopaedia of Islam,* vol. 2, 189).

29a. In the text these lines are quoted in Persian.

30. Sadīd al-Dīn al-Shirāzī: probably a mistake for Sadīd al-Dīn al-Sharghī, of Bukhārā, d. 1177.

31. Lit: scholars from abroad.

32. Maḥ. text differs slightly and is less complete.

33. Fakhr al-Dīn al-Arsābandī, judge in Marw, probably identical with the judge and Ḥanafite leader, Abū Bakr Muḥammad b. al-Ḥusain, d. 1118, who is mentioned by ᶜAbd al-Karim ibn Muḥammad al-Samᶜānī, *The Kitāb al-Ansāb* (Leiden: E. J. Brill, 1912), fols. 25v-26r.

34. Abū Yazīd al-Dabūsī: probably error for Abū Zaid al-Dabūsī, d. in Bukhārā, in 1039.

35. Shams al-Aᵓimma Muḥammad b. Aḥmad al-Ḥulwānī of Bukhārā, legist, d. 1056 or 1057.

36. Abū Bakr al-Zaranjī, mistake for Bakr (b. Muḥammad) al-Zaranjarī, d. 1118, of whom Flügel states expressly that he studied under al-Ḥulwānī (Flügel, Gustav Leberecht. "Die Klassen der Hanefitischen Rechtsgelehrten." *Abhandlungen der Königlichen Sächsischen Gesellschaft der Wissenschaft, Philologisch-Historische Klasse* 3, no. 2 [Leipzig, 1861], 304).

37. 786–809 ad.

38. Al-Aṣmaᶜī, famous grammarian, d. 831.

38a. Belles-lettres and polite deportment.

39. Shams al-aᵓimma Abū Bakr Muḥammad b. Aḥmad al-Sarakhsi, jurist, d. ca. 1106/7.

40. Fakhr al-Dīn al-Ḥasan b. Manṣūr al-Ūzjandī, known as Qādīkhān, jurist, d. 1196.

41. Not identified.

42. I.e., theologians.

43. Not in Maḥ. text.

44. Muḥammad b. Ismāᶜīl al-Bukhārī, one of the greatest traditionists in Islam, d. 870.

45. Qurᵓān 29:69.

46. Qurᵓān 19:13.

47. Al-Mutanabbī, d. 965, one of the outstanding Arabic poets. In the edition by F. Dieterici (Berlin, 1861), 255, 16, p. 677.

48. Ed. Dieterici, 226, 1, 2, p. 548.

49. Raḍī al-Dīn an-Naisābūrī, d. 1149; see Brockelmann, *GAL, Suppl.,* vol. 1, 641, where the title is listed, too.

50. Abū Yūsuf Yaᶜqūb al-Anṣārī, student of Abū Ḥanīfa, Chief Judge of Baghdād, d. 798.

50a. Unidentified.

51. Al-Marghīnānī: *fl. ca.* 1203; cf. Brockelmann, *GAL,* vol. 1, 379.

52. Lit: leading armies.

53. Galenos, [Galen] Greek physician, d. ca. 200 AD.

54. I.e., digestible.

55. Qiwām al-Dīn Aḥmad b. ʿAbdarrashīd al-Bukhārī, legist, 11th cent.; cf. Flügel, "Die Klassen," 310, where no death date is given.

56. Yūsuf al-Hamadāni, Shāfiʿite jurisconsult, d. 1140; on him see Ibn Khallikān, *Biographical Dictionary,* vol. 4, trans. William MacGuckin baron de Slane (Paris: The Oriental Translation Fund of Great Britain and Ireland, 1842–1871), 412–414.

57. Sharaf al-Dīn al-ʿUqailī, jurist, d. 1180/1.

58. Al-Khalīl b. Aḥmad al-Sarahsī, judge, referred to by al-Samʿānī, *al-Ansāb,* fol. 291v. The "al-Sarakhsi" of the Leip. text as well as the al-Sajzarī of the Maḥ. text are misspellings.

58a. The passage: "For discussion . . . and anger," is missing in Leip.

59. Qurʾān 12:76. The translation used is that of R. Bell, Edinburgh, 1937–1939.

60. Fakhr al-Dīn al-Kāshānī (Leip. text wrongly, al-Kisāʾī): F. Abū Bakr al-K., d. 1191, a legist.

61. See al-Zarnūjī, *Taʿlīm,* Introduction I, footnote 34.

62. Abū Ḥafṣ al-Kabīr, Aḥmad b. Fīl, a student of Muḥammad b. al-Ḥasan al-Shaibānī, *fl.* 800.

63. Maḥ. text then suggests: So he was to be thanked for kindness of spirit, learning, and for becoming a source for increase of learning as well.

64. *ahl as-sunna wa'l-jamāʿa*: the term denotes the body of the community of Muslims as opposed to the heretics who seceded from it; cf. *Encyclopaedia of Islam,* 1.1008.

65. This saying not in Maḥ text.

66. Wisdom, *ḥikma,* is somewhat loosely used for the books of the Old and New Testament, the Qurʾān, and the like. Prof. S. I. Feigin, University of Chicago, suggests that the reference is to Prov. 28:20, or possibly to Job 20:18.

67. Sheikh al-Islām Bahāʾ al-Dīn ʿAlī b. Muḥammad b. Ismaʿīl al-Asbījābī (Leip. wrongly: al-Astījābī) al-Samarqandī, famous Ḥanafī legist, d. 1140/1.

68. Not identified.

69. Manṣūr al-Ḥallāj, mystic and theologian, executed in 922.

70. Moses.

71. Qurʾān 18:61.

72. I.e., scholarship.

73. Ibrāhīm b. al-Jarrāḥ, of Kūfa, student of Abū Yūsuf, Ḥanafī judge, d. 832.

74. Throwing of stones during the *ḥajj*: on the 10th of Dhu al-Ḥijja, as part of the *ḥajj* ceremonies, each pilgrim has to throw seven small stones at Mina near Mecca; these stones are said to symbolize the stoning of Satan, once driven off by Abraham at this very place.

75. Ḥasan b. Ziyād al-Luʾluʾī (the Pearl-Merchant), of Kūfa, student of Abū Ḥanīfa, friend of Abū Yūsuf, d. 819.

76. Burhān al-Dīn ʿAbdalʿazīz b. ʿUmar b. Māza, legist; cf. Flügel, "Die Klassen," 311. The text has erroneously Burhān al-Aʾimma, a title which really belongs to [his son, the figure in note] 77.

77. Burhān al-Aʾimma al-Ṣadr al-Shahīd Ḥusām al-Dīn ^{c}Umar b. ^{c}Abdal^{c}aziz b. ^{c}Umar b. Māza, d. 1141/2.

78. Tāj al-Dīn Aḥmad b. ^{c}A. b. ^{c}U. b. Māza; mentioned by Flügel, "Die Klassen," 312.

79. Rukn al-Islām Muḥammad b. Abī Bakr Imāmzāda, Muftī of Bukhārā, d. 1177/8. The mistake of the text in writing "the Imām Khwāhar-Zāda" for "Imāmzāda" is due to the fact that two outstanding Ḥanafite jurists, d. 1090 and 1253, respectively, bore the name Khwāhar-Zāda.

80. Lit: to press the nose of his enemy in the dust.

81. Jesus, Son of Mary.

82. *Dīwān,* 248, 8, 9, pp. 649–50 [see note 47, above].

83. Arabic poet, d. 1010.

84. Lit: inkstand.

85. Maḥ text: Zain al-Islām.

86. Not identified.

87. See footnote 77.

88. ^{c}Isām b. Yūsuf is mentioned by Muḥammad ibn Sa^{c}d (see his *Kitāb al-ṭabaqāt al-kabīr: Biographien Muhammeds, seiner Gefährten und der späteren Träger des Islams,* vol. 7, book 2, ed. Eduard Sachau, et al. [Leiden: Brill, 1905–1940], 108) and characterized as a native of Balkh.

89. Yaḥya b. Mu^{c}ādh al-Rāzī, celebrated preacher, d. 872.

90. al-Imām al-Jalīl Muḥammad b. al-Faḍl: probably Abū Bakr M. b. al-F. al-Kamārī, jurist, d. 981/2.

91. Jurist, theologian, author of a famous creed in the form of a Catechism, d. 1142.

92. Lit: with the eyes.

93. Shaddād b. Ḥakīm, student of Muḥammad b. al-Ḥasan, d. between 825–845.

94. Wakī^{c} b. al-Jarrāḥ, traditionist, d. 813; cf. Ibn Sa^{c}d, *Kitāb al-ṭabaqāt,* vol. 6, 275.

95. Perhaps (white) hellebore, *kundus,* this being used in antiquity to cure headaches, insanity, etc.; text has *kundur,* incense plant.

96. Leip. Text has: eggs.

97. Not identified.

98. The interpretation of this phrase is owed to Professor Nabia Abbott, University of Chicago.

99. Maḥ text has "both power of memory and sustenance."

100. Al-Ḥasan b. ^{c}Alī, son of the Caliph ^{c}Alī, d. probably 669.

101. Lit: Vessels.

102. Qurʾān 56: Chapter of the Event.

103. Qurʾān 67: Kingship.

104. Qurʾān 73: The Heavily Burdened.

105. Qurʾān 92: Sura of the Night.

106. Qurʾān 94: Sura of "Have We Not Expanded."

107. Buzurjmihr, legendary vizier of the Sasanian king, Khosrō I Anūshirwān (531–579), renowned for his wisdom.

108. This sentence is missing in the Maḥ. text.

109. S. 112, 3–4; Bell's translation.

110. On the ceremonial of the *^c^umra,* the so-called Little Pilgrimage, and its relation to the *ḥajj,* cf. R. Paret's article in *Encyclopaedia of Islam,* vol. 4, 1016–1018.

111. Abū al-^c^Abbās al-Mustaghfirī: Abū al-^c^Abbās Ja^c^far b. Muḥammad al-Nasafī al-Mustaghfirī, d. 1040. His *Ṭibb al-Nabī* was printed in Teheran, 1293 (according to *GAL* Suppl., I, 617). Khalifah, *Lexicon,* vol. 4, 132, lists it under *Ṭibb an-nabawī.*

Ibn Jamā^c^ah

1. Qur^ʾ^ān 68:4.

2. The Arabic term *adab,* one of the central values of Islamic culture, does not correspond to any single English term, and so I have had to vary the translation of it according to the context. Originally, the term meant a habit or practical norm of conduct, particularly a good habit or norm of conduct. It could designate the rules of conduct or etiquette governing any learned profession. One could, in this sense, speak of the *adab* of scholars, the *adab* of students, the *adab* of government officials, etc. By extension, *adab* could also mean the knowledge and culture that makes a person courteous and urbane. See F. Gabrieli's article in *EI*^{2}, 1.175–76.

3. "*Madrasah,* in modern usage, is the name of an institution of learning where Islamic sciences are taught, i.e., a college for higher studies, as opposed to an elementary school of traditional type (*kuttāb*); in mediaeval usage, essentially a college of law in which the other Islamic sciences, including literary and philosophical ones, were ancillary subjects only." (J. Pedersen and G. Makdisi in *EI*^{2}, 5.1123.)

4. Qur^ʾ^ān 58:11.

5. ^c^Abdallāh ibn ^c^Abbās, a son of the Prophet's uncle al-^c^Abbās, was one of the greatest scholars of the first generation of Muslims. He died in 68/688.

6. Qur^ʾ^ān 3:18.

7. Qur^ʾ^ān 39:9.

8. Qur^ʾ^ān 16:43. In its original context, "people of the Remembrance" referred to those who knew the Jewish and Christian scriptures, but Ibn Jamā^c^ah extends the meaning to include all scholars.

9. Qur^ʾ^ān 29:43.

10. Qur^ʾ^ān 29:49.

11. Qur^ʾ^ān 35:28.

12. Qur^ʾ^ān 98:7–8.

13. Abū al-Aswad al-Du^ʾ^alī (d. 69/699), known for his loyalty to ^c^Alī, served as judge in al-Baṣrah and was briefly governor of the city.

14. Mu^c^ādh b. Jabal al-Anṣārī (d. 17/638) was a companion of the Prophet.

15. Abū ^c^Īsā Muḥammad b. ^c^Īsā b. Sawra al-Tirmidhī (d. 279/892) was the author of *Al-jāmi^c^ al-ṣaḥīḥ,* one of the six canonical Sunni collections of hadith (sayings of the Prophet).

16. Qurʾān 8:27.

17. Qurʾān 5:44. The verse begins: "Surely We sent down the Torah, wherein is guidance and light; thereby the Prophets who had surrendered themselves gave judgment for those of Jewry, as did the masters and the rabbis, following such portion of God's Book as they were given to keep and were witnesses to. So fear not men, but fear Me."

18. Muḥammad b. Muslim b. ʿUbaydallāh b. ʿAbdallāh b. Shihāb al-Zuhrī (d. 124/741) was one of the most celebrated early collectors and transmitters of traditions. His visits to the Umayyad court earned him the disapproval of some pietists, one of whom is quoted as saying, "What a man is al-Zuhrī, would that he had not harmed himself by intercourse with princes" (quoted in *The Encyclopaedia of Islam*, 1st ed., vol. 8, 1240).

19. The Imam Abū ʿAbdallāh Muḥammad b. Idrīs al-Shāfiʿī (d. 204/820) was the great legal theorist whose teachings formed the basis of one of the four main Sunni legal schools.

20. Ibrāhīm ibn Adham (d. 161/777) was a Ṣūfī ascetic born in Balkh who spent most of his life in Syria. He was widely known for the legend of his conversion, which describes him as a ruler of Balkh who suddenly abdicated his throne to take up the ascetic life.

21. Manṣūr ibn al-Muʿtamir (d. 132/749) was a traditionist of al-Kūfah.

22. Qurʾān 31:17.

23. Abū ʿAbdallāh al-Ḥārith ibn Asad al-Muḥāsibī (d. 243/857) was a Muslim mystic who lived most of his life in Baghdad. His name, al-Muḥāsibī, means "he who calculates his actions," i.e., one who practices examination of conscience. The full title of the book mentioned here is *Kitāb al-Riʿāyah li-ḥuqūq Allāh* (see al-Ḥārith ibn Asad al-Muḥāsibī [d. 857 or 858], *Kitāb al-riʿāyah li-ḥuqūq Allāh*, ed. Margaret Smith [London: Luzac, 1941]).

24. Saʿīd ibn Jubayr b. Hishām al-Asadī al-Wālibī was a *tābiʿī* (son of a companion of the Prophet) who was executed by the Umayyad governor of Iraq, al-Ḥajjāj, in 95/714 for his involvement in the rebellion of Ibn al-Ashʿath.

25. Abū Bakr Aḥmad ibn ʿAlī al-Shāfiʿī, known as al-Khaṭīb al-Baghdādī (d. 463/1071), was the author of the compendious *Tārīkh Baghdād* (History of Baghdad), a biographical encyclopedia of figures connected with the cultural and political life of the city of Baghdad.

26. Mālik ibn Anas (d. 179/796) was a famous Muslim jurist active in Medina. He is considered the imam or founder of the Mālikī school of law, one of the four major Sunni *madhhab*s.

27. I.e., the *wāqif*, the person who established the charitable trust (*waqf*) supporting the institution.

28. The Arabic (literally, "Error is under [the authority] of clamor") contains a play on the similarity of the Arabic words for error and clamor: "*Inna al-ghalaṭ taḥta al-laghaṭ*."

29. Al-Rabīʿ ibn Sulaymān al-Murādī (d. 270/884) was a student of the great jurist al-Shāfiʿī.

30. I.e., he will be fatally disqualified as an authority.

31. Muḥammad [ibn ʿAbdallāh] ibn ʿAbd al-Ḥakam (d. 268/979) was a student of the great jurist al-Shāfiʿī.

32. A *muftī* is a Muslim jurist qualified to issue responses to questions about matters of religious law.

33. Abū Bakr al-Shiblī (d. 334/946) was a Ṣūfī, a pupil of Junayd.

34. Abū Ḥanīfah al-Nu^cmān ibn Thābit (d. 150/767) was an early famous theologian and jurist active in al-Kūfah. He is considered the imam or founder of one of the four major Sunni schools of law (*madhhab*s).

35. In this context Arabic *jalīs* (sitting-companion) probably refers specifically to a student who attends the master's class (*majlis*).

36. *Rabbānī* occurs in the plural three times in the Qur^ʾān (3:79, 5:44, and 5:63), where it refers to scholars, apparently Jewish rabbis, who know one of God's revealed books (Arberry translates it as "masters"). It appears to be derived from Hebrew or Aramaic *rabbān,* a variant on the word that gives us the English word rabbi. An Arabic speaker would most likely connect the word with *Rabb,* Arabic for Lord, a title of God. A *rabbānī* would therefore be "one who devotes himself to religious services or exercises, or applies himself to acts of devotion; who possesses a knowledge of God; or a learned man" (Lane, *Lexicon,* 3:1006). Ibn Jamā^cah here calls attention to an alternative etymology, from the verb *rabbā, yurabbī,* meaning to rear, raise, nourish.

37. I have not been able to identify the maxim to which Ibn Jamā^cah is alluding. *Ḍamān,* in the largest sense, means civil liability, but it often refers specifically to a person's ensuring a financial obligation which is another's (guarantee) or to a person's ensuring the appearance of another person whose presence is required (bail). *Mubāsharah* (the management or conduct of an affair) can have the technical sense of "direct, physical cause." *Sabab* (reason) can refer to any legal reason for an obligation or to its motivating cause.

38. *Qasāmah* was a procedure by which a person suspected of murder could be put to death on the strength of the affirmatory oath of the next of kin of the victim, meaning that in such cases the oath was sworn by the plaintiffs, not the defendant. See J. Schacht, *An Introduction to Islamic Law* (Oxford: Clarendon Press, 1964), 24.

39. Qur^ʾān 26:215.

40. Al-Fuḍayl ibn ^cIyāḍ (d. 187/803) was an early Ṣūfī ascetic and transmitter of hadith. Before his conversion to a pious life, he had been a highway robber.

41. The *kunyah* is a name of honor or nickname added to a Muslim's given name. For men it normally begins with *Abū* ("Father of") and for women *Umm* ("Mother of"), followed by the name of the person's oldest child. However, many *kunyahs* are purely conventional. For example, anyone named Ibrāhīm may be called "Abū Khalīl," because in the Qur^ʾān Ibrāhīm is called "Khalīl Allāh" (the Friend of God). In any case, it is more polite to address a person with his *kunyah* than with his given name.

42. See *Ṣaḥīḥ al-Bukhārī,* 1.2.49.

43. The reference is probably to the Ṣūfī Sahl ibn ^cAbdallāh al-Tustarī (d. 283/896), many of whose dicta concern purification of works and the cleansing of one's state from blemishes and defects.

44. Qur^ʾān 33:4.

45. Sufyān al-Thawrī (d. 161/778) was an important early representative of Islamic law, tradition, and Qur'ānic interpretation.
46. Qur'ān 7:31.
47. Shuᶜbah ibn al-Ḥajjāj (d. 160/776) was an eminent Baṣran scholar and collector of hadith.
48. Arabic: a *wird* of it; normally, one-seventh or one-fourteenth of the text, recited every day or every night, but the word could have the general sense of a portion of the Qur'ān.
49. By verifying (*taṣḥīḥ*) Ibn Jamāᶜah means that the student should find and correct any copyist's errors in his book and that he should check that he is supplying the correct vowels for each word in the unvocalized Arabic script.
50. These two books, both entitled *Ṣaḥīḥ,* are the two most famous Sunni collections of hadith. Muḥammad ibn Ismāᶜīl al-Bukhārī died in 256/870; Muslim ibn al-Ḥajjāj al-Naysablūrī in 261/875.
51. Abū Bakr Aḥmad ibn al-Ḥusayn ibn ᶜAlī b. Mūsá al-Khusrawjirdī (d. 458/1066) was a traditionist and Shāfiᶜī jurist.
52. *Musnad* books are collections in which all the hadiths transmitted on the authority of a particular companion of the Prophet are gathered together.
53. Aḥmad ibn Ḥanbal (d. 241/855), often called "the imām of Baghdad," was a celebrated theologian, jurist, and traditionist. He was the founder of one of the four major Sunni *madhhab*s.
54. The reference is to ᶜAbdallāh ibn al-Zubayr al-Ḥumaydī (d. 219/834).
55. The reference is to Abū Bakr Aḥmad ibn ᶜAmr ibn ᶜAbd al-Khāliq al-Bazzār (d. 292/904–5).
56. Hearing (*samā*ᶜ) includes hearing the teacher read the text, writing it down from dictation, and memorizing it.
57. Arabic, *majālis al-taḥdīth*: the meaning of this is unclear to me.
58. ᶜUmar ibn al-Khaṭṭāb (ruled from 13/634 to 23/644) was the second caliph and a driving force behind the early Islamic conquests.
59. Literally, "someone whose face is weak" (*man raqqa wajhuhu*).
60. Abū al-Ḥajjāj Mujāhid ibn Jabr al-Makkī (died between 100/718 and 104/722) was a *tābi*ᶜ*ī* (member of the generation following that of the companions of the Prophet). He was an early authority on Qur'ān readings and exegesis.
61. Umm Sulaym was the mother of the companion of the Prophet, Anas ibn Mālik.
62. "Black ink, prepared from lampblack bound with plant gum and known in Arabic as *midād,* was appropriate for use on papyrus, but it had notoriously poor adhesion to parchment and tended to flake off. Kufic manuscripts of the Koran were normally copied on parchment in the brownish ink known in Arabic as *ḥibr,* which was made from metal tannates prepared with gallnuts. The metal tannate ink actually penetrated the surface of the parchment like dye. When used on paper, however, the mixture of metal salts and tannins in tannate ink produced acids that eventually destroyed the paper. Carbon ink, by contrast, had no chemical effect on the surface to which it was applied; it was the type of ink secretary-copyists normally used on papyrus and paper." (Jonathan M. Bloom, *Paper Before Print: The History and Impact of Paper in the Islamic World* [New Haven: Yale University Press, 2001], 197.)

63. The saying is attributed to ʿAbd al-Ḥamīd ibn Yaḥyā (d. 132/750), the secretary of the last Umayyad Caliph Marwān II. His epistle of advice to secretaries was frequently quoted.

64. An explanation for readers unacquainted with the Arabic script is in order. Certain letters of the Arabic alphabet have essentially the same shape (*ductus* is the technical term) and normally are differentiated by the presence or absence of a dot or group of dots over or under the letters in question. *Ḥāʾ* (ح) and *jīm* (ج) are two such letters, as are *rāʾ* (ر) and *zāy* (ز). One of the most common mistakes in Arabic manuscripts is the accidental omission of a distinguishing dot on one of these letters.

65. Literally, "he should separate between each two *kalāms* with a circle." Medieval Arabic has no concept that corresponds exactly to the modern paragraph; however, it was normal to separate roughly paragraph-sized sections of text by writing a small circle, usually in red, at the end of the section. *Kalām,* the word used here, means "speech, discourse, argument."

66. Literally, "is a work of supererogation (*nafl*), or it is a *farḍ kifāyah,*" a collective duty the fulfillment of which by a sufficient number of individuals in the community excuses the others from fulfilling it.

67. The translation of this sentence is conjectural as the text is uncertain. The 1974 Beirut edition reads "*li'anna al-ḥumūd ʿalá al-nafs al-masṭūr,*" which means, "because the praiseworthy for the soul is the written." The 1984 Beirut edition reads, "*wa inna al-jumūd ʿalá nafs al-masṭūr,*" which is what I have translated.

68. Reading *yajidu* for *yaḥillu.*

69. The sense (the text is uncertain) would seem to be that although it is best for a resident not to accept a salary or scholarship from the school's endowment, he should, if he is forced by circumstances to accept it, consider it a blessing granted by God and thank God for sending him someone (i.e., the endower of the school) to relieve him from the need to earn a living, with its associated temptations to dishonest gain.

70. The Arabic *murattabīn* is ambiguous. It could mean simply "appointed to a *rutba* or office" and refer to any regularly enrolled student or faculty. Or it could refer specifically to someone given a *rātib* or regular stipend.

71. Arabic *sikkah* "coinage," but also meaning "street, road." The sense is uncertain to me. I conjecture that an idiom is involved and that it has something to do with the fact that coinage and having his name mentioned in the Friday sermon were standard rights of a ruler. Perhaps the meaning is that the resident should accept the political regime and keep to his studies. The 1984 edition reads *masʾalah,* "[legal] problem, question"—most likely a *lectio facilior.*

72. The *ṣuffah* (source of the English word sofa) is a stone bench by the entrance of the mosque. It was a convenient gathering place for visitors.

73. The pronouns in the Arabic are as vague as in the English translation.

74. Taqī al-Dīn Abū ʿAmr ibn al-Ṣalāḥ was a Shāfiʿī scholar who died in Damascus in 643/1245.

Ibn Khaldūn

1. Ibn Khaldūn, *The Muqaddimah: An Introduction to History, Translated from the Arabic by Franz Rosenthal.* Copyright 1958, 1967 by Princeton University Press. Reprinted by permission of Princeton University Press.

2. The first six sections of this chapter are a later addition not yet found in A or B, but appearing in C and D. In their place the earlier text had a much briefer section, printed in Bulaq and depending texts, as also at the end of Vol. 2 of the Paris edition (pp. 407f.). The ideas briefly mentioned there reoccur in the larger text; cf., esp., *Muqaddimah,* Rosenthal trans., 2.417f. What follows is a translation of that earlier section, a few lines of which were translated by Issawi, p. 140.

Science and instruction are natural to human civilization.

This is because all animals share with man his animality, as far as sensual perception, motion, food, shelter, and other such things are concerned. Man is distinguished from them by his ability to think. It enables him to obtain his livelihood, to co-operate to this end with his fellow men, to establish the social organization that makes such co-operation possible, and to accept the divine revelations of the prophets, to act in accordance with them, and to prepare for his salvation in the other world. He thinks about all these things constantly, and does not stop thinking for even so long as it takes the eye to blink. In fact, the action of thinking is faster than the eye can see. Man's ability to think produces the sciences and the afore-mentioned crafts. In connection with the ability to obtain the requirements of nature, which is engrained in man as well as, indeed, in animals, his ability to think desires to obtain perceptions that it does not yet possess. Man, therefore, has recourse to those who preceded him in a science, or had more knowledge or perception than he, or learned a particular science from earlier prophets who transmitted information about it to those whom they met. He takes over such things from them, and is eager to learn and know them. His ability to think and to speculate, then, directs itself to one of the realities. He speculates about every one of the accidents that attach themselves to the essence of (that reality). He persists in doing so until it becomes a habit of his, always to combine all its accidents with a given reality. So, his knowledge of the accidents occurring in connection with a particular reality becomes a specialized knowledge. Members of the next generation desire to obtain that knowledge. Therefore, they repair to the people who know about it. This is the origin of instruction. It has thus become clear that science and instruction are natural to human beings. And God knows better.

3. *Fa-aṣāra*: D.

4. *Leg. malakati.*

5. See Issawi, 167.

6. *Al-mumkināt* "possible": D.

7. See *Muqaddimah,* Rosenthal trans., 1.197, 210, and 3.105, 295.

8. Qurʾān 16.78 (80).

9. See E. I. J. Rosenthal, "Ibn Jaldūn's Attitude to the Falāsifa" in *al-Andalus* 20 (1955): 81.

10. See *Muqaddimah,* Rosenthal trans., 1.198 n. 277.

11. See *Muqaddimah,* Rosenthal trans., 1.211.

12. This is the reading of C (*māddah*). D has "form."

13. The phrasing of the Arabic text calls to mind the famous saying, which is also cited as a *ḥadīth,* that "information (received from others) is not like seeing (things) with one's own eyes."

14. See *Muqaddimah,* Rosenthal trans., 3.81.

15. *Leg. wa-raʾsuhū.*

16. Qurʾān 96.5 (5).

17. See *Muqaddimah,* Rosenthal trans., 1.184ff., and, in particular, 1.194.

18. For the idea expressed in this paragraph, see *Rasāʾil Ikhwān al-ṣafāʾ,* 4.313ff., a passage which at one time provoked an overenthusiastic comparison with Darwinism. F. Dieterici, *Der Darwinismus im X. und XIX. Jahrhundert* (Die Philosophie der Araber, No. 9) (Leipzig, 1878), 29ff., 220ff. See also H. S. Nyberg, *Kleinere Schriften des Ibn al-ʿArabī* (Leiden, 1919), 93f. (Ar. text).

19. See *Muqaddimah,* Rosenthal trans., 1.184f.

20. *Wa-ʿinda*: C.

21. Qurʾān 41.6 (5).

22. See paragraph 1, above.

23. I.e., supernatural, or perceivable by the senses.

24. See Qurʾān 22.5 (5).

25. Qurʾān 16.78 (80).

26. Qurʾān 96.1–5 (1–5), considered to be the first Qurʾānic verses revealed to Muḥammad.

27. Qurʾān 4.17 (20), 92 (94), 104 (105), 111 (111), 170 (168); 48.4 (4).

28. For elementary and higher education, see also paragraph 69ff., and, esp., 93ff.

29. See Issawi, 144f.

30. See *Muqaddimah,* Rosenthal trans., 2.349ff.

31. Ibn Khaldūn refers to the destruction of Almohad rule by the Merinid Abū Yūsuf Yaʿqūb in 1269.

32. Abū l-Qāsim (this is his given name) b. Abī Bakr, born in 621 [1224], traveled in the East in 648 and 656 [1251 and 1258], and died in 691 [1292]. See R. Brunschvig, *La Berbérie orientale,* 2.289.

33. Marginal note in B: This is the imam Fakhr-al-dīn al-Rāzi." See *Muqaddimah,* Rosenthal trans., 1.402.

34. Muḥammad b. Shuʿayb al-Haskūrī, d. 664 [1225]. The ethnical denomination al-Dukkālī seems to be an error. See R. Brunschvig, *loc. cit.* However, Ibn Khaldūn also calls him Dukkālī in the *Autobiography,* 28f.

35. See *Muqaddimah,* Rosenthal trans., 1.xxxix. He was, of course, not personally a pupil of Ibn al-Ḥājib.

36. The famous author of grammatical and legal textbooks studied by Ibn Khaldūn, Abū ʿAmr ʿUthmān b. al-Ḥājib, d. 646 [1249]. See *GAL,* 1.303ff.; *Suppl.*, 1.531ff.

37. The two brothers, Abū Zayd ʿAbd-al-Raḥmān, d. 743 [1342/43], and Abū Mūsá ʿĪsā, d. in the plague of 1348/49. On the former's date, cf. Ibn Farḥūn, *Dībāj,* 152. They belonged to the generation that taught Ibn Khaldūn's teachers. See the *Autobiography,* 28–31, and the literature quoted there.

38. Manṣūr b. Aḥmad, ca. 632–731 [1235–1330/31]. See R. Brunschvig, *op. cit.*, 2.289. The vocalization Mashaddālī is suggested in the *Autobiography,* 59,

and by al-Sakhāwī, *al-Ḍawʾ al-lāmiʿ* (Cairo, 1353–55/1934–36), 8.290. See also *Muqaddimah,* Rosenthal trans., 3.19.

39. The word "east" is found in C and D.

40. Aḥmad b. Idrīs, d. 684 [1285]. See *GAL,* 1.385; *Suppl.,* 1.665f.; also A. M. Sayili in *Isis* 32 (1940):16–26.

41. ʿImrān b. Mūsá, 670–745 [1271/72–1344/45], who was a pupil and son-in-law of Nāṣir-al-dīn. See Ibn al-Khaṭīb, *al-Iḥāṭah,* 2.143, and the *Autobiography,* 59.

42. Qurʾān 12.21 (21).

43. See Issawi, 50–52, 145.

44. Bulaq adds: "it was their original nature which made the people of the East more awake and clever, and . . . "

45. Bulaq adds: "They were biased and partial in this respect . . . "

46. See *Muqaddimah,* Rosenthal trans., 1.168 and 171.

47. See *Muqaddimah,* Rosenthal trans., 2.406f.

48. See R. Dozy in *Journal asiatique* 16, no. 6 (1869): 164.

49. See *Muqaddimah,* Rosenthal trans., 348f.

50. See *Muqaddimah,* Rosenthal trans., 2.406.

51. See *Muqaddimah,* Rosenthal trans., 2.406f.

52. Ibn Khaldūn apparently refers to what he said at the beginning of this chapter. Or, the reference may be to statements such as those made at *Muqaddimah,* Rosenthal trans., 2.353f., or 2.266f.

53. Qurʾān 35.1 (1).

54. Though "terminology" is a closer antecedent for the Arabic suffix than "works," the above translation seems justified. "Method," in this context, is most likely to mean "school system," as shown by the reference to the Qayrawānī, etc., "method" of Mālikism.

55. See Bombaci, 466, who here as above (n. 1133) refers the suffix to "terminology."

56. See *Muqaddimah,* Rosenthal trans., 3.15.

57. See *GAL, Suppl.* 1.662.

58. See *Muqaddimah,* Rosenthal trans., 3.323–24.

59. Muslim scholars considered it necessary to stress the idea that there was constant progress, that the ancients left much for later scholars to do. See, for instance, Franz Rosenthal, "Al-Asturlabi and al-Samawʿal on Scientific Progress." *Osiris* 9 (1950): 559.

60. Qurʾān 5.54 (59); 57.21 (21); 62.4 (4). Needless to say, the word "excellence" does not have the meaning in the Qurʾānic context that it is given here by Ibn Khaldūn.

61. Qurʾān 2.142 (136), 213 (209), etc.

62. See Issawi, pp. 160–61.

63. The word *li-t-tafsīr,* which in this context cannot refer to Qurʾān commentaries, is omitted in A and B, cut off in the margin of C, and missing in D. *Li-t-tafassur,* in the Paris ed., may be a misprint. It may be added here that the word translated "expert knowledge" in the following sentence also has the equivalent meaning of "knowing by heart." See *Muqaddimah,* Rosenthal trans., vol. 3, n. 1362.

64. See *Muqaddimah,* Rosenthal trans., 3.18–19 and 29–30.

65. See *Muqaddimah,* Rosenthal trans., 3.323.
66. See *Muqaddimah,* Rosenthal trans., 3.143.
67. See p. 3.293, below.
68. Bulaq adds: "with great difficulty."
69. Qur'ān 7.185 (185).
70. For the following discussion of education, see L. Buret, "Notes marginales sur les Prolégomènes: Un Pédagogue arabe du XIVe siècle: Ibn Khaldoun," *Revue Tunisienne* 36 (1934): 23–33, and Jamāl al-Muḥāsib, "Ibn Khaldūn's Theory of Education" (in Arabic). *al-Machriq* 43 (1949): 365–98. See also *Muqaddimah,* Rosenthal trans., beginning 3.426.
71. See Issawi, 157–59.
72. Bulaq: "partial."
73. MSS. A, B, C, and D have "students," but one must read "teachers," with Bulaq.
74. Bulaq corrects to "ability."
75. Qur'ān 2.142 (136), 213 (209), etc.
76. Qur'ān 2.239 (240).
77. See paragraph 91, below.
78. The remainder of this section, and the following section down to paragraph 89, are missing in C.
79. Bulaq: "It is the existence (*wijdān*) of a motion." See 1.198, above.
80. See *Muqaddimah,* Rosenthal trans., 1.197, 210, and 2.412 (paragraph 2, above).
81. I.e., the major and minor terms.
82. See Issawi, 168–69.
83. See *Muqaddimah,* Rosenthal trans., 316–17. See also 2.406–407.
84. See *Muqaddimah,* Rosenthal trans., 3.281–82.
85. See Bombaci, 466–67.
86. D: "study."
87. See Qur'ān 2.239 (240).
88. See paragraph 71, above.
89. Notwithstanding the tense used by Ibn Khaldūn, the apodosis would seem to start here (against Bombaci, 467).
90. See paragraph 117, below.
91. See, for instance, *Muqaddimah,* Rosenthal trans., 142.
92. This section is missing in C. See n. 78 to this chapter, above.
93. See Issawi, 162–63.
94. See, for instance, *Muqaddimah,* Rosenthal trans., 3.28 and 49.
95. Or: "In spite of that." But "moreover" seems preferable.
96. See n. 790 to this chapter as published in *Muqaddimah,* Rosenthal trans.
97. Bulaq omits the rest of the sentence. It may be noted that the science of the principles of jurisprudence is not an auxiliary science, and Ibn Khaldūn said so at the beginning of the section.
98. Bulaq: "deductions."
99. The rest of the sentence is not found in Bulaq.
100. See *Muqaddimah,* Rosenthal trans., 2.332, and 109.
101. See *Muqaddimah,* Rosenthal trans., 2.430.

102. See *Muqaddimah,* Rosenthal trans., 1.xxxv–xxxiv.
103. *Muqaddimah,* Rosenthal trans., 2.378.
104. See *Muqaddimah,* Rosenthal trans., 3.394–95.
105. See *Muqaddimah,* Rosenthal trans., 1.446, and 285 (n. 1123). His views on education, from his *Marāqī al-zulfā,* are quoted by I. Goldziher in his article, "Education," in Hastings' *Encyclopedia of Religion and Ethics,* 5.206a. Progressive views on education comparable to those quoted here, are found expressed in the early period of Muslim civilization in the *Nawādir al-falāsifah* by the famous Ḥunayn b. Isḥāq, where he described what he considered to be the curriculum of Greek education.
106. Lit., "he repeated (old things) and brought forth new (original ideas)." Thus, one might translate: "which says everything." See also R. Dozy, *Supplément aux dictionnaires arabes,* 2.186a.
107. See *Muqaddimah,* Rosenthal trans., 2.402 and 3.341, 367, 374, and 410.
108. See *Muqaddimah,* Rosenthal trans., 345–46, and elsewhere.
109. See *Muqaddimah,* Rosenthal trans., 3.194.
110. For this often-used phrase, see, for instance, F. Rosenthal, *A History of the Muslim Historiography,* 297. See also the rather different application of the idea in the verse: *Only the folly of youth is life, And when it is gone, the folly of wine.* See al-Tawḥīdī, *al-Imtā wa-l-mu*ʾ*ānasah* (Cairo, 1939–44), 2.180.
111. Qurʾān 13.41 (41).
112. See Issawi, 161.
113. See, for instance, *Muqaddimah,* Rosenthal trans., 1.257.
114. See Qurʾān 95.5 (5).
115. See Issawi, 61.
116. See *Muqaddimah,* Rosenthal trans., 1.275 and 288.
117. This vocalization is indicated in B, C, and D. However, no such word in the meaning required seems to exist in Arabic dictionaries. Is it, perhaps, a dialectical variant of Arabic *khurq* "charlatanry, foolishness," or a Spanish or Northwest African dialectical expression?
118. See *Muqaddimah,* Rosenthal trans., 1.261, above.
119. Apparently, Ibn Khaldūn interprets this statement to demand that "discipline" (which may mean "education" or "corporal punishment") should be applied only where it is stipulated by the religious law, and not freely meted out by teachers. Actually, it seems to mean that where the religious law prescribes no punishment, none will result in the other world for the individual involved.
120. Khalaf died between 796 and 805; see *GAL, Suppl.,* vol. 1, 111. Ibn Khaldūn's quotation is derived from al-Masʿūdī, *Murūj al-dhahab* (Paris, 1861–77), 6.321–22. See also al-Bayhaqī, *al-Maḥāsin wa-l-masāwī,* ad. Schwally (Giessen, 1902), 617, and al-Sharīshī, *Sharḥ al-Maqāmāt* (Cairo, 1306/1889), 2.300.
121. That is, his ʿAbbāsid relatives.
122. See Issawi, 162.
123. Qurʾān 2.142 (136), etc.
124. See Issawi, 64–66.
125. Qurʾān 12.76 (76).

126. See *Muqaddimah,* Rosenthal trans., 251.

127. In Arabic linguistic usage, the non-Arabs designated by the term *ᶜajam* are primarily Persians. From the title of Ibn Khaldūn's *History* (see *Muqaddimah,* Rosenthal trans., 1.13), one may perhaps conclude that in his mind *ᶜAjam* were mainly eastern non-Arabs, whereas the word Berber, as the most prominent group of western non-Arabs, stands for the latter. But see also *Muqaddimah,* Rosenthal trans., 1.57.

128. See Issawi, pp. 61–64.

129. See *Muqaddimah,* Rosenthal trans., 2.378 and 382–83.

130. The references given in *Concordance,* I, 270a, 1.24, refer to different elaborations of the same theme.

131. The expression of this fear is ascribed to as early a figure as the caliph ᶜUmar b. ᶜAbd-al-ᶜAzīz. See F. Rosenthal, *A History of Muslim Historiography,* 226. Ibn Khaldūn may have in mind the story about Mālik and al-Manṣūr. See *Muqaddimah,* Rosenthal trans., 1.34; also 3.325.

132. See *Muqaddimah,* Rosenthal trans., 2.448–49.

133. See *Muqaddimah,* Rosenthal trans., 3.345–46.

134. See *Muqaddimah,* Rosenthal trans., 2.353–54.

135. Abū Isḥāq Ibrāhīm b. al-Sarī, who died *ca.* 311 [923]. See *GAL*, vol. 1, 110; *Suppl.*, vol. 1, 170. For the other two scholars, see *Muqaddimah,* Rosenthal trans., 3.323 and 3.361.

136. The remainder of the sentence appears only in C and D. D omits: "and the regions beyond."

137. Lit., "people of Fārs.

138. The reference may be to *Muqaddimah,* Rosenthal trans., 1.60. See also 3.410–11.

139. See R. Dozy in *Journal asiatique,* 14, no. 6 (1869): 170–71.

140. See 459–60.

141. See R. Dozy, *loc. cit.*

142. See *Autobiography,* 246; *Muqaddimah,* Rosenthal trans., 1.lviii.

143. See *Muqaddimah,* Rosenthal trans., 3.117.

144. See Bombaci, 467, *Muqaddimah,* Rosenthal trans., 3.148.

145. Qurʾān 3.47 (42), etc., and Qurʾān 2.163 (158), etc.

Bibliography

ᶜAbd al-Raḥmān, Sāliḥ ᶜAbd Allāh. *Educational Theory: A Qurʾānic Outlook.* Mecca: Umm al-Qura University, 1982.

Abū Ḥayyān al-Tawḥīdī, ᶜAlī ibn Muḥammad. *Kitāb al-imtāᶜ wa-al-muʾānasah.* Cairo: Lajnat al-Taʾlīf wa-al-Tarjamah wa-al-Nashr, 1939–.

Afandi, Muhammad Muhammad Hamid and Nabi Bakhshu Khanu Balocu. *Curriculum and Teacher Education.* London: Hodder and Stoughton, 1980.

Alwani, Taha J. "*Taqlīd* and the Stagnation of the Muslim Mind." *The American Journal of Islamic Social Sciences* 8, no. 3 (1991): 513–24.

Ali, Syed Ausaf. "Islam and Modern Education." *Muslim Education Quarterly* 4, no. 2 (1987): 36–44.

Ali, Shahed. "Conflict Between Religion and Secularism in the Modern World and the Role of Education in Preserving, Transmitting and Promoting Islamic Culture," *Muslim Education Quarterly* 2, no. 3 (1984): 51–57.

ᶜAlmawī, ᶜAbd al-Bāsiṭ Ibn Mūsá al-. *Al-muᶜīd fī adab al-mufīd wa-al-mustafīd.* Edited by Shafīq Muḥammad Zayᶜūr. Beirut: Dār Iqraʾ, 1986.

Arkoun, Mohammed. "Textes inédits de Miskawayh," *Annales Islamologiques* 5 (1963): 181–205.

Arnzen, R. Review of "Frammenti e testimonianze di autori antichi nelle Epistole degli Iḫwān aṣ-Ṣafāʾ" by Carmela Baffioni. *Rivista di Filologia* 124 (1996): 359-365.

Ashraf, Syed Ali. "Editorial: Can University Education Be Anything but Liberal?" *Muslim Education Quarterly* 11, no. 1 (1993): 1–2.

ᶜAskarī, Abū Hilāl al-Ḥasan al-. *Al-ḥathth ᶜalá ṭalab al-ᶜilm wa-al-ijtihād fī taᶜlīmihi.* Cairo: Dār al-Faḍīla, 1998.

Attas, Sayed Muhammad Naquib al-, ed. *Aims and Objectives of Islamic Education.* Jeddah: King ᶜAbd al-Aziz University, 1979.

———. *Islam, Secularism and the Philosophy of the Future.* London: Mansell Publishing Ltd., 1985.

———. *Prolegomena to the Metaphysics of Islam: An Exposition of the Fundamental Elements of the Worldview of Islam.* Kuala Lumpur: International Institute of Islamic Thought and Civilization, 1995.

———. "Education and Values: Islamic Vis-a-Vis the Secularist Approaches." *Muslim Education Quarterly* 4, no. 4 (1987): 4–16.

Bailey, Charles. *Beyond the Present and the Particular: A Theory of Liberal Education.* London: Routledge & Kegan Paul, 1984.

Badawī, ᶜAbd al-Raḥmān. *Muʾallafāt al-Ghazālī.* Cairo: al-Majlis al-Aᶜlā li-Riᶜāyat al-Funūn wa-al-Adab wa-al-ᶜUlūm al-Ijtimāᶜīyah, 1961.

Badawi, M.A. Zaki. "Traditional Islamic Education—Its Aims and Purposes in the Present Day." In *Aims and Objectives of Islamic Education*, edited by Sayed Muhammad Naquib al-Attas, 104–17. Jeddah: King ᶜAbd al-Aziz University, 1979.

Barrow, Robin. *Plato, Utilitarianism and Education.* London: Routledge & Kegan Paul, 1975.

Bayhaqī, Ibrāhīm ibn Muḥammad. *Kitāb al-maḥāsin wa-al-masāwī,* edited by Friedrich Schwally. Giessen: J. Ricker, 1902.

Berkey, Jonathan. *The Transmission of Knowledge in Medieval Cairo: A Social History of Islamic Education.* Princeton: Princeton University Press, 1992.

Bewley, Aisha. *Islam: The Empowering of Women.* London: Ta-Ha, 1999.

Biesterfeldt, Hans Hinrich and Dimitri Gutas. "The Malady of Love." *Journal of the American Oriental Society* 104, no. 1 (1984): 21–55.

Bishlawy, Salma S. *The Book of Science by Ghazālī with Translation of the First Three Chapters.* M.A. diss., University of Chicago, 1945.

Black, Deborah L. *Logic and Aristotle's Rhetoric and Poetics in Medieval Arabic Philosophy.* Islamic Philosophy and Theology, vol. 7. Leiden: E. J. Brill, 1990.

Bloom, Jonathan M. *Paper Before Print: The History and Impact of Paper in the Islamic World.* New Haven: Yale University Press, 2001.

Bombaci, A. "Postille alla traduzione De Slane della *Muqqaddimah* di Ibn Ḫaldûn." *Annali dell' Istituto Universitario Orientale di Napoli* 3 (1949): 439–72.

Bouyges, Maurice. *Essai de Chronologie des oeuvres de al-Ghazali.* Edited by Michel Allard. Beirut: Imprimerie Catholique, 1959.

Brockelmann, Carl. *Geschichte der Arabischen Litteratur, Supplement.* Leiden: E. J. Brill, 1937–1940.

Baffioni, C. "The 'General Policy' of the Ikhwān al-Ṣafā: Plato and Aristotle Restated." In *Words, Texts and Concepts Cruising the Mediterranean Sea: Studies on the Sources, Contents and Influences of Islamic Civilization and Arabic Philosophy and Science Dedicated to Gerhard Endress on his Sixty-fifth Birthday.* Edited by R. Arnzen and J. Thielmann. Leuven: Peeters Publishers, 2004.

Buret, L. "Notes marginales sur les Prolégomènes: Un Pédagogue arabe du XIVᵉ siècle: Ibn Khaldoun." *Revue Tunisienne* 36 (1934): 23–33.

Carter, M. G. *Arab Linguistics: An Introductory Classical Text with Translation and Notes.* Studies in the History of Linguistics, vol. 24. Amsterdam: J. Benjamins, 1981.

Cook, Bradley J. "Islamic Versus Western Conceptions of Education: Reflections on Egypt." *International Review of Education* 45, no. 3/4 (1999): 339–58.

———. "Islam." *Encyclopedia of Education.* 2nd ed. Vol. 4. Edited by James W. Guthrie. New York: Macmillan Reference, 2003.

Cook, Michael. *Commanding the Right and Forbidding the Wrong in Islamic Thought.* Cambridge: Cambridge University Press, 2000.

Denny, Frederick. *An Introduction to Islam.* 2nd ed. New York: Macmillan, 1997.
Dhahabī, Muḥammad ibn Aḥmad. *Al-moschtabih.* Edited by P. De Jong. Leiden: E. J. Brill, 1881.
Diels, H., ed. *Commentaria in Aristotelem Graeca.* Berlin: Reimer, 1882–1909.
Dihkhudā, ᶜAli Akbar. *Lughat-nāmah.* Teheran: Chapkhanah-i Majlis, 1946–.
Din El-Shayyal, Gamal el-. "Some Aspects of Intellectual and Social Life in Eighteenth-Century Egypt." In *Political and Social Change in Modern Egypt,* edited by P. M. Holt, 117–32. London: Oxford University Press, 1968.
Dodge, Bayard. *Muslim Education in Medieval Times.* Washington, D. C.: The Middle East Institute, 1962.
Donaldson, Dwight. *Studies in Muslim Ethics.* London: SPCK, 1958.
Dozy, Reinhart Pieter Anne. *Supplément aux dictionnaires arabes.* 2 vols. Leiden: E. J. Brill, 1881.
Duri, A. A. *The Rise of Historical Writing Among the Arabs.* Princeton: Princeton University Press, 1983.
Esposito, John, ed. *The Oxford History of Islam.* New York: Oxford University Press, 1999.
Ess, Josef van. *Theologie und Gesellschaft im 2. und 3. Jahrhundert Hidschra: eine Geschichte des religiösen Denkens im frühen Islam.* 6 vols. New York: Walter de Gruyter, 1992.
Faruqi, Ismail R. al-. *Islamization of Knowledge: General Principles and Work Plan.* Washington D.C.: International Institute of Islamic Thought, 1982.
Faruqi, Ismaᵓil R. al- and Abdullah Omar Nasseef. *Social and Natural Sciences: The Islamic Perspectives.* Sevenoaks, England: Hodder and Stoughton, 1981.
Flügel, Gustav Leberecht. "Die Klassen der Hanefitischen Rechtsgelehrten." *Abhandlungen der Königlichen Sächsischen Gesellschaft der Wissenschaft, Philologische-Historische Klasse* 3, no. 2 (Leipzig: n.p., 1861): 267–358.
Ghazālī, Abū Ḥāmid Muḥammad ibn Muḥammad al-. *Iḥyāᵓ ᶜulūm al-dīn.* Cairo: Būlāq, 1289/1872.
———. *The Incoherence of the Philosophers: A Parallel English-Arabic Text.* Islamic Translation Series. Edited and translated by Michael E. Marmura. Provo, UT: Brigham Young University Press, 1997.
———. *Invocations and Supplications: Book IX of The Revival of the Religious Sciences.* 2nd revised edition. Translated with an introduction and notes by Kōjiro Nakamura. Cambridge: Islamic Texts Society, 1990.
———. *Maqāṣid al-falāsifah.* Lahore: n.p., 1937.
———. *Al-munqidh min al ḍalāl.* Damascus: Maktab al-Nashr al-ᶜArabī, 1939.
———. *Letter to a Disciple: Ayyuhāᵓ 'l-Walad: Bilingual English-Arabic Edition.* Translated by Tobias Mayer. Cambridge: Islamic Texts Society, 2005.
———. *O jeune homme / Ayyuhā al-walad.* Translated by Toufic Sabbagh. Beirut: UNESCO, 1951.
———. *O Youth: Being a Translation of al-Ghazali's Ayyuha ᵓL-walad.* Edited and translated by George H. Scherer. Beirut: American Press, 1933.
———. *On Disciplining the Soul & On Breaking the Two Desires: Books XXII and XXIII of The Revival of the Religious Sciences.* Translated by T. J. Winter. Cambridge: Islamic Texts Society, 1995.
Goldziher, Ignaz. "Muslim Education." *Encyclopedia of Religion and Ethics.* Edited by James Hastings. Vol. 5. Edinburgh: Clark, 1912.

Guthrie, James W., ed. *Encyclopedia of Education*, 2nd ed. Vol. 4. New York: Macmillan Reference, 2003.

Halstead, Mark J. "Toward a Unified View of Islamic Education." *Islam and Christian-Muslim Relations* 6, no. 1 (1995): 25–43.

Hamidullah, M. "Educational System in the Time of the Prophet." *Islamic Culture* 8, no. 1 (1939): 48–59.

Haythamī, Ibn Ḥajar al-. *Taḥrīr al-maqāl fī adab wa-aḥkām wa-fawāʾid yaḥtāju ilayhā muʾaddibū al-aṭfāl*. Cairo: Maktabat al-Qurʿan, 2000.

Hirst, Paul H. *Moral Education in a Secular Society*. London: University of London Press [for the] National Children's Home, 1974.

History and Social Sciences at Secondary Level, Part III. London: Inner London Education Authority, 1983.

Hitti, Philip K. *History of the Arabs*. London: Luzac and Co., 1964.

Hobson, Peter R. and John S. Edwards. *Religious Education in a Pluralist Society: The Key Philosophical Issues*. London: Woburn Press, 1999.

Hourani, George F. "A Revised Chronology of Ghazālī's Writings." *Journal of the American Oriental Society* 104, no. 2 (1982): 289–302.

Husain, Syed Sajjad and Syed Ali Ashraf. *Crisis in Muslim Education*. Sevenoaks, England: Hodder and Stoughton, 1979.

Ibn ʿAbd al-Barr, Yūsuf ibn ʿAbdallāh. *Jāmiʿ bayān al-ʿilm wa-faḍlih, wa-mā yanbaghī fī riwāyatihi wa-ḥamlih*. Beirūt: Dār al-Kutub al-ʿIlmiyah, 1980.

Ibn al-Bayṭār, ʿAbdallāh ibn Aḥmad. *Al-jāmiʿ li-mufradāt al-adwiyah wa-al-aghdiya*. Būlāq: n. p., 1875.

Ibn al-Ṣalāḥ al-Shahrazūrī, ʿUthmān Ibn ʿAbd al-Raḥman. *Adab al-muftī wa-al-mustaftī*. Edited by Muwaffaq ibn ʿAbd Allah Ibn ʿAbd al-Qadir. Beirut?: Maktabat al-ʿUlūm al-Ḥikam, 1986.

Ibn Ḥajar al-ʿAsqalānī, Aḥmad ibn ʿAlī. *Tahdhīb al-tahdhīb*. Hydarabad al-Dakkan: Maṭbaʿat Majlis Dāʾirat al-Maʿārif al-Niẓāmīyah, 1325–27 [1907–1909].

———. *Al-iṣābah fī tamyīz al-ṣaḥābah*. Cairo: Maktabat al-Kullīyāt al-Azharīyah, 1969–.

Ibn Ḥanbal, Aḥmad. *Musnad Ibn Ḥanbal*. Edited by Āḥmad al-Bābī. Cairo: n.p.: 1313/1895.

Ibn Jamāʿah. *Tadhkirat al-sāmiʿ wa-al-mutakallim fī adab al-ʿālim wa-al-mutallim*. Beirut, Dār al-Kutub, n.d.

Ibn Khaldūn. *The Muqaddimah: An Introduction to History*. Translated by Franz Rosenthal. 3 vols. New York: Bollingen Foundation, 1958.

———. *The Muqaddimah: An Introduction to History: Translated from the Arabic by Franz Rosenthal, Abridged and Edited by N. J. Dawood*. Princeton, N.J.: Princeton University Press, 1969.

Ibn Khallikān. *Ibn Khallikan's Biographical Dictionary*. Translated by William MacGuckin Baron de Slane. Paris: The Oriental Translation Fund of Great Britain and Ireland, 1842–1871.

———. *Wafayāt al-aʿyān*. Edited by Iḥsān ʿAbbās. Beirut: Dar Ṣādir, 1968.

Ibn Manẓūr. *Lisān al-ʿArab*. Beirut: Dar Ṣādir, 1955.

Ibn Mūsá, ʿIyāḍ al-Qāḍī. *Tartīb al-madārik wa-taqrīb al-masālik li-maʿrifat aʿlām madhhab Mālik*. Edited by Aḥmad Bukayr Maḥmūd. Beirut: Maktabat al-Ḥayāh, 1968.

Ibn Qayyim al-Jawzīyah. *Miftāḥ dār al-saᶜādah.* Beirut: Dār Ibn Ḥazm, 2003.

Ibn Saᶜd, Muhammad. *Kitāb al-ṭabaqāt al-kabīr: Biographien Muhammeds, seiner Gefährten und der späteren Träger des Islams.* Edited by Eduard Sachau, et al. Leiden: E. J. Brill, 1905–1940.

Ibn Saḥnūn, Muḥammad ibn ᶜAbd al-Salam. *Kitāb adab al-muᶜallimīn.* Edited by Maḥmūd ᶜAbd al-Mawlā. Algiers: al-Sharikah al-Wataniyah, 1973.

———. *Kitāb adab al-muᶜallimīn.* Edited by Muḥammad al-ᶜArūsī Maṭwī. Tūnis: Dār al-Kutub al-Sharqīyah, 1972.

———. "Le livre des règles de conduite des maîtres d'école." Translated by Gérard Lecomte. *Revue des études islamiques* 21 (1953): 77–105.

Ibn Sīnā, Abū ᶜAli Al-Ḥusayn Ibn ᶜAbdallāh. *Kitāb al-siyāsah.* Edited by Fuᵓād ᶜAbd al-Munᶜim Aḥmad. Alexandria: Muᵓassasat Shabāb al-Jāmiᵓah, n.d.

Ikhwān al-Ṣafāᵓ. *Rasāᵓil ikhwān al-ṣafāᵓ wa-khillān al-wafāᵓ.* 4 vols. Beirut: Dar Ṣādir, 1957.

International Institute of Islamic Thought (IIIT). *Islamization of Knowledge.* 3rd ed. Herndon, VA: IIIT, 1995.

Iṣbahānī, Abū al-Faraj al-. *Kitāb al-aghānī.* 20 vols. Bulaq, Egypt: Dār al-Kutub, 1868–1869.

Jaeger, Werner Wilhelm. *Paideia: The Ideals of Greek Culture.* Vol. 1. New York: Oxford University Press, 1939.

Jāḥiẓ, Abū ᶜUthmān al-. *Collection of al-Jāḥiẓ Treatises.* Edited by ᶜAbd al-Salām Hārūn. Cairo: Maktabat al-Khanjī, 1979.

Kaḥḥālah, ᶜUmar Riḍā. *Muᶜjam al-muᵓallifīn.* Beirut: Muᵓassasat al-Risālah, 1993.

Kâtip Çelebi. *Kashf al-ẓunūn ᶜan asāmī al-kutub wa-al-funūn.* Beirut: Dār al-Kutub al-ᶜIlmīya, 1992.

Khalifah, Haji. *Lexicon bibliographicum et encyclopaedicum, ad codicum Vindobonensium, Parisiensium et Berolinensis fidem primum edidit.* Edited by G. L. Flügel. Leipzig: Oriental Translation Fund of Great Britain and Ireland, 1835–1858.

Khalīl, ᶜImād al-Dīn. *Madkhal ilá al-tārīkh wa-al-ḥaḍāra al-Islamīya.* Kuala Lumpur: al-Jāmiᶜah al-Islāmīyah al-ᶜIlmīyah bi-Malīzīah, 2001.

Khan, Mohammed Abdul Muᵓid. "The Muslim Theories of Education During the Middle Ages." *Islamic Culture* 28 (1944): 418–33.

Khaṭīb al-Baghdādī, Abu Bakr Aḥmad ibn ᶜAlī al-. *Al-jāmiᶜ li-akhlāq al-rāwī wa-adab al-sāmiᶜ.* Riyadh: Maktabat al-Maᶜārif, 1983.

Lane, Edward William. *Arabic-English Lexicon.* Cambridge: Islamic Texts Society, 1984.

Landau, J. M. "Kuttāb" *Encyclopaedia of Islam CD-ROM Edition v.1.0.* Edited by P. J. Bearman, et al. Leiden: Brill, 1999.

Leiser, Gary. "Notes on the Madrasa in Medieval Islamic Society." *Muslim World* 76, no. 1 (1986): 16–23.

———. "The *Madrasa* and the Islamization of the Middle East: The Case of Egypt." *Journal of the American Research Center in Egypt* 22 (1985): 29–47.

Lewis, B. "Siyāsa." In *In Quest of an Islamic Humanism: Arabic and Islamic Studies in Memory of Mohamed al-Nowaihi,* edited by Arnold H. Green, 3–14. Cairo: American University in Cairo Press, 1984.

MacDonald, Duncan B. "The Moral Education of the Young among Muslims." *International Journal of Ethics* 15, no. 3 (1905): 286–304.
Mahfuẓ, Muḥammad. *Tarājim al-mu'allifīn al-Tunisiyīn.* Beirut: Dār al-Gharb al-Islāmī, 1984.
Makdisi, George. "Madrasa and the University in the Middle Ages," *Studia Islamica* 32 (1970): 255–64.
———. *The Rise of Colleges: Institutions of Learning in Islam and the West.* Edinburgh: Edinburgh University Press, 1981.
Masᶜūdī. *Les prairies d'or / Murūj al-dhahab wa-maᶜādin al-jawhar.* Paris: Impr. Impériale, 1861–77.
Melchert, Christopher. *The Formation of the Sunni Schools of Law, 9th–10th Centuries* CE. Leiden: E. J. Brill, 1997.
Meyerhof, Max. "Science and Medicine." In *The Legacy of Islam,* edited by Thomas Arnold and Alfred Guillaume, 311–55. London: Oxford University Press, 1931.
Miskawayh, Aḥmad ibn Muḥammad. *Tahdhīb al-akhlāq wa-taṭhīr al-aᶜrāq.* Edited by Ibn al-Khaṭīb. Cairo: al-Maṭbaᶜa al-Miṣrīya wa-Maktabātuhā, 1398 AH.
———. *The Refinement of Character: A Translation of Aḥmad ibn Muḥammad Miskawayh's "Tahdhīb al-akhlāq."* Translated by Constantine K. Zurayk. Beirut: American University of Beirut, 1968.
Mohamed, Yasien. "Islamization: A Revivalist Response to Modernity," *Muslim Education Quarterly* 10, no. 2 (1993): 12–23.
Moussalli, Ahmed. "Sayyid Quṭb's View of Knowledge," *The American Journal of Islamic Social Sciences* 7, no. 3 (1990): 315–34.
Mundhirī, Zakī al-Dīn al-Ḥafiẓ al-, *Al-targhīb wa-al-tarhīb.* Cairo: Dār al-Ḥadīth, n.d.
Mu'nis, Husayn. *Riyād al-nufūs.* Vol. 1. Cairo: Maktabat al-Nahḍa al-Misrīyya, 1951.
Murtada al-Zabīdī, Muḥammad ibn Muḥammad. *Sharh al-qāmūs, al-musammā tāj al-ᶜarūs.* 10 vols. Cairo: Jamālīyat Miṣr al-Maṭbaᶜah al-Khayrīyah, 1888.
Muranyi, M. "Fiqh." In *Grundriss der Arabischen Philologie.* Vol. 2, *Literaturwissenschaft,* edited by H. Gätje. Wiesbaden: Reichert, 1987.
Muḥāsib, Jamâl al-. "Al-tarbiya ᶜind Ibn Khaldūn" [Ibn Khaldūn's theory of education]. *Al-machriq* 43 (1949): 365–98.
Muḥāsibi, al-Ḥārith ibn Asad al-. *Kitāb al-riᶜāyah li-ḥuqūq Allāh.* Edited by Margaret Smith. London: Luzac, 1941.
Nakosteen, Mehdi Khan. *History of Islamic Origins of Western Education,* AD *800–1350.* Boulder, CO: University of Colorado Press, 1964.
Nasr, Seyyed Hossein. "The Islamic Philosophers' Views on Education." *Muslim Education Quarterly* 2, no. 4 (1984): 5–16.
———. *Philosophy, Literature and Fine Arts.* Jeddah: King Abdulaziz University, 1982.
———. *Science and Civilization in Islam.* New York: Praeger, 1968
Nejjar, Zaghloul R. el-. "The Limitations of Science and the Teachings of Science from the Islamic Perspective." *American Journal of Islamic Social Sciences* 3, no. 1 (1986): 59–75.

Netton, I. R. *Muslim Neoplatonists: An Introduction to the Thought of the Brethren of Purity, Ikhwan al-Safaʾ*. London: G. Allen & Unwin, 1982.

Peer, Mohammed. "Muslim Approach to Education: An Overview." *Islamic Culture* 64, nos. 2–3 (1990).

Pederson, J., "Some Aspects of the History of the Madrasa." *Islamic Culture* 3, no. 4 (1929): 527–37.

Qābisī, Abū al-Ḥasan al-. "Al-risālah al-mufaṣṣilah li-aḥwāl al-mutaʿallimīn wa-aḥkām al-muʿallimīn wal-mutaʿallimīn." In *Al-tarbiyah fī al-Islām,* ed. Aḥmad Fuʾād al-Ahwānī. Cairo: Dār al-Kutub al-ʿArabīyah, 1955.

Qaraḍāwī, Yūsuf al-. *Al-muntaqā min al-targhīb wa-al-tarhīb li-al-Mundhirī.* Cairo: Dār al-Wafāʾ, 1993.

———. *Reason and Science in the Holy Qurʾān.* Cairo: Wahba, 1996.

Quṭb, Muḥammad. *Manhaj al-tarbīyah al-islāmiyah.* Cairo: Dār al-Qalam, 1960–1981.

Quṭb, Sayyid. *Al-ʿadāla al-ijtimāʿiyya fī al-Islām.* 7th ed. Cairo: Dār al-Shurūq, 1980.

———. *Al-mustaqbal li-hadhā al-dīn.* 2nd ed. Cairo: Maktabat Wahbah, 1965.

Radwan, Abu al-Futouh Ahmad. *Old and New Forces in Egyptian Education: Proposals for the Reconstruction of the Program of Egyptian Education in the Light of Recent Cultural Trends.* New York: Bureau of Publications, Teachers College, Columbia University, 1951.

Rahman, Fazlur. *Islam and Modernity: Transformation of an Intellectual Tradition.* Chicago: University of Chicago Press, 1982.

———. *Prophecy in Islam: Philosophy and Orthodoxy.* London: Allen & Unwin, 1958.

Rashid, Muḥammad. "Was Muḥammad Literate?" *Islamic Quarterly* 39, no. 1 (1995): 49–55.

Ritter, Helmut, "The Reign of al-Muʿtaṣim," *Oriens* 6 (1953): 157–58.

Rosenthal, E. I. J. *Political Thought in Medieval Islam: An Introductory Outline.* Cambridge: Cambridge University Press, 1958.

Rosenthal, Franz. *A History of Muslim Historiography.* Leiden: E. J. Brill, 1968.

———. "Al-Asturlabi and as-Samawʾal on Scientific Progress." *Osiris* 9 (1950): 555–564.

Sakkākī, Yusūf Ibn Abī Bakr al-. *Miftāḥ al ʿulūm.* Beirut: Dār al-Kutub al-ʿIlmiyya, 1983.

Samʿānī, ʿAbd al-Karīm ibn Muḥammad, al-. *Adab al-imlāʾ wa-al-istimlāʾ.* Beirut: Dār al-Kutub al-ʿIlmīya, 1981.

———. *The "Kitāb al-ansāb."* Leyden: E. J. Brill, 1912.

Saud, al-Faisal al-. "The Glorious Qurʾān is the Foundation of Islamic Education." In Syed Muhammad Naquib al-Attas, ed. *Aims and Objectives of Islamic Education.* Jeddah: King ʿAbd al-Aziz University, 1979: 126–33.

Schacht, Joseph. *An Introduction to Islamic Law.* Oxford: Clarendon Press, 1964.

Schimmel, Annemarie. *Mystical Dimensions of Islam.* Chapel Hill, NC: University of North Carolina Press, 1975.

Sezgin, Fuat. *Geschichte des arabischen Schrifttums.* 9 vols. Leiden: E. J. Brill, 1967.

Shalabi, Aḥmad. *History of Muslim Education.* Beirut: Dār al-Kashshāf, 1954.

Sharīshī, Aḥmad ibn ᶜAbd al-Muʾmin. *Sharḥ al-maqāmāt al-ḥarīrīyah.* Miṣr: Maṭbaᶜat al-Khayrīyah al-Minshāʾt bi-Jamālīyah Miṣr, 1888.

Shāfiᶜī, al-Imām Muḥammad ibn Idrīs al-. *Al-risāla fī uṣūl al-fiqh: Treatise on the Foundations of Islamic Jurisprudence.* Translated by Majid Khadduri. 2nd ed. Cambridge: The Islamic Texts Society, 1987.

Shahi, Ahmed al-. "Educational Cross-Currents." *British Society for Middle Eastern Studies Bulletin* 7, no. 2 (1980): 80–91.

Shawkānī, Muḥammad Ibn ᶜAlī al-. *Al-fawāʾid al-majmūᶜa fī al-aḥādīth al-mawdūᶜa.* Beirut: Dār al-Kitāb al-ᶜArabī, 1986.

Shawkānī, Muḥammad ibn ᶜAlī al-, and ᶜAbd Allah Yahya Sarihi. *Adab al-ṭalab wa-muntahá al-ārab.* 1st ed. Beirut: Dār Ibn Ḥazm, 1998.

Simon, U. G. *Mittelalterliche arabische Sprachbetrachtung zwischen Grammatik und Rhetorik: ᶜIlm al-maᶜānī bei as-Sakkākī.* Heidelberg: Heidelberger Orientverlag, 1993.

Stanton, Charles Michael. *Higher Learning in Islam: The Classical Period A. D. 700–1300.* Savage, MD: Rowman & Littlefield, 1990.

Stoetzer, W. F. G. J. *Theory and Practice in Arabic Metrics.* Leiden: Het Oosters Instituut, 1989.

Sulaiman, Ibrahim. "Education as Imperialism." *Afkar Inquiry* 2, no. 7 (1985): 30–42.

Ṭabarī, Abū Jaᶜfar Muḥammad ibn Jarīr al-. *The History of al-Ṭabarī.* Vol. 5. Translated by C. E. Bosworth. Albany: State University of New York Press, 1999.

Talbani, Aziz. "Pedagogy, Power, and Discourse: Transformation of Islamic Education." *Comparative Education Review* 40, no. 1 (1996): 66–82.

Talbi, M. "Ibn Khaldūn." *Encyclopaedia of Islam CD-ROM Edition v.1.0.* Edited by P. J. Bearman, et al. Leiden: Brill, 1999.

Tawḥīdī, Abū Ḥayyān al-. *Al-muqābasāt.* Ed. Ḥasan al-Sandūbī. Cairo: n.p., 1929.

Tibawi, Abdul Latif. *Islamic Education: Its Traditions and Modernization into the Arab National Systems.* London: Luzac, 1972.

Tīfāshī, Aḥmad ibn Yūsuf al-. *Azhār al-afkār fī jawāhir al-aḥjār.* Edited by M. Y. Hasan and M. B. Khafājī. Cairo: al-Hayʾah al-Miṣriyah al-ᶜĀmmah li'l-Kitāb, 1977.

Tirmidhī, Abū ᶜĪsa al-. *Al-jāmiᶜ al-ṣaḥīḥ wa-huwa sunan al-Tirmidhī.* 5 vols. Beirut: Manshūrāt Muḥammad ᶜAlī Bayḍūn; Dār al-Kutub al-ᶜIlmīyah, 2000.

Totah, Khalil A. *The Contribution of the Arabs to Education.* New York: Teachers College, Columbia University, 1926.

Tritton, A. S. *Materials on Muslim Education in the Middle Ages.* London: Luzac, 1957.

Wasiullah Khan, Mohammad. *Education and Society in the Muslim World.* Sevenoaks, England: Hodder and Stoughton, 1981.

Watson, Brenda. *Education and Belief.* Oxford: Basil Blackwell Ltd., 1987.

Wensinck, A. J. and J. P. Mensing. *Concordance et indices de la tradition musulmane / Al-muᶜjam al-mufahras li-alfāẓ al-ḥadīth al-nabawī.* 8 vols. Leiden: E. J. Brill, 1936–1988.

White, John. *The Aims of Education Restated.* London: Routledge & Kegan Paul, 1982.

———. "A Reply to Raymond Godfrey," *Journal of Philosophy of Education*, 18, no. 1 (1984): 119–21.

Williamson, Bill. *Education and Social Change in Egypt and Turkey: A Study in Historical Sociology*. Houndmills, England: Macmillan, 1987.

Yāqūt ibn ᶜAbdallāh, al-Ḥamawī. *Irshād al-arīb ilá maᶜrifat al-adīb* [Dictionary of Learned Men]. 7 vols. Edited by D. S. Margoliouth. Leiden, E. J. Brill, 1907–1927.

Yūnus, Fatḥī, et al. *Al-tarbīya al-islāmīya bayn al-aṣāla wa-al-maᶜāṣara*. Cairo: ᶜĀlam al-Kutub, 1999.

Zarnūjī, Burhān al-Dīn al-. *Taᶜlīm al-mutaᶜallim: Ṭarīq at-taᶜallum = Instruction of the Student: The Method of Learning*. Translated, with an introduction, by G. E. von Grunebaum and Theodora M. Abel. New York: Kings Crown Press, 1947.

Index

References are to part.verse

About the Editors

DR. BRADLEY J. COOK has been serving as the Provost of Southern Utah University since August of 2009. Prior to this appointment, Cook served as the president of the Abu Dhabi Women's College, an institution serving nearly 3,000 students in the United Arab Emirates. Prior to that he served as vice president for academic affairs at Utah Valley State College in Orem, Utah.

Dr. Cook began his career in higher education in 1990 as the special assistant to the president at the American University in Cairo. Later he became the director of government relations for International Bechtel, Inc. in Kuwait. Upon completing his masters at Stanford University and his doctorate at the University of Oxford, he took a position as an assistant professor in the Department of Educational Leadership and Foundations at Brigham Young University where he taught both undergraduate and graduate courses in international and comparative education, International educational development, and Islamic studies.

He has published numerous articles on Islamic educational theory, comparative religion, and international and comparative education.

FATHI H. MALKAWI is a Jordanian born educator and university professor. He received a B.Sc. in Chemistry from Damascus University in 1966, and an Advance Diploma in Science Education from Reading University in 1972. He also received a Masters degree in Educational Psychology from the University of Jordan in 1978, and a Ph.D. in Science Education and Philosophy of Science from Michigan State University in 1984. He served as a high school teacher, teacher educator, and curriculum specialist at the Ministry of Education in Jordan. He then taught at Yarmouk University in Jordan as a full professor until 1996. More recently he has served as the Executive Director of the International Institute of Islamic Thought in Herndon, Virginia.

A Note on the Types

The English text of this book was set in BASKERVILLE, a typeface originally designed by John Baskerville (1706–1775), a British stonecutter, letter designer, typefounder, and printer. The Baskerville type is considered to be one of the first "transitional" faces—a deliberate move away from the "old style" of the Continental humanist printer. Its rounded letterforms presented a greater differentiation of thick and thin strokes, the serifs on the lowercase letters were more nearly horizontal, and the stress was nearer the vertical—all of which would later influence the "modern" style undertaken by Bodoni and Didot in the 1790s. Because of its high readability, particularly in long texts, the type was subsequently copied by all major typefoundries. (The original punches and matrices still survive today at Cambridge University Press.) This adaptation, designed by the Compugraphic Corporation in the 1960s, is a notable departure from other versions of the Baskerville typeface by its overall typographic evenness and lightness in color. To enhance its range, supplemental diacritics and ligatures were created in 1997 for exclusive use in this series.

The Arabic text was set in NASKH, designed by Thomas Milo (b. 1950), a pioneer of Arabic script research, typeface design, and smart font technology in the digital era. The Naskh calligraphic style arose in Baghdad during the tenth century and became very widespread and refined during the Ottoman period. It has been favored ever since for its clarity, elegance, and versatility. Milo designed and expanded this typeface during 1992–1995 at the request of Microsoft's Middle East Product Development Department and extended its typographic range even further in subsequent editions. Milo's designs pushed the existing typographic possibilities to their limits and led to the creation of a new generation of Arabic typefaces that allowed for a more authentic treatment of the script than had been possible since the advent of moveable type for Arabic.

BOOK DESIGN BY JONATHAN SALTZMAN

◆